Nails

Nail lengths are identified by numbers from 4 to 60 followed by the letter "d," which stands for "penny."

For general framing and repair work, use common or box nails. Common nails are best suited to framing work where strength is important. Box nails are smaller in diameter than common nails, which makes them easier to drive and less likely to split wood. Use box nails for light work and thin materials.

Most common and box nails have a cement or vinyl coating that improves their holding power.

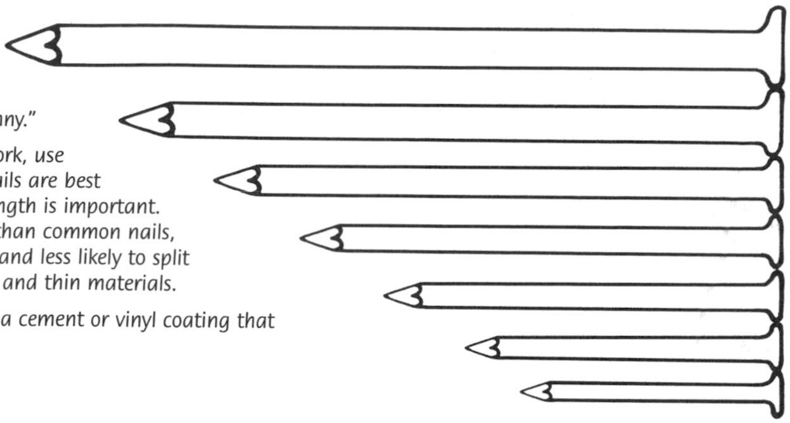

LBS.	MM	IN.
20d	102 mm	4"
16d	89 mm	3½"
10d	76 mm	3"
8d	64 mm	2½"
6d	51 mm	2"
5d	44 mm	1¾"
4d	38 mm	1½"

Lumber Dimensions

NOMINAL - U.S.	ACTUAL - U.S.	METRIC
1 × 2	¾" × 1½"	19 × 38 mm
1 × 3	¾" × 2½"	19 × 64 mm
1 × 4	¾" × 3½"	19 × 89 mm
1 × 5	¾" × 4½"	19 × 114 mm
1 × 6	¾" × 5½"	19 × 140 mm
1 × 7	¾" × 6¼"	19 × 159 mm
1 × 8	¾" × 7¼"	19 × 184 mm
1 × 10	¾" × 9¼"	19 × 235 mm
1 × 12	¾" × 11¼"	19 × 286 mm
1¼ × 4	1" × 3½"	25 × 89 mm
1¼ × 6	1" × 5½"	25 × 140 mm
1¼ × 8	1" × 7¼"	25 × 184 mm
1¼ × 10	1" × 9¼"	25 × 235 mm
1¼ × 12	1" × 11¼"	25 × 286 mm
1½ × 4	1¼" × 3½"	32 × 89 mm
1½ × 6	1¼" × 5½"	32 × 140 mm
1½ × 8	1¼" × 7¼"	32 × 184 mm
1½ × 10	1¼" × 9¼"	32 × 235 mm
1½ × 12	1¼" × 11¼"	32 × 286 mm
2 × 4	1½" × 3½"	38 × 89 mm
2 × 6	1½" × 5½"	38 × 140 mm
2 × 8	1½" × 7¼"	38 × 184 mm
2 × 10	1½" × 9¼"	38 × 235 mm
2 × 12	1½" × 11¼"	38 × 286 mm
3 × 6	2½" × 5½"	64 × 140 mm
4 × 4	3½" × 3½"	89 × 89 mm
4 × 6	3½" × 5½"	89 × 140 mm

Metric Plywood Panels

Metric plywood panels are commonly available in two sizes: 1,200 mm × 2,400 mm and 1,220 mm × 2,400 mm, which is roughly equivalent to a 4 × 8-ft. sheet. Standard and Select sheathing panels come in standard thicknesses, while Sanded grade panels are available in special thicknesses.

STANDARD SHEATHING GRADE		SANDED GRADE	
7.5 mm	(5/16 in.)	6 mm	(4/17 in.)
9.5 mm	(3/8 in.)	8 mm	(5/16 in.)
12.5 mm	(½ in.)	11 mm	(7/16 in.)
15.5 mm	(5/8 in.)	14 mm	(9/16 in.)
18.5 mm	(¾ in.)	17 mm	(2/3 in.)
20.5 mm	(13/16 in.)	19 mm	(¾ in.)
22.5 mm	(7/8 in.)	21 mm	(13/16 in.)
25.5 mm	(1 in.)	24 mm	(15/16 in.)

CREDITS

Creative Director: Tim Himsel
Executive Editor: Bryan Trandem
Editorial Director: Jerri Farris
Managing Editor: Michelle Skudlarek
Lead Editor: Philip Schmidt
Editors: Nancy Baldrica, Paul Gorton, Tom Lemmer, Kathy Zaccaro
Copy Editor: Tracy Stanley
Art Director: Kevin Walton
Lead Mac Designer: Kari Johnston
Mac Designers: Lynne Beckedahl, Janet Rowe, Keith Sellers
Technical Illustrators: Jim Kehnie, Earl Slack, Rich Stromwall
Technical Photo Editor: Keith Thompson
Photo Editors: Julie Caruso, Angela Hartwell, Kathy Zaccaro
Studio Services Manager: Marcia Chambers
Photo Team Leader: Chuck Nields
Photographer: Tate Carlson
Scene Shop Carpenter: Dan Widerski
Production Service Manager: Kim Gerber
Production Staff: Laura Hokkanen, Helga Thielen

CREATIVE PUBLISHING international

President/CEO: Michael Eleftheriou
Vice President/Retail Publishing: Linda Ball
Vice President/Retail Sales & Marketing: Kevin Haas

Printed on American paper by: R. R. Donnelley & Sons Co.
10 9 8 7 6 5 4 3 2

Created by: The Editors of Creative Publishing International, Inc., in cooperation with Black & Decker.® Black & Decker is a trademark of the Black & Decker Corporation and is used under license.

Contributing Editors, Art Directors, Set Builders, and Photographers

Cy DeCosse, William B. Jones,
Gary Branson, Bernice Maehren,
John Riha, Paul Currie,
Greg Breining, Tom Carpenter,
Jim Huntley, Gary Sandin,
Mark Johanson, Dick Sternberg,
John Whitman, Anne Price-Gordon,
Barbara Lund, Dianne Talmage,
Diane Dreon, Carol Harvatin,
Ron Bygness, Kristen Olson,
Lori Holmberg, Greg Pluth,
Rob Johnstone, Dan Cary,
Tom Heck, Mark Biscan,
Abby Gnagey, Joel Schmarje,
Jon Simpson, Dave Mahoney,
Andrew Sweet, Bill Nelson,
Barbara Falk, Dave Schelitzche,
Brad Springer, Lori Swanson,
Daniel London, Jennifer Caliandro
John Hermansen, Geoffrey Kinsey,
Phil Juntti, Tom Cooper,
Earl Lindquist, Curtis Lund,
Tom Rosch, Glenn Terry,
Wayne Wendland, Patrick Kartes,
John Nadeau, Mike Shaw,
Mike Peterson, Troy Johnson,
Jon Hegge, Jim Destiche,
Christopher Wilson, Tony Kubat,
Phil Aarrestad, Kim Bailey, Rex Irmen,
John Lauenstein, Bill Lindner,
Mark Macemon, Charles Nields,
Mette Nielsen, Cathleen Shannon,
Hugh Sherwood, Rudy Calin,
Dave Brus, Paul Najlis,
Mike Parker, Mark Scholtes,
Mike Woodside, Rebecca Hawthorne,
Paul Herda, Brad Parker,
Susan Roth, Ned Scubic,
Stewart Block, Mike Hehner,
Doug Deutscher, Paul Markert,
Steve Smith, Mary Firestone.

Library of Congress Cataloging-in-Publication Data
The complete photo guide to home improvement : over 1700 photos, 250 step-by-step projects.
    p. cm.
    At head of title: Black & Decker.
    Includes index.
    ISBN 0-86573-580-8
    1. Dwellings--Remodeling--Amateurs' manuals. I. Title: Black & Decker, the complete photo guide to home improvement. II. Creative Publishing International. III. Black & Decker Corporation (Towson, Md.)
    TH4816 .C646 2001
    643'.7--dc21
                           2001032451

BLACK & DECKER®

The COMPLETE PHOTO GUIDE TO

HOME
IMPROVEMENT

Over 1700 Photos

250 Step-by-Step Projects

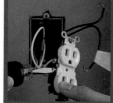

CREATIVE PUBLISHING international

www.howtobookstore.com

CONTENTS

REMODELING PROJECTS

The Complete Photo Guide to Home Improvement

Home improvement has been an obsession of homeowners since the creation of the house. People remodel to improve the quality of their living spaces, to add value to their homes, or simply to change things they never liked about the original designs. Those who do the work themselves find that even big projects can be broken down into a series of manageable tasks. This book can help you do just that.

The first section of the book, Project Planning, shows you the basics of your home's structural and mechanical systems—things you should understand before starting any project. You'll also learn about building codes and building permits. Permits are required by law for most projects, and they ensure that your work and the materials you use comply with the local building codes.

The next section, Basic Techniques, covers the details of carpentry, plumbing, and wiring. There's background information on the specific systems and discussions of the tools, materials, and techniques needed for the projects in the book. You'll also learn how to map and assess your existing plumbing and wiring systems and plan for new installations. In addition, this section acts as a general reference: If a procedure isn't fully explained within a specific project, look for it here.

Before you dive into the work of your project, take the time to make sure that the changes you make will improve not only the appearance of your living space but also its usability. In other words, the designs and products you choose should be safe and easy-to-use for everyone in your home. This will take some thoughtful planning and consideration of how your spaces are used currently as well as how things might change over time. To help you with these decisions, this book features advice for incorporating universal design into your projects. Where traditional design concepts and guidelines provide a good starting point, universal design takes planning one step further to help you create spaces that accommodate people of all sizes, ages and abilities. See page 17 for a list of the universal design topics covered in the book.

Features You'll Find in this Book:

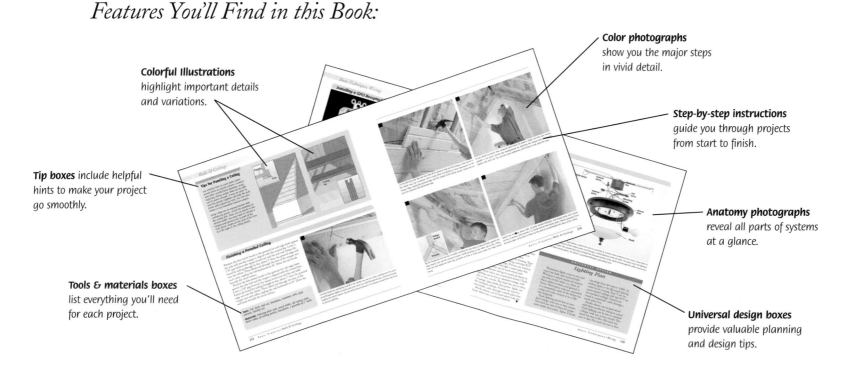

Colorful Illustrations highlight important details and variations.

Color photographs show you the major steps in vivid detail.

Step-by-step instructions guide you through projects from start to finish.

Tip boxes include helpful hints to make your project go smoothly.

Anatomy photographs reveal all parts of systems at a glance.

Tools & materials boxes list everything you'll need for each project.

Universal design boxes provide valuable planning and design tips.

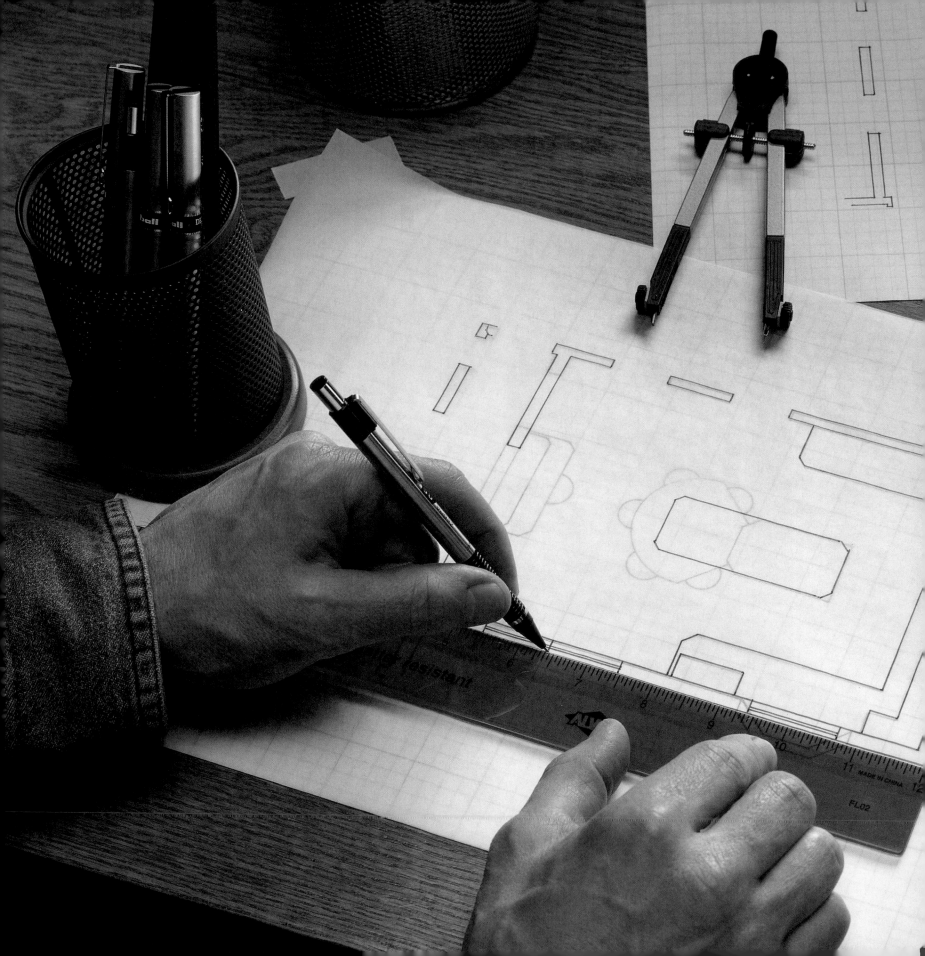

PROJECT
PLANNING

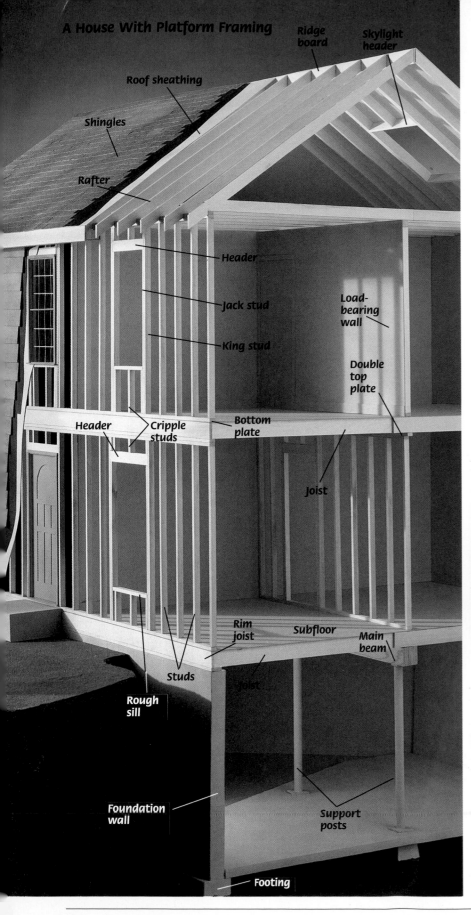

A House With Platform Framing

- Ridge board
- Skylight header
- Roof sheathing
- Shingles
- Rafter
- Header
- Jack stud
- Load-bearing wall
- King stud
- Double top plate
- Header
- Cripple studs
- Bottom plate
- Joist
- Rim joist
- Subfloor
- Main beam
- Studs
- Joist
- Rough sill
- Foundation wall
- Support posts
- Footing

Learning About Your House

Remodeling requires examination of your home's existing structure and various systems—plumbing, wiring, and HVAC (heating, ventilation, and air conditioning). For example, before removing a wall, you must determine whether it is load-bearing and check for service lines running within it. Understanding your home's structure and mapping its systems will help you determine the feasibility of a project and estimate how much work is involved.

House Framing

The basic structure of a house is made up of four systems that work together to form a solid structure: the roof, the walls, the floors, and the foundation. Most houses are built using one of two framing styles—*platform* framing or *balloon* framing. The framing style of your house determines what kind of temporary supports you will need to install while making any changes to the structural framing and can affect the complexity of a project. If you have trouble determining what

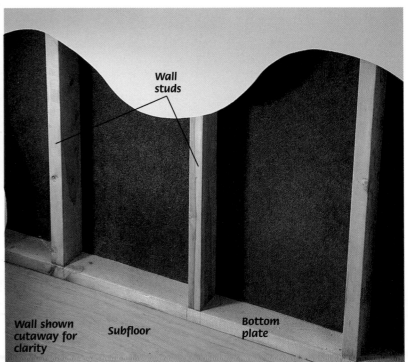

- Wall studs
- Wall shown cutaway for clarity
- Subfloor
- Bottom plate

Platform framing (photos, left and above) is identified by the floor-level bottom plates and ceiling-level top plates to which the wall studs are attached. If you do not have access to unfinished areas, remove the wall surface at the bottom of a wall to determine what kind of framing was used in your home.

type of framing was used in your home, refer to the original blue-prints, if you have them, or consult a building contractor or licensed home inspector.

Platform framing is the style used for most houses built after 1930. It can be identified by its wall studs, which are one story tall and extend from a bottom plate at the floor (or foundation wall) to a top plate attached to the joists above. The floor structures are complete platforms that extend to the perimeter of the building. Platform framing is easy to alter because the support structure starts at the floor for each story.

Balloon framing, commonly used in homes built before 1930, has wall studs that extend from the foundation walls to the roof structure. The first-story floor framing rests on the foundation walls; second- and third-story floors are supported by 1 × 4 ribbons set into notches in the wall studs (see illustration, page 10).

With either framing style, the house frame is supported by the foundation walls and a main beam, or *girder*, in the center of the house; in turn these are supported by the earth around the foundation.

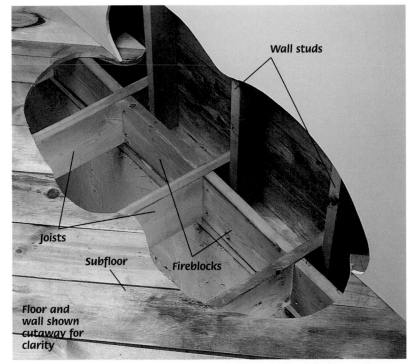

Balloon framing (photos, right and above) is identified by wall studs that run uninterrupted from the roof to a sill plate on the foundation. Full-width 2 × blocking installed between the floor (and ceiling) joists prevent fire from spreading up through the wall-stud cavities.

Floor and Ceiling Framing

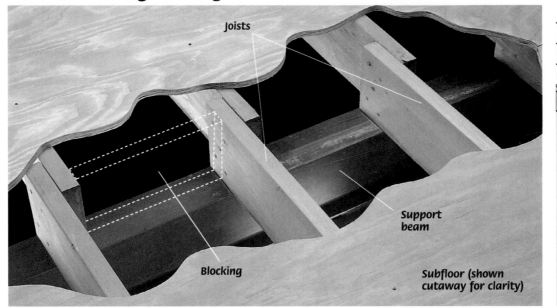

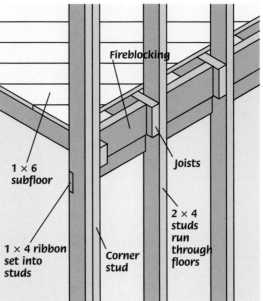

Joists carry the structural load of floors and ceilings. The ends of the joists rest on support beams, foundations, or load-bearing walls; joists always run perpendicular to their supports. Floor joists typically are 2 × 10 or larger lumber. Ceiling joists, which support only a ceiling finish and sometimes limited storage space, may be 2 × 4 or larger. Blocking or X-bridging is often installed between joists to provide additional support.

Floor joists in balloon-frame houses are nailed to the sides of continuous wall studs. Upper-story joists gain additional support from 1 × 4 ribbons notched into the studs. Solid blocking between the joists provides fire protection.

Roof Framing

Rafters, typically made from 2 × 6 or larger lumber, span from the exterior walls to the ridge board (or beam) at the peak of the roof. In most rafter-frame roofs, the ceiling joists link the ends of opposing rafters to create a structural triangle; the frame may also have rafter ties or collar ties for additional support (see page 301). Rafters are usually spaced 16" or 24" apart.

Trusses, prefabricated frames made from 2 × lumber joined with metal plates or fasteners, are found in many houses built after 1950. Standard trusses contain bottom and top cords and interconnecting webs that provide rigidity. Trusses rely on the sum of their parts for support and cannot be cut or altered.

Wall Framing

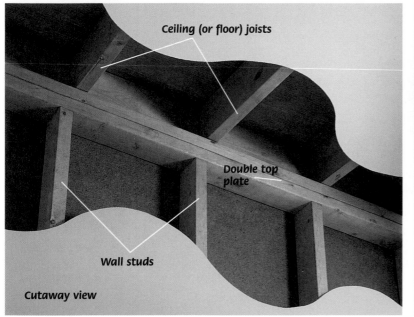

Ceiling (or floor) joists

Double top plate

Wall studs

Cutaway view

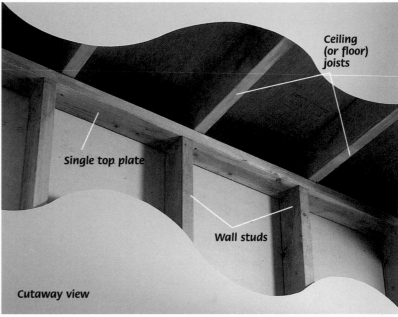

Ceiling (or floor) joists

Single top plate

Wall studs

Cutaway view

Load-bearing walls carry the structural weight of your home. In platform-frame houses, load-bearing walls can be identified by double top plates made from two layers of framing lumber. Load-bearing walls include all exterior walls and any interior walls that are aligned above support beams.

Non-load-bearing, or partition, walls are interior walls that do not carry the structural weight of the house. They have a single top plate and can be perpendicular to floor and ceiling joists but are not aligned above support beams. Any interior wall that is parallel to floor and ceiling joists is a partition wall.

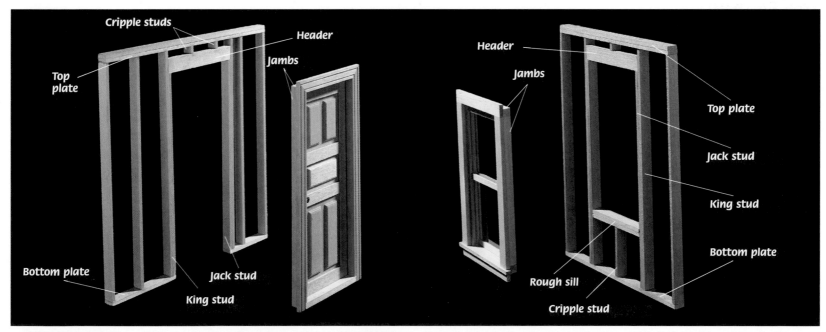

Cripple studs

Header

Top plate

Jambs

Bottom plate

Jack stud

King stud

Header

Jambs

Top plate

Jack stud

King stud

Bottom plate

Rough sill

Cripple stud

Door and window frames, called rough openings, are sized according to the dimensions of the door or window unit. In load bearing walls, the weight from above the opening is borne by the cripple studs, which are supported by a header that spans the opening. A typical header is made with two pieces of 2 × lumber sandwiched around a layer of ½" plywood (see page 52); some builders use oversized headers, which eliminate the need for cripples. Frames in non-load-bearing walls may have only a single 2 × 4 for a header. Each end of the header is supported by a jack stud that extends to the bottom plate and is nailed to a king stud for support. A window frame has a sill that defines the bottom of the opening.

House Systems

Understanding and mapping your plumbing, wiring, and heating systems is an essential step for most remodeling projects. Before you cut into a wall, ceiling, or floor, you'll need to know what's behind the surface. And if your plans call for a systems expansion, finding the best places to join the new lines to the old will influence your design decisions and impact your budget.

Start by drawing a basic map of each of the three main systems. Use the original blueprints of your house or draw new plans for each floor (see pages 18 to 19). The illustrations here show the major elements of typical mechanical systems and demonstrate how smaller lines branch out from the main runs.

Begin your investigation in the basement, if you have one. Otherwise, start in the mechanical or utility room. A crawlspace can reveal a lot, too.

Starting at the systems' sources—water heater, main service panel, or furnace—follow the runs of pipe, cable, or duct as they route between and under floor joists and along walls. Note particularly where lines ascend vertically through walls onto the upper floors. Also note where services enter the house.

Plumbing

Most of the plumbing fixtures in a house are located near the 3" or 4" drain-waste-vent (DWV) pipe known as the *main stack* or the *soil stack,* or near an auxiliary DWV stack. The main stack extends from the basement floor to the roof and serves as both drain and vent for multiple fixtures.

Water supply pipes stem from the water meter and the hot water heater and run together to the various fixtures and appliances.

Because drain pipes rely on gravity to work properly and must be routed according to strict specifications, it's best to position new fixtures near existing drain and vent lines. Supply pipes, by comparison, use pressure to feed the system and can be routed almost anywhere.

Follow the steps on pages 86 to 87 to create a complete map of your plumbing system.

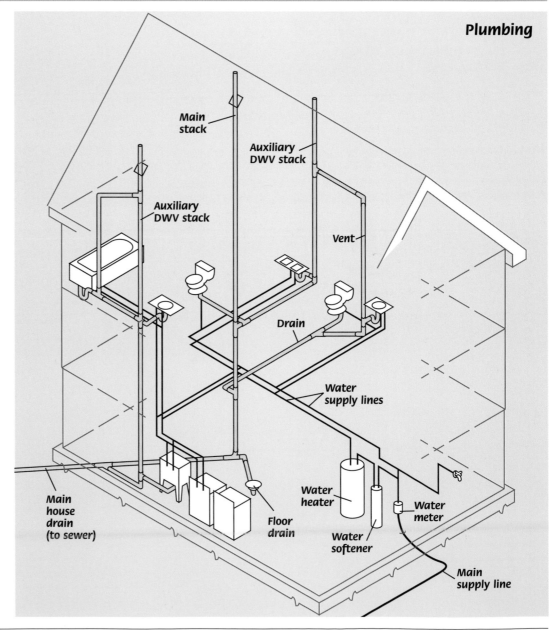

Plumbing

Wiring

A home's electrical system is made up of many circuits, all of which start from the *main service panel*, and in some cases, from a subpanel. Standard electrical cable is slim and flexible and can be routed in almost any configuration; this can make it difficult to follow the exact route of each circuit but makes it easy to add new circuits.

Mapping your electrical system is easy; simply turn each breaker on and off (or remove each fuse) and find which receptacles, fixtures, and appliances shut down. For a general system map it's not necessary to locate every individual cable run, but your notes should include all receptacles, fixtures, switches, and hard-wired devices and appliances.

See page 104 for help with mapping your electrical system.

HVAC

In a forced-air heating system, the furnace feeds a main supply duct, which connects to branch ducts that supply hot air to the rooms. Branch ducts servicing the upper floors of the house typically rise straight up through wall-stud cavities. A second system of ducts circulates cold air back to the furnace.

To map a forced-air system, follow the ducts back from the supply registers and return-air grills to the main ducts in the basement. See pages 310 to 311 for information on expanding a forced-air system.

A hydronic (hot water or steam) heating system has a network of pipes that circulates heated water from the boiler to baseboard heaters, convectors, or radiators. Some systems have one pipe that connects to each fixture; other systems have two.

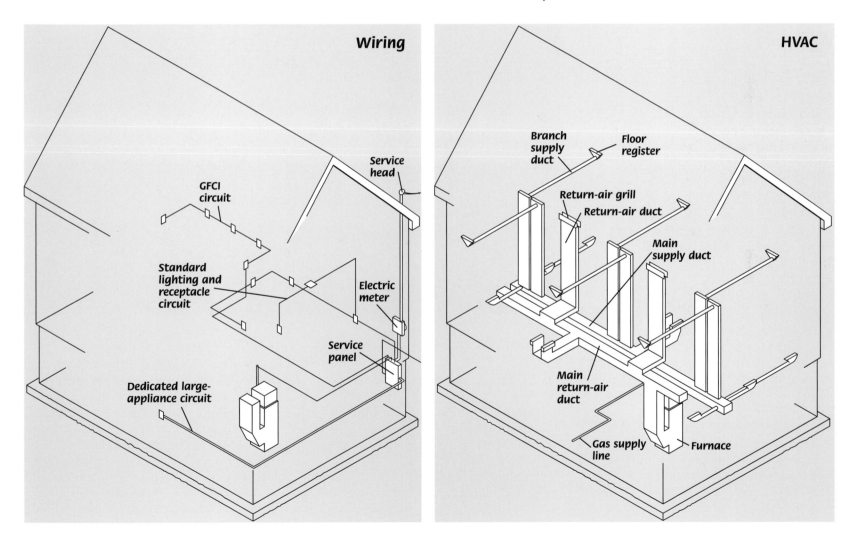

Wiring

- GFCI circuit
- Service head
- Standard lighting and receptacle circuit
- Electric meter
- Service panel
- Dedicated large-appliance circuit

HVAC

- Branch supply duct
- Floor register
- Return-air grill
- Return-air duct
- Main supply duct
- Main return-air duct
- Gas supply line
- Furnace

Building Codes & Permits

Building permits are required for any remodeling project that involves a change or addition to your home's structure or mechanical systems. Building permits are issued to ensure your remodeling project meets local building codes, which establish material standards, structural requirements, and installation guidelines for your project. In short, they ensure that your (or your contractor's) work is done properly.

The areas outlined on pages 15 and 16—room dimensions, exits and openings, light and ventilation, and fire protection—are usually covered by general building permits. If your project involves major changes to your plumbing, electrical, or HVAC systems, you may be required to obtain separate permits from the respective administration departments.

Building permits are required by law, and getting caught without them can result in fines from the city and possibly trouble with your insurance company. Also, work done without permits can cause problems if you try to sell your house.

Most local building codes follow the national codes, such as the National Electrical Code, but are adapted to meet the demands of local conditions and legislation. Keep in mind that local codes always supersede national codes. Always check with your local building department before finalizing your plans.

Before issuing permits, your local building department will require plans and cost estimates for your project. After your plans have been approved, you must pay permit fees, which are based on the cost of the project. You'll also learn what inspections are required and when you should call for inspections.

Once issued, a building permit typically is good for 180 days. You can apply for an extension by submitting a written request showing justifiable cause for the delay.

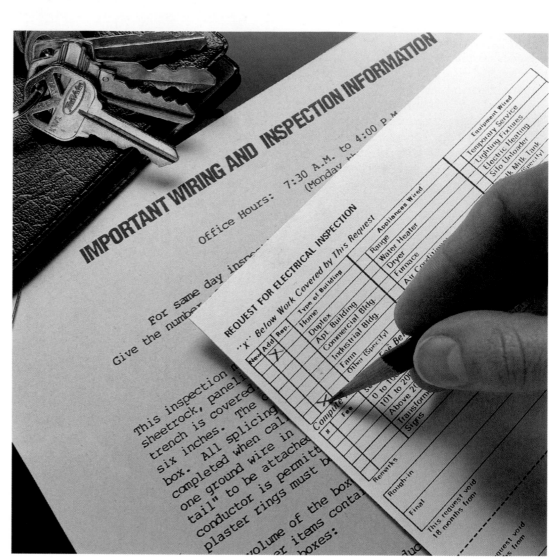

Here are some tips to help you prepare for the permit process:

• To obtain a building permit, you must fill out a form from your local building department that includes a description of the project; your home's address and legal description, and occupancy; and an estimate of the project cost.

• The building department may require two to four sets of construction documents or drawings of your project—including floor and elevation plans—to be submitted for inspection and approval.

• A building inspector will examine all construction plans and stamp or send written notification of approval and acceptance.

• One set of approved documents is kept by the building official, one set is sent to the applicant, and one set is displayed at the site until the project is completed.

• Some permits are granted by phase of construction. After the work for one phase is completed and inspected, a permit for the next phase is issued. However, building officials will not guarantee issuance of subsequent permits.

• All work is inspected by a building official to ensure compliance with codes and permits.

• Your project is complete only after the local building inspector completes a final inspection and gives approval of your site.

Room Dimensions

- Habitable rooms must be at least 7 ft. wide and 7 ft. deep.
- Ceilings in all habitable rooms, hallways, corridors, bathrooms, toilet rooms, laundry rooms, and basements must be at least 7 ft., 6" high, measured from the finished floor to the lowest part of the ceiling.
- Beams, girders, and other obstructions that are spaced more than 4 ft. apart can extend 6" below the required ceiling height.
- In non-habitable rooms, such as unfinished basements, ceilings may be 6 ft., 8" from the floor, and beams, girders, and ducts may be within 6 ft., 4" of the floor.
- Habitable rooms cannot have more than 50% of their floor area under sloped ceilings less than 7 ft., 6" high, and no portion of a floor area can be under a ceiling less than 5 ft. high.
- Finished floor is not considered measurable floor area when it is below sloped ceilings less than 5 ft. high or beneath furred ceilings less than 7 ft., 6" high.
- One habitable room in a home must have at least 120 square feet of gross floor area. Other habitable rooms can have gross floor space of 70 sq. ft. minimum.
- Kitchens cannot have less than 50 sq. ft. of gross floor area.
- Hallways must be at least 3 ft. wide.

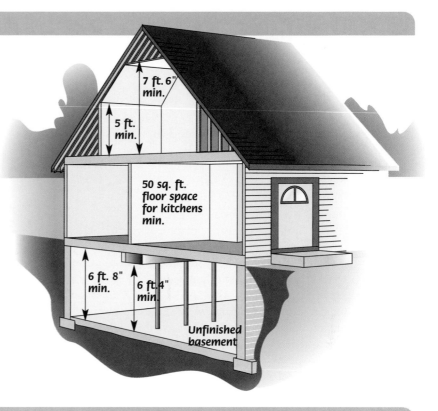

Exits and Openings

- Sleeping rooms and habitable basements must have at least one egress window or exterior door for emergency escape. Occupants must be able to open the exit from inside the home, without a key or tool.
- An egress window must have a net clear opening of at least 5.7 sq. ft., with a minimum height of 24" and a minimum width of 20".
- Window sills on egress windows cannot be more than 44" above the floor.
- Egress windows below ground level must have window wells. If the wells are deeper than 44", they must have permanent ladders or steps. The steps can project up to 6" into the well but must be usable when the window is fully opened. Steps must be at least 12" wide and project at least 3" from the wall. Ladder rungs must be less than 18" apart.
- Screens, bars, grills, and covers on emergency exits must open easily and be removable from inside the home, without tools or keys.
- Exit doors must be at least 3 ft. wide and 6 ft., 8" high. They must provide direct outside access and operate without special knowledge or tools.
- Bulkhead enclosures may serve as emergency exits in habitable basements if they provide direct access to the basement and meet the dimension requirements for emergency exits.

Natural Light and Ventilation

- Ventilation includes windows, doors, louvers, and other approved openings, or mechanical systems.
- Windows must equal at least 8% of the floor area in habitable rooms. The minimum openable area of a window must equal at least 4% of the room's floor area.
- In bathrooms, windows must be at least 3 sq. ft., and at least half of the window must open.
- Windows must open and operate from inside the room, and they must exit to a street, alley, yard, court, or porch.
- Window light can be replaced by an artificial light if it produces 6.46 lux from 30" above the floor.
- Mechanical ventilation can replace operable windows. In bedrooms, ventilation must supply outside air at a rate of 15 cubic ft. per minute (cfm) for each occupant. In primary bedrooms, the rate is based on two occupants. In additional bedrooms, the rate is based on one occupant per room.
- In bathrooms, intermittent mechanical ventilation rates must be 50 cfm, and continuous rates must be 20 cfm. Bathroom ventilation must exhaust to the outside.

Photo courtesy of Andersen Windows, Inc.

Fire Protection

- All concealed and interconnected spaces, such as soffits, drop and cove ceilings, stair stringers, and areas around vents, pipes, ducts, chimneys, and fireplaces must be fireblocked to prevent fire spread.
- Exterior walls must be constructed to resist fire for at least one hour, with exposure from both sides.
- Batts or blankets of fiberglass, mineral wool, or other approved material must be secured between wall studs and partitions, at the ceiling and floor level, and at 10-ft. intervals both vertically and horizontally.
- Foam insulation installed in interior walls covered with ½" wallboard or other approved material must have a flame-spread rating of 75 or less and a smoke-developing index of 450 or less.
- Other insulation, including facings, vapor barriers, and breather papers, must have a flame-spread index of 25 or less and a smoke-developing index of 450 or less.
- Loose-fill insulation mounted with screens or supports must have a flame-spread rating of 25 or less and a smoke-developing index of 450 or less.
- Wall and ceiling finishes must have a flame-classification rating of 200 or less and a smoke-developing index of 450 or less.
- Smoke alarms must be installed in bedrooms, in hallways near bedrooms, and on each full story of a home. Multiple alarms must be wired together so one activation triggers all alarms.

Planning with Universal Design

Universal design is intended for all people. While standard home and product design are based on the "average" person—that is, the average adult male—not everyone fits into that category. Some people are short, some tall; some have difficulty walking, while others walk ably but find bending difficult. And physical abilities change constantly, as do family situations. By incorporating universal design into your remodeling plans, you can create spaces that work better for everyone who lives in or visits your home, regardless of their size, age, or ability.

Universal design is simply good design that improves everyday situations. For example, wide doorways make passage easier for a person carrying a load of laundry as well as for someone in a wheelchair; a lowered countertop enables a child to help prepare dinner and allows a person who tires easily to sit while cooking. More a way of thinking than a set of rules, universal design can be applied to any area of your home—from room layouts to light fixtures to door hardware. In all cases, universal design encourages independence by creating a safe, comfortable environment.

Many people take on remodeling projects to accommodate changes in their households. Perhaps you are remodeling because your aging parents are coming to live with you or your grown children or grandchildren are coming for an extended visit. Or you may be preparing your home for

your own retirement years. Considering both your current and future needs is an essential part of a fundamental universal design concept: creating a *lifespan* home—one that accommodates its residents throughout their lives. A lifespan home enables your aging parents to live comfortably with you now and will allow you to stay in your home as you grow older. And, while universal design makes your everyday life easier, it will also make your home more appealing to a wide range of potential buyers, if you choose to sell.

The universal design boxes featured throughout this book are full of information that will help you plan more thoughtfully; use the page listings below for easy reference. Much of the information provided here comes from universal design specialists, kitchen and bath designers, physical therapists, specialty builders and manufacturers, and organizations such as the National Kitchen and Bath Association (NKBA). Some suggestions are ADA (Americans with Disabilities Act) requirements; while these generally apply to public spaces, they often are used as guidelines for residential design. As always, be sure that all aspects of your project meet local code requirements.

For more help with planning with universal design, contact a qualified professional. Many kitchen and bath designers, home builders, and product manufacturers specialize in universal design. See page 503 for a list of additional resources.

Working with Drawings

Drawings are necessary for any remodeling project that involves construction, enlargement, alteration, repair, demolition, or change to any major system within your home. There are two basic types of construction drawings: *floor plans* and *elevation drawings*.

Floor plans show a room as seen from above. These are useful for showing overall room dimensions, layouts, and the relationships between neighboring rooms. Elevation drawings show a side view of a room, showing one wall per drawing. Elevations are made for both the interior and exterior of a house and generally show more architectural detail than floor plans.

Both floor plans and elevation drawings provide you with a method for planning and recording structural and mechanical systems for your project. They also help the local building department to ensure your project meets code requirements.

Before you draw up new plans, check with your home's architect, builder, or your local building department. These places often have copies of your home's floor plans on file. If your home is a historic building, your plans may be on file at a state or local historic office or university library.

If you are unable to obtain a copy of your home's floor plans, you can draw your own. This process provides you with a wealth of information about your home. Drawings let you see how changes will impact your home's overall layout and feel. They also help you plot your ideas, list materials, and solve design problems.

Follow the steps on page 19 to create floor plans and elevation drawings. Keep in mind that your plans may change as your ideas develop; until you have worked out all the elements of your design, consider your plans to be drafts. When you have arrived at a plan that meets your needs, draw up final floor and elevation plans to submit to your local building department.

Use existing blueprints of your home, if available, to trace original floor plans and elevation drawings onto white paper. Copy the measurement scale of the original blueprints onto the traced drawings. Make photocopies of the traced drawings, then use the photocopies to experiment with remodeling ideas.

To create floor plans, draw one story at a time. First, measure each room on the story from wall to wall. Transfer the rooms' dimensions on ¼" grid paper, using a scale of ¼" = 1 ft. Label each room for its use and note its overall dimensions. Include wall thicknesses, which you can determine by measuring the widths of door and window jambs—do not include the trim.

Next, add these elements to your drawings:

- Windows and doors; note which way the doors swing.
- Stairs and their direction as it relates to each story.
- Permanent features, such as plumbing fixtures, major appliances, countertops, built-in furniture, and fireplaces.
- Overhead features, such as exposed beams, or wall cabinets—use dashed lines.
- Plumbing, electrical, and HVAC elements. You may want a separate set of drawings for these mechanical elements and service lines.
- Overall dimensions measured from outside the house. Use these to check the accuracy of your interior dimensions.

To create elevation drawings, use the same ¼" = 1 ft. scale, and draw everything you see on one wall (each room has four elevations). Include:

- Ceiling heights and the heights of significant features such as soffits and exposed beams.
- Doors, including the heights (from the floor to the top of the opening) and widths.
- Windows, including the height of the sills and tops of the openings, and widths.
- Trim and other decorative elements.

When your initial floor plans and elevations are done, use them to sketch your remodeling layout options. Use tissue overlays to show hidden elements or proposed changes to a plan. Photographs of your home's interior and exterior may also be helpful. Think creatively, and draw many different sketches; the more design options you consider, the better your final plans will be.

When you have completed your remodeling plans, draft your final drawings and create a materials list for the project.

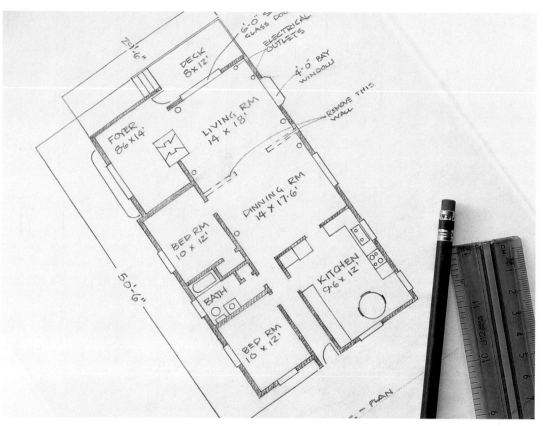

Draft a detailed floor plan showing the layout of the area that will be remodeled, including accurate measurements. Show the location of new and existing doors and windows, wiring, and plumbing fixtures.

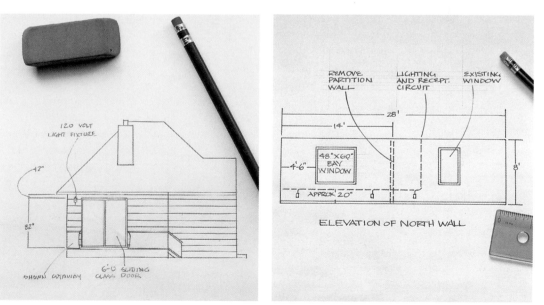

Create elevation drawings showing a side view layout of windows and doors, as viewed from both inside and outside the home. Indicate the size of windows and doors, ceiling heights, and the location of wiring and plumbing fixtures.

Getting Help from Professionals

Many do-it-yourselfers hire professionals to plan or complete the more complex or specialized aspects of their home remodeling project. Tradespeople are available for planning, designing, managing, building, or finishing work. Remodeling professionals generally fall into a few main categories: design professionals, general contractors, and subcontractors.

Design Professionals

Design professionals help you at the planning stages of your project. They are experts at taking ideas and turning them into project plans and blueprints. These professional services are expensive, so it's wise to do some planning of your own before contracting their services. Hourly rates, plus a percentage of materials or total budget are the most common billing arrangements.

Kitchen and bath designers specialize in designing two of the most important areas of your home. They can provide you with detailed help or act as general contractors for your project. Look for certification by the National Kitchen and Bath Association (NKBA), and the initials CKD (certified kitchen designer) or CBD (certified bath designer).

Interior designers work with every room of your home to create a specific style. Designers sometimes work with building contractors and home centers at a lower rate.

Architects are licensed professionals who design and prepare detailed construction plans for homes and buildings. Their services are expensive but warranted and sometimes required for major remodeling projects.

Building designers are similar to architects. They usually have extensive experience in construction and design but less background in engineering.

Design/build firms offer the services of both designers and general contractors to see a project through from start to finish. These firms generally charge one flat fee.

General Contractors

General contractors manage all aspects of a remodeling project. They hire, schedule, coordinate, and supervise the activities of all the professionals working on a job. Good contractors typically charge a percentage of the total budget, and many will take on only major construction projects.

Subcontractors

These professionals provide you with hands-on help. Subcontractors include all the professionals in the various building trades, such as carpenters, plumbers, electricians, and HVAC (heating, ventilation, and air conditioning) specialists. These subcontractors can be hired for specific aspects of a project or to help with planning and problem-solving. Most subcontractors are good at what they do, but it's important to spend some time to find the right people for your project.

Finding Reputable Contractors

Begin your search for a qualified contractor with friends and relatives. Word of mouth is powerful advertising. When you get a referral, ask what type of work the contractor provided, whether there were any problems, if the finished

Call Your Building Inspector

Building inspectors review your project at various stages to ensure it meets local building code requirements. And although inspectors aren't paid as consultants, they are experts in their respective fields and can be excellent resources for specific questions about building, electrical, or plumbing applications.

Inspectors are busy, so keep your questions short. Also request pamphlets or local code summaries, when available.

product was satisfactory, and whether they would hire the contractor again.

You can also find quality contractors by contacting kitchen and bath design centers, design/build firms, builders' associations, local trade guilds, or by talking to your local lumberyard or home center manager. Yellow Pages, home shows, and the Internet are other sources. In general, any contractor you consider should be located close to your home, have at least 5 years' experience with your type of project, and have license and insurance, endorsements or certifications.

Once you have a list of prospective contractors, narrow the field with phone interviews. Tell prospects where you live and what you want done. Then ask whether they are interested in the project. If the contractor seems like a good candidate, schedule a home interview.

A meeting at your home gives you the opportunity to gather information from the contractor, such as estimates or price quotes, license numbers and insurance information, and suppliers and references. It also lets you evaluate the contractor's demeanor and work style. Ask when the job can begin, how many people will be on the job, and who will take care of permits. Also discuss the work you will do yourself.

Before you hire a contractor, check references—including a project currently underway, if possible.

Once you've made a selection, meet with the contractor again to make final arrangements and agree on a contract.

Signing Contracts

A good contract protects both you and the contractor. It spells out the work to be done, the payments to be made, and the responsibilities of each party. A contract can be written to include any pertinent details, but it should include the following information:

- Description of the work at the specified address, including any work that you will complete.
- Itemization of the building permits required and who is responsible for obtaining them.

- Start and completion dates, as well as acceptable reasons for delay.
- Final inspection and "make good" arrangements.
- Amount and due date of each payment (usually $\frac{1}{3}$ to $\frac{1}{2}$ of the down payment, with another payment at the project midpoint, and the last 15% or more paid after the work passes your final inspection).
- Change-order clause, specifying provisions and charges for changes made during the project (a markup of 10%-15% is considered reasonable).
- Cleanup, indicating who is responsible for refuse collection and removal.

Planning a Remodel

The best way to prepare for a remodel project is to create a construction plan. Having a complete construction plan enables you to view your entire project at a glance. It helps you identify potential problems, provides sense of the time involved, and establishes a logical order of steps. Without a construction plan, it's easy to make costly mistakes, such as closing up a wall with wallboard before the rough-ins have been inspected.

The general steps shown here follow a typi-cal construction sequence. Your plan may dif-fer at several points, but thinking through each of these steps will help you create a com-plete schedule.

1. Contact the building department.
To avoid any unpleasant—and expensive—surprises, discuss you project with a building official. Find out about the building codes in your area and what you'll need to obtain the applicable permits. Explain how much of the work you plan to do yourself. In some states, plumbing, electrical, and HVAC work must be done by licensed professionals. Also determine what types of drawings you'll need to get per-mits and whether you'll need engineer's drawings and calculations.

2. Create your drawings.
Make your floor plans and elevation drawings (see pages 18 to 19). This step also involves most of the design work for your project; you may want to get help from a professional for this phase (see pages 20 to 21).

3. Get the permits.
Have your final plans reviewed by the building inspector, and make any necessary adjustments required to obtain all of the permits for your project. This is also the time to schedule inspections. Find out what work must be inspected and when to call for inspections.

4. Hire contractors.
If you're getting help with your project, it's best to find and hire the contractors early in the process, as their schedules will affect yours. It may be necessary for some contractors to obtain their own work permits from the build-ing department. To avoid problems, make sure all of the contractors know exactly what work they are being hired to do and what work you will be doing yourself. Always check contrac-tors' references and make sure they're licensed and insured before hiring them. This is also the time to order materials and arrange for delivery.

5. Complete the framing and major mechanical changes.
Begin the construction work with any major structural or mechanical changes. Move mechanical elements and reroute major service lines. Complete any rough-ins that must happen before the framing goes up, such as

Add vapor barriers as required by local code.

Make sure everything is in place before you cover up the framing, then finish the walls and ceilings. If you're installing wallboard, do the ceilings first, then the walls. Tape and finish the wallboard. Install other finish treatments. Texture, prime, and paint the wallboard when it's convenient. If you are installing a suspended ceiling, do so after you finish the walls.

8. Add the finishing touches.
Install doors, moldings, woodwork, cabinets, and built-in-shelving, and lay the floor coverings. The best order for these tasks will depend on the materials you're using and the desired decorative effects.

Install any new plumbing fixtures you have chosen for bathrooms, and complete the drain and supply hook-ups. Make electrical connections, and install all fixtures, devices, and appliances. Get a final inspection from the building inspector.

adding ducts, installing under-floor drains, or replacing old plumbing. Complete the new framing. Build the rough openings for windows and doors, and install the windows.

6. Complete the rough-ins.
Run drain, waste, and vent (DWV), water, and gas-supply lines. Install electrical boxes, and run the wiring. Complete the HVAC rough-ins. Jot down measurements of pipe and locations of wire, for future reference. Have the building inspector approve your work before you close up the walls. Install any fixtures that go in during the rough-in stage (others will come after the wall surfaces are installed).

7. Finish the walls and ceilings.
After your work has passed inspection, insulate the walls, ceilings, and pipes. Install fiberglass insulation used as fireblocking. Make sure protector plates for pipes and wires running through framing are in place.

BASIC TECHNIQUES

Rough Carpentry

Rough carpentry includes the demolition and framing work that changes the shape of your house: removing old walls, building new ones, and expanding or adding openings for doors and windows. For finish carpentry projects, such as installing paneling and trim, turn to the Walls & Ceilings section of this book.

Many remodeling projects actually begin with demolition, and the basic procedures are the same whether you're working with door and window framing on exterior walls or altering interior walls. The first step is to determine how your house was framed (see pages 8 to 11). This will dictate the proper steps for creating wall openings or removing walls altogether.

After inspecting the walls for hidden mechanicals and rerouting any utility lines in the project area, you're ready to remove the interior wall surfaces (see pages 27 to 31). If you're replacing old windows and doors, now is the time to remove them as well (see pages 146 to 147). Where necessary, you can also remove exterior wall surfaces (see pages 32 to 35), but don't remove any framing members yet.

The next step will depend on the nature of your project. If you're removing a load-bearing wall or creating a new or enlarged opening in one, you'll need to build temporary supports to shore up the ceiling while the work is being done (see pages 36 to 39). Keep in mind that all exterior walls are load-bearing. Temporary supports are not necessary for removing non loadbearing (partition) walls.

With the supports in place, you can safely complete the framing work for the project.

Removing Interior Surfaces

Before you tear into a wall with a hammer or power saw, you need to know what lies inside. Start by checking for hidden mechanicals in the project area. Wiring that's in the way can be moved fairly easily, as can water supply pipes and drain vents. If it's gas piping, drain pipe, or ducting, however, you'll probably have to call a professional before you can move to the next step.

It's also a good idea to locate all of the framing members in the project area. Marking all of the studs, plates, and blocking will help guide your cuts and prevent unpleasant surprises.

When you're ready to begin demolition, prepare the work area to help contain dust and minimize damage to flooring and other surfaces—tearing out wallboard and plaster creates a very fine dust that easily finds its way into neighboring rooms. Cover doorways (even closed ones) and openings with plastic sheeting. Tape plastic over HVAC registers to prevent dust from circulating through the system. Protect floors with cardboard or hardboard and plastic or dropcloths. Also, carefully remove any trim from the project area, cutting painted joints with a utility knife to reduce the damage to the finish.

As an added precaution, turn off the power to all circuits in the work area, and shut off the main water supply if you'll be making cuts near water pipes.

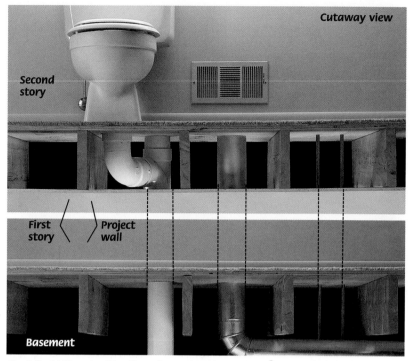

Check for hidden plumbing lines, ductwork, wiring, and gas pipes before cutting into a wall. To locate the lines, examine the areas directly below and above the project wall. In most cases, pipes, utility lines, and ductwork run through the wall vertically between floors. Original blueprints for your house should show the location of many of the utility lines.

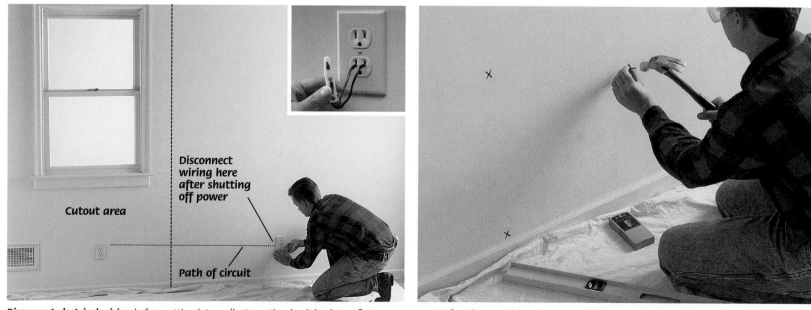

Disconnect electrical wiring before cutting into walls. Trace the circuit back to a fixture outside the cutout area, then shut off the power and disconnect the wires leading into the cutout area. Turn the power back on and test for current with a circuit tester (inset) before cutting into the walls.

Locate framing members using a stud finder or by knocking on the wall and feeling for solid points. Verify the findings by driving finish nails through the wall surface. After finding the center of one stud, measure over 16" to locate neighboring studs.

Removing Wallboard

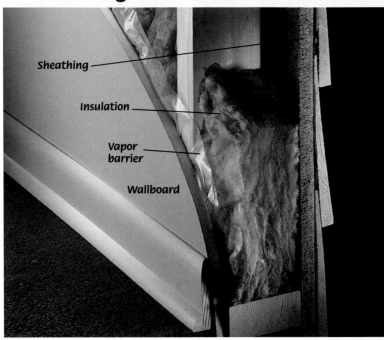

A typical wall consists of wallboard, vapor barrier, insulation, and sheathing. Wallboard in houses typically is between ⅜" and ⅝" thick, with ½" the most common for walls.

Wallboard is easy to remove. For most jobs, it's merely a matter of making cuts at the edges of the planned opening, then smashing up the board in between. Keep in mind that wallboard seams are covered with paper tape and wallboard compound. To make a clean break between panels, cut through the center of the joint with a utility knife (this is especially important at corners).

Remove enough wallboard to make plenty of room to install new framing members. When framing for a window or door, remove the wallboard from floor to ceiling and all the way to the first wall studs on either side of the planned rough opening. If the wallboard was attached with construction adhesive, clean the framing members with a rasp or an old chisel.

Before you start, shut off the power and inspect the wall for wiring and plumbing (see page 27).

Tools: Protective eye wear, dust mask, stud finder, chalk line, circular saw with demolition blade, utility knife, pry bar, drill or screwgun.

Tips for Removing Wallboard

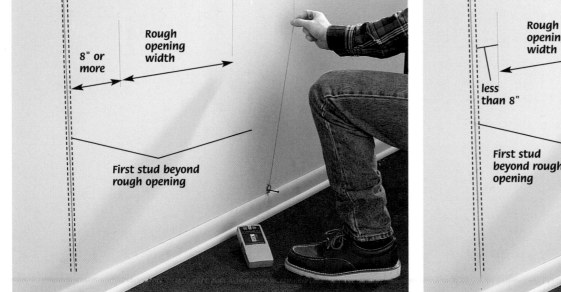

Mark the width of the planned rough opening on the wall, and locate the first stud on either side of the opening. If the rough opening is more than 8" from the next stud, use a chalk line to mark a cutting line on the inside edge of the stud. During framing, an extra stud will be attached to provide backing for the new wallboard (see page 197).

VARIATION: If the rough opening is less than 8" from the next stud, you will not have room to attach an extra stud. Use a chalk line to mark the cutting line down the center of the wall stud. The exposed portion of the stud will provide backing for the new wallboard.

Removing Wallboard

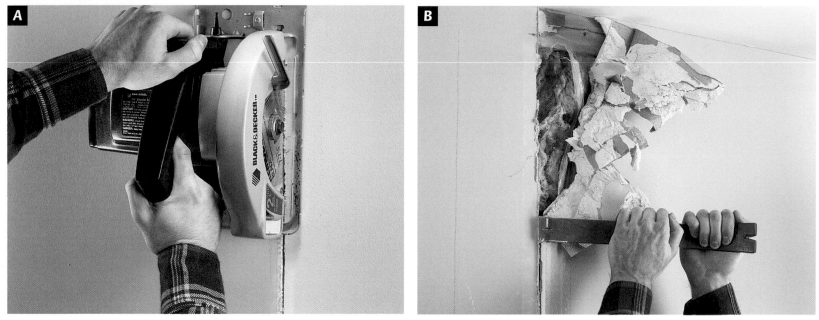

A

Make cutting lines (see page 28). Set a circular saw to the thickness of the wallboard, then cut from floor to ceiling along both cutting lines. Use a utility knife to finish the cuts at the top and bottom and to cut through the taped horizontal seam where the wall meets the ceiling surface. Always wear eye protection and a dust mask when cutting wallboard with a power saw.

B

Insert the end of a pry bar into the cut, near a corner of the opening. Pull the pry bar until the wallboard breaks, then tear away the broken pieces. Take care to avoid damaging the wallboard outside the planned rough opening.

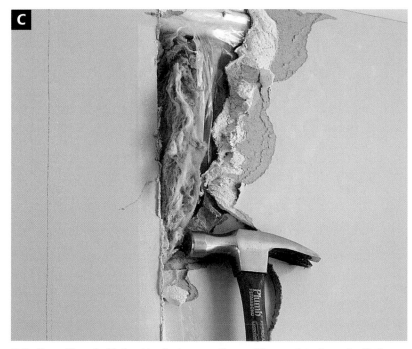

C

Strike the wallboard with the side of a hammer, then pull it away from the wall with the pry bar or your hands.

D

Remove nails, screws, and any remaining wallboard from the framing members, using a pry bar or a drill (or screwgun). Remove any vapor barrier and insulation.

Removing Plaster

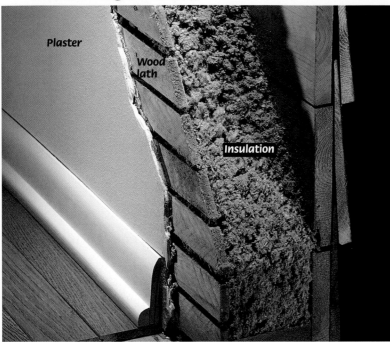

Plaster removal is a dusty job, so always wear eye protection and a dust mask during demolition, and use sheets of plastic to protect furniture and to block open doorways. Also cover the floors well; plaster contains sand and is very abrasive underfoot. Plaster walls are very brittle, so work carefully to avoid cracking the plaster beyond the area to be removed.

If the plaster you're removing covers most of the wall surface, consider removing the whole interior surface of the wall. Replacing the entire wall with wallboard is easier and produces better results than trying to patch around a project area.

Before you start, shut off the power and inspect the wall for wiring and plumbing (see page 27).

Tools: Protective eye wear, dust mask, work gloves, chalk line, straightedge, utility knife, reciprocating saw or jig saw, aviation snips, pry bar.

Materials: Masking tape, scrap 2 × 4.

Plaster walls usually consist of three layers: plaster surface, wood lath, and insulation. Sometimes these walls include a layer of metal lath over the wood lath (see variation, page 31).

Removing Plaster

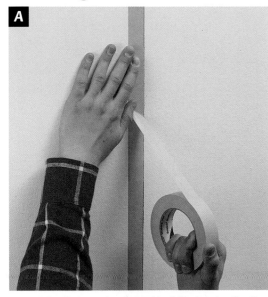

A

Mark the wall area to be removed by following the directions on page 28. Apply a double layer of masking tape along the outside edge of each cutting line.

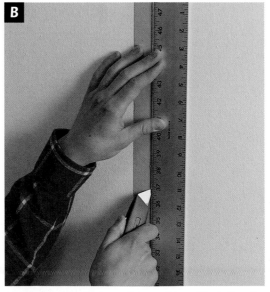

B

Score each cutting line several times with a utility knife, using a straightedge as a guide. The lines should be at least ⅛" deep.

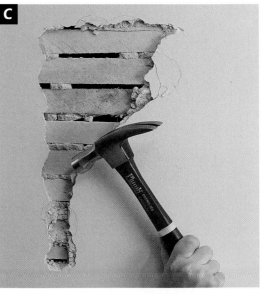

C

Beginning at the top of the wall in the center of the planned opening, break up the plaster by striking the wall lightly with the side of a hammer. Clear away all plaster—from floor to ceiling—within 3" of the cutting lines.

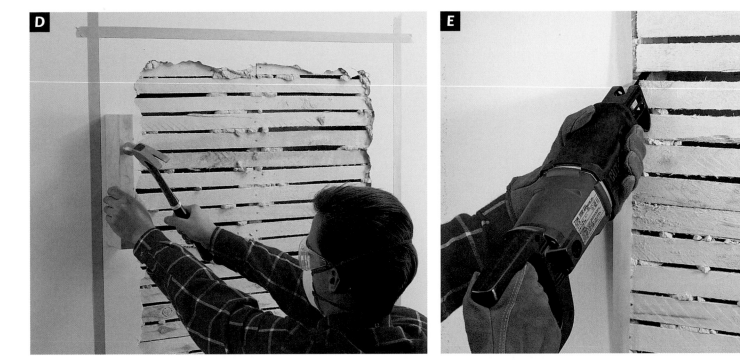

Break the plaster along the edges by holding a scrap piece of 2 × 4 on edge just inside the scored lines, and rapping it with a hammer. Use a pry bar to remove the remaining plaster.

Cut through the lath along the edges of the plaster, using a reciprocating saw or jig saw.

Metal lath

VARIATION: If the wall has metal lath laid over the wood lath, use aviation snips to clip the edges of the metal lath. Press the jagged edges of the lath flat against the stud. The cut edges of metal lath are very sharp; be sure to wear heavy work gloves.

Remove the lath from the studs, using a pry bar. Pry away any remaining nails, and remove any vapor barrier and insulation.

Removing Exterior Surfaces

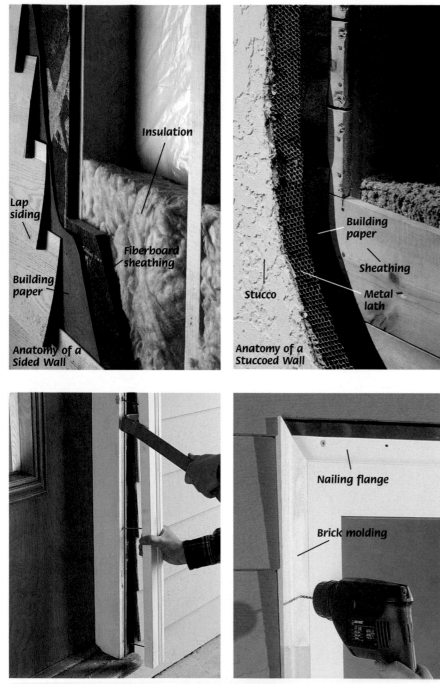

Anatomy of a Sided Wall

Insulation

Lap siding

Fiberboard sheathing

Building paper

Anatomy of a Stuccoed Wall

Building paper

Sheathing

Stucco

Metal lath

Brick molding *comes preattached to most wood-frame window and door units. To remove the molding, pry along the outside of the frame to avoid marring the exposed parts of the jambs and molding.*

Nailing flange

Brick molding

Nailing flanges *provide means of attachment for most vinyl windows. After installation, the nailing flanges are covered with brick molding, 1 × exterior trim, or channel trim for vinyl or metal siding.*

Exterior surfaces must be removed when you create or enlarge an opening for a door or window in an exterior wall. Determine the best method for your project based on the exterior surface you have and the type of door or window unit you plan to install.

Wood siding can be cut in place or removed in full pieces to expose the area for the door or window opening. For doors and windows with brick molding, you can temporarily set the unit in place, trace around the brick molding onto the wood siding, then cut the siding to fit exactly around the molding. This method is shown on pages 148 to 149.

An alternative method is to remove the brick molding from the door or window unit, then cut the siding roughly flush with the framed rough opening. After the unit is installed, temporarily set the molding in place and trace around it onto the siding. Cut the siding, then permanently attach the molding to the unit frame. Use this method to install a window with nailing flanges, but be sure to remove enough siding during the initial cut to provide room for the flanges.

With vinyl or metal siding, it's best to remove whole pieces of siding to expose the opening, then cut them to fit after the unit and molding are installed. Be aware that vinyl and metal siding typically require special trim around openings. Check with the siding manufacturer before cutting anything, to make sure all of the necessary pieces are available.

Stucco surfaces can be cut away so that brick molding is recessed into the wall surface and makes contact with the sheathing. Or, you can use masonry clips (see page 165) and install the unit with the molding on top of the stucco. (See pages 188 to 189 for more information on stucco construction.)

If you're installing a door or window in a new framed opening, don't remove the exterior surface until the framing is complete. Always shut off the power and reroute utility lines before cutting into a wall. To protect the wall cavities against moisture, cover new openings as soon as you remove the exterior surface.

Tools: *Stapler, flat pry bar, zip tool, drill, chalk line, circular saw, reciprocating saw, masonry chisel and hammer, masonry-cutting blade, masonry bit, aviation snips.*

Materials: *Building paper, nails, 1 × 4.*

Tips for Removing Siding

Remove whole pieces of siding to expose the area around a door or window opening. Siding is installed in a staggered pattern so that joints between successive rows do not line up. Number the siding pieces as you remove them to simplify reinstallation.

Patch-in building paper after removing siding. Loosen the building paper above the patch area, slip the top of the patch underneath, and attach it with staples. Use roofing cement to patch small holes or tears. Do not leave any sheathing exposed to the elements.

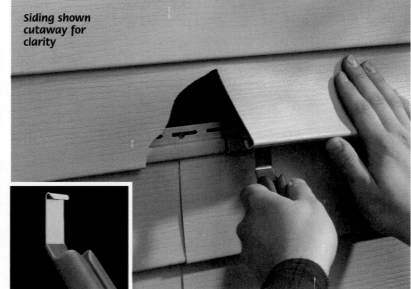

Siding shown cutaway for clarity

To remove a piece of wood siding, start by prying up the piece above, using a flat pry bar near nail locations. Knock the top piece back down with a hammer to expose the raised nails, then pull the nails. Insert spacers between the siding and sheathing to make it easier to access work areas. Use a hacksaw blade or a cold chisel to shear any difficult nails.

Vinyl and metal siding pieces have a locking J-channel that fits over the bottom of the nailing strip on the piece below. Use a zip tool (inset) to separate the siding panels. Insert the zip tool at the overlapping seam nearest the removal area. Slide the zip tool over the J-channel, pulling outward slightly, to unlock the joint from the siding below. Remove nails from the panel, then push the panel down to unlock it. **Caution:** Metal siding will buckle if bent too far.

Cutting Wood Siding

A

To cut wood siding to expose a framed opening start from inside the house. Drill through the wall at the corners of the framed opening. Then push nails through the holes to mark their locations. For round-top windows, drill holes around the curved outline.

B

Now from the outside, measure the distance between the nails to make sure the dimensions are accurate. Mark the cutting lines with a chalk line stretched between the nails. Push the nails back through the wall.

C

Nail a straight 1 × 4 flush with the inside edge of the right cutting line. Sink the nail heads with a nail set to keep them from scratching the foot of the saw. Set the depth of the circular saw blade so it will cut through the siding only.

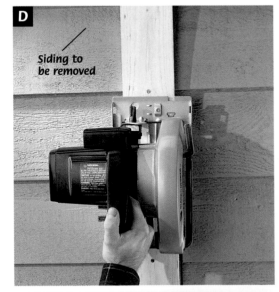

D

Siding to be removed

Rest the saw on the 1 × 4, and cut along the line, using the edge of the board as a guide. Stop the cuts about 1" short of the corners to prevent cutting into the framing members.

E

Siding to be removed

Reposition the board, and make the remaining cuts. To make the final cut, position the board on the outside of the cutout. Drive the nails within 1½" of the inside edge of the board, because the siding under this area will be removed to make room for the door or window trim.

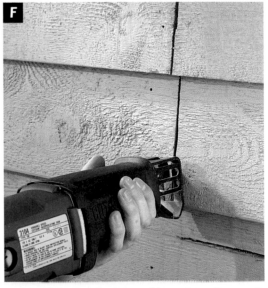

F

Complete the cuts at the corners with a reciprocating saw, jig saw, or chisel. Remove the cut-out wall section. If you wish, remove the siding pieces from the sheathing and save them for future use.

Removing Stucco

Drill corners and mark cutting lines with a chalk line (see page 34). Measure out from the chalk line the same distance as the width of the molding on the window or door unit. Make a second set of lines at the outer marks (the added margin will allow the brick molding to fit tight against the wall sheathing). Score the stucco surface around the outer lines, using a masonry chisel and hammer. The scored grooves should be at least ⅛" deep.

Make straight cuts using a circular saw and masonry-cutting blade. Make several passes with the saw, gradually deepening the cuts until the blade just cuts through the metal lath, causing sparks to fly. Stop the cuts just ahead of the corners to avoid damaging the stucco past the cutting line; complete the cuts with a masonry chisel.

VARIATION: For round-top windows, mark the outline on the stucco, using a cardboard template. Drill a series of holes around the outline, using a masonry bit. Complete the cut with a masonry chisel.

Break up the stucco with a masonry hammer or sledgehammer, exposing the underlying metal lath. Use aviation snips to cut through the lath around the opening. Use a pry bar to pull away the lath and attached stucco.

Outline the rough opening on the sheathing, using a straightedge as a guide. Cut the rough opening along the inside edge of the framing members, using a circular saw or reciprocating saw. Remove the cut section of sheathing.

Making Temporary Supports

Temporary top plate

Bottom plate (found only in platform framing)

Hydraulic jacks

Temporary bottom plate

Temporary supports for a platform-frame house must support the ceiling joists, since the ceiling platform carries the load of the upper floors. Platform framing can be identified by the bottom plate to which the wall studs are nailed.

Whaler

Braces

Planned rough opening

Temporary supports for a balloon-frame house support the wall studs, which carry the upstairs load. The temporary support header, called a *whaler*, is anchored to the wall studs above the planned rough opening, and is supported by wall studs and bracing adjacent to the rough opening. Balloon framing can be identified by long wall studs that pass uncut through the floor to a sill plate resting on the foundation.

If your project involves removing more than one stud in a load-bearing wall, you'll need to build temporary supports before making any changes to the framing. To identify a load-bearing wall, see page 11. The techniques for making temporary supports vary, depending on whether your house is built with platform framing or balloon framing.

Platform framing is found in most homes built after 1930. To make temporary supports, use hydraulic jacks (see page 37) or a temporary stud wall (see page 38). The stud-wall method is a better choice if the supports must remain in place for more than one day.

If the ceiling and floor joists run parallel to the wall you are working on, use the method shown at the bottom of page 38.

Balloon framing is found in many homes built before 1930. To make temporary supports in a balloon-frame house, use the method shown on page 39. The project shown involves building a support structure for an exterior wall on the first floor of a balloon-frame house. Consult a professional if you want to make changes to an interior load-bearing wall or an exterior wall on an upper floor of a balloon-frame house.

Some remodeling jobs require two temporary supports. For example, when making a large opening in or removing an interior load-bearing wall, you must install supports on both sides of the wall (see page 42).

NOTE: Load-bearing walls longer than 12 ft. should be removed only by professionals.

Tools: Circular saw, hydraulic jacks, level, drill and $\frac{3}{16}$" bit and spade bit, ratchet wrench.

Materials: 2 × 4 lumber, 10d nails, $\frac{3}{8}$ × 3" and $\frac{3}{8}$ × 4" lag screws, cloth, tapered wood shims, 2 × 8 lumber, 2" wallboard screws, nailing plates.

Supporting Platform Framing with Jacks (joists perpendicular to project wall)

A

Measure the width of the planned rough opening and add 4 ft. so the temporary support will reach well past the rough opening. Cut three 2 × 4s to that length. Nail two of the 2 × 4s together with 10d nails to make a top plate for the temporary support; the remaining 2 × 4 will be the bottom plate. Place the temporary bottom plate on the floor, 3 ft. from the wall, centering it on the planned rough opening.

B

Set the hydraulic jacks on the temporary bottom plate, 2 ft. in from the ends. (Use three jacks if the opening will be more than 8 ft. wide.) For each jack, build a post by nailing together a pair of 2 × 4s. The posts should be about 4" shorter than the distance between the ceiling and the top of the jacks. Attach the posts to the top plate, 2 ft. from the ends, using countersunk 3" lag screws.

C

Direction of joists

Cover the top plate with a thick layer of cloth to protect the ceiling from marks and cracks, then lift the support structure onto the hydraulic jacks.

D

Adjust the support structure so the posts are exactly plumb, and raise the hydraulic jacks until the top plate just begins to lift the ceiling. Do not lift too far or you may damage the floor or ceiling.

Supporting Platform Framing with a Stud Wall (joists perpendicular to project wall)

Build a 2 × 4 stud wall that is 4 ft. wider than the planned wall opening and 1¾" shorter than the distance from the floor to the ceiling. Space the studs about 16" on-center.

Raise up the stud wall and position it 3 ft. from the project wall, centered on the planned rough opening.

Slide a 2 × 4 top plate between the temporary wall and the ceiling. Check to make sure the wall is plumb, and drive shims under the top plate at 12" intervals until the wall is wedged tightly in place.

Supporting Platform Framing with Jacks (joists parallel to project wall)

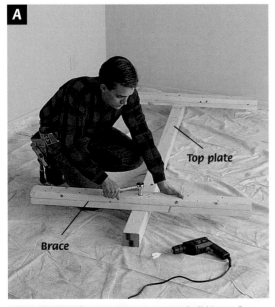

Follow the directions on page 37, except: build two 4-ft.-long cross braces, using pairs of 2 × 4s nailed together. Attach the cross braces to the double top plate, 1 ft. from the ends, using countersunk 3" lag screws.

Place a 2 × 4 bottom plate directly over a floor joist, then set hydraulic jacks on it. For each jack, nail together two 2 × 4s, 8" shorter than the jack-to-ceiling distance. Nail these posts to the top plate, 2 ft. from the ends. Cover the braces with thick cloth, and set the support structure on the jacks.

Adjust the support structure so the posts are exactly plumb, and pump the hydraulic jacks until the cross braces just begin to lift the ceiling. Do not lift too far or you may damage the ceiling or floor.

Supporting Balloon Framing

A

Whaler

Planned rough opening

Remove the wall surfaces around the rough opening from floor to ceiling (see pages 27 to 31). Make a whaler by cutting a 2 × 8 long enough to extend at least 20" past each side of the planned rough opening. Center the whaler against the wall studs, flush with the ceiling. Tack the whaler in place with 2" wallboard screws.

B

Nailing plate

Cut two lengths of 2 × 4 to fit snugly between the bottom of the whaler and the floor. Slide the 2 × 4s into place at the ends of the whaler, and attach them with nailing plates and 10d nails.

C

Drill two ³⁄₁₆" holes through the whaler and into each stud it spans. Secure the whaler with ³⁄₈ × 4" lag screws.

D

Drive tapered shims between the bottom of each temporary 2 × 4 and the floor to help secure the support structure.

After

Header made
from two pieces
of MicroLam®

Post

Post

Spacing
blocks

Spacing
blocks

Nailing strip

Before

Removing a wall can open up a room, join two rooms, or add usable living space. A load-bearing wall must be replaced by a header and posts to carry the weight once borne by the wall. You may have to remove the wall surface to determine if the wall is load-bearing. **NOTE:** Load-bearing walls over 12 ft. long should be removed only by professionals.

Removing Walls

Removing an existing wall dramatically changes a room. The project is not complicated, but it may involve serious structural considerations. The first step is to determine whether the wall you want to remove is load-bearing or non-load-bearing (see page 11). You'll also need to check for mechanical lines in the wall and decide whether the lines can be moved (see page 27).

If the wall is non-load-bearing, you can simply tear it out once the mechanicals are dealt with. If it's load-bearing, you must build a temporary support on both sides of the wall to carry the floor joists above before removing the wall (see pages 36 to 39). With the wall gone, you're ready to install a permanent beam, or *header*, to span the new opening. A typical header is 3½" wide—the same as standard wall framing—and is supported on both ends by posts made from two 2 × 4s. The posts are hidden inside the adjacent walls; the header remains visible, but covering it with wallboard helps it blend with the ceiling.

Sizing the header (width) for your project is critical: it's based on the length of the header, the material it's made from, and the weight of the load it must support (the number of floors above).

In the projects that follow, you'll see how to remove a wall and install a permanent header to replace a load-bearing wall in a platform-frame house. The procedures for removing a load-bearing wall in a balloon-frame house are quite different, and you should consult a professional for help with that type of project.

Header Sizes

The recommended header sizes shown here are suitable for projects where a full story and roof are located above the rough opening. This chart is intended for rough estimations only. For actual requirements, contact your local building department.

Rough Opening Width	Header Size & Construction
Up to 3 ft.	½" plywood between two 2 × 4s
3 ft. to 4 ft.	½" plywood between two 2 × 6s
4 ft. to 6 ft.	½" plywood between two 2 × 8s
6 ft. to 7 ft.	½" plywood between two 2 × 10s
7 ft. to 8 ft.	½" plywood between two 2 × 12s
8 ft. to 12 ft.	*See Header Materials, below*

Tools: Protective eye wear, dust mask, stud finder, chalk line, circular saw with demolition and standard blades, utility knife, pry bar, drill, reciprocating saw, hydraulic jacks, ratchet wrench, level.

Materials (for installing a header): 2 × dimension lumber, ⅜ × 3" lag screws, cloth, MicroLam® framing members, 10d common nails, wood glue.

Header Materials

Beam made from 2 × 12s and plywood: 8-ft. maximum recommended span.

Double 9½" MicroLam beam: 10-ft. maximum recommended span. MicroLam framing members are made from thin layers of wood laminate glued together.

Double 11⅜" MicroLam beam: 11-ft. maximum recommended span.

12" Glue-lam beam: 12-ft. maximum recommended span. Glue-lam beams are made from layers of dimension lumber laminated together.

Wood beams for headers *can be made in a variety of ways. Manufactured beams are stronger and more durable than those made from dimension lumber, and they can carry more weight in smaller sizes. Consult your local building department or a qualified contractor when choosing materials and sizes for a header.*

Removing a Wall (platform framing)

Turn off power and water to the area. Prepare the project site. Remove or reroute any wiring, plumbing lines, or ductwork. Remove the wall surfaces (see pages 27 to 31).

Remove enough of the surface of the adjoining walls to expose the permanent studs.

Determine if the wall being removed is load-bearing (see page 11). If the wall is load-bearing, install temporary supports on each side (see pages 36 to 39).

Remove the studs by cutting them through the middle with a reciprocating saw and prying them away from the bottom and top plates.

Remove the final stud on each end of the wall. If the wall being removed is load-bearing, also remove any nailing studs or blocking in the adjoining walls directly behind the removed wall.

Make two cuts through the top plate, at least 3" apart. Remove the cut section with a pry bar.

Remove the remaining sections of the top plate, using a pry bar.

Cut out a 3"-wide section of the bottom plate. Pry out the entire bottom plate. If the removed wall was load-bearing, install a permanent header (see pages 44 to 45).

Tips For Removing a Section of Wall

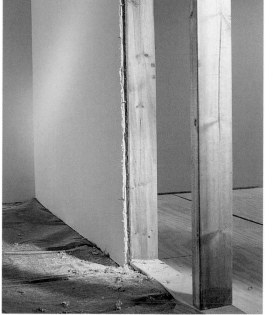

When removing wall surfaces, expose the wall to the first permanent stud at each side of the opening.

Leave a small portion of exposed bottom plate to serve as the base for posts. In a load-bearing wall, leave 3" of bottom plate to hold the double 2 × 4 post that will support the permanent header. In a non-load-bearing wall, leave 1½" of exposed bottom plate to hold one extra wall stud. Remove the top plates over the entire width of the opening. (See Tip, page 45).

Installing a Permanent Header (platform framing)

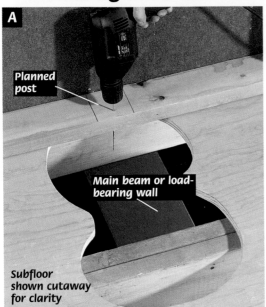

A

Planned post

Main beam or load-bearing wall

Subfloor shown cutaway for clarity

Mark the location of the planned support posts on the bottom plate. Drill through the bottom plate where the support posts will rest to make sure there is a joist directly underneath. If not, install blocking under the post locations (step B).

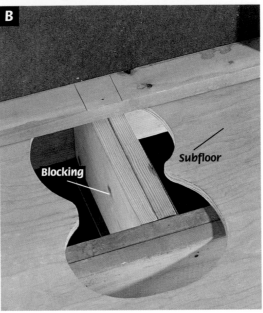

B

Blocking

Subfloor

If necessary, cut and install double 2 × blocking between joists. (You may need to cut into a finished ceiling to gain access to this space.) The blocking should be the same size lumber as the joists. Attach blocks to the joists with 10d nails.

C

Build a support header to span the width of the removed wall, including the width of the support posts. (See page 41 for header recommendations.) In this project, the header is built with two lengths of MicroLam® joined with 10d nails.

D

Temporary supports not shown for clarity

First ceiling joist

Lay the ends of the header on the bottom plates. Find the length for each support post by measuring between the top of the header and the bottom of the first ceiling joist in from the wall.

E

Make support posts by cutting pairs of 2 × 4s to length and joining them side by side with wood glue and 10d nails.

F

A

B

A

B

Measure the thickness (A) and width (B) of the top plate at each end, then notch the top corners of the header to fit around the top plates, using a reciprocating saw (inset).

Lift the header against the ceiling joists, then set the posts under the ends of the header. If the header will not fit due to sagging ceiling joists, raise the joists by jacking up or shimming the temporary supports (see page 37).

Toenail the posts to the header with 10d nails.

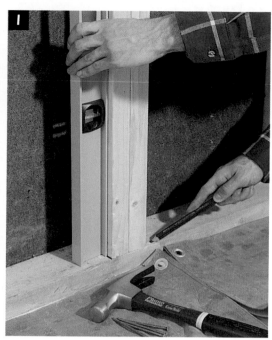

Check each post for plumb with a level. Adjust the post if necessary by tapping the bottom with a hammer. When the post is plumb, mark a reference line on the bottom plate, and toenail each post to the bottom plate.

Cut 2 × 4 nailing strips and attach them to each side of the post and header with 10d nails. Nailing strips provide a surface for attaching new wallboard.

Temporary supports not shown for clarity

Cut and toenail spacing blocks to fit into the gaps between the permanent studs and the nailing strips. Remove the temporary supports. Patch the wall and, if desired, finish the header with wallboard (see pages 196 to 202).

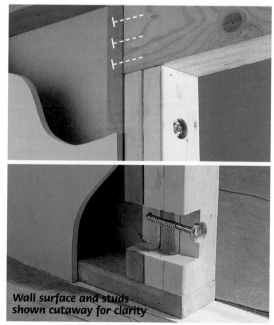

Wall surface and studs shown cutaway for clarity

TIP: When removing a section of a wall, endnail the wall studs to the header with 10d nails, (top) and attach the posts to the wall studs with countersunk lag screws (bottom).

Building Partition Walls

Wall studs · Top plate · Cripple stud · Header · Jack stud · King stud · Bottom plate

A typical partition wall consists of top and bottom plates and 2 × 4 studs spaced 16" on center, and may contain a door frame. 2 × 6 walls provide more space for large pipes (inset).

Partition walls are non-load-bearing walls used to define many of the rooms in your house. While interior load-bearing walls are always perpendicular to floor joists, partition walls can run perpendicular or parallel to joists. Partition walls are typically built with 2 × 4 lumber but can also be built with 3⅝" steel studs (see pages 50 to 51). Walls that will hold large plumbing pipes can be framed with 2 × 6 lumber. For basement walls that sit on bare concrete, use pressure-treated lumber for the bottom plates. Partition walls need only support their own weight, but they must be installed over joists or be supported by blocking between joists.

This project involves building a partition wall in place, rather than framing a complete wall on the floor and tilting it upright, as in new construction. The build-in-place method allows for variations in floor and ceiling levels and is generally much easier for remodeling projects.

If your wall will include a door or other opening, see pages 52 to 54 before laying out the wall. Check the local building codes for requirements about fireblocking in partition walls. And after your walls are framed and the mechanical rough-ins are completed, install metal protector plates where pipes and wires run through framing members (see page 196).

> **Tools:** Chalk line, circular saw, framing square, combination square, plumb bob, powder-actuated nailer, T-bevel.
>
> **Materials:** 2 × 4 lumber, 2 × blocking lumber, 16d and 8d common nails, concrete fasteners, wallboard screws.

Tips for Supporting Top Plates

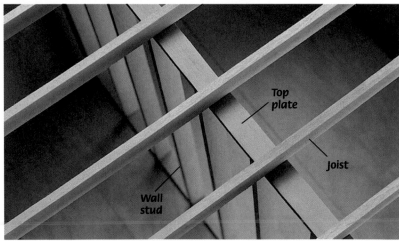

Top plate · Joist · Wall stud

When a new wall is perpendicular to the ceiling or floor joists above, attach the top plate directly to the joists, using 16d nails.

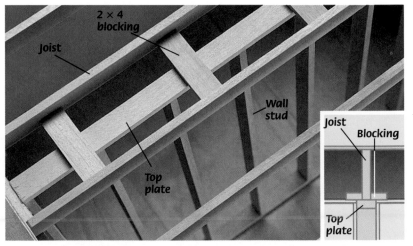

2 × 4 blocking · Joist · Wall stud · Top plate · Joist · Blocking · Top plate

When a new wall falls between parallel joists, install 2 × 4 blocking between the joists every 24". The blocking supports the new wall's top plate and provides backing for the ceiling wallboard. If the new wall is aligned with a parallel joist, install blocking on both sides of the wall, and attach the top plate to the joist (inset).

Tips for Supporting Bottom Plates

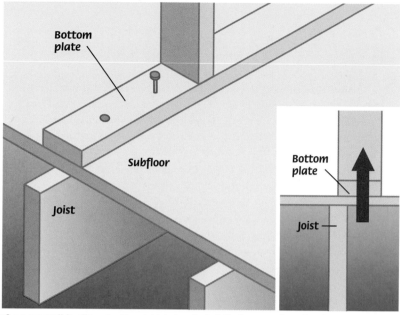

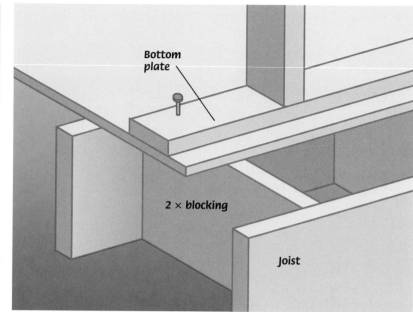

If a new wall is aligned with a joist below, install the bottom plate directly over the joist or off-center over the joist (inset). Off-center placement allows you to nail into the joist but provides room underneath the plate for pipes or wiring to go up into the wall.

If a new wall falls between parallel joists, install 2 × 6 or larger blocking between the two joists below, spaced 24" on center. Nail the bottom plate through the subfloor and into the blocking.

Framing a Partition Wall

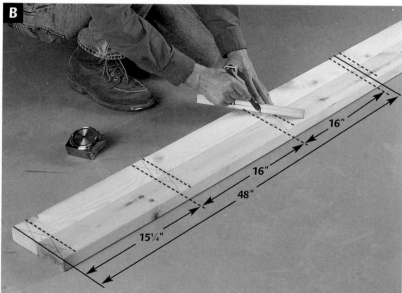

Mark the location of the leading edge of the new wall's top plate, then snap a chalk line through the marks across the joists or blocks. Use a framing square, or take measurements, to make sure the line is perpendicular to any intersecting walls. Cut the top and bottom plates to length.

Set the plates together with their ends flush. Measure from the end of one plate, and make marks for the location of each stud. The first stud should fall 15¼" from the end; every stud thereafter should fall 16" on center. Thus, the first 4 × 8-ft. wallboard panel will cover the first stud and "break" in the center of the fourth stud. Use a square to extend the marks across both plates. Draw an "X" at each stud location.

Continued on next page

Framing a Partition Wall (cont.)

Position the top plate against the joists, aligning its leading edge with the chalk line. Attach the plate with two 16d nails driven into each joist. Start at one end, and adjust the plate as you go to keep the leading edge flush with the chalk line.

To position the bottom plate, hang a plumb bob from the side edge of the top plate so the point nearly touches the floor. When it hangs motionless, mark the point's location on the floor. Make plumb markings at each end of the top plate, then snap a chalk line between the marks. Position the bottom plate along the chalk line, and use the plumb bob to align the stud markings between the two plates.

Fasten the bottom plate to the floor. On concrete, use a powder-actuated nailer or masonry screws (see pages 323 to 324), driving a pin or screw every 16". On wood floors, use 16d nails driven into the joists below.

Measure between the plates for the length of each stud. Cut each stud so it fits snugly in place but is not so tight that it bows the joists above. If you cut a stud too short, see if it will fit somewhere else down the wall.

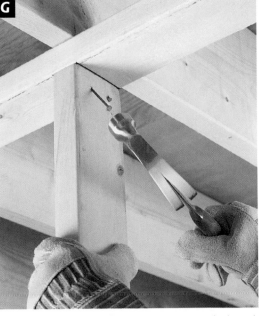

Install the studs by toenailing them at a 60° angle through the sides of the studs and into the plates. At each end, drive two 8d nails through one side of the stud and one more through the center on the other side.

Tips for Framing Corners

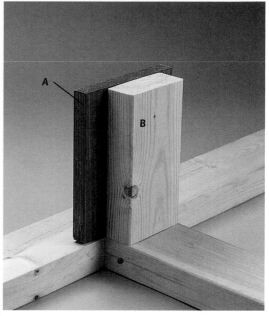

L-corners: Nail 2 × 4 spacers (A) to the inside of the end stud. Nail an extra stud (B) to the spacers. The extra stud provides a surface to attach wallboard at the inside corner.

T-corner meets stud: Fasten 2 × 2 backers (A) to each side of the side-wall stud (B). The backers provide a nailing surface for wallboard.

T-corner between studs: Fasten a 1 × 6 backer (A) to the end stud (B) with wallboard screws. The backer provides a nailing surface for wallboard.

Framing an Angled Partition Wall in an Attic

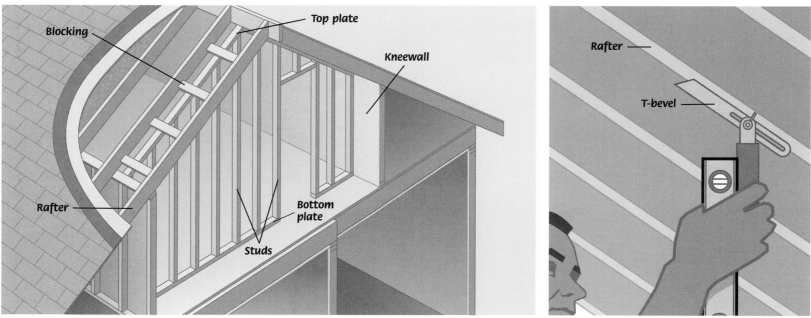

Full-size attic partition walls typically run parallel to the rafters and have sloping top plates that extend down to knee walls on either side. To build one, cut the top and bottom plates, and mark the stud locations on the bottom plate only. Nail the top plates in place, and use a plumb bob to position the bottom plate, as with a standard wall. Use the plumb bob again to transfer the stud layout marks from the bottom to the top plate. To find the proper angle for cutting the top ends of the studs, set a level against the top plate (or rafter) and hold it plumb. Then, rest the handle of a T-bevel against the level, and adjust the T-bevel blade to follow the plate. Transfer the angle to the stud ends, and cut them to length.

Framing with Steel

Steel framing is quickly becoming a popular alternative to wood in residential construction due to the rising cost of wood and the advantages that steel offers. Steel framing is fireproof, insect proof, highly rot-resistant, and usable almost anywhere wood framing would normally be used.

Available in different widths and thicknesses at most home centers, the most common steel studs and tracks (plates) are 25-ga. steel and are designed for non-load-bearing partition walls and soffits. Consult a professional if you plan to build a steel-frame load-bearing wall.

With a few exceptions, the layout and framing methods used for a steel-frame partition wall are the same as for a wood-frame wall. For more information on framing partition walls see page 46; see pages 327 to 329 for help with framing soffits.

However, there are a few things to keep in mind when working with steel:
• Steel framing is fastened together with screws, not nails. Attach steel tracks to existing wood framing using long wallboard screws. Use locking C-clamp pliers to hold the tracks and studs together while screwing the steel framing together.

• Even pressure and slow drill speed make it easy to start screws. Drive the screws down tight, but be careful not to strip the steel. Do not use drill-point screws with 25-gauge steel, which can strip easily.
• Most steel studs have punch-outs for running plumbing and electrical lines through the framing. These punch-outs need to be lined up to work properly. Cut each stud to length from the same end, to keep the punch-outs lined up.
• The hand-cut edges of steel framing are very sharp; wear heavy gloves when handling them.

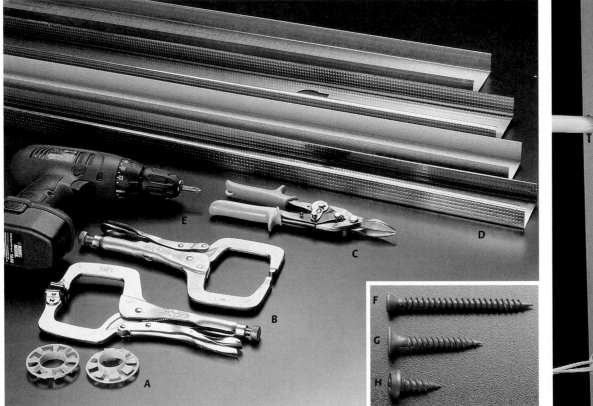

Steel framing tools and materials include: plastic spacers (A), locking C-clamp pliers (B), aviation snips (C), 25-ga. track and studs (D), and drill or screwgun (E). Use self-tapping screws (inset) to fasten steel components. To install moldings and casings, use a type S trim-head screw (F). To fasten drywall, use a type S bugle-head wallboard screw (G). To fasten studs and tracks together use a 7/16" type S pan-head screw (often called a framing screw) (H).

Run electrical and plumbing lines through pre-formed punch-outs in each stud. Building codes require that metal plumbing pipe and electrical cable be run through a plastic spacer in each punch-out—to prevent galvanic action and electrification of the wall. Install the studs 16" on center, taking care to align the punch-outs. Install wood blocking where needed for hanging decorative accessories or wainscoting.

Tips for Framing with Steel

Cut steel tracks and studs to size with aviation snips. Cut through the side flanges first, then bend the waste piece back and cut across the web.

Install the studs by clamping them to the track with locking C-clamp pliers. Then, drive a screw through the track into the stud. Drive one screw at the top and bottom of each side of the stud.

Frame door openings 3" wider and 1½" taller than normal, then wrap the openings with 2 × 4s to simplify hanging the door. Use track for the steel header piece: Make fastening tabs by cutting the flanges and bending down the ends at 90°.

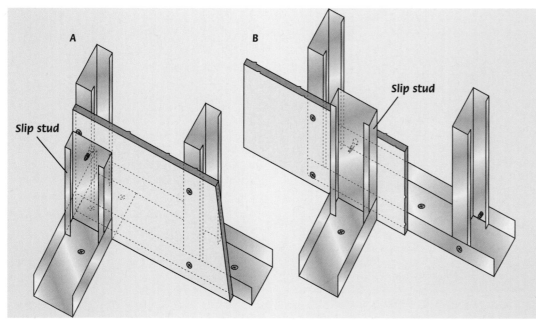

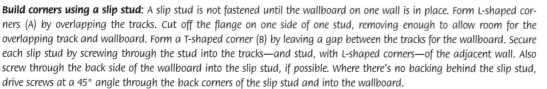

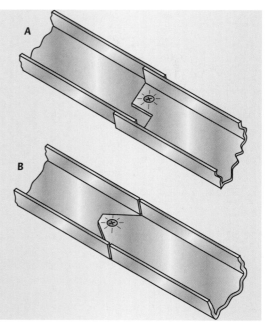

Build corners using a slip stud: A slip stud is not fastened until the wallboard on one wall is in place. Form L-shaped corners (A) by overlapping the tracks. Cut off the flange on one side of one stud, removing enough to allow room for the overlapping track and wallboard. Form a T-shaped corner (B) by leaving a gap between the tracks for the wallboard. Secure each slip stud by screwing through the stud into the tracks—and stud, with L-shaped corners—of the adjacent wall. Also screw through the back side of the wallboard into the slip stud, if possible. Where there's no backing behind the slip stud, drive screws at a 45° angle through the back corners of the slip stud and into the wallboard.

Join sections of track with a spliced joint (A) or notched joint (B). Make a spliced joint by cutting a 2" slit down the center of the web of one track. Slip the other track into the slit and secure them both with a screw. Make a notched joint by cutting back the flanges of one track and tapering the web so it fits into the other track; secure both with a single screw.

Framing for Doors & Windows

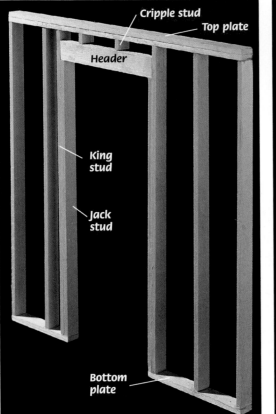

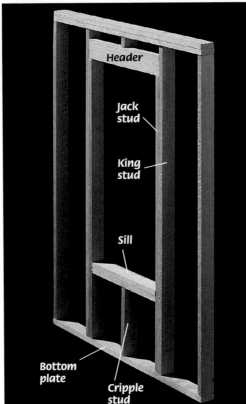

The projects that follow show you how to build door frames in new partition walls and new frames in existing exterior walls for both platform- and balloon-frame houses. You'll also see how to build a window frame in an exterior wall. The window project shown involves platform framing; if your house is balloon-frame, follow steps A through I on pages 56-58 to install the header for your window. (Consult a professional to install a window on the second story of a balloon-frame house.)

Because exterior walls are load-bearing, their door and window frames must have headers at the top to carry the weight from above. For standard doors and windows, construct the header using 2 × lumber and plywood—called a *built-up header*. Consult the chart on page 41 for the recommended size of lumber required for your header.

When planning the placement of a window, remember that the bottom of an egress window can be no higher than 44" from the finished floor (see page 15), and windows lower than 24" may require tempered glazing. See page 53 for more layout considerations.

All of the projects include frames for prehung door and window units, meaning the doors or windows are already mounted in their jambs. To lay out and build a door or window frame, you'll need the exact dimensions of the door or window unit. If you don't have the unit on-hand, contact the manufacturer to get the exact dimensions. Follow the manufacturer's specifications for rough opening size when framing a window. The listed opening usually is 1" wider and ½" taller than the actual dimensions of the window unit.

Built-up Header

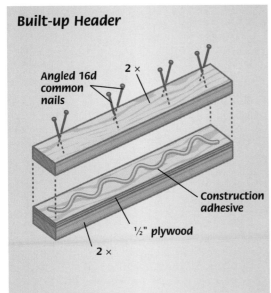

Door frames (above left) have king studs attached to the wall plates, and jack studs that support the header. Cripple studs transfer the load from above onto the header, and are placed to maintain the stud layout. The dimensions of the framed opening are called the *rough opening*.

Window frames (above) have full-length king studs, as well as jack studs that support the header. They also have a sill (often a double-sill) that defines the bottom of the rough opening.

Tools: Circular saw, handsaw, 4-ft. level, pry bar, reciprocating saw, nippers, plumb bob, combination square.

Materials: Door or window unit; 2 × lumber; 16d, 10d, and 8d common nails; ½"- and ¾"-thick plywood; construction adhesive.

Framing for Accessibility

Careful planning can make your new doors and windows more accessible and easier to operate. Make sure all doors and windows have clear approach spaces and that windows are positioned at heights that accommodate small people and people in wheelchairs. See pages 142 to 143 for tips on choosing new doors, windows, and hardware.

- Provide a clear approach space in front of each door that is 48 × 48". This includes an 18"- to 24"-wide space between the latch side of the door and an adjacent wall—to allow users room to maneuver.
- Frame doorless openings at a minimum of 32" wide (36" preferred).

- Plan a clear approach space to each window, 30" deep × 48" wide.
- Position view windows at a maximum sill height of 30" to 36", so that children and seated people can see out.
- Position windows so that hardware is at a maximum height of 48" if the window is operable.

NOTE: Lower sills may pose a safety risk to children; be sure to choose your window heights accordingly, and choose tempered glass for lower windows, when required by local building codes.

Framing a Door Opening in a Partition Wall (non-load-bearing)

A

Measure the width of the door unit along the bottom. Add 1" to this dimension to calculate the width of the rough opening (the distance between the jack studs). This gives you a ½" gap on each side for adjusting the door frame during installation. Mark the top and bottom plates for the jack and king studs. Install the plates as shown on page 48.

Continued on next page

Framing a Door Opening in a Partition Wall (platform framing) (cont.)

B

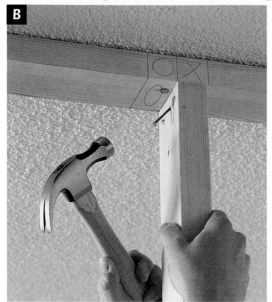

After you've installed the plates, cut the king studs and toe-nail them in place at the appropriate markings.

C

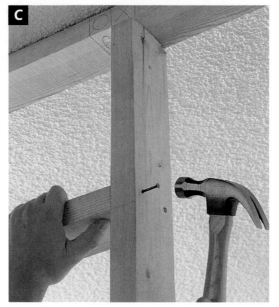

Measure the full length of the door unit, and add ½" to determine the height of the rough opening. Measure up from the floor and mark the rough opening height onto the king studs. Cut a 2 × 4 header to fit between the king studs. Position the header flat with its bottom face at the marks, and secure it to the king studs with 16d nails.

D

Cut and install a cripple stud above the header, centered between the king studs. Install any additional cripples required to maintain the standard 16"-on-center layout of the wall studs.

E

Cut the jack studs to fit snugly under the header. Fasten them in place by nailing down through the header, then drive 10d nails through the faces of the jack studs and into the king studs, spacing the nails 16" apart.

F

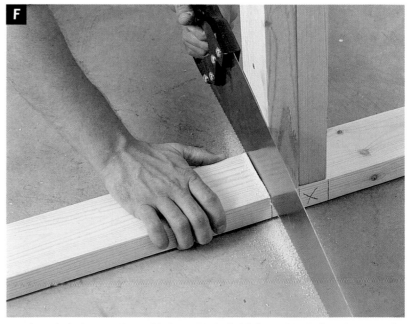

Saw through the bottom plate so it's flush with the inside faces of the jack studs. Remove the cut-out portion of the plate. NOTE: If the wall will be finished with wallboard, install the door after the wallboard is installed.

Framing a Door Opening in an Exterior Wall (platform framing)

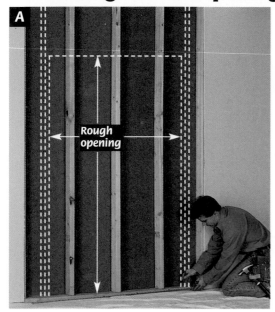

After you remove the interior wall surfaces (see pages 27 to 31), measure and mark the rough opening width on the bottom plate (see step A, page 53). Mark the locations of the jack studs and king studs on the sole plate. (Where practical, use existing studs as king studs.)

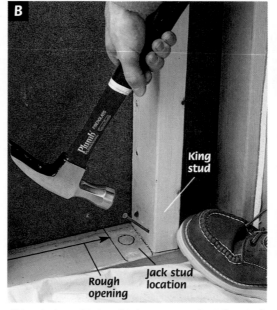

If king studs need to be added, measure and cut them to fit between the bottom plate and top plate. Position the king studs and toenail them to the bottom plate with 10d nails.

Check the king studs with a level to make sure they are plumb, then toenail them to the top plate with 10d nails.

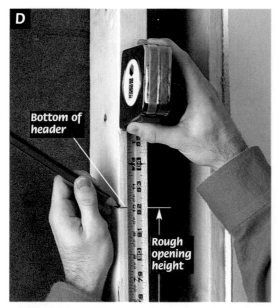

Measuring from the floor, mark the rough opening height on one king stud (see step C, page 54). This line marks the bottom of the door header.

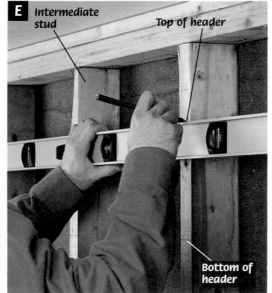

Determine the size of the header needed (see page 41). Measure and mark where the top of the header will fit against a king stud. Use a level to extend the lines across the intermediate studs to the opposite king stud.

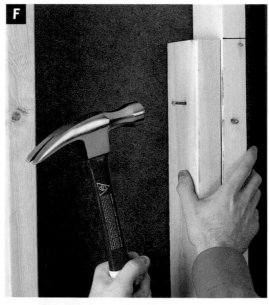

Cut two jack studs to reach from the top of the bottom plate to the bottom of the header as marked on the king studs. Nail the jack studs to the king studs with 10d nails driven every 12". **Make temporary supports** (see pages 36 to 39) if you are removing more than one stud.

Continued on next page

Framing a Door Opening in an Exterior Wall (platform framing) (cont.)

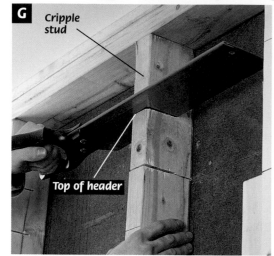

Use a circular saw to start cuts at the top header marks on the intermediate studs. (Do not cut king studs.) Make additional cuts 3" below the initial cuts. Finish each cut with a handsaw. Knock out the 3" sections, then remove the cut studs, using a pry bar. The remaining stud sections will serve as cripple studs.

Build a header to fit between the king studs, on top of the jack studs. Use two pieces of 2 × lumber sandwiched around ½" plywood (see page 52). Attach the header to the jack studs, king studs, and cripple studs, using 10d nails.

Use a reciprocating saw to cut through the bottom plate next to each jack stud, then remove the bottom plate with a pry bar. Cut off any exposed nails, using nippers. When you're ready to install the door, remove the exterior wall surface (see pages 32 to 35).

Framing a Door Opening in an Exterior Wall (balloon framing)

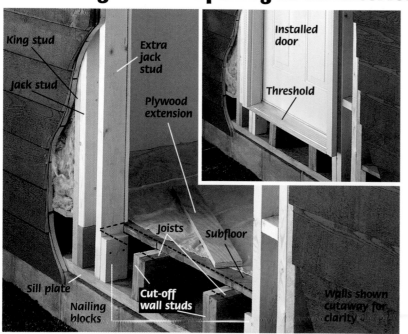

A **new door opening in a balloon-frame house** has studs extending past the subfloor to rest on the sill plate. Jack studs rest either on the sill plate or on top of the joists. To provide a surface for the door threshold, install nailing blocks, and add plywood to extend the subfloor out to the ends of the joists.

Remove the interior wall surfaces (see pages 27 to 31). Select two existing studs to use as king studs. The distance between selected studs must be at least 3" wider than the planned rough opening. Measuring from the floor, mark the rough opening height on a king stud (see step C, page 54).

Determine the header size (see page 41) and measure and mark where the top of it will fit against a king stud. Use a level to extend the line across the intermediate studs to the opposite king stud.

Use a reciprocating saw to cut open the subfloor between the studs, and remove any fire blocking in the stud cavities. This allows access to the sill plate when installing the jack studs. **Make temporary supports** if you will be removing more than one wall stud, (see pages 36 to 39).

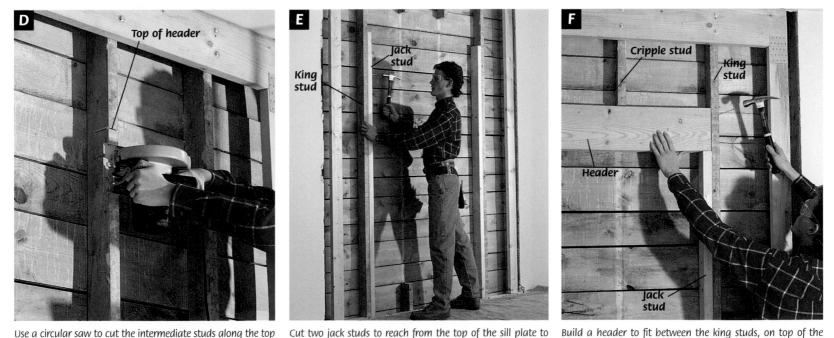

Use a circular saw to cut the intermediate studs along the top header markings. (Do not cut the king studs.) Make two additional cuts on each stud, 3" below the first cut and 6" above the floor. Finish the cuts with a handsaw, then knock out the 3" sections with a hammer. Remove the studs with a pry bar.

Cut two jack studs to reach from the top of the sill plate to the rough opening marks on the king studs. Nail the jack studs to the king studs with 10d nails driven every 12".

Build a header to fit between the king studs, on top of the jack studs, using two pieces of 2 × lumber sandwiched around ½" plywood (see page 41). Attach the header to the jack studs, king studs, and cripple studs, using 10d nails.

Continued on next page

Framing a Door Opening in an Exterior Wall (balloon framing) (cont.)

G

Sill
plate

Measure the rough opening width of the door (see step A, page 53) and mark it on the header. Use a plumb bob to mark the rough opening on the sill plate (inset).

H

Additional
jack stud

Cut and install additional jack studs, as necessary, to frame the sides of the rough opening. Toenail the jack studs to the header and the sill plate, using 10d nails. NOTE: You may have to go to the basement to do this.

I

Blocking

Additional
jack studs

Install horizontal 2 × 4 blocking between the studs on each side of the rough opening, using 10d nails. Install blocking at the lockset and hinge locations on the new door.

J

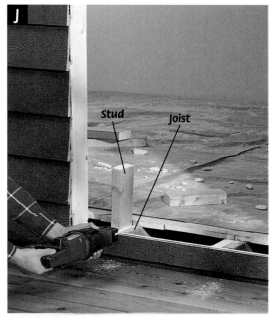

Stud

Joist

NOTE: Do not begin this step until you are ready to install the door. Remove the exterior wall surface (see pages 32 to 35), and cut off the ends of the exposed studs flush with the tops of the floor joists, using a reciprocating saw or handsaw.

K

Nailing blocks

Install 2 × 4 nailing blocks next to the jack studs and joists, flush with the tops of the floor joists. Replace any fire-blocking that was removed. Patch the subfloor area between the jack studs with plywood to form a flat, level surface for the door threshold.

Framing Window Openings

A

Prepare the project site, and remove the interior wall surfaces (see pages 27 to 31). Measure and mark the rough opening width on the bottom plate (see page 52). Mark the locations of the jack studs and king studs on the bottom plate. Where practical, use the existing studs as king studs.

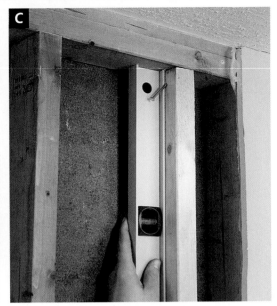

B

Measure and cut king studs, as needed, to fit between the bottom plate and the top plate. Position the king studs and toenail them to the bottom plate with 10d nails.

C

Check the king studs with a level to make sure they are plumb, then toenail them to the top plate with 10d nails.

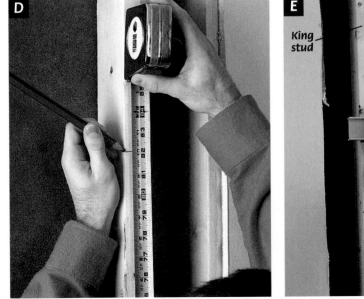

D

Measuring from the floor, mark the rough opening height on one of the king studs. This line marks the bottom of the window header. For most windows, the recommended rough opening is ½" taller than the height of the window unit.

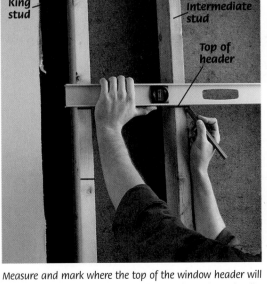

E

King stud

Intermediate stud

Top of header

Measure and mark where the top of the window header will fit against the king stud. The header size depends on the distance between the king studs (see page 41). Use a level to extend the lines across the intermediate studs to the opposite king stud.

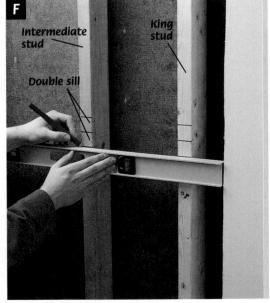

F

Intermediate stud

King stud

Double sill

Measure down from the bottom header line, and outline the rough double sill on the king stud. Use a level to extend the lines across the intermediate studs to the opposite king stud. **Make temporary supports** (see pages 36 to 39) if you will be removing more than one stud.

Continued on next page

Framing Window Openings (cont.)

Set a circular saw to its maximum blade depth, then cut through the intermediate studs along the lines marking the bottom of the rough sill and along the lines marking the top of the header. (Do not cut the king studs.) On each stud, make an additional cut about 3" above each sill cut. Finish the cuts with a handsaw.

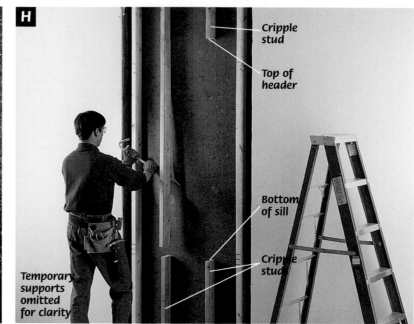

Knock out the 3" stud sections, then tear out the intermediate studs inside the rough opening, using a pry bar. Use nippers to clip away any exposed nails. The remaining sections of the cut studs will serve as cripple studs for the window.

Cut two jack studs to reach from the top of the bottom plate to the bottom header lines on the king studs. Nail the jack studs to the king studs with 10d nails driven every 12". NOTE: On a balloon-frame house, the jack studs will reach to the sill plate.

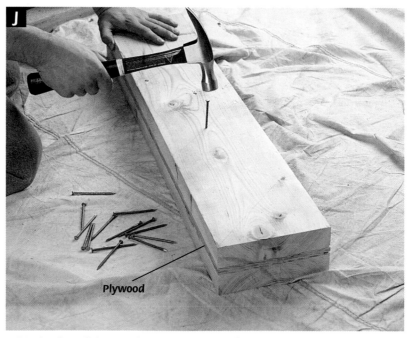

Build a header to fit between the king studs on top of the jack studs, using two pieces of 2 × lumber sandwiched around ½" plywood (see page 52).

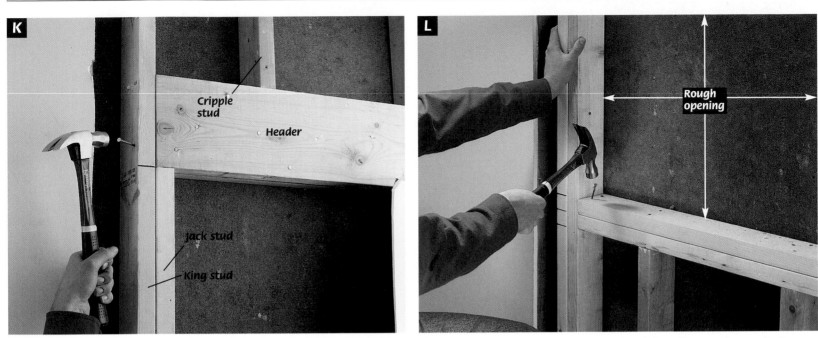

Position the header on the jack studs, using a hammer if necessary. Attach the header to the king studs, jack studs, and cripple studs, using 10d nails.

Build the rough sill to reach between the jack studs by nailing together a pair of 2 × 4s. Position the rough sill on the cripple studs, and nail it to the jack studs and cripple studs with 10d nails. When you're ready to install the window, remove the exterior wall surface (see pages 32 to 35).

Variation For Round-top Windows

Create a template to help with the framing and marking of the rough opening on the sheathing. Scribe the outline of the curved frame on cardboard, allowing an extra ½" for adjustments within the rough opening. (A ¼ × 1¼" metal washer makes a good spacer for scribing the outline.) Cut out the template along the scribed line.

Tape the template to the sheathing, with the top touching the header. Use the template as a guide for attaching diagonal framing members across the top corners of the framed opening. The diagonal members should just touch the template. Outline the template on the sheathing as a guide for cutting the exterior wall surface (see pages 32 to 35).

Plumbing

Your remodeling project may involve installing all-new plumbing lines, branching from existing lines, and even replacing portions of an older system.

This section of the book covers the basic plumbing system (pages 62 to 63), the tools and materials used in common plumbing projects (pages 64 to 69), and how to work with those materials (pages 70 to 85). Tips on planning your new plumbing and working within plumbing code guidelines (pages 86 to 93) are also provided.

Plumbing Basics

Home Plumbing Systems

A typical home plumbing system includes three basic parts: a water supply system, fixtures and appliances, and a drain system. Fresh water enters a home through a main supply line (1). The water may pass through a meter (2) that registers the amount used.

Immediately after entering the house, a branch line (3) splits off and feeds a hot water heater (4). From there, a hot water line runs parallel to the cold water line to bring water to fixtures and appliances in the home.

Waste water from each fixture flows into a trap (5), then into the drain system, which works entirely by gravity. The waste water flows downhill through a series of large-diameter drain pipes attached to a system of vent pipes (6), which allow air to enter the system via a roof vent (7). The fresh air prevents suction that would slow or stop drain water from flowing freely.

All waste water eventually reaches the main waste and vent stack (8), which flows into the sewer line (9) that exits the house near the foundation and empties into a municipal sewer system or septic tank. Sewer gases rise through the vent stack to escape the house.

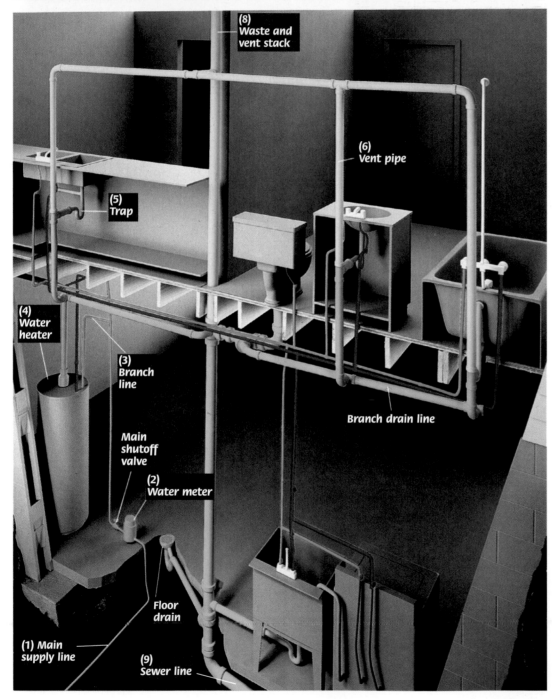

The Supply System

Supply pipes deliver hot and cold water throughout a home's plumbing system. Prior to 1950, supply pipes were often made of galvanized iron; in newer homes supply pipes typically are copper, although plastic (CPVC) pipes are gaining acceptance by many local plumbing codes. A remodeling project can be a great opportunity to replace old pipes with newer, more durable materials.

Water supply pipes are made to withstand the high pressures of a water supply system. They have small diameters, usually ½" to 1", and are joined with strong, watertight fittings. The hot and cold lines run in tandem to fixtures and appliances and are generally located inside wall cavities or strapped to the undersides of floor joists.

Water supplies are controlled by valves that are connected to the main line and branch lines, and near each fixture.

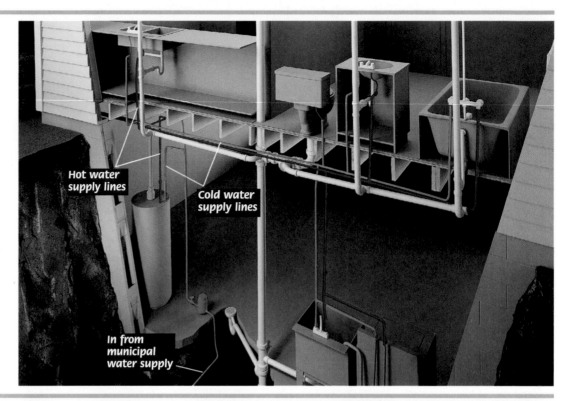

Hot water supply lines

Cold water supply lines

In from municipal water supply

The Drain-Waste-Vent System

Waste water is carried out of the house by the drain-waste-vent (DWV) system. This system takes advantage of gravity, drawing waste water down vertical or sloped pipes and into a municipal sewer system or septic tank. Drainpipe slope is governed by local building codes, but typically is ¼" per ft.

Made of plastic or cast iron, drain pipes are larger in diameter than supply pipes, ranging from 1¼" to 4", to allow easy passage of waste water through the system. In older homes, drain pipes may be copper or lead.

Every drain must have a *trap*, a curved section of pipe that holds standing water and prevents sewer gases from entering the house. Each time a drain is used, the standing water is flushed away and replaced by new water.

For waste water to flow freely, drain pipes are joined to a vent system that brings outdoor air into the house to lower the pressure in the pipes, usually through one or more rooftop vent stacks. Inadequately vented lines can interfere with toilet flushing and drain function, and allow sewer gas backup.

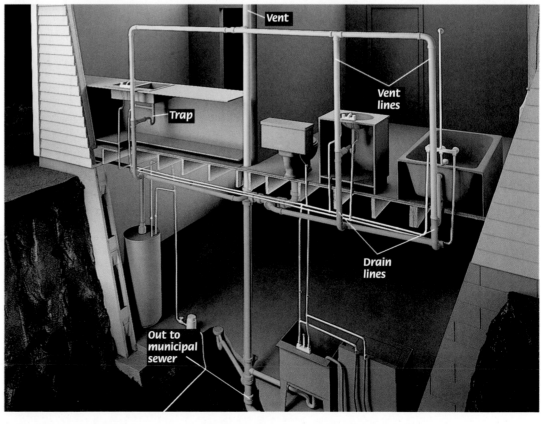

Vent

Trap

Vent lines

Drain lines

Out to municipal sewer

Tools and Pipe Materials

Recognizing the different types of piping used in plumbing systems is important for trouble shooting and crucial when purchasing supplies or making repairs. The materials used in home plumbing systems are closely regulated by building codes, so look for product standard codes and check local plumbing regulations prior to making purchases.

Cast iron is commonly used for drain-waste-vent (DWV) purposes. Though it is the strongest piping, it's very heavy and somewhat difficult to join and install. Its thickness helps contain the noise inherent in drain systems.

Plastic piping is often used for water supply pipes where permitted by local code. It's inexpensive, easy to handle, doesn't corrode or rust, and has insulating properties. Plastic pipe is available in four types: ABS and PVC are used exclusively in home drain systems, CPVC is suitable for water supply lines, and PE is used for outdoor water supply pipes.

Brass, and the more expensive but attractive chromed brass, are durable plumbing materials used for drains, valves, and shutoffs.

Galvanized iron, suitable for supply and DWV purposes, is rarely used today because it corrodes and is difficult to install.

Copper is considered the best choice for water supply lines and parts of some DWV systems. It resists scale deposits, maintains water flow and pressure, is lightweight, and is easily installed. Copper is more expensive than plastic.

Helpful Hint

When pipes of different metals touch each other, a process called galvanic action *can lead to premature corrosion. Use only brackets and straps made of the same material as your pipes. To join dissimilar metals, such as galvanized iron and copper, you must use* dielectric fittings.

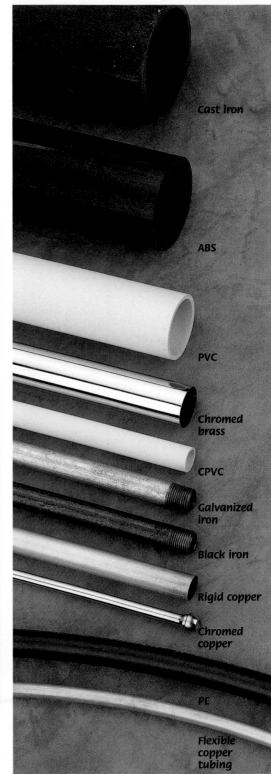

Cast iron

ABS

PVC

Chromed brass

CPVC

Galvanized iron

Black iron

Rigid copper

Chromed copper

PE

Flexible copper tubing

Plumbing tools include: *Propane torch with starter, solder paste, and lead-free solder (A), ratchet wrench with sockets (B), hacksaw (C), tubing cutter (D), ball peen hammer (E), wire brush (F), rubber mallet (G), file (H), channel-type pliers (I), adjustable wrenches (J), and pipe wrenches (K). You will use these tools extensively during remodeling projects and when making future repairs. Specialty and power tools for plumbing projects can be rented from rental centers.*

Benefits & Characteristics	Common Uses	Fitting Methods	Tools for Cutting
Cast iron is very strong but is difficult to cut and fit. Repairs and replacements should be made with plastic pipe, if allowed by code.	Main drain-waste-vent pipes	Joined with hubbed fittings or banded couplings	Cast iron cutter or hacksaw
ABS (Acrylonitrile-Butadiene-Styrene) was the first rigid plastic approved for use in home drain systems. Some local plumbing codes now restrict the use of ABS in new installations.	Drain & vent pipes; drain traps	Joined with solvent glue and plastic fittings	Tubing cutter, miter saw, or hacksaw
PVC (Poly-Vinyl-Chloride) is a modern rigid plastic that is highly resistant to damage by heat or chemicals. It is the best material for drain-waste-vent (DWV) pipes.	Drain & vent pipes; drain traps	Joined with solvent glue and plastic fittings	Tubing cutter, miter saw, or hacksaw
Chromed brass has an attractive, shiny surface and is used for drain traps where appearance is important.	Valves & shutoffs; chromed drain traps	Joined with compression fittings, or with metal solder	Tubing cutter, hacksaw, or reciprocating saw
CPVC (Chlorinated-Poly-Vinyl-Chloride) rigid plastic is chemically formulated to withstand the high temperatures and pressures of water supply systems. Pipes and fittings are inexpensive.	Hot & cold water supply pipes	Joined with solvent glue and plastic fittings, or with plastic compression fittings	Tubing cutter, miter saw, or hacksaw
Galvanized iron is very strong but gradually will corrode. Not advised for new installation. Galvanized iron is difficult to cut and fit; large jobs are best left to professionals.	Drains; hot & cold water supply pipes	Joined with galvanized threaded fittings	Hacksaw or reciprocating saw
Black iron looks much like galvanized iron, but there is an important difference. Black iron is used for gas piping, not for plumbing. Repairs should be handled by professionals.	Gas piping	Joined with black iron threaded fittings	Hacksaw or reciprocating saw
Rigid copper is the best material for water supply pipes. It resists corrosion and has smooth surfaces that provide good water flow. Soldered copper joints are very durable.	Hot & cold water supply pipes	Joined with metal solder or compression fittings	Tubing cutter, hacksaw, or jig saw
Chromed copper has an attractive, shiny surface and is used in areas where appearance is important. Chromed copper is durable and easy to bend and fit.	Supply tubing for plumbing fixtures	Joined with brass compression fittings	Tubing cutter or hacksaw
PE (polyethylene) plastic is a black or bluish flexible pipe sometimes used for main water service lines as well as irrigation systems.	Outdoor cold water supply pipes	Joined with rigid PVC fittings and stainless steel hose clamps	Ratchet-style plastic pipe cutter or miter saw
Flexible copper tubing is easy to shape and will withstand a slight frost without rupturing. Flexible copper bends easily around corners, so it requires fewer fittings than rigid copper.	Gas tubing, hot & cold water supply tubing	Joined with brass flare fittings, compression fittings, or metal solder	Tubing cutter or hacksaw

Valves & Fittings

Always use fittings made from the same materials as your pipes. If unlike materials are to be joined, use a transition fitting.

Fittings come in many sizes, but the basic shapes are standard to all metal and plastic pipes. In general, fittings used to connect drain-waste-vent (DWV) pipes have gradual bends for a smooth flow of waste water from drains. Because water in supply lines moves under pressure, the bends in water supply fittings can be sharper, conserving space.

90° elbows make right-angle bends in a pipe run. DWV elbows are curved so debris doesn't get trapped in the bends. Elbows are also available in 22½°, 45°, and 60° bends to create gradual bends in pipe runs.

T-fittings connect branch lines in water supply and DWV systems. In a DWV system they are called *waste Ts* or *sanitary Ts*.

Couplings join two straight pipes. Special transition fittings (opposite page) are used to join two pipes of different materials.

Reducers connect pipes of different diameters. Reducing T-fittings and elbows are also available.

Caps close off unused sections of pipe.

Y-fittings join intersecting DWV pipes.

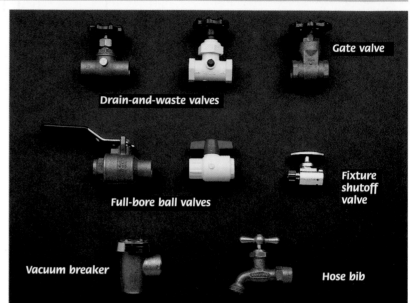

Gate valve

Drain-and-waste valves

Full-bore ball valves

Fixture shutoff valve

Vacuum breaker

Hose bib

Standard Fittings

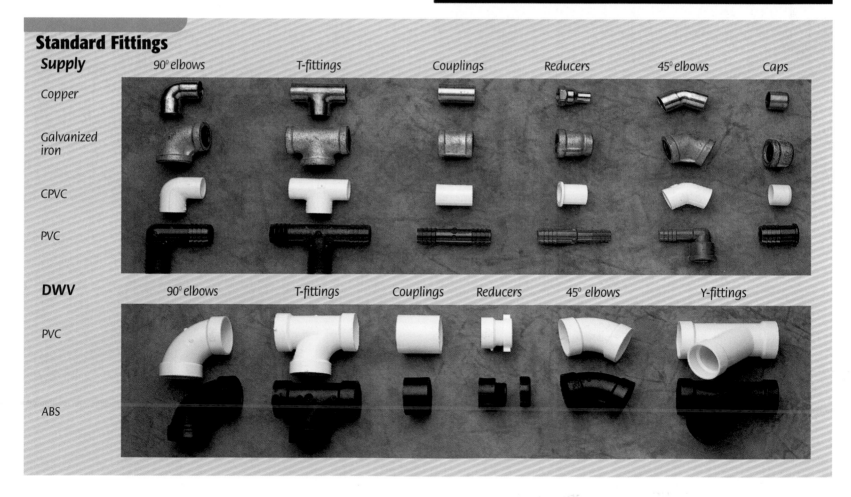

Supply	90° elbows	T-fittings	Couplings	Reducers	45° elbows	Caps
Copper						
Galvanized iron						
CPVC						
PVC						

DWV	90° elbows	T-fittings	Couplings	Reducers	45° elbows	Y-fittings
PVC						
ABS						

Using Transition Fittings

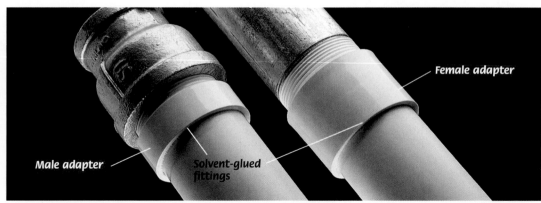

Female adapter

Male adapter

Solvent-glued fittings

Connect plastic to cast iron with banded couplings. Rubber sleeves cover the ends of the pipes for a watertight joint.

Connect plastic to threaded metal pipes with male and female threaded adapters. Glue a plastic adapter to the plastic pipe with solvent-based glue. Wrap the threads of the pipe with Teflon® tape, then screw the metal pipe directly to the adapter.

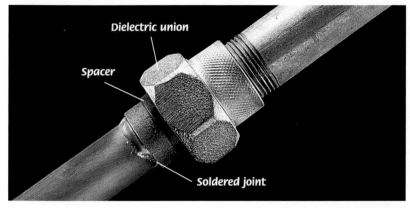

Dielectric union

Spacer

Soldered joint

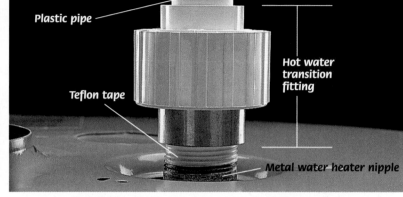

Plastic pipe

Hot water transition fitting

Teflon tape

Metal water heater nipple

Connect copper to galvanized iron with a dielectric union. Attach the threaded end of the union to the iron pipe and solder the other end to the copper pipe. A dielectric union has a plastic spacer that prevents corrosion caused by galvanic action.

Connect metal hot water pipe to plastic with a hot water transition fitting that prevents leaks caused by different expansion rates of materials. Wrap the metal pipe threads of the water heater nipple with Teflon tape, and attach the threaded end of the fitting. Solvent-glue the other end of the fitting to the plastic pipe.

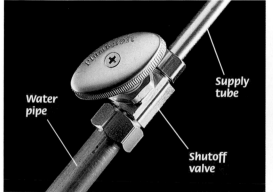

Water pipe

Supply tube

Shutoff valve

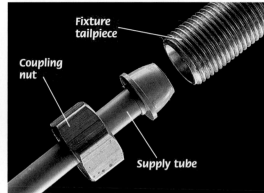

Fixture tailpiece

Coupling nut

Supply tube

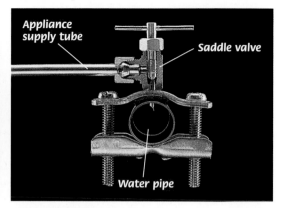

Appliance supply tube

Saddle valve

Water pipe

Connect a water pipe to any fixture supply tube with a shutoff valve. Be sure that the diameter of the valve matches that of the water pipe. Tighten the valve and check for leaks.

Connect any supply tube to a fixture tailpiece with a coupling nut. A coupling nut seals the bell-shaped end of the supply tube against the fixture tailpiece.

Connect an appliance supply tube to a copper water pipe with a saddle valve. Saddle valves (shown here cutaway) often are used to connect refrigerator icemakers.

DWV Fittings

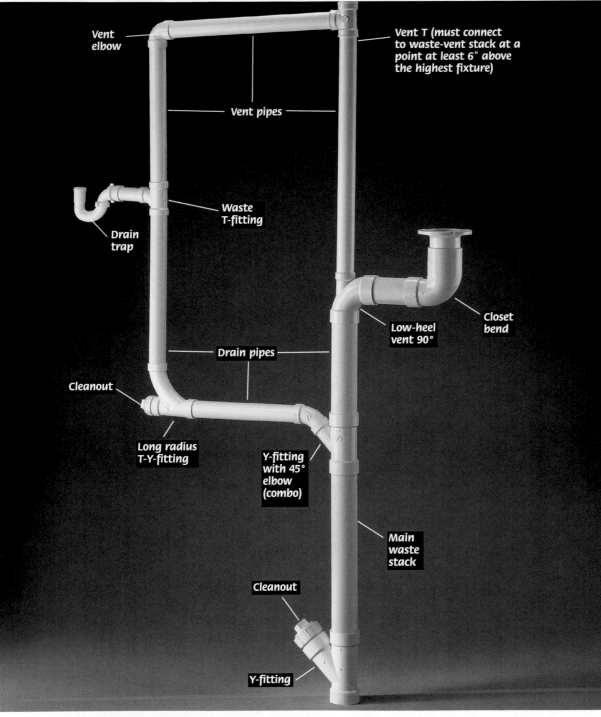

Vent elbow

Vent T (must connect to waste-vent stack at a point at least 6" above the highest fixture)

Vent pipes

Waste T-fitting

Drain trap

Closet bend

Low-heel vent 90°

Drain pipes

Cleanout

Long radius T-Y-fitting

Y-fitting with 45° elbow (combo)

Main waste stack

Cleanout

Y-fitting

A basic DWV tree shows the correct orientation of drain and vent fittings in a plumbing system. Bends in vent pipes can be very sharp, but drain pipes should use fittings with a noticeable sweep. Fittings used to direct falling waste water from a vertical to a horizontal pipe should have bends that are even more sweeping. Local plumbing code may require that you install cleanout fittings where vertical drain pipes meet horizontal runs.

DWV fittings come in a variety of shapes to serve different functions within the plumbing system. Each fitting is available in a variety of sizes to match your needs. Always use fittings made from the same material as your DWV pipes.

Vents: In general, the fittings used to connect vent pipes have very sharp bends with no sweep. Vent fittings include the vent T and vent 90° elbow. Standard drain pipe fittings can also be used to join vent pipes.

Horizontal-to-vertical drains: To change directions in a drain pipe from the horizontal to the vertical, use fittings with a noticeable sweep. Standard fittings for this use include waste T-fittings and 90° elbows. Y-fittings and 45° and 22½° elbows can also be used for this purpose.

Vertical-to-horizontal drains: To change directions from the vertical to the horizontal, use fittings with a long, gradual sweep. Common fittings for this purpose include the combination Y-fitting with 45° elbow (often called a *combo*), and the long radius T-Y-fitting.

Horizontal offsets in drains: Y-fittings, 45° elbows, 22½° elbows, and long sweep 90° elbows are used when changing directions in horizontal pipe runs. Whenever possible, horizontal drain pipes should use gradual, sweeping bends rather than sharp turns.

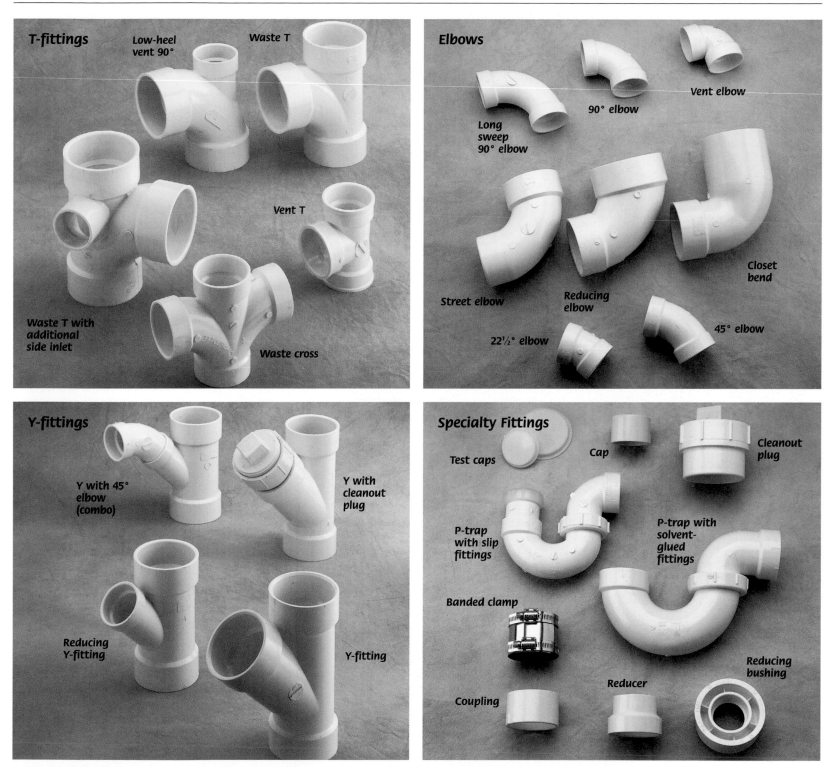

T-fittings

Low-heel vent 90°

Waste T

Vent T

Waste T with additional side inlet

Waste cross

Elbows

90° elbow

Vent elbow

Long sweep 90° elbow

Closet bend

Street elbow

Reducing elbow

45° elbow

22½° elbow

Y-fittings

Y with 45° elbow (combo)

Y with cleanout plug

Reducing Y-fitting

Y-fitting

Specialty Fittings

Test caps

Cap

Cleanout plug

P-trap with slip fittings

P-trap with solvent-glued fittings

Banded clamp

Coupling

Reducer

Reducing bushing

Fittings for DWV pipes *are available in many configurations, with openings that range from 1¼" to 4" in diameter. When planning your project, buy a large supply of DWV and water supply fittings from a reputable retailer with a good return policy. It is much more efficient to* return leftover materials after you complete your project than it is to interrupt your work each time you need to shop for an additional fitting.

Working with Copper Pipe

Copper is the ideal material for water supply pipes. It resists corrosion and has smooth surfaces that provide good water flow. Copper pipes are available in several diameters, but most home water supply systems use ½" or ¾" pipe. Copper pipe is manufactured in rigid and flexible forms.

Rigid copper, sometimes called *hard copper*, is approved for home water supply systems by all local codes. It comes in three wall-thickness grades: Types M, L, and K. Type M is thin and inexpensive, which makes it a good choice for do-it-yourself home plumbing.

Rigid Type L usually is required by codes for commercial plumbing systems. Because it is strong and solders easily, Type L may be preferred by some professional plumbers, and by do-it-yourselfers for home use. Type K has the heaviest wall thickness, and most often is used for underground water service lines.

Flexible copper, also called *soft copper*, comes in two wall-thickness grades: Types L and K. Both are approved for most home water supply systems, although flexible Type L copper is used primarily for gas service lines. Because it is bendable and resists mild frosts, Type L may be installed as part of a water supply system in unheated indoor areas, such as crawlspaces. Type K is used for underground water service lines.

A third form of copper, called DWV, is used for drain systems. Because most codes now allow low-cost plastic pipes for drain systems, DWV copper is seldom used.

Copper pipes are usually connected with soldered fittings. Correctly soldered fittings are strong and trouble-free. Copper pipe can also be joined with compression fittings, which are more expensive than soldered joints, but which allow pipes or fixtures to be repaired or replaced readily. Flare fittings are used only with flexible copper pipes, usually as a gas-line fitting; it's best to leave these to professionals.

Many remodeling projects involve separating existing joints to extend copper lines or remove defective pipes; this isn't difficult, but it's important to work carefully.

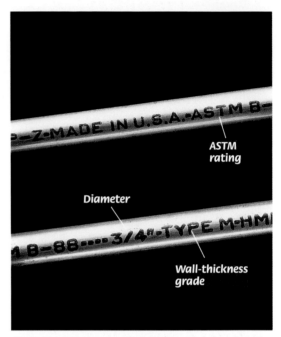

Check the grade stamp information for pipe diameter, wall-thickness grade, and stamp of approval from the American Society for Testing and Materials (ASTM). Type M pipe is identified by red lettering, Type L by blue lettering.

Tips for Working with Copper Pipe

Bend flexible copper pipe with a coil-spring tubing bender to avoid kinks. Use a bender that matches the outside pipe diameter; slip it over the pipe with a twisting motion, and bend slowly into the correct angle, but not more than 90°.

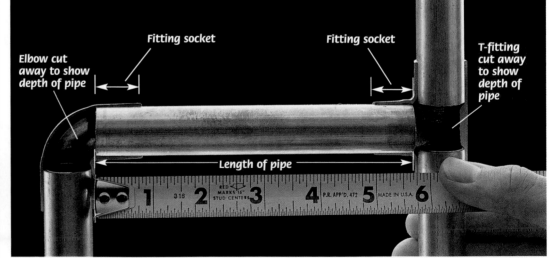

Determine the length of copper pipe needed by measuring between the bottom of the copper fitting sockets (fittings shown here cutaway). Mark the length on the pipe with a felt-tipped pen.

Copper Pipe & Fitting Chart

Fitting Method	Rigid Copper			Flexible Copper		General Comments
	Type M	Type L	Type K	Type L	Type K	
Soldered	yes	yes	yes	yes	yes	Inexpensive, strong, and trouble-free fitting method. Requires some skill.
Compression	yes	not recommended		yes	yes	Easy to use. Allows pipes or fixtures to be repaired or replaced readily. More expensive than solder. Best used on flexible copper.
Flare	no	no	no	yes	yes	Use only with flexible copper pipes. Usually used as a gas-line fitting. Requires some skill.

Taking Apart Soldered Joints

A	B	C	D

A Turn off the water at the main shutoff valve (see page 62) and drain the pipes by opening the highest and lowest faucets in the house. Light a propane torch (see page 74) and hold the flame tip to the fitting until the solder becomes shiny and begins to melt.

B Separate the pipes from the fitting with channel-type pliers. Discard the old fittings—they should not be reused.

C Remove the old solder by heating the ends of the pipe with the propane torch. Carefully wipe away the melted solder with a dry rag. Work quickly, but cautiously. The pipes will be hot.

D Allow the pipes to cool, then use an emery cloth to polish the ends down to the bare metal. Any residual solder or metal burrs left on the pipe may cause the new joint to leak.

Cutting & Soldering Copper Pipe

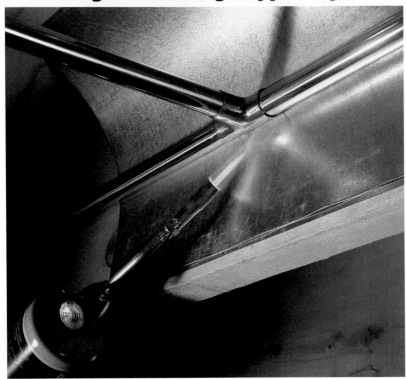

The best way to cut rigid and flexible copper pipe is with a tubing cutter. A tubing cutter makes a smooth, straight cut—an important first step toward making a watertight joint. Remove any metal burrs on the cut edges with a reaming tool or round file.

Copper also can be cut with a hacksaw, which is useful in tight areas where a tubing cutter won't fit. Since it is more difficult to be accurate with a hacksaw, take care to make smooth, straight cuts.

To form a watertight seal, start with copper pipes and fittings that are clean and dry. Practice soldering scrap pipe before starting your project. Protect flammable surfaces with a double layer of 26-gauge sheet metal or a heat-absorbent pad.

A soldered pipe joint, also called a *sweated joint*, is made by heating a copper or brass fitting with a propane torch until the fitting is just hot enough to melt metal solder. The heat draws the solder into the gap between the fitting and the pipe to form a watertight seal. A fitting that is overheated or unevenly heated will not draw in solder. The tip of the torch's inner flame produces the most heat.

Tools: Tubing cutter with reaming tip (or hacksaw and round file), wire brush, flux brush, propane torch, spark lighter (or matches), adjustable wrench.

Materials: Copper pipe, copper fittings (or brass valve), emery cloth, soldering paste (flux), lead-free solder, dry rag.

Protect wood from the heat of the torch flame while soldering, using a double layer (two 18 × 18" pieces) of 26-gauge sheet metal available at hardware stores or home centers.

Tips for Soldering Copper Pipe

Use caution when soldering copper. Allow pipes and fittings time to cool before handling them.

Keep joints dry when soldering existing water pipes by plugging the pipe ends with bread. Bread absorbs moisture that would ruin the soldering process and cause pinhole leaks. The bread dissolves when the water is turned back on.

Prevent accidents by shutting off the propane torch immediately after use; make sure the valve is completely closed.

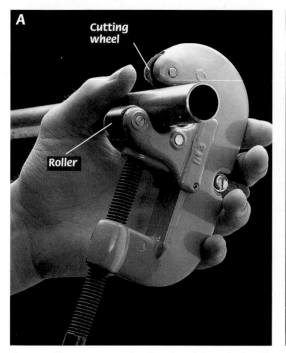

A

Cutting wheel

Roller

Place a tubing cutter over the pipe, then tighten the handle so the pipe rests on both rollers, and the cutting wheel is on the marked line.

B

Turn the tubing cutter one rotation to score a continuous straight line around the pipe.

C

Rotate the cutter in the opposite direction, tightening the handle slightly after every two rotations, until the cut is complete.

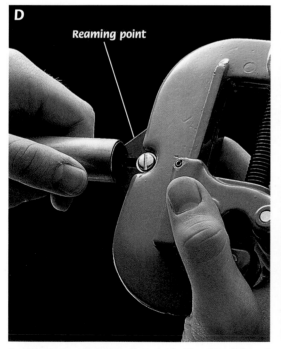

D

Reaming point

Remove sharp metal burrs from the inside edge of the cut pipe, using the reaming point on the tubing cutter or a round file.

E

Emery cloth

Clean the end of each pipe by sanding it with emery cloth. The ends must be free of dirt and grease to ensure that the solder forms a good seal.

F

Clean inside each fitting by scouring with a wire brush or emery cloth.

Continued on next page

Cutting & Soldering Copper Pipe (cont.)

Flux brush

Apply a thin layer of soldering paste (flux) to the end of each pipe, using a flux brush. Cover about 1" of the end of the pipe with the paste.

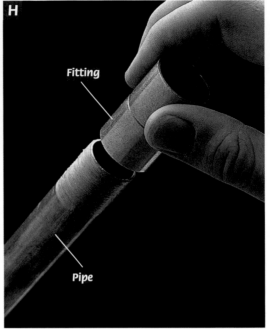

Fitting

Pipe

Assemble each joint by inserting the pipe into the fitting so it is tight against the bottom of the fitting sockets. Twist the fitting slightly to spread the soldering paste.

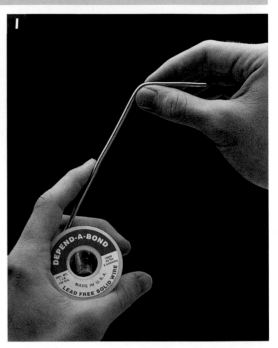

Prepare the wire solder by unwinding 8" to 10" of wire from the spool. Bend the first 2" of the wire to a 90° angle.

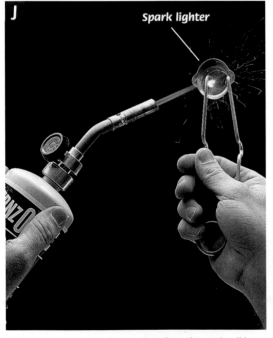

Spark lighter

Light a propane torch by opening the valve and striking a spark lighter or match next to the torch nozzle until the gas ignites.

Adjust the torch valve until the inner portion of the flame is 1" to 2" long.

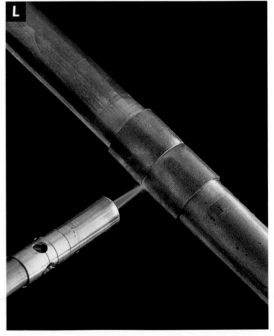

Hold the flame tip against the middle of the fitting for 4 to 5 seconds, until the soldering paste begins to sizzle.

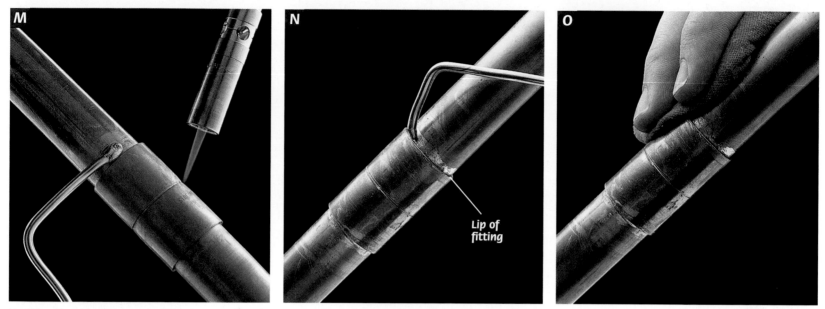

M

N

O

Lip of fitting

Heat the other side of the copper fitting to ensure that the heat is distributed evenly. Touch the solder to the pipe. If the solder melts, the joint is ready to be soldered.

Remove the torch and quickly push ½" to ¾" of solder into each joint. Capillary action fills the joint with liquid solder. A correctly soldered joint shows a thin bead of solder around the lip of the fitting.

Carefully wipe away excess solder with a dry rag. (The pipes will be hot.) When all joints have cooled, turn on the water and check for leaks. If a joint leaks, drain the pipes, disassemble and clean the pipe and fittings, then resolder the joint.

Soldering Brass Valves

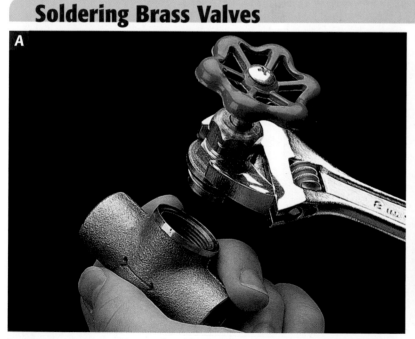

A

B

Remove the valve stem with an adjustable wrench to prevent heat damage to rubber or plastic stem parts while soldering. Prepare the copper pipes (see pages 73 to 74) and assemble the joints.

Light a propane torch. Heat the body of the valve, moving the flame to distribute the heat evenly. Concentrate the flame on the brass—it is denser than copper and requires more heat before the joints will draw solder. Apply the solder (steps M through O, above). Let the joint cool, then reassemble the valve.

Using Compression Fittings

When cramped or poorly ventilated spaces make it difficult or unsafe to solder, compression fittings are a good choice. They're also appropriate for connections that may need to be taken apart at a later date. Because they're easy to disconnect, compression fittings often are used to install supply tubes and fixture shutoff valves.

Compression fittings work well with flexible copper pipe, which is soft enough to allow the compression ring to seat snugly, creating a watertight seal. They are also used to make connections with Type M rigid copper pipe.

Compression fittings are available in unions, 90° elbows, tees, straight and angled shut-off valves, and hose bibs. They usually have flat sides that can be gripped with an adjustable wrench.

When measuring copper tubing to be used with compression fittings, add ½" for the length of pipe that must fit inside the valve. As with all plumbing joints, smooth, straight cuts are vital to forming watertight seals. Cut tubing with a tubing cutter or a hacksaw (see page 73) and remove any metal burrs on the cut edges, using a reaming tool or round file.

Compression fittings tend to cross thread, so check the fittings for leaks after the assembly. To ensure a watertight seal, cover compression rings with pipe joint compound before assembling the fittings.

Tools: Felt-tipped pen, tubing cutter or hacksaw, basin wrench, adjustable wrenches.

Materials: Brass compression fittings, pipe joint compound.

A **compression fitting** (shown here cutaway) has a compression ring and a compression nut, which forms a tight seal by forcing the ring against the inner portion of the fitting.

Joining Two Copper Pipes with a Compression Union Fitting

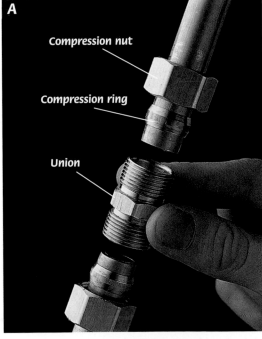

A

Compression nut

Compression ring

Union

Slide the compression nuts and rings over the ends of the pipes. Place the threaded union between the pipes.

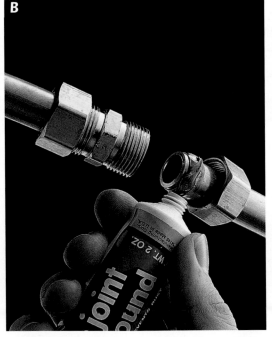

B

Apply a layer of pipe joint compound to the compression rings, then screw the compression nuts onto the threaded union. Hand-tighten the nuts.

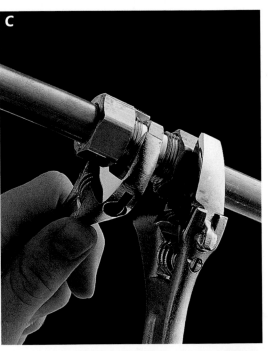

C

Hold the center of the union fitting with an adjustable wrench. Use another wrench to tighten each compression nut one complete turn. Turn on the water. If the fitting leaks, gently tighten the nuts.

Installing Shutoff Valves & Supply Tubes

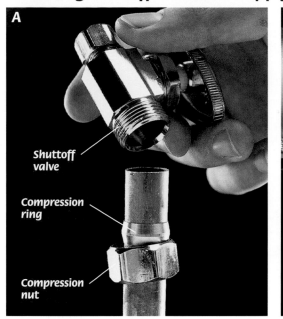

A

Slide a compression nut and ring over the copper water pipe, with the nut threads facing the end of the pipe. Fit the shutoff valve onto the pipe. Apply a layer of pipe joint compound to the compression ring. Screw the nut onto the shutoff valve and tighten it with an adjustable wrench.

Labels: Shuttoff valve, Compression ring, Compression nut

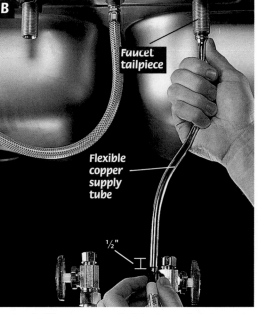

B

Bend a flexible copper supply tube to reach between the faucet tailpiece and the shutoff valve (see page 70). Fit the bell-shaped end of the supply tube into the end of the tailpiece, and mark the other end to length. Include a ½" portion that will fit inside the valve. Cut the tube (see page 73).

Labels: Faucet tailpiece, Flexible copper supply tube, ½"

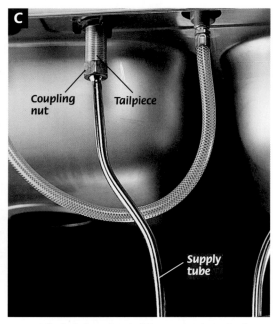

C

Connect the bell-shaped end of the supply tube to the faucet tailpiece, using a coupling nut. Tighten the nut with a basin wrench (see page 482) or channel-type pliers.

Labels: Coupling nut, Tailpiece, Supply tube

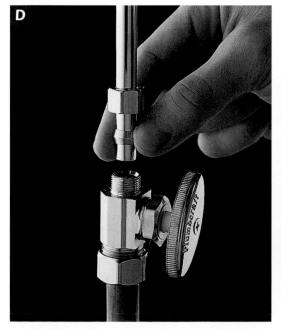

D

To connect the supply tube to the valve, slide a compression nut over the end of the pipe, with the threads facing the valve, then slide on the compression ring.

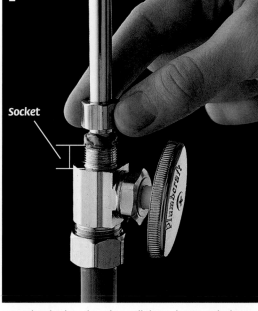

E

Insert the pipe into the valve until the end rests at the bottom of the fitting socket. Apply a layer of joint compound over the compression ring and hand-tighten the nut onto the valve.

Label: Socket

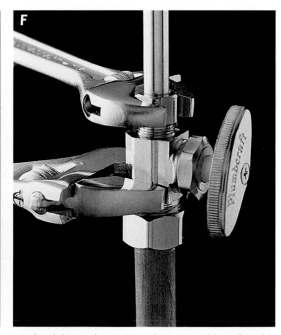

F

Gently tighten the compression nut with adjustable wrenches. Do not overtighten. Turn on the water and check for leaks. If the fitting leaks, carefully tighten the nut.

Working with Plastic Pipe

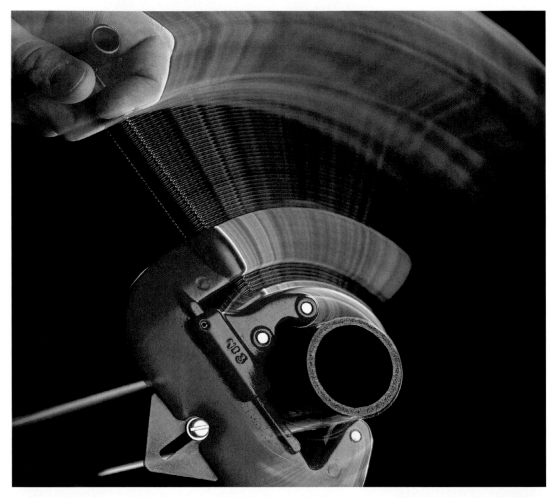

Plastic pipes and fittings are popular because they are lightweight, inexpensive, and easy to use. Local plumbing codes increasingly are approving their use for home plumbing.

Plastic pipes are available in rigid and flexible forms. ABS and PVC are used in drain systems. PVC resists chemical damage and heat better than ABS, and is approved for above-ground use by all plumbing codes. However, some codes still require cast-iron pipe for main drains running under concrete slabs.

PE is often used for underground cold water lines, such as those found in sprinkling systems.

CPVC is used for both cold and hot water supply lines. Plastic pipes can be joined to iron or copper pipes with transition fittings, but different types of plastic should not be joined.

PB flexible plastic is no longer considered reliable and isn't widely available. If problems develop with PB pipe or fittings, consult a licensed plumber for advice.

Prolonged exposure to sunlight eventually can weaken plastic plumbing pipe, so do not install or store it in areas that receive constant, direct sunlight.

Use PVC or ABS pipe for sink traps and drain pipes. Use CPVC pipe for water supply lines. PVC and ABS pipes used for drains usually have an inside diameter of $1\frac{1}{4}$" to 4". CPVC pipes for water supply usually have an inside diameter of $\frac{1}{2}$" or $\frac{3}{4}$". For sink traps and drains, choose PVC or ABS pipe with DWV ratings from the National Sanitation Foundation (NSF). For water supply pipes, choose CPVC with PW (pressurized water) ratings.

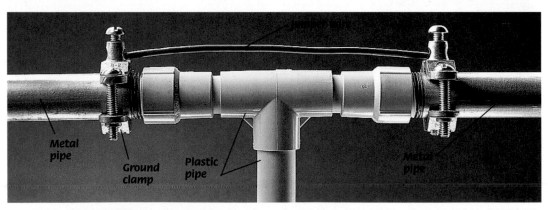

Your home's electrical system may be grounded through metal water pipes. When adding plastic pipes to a metal plumbing system, make sure the electrical ground circuit remains intact. Use ground clamps and jumper wires (available at hardware stores) to bypass the plastic transition and complete the electrical ground circuit. Make sure the clamps are firmly attached to bare metal on both sides of the plastic pipe.

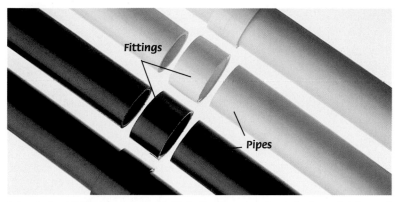

Solvent-glued fittings are used on rigid plastic pipes. The solvent dissolves a thin layer of plastic and bonds the pipe and fitting together.

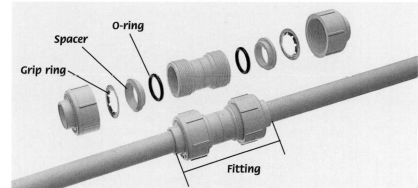

Plastic compression fittings (or grip fittings) are used to join CPVC pipe. Some types have a rubber O-ring, instead of a compression ring, that makes the watertight seal.

Plastic Pipe Grade Stamps

Material Identification: For sink traps and drain pipes, use PVC or ABS pipe. For water supply pipes, use CPVC pipe. PE is used for outdoor cold water supply. PB is not widely available and is prohibited by many local codes.

NSF rating: For sink traps and drains, choose PVC or ABS pipe that has a DWV rating from the NSF. For water supply pipes, choose CPVC pipe that has a PW rating.

Pipe diameter: PVC and ABS pipes for drains usually have an inside diameter of 1¼" to 4". CPVC pipes for water supply usually have an inside diameter of ½" or ¾".

Cutting and Fitting Plastic Pipe

Rigid ABS, PVC, or CPVC pipes can be cut with a tubing cutter or saw. Flexible PE pipes can be cut with a plastic tubing cutter or knife. When cutting any type of plastic pipe, make sure all cuts are level and straight to ensure watertight joints.

There are a variety of fittings available for joining plastic pipes. Plastic compression fittings are used to join rigid plastic pipes to copper pipes. Barbed, rigid PVC fittings and stainless steel hose clamps connect PE pipe. Rigid plastics are joined using plastic fittings and primer and solvent glue specifically made for the pipe material being joined. All-purpose or universal solvents may be used on all types of rigid plastic pipe. Solvent glue hardens in about 30 seconds, so test-fit all the plastic pipe and fittings before gluing the first joint. For best results, the pipe and fittings should be dulled with an emery cloth and liquid primer before they are joined.

Liquid solvent glues and primers are toxic and flammable. Always provide adequate ventilation when fitting plastics, and store the products away from heat.

Tools: Tubing cutter (or saw), felt-tipped pen, utility knife.

Materials: Plastic pipe and fittings, emery cloth, petroleum jelly, plastic-pipe primer, solvent glue, rag.

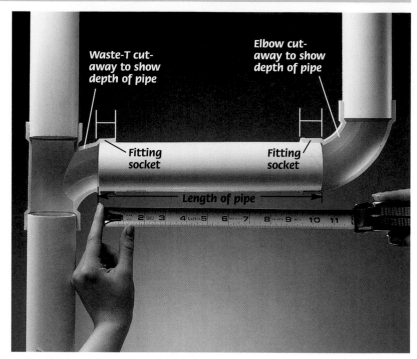

Find the length of plastic pipe needed by measuring between the bottoms of the fitting sockets (fittings shown here cutaway). Mark the length on the pipe with a felt-tipped pen.

Cutting Rigid Plastic Pipe

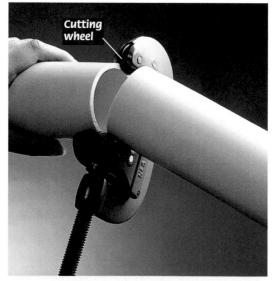

Tubing cutter: Tighten the tool around the pipe so the cutting wheel is on the marked line. Rotate the tool around the pipe, tightening the screw every two rotations, until the pipe snaps.

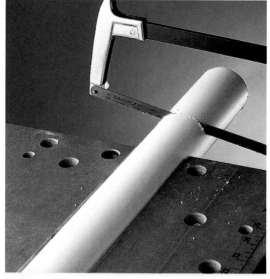

Hacksaw: Clamp the plastic pipe in a portable gripping bench or a vise, and keep the hacksaw blade straight while sawing. TIP: To draw a straight cutting line around the circumference of a pipe, wrap a sheet of paper around the pipe and line up the paper edges. Then, trace along the edge.

Miter box: Make straight cuts on all types of plastic pipe with a power miter saw or hand miter box (see page 226). With a hand miter box, use a hacksaw rather than a back saw.

Fitting Rigid Plastic Pipe with Solvent Glue

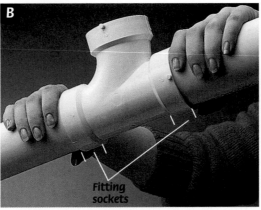

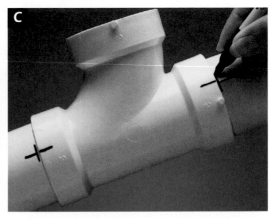

Measure and cut the pipe to length. Remove rough burrs on the cut ends, using a utility knife.

Test-fit all pipes and fittings. The pipes should fit tightly against the bottom of the fitting sockets.

Make alignment and depth marks across each pipe joint, using a felt-tipped pen. Disassemble the pipes.

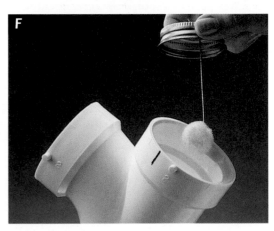

Clean the ends of the pipes and the fitting sockets, using an emery cloth.

Apply plastic-pipe primer to one end of a pipe.

Apply plastic-pipe primer inside the fitting socket.

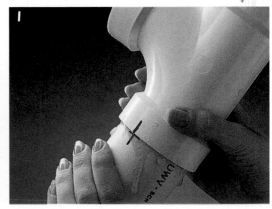

Apply a thick coat of solvent glue to the end of the pipe, and a thin coat to the inside surface of the fitting socket. Work quickly. Solvent glue hardens in about 30 seconds.

Quickly position the pipe and fitting so the alignment marks are offset by about 2" and the end of the pipe fits flush against the bottom of the socket.

Twist the pipe until the marks are aligned. Hold the pipe in place for about 20 seconds, then wipe away any excess glue with a rag. Let the joint dry undisturbed for 30 minutes.

Working with Galvanized Iron Pipe

Galvanized iron pipe often is found in older homes, where it's used for water supply and small drain lines. It can be identified by the zinc coating that gives it a silver color and by the threaded fittings used to connect the pipes.

Galvanized iron pipes and fittings corrode with age and eventually must be replaced. Low water pressure may be a sign that rust has built up inside galvanized pipes. Blockages usually occur in elbow fittings. Don't try to clean galvanized pipes—replace them instead.

Galvanized iron pipe and fittings are available at hardware stores and home centers. When purchasing, specify the interior diameter (I.D.) of the pipe and fittings. Pre-threaded pipes, called *nipples*, are available in lengths from 1" to 12". If a project requires longer pipes, have a hardware or plumbing supply store cut and thread them to your specifications.

Old galvanized iron systems can be difficult to repair or replace. When fittings are rusted in place, what seems like a small job may quickly become a much larger project. Cutting apart a section of pipe often reveals adjacent pipes that also need to be replaced. If your project involves extensive changes, consult a plumber; it may be easier to replace the old pipes.

When disassembling a run of pipe and fittings, start at the end of the run and unscrew each piece in turn. Reaching the middle of a run to replace a section of pipe can be a long, tedious job. However, a three-piece fitting, called a *union*, makes it possible to remove a section of pipe or a fitting without taking apart the entire system.

While detaching pipes, use two wrenches, one stationary and one moving. Position the wrenches so the jaws face opposite directions, and move the one wrench handle toward the opening of its jaws.

Don't confuse galvanized iron with black iron, which is available in similar sizes and has similar fittings. Black iron is used only for gas lines.

> **Tools:** Reciprocating saw with metal-cutting blade or hacksaw, wire brush, pipe wrenches, propane torch.
>
> **Materials:** Nipples, end caps, union fitting, pipe joint compound, replacement fittings (if needed).

Tips for Working with Galvanized Iron Pipe

Measure old pipe before replacing it. Add ½" at each end for the pipe threads that extend inside the fitting. Bring the overall measurement to the store when buying parts.

Use a union fitting and two threaded pipe nipples to replace a section of old pipe. When assembled, the union and nipples must equal the length of the pipe being replaced.

Replacing a Section of Galvanized Iron Pipe

A

Cut through the section of pipe, using a reciprocating saw with a metal-cutting blade or a hacksaw.

B

Hold the fitting stationary with one pipe wrench, and use another to unscrew the old pipe. The jaws of the wrenches should face opposite directions.

C

Remove any corroded fittings using two pipe wrenches, one to turn the fitting and the other to hold the pipe. Clean the threads with a wire brush.

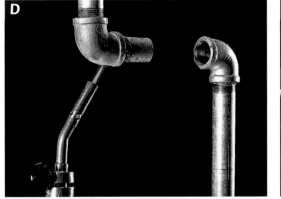

D

Heat stubborn fittings with a propane torch for easy removal. Shield flammable materials with a double layer of sheet metal, and apply the flame for 5 to 10 seconds.

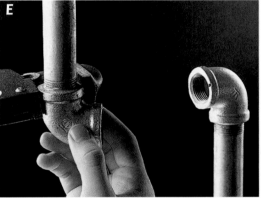

E

Spread pipe joint compound evenly over the threads of all pipes and nipples. Use two wrenches to tighten the new fittings onto the pipes, leaving them ⅛ turn out of alignment.

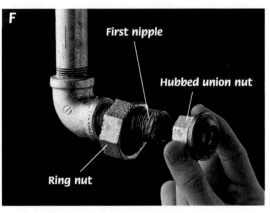

F

First nipple

Hubbed union nut

Ring nut

Screw the first nipple into a fitting and tighten it with a pipe wrench. Slide a ring nut onto the nipple, screw the hubbed union nut onto the nipple and tighten it with a pipe wrench.

G

Second nipple

Screw a second nipple onto the other fitting and tighten it with a pipe wrench.

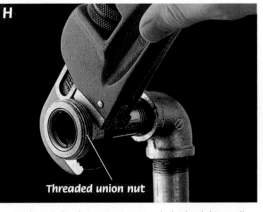

H

Threaded union nut

Screw threaded union nut onto second nipple; tighten. Align pipes so lip of hubbed nut fits inside threaded union nut.

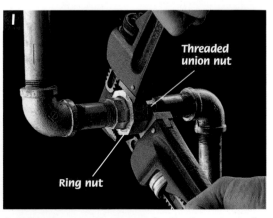

I

Threaded union nut

Ring nut

Complete the connection by screwing the ring nut onto the threaded union nut. Tighten the ring nut.

Working with Cast-iron Pipe

Cast-iron pipe is rarely installed these days, but years ago it was commonly used within DWV systems. It can be identified by its dark color, rough surface, and large size—usually 3" or more in diameter.

Cast-iron pipe is often joined with *hubbed fittings* (see step A, below), made by inserting the straight end of one pipe into the flared, or *hubbed*, end of another pipe. The joints are sealed with packing material (called *oakum*) and lead.

Hubbed fittings sometimes develop leaks, and pipes can rust through. You can replace a leaky fitting with a section of plastic pipe. You can also connect a new drain pipe to a cast-iron stack using a plastic waste fitting. The basic steps are the same for both projects.

A special fitting called a *banded coupling* is used to connect new plastic pipe to existing cast iron. A banded coupling has a neoprene sleeve that seals the joint and stainless steel bands and screw clamps that hold the pipes together. These couplings come in different styles, so check the local plumbing code to determine which types are approved in your area.

The best way to cut cast-iron pipe is with a rental tool called a *snap cutter*. Snap cutter designs vary, so be sure to follow the rental dealer's instructions for using the tool. Also be aware that using a snap cutter on weakened, brittle, or very old pipe can cause the pipe to crumble or shatter. Before you cut, have a professional inspect the pipe and recommend the best method for cutting it.

Cast-iron pipe is heavy, and you must provide permanent support on both sides of a pipe before cutting it (see photos, right).

Tools: Chalk, adjustable wrench, cast iron snap cutter, hacksaw, ratchet wrench.

Materials: Riser clamps or strap hangers, wood blocks, 2½" wallboard screws, banded couplings, plastic pipe.

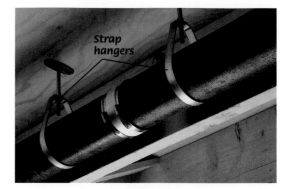

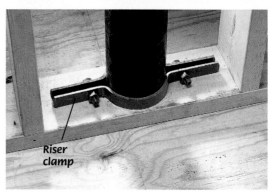

Install supports for cast-iron pipe before cutting. Support horizontal pipe with strap hangers every 5 ft. and at every joint connection (top). Support vertical pipe at every floor level and above every cut, using riser clamps (bottom).

Replacing a Section of Cast-iron Pipe

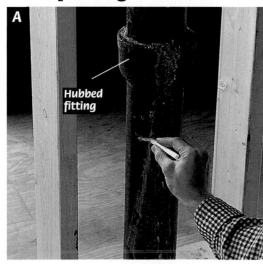

A

Hubbed fitting

Use chalk to mark cutting lines on the cast-iron pipe. If you're replacing a leaky hubbed fitting, mark at least 6" above and below the fitting.

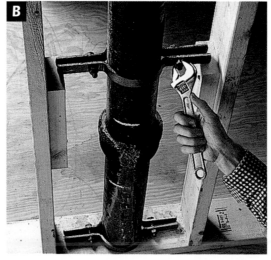

B

Support the lower section of pipe by installing a riser clamp flush against the bottom plate or floor. Install a riser clamp 6" to 12" above the section being replaced. Attach wood blocks to the studs with 2½" wallboard screws, so that the riser clamp rests securely on the tops of the blocks.

C

Wrap the chain of the snap cutter around the pipe so the cutting wheels align with the chalk line. Tighten the chain and then snap the pipe according to the tool manufacturer's directions.

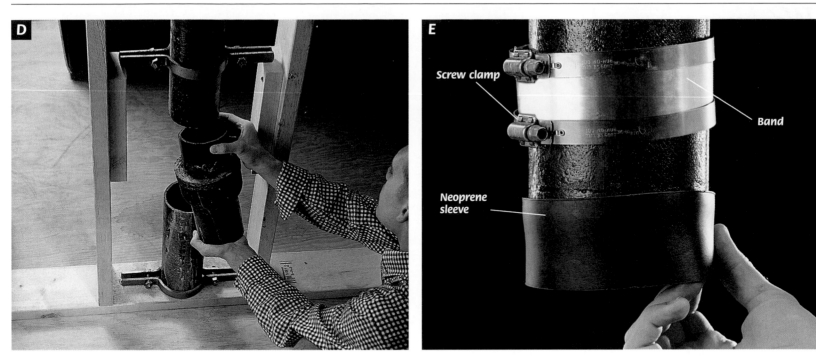

D

Make a second cut at the other chalk line, and remove the section of pipe. Cut a length of PVC or ABS plastic pipe 1" shorter than the section of cast-iron pipe that has been cut away (see page 80).

E

Screw clamp

Band

Neoprene sleeve

Slip a band and neoprene sleeve of a banded coupling onto each end of the cast-iron pipe. Make sure the cast-iron pipe is seated snugly against the rubber separator ring molded into the interior of the sleeve (see step F).

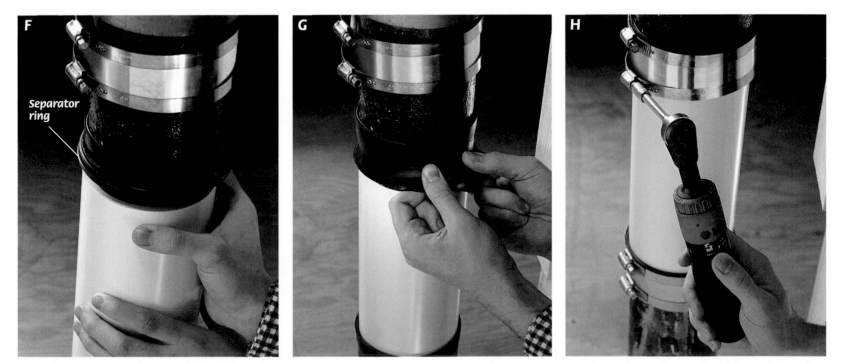

F

Separator ring

Fold back the end of each neoprene sleeve until the molded separator ring on the inside of the sleeve is visible. Position the new plastic pipe so it is aligned with the cast-iron pipes.

G

Roll the ends of the neoprene sleeves over the new plastic pipe.

H

Slide the bands over the neoprene sleeves and tighten the screw clamps with a ratchet wrench or screwdriver.

Installing New Plumbing

A major plumbing project can be a complicated affair that often requires demolition and carpentry work. In addition, your bathroom or kitchen plumbing may be unusable for several days while you complete the work, so arrange backup facilities to use during this time.

The how-to projects shown here demonstrate standard plumbing techniques but should not be used as exact models for your own projects. Pipe and fitting sizes, fixture layouts, and pipe routing will vary according to individual circumstances.

Before you begin work, create a detailed map of your plumbing system to guide your work and help you obtain the required permits. Determine the scope of your project and develop a working plan, allowing for minimum code clearances and comfort. Many of

the standard code specifications are shown on pages 88 to 92. As with any construction project, always consult the local building codes before finalizing your plans.

To ensure that your project goes quickly, always buy plenty of pipe and fittings—at least 25% more than you think you'll need. Making extra trips to the store for last-minute supplies is a nuisance and can add many hours to your project. Always purchase from a reputable retailer who will allow you to return leftover fittings for credit.

When scheduling your project, be sure to allow time for inspections. Find out whether the inspector will require a pressure test of the new plumbing; if a test is required, perform your own test beforehand (see page 93).

Mapping Your Plumbing System

Mapping your plumbing system is a good way to familiarize yourself with your home's plumbing layout, and it can help you plan your plumbing renovation project.

With a good map, you can envision the best spots for new fixtures and plan new pipe routes more efficiently. Maps also help in emergencies, when you need to locate burst or leaking pipes quickly.

Draw a plumbing map for each floor of your home, using the original floor plans of your house or your own drawings (see pages 18 to 19). Convert the general outlines for each floor to tracing paper, so you can overlay the drawings and still read the underlying information.

Walls on your map can be drawn larger than scale to fit all the plumbing symbols you need to map, but keep overall room dimensions and plumbing fixtures to scale. Fixture templates and tracing paper are available at drafting supply stores.

Be sure to include diagrams for basements and attic spaces in your plumbing map.

Map your plumbing system using a separate diagram for each floor, starting with the basement diagram. Mark the location of the water meter, found on the main supply line. If your house doesn't have a basement, start your mapping at the meter or water heater.

Create a tracing-paper diagram for each floor of the house. Complete the mapping for one floor, then lay the diagram for the next floor over the lower floor. Transfer the locations of pipes that carry through from one floor to the next.

Locate all water supply runs by following the cold water pipe leading from the water meter. Follow all branch supply lines until they terminate at an outdoor faucet, or a fixture, or until they connect to a vertical riser leading to the next floor.

Determine the path of vertical supply risers by measuring from the nearest outside wall to the riser. Do the same at the respective fixture on the next floor up. If the measurements are not the same, there is a hidden offset in the pipe route.

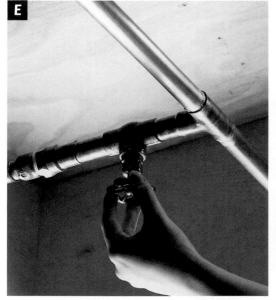

Locate and map all valves throughout the supply lines. This will allow you to shut off the water to pipes you're working on while maintaining service to the rest of the house. Use the symbols shown in the Standard Plumbing Symbols chart (right) to identify different valve types (see page 66).

Map all waste and vent pipes, starting with the main waste-vent stack, found in the basement. Note horizontal drain pipes on all floors, and the points where vertical drains extend between floors. Note auxiliary waste-vent stacks (typically 2" vertical pipes often found near basement utility sinks or below a kitchen).

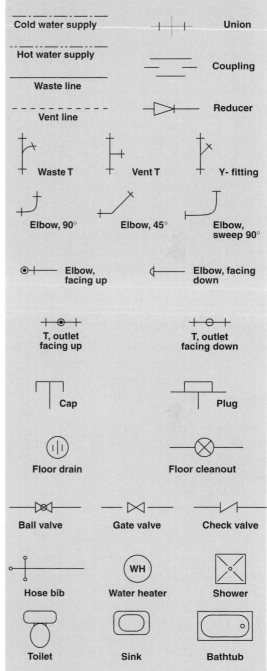

Standard Plumbing Symbols

Cold water supply

Hot water supply

Waste line

Vent line

Union

Coupling

Reducer

Waste T   Vent T   Y- fitting

Elbow, 90°   Elbow, 45°   Elbow, sweep 90°

Elbow, facing up   Elbow, facing down

T, outlet facing up   T, outlet facing down

Cap   Plug

Floor drain   Floor cleanout

Ball valve   Gate valve   Check valve

Hose bib   Water heater (WH)   Shower

Toilet   Sink   Bathtub

TIP: Use standard plumbing symbols on your map to identify the components of your plumbing system. These symbols will help you and the building inspector follow connections and transitions more easily.

Plumbing Codes & Permits

The Plumbing Code is the set of regulations that building officials and inspectors use to evaluate your project plans and the quality of your work. Codes vary from region to region, but most are based on the National Uniform Plumbing Code, a highly technical, difficult-to-read manual. More user-friendly code handbooks are available at bookstores and libraries. These handbooks are based on the National Uniform Plumbing Code, but they are easier to read and include diagrams and photos.

Sometimes these handbooks discuss three different plumbing zones in an effort to accommodate state variations in regulations. Remember that local plumbing code always supersedes national code. Your local building inspector can be a valuable source of information and may provide you with a convenient summary sheet of the regulations that apply to your project.

As part of its effort to ensure public safety, your community building department requires a permit for most plumbing projects. When you apply for a permit, the building official will want to review three drawings of your plumbing project: a site plan, a water supply diagram, and a drain-waste-vent diagram. If the official is satisfied that your project meets code requirements, you will be issued a plumbing permit, which is your legal permission to begin work. As your project nears completion, the inspector will visit your home to check your work.

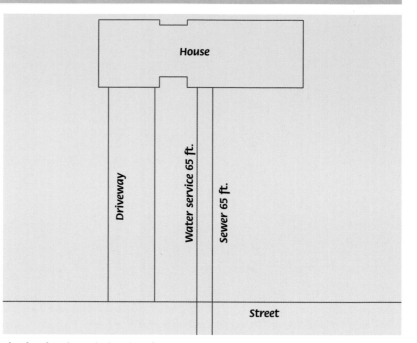

The site plan shows the location of the water main and sewer main with respect to your yard and home. The distances from your foundation to the water main and from the foundation to the main sewer should be indicated on the site map.

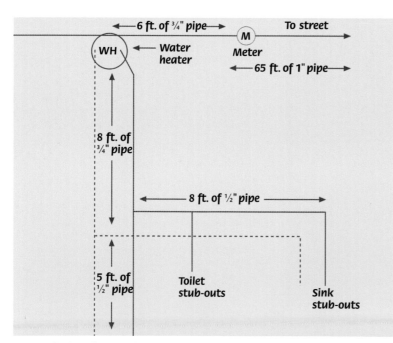

The supply riser diagram shows the length of the hot and cold water pipes and the relation of the fixtures to one another. The inspector will use this diagram to determine the proper size for the new water supply pipes in your system.

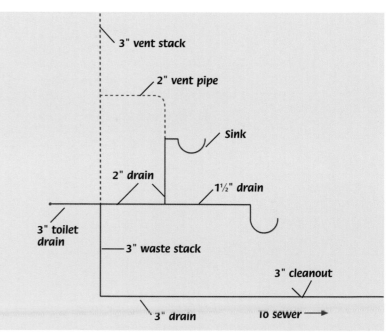

A DWV diagram shows the routing of drain and vent pipes in your system. Indicate the lengths of drain pipes and the distances between fixtures. The inspector will use this diagram to determine if you have properly sized the drain traps, drain pipes, and vent pipes.

Sizing for Water Distribution Pipes

Fixture	Unit rating	Size of service pipe from street	Size of distribution pipe from water meter	Maximum length (ft.)—total fixture units					
				40	60	80	100	150	200
Toilet	3								
Vanity sink	1								
Shower	2	³⁄₄"	½"	9	8	7	6	5	4
Bathtub	2								
Dishwasher	2	³⁄₄"	³⁄₄"	27	23	19	17	14	11
Kitchen sink	2	³⁄₄"	1"	44	40	36	33	28	23
Clothes washer	2								
Utility sink	2	1"	1"	60	47	41	36	30	25
Sillcock	3	1"	1¼"	102	87	76	67	52	44

Water distribution pipes are the main pipes extending from the water meter throughout the house, supplying water to the branch pipes leading to individual fixtures. To determine the size of the distribution pipes, you must first calculate the total demand in "fixture units" (above left) and the overall length of the water supply lines, from the street hookup through the water meter and to the most distant fixture in the house. Then, use the second table (above, right) to calculate the minimum size for the water distribution pipes. Note that the fixture unit capacity depends partly on the size of the street-side pipe that delivers water to your meter.

Sizing for Branch Pipes & Supply Tubes

Fixture	Min. branch pipe size	Min. supply tube size
Toilet	½"	³⁄₈"
Vanity sink	½"	³⁄₈"
Shower	½"	½"
Bathtub	½"	½"
Dishwasher	½"	½"
Kitchen sink	½"	½"
Clothes washer	½"	½"
Utility sink	½"	½"
Sillcock	³⁄₄"	N.A.
Water heater	³⁄₄"	N.A.

Branch pipes are the water supply lines that run from the distribution pipes toward the individual fixtures. **Supply tubes** are the vinyl, chromed copper, or mesh tubes that carry water from the branch pipes to the fixtures. Use the chart above as a guide when sizing branch pipes and supply tubes.

Valve Requirements

Full-bore gate valves or ball valves are required in the following locations: on both the street side and house side of the water meter; on the inlet pipes for water heaters and heating system boilers. Individual fixtures should have accessible shutoff valves, but these need not be full-bore valves. All sillcocks must have individual control valves located inside the house.

Plumbing Codes & Permits (cont.)

Preventing Water Hammer

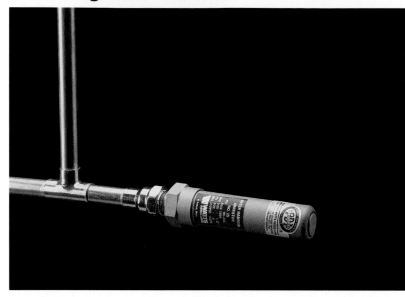

Water hammer arresters may be required by code. Water hammer is a problem that may occur when the fast-acting valves on washing machines or other appliances cause pipes to vibrate against framing members. The arrester works as a shock absorber, with a watertight diaphragm inside. It is mounted to a T-fitting installed near the appliance.

Anti-siphon Devices

Vacuum breakers must be installed on all indoor and outdoor hose bibs and any outdoor branch pipes that run underground. By allowing air to enter the pipes, vacuum breakers prevent contaminated water from being drawn into the water supply pipes in the event of a sudden drop in water pressure in the water main.

Maximum Hole and Notch Sizes for Framing Members

Framing member	Maximum hole size	Maximum notch size
2 × 4 load-bearing stud	1⁷⁄₁₆" diameter	⅞" deep
2 × 4 non-load-bearing stud	2½" diameter	1⁷⁄₁₆" deep
2 × 6 load-bearing stud	2¼" diameter	1⅜" deep
2 × 6 non-load-bearing stud	3⁵⁄₁₆" diameter	2³⁄₁₆" deep
2 × 6 joists	1½" diameter	⅞" deep
2 × 8 joists	2⅜" diameter	1¼" deep
2 × 10 joists	3¹⁄₁₆" diameter	1½" deep
2 × 12 joists	3¾" diameter	1⅞" deep

A framing member chart shows the maximum sizes for holes and notches that can be cut into studs and joists when running pipes. Where possible, use notches rather than bored holes because pipe installation is usually easier. When boring holes, there must be at least ⅝" of wood between the edge of a stud and the hole, and at least 2" between the edge of a joist and the hole. Joists can be notched only in the end one-third of the overall span; never in the middle one-third of the joist. When two pipes are run through a stud, the pipes should be stacked one over the other, never side by side.

NOTE: This chart is shown for general reference, and its specifications may not conform to all building codes; check with the local building department regarding regulations in your area.

Drain Cleanouts

Drain cleanouts make your DWV system easier to service. In most areas, the plumbing code requires that you place cleanouts at the end of every horizontal drain run. Where horizontal runs are not accessible, removable drain traps will suffice as cleanouts.

Pipe Support Intervals

Type of pipe	Vertical support interval	Horizontal support interval
Copper	6 ft.	10 ft.
ABS	4 ft.	4 ft.
CPVC	3 ft.	3 ft.
PVC	4 ft.	4 ft.
Galvanized Iron	12 ft.	15 ft.
Cast Iron	5 ft.	15 ft.

Minimum intervals for supporting pipes are determined by the type of pipe and its orientation in the system. Use only brackets and supports made of the same (or compatible) materials as the pipes. Remember that the measurements shown above are minimum requirements; many plumbers install pipe supports at closer intervals.

Fixture Units & Minimum Trap Size

Fixture	Fixture units	Min. trap size
Shower	2	2"
Vanity sink	1	1¼"
Bathtub	2	1½"
Dishwasher	2	1½"
Kitchen sink	2	1½"
Kitchen sink*	3	1½"
Clothes washer	2	1½"
Utility sink	2	1½"
Floor drain	1	2"

*Kitchen sink with attached food disposer

Minimum trap size for fixtures is determined by the drain fixture unit rating, a unit of measure assigned by the plumbing code. NOTE: Kitchen sinks rate 3 units if they include an attached food disposer, 2 units otherwise.

Sizes for Horizontal & Vertical Drain Pipes

Pipe size	Maximum fixture units for horizontal branch drain	Maximum fixture units for vertical drain stacks
1¼"	1	2
1½"	3	4
2"	6	10
2½"	12	20
3"	20	30
4"	160	240

Drain pipe sizes are determined by the load on the pipes, as measured by the total fixture units. Horizontal drain pipes less than 3" in diameter should slope ¼" per foot toward the main drain. Pipes 3" or more in diameter should slope ⅛" per foot. NOTE: Horizontal or vertical drain pipes for a toilet must be 3" or larger.

Plumbing Codes & Permits (cont.)

Vent Pipe Sizes, Critical Distances

Size of fixture drain	Minimum vent pipe size	Maximum trap-to-vent distance
1¼"	1¼"	2½ ft.
1½"	1¼"	3½ ft.
2"	1½"	5 ft.
3"	2"	6 ft.
4"	3"	10 ft.

Vent pipes are usually one pipe size smaller than the drain pipes they serve. Code requires that the distance between the drain trap and the vent pipe fall within a maximum "critical distance," a measurement that is determined by the size of the fixture drain. Use this chart to determine both the minimum size for the vent pipe and the maximum critical distance.

Vent Pipe Orientation to Drain Pipe

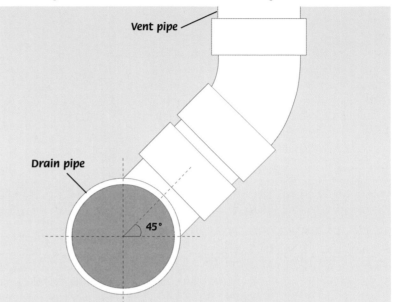

Vent pipes must extend in an upward direction from drains, no less than 45° from horizontal. This ensures that waste water cannot flow into the vent pipe and block it. At the opposite end, a new vent pipe should connect to an existing vent pipe or main waste-vent stack at a point at least 6" above the highest fixture draining into the system.

Wet Venting

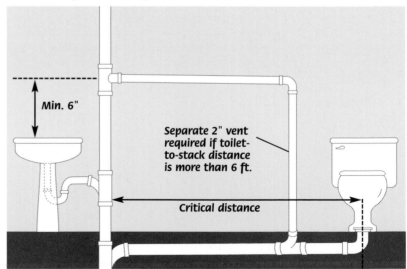

Wet vents are pipes that serve as a vent for one fixture and a drain for another. The sizing of a wet vent is based on the total fixture units it supports (see pages 89 and 91): a 3" wet vent can serve up to 12 fixture units; a 2" wet vent is rated for 4 fixture units; a 1½" wet vent, for only 1 fixture unit. NOTE: The distance between the wet-vented fixture and the wet vent itself must be no more than the maximum critical distance.

Auxiliary Venting

Fixtures must have auxiliary vents if the distance to the main waste-vent stack exceeds the critical distance. A toilet, for example, should have a separate vent pipe if it is located more than 6 ft. from the main waste-vent stack. This secondary vent pipe should connect to the stack or an existing vent pipe at a point at least 6" above the highest fixture on the system.

Testing New Plumbing Pipes

When the building inspector comes to review your new plumbing, he or she may require that you perform a pressure test on the DWV and water supply lines. The inspection and test should be performed after the system is completed, but before the new pipes are covered with wallboard. To ensure that the inspection goes smoothly, perform your own preliminary test, so you can locate and repair any problems before the inspection.

The DWV system is tested by blocking off the new drain and vent pipes, then pressurizing the system with air to see if it leaks. At the fixture stub-outs, the DWV pipes can be capped off or plugged with test balloons designed for this purpose. The air pump, pressure gauge, and test balloons required to test the DWV system can be obtained at tool rental centers.

Testing the water supply lines is a simple matter of turning on the water and examining the joints for leaks. If you find a leak, drain the pipes, disassemble and resolder the faulty joints.

*A **pressure gauge and air pump** are used to test DWV lines. The system is blocked off at each fixture and at points near where the new drain and vent pipes connect to the main stack. A weenie—a special test balloon with an air gauge and inflation valve—is inserted at a cleanout valve. An air pump is attached to the weenie, and the pipe is pressurized to 5 pounds per square inch (psi). To pass inspection, the system must hold this pressure for 15 minutes.*

Testing New DWV Pipes

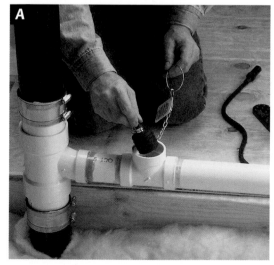

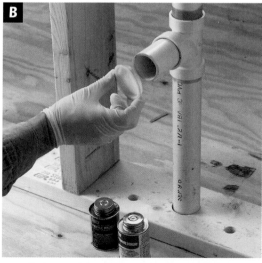

Insert test balloons into test T-fittings at the top and bottom of new DWV lines, blocking the pipes entirely. NOTE: Ordinary T-fittings installed near the bottom of drain lines and near the top of vent lines are generally used for test fittings. Use large balloons for toilet drains, and inflate them with an air pump.

Cap off the remaining fixture drains by solvent-gluing test caps onto the stub-outs. If the DWV system loses air when pressurized, check joints for leaks by rubbing soapy water over the fittings and looking for active bubbles. Cut out problem joints from the existing fitting and solvent-glue a new fitting in place, using couplings and short lengths of pipe.

After the DWV system has been inspected and approved by a building official, remove the test balloons and close the test T-fittings by solvent-gluing caps onto the open lines. Remove test caps by knocking them loose with a hammer.

Wiring

Many home improvement projects require some kind of electrical work. This work can always be hired out to a professional, but with a basic understanding of your home electrical system, you can easily complete many of the jobs yourself.

This section discusses the basics of an electrical system (pages 94 to 98), the tools and materials used in home wiring projects (pages 99 to 103), and how to plan your wiring project (pages 104 to 107). Also included are installation tips for household electrical devices and 15 circuit maps (pages 108 to 115) that show common wiring configurations.

Wiring Basics

Home Wiring Systems

Before starting a project that requires any electrical work, make sure you have a basic understanding of your home's electrical system.

The *service head* (photo, right), or weather head, anchors the power supplied by overhead *service wires* to your house. Standard 240-volt service is delivered by three wires: two wires of 120-volt current and a grounded neutral wire.

The *electric meter* measures every watt of power consumed by your electrical system. It's usually attached to the side of the house and is connected to the service head or buried power lines.

The *main service panel,* also called the breaker box or fuse box, distributes power to individual circuits. Each circuit breaker or fuse is designed to shut down the circuit in the event of an overload or a short circuit.

NOTE: The wires to the service head, electric meter, and service panel are always live unless the utility company turns them off. Never attempt to inspect or repair any of these devices. If you suspect a problem with them, contact the utility company.

Electrical boxes enclose wire connections. The National Electrical Code requires that

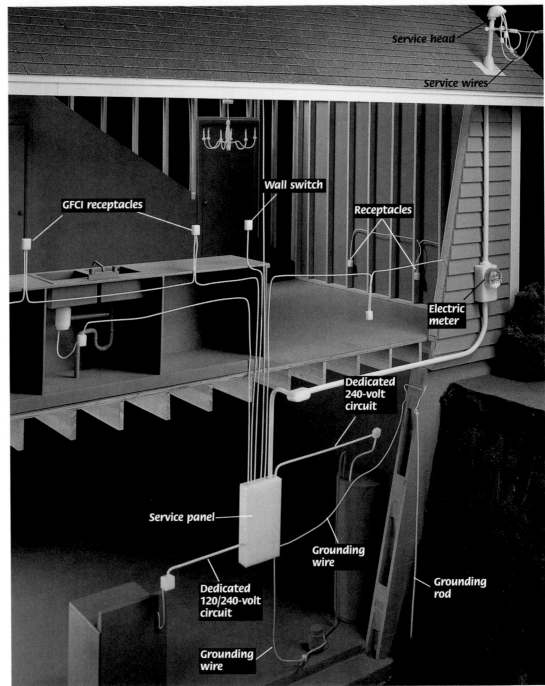

every wire connection and splice be contained within a plastic or metal electrical box.

Receptacles, or outlets, provide plug-in access to power. 125-volt, 15-amp three-prong receptacles are the most typical in wiring systems installed after 1965.

Switches control the current leading to light

fixtures, appliances, and receptacles. Light fixtures are wired directly into circuits.

The grounding wire connects the entire system to the earth through a metal water pipe or grounding rod. In the case of an overload or short circuit, it channels excess current harmlessly into the earth.

Understanding Circuits

If you look up the word *circuit* in the dictionary, you'll find the definition: "a regular tour around an assigned territory." As this indicates, household circuits carry electricity along a regular route from the main service panel, through the house, and back to the service panel. For the circuit to function properly, this loop must remain uninterrupted.

Current travels outward to electrical devices on "hot" wires and returns along "neutral" wires. The two kinds of wires are color coded: hot wires are black or red, and neutral wires typically are white or light gray.

For safety, most circuits also include a bare copper or green insulated grounding wire. The grounding wire helps reduce the chance of electrical shock and carries any excess current in the case of a short circuit or overload.

Circuits are rated according to the amount of power they can carry without overheating. If the devices on a circuit try to draw more power than that amount, the fuse or circuit breaker is triggered and automatically shuts down the circuit.

Usually, several switches, receptacles, fixtures,

or appliances are connected to each circuit, and a loose connection at any device can cause electricity to flow outside the circuit wires. The resulting reduction in resistance, called a *short circuit*, triggers the circuit breaker or fuse, and the circuit shuts down.

After passing through the electrical devices, current returns to the service panel along a neutral circuit wire. There it merges with a main circuit wire and leaves the house on a neutral service line that returns it to the transformer on the utility pole.

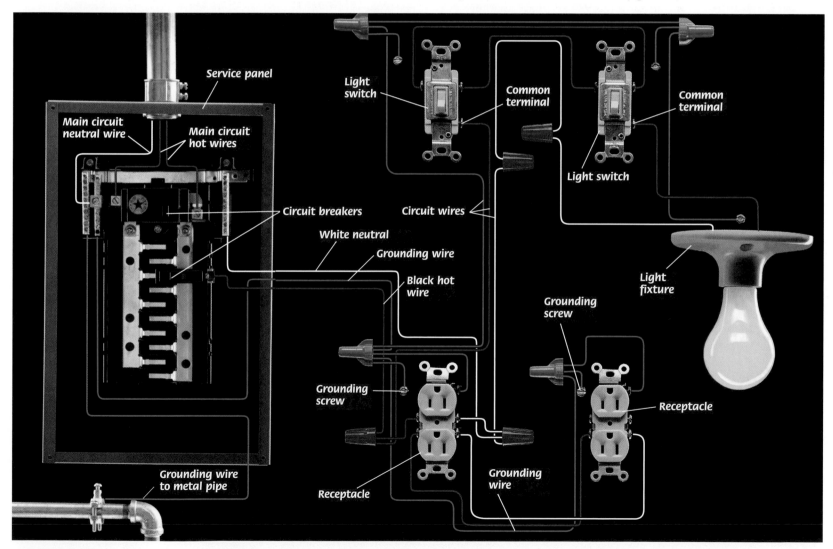

Household circuits carry electrical current through the house in a continuous loop. Power enters the system on hot wires (shown here in red) and returns along neutral wires (white). The system also includes grounding wires (green) for safety.

Grounding & Polarization

Electricity always seeks to return to its source and complete a continuous circuit. In a household wiring system, the return path is provided by neutral wires (usually white) that return the current to the main service panel.

When working with wiring, remember that electric current always seeks the path of least resistance. When you touch a device, tool, or appliance that has a short circuit, the current may attempt to return to its source by passing through your body.

Grounding wires are designed to minimize this danger by providing a safe, easy path for the current to follow back to its source. If you touch a short-circuited device that has a properly installed grounding wire, your chance of receiving a severe shock is greatly reduced.

Most electrical systems installed since 1920 also have another safety measure—receptacles that accept polarized plugs. While it's not a true grounding method, polarization is designed to keep the current flowing along the proper wires within the circuit.

In the 1940s, armored cable (also called BX or Greenfield cable) was installed in many homes. Armored cable has a metal sheath that, when connected to a metal junction box, provides a true grounding path back to the service panel.

Most wiring systems installed since 1965 contain NM (nonmetallic) cable that has a bare or green insulated copper wire that serves as a continuous grounding path for excess current. These circuits are usually equipped with three-slot receptacles, which have direct connections to the circuit grounding wire. This protects appliances, tools, and people from short circuits.

If a two-slot receptacle is connected to a grounded electrical box, you can plug three-prong plugs into it by using a receptacle adapter. To connect the adapter to the grounded metal electrical box, attach the short grounding wire or wire loop on the adapter to the receptacle's coverplate mounting screw.

Another safety precaution is the use of double-insulated tools. These devices have nonconductive plastic bodies that prevent shocks caused by short circuits. Because of these features, double-insulated tools can be used safely with two-slot receptacles.

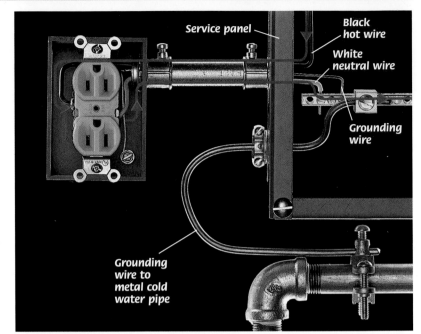

Normal current flow: *Current enters the electrical box along a black hot wire, then returns to the service panel along a white neutral wire. Any excess current passes into the earth via a grounding wire attached to a metal water pipe or grounding rod.*

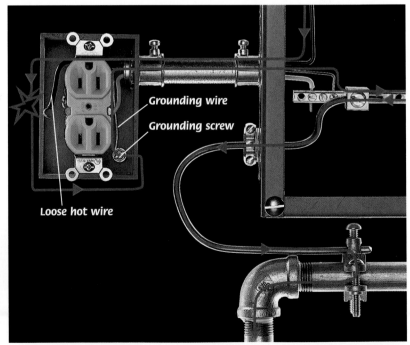

Short circuit: *Current is detoured by a loose wire in contact with the metal box. The grounding wire picks it up and channels it safely back to the main service panel. There, it returns to its source along a neutral service cable or enters the earth via the grounding system.*

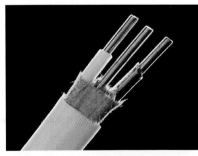

Nonmetallic (NM) cable *contains a bare copper wire that provides grounding.*

Armored (BX or Greenfield) cable *has a metal sheath that serves as a ground.*

Service Panels

Circuit breaker panel: Circuit breaker panels that provide 100 amps of power or more are common in wiring systems installed since the 1960s. They're usually housed in a gray metal cabinet that holds two rows of circuit breakers. The size of the service can be identified by the amperage rating stamped on the main circuit breaker, which is located at the top of the service panel.

A 100-amp service panel is now the standard minimum for new home construction and is considered adequate for medium-sized homes with up to three major electric appliances. Larger homes with more major appliances require a service panel that provides 150 amps or more.

If the main circuit breaker panel does not have enough open breaker slots for the new circuits you are planning, have an electrician install a circuit breaker subpanel. The subpanel serves as a second distribution center for connecting circuits. It receives power from a double-pole "feeder" circuit breaker installed in the main circuit breaker panel.

To shut off power to an individual circuit, flip the lever on the appropriate circuit breaker to the OFF position. To shut off power to the entire house, flip the lever on the main circuit breaker to the OFF position.

60-amp fuse panel: Sixty-amp fuse panels are common in wiring systems installed between 1950 and 1965. They're usually housed in a gray metal cabinet that holds four plug fuses and one or two pull-out fuse blocks for cartridge fuses.

A 60-amp fuse panel is adequate for small homes (up to 1100 sq. ft.) that have no more than one 240-volt appliance. Many homeowners upgrade 60-amp service to 100 amps or more to accommodate additional circuits.

To shut off power to an individual circuit, carefully unscrew the appropriate fuse, touching only its insulated rim. To shut off power to the entire house, grasp the handle of the main fuse block and pull sharply to remove it; shut off power to major appliances by removing the appliance fuse box in the same way.

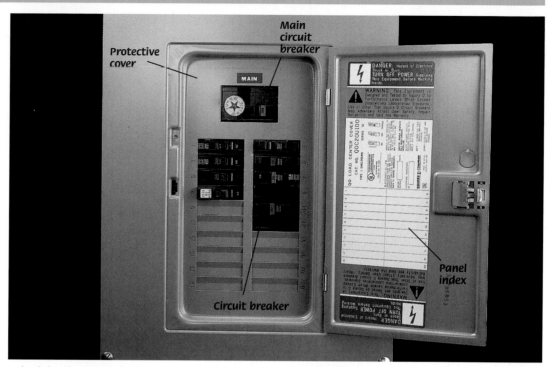

A circuit breaker panel of 100 amps or more holds two rows of individual circuit breakers. The size of the service is indicated on the main circuit breaker.

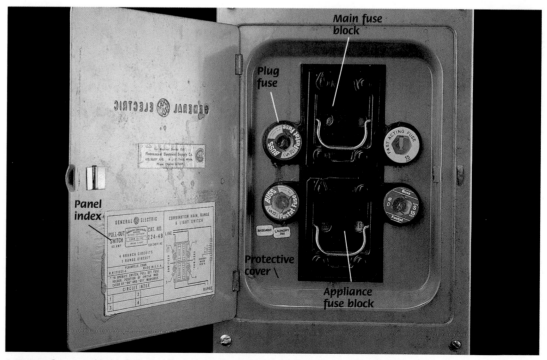

A 60-amp fuse panel holds four plug fuses plus one or two pull-out fuse blocks. This panel is adequate for a small home that has no more than one 240-volt appliance.

Electrical Safety

Turn off the power at the service panel before you start work. Switch the appropriate breaker to the OFF position.

Post a sign to keep others from turning the power on. Turn power back on only when you are done working.

After shutting off the power at the service panel, test receptacles twice with a neon circuit tester.

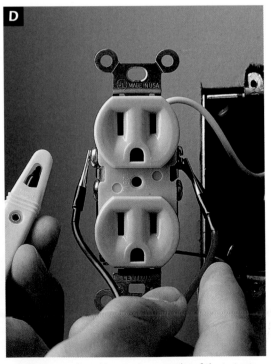

Test the receptacle again. Touch one probe of the tester to a brass screw terminal and the other to a silver terminal.

When working with electricity, safety is always a primary concern. An electric current follows its own rules, and the best way to ensure safety is to respect those rules and take a few commonsense precautions.

Before starting any electrical work, always turn off power to the area in which you're working. In the main service panel, shut off the breaker or remove the fuse that controls the circuit involved (photo A). A circuit map (see page 104) will help you locate the correct fuses or breakers. Leave a note on the service panel to prevent others from turning on the power while you're working (photo B).

After shutting off the circuit, use a neon circuit tester to confirm the power is off before working with a device. To test receptacles, place one probe of the tester in each slot (photo C). If the tester light glows, the receptacle is receiving current. Return to the panel and shut off the correct circuit. Always check both outlets of a duplex receptacle.

Before touching any wires, test the receptacle again. Remove the coverplate and receptacle mounting screws, and carefully pull the receptacle from the box. Test both a brass and silver screw terminal (photo D). If the tester glows, return to the service panel. If wires are connected to both sets of screw terminals, test both sets.

Test light fixtures for power by touching one tester probe to the grounding screw, bare copper grounding wire, or a grounded metal box, and touching the other probe to the hot and neutral wires, in turn. Test switches by touching one probe to a ground and the other to each screw terminal on the switch.

Here are a few more basic safety rules:
• Use the correct fuses or breakers in the service panel. Never install a fuse or breaker with a higher amperage than the circuit.
• Use tools with insulated handles.
• Don't touch metal pipes, faucets, or fixtures while working with electricity.
• Don't drill into walls or ceilings without shutting off electrical power to the area.
• Use only UL-approved electrical parts or devices (they have been tested for safety).

Tools & Materials for Projects

Unlike some other kinds of projects, home electrical projects require tools that are simple, inexpensive, and widely available. The set shown below includes the basic tools you'll need for most home improvement projects.

Neon circuit testers (A) check wires, receptacles, fixtures, and switches for power. This inexpensive device has two probes attached to a light. When the probes are in place and a circuit is live, the tester light is activated. Always make sure the bulb is working on a circuit tester by "testing" a receptacle you know to be live.

Cable rippers (B) remove the outer sheath from nonmetallic (NM) cable, without cutting the insulation on the individual wires inside.

The tool is squeezed to force a small cutting point through plastic vinyl sheath, then pulled along the cable to tear it open.

Combination tools (C) cut cables and wires, measure wire gauges, and strip insulation from individual wires. These tools are also useful for crimping special fasteners. Their insulated handles ensure safety when working with electrical wires.

Needlenose pliers (D) bend and shape wires, and are especially useful for making loops for screw terminal connections. Some have cutting jaws for clipping wires. The fine tip of this tool also provides access in narrow spaces.

Linesman's pliers (E) are better than needlenose for cutting and pulling wire. The heavy, square jaws of this tool make it ideal for twisting wires together.

Insulated screwdrivers (F) have rubber- or plastic-coated handles to reduce the risk of shock. For the many different screws common to electrical work, it helps to have several sizes of both slotted and Phillips screwdrivers.

Fish tape (G), available both with and without a reel, is a good tool to have on hand for running wire through finished walls. The thin metal tape is threaded through a wall, wire is attached to its end, and the fish tape is pulled back out, threading the wire as it comes.

Utility knives (H) are handy for slitting sheathing on nonmetallic cable and for general-purpose cutting. The thin blades are razor sharp and can be replaced easily when they become dull.

Fuse pullers (I) help remove individual cartridge-type fuses from fuse blocks in older service panels.

Continuity testers (J) are battery-operated tools that check for broken circuitry paths, such as short circuits and wiring flaws in switches, sockets, wiring, and fuse elements. They can help determine whether a fuse must be replaced and give a reading on a fuse's resistance.

Tools & Materials: Boxes

Use the chart below to select the proper type of box for your wiring project. For most indoor wiring done with NM cable, use plastic electrical boxes. Plastic boxes are inexpensive, lightweight, and easy to install.

Metal boxes also can be used for indoor NM cable installations and are still favored by some electricians, especially for supporting heavy ceiling light fixtures.

If you have a choice of box depths, always choose the deepest size available. Wire connections are easier to make if boxes are roomy. Forcing wires into an undersized box can damage wires and disturb their connections, creating a potential fire hazard. Check with your local inspector if you have questions regarding proper box size.

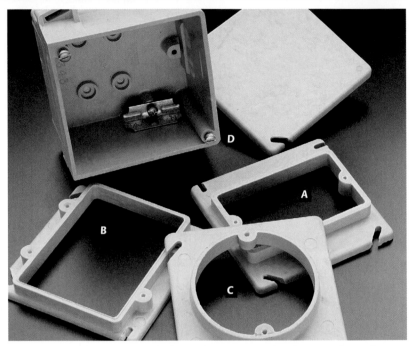

Box type	Typical Uses
Plastic	• Protected indoor wiring, used with NM cable • Not suited for heavy light fixtures and fans
Metal	• Exposed indoor wiring, used with metal conduit • Protected indoor wiring, used with NM cable
Cast aluminum	• Outdoor wiring, used with metal conduit
PVC plastic	• Outdoor wiring, used with PVC conduit • Exposed indoor wiring, used with PVC conduit

A square plastic box, 4 × 4" (3" deep), provides extra space for wire connections. It has pre-attached nails for easy mounting. A variety of adapter plates are available for 4 × 4" boxes, including single-gang (A), double-gang (B), light fixture (C), and junction box coverplate (D). Adapter plates come in several thicknesses to match different wall surfaces.

3½"-deep plastic boxes with preattached mounting nails are used for any indoor wiring project that will be protected by finished walls, such as a room addition or a rewired kitchen. Common styles include single-gang (A), double-gang (B), and triple-gang (C). Double-gang and triple-gang boxes require internal cable clamps.

Metal boxes should be used for exposed indoor wiring, such as conduit installations in an unfinished basement. Metal boxes are available in the same variety of sizes and shapes as plastic boxes and can also be used for wiring that will be covered by finished walls. Metal boxes are good electrical conductors, so they must be pigtailed to the circuit grounding wires to reduce the chance of shock caused by a short circuit.

Plastic retrofit boxes are used when a new switch or receptacle must fit inside a finished wall. Use internal cable clamps with these boxes.

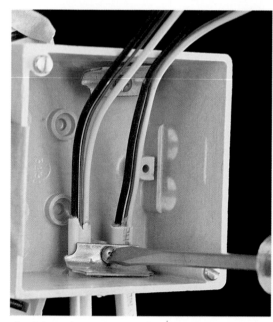

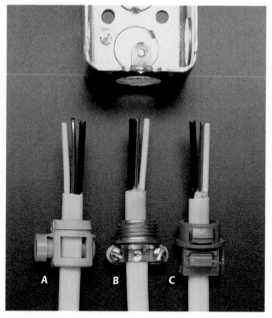

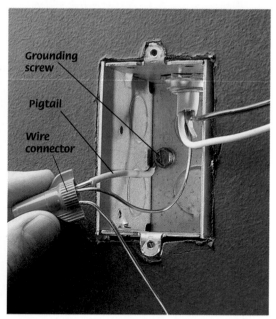

Plastic boxes larger than 2 × 4", and all retrofit boxes, must have internal cable clamps. After installing cables in the box, tighten the cable clamps over the cables so they are gripped firmly, but not so tightly that the cable sheathing is crushed.

Cables entering a metal box must be clamped. A variety of clamps are available, including plastic clamps (A, C) and threaded metal clamps (B).

Metal boxes must be grounded to the circuit grounding system. Connect the circuit grounding wires to the box with a green insulated pigtail wire and wire connector (as shown) or with a grounding clip (see page 120).

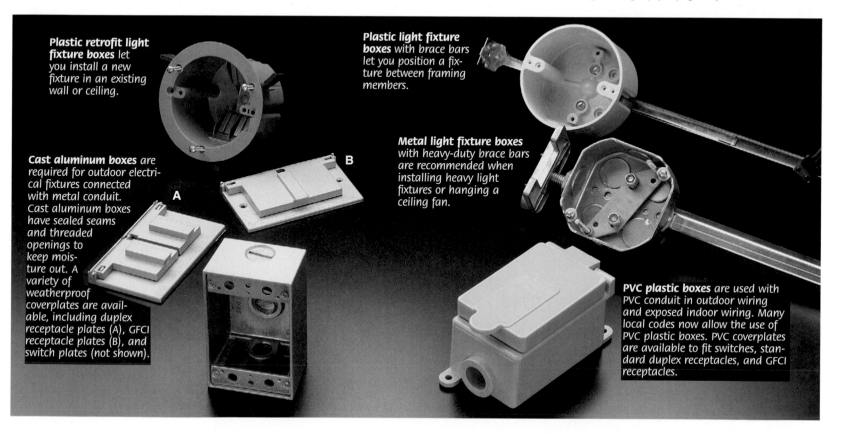

Plastic retrofit light fixture boxes let you install a new fixture in an existing wall or ceiling.

Plastic light fixture boxes with brace bars let you position a fixture between framing members.

Cast aluminum boxes are required for outdoor electrical fixtures connected with metal conduit. Cast aluminum boxes have sealed seams and threaded openings to keep moisture out. A variety of weatherproof coverplates are available, including duplex receptacle plates (A), GFCI receptacle plates (B), and switch plates (not shown).

Metal light fixture boxes with heavy-duty brace bars are recommended when installing heavy light fixtures or hanging a ceiling fan.

PVC plastic boxes are used with PVC conduit in outdoor wiring and exposed indoor wiring. Many local codes now allow the use of PVC plastic boxes. PVC coverplates are available to fit switches, standard duplex receptacles, and GFCI receptacles.

Tools & Materials: Wire & Cables

Many types of wire and cable are available at home centers, but only a few are used in most home wiring projects. Modern wire is solid copper, and individual wires are insulated with colored rubber or plastic to identify the wires as hot (black or red), neutral (white or gray), or grounding (green or bare).

In the past, some wire was made from aluminum or aluminum covered with a thin layer of copper (see page 103). Aluminum wiring requires special tools available only to licensed electricians.

Choose wire large enough for the circuit "ampacity," a measurement of how much current a wire can carry safely. Check your local electrical code to learn which type of wire to use.

Cables are identified by the wire gauge and the number of insulated circuit wires they contain. In addition, all cables have a grounding wire.

For example, a cable labeled "12/2 W G" contains two insulated 12-gauge wires, plus a grounding wire.

Use NM cable for new wiring installed inside walls. NM cable is easy to install when walls and ceilings are unfinished. Running cable in finished walls requires extra planning, and often is easier with a helper (see pages 121 to 122).

The growing need to send and receive electronic information has created a demand for high-performance, low-voltage cabling which can carry larger amounts of information faster. Coaxial cable carries audio/video signals throughout your home. Category 5 cable is similar to telephone cable but can transmit digital information six times faster than standard phone wire, providing high-speed connections between phones, computers, fax machines, and other equipment.

NM (nonmetallic) sheathed cable should be used for most indoor wiring projects in dry locations, such as a room addition or kitchen. NM cable is available in a wide range of wire sizes, and in either "2-wire with ground" or "3-wire with ground" types. NM cable is sold in boxed rolls that contain from 25 to 250 ft. of cable.

Large-appliance cable is used for kitchen ranges and other 40-amp or 50-amp appliances that require 8-gauge or 6-gauge wire. Large-appliance cable is similar to NM cable, but each individual conducting wire is made from fine stranded copper wires so the cable is easier to bend. Large-appliance cable is available in both 2-wire and 3-wire types.

UF (underground feeder) cable is used for wiring in damp or wet locations, such as in an outdoor circuit. It has a white or gray solid-core vinyl sheathing that protects the conducting wires and ground wire inside. Most codes allow UF cable to be buried directly in the ground. It also can be used indoors wherever NM cable is allowed.

Coaxial cable is used to transmit video signals. Coaxial cable is available in lengths up to 25 ft. You can buy coaxial cable with preattached fittings called F-connectors, or buy bulk cable in any length and attach your own F-connectors.

THHN/THWN wire is a versatile product that can be used in all conduit applications. Each conducting wire, purchased individually, is covered with a color-coded thermoplastic insulating jacket similar to the insulation on the wires inside NM cable. Make sure the wire you buy has the thhn/thwn rating. Other wire types have a similar appearance but are less resistant to heat and moisture than thhn/thwn wire.

Telephone cable is used to connect telephone jacks (see page 132). Four-wire cable (shown below) is commonly used, but eight-wire cable, an unshielded twisted pair (UTP) cable, is becoming the standard due to its ability to carry greater amounts of telecommunication information. Category 5 cable is the most common UTP cable in use.

Aluminum Wire

Inexpensive aluminum wire was used in place of copper in many wiring systems installed during the late 1960s and early 1970s, when copper prices were high.

Aluminum wire is identified by its silver color and by the "AL" stamp on the cable sheathing. A variation—copper-clad aluminum wire—has a thin coating of copper bonded to a solid aluminum core.

Circuit cables marked AL or CU-CLAD, and devices marked CU-CLAD ONLY or CO/ALR indicate aluminum wiring. Existing aluminum wiring in homes is considered safe if proper installation methods have been followed, and if the wires are connected to special switches and receptacles designed to be used with aluminum wire. If your home has aluminum wiring, hire a licensed electrician to make changes to the electrical system.

Wire Size Chart

Wire gauge	Wire capacity & use
#6	60 amps, 240 volts; central air conditioner, electric furnace.
#8	40 amps, 240 volts; electric range, central air conditioner.
#10	30 amps, 240 volts; window air conditioner, clothes dryer.
#12	20 amps, 120 volts; light fixtures, receptacles, microwave oven.
#14	15 amps, 120 volts; light fixtures, receptacles.
#16	Light-duty extension cords.
#18 to 22	Thermostats, doorbells, security systems.

Identifying Electrical Devices

Read the markings on replacement devices to make sure they match the originals. Switches and receptacles marked CU or COPPER are for solid copper wire. Those marked CU-CLAD ONLY are for copper-clad aluminum wire. Devices marked AL/CU are no longer acceptable for use with any type of wire, according to the National Electrical Code. Standard devices carry amp and voltage ratings of 15A, 125V. For switches and receptacles, voltage ratings of 110, 120, and 125 are considered identical for replacement purposes. You'll also find a specification for wire gauge (size). Standard-voltage devices for 20-amp circuits accept #12 wire; those for 15-amp circuits, #14 wire. The abbreviation UL or UND. LAB. INC. LIST means the device meets the safety standards of Underwriters Laboratories.

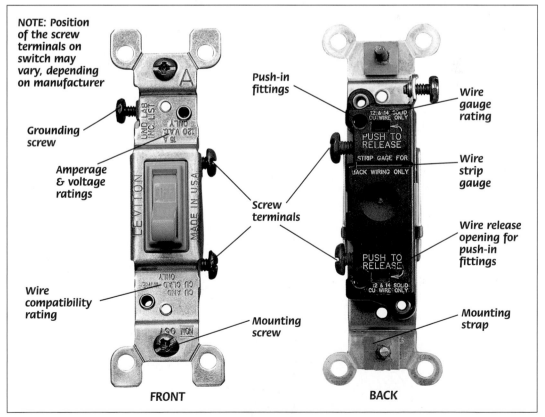

NOTE: Position of the screw terminals on switch may vary, depending on manufacturer

Push-in fittings

Grounding screw

Amperage & voltage ratings

Screw terminals

Wire compatibility rating

Mounting screw

Wire gauge rating

Wire strip gauge

Wire release opening for push-in fittings

Mounting strap

FRONT

BACK

Planning a Wiring Project

Careful planning of a wiring project ensures you will have plenty of power for present and future needs. Consider all possible ways a space might be used, and plan for enough electrical service to meet peak needs. For example, a single 15-amp circuit provides plenty of power to a new spare bedroom, but if you ever choose to convert that room into a family recreation space, it will need at least two 20-amp circuits.

Begin with evaluating your electrical loads (see page 106) to ensure the total load of the existing wiring and the planned new circuits will not exceed the main service capacity. A professional can recommend upgrades to improve service and safety.

A large wiring project adds a considerable load to your main electrical service. In about 25% of all homes, some type of service upgrade is needed before new wiring can be installed. Many homeowners will need to replace an older 60-amp electrical service with a new service rated for 150 amps or more. This is a job for a licensed electrician but is well worth the investment. In other cases, the existing main service provides adequate power, but the main circuit breaker panel is too full to hold any new circuit breakers. In this case it is necessary to install a circuit breaker subpanel to provide for added circuits.

Next, draw a wiring diagram, get a permit, and plan for inspections. Inspectors need to see an accurate wiring diagram and materials list before issuing a permit.

Mapping Your System

Adding to your electrical system will be easier and safer if you have an up-to-date map of your circuits. A circuit map shows all the lights, appliances, switches, and receptacles connected to each circuit. It also allows you to index the main service panel so that the correct circuit can be shut off for repairs.

The easiest way to map circuits is to turn on one circuit at a time and check which fixtures, receptacles, and appliances are affected. Start by making a sketch of every room in the house on graph paper. Include the hallways, basement, attic, and all utility areas. (You can use a blueprint of your home, if you have one.) Also sketch the exterior of the house, the garage, and any other structures that are wired for electricity.

Indicate the location of all electrical devices, including receptacles, light fixtures, switches, appliances, doorbells, thermostats, heaters, fans, and air conditioners; it may help to use standard plan symbols (see page 107).

At the main service panel, label each circuit with masking tape. Turn off all the circuits, then turn on one circuit at a time. Note the amperage of each circuit.

Turn on switches, lights, and appliances throughout the house, and identify those that are powered by the circuit. Label each device with a piece of masking tape noting the circuit number and amperage rating.

Test receptacles for power, using a neon circuit tester. Check both halves of receptacles, as some may be wired on two circuits.

Check the furnace and electric water heater for power by turning their thermostats to the highest settings; turn down the thermostat to check central air-conditioning.

Tape an index summary of your map on the door of the main service panel, and attach the completed circuit maps to the main service panel. Turn all the circuits back on.

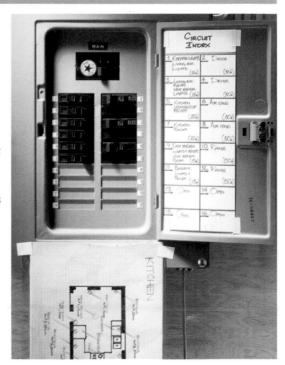

Learning about Codes

When you install new wiring, you are required to get a permit and have the completed work reviewed for safety by an appointed inspector.

Electrical inspectors use the National Electrical Code (NEC) as the authority for evaluating wiring, but they also follow local building and electrical code standards.

As you begin planning new circuits, call or visit your local electrical inspector to discuss your project. Inspectors are the final authority on code requirements. They can tell you which code requirements apply to your job and may have a packet of information summarizing these regulations. Although they are busy, most inspectors will answer questions and help you design well-planned circuits.

When you apply for a work permit, the inspector may expect you to understand local electrical guidelines, as well as some basic NEC requirements. Some of the most common code issues are shown here.

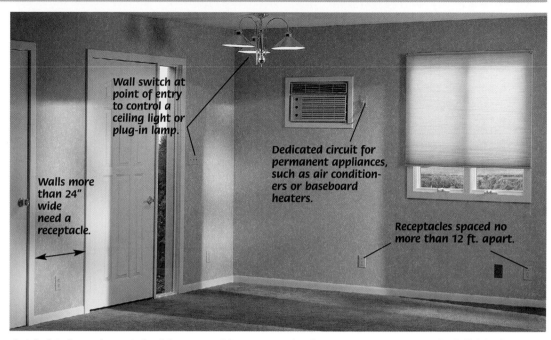

Electrical Code requirements for living areas: Living areas need at least one 15-amp or 20-amp basic lighting/receptacle circuit for each 600 square ft. of living space. Kitchens and bathrooms must have a ceiling-mounted light fixture.

Cables must be protected against damage by nails and screws by at least 1¼" of wood (top). When cables pass through 2 × 2 furring strips (bottom), protect the cables with metal protector plates.

Kitchen and bathroom receptacles must be protected by a GFCI (see page 130). Also, all outdoor receptacles and general-use receptacles in an unfinished basement or crawl-space must be protected by a GFCI.

Amp ratings of receptacles and other devices must match the size of the circuit. A common mistake is to use 20-amp receptacles (top) on 15-amp circuits—a potential cause of dangerous circuit overloads.

Calculating Circuit Loads

Calculating supply and demand—for each circuit and for the entire house—is an essential part of any wiring plan. This ensures that you'll have properly sized circuits for the fixtures and appliances they supply, as well as an adequate main power supply to feed all of the circuits.

Whole-house demand is based on the maximum amount of electricity your house is likely to use at any one time. You'll probably need the help of an electrician or electrical inspector to determine if your main power supply is adequate to cover the additions you're planning. If you have an old 60-amp service panel, you may be required by the building department to upgrade your electrical service before making any changes to the house wiring.

To calculate the supply and demand for a specific circuit, first determine the safe capacity of the circuit, then calculate the load of all the fixtures and appliances (new or existing) that will run on the circuit. This will help you plan the number and type of new circuits you will need, if any, and it can help you troubleshoot existing circuits that are prone to tripping. Frequent trippings may indicate a short circuit or other problem, but in most cases the circuit is merely overloaded.

Find the safe capacity of a circuit by multiplying the voltage by the amperage, yielding the total capacity—in watts. Then multiply the total capacity by 0.8 to find the safe capacity. The chart at right shows the capacities of the most common household circuits. If the amp ratings for the circuits aren't listed on the index map inside the main service panel, look for a number on the end of each breaker lever or on the rim of each fuse. As for voltage, all single-pole breakers and plug fuses are 120-volt; double-pole breakers and cartridge fuses should be 240-volts.

To calculate the load on a specific circuit, add up the wattage ratings for all the fixtures and appliances on the circuit. Wattage ratings are found on appliance nameplates and on the light bulbs used by fixtures. If the wattage rating is not given for an appliance, multiply the amp rating for the appliance by the voltage of the circuit (for example, a 4-amp blender on a 120-volt circuit uses 480 watts). Ratings can also be found in owner's manuals or by calling the manufacturer.

Compare the circuit load to the safe capacity of the circuit: The load must not exceed the safe capacity. Overloaded circuits not only blow fuses and trip breakers, but frequent overloads can damage circuit wiring and lead to short circuits. Also keep in mind that most permanent appliances, like water heaters, dryers, and disposers, require their own "dedicated" circuits.

Converting Amps/Volts/Watts

Amps × Volts	Total capacity	Safe capacity
15 A × 120 V =	1800 watts	1440 watts
20 A × 120 V =	2400 watts	1920 watts
25 A × 120 V =	3000 watts	2400 watts
30 A × 120 V =	3600 watts	2880 watts
20 A × 240 V =	4800 watts	3840 watts
30 A × 240 V =	7200 watts	5760 watts

Amperage ratings *are stamped on the end of circuit breaker levers. Standard single-pole breakers are 120-volts. Double-pole breakers (240-volt) are much wider than single-poles, and may be rated between 20 and 50 amps.*

Circuit ratings in older service panels *can be identified by reading the lettering on the fuses or cartridges. Plug fuses (shown above) are typical for 120-volt circuits. Cartridge fuses control 240-volt circuits and are housed in a fuse block.*

Wattage ratings for appliances *appear on manufacturers' nameplates. If the rating is in kilowatts, find watts by multiplying times 1000. If only amps are given, find watts by multiplying the amps times the voltage—120 or 240.*

Drawing a Wiring Diagram

Drawing a wiring diagram is the last step in planning a circuit installation. A detailed wiring diagram helps you get a work permit, makes it easy to create a list of materials, and serves as a guide for laying out circuits and installing cables and fixtures. Use the circuit maps on pages 108 to 115 to help you plan wiring configurations and cable runs.

Begin by drawing a scaled diagram of the space you'll be wiring. Show walls, doors, windows, plumbing pipes and fixtures, and heating ducts. Calculate the floor space by multiplying room length by width (don't include closets or storage areas), and indicate this on the diagram.

Next, mark the locations of all switches, receptacles, light fixtures, and permanent appliances, using the electrical symbols shown below. Where you position these devices along the cable run determines how they are wired. Draw cable runs between devices and indicate cable size and type and circuit amperage. Identify each circuit with colored pencil.

Last, identify the wattages for light fixtures and permanent appliances, and the type and size of each electrical box. Then create a detailed materials list.

Bring the diagram and materials list when you visit the electrical inspector to apply for a work permit. Never install new wiring without following your community's permit and inspection procedure. A work permit is not expensive, and it ensures that your work will be reviewed by a qualified inspector to guarantee its safety.

The electrical inspector will look over your wiring diagram, and may ask questions to see if you have a basic understanding of the electrical code and fundamental wiring skills.

You may be allowed to do some, if not all, of the work. A few communities allow you to install wiring only when supervised by an electrician. This means you must hire a licensed electrician to apply for the work permit and to check your work before the inspector arrives. The electrician is held responsible for the quality of your job.

Electrical Symbol Key

	240-volt receptacle
	Isolated ground receptacle
	Duplex receptacle
	240-volt dryer receptacle
	Singleplex receptacle
	Fourplex receptacle
GFCI	GFCI duplex receptacle
	Switched receptacle
WP	Weatherproof receptacle
S_{TH}	Thermostat
S_P	Pilot-light switch
S	Single-pole switch
S_T	Timer switch
S_3	Three-way switch
J	Junction box
S	Ceiling pull switch
	Surface-mounted light fixture
R	Recessed light fixture
	Fluorescent light fixture
	Wall-mounted light fixture
WP	Weatherproof light fixture
CF	Ceiling fan
D	Electric door opener
BT	Low-voltage transformer
TV	Television jack
	Telephone outlet
D	Smoke detector
VF	Vent fan

Common Circuit Layouts

The arrangement of switches and appliances along an electrical circuit differs for every project. This means that the configuration of wires inside an electrical box can vary greatly, even when fixtures are identical.

The circuit maps on the following pages show some of the most common wiring variations for typical electrical devices. Most new wiring you install will match one or more of the examples shown. By finding the examples that match your situation, you can use these maps to plan circuit layouts.

The 120-volt circuits shown on the following pages are wired for 15 amps, using 14-gauge wire and receptacles rated at 15 amps. If you are installing a 20-amp circuit, substitute 12-gauge cables and use receptacles rated for 20 amps.

In configurations where a white wire serves as a hot wire instead of a neutral, both ends of the wire are coded with black tape to identify it as hot. In addition, each of the circuit maps shows a box grounding screw. This grounding screw is required in all metal boxes, but plastic electrical boxes do not need to be grounded.

NOTE: For clarity, all grounding conductors in the circuit maps are colored green. In practice, the grounding wires inside sheathed cables usually are bare copper.

The Grounding System

Several switches, receptacles, light fixtures, or appliances may be connected to a single circuit. For safety, most circuits include a bare copper or green insulated grounding wire, and many switches, receptacles, light fixtures, metal boxes, and appliances include a green grounding screw to which the wire is attached.

Individual grounding wires conduct current in the event of a short circuit or overload. This grounding system helps reduce the chance of fire in your home and minimizes the risk of severe electrical shock to people, appliances, and fixtures.

From each electrical device the wires are run back to the ground bar in your service panel. From there, the wire is directed out of the house on a grounding rod, returning any overload safely to the earth.

The grounding system is an important safety feature of your home. Remember to reattach all grounding wires after completing electrical installation or repair work.

1. 120-volt Duplex Receptacles Wired in Sequence

Use this layout to link any number of duplex receptacles in a basic lighting/receptacle circuit. The last receptacle in the cable run is connected like the receptacle shown at the right side of the circuit map below. All other receptacles are wired like the receptacle shown on the left side. Requires two-wire cables.

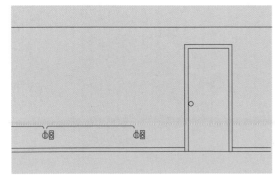

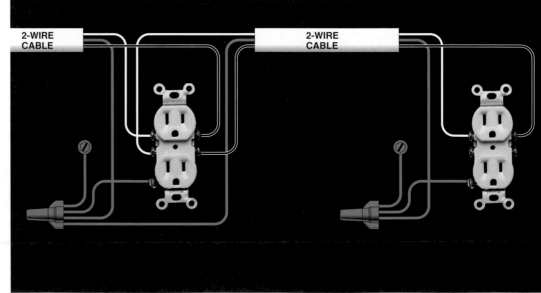

2. GFCI Receptacles (Single-location Protection)

Use this layout when receptacles are within 6 ft. of a water source, and where required in kitchens and bathrooms. To prevent "nuisance tripping" caused by normal power surges, GFCIs should be connected only at the LINE screw terminals, so they protect a single location and not the fixtures on the LOAD side of the circuit. Requires two-wire cables. Where a GFCI must protect other fixtures, use circuit map 3.

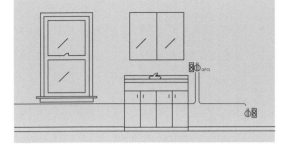

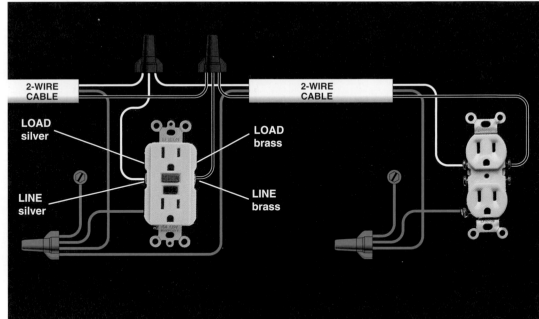

3. GFCI Receptacle, Switch & Light Fixture (Multiple-location Protection)

In some locations, such as an outdoor circuit, it's a good idea to connect a GFCI receptacle so it also provides shock protection to the wires and fixtures that continue to the end of the circuit. Wires from the power source are connected to the LINE screw terminals; outgoing wires are connected to the LOAD screws. Requires two-wire cables.

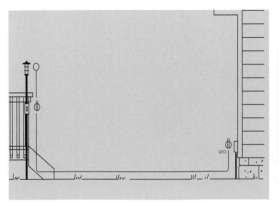

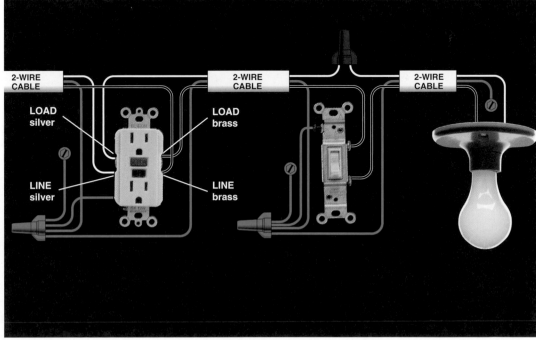

Continued on next page

Common Circuit Layouts (cont.)

4. Single Pole Switch & Light Fixture (Light Fixture at End of Cable Run)

Use this layout for light fixtures in basic lighting/receptacle circuits throughout the home. It is often used as an extension to a series of receptacles (circuit map 1). Requires two-wire cables.

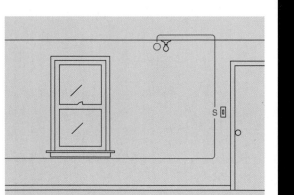

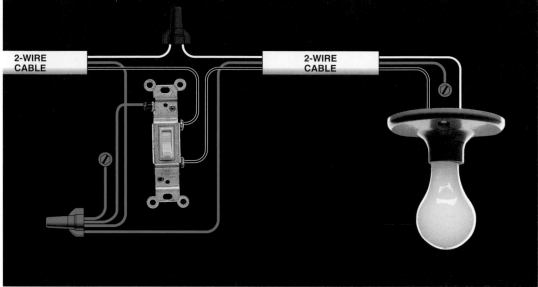

5. Single-pole Switch and Light Fixture, Duplex Receptacle (Switch at Start of Cable Run)

Use this layout to continue a circuit past a switched light fixture to one or more duplex receptacles. To add multiple receptacles to the circuit, see circuit map 1. Requires two-wire and three-wire cables.

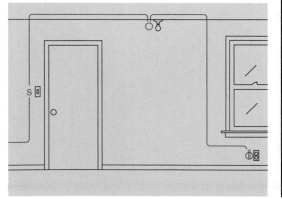

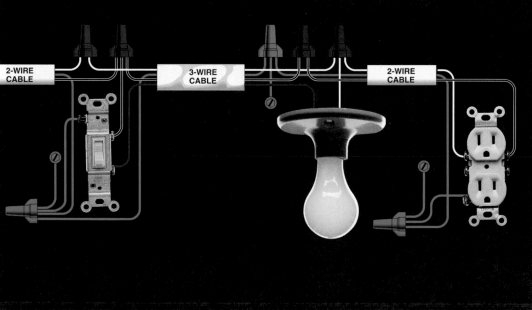

6. Switch-controlled Split Receptacle, Duplex Receptacle (Switch at Start of Cable Run)

This layout lets you use a wall switch to control a lamp plugged into a wall receptacle. This configuration is required by code for any room that does not have a switch-controlled ceiling fixture. Only the bottom half of the first receptacle is controlled by the wall switch; the top half of the receptacle and all additional receptacles on the circuit are always hot. Requires two-wire and three-wire cables.

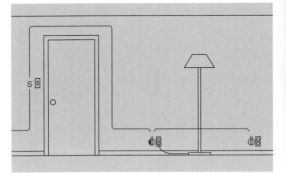

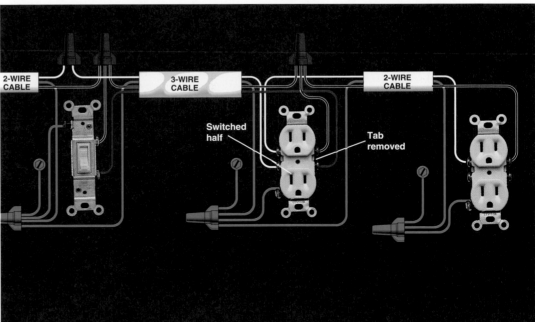

7. Switch-controlled Split Receptacle, Duplex Receptacle (Split Receptacle at Start of Run)

Use this variation of circuit map 6 where it is more practical to locate a switch-controlled receptacle at the start of a cable run. Only the bottom half of the first receptacle is controlled by the wall switch; the top half of the receptacle, and all other receptacles on the circuit, are always hot. Requires two-wire cables.

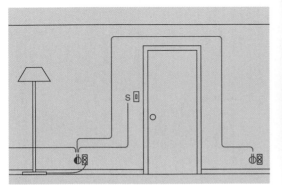

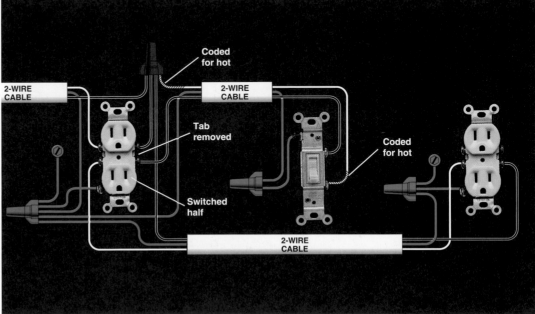

Continued on next page

Common Circuit Layouts (cont.)

8. 240-volt Appliance Receptacle

This layout represents a 20-amp, 240-volt dedicated appliance circuit wired with 12/2 cable, as required by code for a large window air conditioner. Receptacles are available in both singleplex (shown) and duplex styles. The black and white circuit wires connected to a double-pole breaker each bring 120 volts of power to the receptacle. The white wire is tagged (coded) with black tape to indicate it is hot.

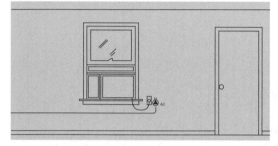

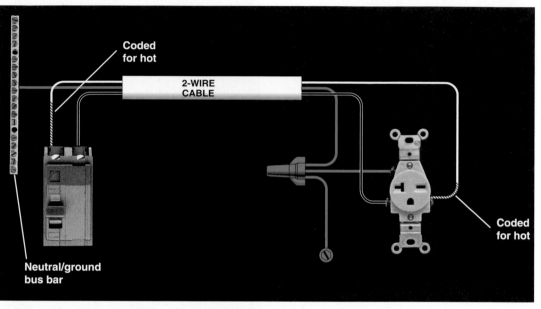

9. Double Receptacle Circuit with Shared Neutral Wire (Receptacles Alternate Circuits)

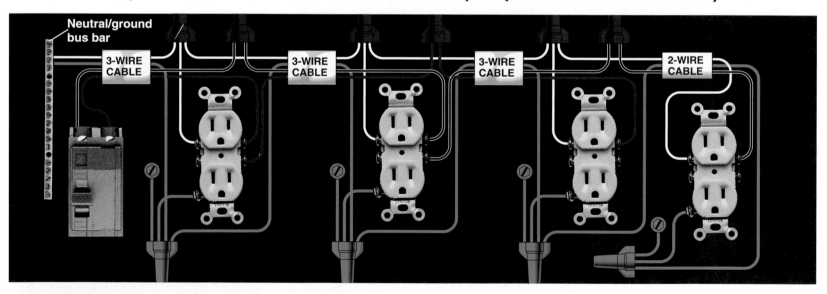

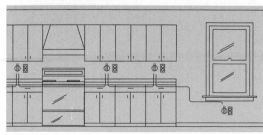

This layout features two 120-volt circuits wired with one three-wire cable connected to a double-pole circuit breaker. The black hot wire powers one circuit; the red wire powers the other. The white wire is a shared neutral that serves both circuits. When wired with 12/2 and 12/3 cable, and GFCI receptacles rated for 20 amps, this layout can be used for the two small-appliance circuits required in a kitchen.

10. 240-volt Baseboard Heaters, Thermostat

This layout is typical for a series of 240-volt baseboard heaters controlled by a wall thermostat. Except for the last heater in the circuit, all heaters are wired as shown here. The last heater is connected to only one cable. The size of the circuit and cables are determined by finding the total wattage of all heaters (see page 106). Requires two-wire cable.

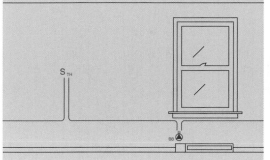

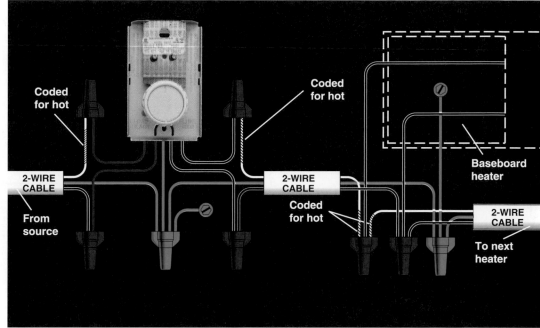

Coded for hot

Coded for hot

Baseboard heater

2-WIRE CABLE

2-WIRE CABLE

Coded for hot

2-WIRE CABLE

From source

To next heater

11. 120/240-volt Appliance Receptacle

This layout is for a 50-amp, 120/240-volt dedicated appliance circuit wired with 6/3 cable, as required by code for a large kitchen range. The black and red circuit wires, connected to a double-pole circuit breaker in the circuit breaker panel, each bring 120 volts of power to the setscrew terminals on the receptacle. The white circuit wire attached to the neutral bus bar in the circuit breaker panel is connected to the neutral setscrew terminal on the receptacle.

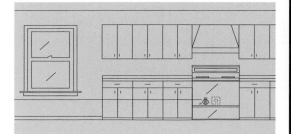

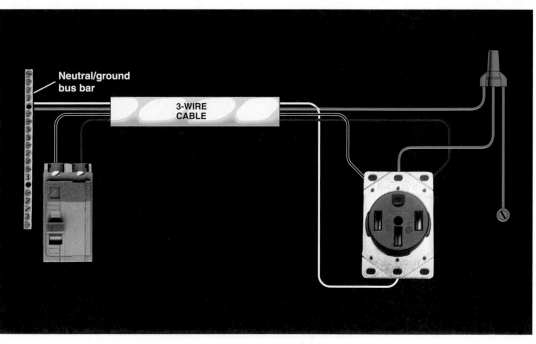

Neutral/ground bus bar

3-WIRE CABLE

Continued on next page

Common Circuit Layouts (cont.)

12. Three-way Switches & Light Fixture (Fixture Between Switches)

This layout for three-way switches lets you control a light fixture from two locations. Each switch has one COMMON screw terminal and two TRAVELER screws. Circuit wires attached to the TRAVELER screws run between the switches, and hot wires attached to the COMMON screws bring current from the power source and carry it to the light fixture. Requires two-wire and three-wire cables.

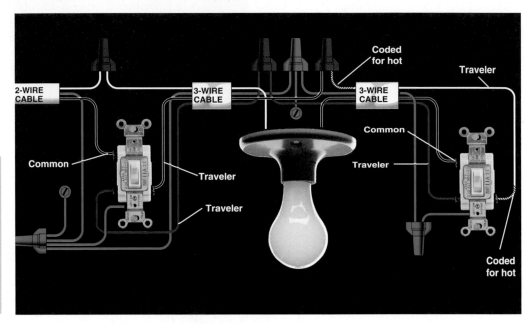

13. Three-way Switches & Light Fixture (Fixture at Start of Cable Run)

Use this layout variation of circuit map 12 where it is more convenient to locate the fixture ahead of the three-way switches in the cable run. Requires two-wire and three-wire cables.

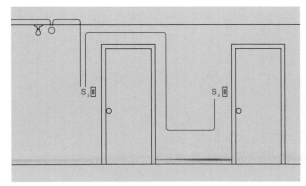

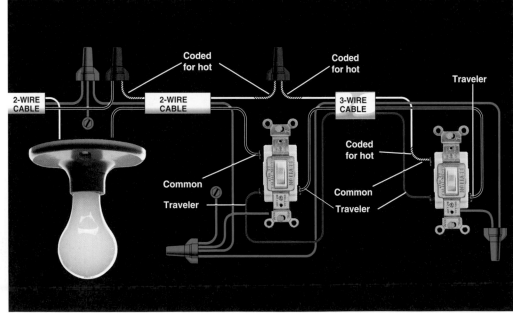

14. Three-way Switches & Light Fixture with Duplex Receptacle

Use this layout to add a receptacle to a three-way switch configuration (circuit map 12). Requires two-wire and three-wire cables.

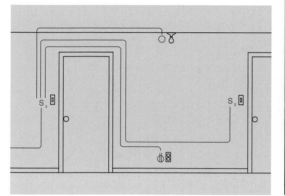

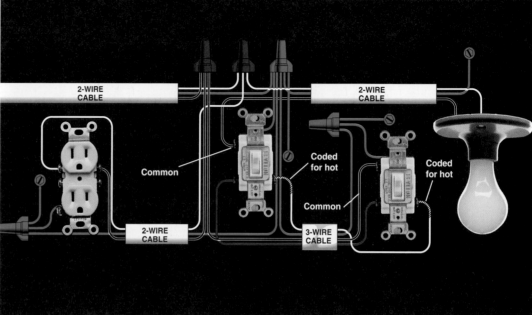

15. Four-way Switch & Light Fixture (Fixture at End of Cable Run)

This layout for a four-way switch lets you control a light fixture from three locations. A pair of three-wire cables enter the box of the four-way switch. The black and the red wires from one cable attach to the top pair of screw terminals (LINE 1), and the black and red wires from the other cable attach to the bottom screw terminals (LINE 2). Requires two-wire and three-wire cables.

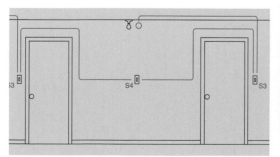

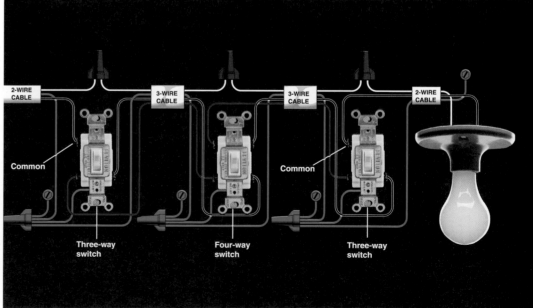

Installing Electrical Boxes & Cables

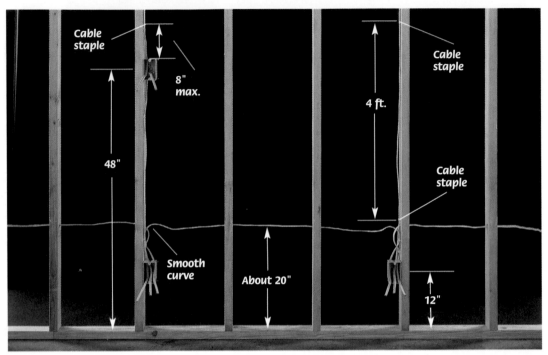

Install electrical boxes for all devices only after your wiring plan has been approved by an inspector. Use your plan as a guide and follow electrical code guidelines when laying out box positions (see photo, left). Some electrical fixtures, like recessed lights and exhaust fans, have their own wire connection boxes; install these along with the other electrical boxes.

After your boxes are installed, run all of the NM cables. Start each new circuit near the service panel or subpanel, and run them to the first boxes in the circuit. Also run any branch cables between boxes on the same circuit. Schedule a rough-in inspection after the cables are run. When the rough-in wiring has been approved, you can close up the walls and install the electrical devices. Then, hire an electrician to make the final connections at the service panel or subpanel.

Tools: Screwdrivers, drill, ⅝" and 1" bits, bit extender, needlenose pliers, fish tape, cable ripper, combination tool.

Materials: Electrical boxes, NM cable, cable clamps and staples, cable lubricant, masking and electrical tape, grounding pigtails, wire connectors.

Standard heights for electrical boxes are as follows (measured to the box centers): receptacle boxes in living areas are 12" above the finished floor; switches are at 48". GFCI boxes in bathrooms should be about 10" above the countertop, and thermostats between 48" to 60". Switch boxes should be at accessible locations, such as on the latch sides of doors. Cables should be stapled within 8" of each box, and every 4 ft. thereafter when they run along studs. Cables should not be crimped or bent sharply or be installed diagonally between framing members. Some inspectors specify that cables running between receptacle boxes should be about 20" above the floor. For special circumstances, inspectors may allow changes to these measurements (see Universal Design tip, opposite page).

Tips for Installing Electrical Boxes

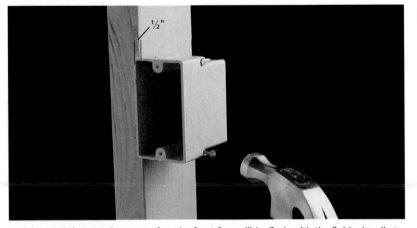

Position each box against a stud so the front face will be flush with the finished wall. For example, if you will be installing ½" wallboard, position the box so it extends ½" past the front edge of the stud. Anchor the box by driving the mounting nails into the stud.

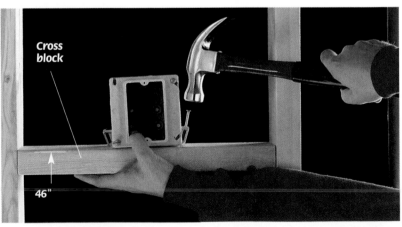

To install a switch box between studs, first install a cross block between the studs, with the top edge 46" above the floor. Position the box on the cross block so the front face will be flush with the finished wall, and drive the mounting nails into the cross block.

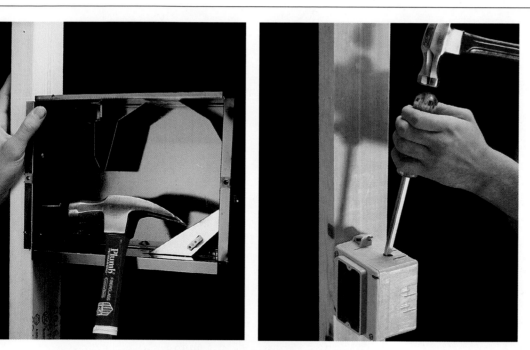

Recessed fixtures that fit inside wall cavities (far left) have built-in wire connection boxes, and require no additional electrical boxes. Common recessed fixtures include electric blower-heaters (shown here), bathroom vent fans, and recessed light fixtures. Surface mounted fixtures, such as electric baseboard heaters and fluorescent lights, have wire connection boxes that are integral to the fixtures; they need no boxes installed during the rough-in.

Open one knockout for each cable (left) that will enter the box. You can open the knockouts as you install the boxes or wait until you run cable to each box. Open a knockout by striking inside the scored lines of the knockout with a screwdriver and hammer. Then, use the screwdriver to break off any sharp edges that might damage the vinyl sheathing of the cable.

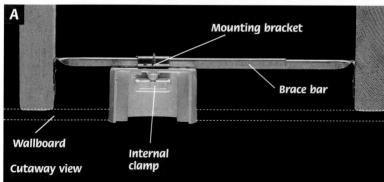

A

Mounting bracket

Brace bar

Wallboard

Cutaway view

Internal clamp

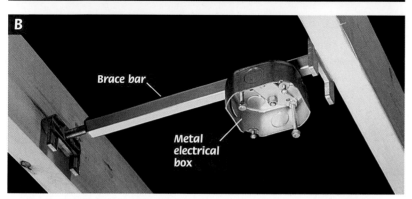

B

Brace bar

Metal electrical box

To mount a light fixture between joists, attach an electrical box to an adjustable brace bar (photo A). Nail the ends of the brace bar to the joists so the face of the box will be flush with the finished ceiling surface. Slide the box along the brace bar to the desired position, then tighten the mounting screws. Use internal cable clamps for boxes mounted with a brace bar. NOTE: For ceiling fans and heavy light fixtures, use a metal box and heavy-duty brace bar rated for heavy loads (photo B).

Accessible Box Heights

Following a few simple guidelines will enable everyone to reach and use light switches, electrical receptacles, and climate control devices.

- Plan a clear approach space of 30 × 48" in front of electrical panels, thermostats, intercoms, and security system controls.
- Locate light switches and intercoms at a height of 40" to 48", within the reach of children and seated users.
- Consider the heights of thermostats—they should be low enough for an adult in a wheelchair, but too high for a young child.
- Install receptacles at a minimum height of 18", although 20" to 40" may be preferred. This makes it easy for seated users and standing users who have trouble bending.
- Consider the height and placement of receptacles in kitchens or bathrooms. See pages 368 to 371 and 447 to 451.

Installing NM Cables

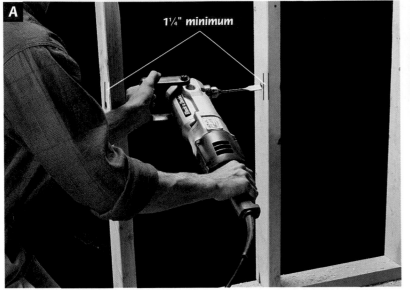

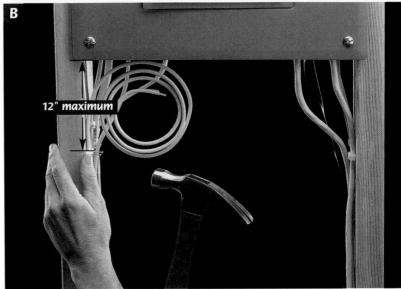

A 1¼" minimum

B 12" maximum

Drill ⅝" holes in framing members for the cable runs. This is done easily with a right-angle drill (available at rental centers). Set back holes at least 1¼" from the front edges of the framing members. Where cables will turn corners, drill intersecting holes in adjoining faces of studs (see step C, below). Measure and cut all cables, allowing 2 ft. extra at ends entering the service panel, and 1 ft. extra for ends entering an electrical box.

Staple one end of each new circuit cable within 12" of the service panel or subpanel, leaving 2 ft. of extra cable for entering the panel. Loosely coil the extra cable to keep it out of the way. Run the cable to the first electrical box. Where the cable runs along the sides of framing members, anchor it with cable staples no more than 4 ft. apart.

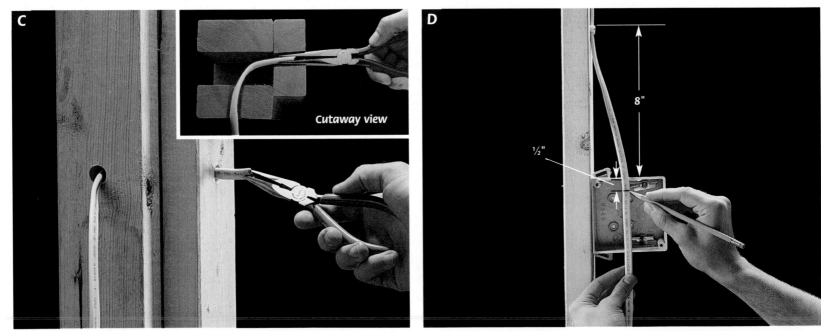

C Cutaway view

D 8" ½"

At corners, form a slight L-shaped bend in the end of the cable and insert it into one hole. Retrieve the cable through the other hole, using needlenose pliers (inset).

At each electrical box, staple the cable to a framing member 8" from the box. Hold the cable taut against the front of the box, aligning it with the knockout, and mark a point on the sheathing ½" past the box edge. Strip cable from the marked line to the end, and clip away excess sheathing (see page 123). Insert the cable through the knockout in the box. If required, clamp the cable in place (see page 101).

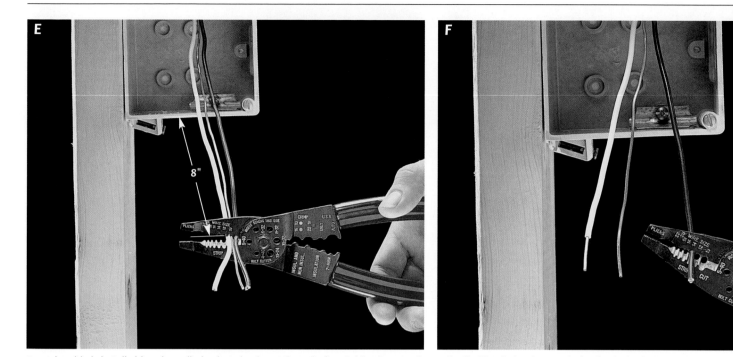

As each cable is installed in a box, clip back each wire so that 8" of workable wire extends past the front edge of the box.

Strip ¾" of insulation from each circuit wire in the box, using a combination tool. Choose the opening that matches the gauge of the wire, and take care not to nick the copper.

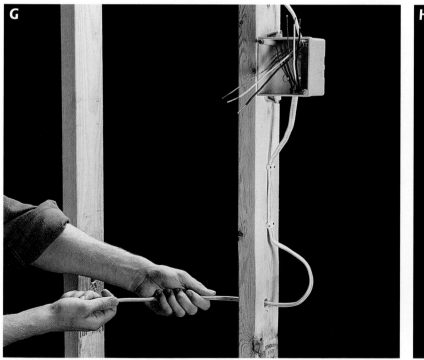

Continue the circuit by running cable between each pair of electrical boxes, leaving an extra 1 ft. of cable at each end.

At metal boxes and recessed fixtures, open knockouts and attach cables with cable clamps. From inside the fixture, strip away all but ¼" of sheathing. Clip back wires so there is 8" of workable length, then strip ¾" of insulation from each wire.

Continued on next page

Installing NM Cables (cont.)

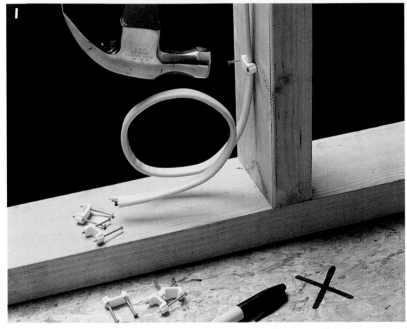

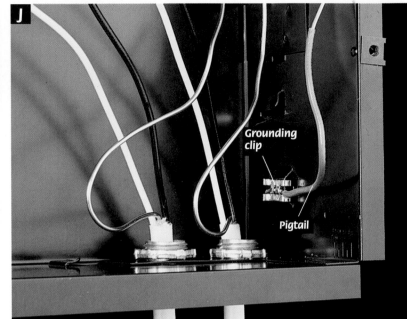

For a surface-mounted fixture, such as a baseboard heater or fluorescent light fixture, staple the cable to a stud near the fixture location, leaving plenty of excess cable. Mark the floor so the cable will be easy to find if it accidentally gets covered.

At each recessed fixture and metal electrical box, connect one end of a grounding pigtail to the metal frame, using a grounding clip attached to the frame (shown here) or a green grounding screw (see page 101).

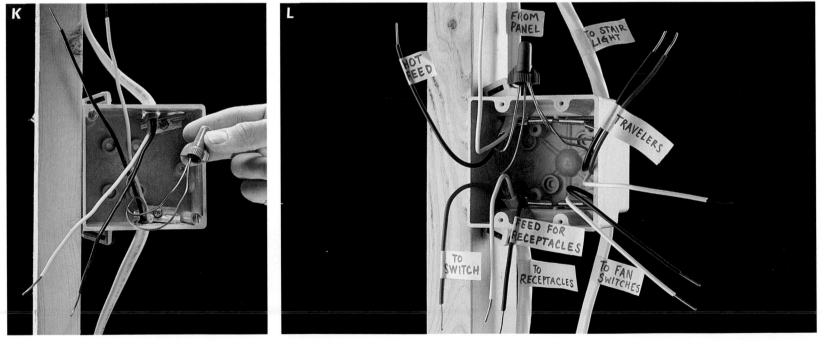

At each electrical box and recessed fixture, join the grounding wires together with a wire connector.

Label the cables entering each box to indicate their destinations. In boxes with complex wiring configurations, also tag the individual wires to simplify the final hookups. After all cables are installed, your rough-in work is ready to be reviewed by an electrical inspector.

Installing Cable Inside a Finished Wall

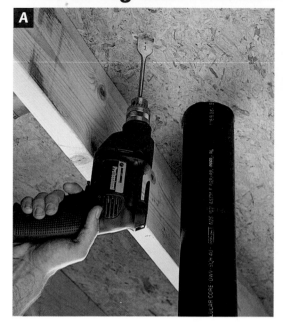

A

From the unfinished space below the finished wall, look for reference points, like plumbing pipes or electrical cables, that indicate the location of the wall above. Choose a location for the new cable that does not interfere with existing utilities. Drill a 1" hole up into the stud cavity.

B Attic

Cutaway view · Drill bit extender · Bottom plate · Top plate

From the unfinished space above the finished wall, find the top of the stud cavity by measuring from the same fixed reference point used in step A. Drill a 1" hole down through the top plate and into the stud cavity, using a drill bit extender.

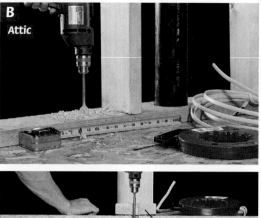

C Attic · Cutaway view · Top plate · Bottom plate · Basement

Extend a fish tape down through the top plate, twisting the tape until it reaches the bottom of the stud cavity. From the unfinished space below the wall, use a piece of stiff wire with a hook on one end to retrieve the fish tape through the drilled hole in the bottom plate.

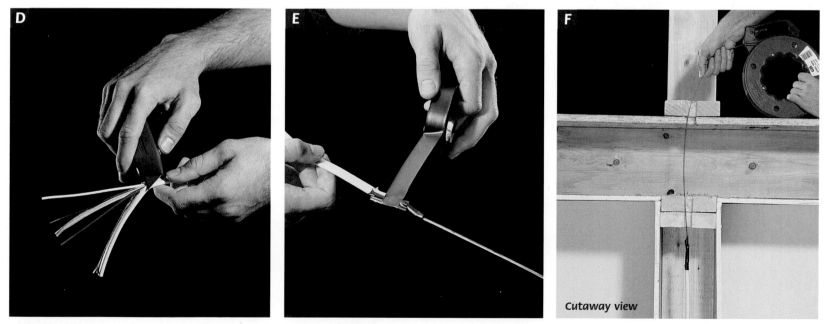

D

Trim back 3" of outer insulation from the end of the NM cable, then insert the wires through the loop at the end of the fish tape.

E

Bend the wires against the cable, then use electrical tape to bind them tightly. Apply cable-pulling lubricant to the taped end of the fish tape (see page 122).

F Cutaway view

From above the finished wall, pull steadily on the fish tape to draw the cable up through the stud cavity. To make this job easier, have a helper feed the cable from below as you pull.

Continued on next page

Installing Cable Inside a Finished Wall (cont.)

Tips for Installing Cable Inside a Finished Wall

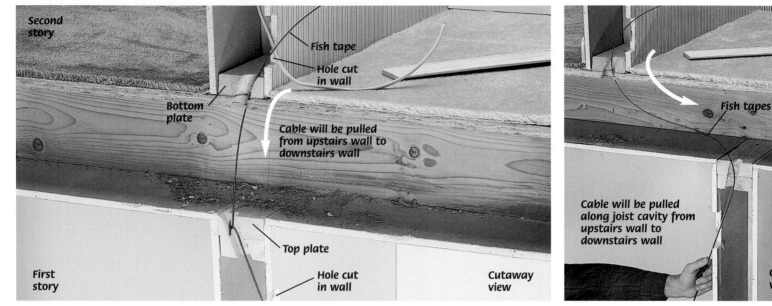

If there is no access space above and below a wall, cut openings in the finished walls to run a cable. This often occurs in two-story homes when a cable is extended from an upstairs wall to a downstairs wall. Cut small openings in the wall near the top and bottom plates, then drill an angled 1" hole through each plate. Extend a fish tape into the joist cavity between the walls and use it to pull the cable from one wall to the next. If the walls line up one over the other, you can retrieve the fish tape using a piece of stiff wire.

VARIATION: If the walls do not line up, use a second fish tape. After running the cable, repair the holes in the walls with patching plaster, or wallboard scraps and taping compound.

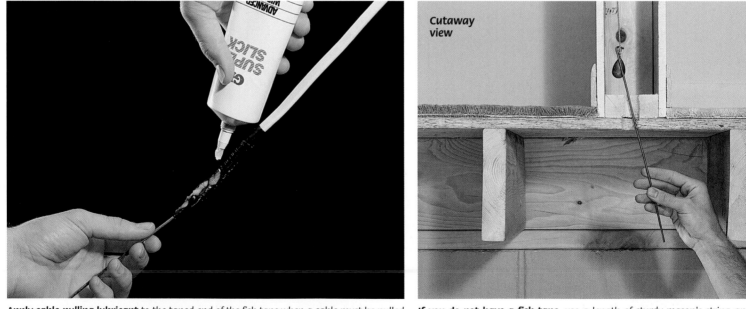

Apply cable-pulling lubricant to the taped end of the fish tape when a cable must be pulled through a sharp bend. Do not use oil or petroleum jelly as a lubricant, because they can damage the thermoplastic cable sheathing.

If you do not have a fish tape, use a length of sturdy mason's string and a lead fishing weight or heavy washer to fish down through a stud cavity. Drop the line into the stud cavity from above, then use a piece of stiff wire to hook the line from below.

Stripping NM Cable & Wires

A

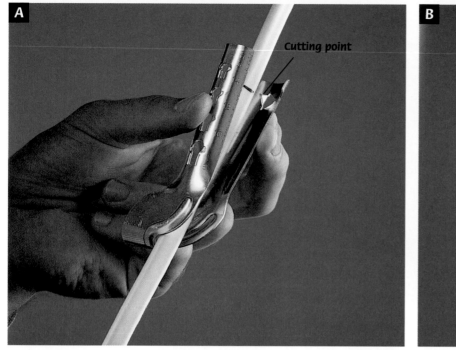

Cutting point

Measure and mark the cable 8" to 10" from the end. Slide the cable ripper onto the cable, and squeeze the tool firmly to force the cutting point through the plastic sheathing.

B

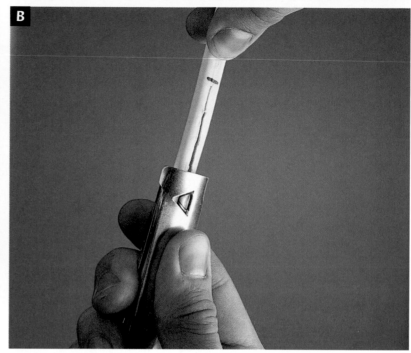

Grip the cable tightly with one hand, and pull the cable ripper toward the end of the cable to cut open the plastic sheathing.

C

Peel back the plastic sheathing and the paper wrapping from the individual wires.

D

Cut away the excess plastic sheathing and paper wrapping, using the cutting jaws of a combination tool.

E

Strip insulation from each wire, using the stripper openings. Choose the opening that matches the gauge of the wire, and take care not to nick or scratch the ends of the wires.

Installing Electrical Devices

Common household electrical devices include switches, receptacles, light fixtures, smoke alarms, and specialty items that are permanently connected to an electrical circuit. Most devices are easy to install and often include directions or color-coding to simplify the connections. Specific wiring will vary, based on the type of device, the manufacturer, and the wiring configuration (where it lies in the circuit), but there are a few general rules to follow when purchasing and installing devices.

Always use devices that have the same amp and voltage ratings as the circuit they will run on (see page 103). Devices with the wrong ratings can lead to dangerous circuit overloads.

Be sure the power to a circuit is shut off before beginning any electrical work (see page 98). And always complete the installation before restoring power to the circuit. When working on new circuits, install the devices before connecting the circuits at the service panel.

Most electrical devices are connected to circuit wires with screw terminals, push-in fittings, or wire *leads*—short wires permanently attached to the device.

Use a *wire connector* (right) to join circuit wires to leads, or to connect pigtail wires. Wire connectors come in several sizes that are colored for identification. Always use the right size of connector for the number and gauge of wires you're working with (follow the chart on the package).

To make the connection, cut the wire ends even, then strip about ½" of insulation from each wire. Insert the wires into the connector and screw the connector clockwise until it's snug (there's no need to pre-twist the wires). Tug gently on each wire to make sure it's secure, then make sure no bare wire is visible outside the connector.

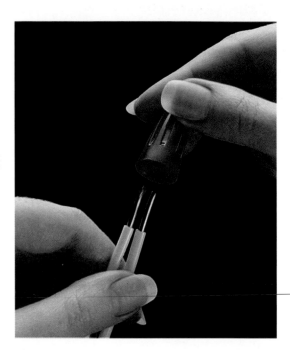

Connecting Wires to Screw Terminals

A

Strip about ¾" of insulation from each wire, using a combination tool. Choose the stripper opening that matches the gauge of the wire, then clamp the wire in the tool. Pull the wire firmly to remove the plastic insulation.

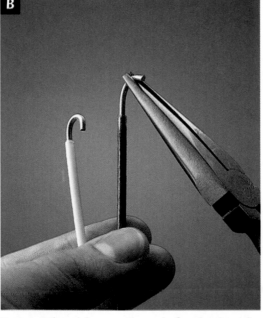

B

Form a C-shaped loop on the end of each wire, using needlenose pliers. The wire should be free of scratches and nicks.

C

Hook each wire around a screw terminal so it forms a clockwise loop. Tighten the screw firmly. The wire insulation should just touch the head of the screw. Never attach two wires to a single screw terminal. Instead, use a pigtail wire (see page 125).

Connecting Wires to Push-in Fittings

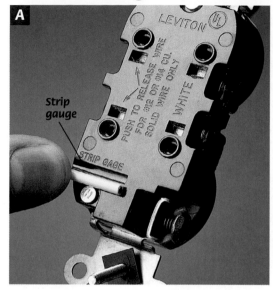

A

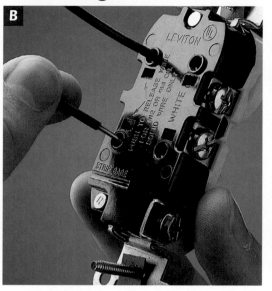

B

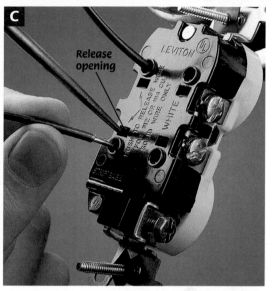

C

Mark the amount of insulation to be stripped from each wire, using the strip gauge on the back of the switch or receptacle. Strip the wires using a combination tool (see step A, page 124). NOTE: Never use push-in fittings with aluminum wiring.

Insert the bare copper wires firmly into the push-in fittings on the back of the switch or receptacle. When connected, the wires should have no bare copper exposed.

Remove a wire from a push-in fitting by inserting a small nail or screwdriver into the release opening next to the wire. Pull out the wire to remove it.

Pigtailing Wires

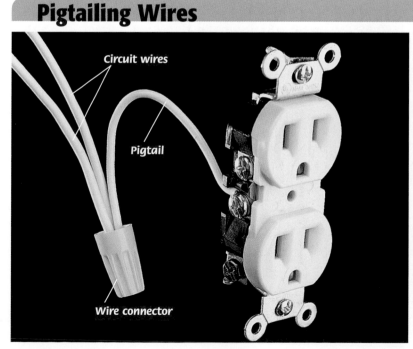

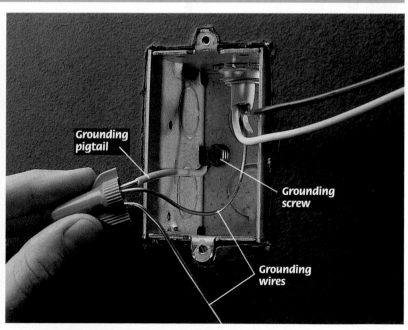

Connect two or more wires to a single screw terminal with a pigtail. A pigtail is a short piece of wire. Connect one end of the pigtail to a screw terminal, and the other end to the circuit wires, using a wire connector. You can also use pigtails to lengthen circuit wires that are too short. NOTE: The pigtail must be of the same type and gauge as the circuit wires.

Use a grounding pigtail to connect circuit grounding wires to a grounded metal electrical box. Grounding pigtails have green insulation and are available with preattached grounding screws. Attach the grounding screw to the box, and join the end of the pigtail to the bare copper grounding wires with a wire connector.

Installing Switches

There are three standard types of wall switches: single-pole, three-way, and four-way; all are shown here. Each type can be identified by the number of screw terminals it has. Newer switches may also have push fittings in addition to screw terminals.

Most switches include a grounding terminal, which is identified by its green color. When pigtailed to the grounding wires, the grounding screw provides added protection against shock. If a switch doesn't have a grounding screw, it must be contained in a grounded metal electrical box.

Also available are specialty switches that are designed to add convenience and security to your home. The most common are dimmer switches, combination switch/receptacles, and pilot-light switches. More sophisticated types include motion-sensing switches with an infrared beam that detects nearby movement and turns the switches on or off, and pro-grammable switches with digital controls that can store up to four ON-OFF cycles per day.

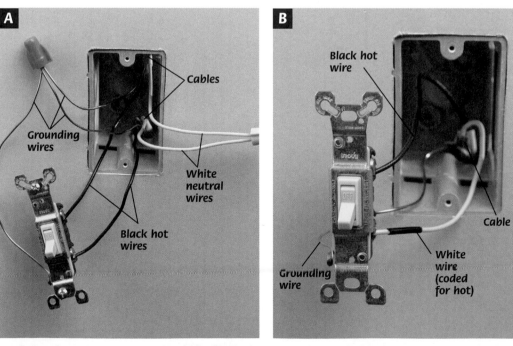

UNIVERSAL DESIGN

Simpler Switches

Conventional toggle-type switches can be difficult to use—whether your arms are full of grocery bags or you have limited dexterity. Consider installing alternative switches, where appropriate:

- Rocker switches (photo, right) can be operated simply by pressing one side of a large rocker panel.
- Switches with internal lights help users locate the switch and may help orient someone in the dark.
- Remote switches allow a person to control lighting before entering a room and after leaving it.
- Motion- and sound-activated switches provide on-demand power.
- Switch coverplates in colors that contrast with the walls are easier to see in low light.

Single-pole Switches

A single-pole switch is the most common type of wall switch. It usually has ON-OFF markings on the switch lever, and is used to control a set of lights, an appliance, or a receptacle from a single location. A single-pole switch has two screw terminals. Most types also have a grounding screw.

In a correctly wired single-pole switch, a hot circuit wire is attached to each screw terminal. However, the color and number of wires inside the switch box will vary, depending on the switch location along the electrical circuit.

If two cables enter the box, the switch lies in the middle of the circuit (photo A). In this installation, both of the hot wires attached to the switch are black.

If only one cable enters the box, the switch lies at the end of the circuit (photo B). In this installation (sometimes called a *switch loop*), one of the hot wires is black, but the other hot wire usually is white. A white hot wire should be coded with black tape or paint.

A — Cables / Grounding wires / White neutral wires / Black hot wires

B — Black hot wire / Cable / White wire (coded for hot) / Grounding wire

Installation of a single-pole switch in the middle of a circuit.

Installation of a single-pole switch at the end of a circuit.

Three-way Switches

Three-way switches have three screw terminals and do not have ON-OFF markings. They are always installed in pairs and are used to control a set of lights from two locations.

One of the screw terminals on a three-way switch is darker than the others. This is the *common* screw terminal; its position may vary by manufacturer. The two lighter-colored screw terminals on a three-way switch are called *traveler* screw terminals. These terminals are interchangeable.

If a switch lies in the middle of a circuit, the box should have two cables: one 2-wire cable, and one 3-wire cable (photo A). The black (hot) wire from the 2-wire cable is connected to the common screw terminal, and the red and black wires from the 3-wire cable connect to the traveler terminals.

At the end of a circuit, a three-way switch is connected to one 3-wire cable (photo B). The white wire is coded black for hot.

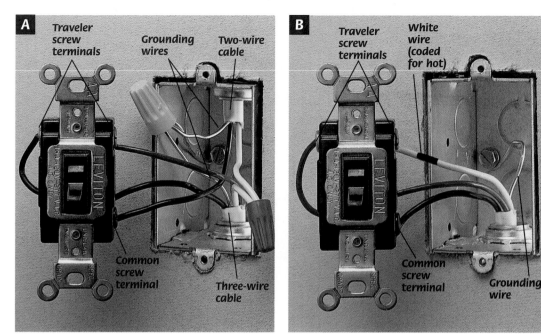

Installation of a three-way switch in the middle of a circuit.

Installation of a three-way switch at the end of a circuit.

Four-way Switches

Four-way switches have four screw terminals and do not have ON-OFF markings. They are always installed between a pair of three-way switches, making it possible to control a set of lights from three or more locations. Four-way switches are common in homes where large rooms contain multiple living areas, such as where a kitchen opens into a dining room.

In a typical four-way switch installation, there will be a pair of 3-wire cables that enter the switch box. With most switches, the hot wires from one cable should be attached to the bottom or top pair of screw terminals, and the hot wires from the other cable should be attached to the remaining pair of screw terminals.

However, not all switches are designed the same way, and the wiring configurations in the boxes may vary, as well. Always study the wiring diagram that comes with the switch. Some four-way switches have a wiring guide stamped on the back of the device.

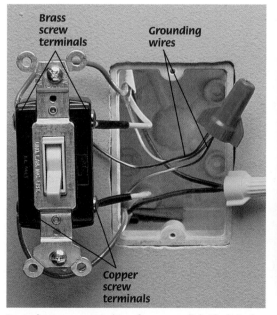

Four wires are connected to a four-way switch. The hot wires from one cable are attached to the top pair of screw terminals, while the hot wires from the other cable are attached to the bottom screw terminals.

VARIATION: For the switch shown above, one pair of color-matched circuit wires will be connected to the screw terminals marked LINE 1; the other pair will be attached to the screw terminals marked LINE 2.

Installing Receptacles

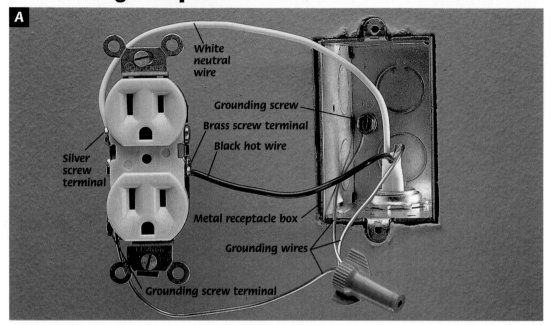

Single cable entering the box indicates end-of-run wiring. The black hot wire is attached to a brass screw terminal, and the white neutral wire is connected to a silver screw terminal. If the box is metal, the grounding wire is pigtailed to the grounding screws of the receptacle and the box. In a plastic box, the grounding wire is attached directly to the grounding screw terminal of the receptacle.

A standard duplex receptacle has two halves that receive plugs. Each half has a long (neutral) slot, a short (hot) slot, and a U-shaped grounding hole. The three slots fit the wide prong, the narrow prong, and the grounding prong of a three-prong plug. This ensures the connection will be polarized and grounded.

A 125-volt duplex receptacle can be wired to the electrical system in a number of ways. The most common are shown on these pages.

Receptacles are wired as either *end-of-run* or *middle-of-run*. These configurations are easily identified by counting the number of cables entering the receptacle box. End-of-run wiring (photo A) has only one cable, indicating that the circuit ends. Middle-of-run wiring (photo B) has two cables, indicating that the circuit continues on to other receptacles, switches, or fixtures.

In a *split-circuit receptacle* (photo C), each half of the receptacle is wired to a separate circuit. This allows two appliances of high wattage to be plugged into the same receptacle without blowing a fuse or tripping a breaker. This wiring configuration is similar to a receptacle that is controlled by a wall switch. Most electrical codes require a switch-controlled receptacle in any room that does not have a built-in light fixture operated by a wall switch.

Split-circuit and switch-controlled receptacles are connected to two hot wires, so use caution during repairs and replacements. And make sure the connecting tab between the hot screw terminals is removed.

Two-slot receptacles (photo D) are common in older homes. There is no grounding wire attached to the receptacle, but the box may be grounded with armored cable or conduit.

Ground-fault circuit-interrupter (GFCI) receptacles (see page 130) are required by code in rooms where water may be present and in outside locations. GFCIs can be wired to protect one or more receptacles on a single circuit.

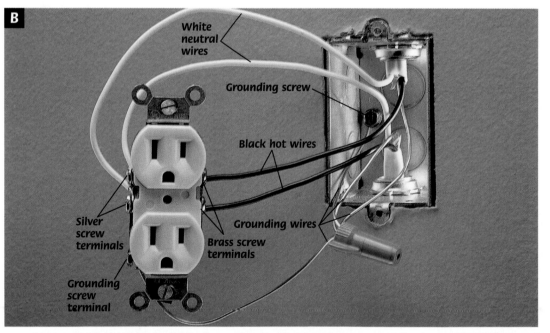

Two cables entering the box indicate middle-of-run wiring. The black hot wires are connected to brass screw terminals, and the white neutral wires are connected to the silver screw terminals. The grounding wire is pigtailed to the grounding screws of the receptacle and the box.

A split-circuit receptacle is attached to a black hot wire, a red hot wire, a white neutral wire, and a bare grounding wire. The wiring is similar to a switch-controlled receptacle.

The hot wires are attached to the brass screw terminals, and the connecting tab or fin between the brass terminals is removed. The white wire is attached to a silver screw terminal, and the connecting tab on the neutral side remains intact. The grounding wire is pigtailed to the grounding screw terminal of the receptacle and to the grounding screw attached to the box.

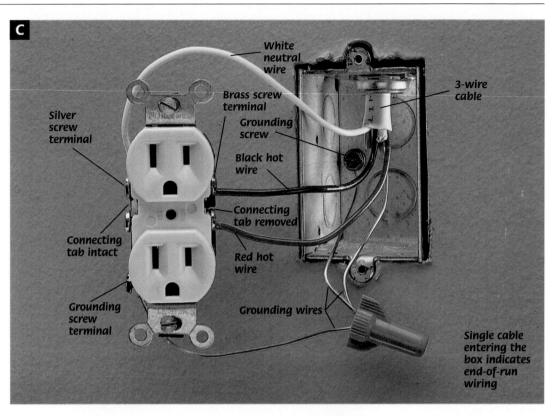

C

White neutral wire

Brass screw terminal

Silver screw terminal

Grounding screw

Black hot wire

3-wire cable

Connecting tab removed

Connecting tab intact

Red hot wire

Grounding screw terminal

Grounding wires

Single cable entering the box indicates end-of-run wiring

A two-slot receptacle is often found in older homes. The black hot wires are connected to the brass screw terminals, and the white neutral wires are pigtailed to a silver screw terminal.

Two-slot receptacles may be replaced with three-slot types, but only if a means of grounding exists at the receptacle box.

NOTE: If you have a remodeling project that involves installing additional receptacles to a circuit containing two-slot receptacles, you may be required by code to replace the two-slot receptacles with standard three-slot receptacles. Check with your electrical inspector for code restrictions in your area.

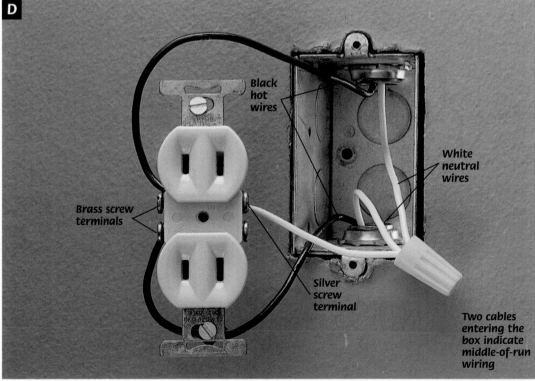

D

Black hot wires

White neutral wires

Brass screw terminals

Silver screw terminal

Two cables entering the box indicate middle-of-run wiring

Installing a GFCI Receptacle

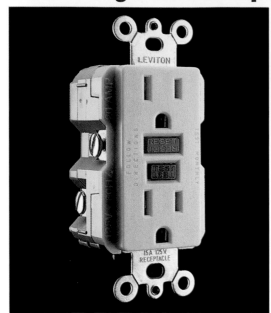

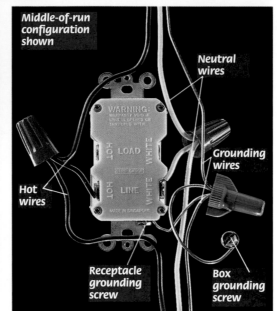

Middle-of-run configuration shown

Neutral wires

Grounding wires

Hot wires

Receptacle grounding screw

Box grounding screw

A GFCI receptacle has a red RESET button and a black TEST button on its face. Test a GFCI monthly by pressing the black button: The red button should click out and shut off the power. Restore power by depressing the red button.

Wired for single-location protection, a GFCI (shown from the back) has hot and neutral wires connected only to the screw terminals marked LINE. The circuit grounding wires are pigtailed to the grounding screw on the receptacle.

GFCI (Ground-fault circuit-interrupter) receptacles protect against electrical shock caused by common hazards such as faulty appliances, worn cords, or wet plugs. They are required by code for receptacle installations where water may be present, such as in bathrooms, kitchens, garages, crawlspaces, unfinished basements, and outside locations.

GFCIs automatically shut off power when there are changes in current flow. Because of this, GFCIs provide security even if they're not grounded. This makes them suitable for replacing old duplex receptacles where no grounding path exists.

A GFCI can be wired to protect only itself (single-location) or to protect itself and all devices "down-stream" to the end of the circuit (multiple-location). It cannot protect devices between itself and the main service panel.

Single-location wiring is preferable, since multiple devices may make a GFCI overly sensitive to false trippings. Consult an electrician for help with multiple-location wiring.

Installing a GFCI Receptacle for Single-location Protection

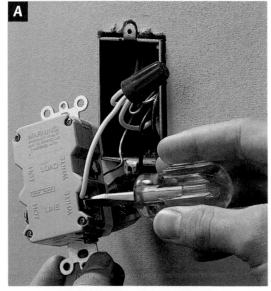

A

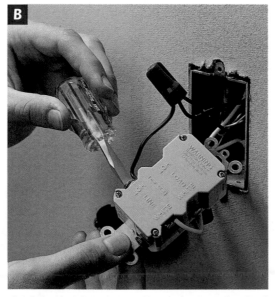

B

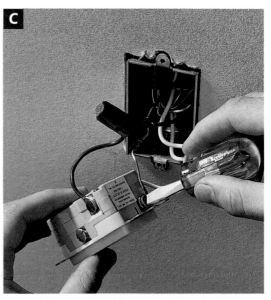

C

Shut off power to the circuit at the main service panel. Pigtail the white neutral wires together (see page 125), and connect the pigtail to the terminal marked WHITE LINE on the GFCI.

Pigtail the black hot wires together, and connect the pigtail to the terminal marked HOT LINE on the GFCI.

Connect the grounding wire to the green grounding screw terminal on the GFCI. Mount the GFCI to the box, and attach the coverplate. Restore power and test the GFCI according to the manufacturer's instructions.

Installing Light Fixtures & Smoke Alarms

Light fixtures and smoke alarms typically run on standard, 120-volt circuits. Often, all of the fixtures for a room and neighboring hallway can be powered by one circuit.

Most light fixtures come with their own internal wiring, and connecting them is simply a matter of joining the fixture leads to the circuit wires. Fixtures must be attached to properly anchored electrical boxes by means of a mounting strap.

In remodeling work, new smoke alarms must be hard-wired, meaning they are powered by a circuit (not a battery). However, some codes require hard-wired alarms to have a battery back-up. Hard-wired alarms also must be wired in series, so that if one alarm triggers, it sets off all of the other alarms automatically.

To wire alarms in series, run three-wire cable between the various alarms, using the red cable wire to join the trigger wires of the different units.

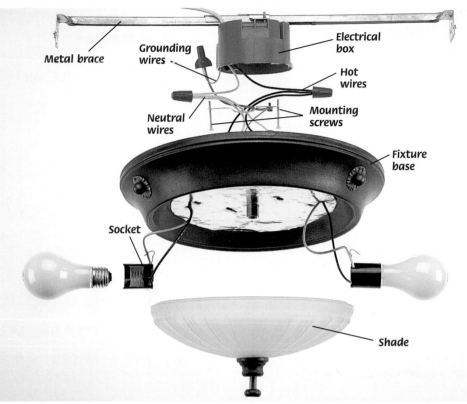

A typical incandescent light fixture has hot and neutral leads that connect to circuit wires with wire connectors. Electrical boxes for fixtures must be attached directly to framing or to metal braces that span between framing members.

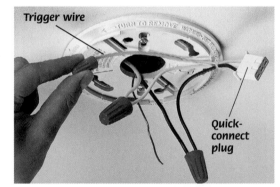

Smoke alarms for hard-wiring have a trigger wire for connecting multiple alarms in a series. Some models have quick-connect plugs for easy connection to the alarm body.

Fixtures for a Lifespan Home

A universal lighting plan includes fixtures that provide appropriate light levels and require minimal effort to operate and maintain. Distribute overhead, wall, and task lighting evenly in order to create a safe environment, especially for people with vision limitations.

- Choose fixtures with bulbs that can be changed easily. Some fixtures have retractable cords that let you pull the fixture close for changing bulbs.
- Look for fixtures that have at least two bulbs; this ensures there will be a light source even when one bulb burns out.
- Choose timed, motion- or voice-activated lights where appropriate. These lights eliminate the need to find and operate switches. (Make sure the fixture settings are easily adjustable.)

- Consider touch-controlled light fixtures, which don't require precise hand movements for operation.
- Install a power-failure light in each room.
- Consider using fluorescent bulbs where appropriate. They last longer and cost less than incandescents, and newer fluorescent bulbs come in colors that are pleasing to the eye.

Installing Telephone Wires

Your telephone company owns and maintains the telephone wires entering your house up to the *demarcation jack*. The wiring and jacks installed beyond this point are your responsibility, and you can expand or update your system to accommodate your changing needs. Common improvements to a standard telephone system include replacing older jacks with modern modular jacks, and installing a distribution hub—known as a *junction box*—to accommodate new phone lines. (For an upgrade that goes beyond adding phone lines, consider installing a home network system—see pages 134 to 139.)

Modern phone systems typically use a junction box that feeds individual lines to the phone jacks in your house. This wiring method is called the "home run" or "star" method. One advantage of this system is that if one line is damaged, the others remain operable. If your system has a junction box, you can easily add a new jack by running new wiring from this junction box. It's also easy to install a junction box, if your system doesn't have one.

Older phone systems may be wired using the "continuous loop" method, in which all of the jacks are connected along a single loop of wire running through the house. These older systems may also have outdated phone jacks that don't accept modern line connectors. A simple way to update an older system is to install new jacks that can serve as junction boxes for additional lines.

Telephone jacks are color-coded to match the colors of the four main wires in standard telephone cable. However, there may be differences in the color-coding systems; the chart below lists the most common connections.

Telephone wires are low voltage and can be worked on with little risk of shock, but, as an added precaution, it's a good idea to unplug the service line from the demarcation jack before you begin.

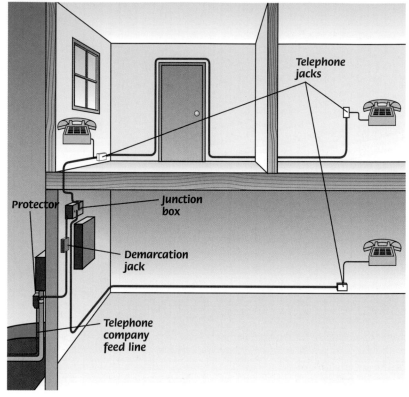

The telephone system *inside your home starts at the demarcation jack, which is connected to the main feed line. Individual lines may stem from a junction box or from another jack.*

The red terminal will accept:
- a red wire
- a blue wire
- a blue wire with a white stripe

The yellow terminal will accept:
- a yellow wire
- an orange wire
- an orange wire with a white stripe

The green terminal will accept:
- a green wire
- a white wire with a blue stripe

The black terminal will accept:
- a black wire
- a white wire with orange stripes

Note: If there are extra wires (usually green or white) leave them unconnected and tuck them into the jack.

Tools: *Screwdriver, wire cutters.*

Materials: *Modular jack, junction box.*

Adding Phone Lines for Safety and Convenience

Installing at least one phone line in each room will afford your family flexibility, safety, and convenience.

A bathroom is an especially good place for a phone. Because wet surfaces make bathrooms likely places for accidents, a bathroom phone can be an important safety feature. It enables a person to call for assistance, should he or she fall while home alone.

A guest suite can also benefit from additional phone lines; your visitors will appreciate the convenience and security. And because guest rooms often serve many different functions for the family, having phone lines in place makes them more versatile.

Keep in mind that the small buttons on standard telephones can be difficult to read and use, so consider installing large-button phones instead.

Installing a Modular Jack

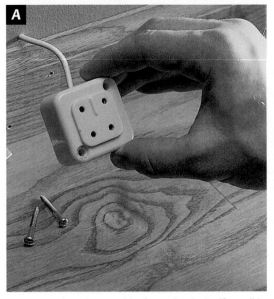
A

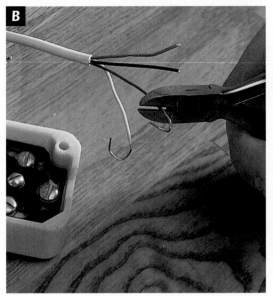
B

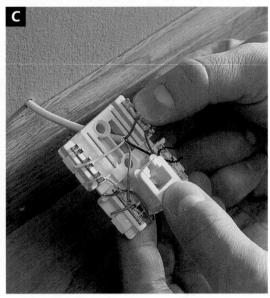
C

Disconnect the phone cable from the jack, if possible. Unscrew the jack from the wall (you may have to remove a coverplate), and carefully pull the jack from the wall.

Disconnect the wires from the jack terminals. Clip off the bare copper end of each cable wire, using a wire cutter.

Feed the cable through the back of the new jack. Force each colored wire into one of the free metal slots on the terminal block that has a wire of the same color. Fasten the jack to the wall, and attach the coverplate.

Installing a Junction Box

A

B

C

Determine the location for the junction box on a wall or framing member near the demarcation jack. Mount the junction box with screws.

Using standard phone cable, strip the end of each wire and attach it to the color-matched terminal on the demarcation jack. Run the cable into the junction box, securing it with staples every 2 ft. Attach each wire to the appropriate screw terminal on the junction box.

Connect the cables for each phone line to the slotted terminals in the junction box. Test the system to make sure the lines are working, then install the junction-box coverplate.

Home Network Wiring

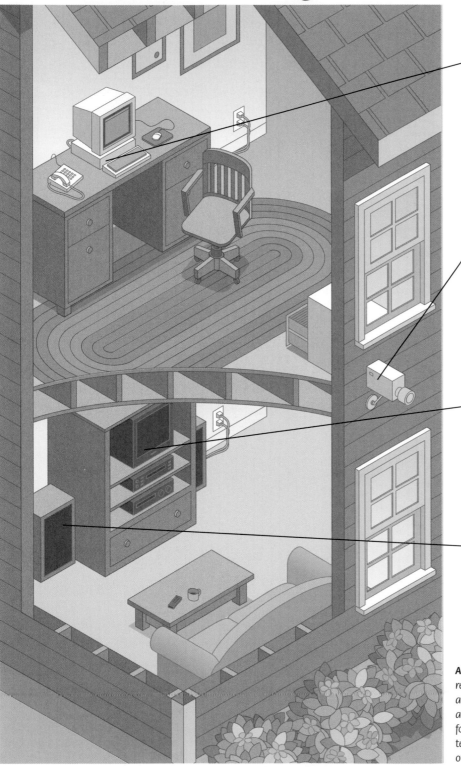

Voice/data (RJ45) *jacks can accept any pin-size telecommunication jack, including standard phone and data lines, as well as multi-line computer data connections for a home office.*

Accessories, *such as closed-circuit cameras, allows homeowners to tailor a system to their specific needs.*

Video (F-connector) jacks *provide connections for receiving and redistributing TV, VCR, DVD, and closed-circuit camera signals.*

Audio terminals *or a recessed speaker system can enhance a home theater system or be used to create a whole-house audio system with localized volume control.*

A **home network wiring system** *allows you to receive and distribute voice, data, and video signals anywhere inside your home. The network is accessed at various outlets that contain jacks and connectors for plug-and-play connection of phones, computers, televisions, VCRs, DVDs, stereo systems, and many other electronic devices.*

Photos this page courtesy of Pass & Seymour/egrand

Home Network Wiring

The ability to send and receive electronic information has become an important part of our lives. Internet access, multiple phone lines, cable television, satellites, home computer networks, and security systems are now commonplace in many homes. And as our telecommunications needs grow, a better, faster, and more convenient way to manage these separate systems becomes increasingly necessary.

A home network system brings all these single systems together at one central location. Just as an electrical system starts at a service panel and has circuit wiring to supply electricity to the various rooms, a network wiring system has a distribution hub and specialty cables to carry voice, video, audio, and computer data to wherever you need it.

The whole system revolves around the hub, or *distribution center* (photo A). This is mounted in a basement or a utility closet, and it receives all of the input connections from outside the home, such as phone, Internet, and cable or satellite T.V. lines, as well as stereo and video connections from an entertainment center inside the home. The distribution center contains various *distribution modules* (photo B), each designed to transmit specific voice, data, and video (VDV) signals. Some modules receive electrical power from a receptacle mounted inside the distribution box, allowing them to send strong signals to multiple outlets. From the modules, high-performance cabling and wire (photo C) are routed to any room in the house, where they connect to specialty outlets (photo D). The outlets are said to be "plug-and-play," meaning they contain jacks that accept standard plugs for audio/video, computer, phone, and other household equipment.

Many home centers carry the components, materials, and specialty tools for home network systems; you can purchase an entire system at once or build one over time. The following pages provide an overview of the planning and installation of a basic network system.

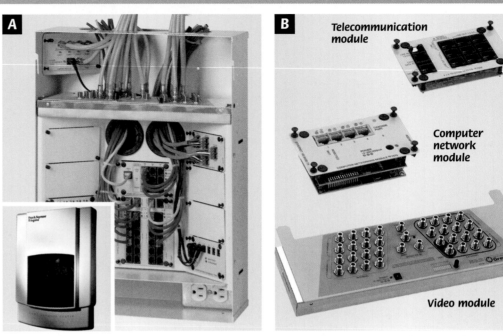

The distribution center houses all of the modules, cable and wire connections, and the power supply for the entire network system. A plastic cover (inset) provides protection and allows easy access to the modules and cable connections, making it easy to reconfigure outlets or make any system changes.

Distribution modules are interface devices that maintain the strength of incoming signals for distribution throughout the system. Modules can also redistribute internal signals to create in-home camera monitoring systems or to route DVD, VCR, or audio signals from a single location to any room in the house.

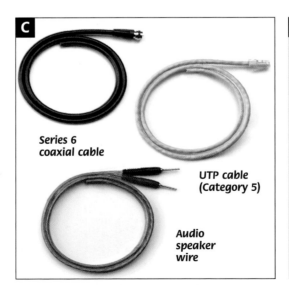

High-performance cabling and wire carry signals between the modules, outlets, and equipment. Series 6 coaxial cable distributes audio/video signals, category 5 cabling carries phone and data signals, and high-grade audio speaker wire routes audio signals throughout the system.

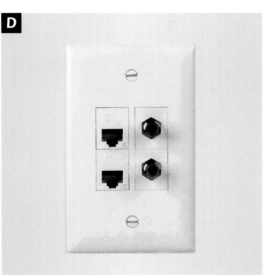

Multimedia outlets can be tailored to the specific needs of each room. Outlets contain a series of jacks and connectors (see page 134) for plug-and-play connection. For convenience, many outlets can be installed next to standard electrical receptacles.

Planning a Home Network System

Installing a home network system is a project that any homeowner can accomplish. Though it is easier to run cables and wires in the construction phase before the walls are finished, retrofit installations are quite manageable if you carefully plan the system needs, determine the optimal location for each component, and map out the cable and wire routes.

As a general rule, it's a good idea to plan for more cabling and multimedia outlets than you think you will currently use (a teenager's bedroom may become a home office in a few years).

The living room, home office, bedroom, entertainment and recreation rooms, and den are all obvious places for outlets, but outlets in rooms such as the kitchen, bathroom, laundry and utility room, or at locations near large appliances, will help prepare your home for future conveniences and home automation features.

Include multiple outlets in various locations of specific rooms, especially in entertainment areas and the home office. A home office will also benefit from multiple phone and data lines for Internet access on the computer. Locate these outlets near receptacles to simplify computer connections.

Sketches and routing maps will help you plan the wire and cable runs. Installing network system lines is similar to running electrical cable (see pages 116 to 122). To maximize cable performance, plan the runs with as few turns and bends as possible.

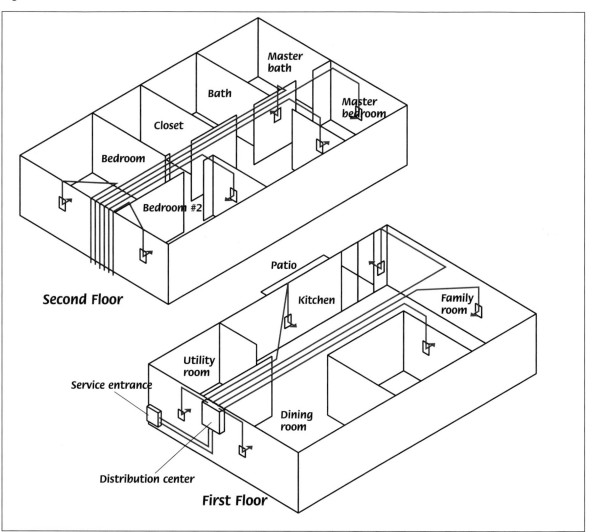

The distribution center *should be installed in an accessible, central location (such as a basement or utility room) and near the service entrance. Easy access to the center will not only simplify the current installation, but also future alterations to the system. The central location will make cable lengths less likely to extend past their recommended routing length (295 ft.).*

Building Codes

With the increasing need for networking capabilities in the home, standards have been developed by the Telecommunications Industry Association (TIA) and the Electronic Industry Alliance (EIA) in accordance with the Federal Communications Commission (FCC). These standards are becoming the code requirements for home network wiring installation across the country.

Make sure to check with your local building inspector for the current codes in this new and changing area of home wiring.

Preparing Multimedia Outlets

In new construction, use extension brackets to install multimedia outlets next to existing electrical receptacles. Fit the bracket over the receptacle, and fasten it to the stud with screws, then install the new outlet box. Use standard double-gang boxes or hollow-backed boxes (see photo, right) for single outlets; this prevents bending and twisting that can damage the wiring. Mount individual outlet boxes 12" from the floor, measured to the box center.

For retrofit installations, use plastic retrofit boxes (hollow-backed or double-gang). Cut a hole in the wallboard and insert the box, then turn the mounting screws until the ears clamp snugly to the back of the wallboard (inset). Route all wiring to the boxes (see page 138), leaving at least 12" of slack at each box.

Mounting the Distribution Center

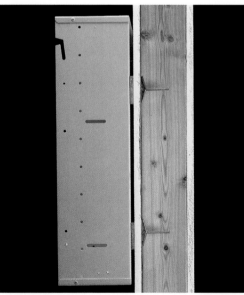

Mount the distribution center at least 48" above the floor, in an easily accessible location. Many units can be recess-mounted between studs with 16" on-center spacing.

Distribution centers can also be surface mounted on finished walls, or attached to a wood backer board. Leave at least ¼" gap between the unit and wall to accommodate module installation and fastening hardware.

Install a dedicated 15-amp, 120-volt, non-switchable duplex receptacle either in the enclosure itself, or within 60" of the distribution center. A transformer will be used to distribute power to the modules that require it.

Routing Cables & Wires

Drill holes in the top plate *above the distribution center for routing wiring into the enclosure. Where network wiring runs next to electrical cables in long stretches, maintain a 6" space between them. Feed cables from the outlet locations to the distribution center. See pages 118 to 122 for tips on installing cable in finished walls and unfinished walls.*

Label each run of cable *at both the distribution center and the room outlet. At the distribution center, cut each cable to hang even with the bottom of the enclosure. Attach a label with its room location and the specified module connection. At the outlet end of the cable, label it according to its module connection.*

Attaching Connectors to Cable Ends

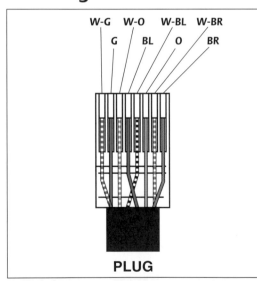

Category 5 cable *carries voice and data signals. It contains four twisted pairs of color-coded wires. To attach a RJ45 plug (see photo, right), untwist the wires and arrange them in the plug according to the wiring assignment chart provided by the manufacturer.*

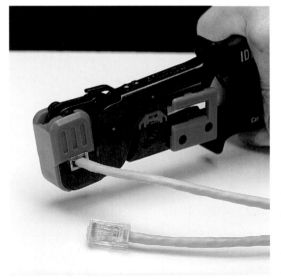

Install plugs *using a crimping tool. Make sure that each wire is matched to the proper conductor and that ½" of outer insulation is inside the plug, then crimp the plug to secure it.*

Use F-connector fittings *to connect coaxial cable to F-connector video terminals. Slide the connector over the stripped end of the cable, and attach it with an F-connector crimping tool.*

Terminating the Connectors

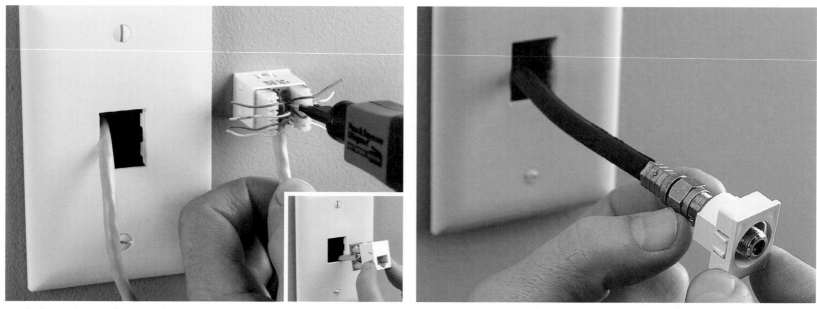

RJ45 jacks are the ports for connecting phone and data devices to the network system. The jacks are wired to a universal pin/pair assignment standard (standard T568A), which allows any size telecommunication plug to be used with the jack. The back side of RJ45 jacks are color-coded to simplify installation. Use a punchdown tool to connect the wires to the terminals, then snap the jack into the outlet (inset).

F-connector terminals provide every room in your house with the ability to receive and distribute antenna, cable TV, and satellite signals, as well as internal transmission signals from DVDs, VCRs, and closed-circuit cameras. The f-connector fittings on coaxial cable ends are threaded and screw onto the f-connector terminals.

Making the Final Connections

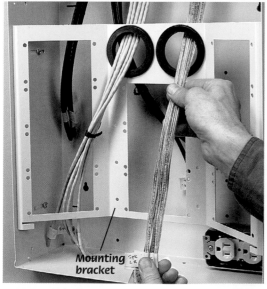

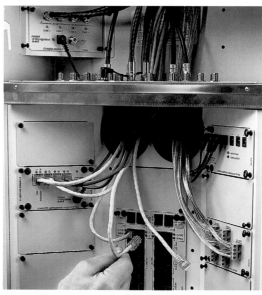

Install a mounting bracket (if required) to the distribution center for mounting the various modules. Determine where each module will be placed and route the appropriate cables to their corresponding module.

Attach the modules using push-pin grommets or screws. Install a power module to supply modules that require electrical current. A power module connects to a transformer that's plugged into the distribution-center receptacle.

Connect the cables to the proper module, using the labels for guidance. Connect cables for incoming service and internal networks to INPUT ports, and those routed to outlets to OUTPUT ports. Finally, test the system, then attach the cover.

$\mathcal{D}$OORS &
WINDOWS

Selecting Doors & Windows

Because doors and windows serve very basic purposes, consider your options carefully before making any purchases (some designs are far from universal). Lever door handles and remote or slide-bolt locks are good examples of universal design: They make opening a door easier for a person carrying packages as well as for someone lacking manual dexterity.

Hardware is also an important consideration, as it alone can make the difference between a door that serves as a passageway and one that acts only as a barrier. The type of doors or windows you select may dictate the general style of hardware you install; hardware types are discussed below. As a general rule, installing hardware at a maximum height of 44" to 48" makes it easy to use for people of various heights.

As with doors, your design considerations will affect which window styles you select; consider your family's situation before purchasing. Keep in mind the size and strength of those who will operate the windows, and remember that the hardware must be reachable by those users.

Hinged Doors

A hinged door requires swing space equal to the width of the door plus 18" to 24" of clear space on the latch side for maneuvering (see page 53). Consider the swing direction, available swing space, and whether the swing of the door will interrupt the flow of traffic in a hallway.

Many experts recommend that hinged bathroom doors swing outward, so a person who has fallen inside the bathroom cannot block the door.

Choose entry doors with low thresholds or no thresholds. The front edge of the threshold should be no more than $\frac{1}{4}$" high if it's square, $\frac{1}{2}$" high if it's beveled.

Hinged-door hardware

Select lever handles; they require less exacting hand placement and are easier to use than knobs or pulls. Locks vary widely. For exterior locks, a keyless entry system is an ideal way to eliminate fumbling with keys in cold weather. For interior locks, slide bolts typically are preferred over standard deadbolts, because they are easier to operate. Avoid chain locks, which are difficult to use.

Handle photos courtesy of Kwikset

Remote locks and other keyless entry systems improve the safety and convenience of entry doors.

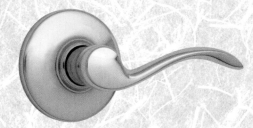

Adding lever door handles is an easy way to make your doors more accessible.

You can gain space in all hinged-door openings by installing swing-clear hinges. These have L-shaped leaves that allow the door to swing away from the jamb, increasing the clear opening by the thickness of the door.

Swinging Doors

A swinging door with no latch requires swing space on both sides. Because they require no hardware to open and close, swinging doors may be a good option in situations where

latches or locks are unnecessary. As with a standard hinged door, consider the door's swing space and whether the swing will interrupt traffic flow.

Sliding Glass Doors

Sliding doors present several problems. Glass doors are dangerous to some because they can appear to be open when they aren't. They can be difficult to operate from a seated position, and as doors age and dirt accumulates in the tracks, they become even more difficult to open. Finally, thresholds on sliding doors typically are high, which creates barriers for walkers and wheelchairs.

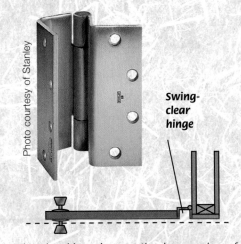

Photo courtesy of Stanley

Swing-clear hinge

Swing-clear hinges increase the clear openings of doorways; they are mounted like standard hinges.

Pocket Doors

Perhaps the best alternative to a hinged or sliding door is a pocket door. It saves space, requires no threshold, and can be equipped with hardware that is easy to use. Pocket doors require special framing considerations; because the door slides into the wall, the rough opening is roughly twice the width of a standard door opening. Door units can be custom-built or purchased as prehung units (see illustration at right).

Standard recessed hardware for pocket doors is difficult to use, so install D-pulls instead. Mount the pulls 1½" from the edge of the door (to provide room for fingers when the door is closed). Also, install a stop at the back of the frame, so the door stops 1½" short of the D-pull (to provide room for fingers when the door is open) (see the drawings at far right). Keep in mind that this design reduces the width of the door opening by 3". An alternative is to build recesses into the wall that accept the D-pulls, so the door is flush with the jamb when fully opened.

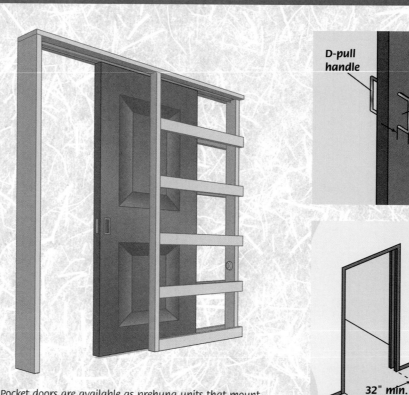

Pocket doors are available as prehung units that mount into framed openings. Mount 1½" D-pull or lever handles leaving 1½" of clearance. Make sure all doors have a 32" (min.) clear opening and a 48"-deep approach space.

Photos courtesy of Andersen Windows, Inc.

Single-lever latches and automatic openers make casement windows easier to operate.

Casement Windows

Casement windows offer many attractive design features. Well-built models are easy to operate, and some come equipped with tandem latches or single-lever locking systems. Unfortunately, casement windows do not accept window air conditioners.

Horizontal Sliding Sash

Many horizontal sliding sash windows have improved in recent years. Some manufacturers now produce models with quality sliding mechanisms and offset hardware. These windows can accept air conditioners and screens.

Window Hardware

Although the type of window you select determines the hardware that is available, keep the following guidelines in mind.

Tandem latches, which operate multiple locks on a window with one motion, may be optional on some models; they simplify use considerably. Where possible, opt for larger handles or automatic openers. For other types of hardware, investigate adapters that make windows easier to operate.

Vertical Sliding Sash

Vertical sliding sash windows may be good options due to their availability and affordability, and they accept air conditioners and screens. High-quality models are easy to operate and many come with convenient features, such as tilt-in design for easy cleaning.

Installing a Prehung Interior Door

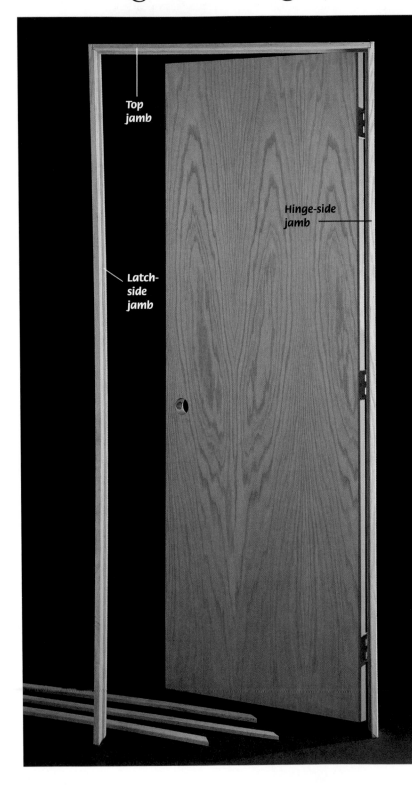

Prehung doors come as single units with the door already hung on hinges attached to a factory-built frame. To secure the unit during shipping, most prehung doors are nailed shut with a couple of duplex nails driven through the jambs and into the door edge. These nails must be removed before you install the door.

The key to installing doors is to plumb and fasten the hinge-side jamb first. After that's in place, you can position the top and latch-side jambs by checking the *reveal*—the gap between the closed door and the jamb.

Standard prehung doors have 4½"-wide jambs and are sized to fit walls with 2 × 4 construction and ½" wallboard. If you have thicker walls, you can special-order doors to match, or you can add jamb extensions to standard-size doors.

Tools: 4-ft. level, nail set, handsaw.

Materials: Prehung door unit, wood shims, 8d casing nails.

TIP: If your walls are built with 2 × 6 studs, extend the jambs by attaching 1"-thick wood strips to the jamb edges on both sides. Use glue and 4d casing nails to attach these extensions to the jambs.

Installing a Prehung Interior Door

A

Set the door unit into the framed opening so the jamb edges are flush with the wall surfaces and the unit is centered from side to side. Using a level, adjust the unit so the hinge-side jamb is plumb.

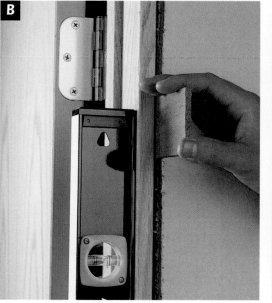

B

Starting near the top hinge, insert pairs of shims driven from opposite directions into the gap between the framing and the jamb, sliding the shims in until they are snug. Check the jamb to make sure it remains plumb and does not bow inward. Install shims near each hinge.

C

Anchor the hinge-side jamb with 8d casing nails driven through the jamb and shims and into the framing. Drive nails only at the shim locations.

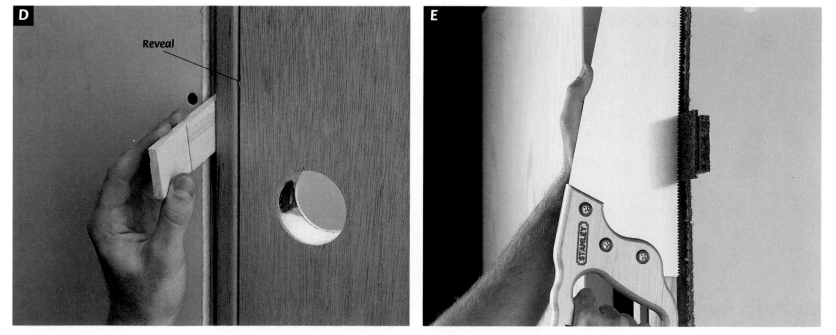

D

Reveal

Insert pairs of shims into the gap between the framing members and the top jamb and latch-side jamb, aligning them roughly with the hinge-side shims. With the door closed, adjust the shims so the reveal is ⅛" to ⅛" wide. Drive casing nails through the jambs and shims and into the framing members.

E

Set all nails below the surface of the wood with a nail set, then cut off the shims flush with the wall surface, using a handsaw or utility knife. Hold the saw vertically to prevent damage to the door jamb or wall. See pages 230 to 231 to install the door casing.

Masking tape used to keep windows from shattering

Removing Doors & Windows

If your remodeling project requires removing old doors and windows, do not start this work until all the preparation work is finished and the interior wall surfaces and trim have been removed. You will need to close up the wall openings as soon as possible, so make sure you have all the necessary tools, framing lumber, and new window or door units on hand before starting the final stages of demolition. Be prepared to finish the work as quickly as possible.

Doors and windows are removed using the same basic procedures. In many cases, old units can be salvaged for resale or later use, so use care when removing them.

Tools: Utility knife, flat pry bar, screwdriver, reciprocating saw.
Materials: Masking tape, plywood sheets, screws.

TIP: *If you can't fill the wall openings immediately, cover the openings with scrap pieces of plywood screwed to the framing members. Staple plastic sheeting to the outside of the openings to prevent moisture damage.*

Removing Doors

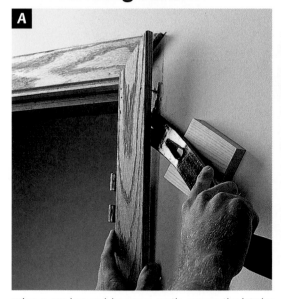

A Using a pry bar and hammer, gently remove the interior door trim. Save the trim to use after the new door is installed.

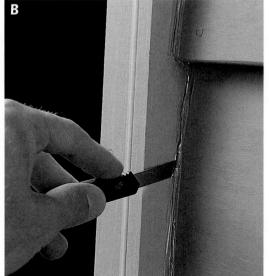

B Cut away the old caulk between the exterior siding and the brick molding on the door frame, using a utility knife.

C Use a flat pry bar or a cat's paw to remove the casing nails securing the door jambs to the framing. Cut stubborn nails with a reciprocating saw (see step B, below). Remove the door from the opening.

Removing Windows

A Carefully pry off the interior trim around the window frame. For double-hung windows with sash weights, remove the weights by cutting the cords and pulling the weights from the weight pockets near the bottoms of the side jambs.

B Cut through the nails holding the window jambs to the framing members, using a reciprocating saw. Place tape over the window panes to prevent shattering, then remove the window unit from the opening.

Nailing flange

VARIATION: For windows and doors attached with nailing flanges, cut or pry loose the siding material, then remove the nails holding the unit to the sheathing. See pages 32 to 35 for more information on removing siding.

Installing an Entry Door

Prehung entry doors come in many styles, but most are installed using the same basic methods. Because entry doors are very heavy—some large units weigh several hundred pounds—make sure you have help for this project.

To speed your work, complete the interior surface removal (see pages 28 to 31) and framing work (see pages 55 to 58) in advance.

In this installation project, the new door is set into the framed opening, and the siding is marked and then cut to accept the door molding. See pages 32 to 35 for more information on cutting or removing exterior wall surfaces in preparation for a new door or window.

Before installing the door, make sure you have all the necessary hardware. Protect the door against the weather by painting or staining it and by adding a storm door, if desired.

Tools: Aviation snips, 4-ft. level, circular saw, wood chisel, stapler, caulk gun, nail set, drill, handsaw.

Materials: Door unit, tapered wood shims, building paper, drip edge, paintable silicone caulk, fiberglass insulation, 10d galvanized casing nails.

Installing an Entry Door

A

Remove the door unit from its packing. Do not remove the retaining brackets that hold the door closed.

B

Test-fit the door unit, centering it within the rough opening. Check to make sure door is plumb. If necessary, shim underneath the side door jambs until the door is plumb and level.

C

Brick molding

Trace an outline of the brick molding onto the siding, then remove the door unit and set it aside.

D Cut the siding along the outline, just down to the sheathing, using a circular saw. You may want to use a 1 × 4 to provide a flat base for the saw (see pages 34 to 35). Stop just short of the corners to prevent damage to the siding that will remain.

E Finish the cuts at the corners with a sharp wood chisel.

F Slide 8"-wide strips of building paper between the siding and sheathing at the top and sides of the opening, to shield the framing members from moisture. Wrap the paper around the framing members and staple it in place.

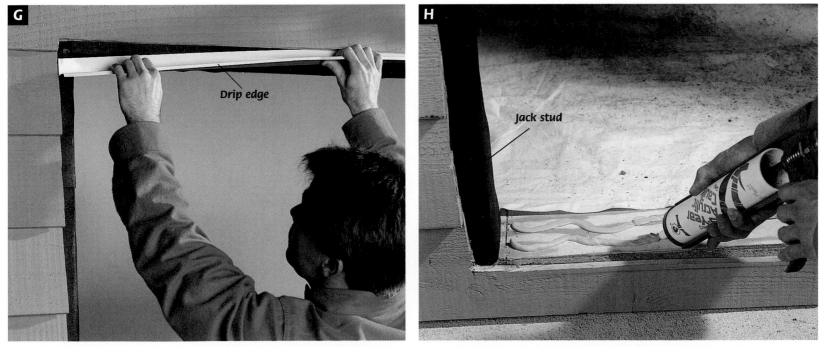

G To provide an added moisture barrier, cut a piece of drip edge to fit the width of the rough opening, then slide it between the siding and the building paper at the top of the opening. Do not nail the drip edge.

Drip edge

H Apply several thick beads of silicone caulk to the subfloor at the bottom of the door opening. Also apply silicone caulk over the building paper on the front (outside) edges of the jack studs and header.

Jack stud

Continued on next page

Installing an Entry Door (cont.)

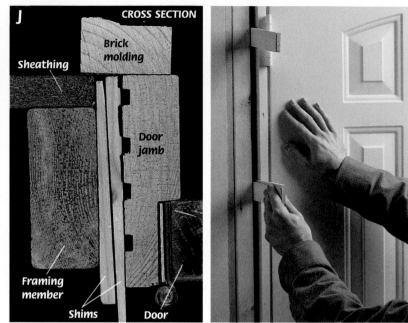

Center the door unit in the rough opening, and push the brick molding tight against the sheathing. Have a helper hold the door unit steady until it is nailed in place.

From inside, place pairs of tapered shims together to form flat shims (left), and insert the shims into the gaps between the door jambs and framing members. Insert the shims at the lockset and hinge locations and every 12" thereafter.

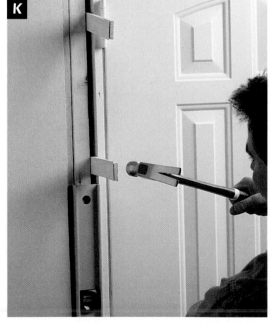

Make sure the door unit is plumb. Adjust the shims, if necessary, until the door is plumb and level. Fill the gaps between the jambs and the framing members with loosely packed fiberglass insulation.

From outside, drive 10d galvanized casing nails through the door jambs and into the framing members at each shim location. If necessary, drill pilot holes to prevent splitting. Use a nail set to drive the nail heads below the surface.

Remove the retaining brackets installed by the manufacturer, then open and close the door to make sure it works properly.

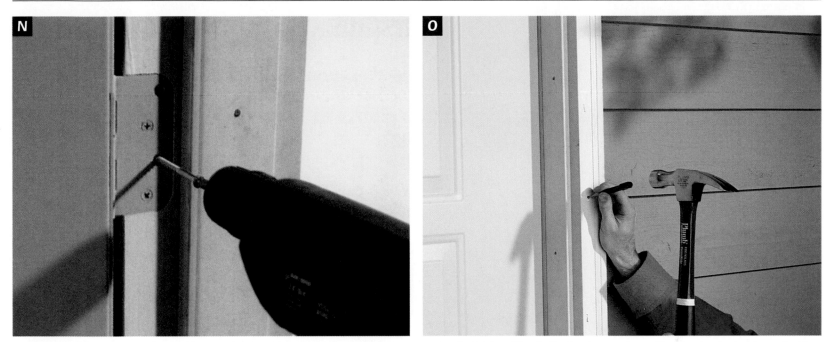

Remove two of the screws on the top hinge, and replace them with long anchor screws (usually included with the unit). These anchor screws strengthen the installation by penetrating the framing members.

Anchor the brick molding to the framing members with 10d galvanized casing nails driven every 12". Use a nail set to drive the nail heads below the surface.

Adjust the door threshold to create a tight seal along the bottom of the door, following the manufacturer's recommendations. Be careful not to strip the adjusting screws.

Cut off the shims flush with the framing members, using a handsaw or utility knife.

Apply paintable silicone caulk around the entire door unit. Fill the nail holes with caulk if you plan on painting the area. Finish the door and install the lockset as directed by the manufacturer.

Installing a Patio Door

For easy installation, buy a patio door with the door panels mounted in a preassembled frame. Try to avoid patio doors sold with frame kits that require complicated assembly.

Because patio doors have very long bottom sills and top jambs, they are susceptible to bowing and warping. To avoid these problems, be very careful to install the patio door so it is level and plumb, and to anchor the unit securely to framing members. Yearly caulking and touch-up painting help prevent moisture from warping the jambs.

In this installation project, the new door is set into the framed opening and the siding is marked and then cut to accept the door molding. See pages 32 to 35 for more information on cutting or removing exterior wall surfaces in preparation for a new door or window.

Tools: Flat pry bar, 4-ft. level, circular saw, wood chisel, stapler, caulk gun, drill, handsaw, nail set.

Materials: Door unit, tapered wood shims, drip edge, building paper, paintable silicone caulk, 10d casing nails (galvanized and standard), 3" wood screws, fiberglass insulation, sill nosing.

Purchase screen doors from the door manufacturer, if they are not included with your new door unit. Most screen doors have spring-mounted rollers that fit into a narrow track on the outside of the patio door threshold.

Tips for Installing Sliding Doors

Remove heavy glass panels if you are installing the door without help. Reinstall the panels after the frame has been placed in the rough opening and nailed at opposite corners. To remove and install the panels, remove the stop rail found on the top jamb of the door unit.

Adjust the bottom rollers after installation is complete. Remove the coverplate on the adjusting screw, found on the inside edge of the bottom rail. Turn the screw in small increments until the door rolls smoothly along the track without binding when it is opened and closed.

Tips for Installing French-style Patio Doors

Shown cutaway for clarity

$\frac{1}{8}$" gap

Provide extra support for door hinges by replacing the center mounting screw on each hinge with a 3" wood screw. These long screws extend through the side jambs and deep into the framing members.

Keep a uniform $\frac{1}{8}$" gap between the door, side jambs, and top jamb to ensure that the doors will swing freely without binding. Check this gap frequently as you shim around the door unit. For more information on shimming and fastening hinged entry doors, see pages 150 to 151.

Installing a Patio Door

Prepare the work area and remove the interior wall surfaces (see pages 27 to 31), then frame the rough opening for the patio door (see pages 52 to 58). Remove the exterior surfaces inside the framed opening (see pages 32 to 35).

Test-fit the door unit, centering it within the rough opening. Check to make sure door is plumb. If necessary, shim underneath the side jambs until the door is plumb and level. Have a helper hold the door in place while you adjust it.

Trace the outline of the brick molding onto the siding, then remove the door unit.

Cut the siding along the outline, just down to the sheathing, using a circular saw. You may want to use a 1 × 4 to provide a flat base for the saw (see pages 34 to 35). Stop just short of the corners to prevent damage to the remaining siding. Finish the cuts at the corners with a sharp wood chisel.

Drip edge

To provide an added moisture barrier, cut a piece of drip edge to fit the width of the rough opening, then slide it between the siding and the existing building paper at the top of the opening. Do not nail the drip edge.

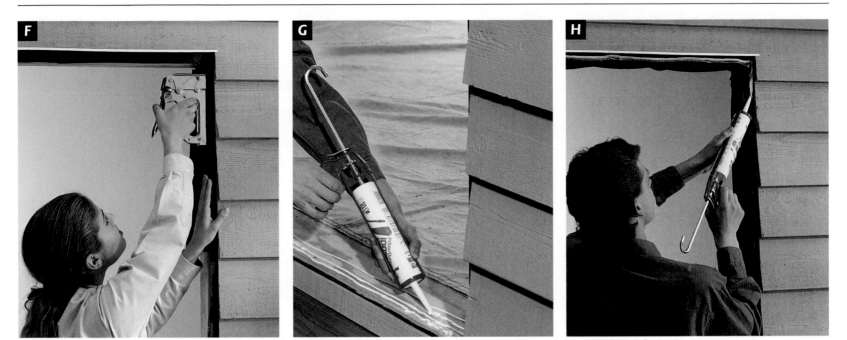

Slide 8"-wide strips of building paper between the siding and the sheathing. Wrap the paper around the framing members, and staple it in place.

Apply several thick beads of silicone caulk to the subfloor at the bottom of the door opening.

Apply silicone caulk around the front edge of the framing members, where the siding meets the building paper.

Center the patio door unit in the rough opening so the brick molding is tight against the sheathing. Have a helper hold the door unit from outside until it is shimmed and nailed in place.

Check the door threshold to make sure it is level. If necessary, shim underneath the side jambs until the patio door unit is level.

Continued on next page

Installing a Patio Door (cont.)

If there are gaps between the threshold and subfloor, insert shims coated with caulk into the gaps, spaced every 6". Shims should be snug, but not so tight that they cause the threshold to bow. Remove excess caulk immediately.

Place pairs of tapered shims together to form flat shims (see page 150). Insert the shims every 12" into the gaps between the side jambs and the jack studs. For sliding doors, shim behind the strike plate for the door latch.

Insert shims every 12" into the gap between the top jamb and the header.

From outside, drive 10d galvanized casing nails, spaced every 12", through the brick molding and into the framing members. If necessary, drill pilot holes to prevent splitting. Use a nail set to drive the nail heads below the surface.

From inside, drive 10d casing nails through the door jambs and into the framing members at each shim location. Use a nail set to drive the nail heads below the surface.

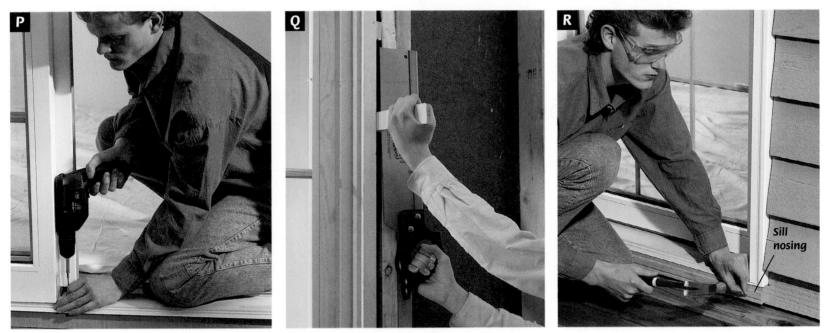

P Remove one of the screws on the stop block found in the center of the threshold. Replace the screw with a 3" wood screw driven into the subfloor as an anchor.

Q Cut off the shims flush with the face of the framing members, using a handsaw or utility knife. Fill the gaps around the door jambs and beneath the threshold with loosely packed fiberglass insulation.

R Reinforce and seal the edge of the threshold by installing sill nosing under the threshold and against the wall. Drill pilot holes, and attach the nosing with 10d galvanized casing nails.

sill nosing

S Make sure the drip edge is tight against the top brick molding, then apply paintable silicone caulk along the top of the drip edge and along the outside edge of the side brick moldings. Fill all exterior nail holes with caulk if you plan to paint over the area.

T Caulk completely around the sill nosing, using your finger to press the caulk into any cracks. As soon as the caulk is dry, paint the sill nosing. Finish the door and install the lockset as directed by the manufacturer. See pages 196 to 203 to finish the walls, and pages 230 to 231 to trim the interior of the door.

Installing Replacement Windows

If you're looking to replace or improve old single- or double-hung windows, consider using sash-replacement kits. They can give you energy-efficient, maintenance-free windows without changing the outward appearance of your home or breaking your budget.

Unlike *prime* window replacement, which changes the entire window and frame, or *pocket* window replacement, in which a complete window unit is set into the existing frame, sash replacement uses your home's original window jambs, eliminating the need to alter exterior or interior walls or trim. Installing a sash-replacement kit involves little more than removing the old window stops and sash and installing new vinyl jamb liners and wood or vinyl sash. And all of the work can be done from inside your house.

Most sash-replacement kits offer tilt features and other contemporary conveniences. Kits are available in vinyl, aluminum, or wood construction, with various options for color and glazing, energy-efficiency, security features, and noise-reduction.

Nearly all major window manufacturers offer sash replacement kits designed to fit their own windows. You can also order custom kits that are sized to your specific window dimensions. A good fit is essential to the performance of your new windows. Review the tips shown on page 159 for measuring your existing windows, and follow the manufacturer's instructions for the best fit.

Tools: *Sill-bevel gauge, flat pry bar, scissors, screwdriver, nail set.*

Materials: *Sash replacement kit, fiberglass insulation, 1" galvanized roofing nails, finish nails, wood-finishing materials.*

Photo courtesy of Marvin Windows and Doors

Upgrade old, leaky windows with new, energy-efficient sash replacement kits. Kits are available in a variety of styles to match your existing windows or to add a new decorative accent to your home. Most kits offer natural or painted interior surfaces and a choice of outdoor surface finishes.

Tips for Measuring for Sash-replacement Kits

Head jamb

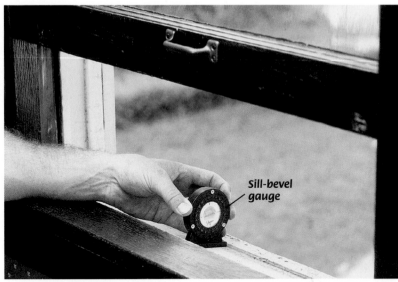

Sill-bevel gauge

Measure the width of the existing window at the top, middle, and bottom of the frame. Use the smallest measurement, then reduce the figure by ⅜". Measure the height of the existing window from the head jamb to the point where the outside edge of the bottom sash meets the sill. Reduce the figure by ⅜". NOTE: Manufacturers' specifications for window sizing may vary.

Use a sill-bevel gauge to determine the bevel of the existing window sill. This helps ensure the sash kit will fit properly. Also make sure that the sill, side, and head jambs are straight, level, and plumb. Measure the frame diagonally to check for square (if the diagonal measurements are equal, the frame is square). If the frame is not square, check with the sash-kit manufacturer: Most window kits can accommodate some deviation in frame dimensions.

Installing a Sash-replacement Kit

Photos this page courtesy of Marvin Windows and Doors

A

Carefully remove the interior stops from the side jambs, using a putty knife or pry bar. Save the stops for reinstallation.

B

With the bottom sash down, cut the cord holding the sash balancing weight on each side of the sash. Let the weights and cords fall into the weight pockets.

Continued on next page

Installing a Sash-replacement Kit (cont.)

C Lift out the bottom sash. Remove the parting stops from the head and side jambs. (The parting stops are the strips of wood that separate the top and bottom sash.) Cut the sash cords for the top sash, then lift out the top sash. Remove the sash-cord pulleys. If possible, pull the weights from the weight pockets at the bottom of the side jambs, then fill the weight pockets with fiberglass insulation. Repair any parts of the jambs that are rotted or damaged.

D Position the jamb-liner brackets, and fasten them to the jambs with 1" galvanized roofing nails. Place one bracket approximately 4" from head jam, and one 4" from the sill. Leave ¹⁄₁₆" clearance between the blind stop and the jamb-liner bracket. Install any remaining brackets, spacing them evenly along the jambs.

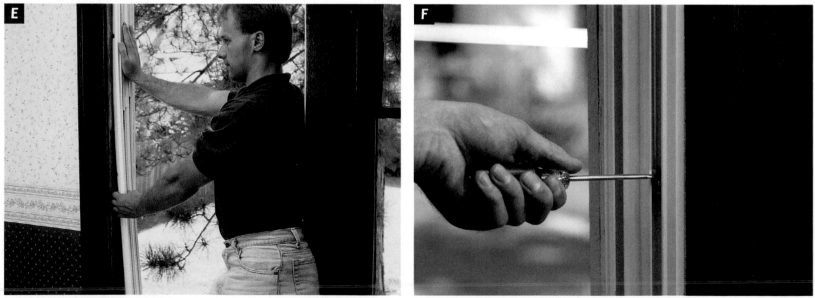

E Position any gaskets or weatherstripping provided for the jamb liners. Carefully position each jamb liner against its brackets and snap it into place. When both liners are installed, set the new parting stop into the groove of the existing head jamb, and fasten it with small finish nails. Install a vinyl sash stop in the interior track at the top of each jamb liner. These stops prevent the bottom sash from being opened too far.

F Set the sash control mechanisms, using a slotted screwdriver. Gripping the screwdriver firmly, slide down the mechanism until it is about 9" above the sill, then turn the screwdriver to lock the mechanism and prevent it from springing upward. The control mechanisms are spring-loaded—do not let them go until they are locked in place. Set the mechanism in each of the four sash channels.

Install the top sash into the jamb liners. Set the cam pivot on one side of the sash into the outside sash channel. Tilt the sash, and set the cam pivot on the other side of the sash. Make sure both cam pivots are set above the sash control mechanisms. Holding the sash level, tilt it up, then depress the jamb liners on both sides and set the sash in the vertical position in the jamb liners. Once the sash is in position, slide it down until the cam pivots contact the locking terminal assemblies. This will engage the control mechanisms.

Install the bottom sash into the jamb liners, setting it into the inside sash channels. When the bottom sash is set in the vertical position, slide it down until it engages the control mechanisms. Open and close both sashes to make sure they operate properly.

Reinstall the stops that you removed in step A. Fasten them with finish nails, using the old nail holes, or drill new pilot holes for the nails.

Check the tilt operation of the bottom sash to make sure the stops do not interfere. Remove the labels, and clean the windows. Paint or varnish the new sash as desired.

Installing New Windows

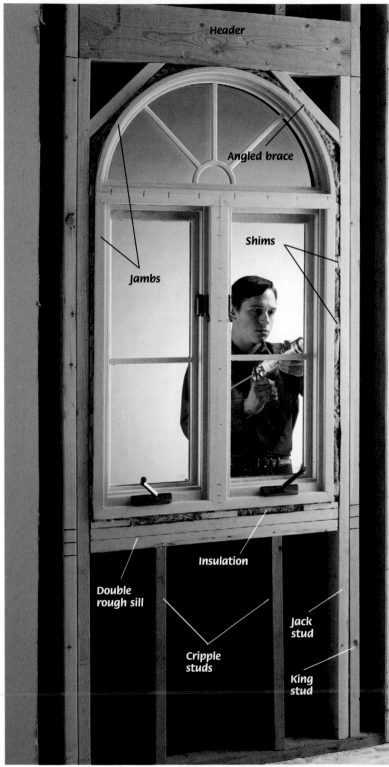

- Header
- Angled brace
- Jambs
- Shims
- Double rough sill
- Insulation
- Cripple studs
- Jack stud
- King stud

In this project, the new window is set into a framed opening, the unit is plumbed and leveled, then the exterior siding is marked and cut to accept the exterior window molding. For more information on cutting or removing exterior wall surfaces, see pages 32 to 35. If your house has masonry walls, or if you are installing polymer-coated windows, you may want to attach your window using masonry clips instead of nails (see page 165).

Many windows must be custom-ordered several weeks in advance. To save time, you can complete the interior framing before the window unit arrives, but be sure you have the exact dimensions of the window unit before building the frame. Leave the exterior wall surface intact until you have the window and accessories and are ready to install them. If you're installing a new window in an existing opening, remove the old window (see pages 146 to 147), and make any necessary changes to the framing.

Tools: Level, pry bar, reciprocating saw, circular saw, wood chisel, stapler, nail set, handsaw, caulk gun.

Materials: Window unit, wood blocks (if needed), wood shims, building paper, drip edge, 10d galvanized casing nails, 8d casing nails, fiberglass insulation, paintable silicone caulk.

Installing New Windows

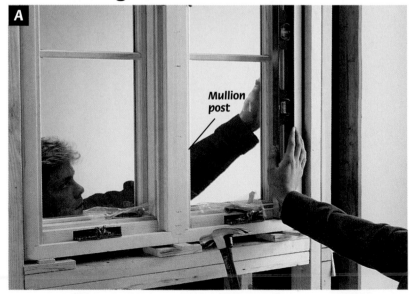

A

- Mullion post

Remove the exterior wall surface as directed on pages 32 to 35, then test-fit the window, centering it within the rough opening. Support the window with wood blocks and shims placed under the side jambs and mullion post. Check to make sure the window is plumb and level, and adjust the shims, if necessary.

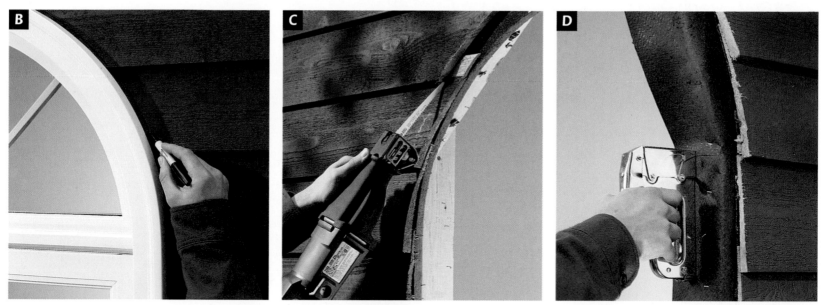

B	C	D
Trace the outline of the brick molding on the siding. Remove the window after finishing the outline.	Cut the siding along the outline, just down to the sheathing. For a round-top window, use a reciprocating saw held at a low angle. Use a circular saw for straight cuts. You may want to use a 1 × 4 to provide a flat base for the saw (see pages 34 to 35). Complete the cuts at the corners with a sharp chisel.	Cut 8"-wide strips of building paper, and slide them between the siding and sheathing around the entire window opening. Wrap the paper around the framing members and staple it in place.

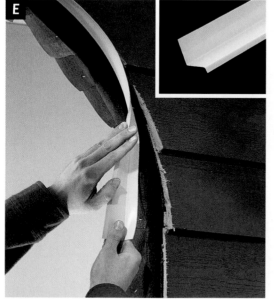

E — Cut a length of drip edge to fit over the top of the window, then slide it between the siding and building paper. For round-top windows, use flexible vinyl drip edge; for rectangular windows, use rigid metal drip edge (inset).

F — Insert the window in the opening, and push the brick molding tight against the sheathing. Check to make sure the window is level.

G — If the window is level, nail both bottom corners of the brick molding with 10d galvanized casing nails. If it's not level, nail only at the higher of the two bottom corners, and have a helper shim under the lower corner from inside. When the window is level, drive nails from the outside through the brick molding and into the framing at the remaining corners.

Continued on next page

Installing New Windows (cont.)

Place pairs of shims together to form flat shims. From inside, insert shims into the gaps between the jambs and framing members, spaced every 12". On round-top windows, also shim between the angled braces and the curved jamb.

Adjust the shims so they are snug, but not so tight that they cause the jambs to bow. On multiple-unit windows, make sure the shims under the mullion post are tight.

Use a level to check the side jambs to make sure they do not bow. If necessary, adjust the shims until the jambs are flat. Open and close the window to make sure it works properly.

At each shim location, drill a pilot hole, then drive an 8d casing nail through the jamb and shims. Be careful not to damage the window. Drive the nail heads below the surface with a nail set.

Fill the gaps between the window jambs and the framing members with loosely packed fiberglass insulation.

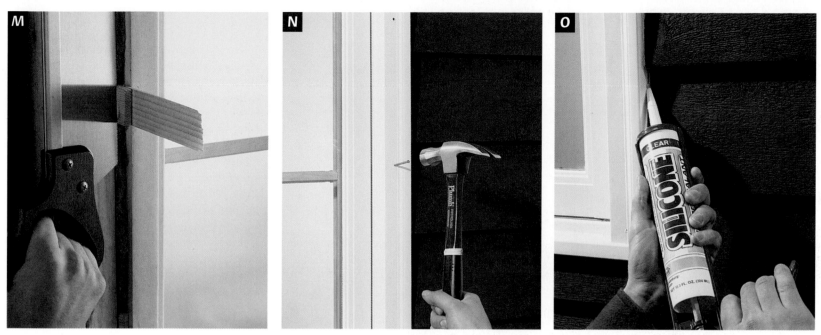

Trim the shims flush with the framing members, using a handsaw or utility knife.

From outside, drive 10d galvanized casing nails, spaced every 12", through the brick moldings and into the framing members. Drive all nail heads below the surface with a nail set.

Apply paintable silicone caulk around the entire window unit. Fill the nail holes with caulk. See pages 196 to 203 to finish the interior walls, and pages 230 to 231 to trim the interior of the window.

Installation Variation: Masonry Clips

Use metal masonry clips when the brick molding on a window cannot be nailed because it rests against a masonry or brick surface. Masonry clips hook into precut grooves in the window jambs (above, left) and are attached to the jambs with screws. After setting the window unit in the rough opening, bend the masonry clips around the framing members and anchor them with screws (above, right). NOTE: Masonry clips also can be used in ordinary lap siding installations if you want to avoid making nail holes in the smooth surface of the brick moldings. For example, windows that are precoated with polymer-based paint can be installed with masonry clips so the brick moldings are not punctured by nails.

Installing a Bay Window

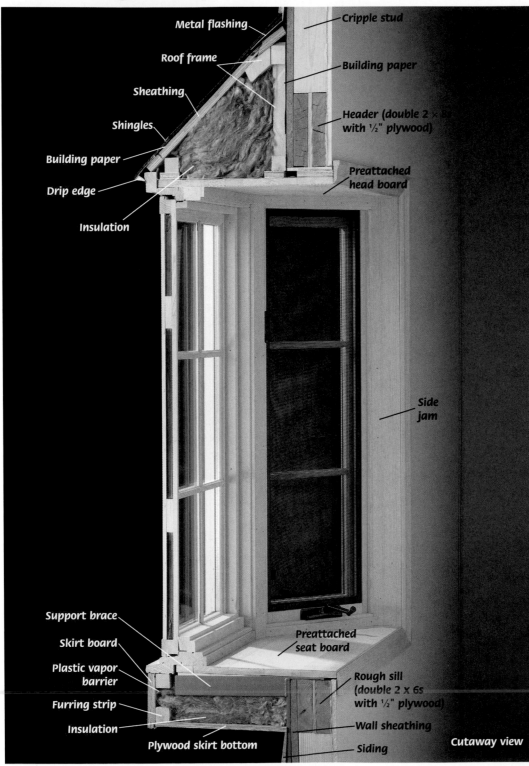

Metal flashing

Roof frame

Sheathing

Shingles

Building paper

Drip edge

Insulation

Cripple stud

Building paper

Header (double 2 × 8s with ½" plywood)

Preattached head board

Side jam

Support brace

Skirt board

Plastic vapor barrier

Furring strip

Insulation

Plywood skirt bottom

Preattached seat board

Rough sill (double 2 × 6s with ½" plywood)

Wall sheathing

Siding

Cutaway view

Modern bay windows are preassembled for easy installation, but it still will take several days to complete an installation. Bay windows are large and heavy, and installing them requires special techniques. Have at least one helper to assist you, and try to schedule the work when there's little chance of rain. Using prebuilt bay window accessories will speed your work (see page 167).

A large bay window can weigh several hundred pounds, so it must be anchored securely to framing members in the wall and supported by braces attached to framing members below the window. Some window manufacturers include cable-support hardware that can be used instead of metal support braces.

Before purchasing a bay window unit, check with the local building department regarding the code requirements. Many local codes require large windows and low bay windows with window seats to be glazed with tempered glass for safety.

Tools: Straightedge, circular saw, wood chisel, pry bar, drill, level, nail set, stapler, aviation snips, roofing knife, caulk gun, utility knife, T-bevel.

Materials: Bay window unit, prebuilt roof frame kit, metal support brackets, 2 × lumber, 16d galvanized common nails, 16d and 8d galvanized casing nails, 3" and 2" galvanized utility screws, 16d casing nails, tapered wood shims, building paper, fiberglass insulation, 6-mil polyethylene sheeting, drip edge, 1" roofing nails, step flashing, shingles, top flashing, roofing cement, 2 × 2 lumber, 5½" skirt boards, window trim, ¾" exterior-grade plywood, paintable silicone caulk.

Tips for Installing a Bay Window

Use prebuilt accessories to ease installation of a bay window. Roof frames (A) come complete with sheathing (B), metal top flashing (C) and step flashing (D) and can be special-ordered at most home centers. You will have to specify the exact size of your window unit and the angle (pitch) you want for the roof. You can cover the roof inexpensively with building paper and shingles or order a copper or aluminum shell. Metal support braces (E) and skirt boards (F) can be ordered at your home center if they are not included with the window unit. Use two braces for bay windows up to 5 ft. wide and three braces for larger windows. Skirt boards are clad with aluminum or vinyl and can be cut to fit with a circular saw or power miter saw.

Construct a bay window frame similar to that for a standard window (see pages 59 to 61) but use a built-up sill made from two 2 × 6s sandwiched around ½" plywood (see page 52). Install extra jack studs under the sill ends to help carry the window's weight.

Build an enclosure above the bay window if the roof soffit overhangs the window. Build a 2 × 2 frame (above, left) to match the angles of the bay window, and attach the frame securely to the wall and overhanging soffit. Install a vapor barrier and insulation (see page 171), then finish the enclosure so it matches the house siding (above, right).

Installing a Bay Window

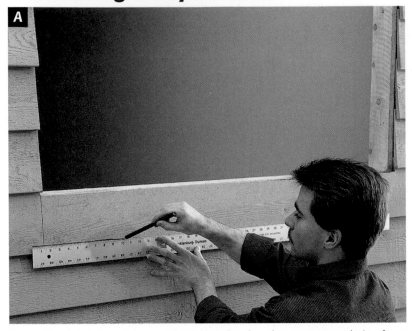

Prepare the project site and remove the interior wall surfaces (see pages 27 to 31), then frame the rough opening. Remove the exterior wall surfaces as directed on pages 32 to 35. Mark for removal a section of siding directly below rough opening. The width of the marked area should equal that of the window unit and the height should equal that of the skirt board.

Set the blade on a circular saw just deep enough to cut through the siding, then cut along the outline. Stop just short of the corners to avoid damaging the siding outside the outline. Use a sharp chisel to complete the corner cuts. Remove the cut siding inside the outline.

Position the support braces along the rough sill within the widest part of the bay window and above the cripple stud locations. Add cripple studs to match the support brace locations, if necessary. Draw outlines of the braces on the top of the sill. Use a chisel or circular saw to notch the sill to a depth equal to the thickness of the top arm of the support braces.

Slide the support braces down between the siding and the sheathing. Pry the siding material away from the sheathing slightly to make room for the braces, if necessary. NOTE: On stucco, you will need to chisel notches in the masonry surface to fit the support braces.

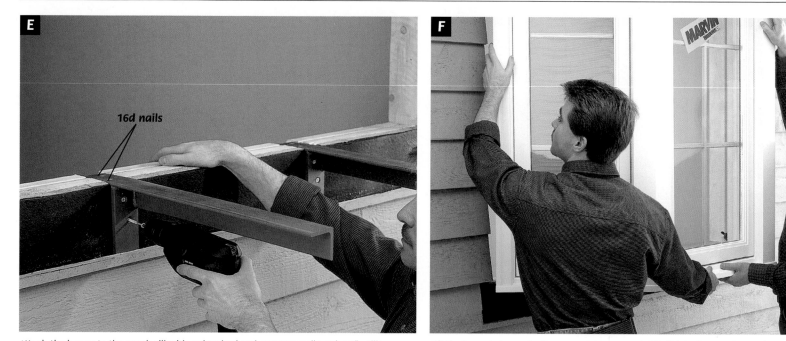

Attach the braces to the rough sill with galvanized 16d common nails. Drive 3" utility screws through the front of the braces and into the rough sill to prevent twisting.

Lift the bay window onto the support braces and slide it into the rough opening. Center the unit within the opening.

Check the window unit to make sure it is level. If necessary, drive shims under the low side to level the window. Temporarily brace the outside bottom edge of the unit with 2 × 4s to keep it from moving on the braces.

Set the roof frame on top of the window, with the sheathing loosely tacked in place. Trace the outline of the window and roof unit onto the siding. Leave a gap of about ½" around the roof unit to allow room for the flashing and shingles.

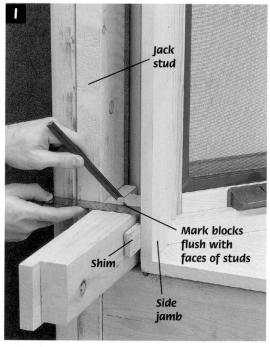

If the gap between the side jambs and jack studs is more than 1" wide, mark and cut wood blocks to bridge the gap (smaller gaps require no blocks). Leave a small space for inserting wood shims. Remove the window, then attach blocks every 12" along the studs.

Continued on next page

Installing a Bay Window (cont.)

Cut the siding just down to the sheathing along the outline, using a circular saw. You may want to use a 1 × 4 to provide a flat base for the saw (see pages 34 to 35). Stop just short of corners, then use a wood chisel to complete the corner cuts. Remove the cut siding. Pry the remaining siding slightly away from the sheathing around the roof outline to allow for easy installation of the metal flashing. Cover the exposed sheathing with 8"-wide strips of building paper (see step D, page 163).

Set the bay window unit back on the braces, and slide it back into the rough opening until the brick moldings are tight against the sheathing. Insert wood shims between the outside end of the metal braces and the seat board (inset). Check the unit to make sure it is level, and adjust the shims, if necessary.

Anchor the window by driving 16d galvanized casing nails through the outside brick molding and into the framing members. Space the nails every 12", and use a nail set to drive the nail heads below the surface of the wood. If necessary, drill pilot holes to prevent splitting the wood.

Drive wood shims into the spaces between the side jambs and the blocking or jack studs and between the headboard and header, spacing the shims every 12". Fill the spaces around the window with loosely packed fiberglass insulation. At each shim location, drive 16d casing nails through the jambs and shims and into the framing members. Cut off the shims flush with the framing members, using a handsaw or utility knife. Use a nail set to drive the nail heads below the surface. If necessary, drill pilot holes to prevent splitting the wood.

Staple sheet plastic over the top of the window unit to serve as a vapor barrier. Trim the edges of the plastic around the top of the window, using a utility knife.

Remove the sheathing pieces from the roof frame, then position the frame on top of the window unit. Attach the roof frame to the window and to the wall at stud locations, using 3" utility screws.

Fill the empty space inside the roof frame with loosely packed fiberglass insulation. Screw the sheathing back onto the roof frame, using 2" utility screws.

Staple asphalt building paper over the roof sheathing. Make sure each piece of building paper overlaps the one below by at least 5".

Cut drip edges with aviation snips, then attach them around the edge of the roof sheathing, using roofing nails.

Continued on next page

Installing a Bay Window (cont.)

Cut and fit a piece of step flashing on each side of the roof frame. Adjust the flashing so it overhangs the drip edge by ¼". Flashings help guard against moisture damage.

Trim the end of the flashing to the same angle as the drip edge. Nail the flashing to the sheathing with roofing nails.

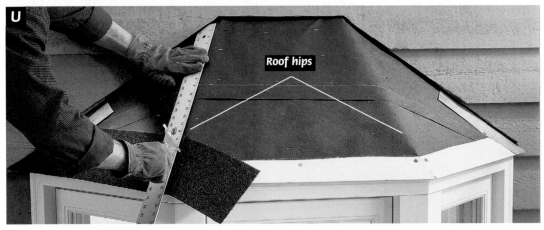

Cut 6"-wide strips of shingles for the starter row. Use roofing nails to attach the starter row shingles so they overhang the drip edge by about ½". Cut the shingles along the roof hips with a straightedge and roofing knife.

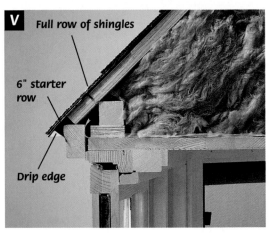

Nail a full row of shingles over the starter row, aligning the bottom edges of the full shingles with the bottom edge of the starter row. Make sure the shingle notches are not aligned.

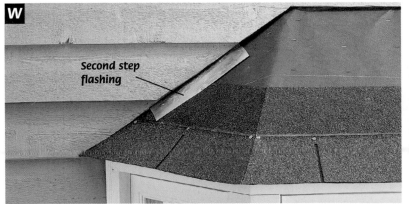

Install another piece of step flashing on each side of the roof, overlapping the first piece of flashing by about 5".

Cut and install another row of full shingles. The bottom edges should overlap the tops of the notches on the previous row by ½". Attach the shingles with roofing nails driven just above the notches.

Continue installing alternate rows of step flashing and shingles to the top of the roof. Bend the last pieces of step flashing to fit over the roof hips.

When the roof sheathing is covered with shingles, install the top flashing. Cut and bend the ends over the roof hips, and attach it with roofing nails. Attach the remaining rows of shingles over the top flashing.

Find the height of the final rows of shingles by measuring from the top of the roof to a point ½" below the top of the notches on the last installed shingle. Trim the shingles to fit.

Attach the final row of shingles with a thick bead of roofing cement—not nails. Press firmly to ensure a good bond.

Make ridge caps by cutting shingles into 1-ft.-long sections. Use a roofing knife to trim off the top corners of each piece, so the ridge caps will be narrower at the top than at the bottom.

Install the ridge caps over the roof hips, beginning at the bottom of the roof. Trim the bottom ridge caps to match the edges of the roof. Keep the same amount of overlap with each layer.

Continued on next page

Installing a Bay Window (cont.)

EE

At the top of the roof hips, use a roofing knife to cut the shingles to fit flush with the wall. Attach the shingles with roofing cement—do not use any nails.

FF

Staple sheet plastic over the bottom of the window unit to serve as a vapor barrier. Trim the plastic around the bottom of the window.

GG

Cut and attach a 2 × 2 skirt frame around the bottom of the bay window, using 3" galvanized utility screws. Set the skirt frame back about 1" from the edges of the window.

HH

Cut skirt boards to match the shape of the bay window bottom, mitering the ends to ensure a tight fit. Test-fit the skirt board pieces to make sure they match the bay window bottom.

II

Cut a 2 × 2 furring strip for each skirt board. Miter the ends to the same angles as the skirt boards. Attach the furring strips to the back of the skirt boards, 1" from the bottom edges, using 2" galvanized utility screws.

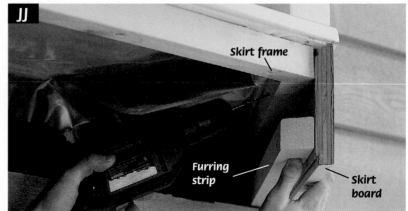

JJ

Skirt frame

Furring strip

Skirt board

Attach the skirt board pieces to the skirt frame. Drill ⅛" pilot holes every 6" through the back of the skirt frame and into the skirt boards, then attach the skirt boards with 2" galvanized utility screws.

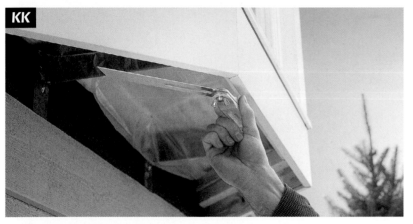

KK

Measure the space inside the skirt boards, using a T-bevel to duplicate the angles. Cut a skirt bottom from ¾" exterior-grade plywood to fit this space.

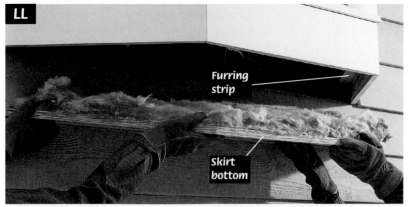

LL

Furring strip

Skirt bottom

Lay fiberglass insulation on the skirt bottom. Position the skirt bottom against the furring strips and attach it by driving 2" galvanized utility screws every 6" through the bottom and into the furring strips.

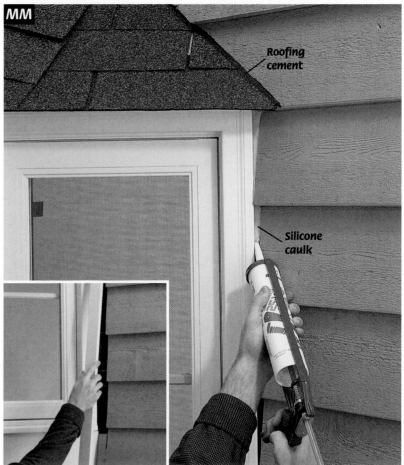

MM

Roofing cement

Silicone caulk

Install any additional trim pieces (inset) specified by your window manufacturer, using 8d galvanized casing nails. Seal roof edges with roofing cement, and seal around the rest of the window with paintable silicone caulk. See pages 196 to 203 to finish the walls, and pages 230 to 231 to trim the interior of the window.

Installing a Skylight

Depending on the model you choose and where you place it, a skylight can offer warmth in the winter, cooling ventilation in the summer, and a view of the sky or the tree-tops around your house during any season. And, of course, skylights provide natural light.

Because a skylight lets in so much light, the sizing and placement of the unit are important considerations. A skylight that's too big can quickly overheat a space, especially in an attic. The same is true of using too many skylights in any one room. For that reason it's often best to position a skylight away from the day's brightest sun. Other ways to avoid overheating include choosing a model with tinted glazing or a low solar-heat-gain coefficient (between .30 and .50), or simply covering the skylight with a shade during the hottest hours of the day.

You may want to select an operable skylight that opens and closes to vent warm air. In finished attics, operable skylights help draw cooler air from the floors below. In addition, some operable models open far enough to serve as egress windows—an important consideration for installations in finished attics.

When a skylight is installed above an unfinished attic space, a special skylight shaft must be constructed to channel light directly to the room below. To install a skylight shaft, see pages 182 to 185.

Installing a skylight above finished space involves other considerations. First, the ceiling surface must be removed to expose the rafters. For information on removing wall and ceiling surfaces, see pages 27 to 31.

A skylight frame is similar to a standard window frame (see page 52). It has a header and sill, like a window frame, but has *king rafters*, rather than king studs. Skylight frames also have *trimmers* that define the sides of the rough opening. Refer to the manufacturer's instructions to determine what size to make the opening for the skylight you select.

With standard rafter-frame roof construction, you can safely cut into one or two rafters

Photo courtesy of Velux-America, Inc.

as long as you permanently support the cut rafters, as shown in the following steps. If your skylight requires alteration of more than two rafters or if your roofing is made with unusually heavy material, such as clay tile or slate, consult an architect or engineer before starting the project.

Today's good-quality skylight units are unlikely to leak, but a skylight is only as leakproof as its installation. Follow the manufacturer's instructions, and install the flashing meticulously, as it will last a lot longer than any sealant.

Tools: 4-ft. level, circular saw, drill, combination square, reciprocating saw, pry bar, chalk line, stapler, caulk gun, utility knife, tin snips, plumb bob, jig saw, wallboard tools.

Materials: 2 x lumber; 16d and 10d common nails; 1 x 4; building paper; roofing cement; skylight flashing; 2", 1¼", and ¾" roofing nails; finish nails; fiberglass insulation; twine; 6-mil polyethylene sheeting; ½" wallboard; wallboard screws; finishing materials.

Installing a Skylight

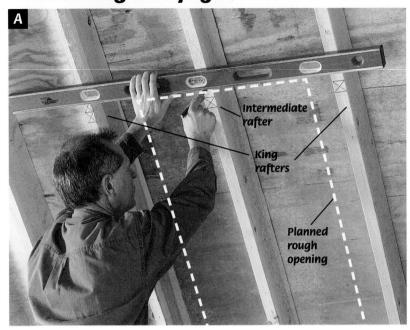

A

Use the first rafter on each side of the planned rough opening as a king rafter. Measure and mark where the double header and sill will fit against the king rafters. Then, use a level as a straightedge to extend the marks across the intermediate rafter.

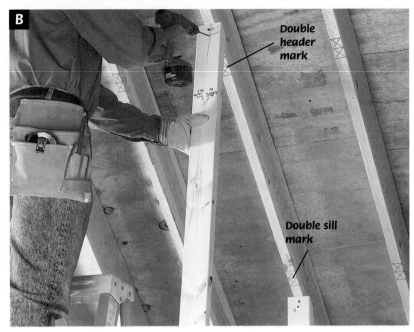

B

Brace the intermediate rafter by installing two 2 × 4s between the rafter and the attic floor. Position the braces just above the header marks and just below the sill marks. Secure them temporarily to the rafter and subfloor (or joists) with screws.

C

Reinforce each king rafter by attaching a full-length "sister" rafter against its outside face. Cut the sister rafters from the same size of lumber as the existing rafters, matching the lengths and end cuts exactly. Work each sister rafter into position, flush against the outside face of the king rafters, then nail the sisters to the kings with pairs of 10d common nails, spaced 12" apart.

D

Use a combination square to transfer the sill and header marks across the face of the intermediate rafter, then cut along the outermost lines with a reciprocating saw. Do not cut into the roof sheathing. Carefully remove the cut-out section with a pry bar. The remaining rafter portions will serve as cripple rafters.

Continued on next page

Installing a Skylight (cont.)

Build a double header and double sill to fit snugly between the king rafters, using 2 × lumber that is the same size as the rafters. Nail the header pieces together using pairs of 10d nails, spaced 6" apart.

Install the header and sill, anchoring them to the king rafters and cripple rafters with 16d common nails. Make sure the ends of the header and sill are aligned with the appropriate marks on the king rafters.

If your skylight unit is narrower than the opening between the king studs, measure and make marks for the trimmers: They should be centered in the opening and spaced according to the manufacturer's specifications. Cut the trimmers from the same 2 × lumber used for the rest of the frame, and nail them in place with 10d common nails. Remove the 2 × 4 braces.

Mark the opening for the roof cutout by driving a screw through the sheathing at each corner of the frame. Then, tack a couple of scrap boards across the opening to prevent the roof cutout from falling and causing damage below.

From the roof, measure between the screws to make sure the rough opening dimensions are accurate. Snap chalk lines between the screws to mark the rough opening, then remove the screws.

Tack a straight 1 × 4 to the roof, aligned with the inside edge of one chalk line. Make sure the nail heads are flush with the surface of the board.

Cut through the shingles and sheathing along the chalk line, using a circular saw and an old blade or a remodeling blade. Rest the saw foot on the 1 × 4, and use the edge of the board as a guide. Reposition the 1 × 4, and cut along the remaining lines. Remove the cut-out roof section.

Remove the shingles around the rough opening with a flat pry bar, exposing at least 9" of building paper on all sides of the opening. Remove whole shingles, rather than cutting them.

Continued on next page

Installing a Skylight (cont.)

M

Cut strips of building paper and slide them between the shingles and existing building paper. Wrap the paper around so that it covers the faces of the framing members, and staple it in place.

N

Nailing flange

Spread a 5"-wide layer of roofing cement around the roof opening. Set the skylight into the opening so that the nailing flange rests on the roof. Adjust the unit so that it sits squarely in the opening.

O

Nail through the nailing flange and into the sheathing and framing members with 2" galvanized roofing nails spaced every 6". Note: If your skylight uses L-shaped brackets instead of a nailing flange, follow the manufacturer's instructions.

P

Adhesive strip

Patch in shingles up to the bottom edge of the skylight unit. Attach the shingles with 1¼" roofing nails driven just below the adhesive strip. If necessary, cut the shingles with a utility knife so that they fit against the bottom of the skylight.

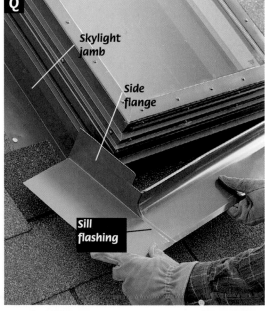

Q

Skylight jamb

Side flange

Sill flashing

Spread roofing cement on the bottom edge of the sill flashing, then fit the flashing around the bottom of the unit. Attach the flashing by driving ¾" galvanized roofing nails through the vertical side flange (near the top of the flashing) and into the skylight jambs.

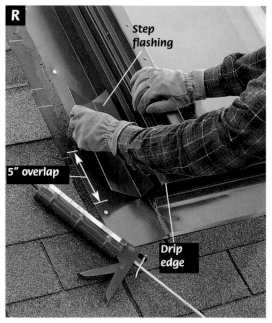

R

Step flashing

5" overlap

Drip edge

Spread roofing cement on the bottom of a piece of step flashing, then slide the flashing under the drip edge on one side of the skylight. The step flashing should overlap the sill flashing by 5". Press the step flashing down to bond it. Do the same on the opposite side of the skylight.

S

Patch in the next row of shingles on each side of the skylight, following the existing shingle pattern. Drive a 1¼" roofing nail through each shingle and the step flashing and into the sheathing. Drive additional nails just above the notches in the shingles.

T

Continue applying alternate rows of step flashing and shingles, using roofing cement and roofing nails. Each piece of flashing should overlap the preceding piece by 5".

U

At the top of the skylight, cut and bend the last piece of step flashing on each side, so the vertical flange wraps around the corner of the skylight. Patch in the next row of shingles.

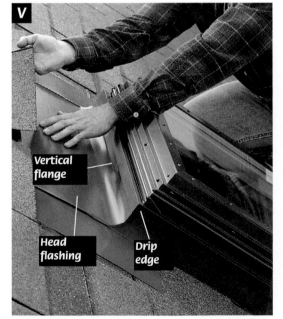

V

Spread roofing cement on the bottom of the head flashing, to bond it to the roof. Position the flashing against the top of the skylight so the vertical flange fits under the drip edge and the horizontal flange fits under the shingles above the skylight.

W

Fill in the remaining shingles, cutting them to fit, if necessary. Attach the shingles with roofing nails driven just above the notches.

X

Apply a continuous bead of roofing cement along the joint between the shingles and skylight. Finish the interior of the framed opening as desired.

Building a Skylight Shaft

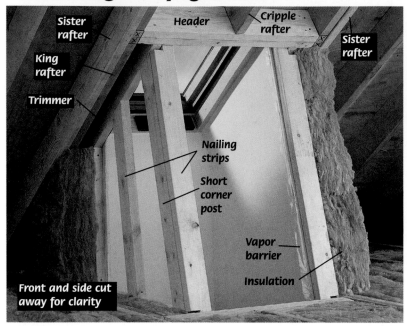

Sister rafter

Header

Cripple rafter

King rafter

Sister rafter

Trimmer

Nailing strips

Short corner post

Vapor barrier

Insulation

Front and side cut away for clarity

A

A skylight shaft is made with 2 × 4 lumber and wallboard, and includes a vapor barrier and fiberglass insulation. You can build a straight shaft with four vertical sides or an angled shaft that has a longer frame at the ceiling level and one or more sides set at an angle. Since the ceiling opening is larger, an angled shaft lets in more direct light than a straight shaft.

Remove any insulation in the area where the skylight will be located; turn off and re-route electrical circuits as necessary. Use a plumb bob as a guide to mark reference points on the ceiling surface, directly below the inside corners of the skylight frame.

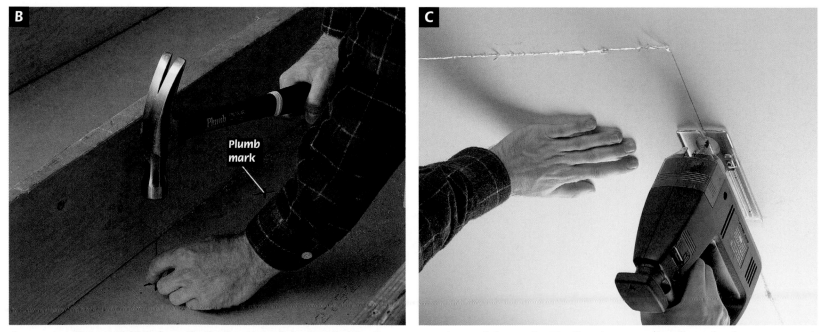

B

Plumb mark

C

If you are installing a straight shaft, use the plumb marks made in step A to define the corners of the ceiling opening; drive a finish nail through the ceiling surface at each mark. If you are installing an angled shaft, measure out from the plumb marks and make new marks that define the corners of the ceiling opening; drive finish nails at the new marks.

From the room below, mark cutting lines, then remove the ceiling surface (see pages 27 to 31).

Use the nearest joists on either side of the ceiling opening to serve as king joists. Measure and mark where the double header and double sill will fit against the king joists, and where the outside edge of the header and sill will cross any intermediate joists.

If you will be removing a section of an intermediate joist, reinforce the king joists by nailing full-length "sister" joists to the outside faces of the king joists, using 10d nails. See pages 318 to 319 for more information on installing sister joists.

Install temporary supports below the project area to support the intermediate rafter on both sides of the opening (see pages 36 to 39). Use a combination square to extend the cutting lines down the sides of the intermediate joist, then cut out the joist section with a reciprocating saw. Pry loose the cut-out portion of the joist, being careful not to damage the ceiling surface.

Build a double header and double sill to span the distance between the king joists, using 2 × dimension lumber the same size as the joists.

Continued on next page

Building a Skylight Shaft (cont.)

Install the double header and double sill, anchoring them to the king joists and cripple joists with 10d nails. The inside edges of the header and sill should be aligned with the edge of the ceiling cutout.

Complete the ceiling opening by cutting and attaching trimmers, if required, along the sides of the ceiling cutout between the header and sill. Toenail the trimmers to the header and sill with 10d nails.

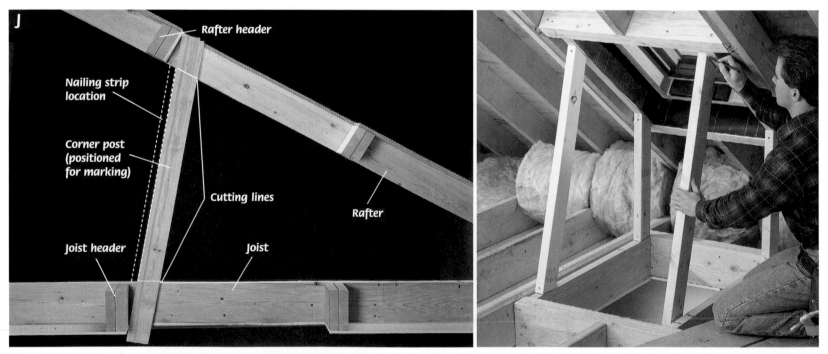

Install 2 × 4 corner posts for the skylight shaft. To measure for the posts, begin with a 2 × 4 that is long enough to reach from the top to the bottom of the shaft. Hold the 2 × 4 against the inside of the framed openings, so it is flush with the top of the rafter header and the bottom of the joist header (left photo). Mark cutting lines where the 2 × 4 meets the top of the joist or trimmer, and the bottom of the rafter or trimmer (right photo). Cut along the lines, then toenail the posts to the top and bottom of the frame with 10d nails.

Attach a 2 × 4 nailing strip to the outside edge of each corner post to provide a nailing surface for attaching the wallboard. Notch the ends of the nailing strips to fit around the trimmers; a perfect fit is not necessary.

Install additional 2 × 4 nailing strips between the corner posts if the distances between posts are more than 24". Miter the top ends of the nailing strips to fit against the rafter trimmers.

Wrap the skylight shaft with fiberglass insulation. Secure the insulation by wrapping twine around the shaft and insulation.

From inside the shaft, staple a plastic vapor barrier of 6-mil polyethylene sheeting over the insulation.

Finish the inside of the shaft with wallboard (see pages 196 to 202). Tip: To reflect light, paint the shaft interior with a light-colored, semi-gloss paint.

Patching Exterior Walls

Many remodeling projects involve patching or repairing exterior wall surfaces, and the key to a successful job is to follow the original work. This will help you determine the best installation method and make sure the patch blends in well with the surrounding area.

To patch siding, it's important to use a staggered pattern where vertical end-joints are not aligned between rows. If you've installed a window or door into an existing opening, you may have to remove some siding pieces before patching in new ones to maintain the staggered installation (see right).

Wood siding generally is easy to match with new material from a lumber yard. Vinyl and metal siding can be more difficult to match, so contact the siding manufacturer before making any changes to your existing surfaces. It's also important that you have the right trim pieces to make sure the patch looks good and creates a weather-proof barrier.

If you're patching a stucco wall (see pages 188 to 189), practice first on scrap materials, because duplicating stucco textures takes some skill.

Windows and doors with nailing flanges must be covered with wood or metal molding, usually purchased separately. After the window is installed, hold the trim pieces in place, then mark an outline around the trim onto the siding. Trim the siding to fit. The window shown here was installed in an old door opening, which required patching beneath the window with sheathing, building paper, and siding.

Tools: Circular saw, flat pry bar, aviation snips, trowel, scratching tool, whisk broom.

Materials: Exterior-wall sheathing, building paper, siding, 6d siding nails, paintable silicone caulk, stucco mix, tint (optional), self-furring metal lath, spray bottle.

Tips for Installing Vinyl Siding

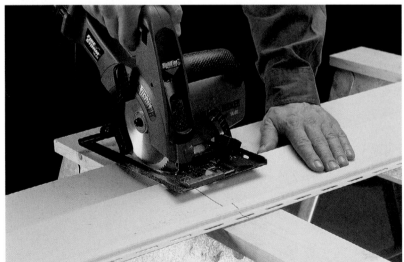

Cut vinyl siding using a circular saw, metal snips, or a utility knife. Outfit a circular saw with a plywood blade (fine-toothed), and install the blade backwards so the teeth point down. Make the cuts slowly, using standard cutting techniques. **Note:** Do not cut any material other than vinyl siding with the saw blade installed backwards. When cutting siding with a utility knife, score the panels using a framing square as a guide, then snap along the scored line.

Attach siding panels so they can expand and contract with temperature changes. Lock the bottom edge underneath the nailing strip of the panel below, using a zip tool (see page 33) if necessary. Hold the panel flat to the sheathing without stretching it upward and nail through the centers of the nailing-strip slots, leaving about 1/32" between the nail head and the panel. Fasten the middle of the panel first, and space the nails following manufacturer's instructions.

Patching Wood Lap Siding

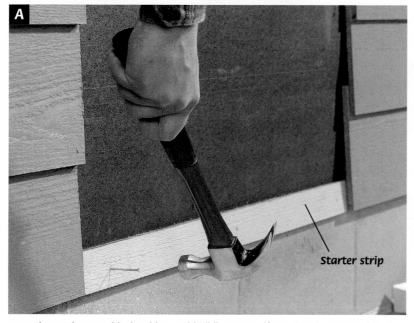

Starter strip

Cover the patch area with sheathing and building paper, if not already present. If the bottom row of siding is missing, nail a starter strip cut from a piece of siding along the bottom of the patch area, using 6d siding nails. Leave a ¼" gap at each joint in the starter strip to allow for expansion.

Use a flat pry bar to remove lengths of lap siding on both sides of the patch area, creating a staggered pattern. When new siding is installed, the end joints will be offset for a less conspicuous appearance.

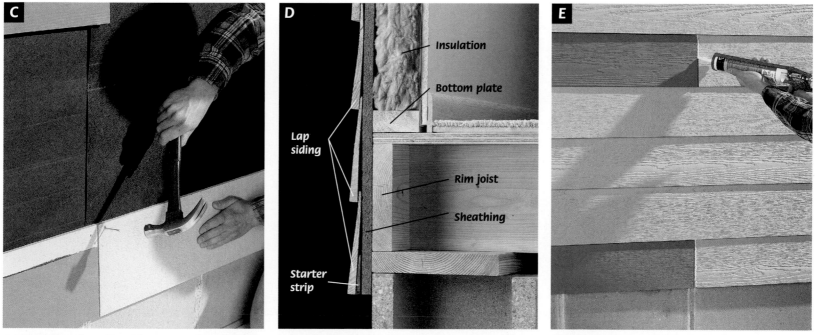

Insulation

Bottom plate

Lap siding

Rim joist

Sheathing

Starter strip

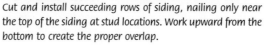

Cut the bottom piece of lap siding to span the entire opening, and lay it over the starter strip. Allow a ¼" expansion gap between board ends. Attach the siding with pairs of 6d siding nails driven at each stud location.

Cut and install succeeding rows of siding, nailing only near the top of the siding at stud locations. Work upward from the bottom to create the proper overlap.

Fill joints between the siding pieces with paintable silicone caulk. Repaint the entire wall surface as soon as the caulk dries to protect the new siding against weather.

Patching Stucco

Ingredients of Scratch (base) Coat, and Brown Coat Stucco

3 parts sand

2 parts portland cement

1 part masonry cement

water

Ingredients of Finish Coat Stucco

1 part lime

3 parts sand

6 parts white cement

tint (as desired)

water

For small jobs, use pre-mixed stucco, available at building centers. For best results, apply the stucco in two or three layers, letting each layer dry completely between applications. Pre-mixed stucco also can be used on larger areas, but it is more expensive than mixing your own ingredients.

For large jobs, combine dry stucco mix with water, following the manufacturer's directions, or use the ingredients lists shown here. A stucco finish typically contains two or three layers, depending on the application (see below). The mixtures for the *base* and *brown* coats should be just moist enough to hold their shape when squeezed (inset). A finish-coat mix requires slightly more water than other coats. If you need to color the finish coat, mix test batches first, adding measured amounts of tint to each batch. Let the test batches dry for at least an hour to get an accurate indication of the final color.

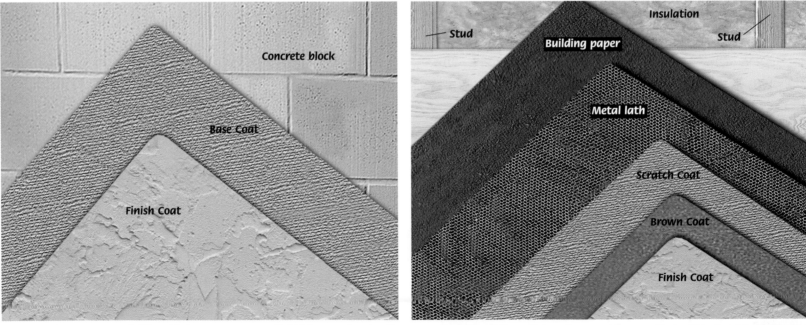

When applying stucco over brick or block, use two coats: a ⅜"-thick base coat and a ¼"-thick finish coat (left photo). Do not apply stucco directly over painted concrete block. **On wood-frame construction or an insulation-board surface,** cover the area first with building paper and metal lath. Then apply three coats of stucco: a scratch coat (⅜"-½" thick), a brown coat (⅜" thick), and a finish coat (⅛" thick) (right photo). Both the base coat on

masonry walls and the scratch coat on wood-frame walls should be "scratched" after they are applied. This involves etching horizontal grooves into the partially set stucco using a scratching tool. You can make your own scratching tool by driving a row of 1½" wire nails through a piece of 1 × 2. The grooves provide a gripping surface for the next stucco layer.

Applying Stucco onto a Wood-frame Wall

Cover the patch area with sheathing and building paper, if not already present. Cut self-furring metal lath, using aviation snips, and attach it to the sheathing with 1½" galvanized roofing nails, driven into the wall studs every 6". Overlap pieces of lath by 2". NOTE: If the patch area extends to the base of the wall, install a metal *stop bead* at the bottom of the wall.

Mix a batch of stucco for the scratch coat (see page 188). Apply a ⅜"-thick layer of stucco over the lath, using a trowel. Press firmly to fill any voids, and cover the lath completely. Let the stucco dry until it will hold the impression of a thumbprint, then use a scratching tool to make shallow grooves across the entire surface. Let the stucco set for two days, dampening it every few hours with fine spray to help it cure evenly.

Mix a batch of stucco for the brown coat (see page 188), and apply it in a ⅜"-thick layer or until the patch area is within ¼"-⅛" of the surrounding surface. Let the coat cure for two days, dampening it every few hours.

Mix a stucco finish coat (see page 188). Dampen the wall, then apply the finish coat to match the surrounding stucco. The texture for the finish coat above was dashed on with a flick of a whisk broom, then flattened with a trowel. Keep the finish coat damp for a week while it cures. Let the stucco dry for several more days if you plan to paint it.

WALLS & CEILINGS

Installing Fiberglass Insulation

Before you insulate your walls, ceilings, or floors (or even buy insulation), ask the local building department about two things: *R-value* and *vapor barriers*. All insulation has an R-value clearly printed on its packaging. This is the measure of how well the insulation keeps in the heat and keeps out the cold, and vice versa. The higher the R-value, the better the insulation works—and the thicker it is. The building department will tell you what R-values you need for your walls, ceilings, and floors, and whether the insulation job must be inspected before you cover it.

Vapor barriers come in a few different forms, but all have a common purpose. They prevent the water vapor present in warm indoor air from passing beyond wall or ceiling surfaces and through the framing, where it would contact cold exterior surfaces and condense. This condensation promotes mildew growth that can rot the framing and insulation. Vapor barriers are required in most climates and are typically installed on the "warm-in-winter" side of exterior walls and ceilings, between the insulation and the interior finish material.

Paper-faced, foil-faced, and encapsulated insulation have their own vapor barriers, but a layer of 6-mil polyethylene sheeting stapled to framing members over unfaced insulation provides a more effective, continuous barrier. If you decide to use faced insulation be aware that it comes with a few drawbacks: The paper tears easily, and facings make it difficult to cut around obstacles. Also, if you trim a batt to fit into a narrow bay, you lose the facing flange—and thus the vapor seal—on one side. Most facings are flammable and must be covered with wallboard or another approved finish, even in unfinished areas, such as storage rooms. One alternative is to use insulation with an approved flame-resistant foil facing.

When installing insulation, make sure there are no gaps between the insulation and framing, around obstructions, or between pieces of insulation. The idea is to create a continuous "thermal envelope" that keeps interior air from coming into contact with outdoor temperatures.

Fiberglass insulation comes in *batts* cut to length for standard stud-wall bays, as well as long rolls. Various options include: kraft-paper and foil facings (A), which serve as vapor barriers (some foils are flame-resistant); plastic-encapsulated blankets (B); high density blankets (for rafters) (C); and standard, unfaced rolls and batts (D). Standard widths fit between 16"- or 24"-on-center framing.

Tools: Utility knife, stapler.

Materials: Fiberglass insulation, 6-mil polyethylene sheeting, staples, packing tape.

Handling fiberglass is a lot less uncomfortable when you're dressed for it. Wear pants, a long-sleeve shirt, gloves, goggles, and a good-quality dust mask or respirator. Shower as soon as you finish working.

Tips for Installing Fiberglass Insulation

Never compress insulation to fit into a narrow space. Instead, use a sharp utility knife to trim the blanket about ¼" wider and longer than the space. To trim, hold the blanket in place and use a wall stud as a straightedge and cutting surface.

Insulate around pipes, wires, and electrical boxes by peeling the blanket in half and sliding the back half behind the obstruction. Then, lay the front half in front of the obstruction. Trim the front half to fit snugly around boxes.

Use scraps of insulation to fill gaps around window and door jambs. Fill the cavities loosely to avoid compressing the insulation. Fill narrow gaps with expanding spray-foam insulation, following manufacturer's instructions.

Tips for Adding Vapor Barriers

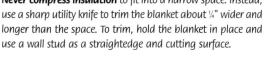

Facing flange

Provide a vapor barrier using faced insulation by tucking in the edges of the insulation until the facing flanges are flush with the edges of the framing. Make sure the flanges lie flat, with no wrinkles or gaps, and staple them to the faces of the framing members about every 8". Patch any gaps or facing tears with packing tape or a construction tape supplied by the manufacturer.

Install a polyethylene vapor barrier by draping the sheeting over the entire wall or ceiling, extending it a few inches beyond the perimeter and overlapping the sheets at least 12". Staple the sheeting to the framing, then carefully cut around obstructions. Seal around electrical boxes and other penetrations with packing tape. Trim excess sheeting along the ceiling and floor after you install the surface material.

Soundproofing Walls & Ceilings

One of the more common reasons people remodel is to create spaces where they can get away from everyday household activity and noise. Perhaps you're planning a quiet reading space, a home office, or a home theater. These rooms will be more enjoyable if their walls and ceilings are properly soundproofed.

Wall and ceiling construction is rated for sound transmission by a system called Sound Transmission Class (STC). The higher the STC rating, the quieter the house. For example, if a wall is rated at 30 to 35 STC, loud speech can be understood through the wall. At 42 STC, loud speech is reduced to a murmur. At 50 STC, loud speech cannot be heard. Standard construction methods typically result in a 32 STC rating, while soundproofed walls and ceilings can carry a rating of up to 48 STC.

Basic soundproofing materials include fiberglass insulation, acoustical tile, soundboard, ⅝" wallboard, and resilient steel channels or *sound channels*. Sound channels, used to anchor wallboard to walls and ceilings, reduce sound transmission by absorbing vibrations.

In addition to using soundproofing materials in your walls and ceilings, it's important to seal any air leaks between rooms. Sound travels through air, and even small air passages between rooms can destroy your efforts at soundproofing. Block air by caulking around electrical boxes and other penetrations after the finish materials are in place. Also seal along the bottoms and tops of walls and around door jambs. Install door sweeps to stop air flow beneath doors.

Soundproofing Walls & Ceilings (walls shown cut away)	Sound Transmission Class
Typical utility area stud wall, unfinished on one side.	28 STC
Spaces between framing members filled with fiberglass insulation (A) and stud wall covered with wallboard on both sides.	39 STC
Extra layer of wallboard attached to wall, using sound channels (B).	44 STC
Acoustical tile (C) attached to an insulated stud wall, using construction adhesive or staples.	46 STC

Soundproofing New Walls

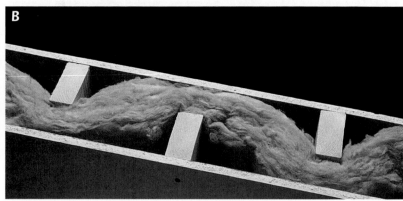

Build walls with 2 × 6 top and bottom plates. Position 2 × 4 studs every 12", staggering them flush with alternate edges of the plates.

Weave 3½" unfaced fiberglass blanket insulation horizontally between the 2 × 4 studs. When covered with ½" wallboard, this wall has a rating of 48 STC.

Soundproofing Existing Walls & Ceilings

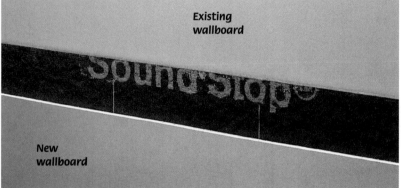

Existing
wallboard

New
wallboard

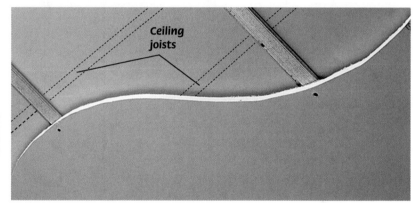

Ceiling
joists

Install ½" sound board over an existing layer of wallboard using 1½" wallboard screws. Glue ½" wallboard over the sound board with construction adhesive. The sound rating for this construction is 46 STC.

Screw resilient steel channels over the ceiling or wall, spaced 24" on center, perpendicular to the existing framing. Attach ⅝" wallboard to the channels with 1" wallboard screws. The sound rating for this construction is 44 STC.

Reducing Air Flow

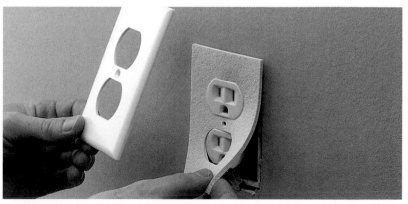

Seal the joints where walls meet floors to stop air flow between rooms. With new framing, caulk any gaps along the subfloor. With finished walls, remove shoe molding and spray insulating foam under the baseboards. Also seal gaps around door frames.

Use caulk or neoprene slips to seal holes cut into wall surfaces, such as cutouts for electrical boxes. Reinstall the coverplates over the neoprene seals.

Installing & Finishing Wallboard

Wallboard is commonly available in 4 × 8-ft. and 4 × 12-ft. panels, in thicknesses ranging from ¼" to ¾". The panels are tapered along their long edges so that adjoining panels form a slightly recessed seam that you finish with paper tape and wallboard compound. End-to-end joints are more difficult to finish, so avoid end-butted seams whenever possible. To minimize the number of joints that need finishing, use the longest panels you can safely handle; just make sure you can get them into the workspace.

Use ½"- or ⅝"-thick panels on ceilings. Thinner panels are lighter and easier to work with, but ⅝" wallboard provides better sound insulation and is less likely to sag over time. Use ½" panels on walls. Install wallboard on the ceiling first, then finish the walls, butting the wall panels snug against the ceiling panels to give them extra support.

Unless you're experienced at finishing wallboard, start your finishing in inconspicuous areas. Take the time to make sure your joints are flat and smooth, as paint does little to hide imperfections.

Tools: Wallboard T-square; utility knife; jig saw; wallboard compass; chalk line; wallboard lift (available at rental centers); drill or screwgun; wallboard lifter; 4-ft. level; 4", 6", 10" and 12" wallboard knives; pole sander.

Materials: Wallboard, 1¼" wallboard screws, wallboard compound, joint tape, corner bead, sandpaper or sanding screen.

Tips for Installing & Finishing Wallboard

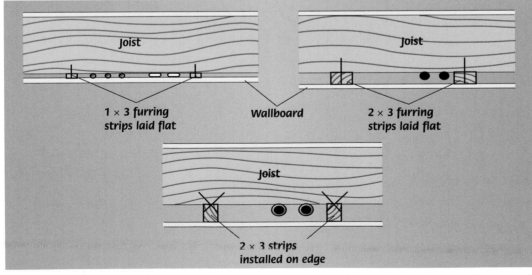

Attach furring strips to framing where service lines and other obstacles project beyond the framing. The strips create a flat surface for attaching wallboard. Use 1 × 3 or 2 × 3 furring strips, and attach them perpendicular to the framing, using wallboard screws. Space the strips 16" or 24" on center so they provide support for the wallboard edges. NOTE: Insulate cold water pipes before wallboarding to prevent water stains caused by condensation.

Use protector plates where wires or pipes pass through framing members and are less than 1¼" from the front edges. The plates prevent wallboard screws from puncturing wires or pipes.

Mark the locations of the studs and other framing members so you'll know where to drive fasteners during installation.

Add 1 × or 2 × backing in situations where additional support is necessary to support wallboard edges.

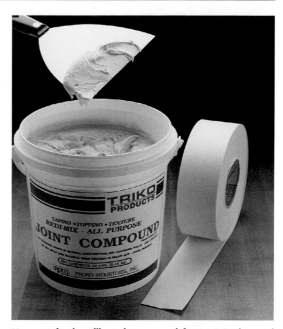

Use premixed wallboard compound for most taping and finishing jobs to eliminate messy mixing and lumpy results. Use paper joint tape with premixed compound.

Cutting Wallboard: Straight Cuts

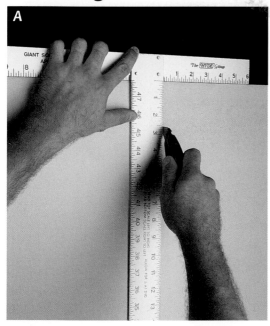

A

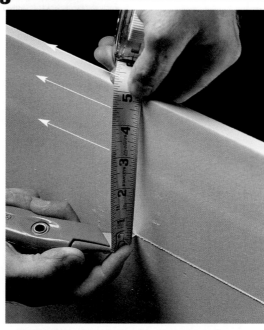

B

To make vertical cuts, set the wallboard panel against a wall with the front side facing out. Mark the desired length on the face, then position a wallboard T-square at the mark. Hold the square in place with your hand and foot, and cut through the face paper, using a utility knife.

VARIATION: Make horizontal cuts by extending a tape measure to the desired width of the cut, and hooking a utility knife blade under the end of the tape. Grip the tape tightly in one hand and the utility knife in the other, and move both hands along the panel to cut through the face paper.

Bend the scored section backwards with both hands to break the gypsum core of the wallboard. Fold back the unwanted piece, and cut through the back paper with the utility knife.

Cutting Wallboard: Notches

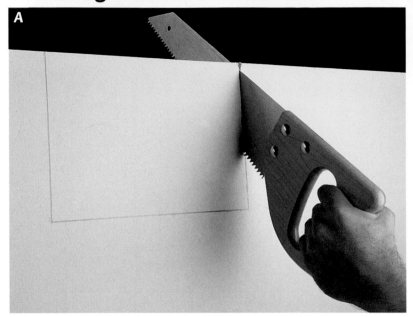

For large notches or long, straight cuts, use a large wallboard saw. These saws are also handy for cutting out door and window openings after the wallboard is attached to the wall. Make notches by sawing down to the bottom of the notch on both sides.

Finish by cutting the face paper along the bottom of the notch, using a utility knife. Snap the cutout backwards to break the wallboard core, then cut the back paper.

Cutting Wallboard: Holes

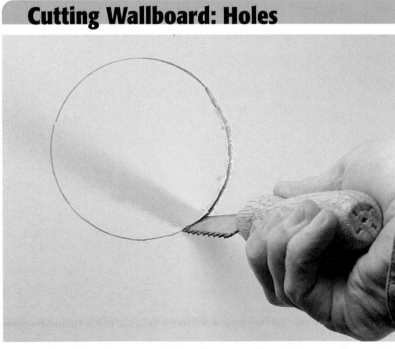

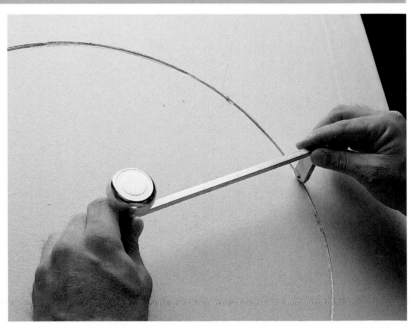

Use a small wallboard saw to make internal cuts in wallboard. These saws have pointed ends so the blade can be driven through the board to begin the cut.

Make clean circular cutouts using a wallboard compass. Mark the centerpoint of the cutout, then set the compass point on the mark. Press down and rotate the compass wheel to score through the face paper. Tap a nail through the centerpoint to mark the other side. Score the back paper, then knock out the hole through the front side with a hammer.

Installing Wallboard on Ceilings

Create a control line by measuring out from the top plate of the adjoining wall. Make a mark on the outermost joists (or rafters) at 48⅛", then snap a chalk line through the marks. The line should be perpendicular to the joists. Use the control line to align the first row of panels and to measure for cutouts.

Measure across the joists to make sure the first panel will "break" on the center of a joist. If necessary, cut the panel from the end that abuts the side wall so that the panel breaks on the next farthest joist. Load the panel onto a rented wallboard lift, and hoist the panel until it rests flat against the joists.

Position the panel so the side edge is even with the control line and the leading end is centered on a joist. Fasten the panel using 1¼" wallboard screws (see page 200). Drive a screw every 8" along the edges and every 12" in the field of the panel (consult the local building department for fastening requirements in your area).

After the first row of panels is installed, begin the next row with a half-panel. This ensures that the butted end joints will be staggered between rows.

Installing Wallboard on Walls

A

Plan the wallboard placement so there are no joints at the corners of doors or windows. Wallboard joints at corners often crack or cause bulges that interfere with window and door trim.

B

Wallboard lifter

Install wallboard panels vertically unless the panels are long enough to span the wall horizontally. Lift the panels tight against the ceiling with a wallboard lifter. Plumb the first panel with a 4-ft. level, making sure the panel breaks on the center of a stud.

C

Anchor the panels to the framing with 1¼" wallboard screws. Drive a screw every 8" along the edges and every 12" in the field of the panel. Drive the screws so their heads are just below the surface. A wallboard screwgun with an adjustable screw-depth setter (shown here) is the best tool for big jobs. If you use a drill, pay close attention to the screw depth. You can also buy a depth setter attachment for standard drills.

TIP:

With their bugle-shaped heads, wallboard screws are designed to dimple the surface of wallboard without ripping the face paper. All wallboard fasteners must be recessed to provide a space for the finishing compound. However, driving the fastener too far and breaking the paper renders the fastener useless. If this happens, drive another fastener about 2" from the first.

As you make the first pass in the finishing process, keep a screwdriver in your pocket for driving any screws that aren't recessed.

Finishing Wallboard: Butt Joints

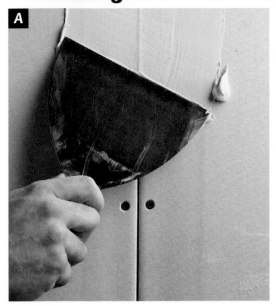

A Load a 4" or 6" wallboard knife by dipping it into a mud pan filled with wallboard compound. Apply a thin layer of wallboard compound over the joint.

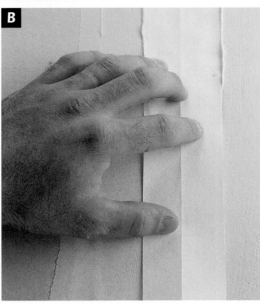

B Press the wallboard tape into the compound immediately, centering the tape over the joint. Smooth the tape firmly with the knife to flatten the tape and squeeze out excess compound. Let the compound dry completely.

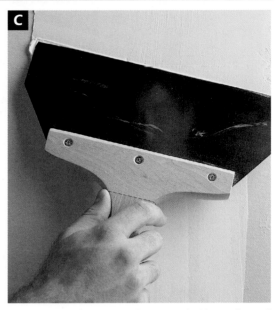

C Apply two thin finish coats of compound with a 10" or 12" wallboard knife. Allow the first finish coat to dry and shrink overnight before applying the final coat. Let the final coat dry completely before sanding (see page 202).

Finishing Wallboard: Inside Corners

A Fold a strip of paper wallboard tape in half by pinching the strip and pulling it between your thumb and forefinger. Apply a thin layer of wallboard compound to both sides of the inside corner, using a 4" or 6" wallboard knife.

B Position the end of the folded tape strip at the top of the joint and press the tape into the wet compound with the knife. Smooth both sides of the corner to flatten the tape and remove excess compound.

C Apply second coat of compound to one side of corner at a time. When the first side of the corner is dry, finish the opposite corner. After the second coat dries, apply a final coat of compound. Sand the final coat smooth (see page 202).

Finishing Wallboard: Outside Corners

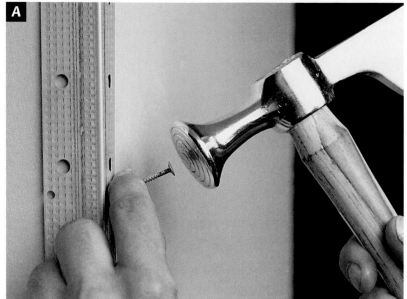

A

Position metal corner bead on the outside corners, making sure the bead is centered along the edge. Attach the bead with 1¼" wallboard nails or screws spaced 8" apart.

B

Cover the corner bead with three coats of wallboard compound, using a 6" or 10" wallboard knife. Let each coat dry and shrink overnight before applying the next coat. Sand the final coat smooth.

Covering Fastener Heads

Cover screw or nail heads with three coats of wallboard compound, using a 4" or 6" wallboard knife. Allow each coat to dry overnight before applying the next.

Sanding the Finish Work

Sand all finished joints lightly after the wallboard compound dries, using a pole sander and wallboard sandpaper (sanding screen) or a sanding sponge. Wear a dust mask and goggles when sanding.

Texturing Walls & Ceilings

With a little creativity, you can recreate almost any texture using texture paint or diluted wallboard compound. Texture paints come in various thicknesses, and some contain additives, such as sand and polystyrene beads, for specific effects. Aerosol cans and hand-operated pump guns make it easy to create modern textures without special spray equipment. You can leave a texture paint as-is or apply a top coat of a different color. Like other paints, texture paints may not cover all stains, so prime the surface before you paint it.

Practice texturing on a sheet of cardboard or wallboard, and try different tools (or your hands) and material thicknesses until you find the right combination. Whatever the design, apply it carefully but with confidence; a tentative, sketchy texture job will be more noticeable than one done with bold strokes. Remember, you can always scrape it off while it's still wet and start over.

Tools & materials for texturing include: *spray-on texture (A), all-purpose wallboard compound (B), texture paint (C), texture roller (D), whisk broom (E), wallboard knife (F), sponge (G), and trowel (H).*

Tips for Texturing

Use a whisk broom *for various lined patterns. Apply the texture material with a paint roller, then create the pattern with the broom.*

Smooth a trowel *or a wallboard knife over a partially dried texture for a "knockdown" effect.*

Dilute wallboard compound *with water, and apply it with a texture roller or any other tool.*

Installing Ceramic Wall Tile

Ceramic wall tile is one of the most durable surface materials for walls and ceilings. It's popular in bathrooms and other wet areas because it's virtually impervious to water and easy to clean. However, a tiled surface in a bathroom or shower must be prepared using the proper materials to ensure that the wall system will be protected if water does get through the surface.

In high-moisture areas, install your tile over cementboard. Made from cement and fiberglass, cementboard panels are screwed to wall framing just like standard wallboard. Be sure to tape and finish the seams between cementboard panels before laying the tile. Use thin-set mortar (see page 265) as an adhesive for tile laid over cementboard.

NOTE: In some areas, building codes require the installation of a waterproof membrane, such as roofing felt or polyethylene sheeting, between the framing members and the cementboard; check your local code requirements and the recommendations of the tile manufacturer.

For walls and ceilings that will remain dry most of the time, you can install your tile over standard wallboard, or use water-resistant wallboard for a little added protection from moisture damage. Pre-mixed, latex mastic adhesives generally are acceptable for wall tile in dry areas. When shopping for tile, keep in mind that tiles that are at least 4 × 6" are easier to install than small tile, because they require less cutting and cover more surface area. Larger tiles also have fewer grout

lines that must be cleaned and maintained. Check out the selection of trim and specialty tiles and ceramic accessories that are available to help you customize your project.

Most wall tile is designed to have narrow grout lines (less than $\frac{1}{8}$" wide) filled with unsanded grout. Grout lines wider than $\frac{1}{8}$" should be filled with sanded floor-tile grout. Either type will last longer if it contains, or is mixed with, a latex additive. To prevent staining, it's a good idea to seal your grout after it fully cures, then once a year thereafter.

> **Tools:** Tile-cutting tools (see pages 266 to 267), marker, tape measure, carpenter's level, notched trowel, rod saw, drill with masonry bit, clamps, grout float, sponge, small paint brush, caulk gun, utility knife, cementboard, scoring tool, jig saw, screwdriver, hammer, wallboard knife.
>
> **Materials:** Straight 1 × 2, dry-set tile mortar with latex additive, ceramic wall tile, ceramic trim tile (as needed), tile grout with latex additive, tub & tile caulk, alkaline grout sealer, cardboard, fiberglass wallboard tape, wallboard screws and nails, wallboard corner bead, wallboard compound.

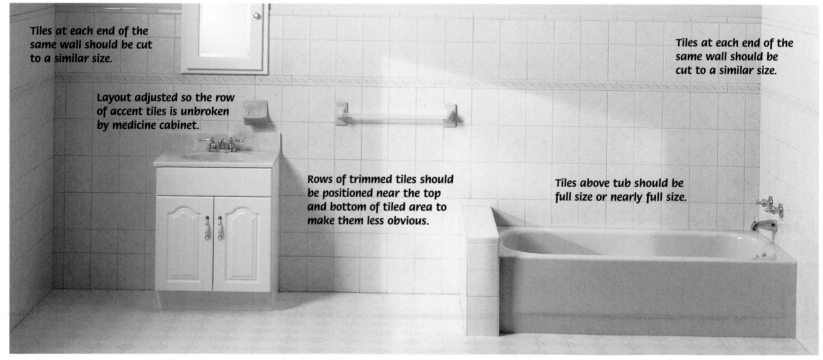

Tiles at each end of the same wall should be cut to a similar size.

Layout adjusted so the row of accent tiles is unbroken by medicine cabinet.

Tiles at each end of the same wall should be cut to a similar size.

Rows of trimmed tiles should be positioned near the top and bottom of tiled area to make them less obvious.

Tiles above tub should be full size or nearly full size.

A *good layout* is the key to a successful wall-tile project. The project shown here was planned so that the tiles directly above the most visible surface (in this case, the bathtub) are nearly full-height. To accomplish this, cut tiles were used in the second row up from the floor.

The short second row also allows the row of accent tiles to run uninterrupted below the medicine cabinet. Cut tiles in both corners should be of similar width to maintain a symmetrical look in the room.

Tips for Installing Ceramic Wall Tile

Make a storyboard to mark layout patterns on walls. For square tiles, set a row of tiles (and plastic spacers, if they will be used) in the selected pattern on a flat surface. Mark a straight 1 × 2 to match the tile spacing. Include any narrow trim tiles or accent tiles. For rectangular and odd-shaped tiles, make separate sticks for the horizontal and vertical layouts.

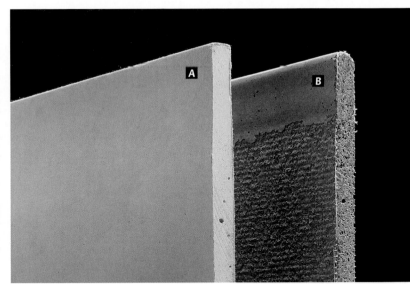

Choose moisture-resistant backing materials. Water-resistant wallboard (A) is made from gypsum, and has a water-resistant facing. Use it only in moderately damp or dry areas. Cementboard (B) is a rigid material with a fiberglass facing and a cement core. Water does not damage cementboard and it is the most appropriate backing material for bathroom tile.

Installing Cementboard

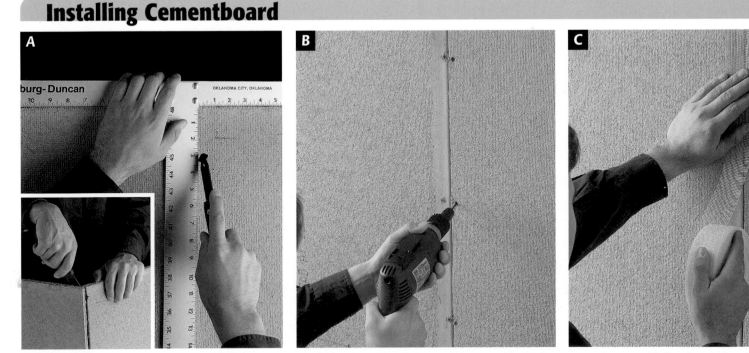

Cut cementboard by scoring through the fiberglass-mesh layer just beneath the surface, using a cementboard scoring tool or a utility knife. Snap the panel along the scored line, then cut the back surface (inset).

Lay the panels over the wall studs with the rough sides facing out. Attach the panels with 1½" galvanized deck screws. If necessary, drill pilot holes along the edges to prevent crumbling. Leave a ⅛" gap between panels and a ¼" gap along the perimeter. Drive a screw every 6".

Cover all seams with fiberglass-mesh wallboard tape. Use a wallboard knife to apply thin-set mortar to the seams, filling the gaps between sheets and spreading a thin layer of mortar over the tape. Allow the mortar to cure for two days before starting the tile installation.

Marking a Layout for Wall Tile

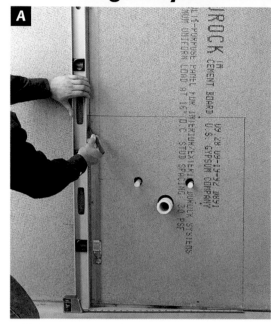

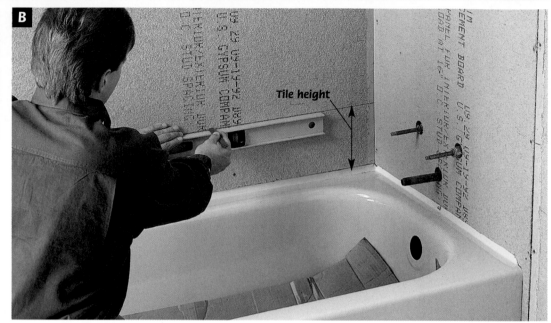

Mark the wall to show the planned location of all vanities, wall cabinets, recessed fixtures, and ceramic wall accessories, such as soap and toothbrush holders or towel rods.

Locate the most visible horizontal line in the bathroom (usually the top edge of the bathtub). Measure up and mark a point at a distance equal to the height of one ceramic tile (if the tub edge is not level, measure up from the lowest spot). Draw a level line through this point, around the entire room. This line represents a tile grout line and will be used as a reference line for making the entire tile layout.

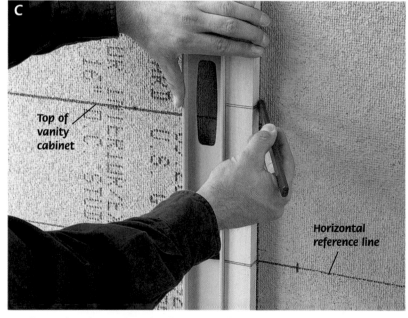

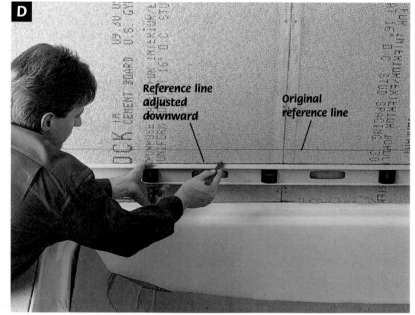

Use the storyboard to see how the tile pattern will run in relation to other features in the room, such as countertops, window and door frames, and wall cabinets. Hold the storyboard so it is perpendicular to the horizontal reference line, with one joint mark touching the line; mark the locations of the tile joints.

Adjust the horizontal reference line if the storyboard shows that tile joints will fall in undesirable locations. In the bathroom shown above, adjusting the reference line downward allowed an unbroken row of accent tiles to span the wall under the medicine cabinet (see photo, page 204).

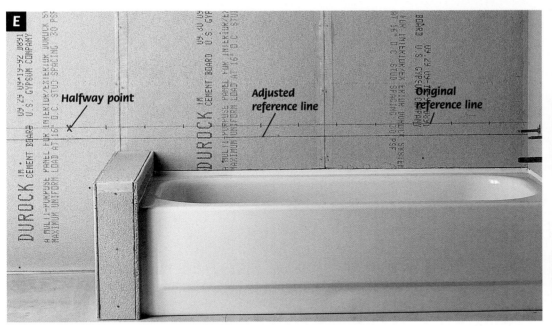

E

Halfway point

Adjusted reference line

Original reference line

On each wall, measure and mark the halfway point along the original horizontal reference line. Using the storyboard as a guide, mark lines in each direction from the halfway point to show where the vertical grout joints will be located. If the storyboard shows that the corner tiles will be less than half of a full tile width, adjust the layout as shown in the next step.

F

Adjust the layout of the vertical joints by moving the halfway point (step E) half the width of a tile in either direction. Mark the new point onto the adjusted horizontal reference line. Use a level to draw a vertical reference line through this point, from the floor to the top tile row.

G

Use the storyboard to measure up from the floor along the vertical reference line, a distance equal to the height of one tile plus 1/8", and mark a point on the wall. Draw a level reference line through this point, across the wall.

H

Bullnose border tiles

Cut tiles

Accent tiles

Cut tiles

Mark reference lines to show where the remaining tile joints will be located, starting at the point where the vertical and horizontal reference lines meet. Include any decorative border or accent tiles. If a row of cut tiles is unavoidable, position it near the floor, between the first and third rows, or at the top, near the border tiles. Extend all horizontal reference lines onto adjoining walls that will be tiled, then repeat steps E through H for all other walls being tiled.

Installing Ceramic Wall Tile

A

Mark the layout pattern (see pages 206 to 207), then begin installation with the second row of tiles above the floor. If the layout requires cut tiles for this row, mark and cut the tiles for the entire row at one time.

B

Make straight cuts with a tile cutter. Place the tile faceup on the tile cutter, with one side flush against the cutting guide. Adjust the cutting tool to the desired width, then score a groove by pulling the cutting wheel firmly across the tile. Snap the tile along the scored line, as directed by the tool manufacturer.

C

Mix a small batch of thin-set mortar containing a latex additive. (Some mortar has additive mixed in by the manufacturer and some must have additive mixed in separately.) Cover the back of the first tile with adhesive, using a ¼" notched trowel.

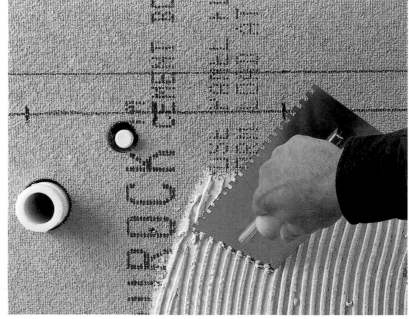

VARIATION: Spread adhesive on a small section of the wall, then set the tiles into the adhesive. Thin-set adhesive sets quickly, so work quickly if you choose this installation method.

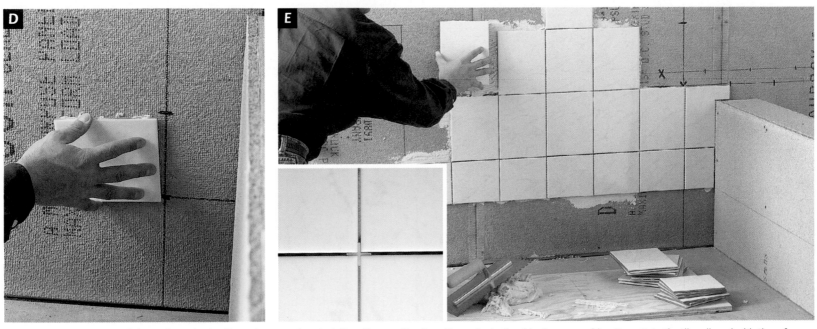

Beginning near the center of the wall, apply the tile to the wall with a slight twisting motion, aligning it exactly with the horizontal and vertical reference lines. When placing cut tiles, position the cut edges where they will be least visible.

Continue installing tiles, working from the center to the sides in a pyramid pattern. Keep the tiles aligned with the reference lines. If the tiles are not self-spacing, use plastic spacers inserted in the corner joints to maintain even grout lines (inset). The base row should be the last row of full tiles installed. To cut tiles at inside corners, see page 210.

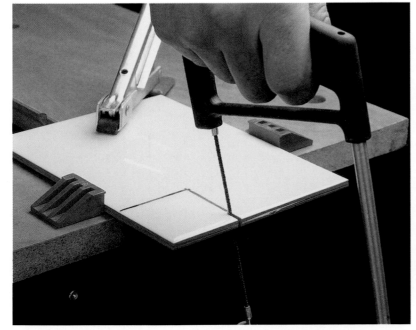

TIP: Make notches and curved cuts in tile by clamping the tile to a flat surface, then cutting it with a rod saw (a specialty saw with an abrasive blade designed for cutting tile).

TIP: Cut holes for plumbing stub-outs by marking the outline of the hole on the tile, then drilling around the edges of the outline, using a ceramic-tile bit. Gently knock out the waste material with a hammer. Rough edges of the hole will be covered by protective plates on the plumbing fixtures (called escutcheons).

Continued on next page

Installing Ceramic Wall Tile (cont.)

As small sections of tile are completed, "set" the tile by laying a scrap of 2 × 4 wrapped with carpet onto the tile and rapping it lightly with a mallet. This embeds the tile solidly in the adhesive and creates a flat, even surface.

To mark tiles for straight cuts, begin by taping ⅛" spacers against the surfaces below and to the side of the tile. Position a tile directly over the last full tile installed, then place a third tile so the edge butts against the spacers. Trace the edge of the top tile onto the middle tile to mark it for cutting.

Install trim tiles, such as the bullnose edge tiles shown above, at border areas. Wipe away excess mortar along the top edges of the edge tiles.

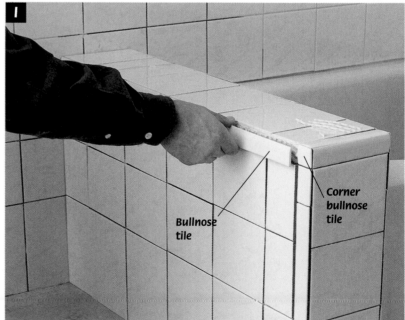

Use bullnose and corner bullnose (with two adjacent bullnose edges) tiles at outside corners to cover the rough edges of the adjoining tiles.

Install any ceramic accessories by applying thin-set mortar to the back side, then pressing the accessory into place. Use masking tape to support the weight until the adhesive dries (inset).

Let mortar dry completely (12 to 24 hours), then mix a batch of grout containing latex additive. Apply the grout with a rubber grout float, using a sweeping motion to force it deep into the joints (see page 270). Do not grout the joints adjoining the bathtub, floor, and room corners. These will serve as expansion joints and will be caulked later.

Wipe a damp grout sponge diagonally over the tile, rinsing the sponge in cool water between wipes. Wipe each area only once; repeated wiping can pull grout from the joints. Allow the grout to dry for about 4 hours, then use a soft cloth to buff the tile surface and remove any remaining grout film.

When the grout has cured completely, use a small foam brush to apply grout sealer to the joints, following the manufacturer's directions. Avoid brushing sealer on the tile surfaces, and wipe up excess sealer immediately.

Fill the tub with water, then seal expansion joints around the bathtub, floor, and room corners with silicone caulk. After the caulk dries, buff the tile with a dry, soft cloth.

Applying Tongue & Groove Wainscoting

Wainscoting refers to virtually any specialized finish of the lower three to four feet of interior walls. The form demonstrated here, using tongue-and-groove boards, is a popular way to dress up a room.

Typical tongue-and-groove boards for wainscoting are made of pine, fir, or other softwoods, and measure ¼" to ¾" thick. Each board has a tongue on one edge, a groove on the other, and usually a decorative bevel or bead along the edges and in the middle of the board.

There are two basic methods for installing wainscoting. Thinner material can be glued to finished wallboard, using construction adhesive or a trowel-applied panel adhesive. It can also be nailed to the wall; thicker wainscoting material always should be fastened with nails. However, in order to use nails, you need to install backing, which can be done in a few simple ways. One method is to install plywood over the wall studs, and cover the rest of the wall with wallboard of the same thickness. Or, you can simply install 2 × 4 blocks between the studs before hanging the wallboard. If the wall is already finished with wallboard, cut out horizontal strips of wallboard to create channels, then screw strips of ½" plywood directly to the studs.

Some tongue-and-groove wainscoting can be *blind-nailed*, a technique in which angled nails are driven into the board at the base of the tongue (see step E, page 218). The advantage of blind-nailing is that the groove of the next board hides the nails. If your wainscoting material is very thin, however, you may have to face-nail all of the boards rather than risk splitting the edges.

Once the boards are installed, you can trim your wainscoting with molding called *cap rail*. When installed to the height of the furniture in the room, wainscoting provides visual symmetry. It also allows the cap rail to double as a chair rail, protecting the lower portion of the walls from damage.

Wainscoting can be painted or stained. Oil-based stains can be applied before or after installation, since most of the stain will be absorbed into the wood and won't interfere with the tongue-and-groove joints. For staining, choose a wood species with a pronounced grain. For painting, poplar is a good choice, since it has few knots and a highly consistent grain. If you're painting, choose a latex-based paint; it will resist cracking as the joints expand and contract with changes in humidity.

In a typical application, wainscoting adds thickness to a wall surface. This can cause problems where the wainscoting meets other trim, such as window and door casing and baseboard. Before the installation, go around the room with a piece of the wainscoting and any trim you plan to install on top of it, and butt the pieces up to the existing trim. Making everything blend attractively may require additional molding (see page 215), or you might decide to install new molding that matches the wainscot trim.

Tools: 4-ft. level, circular saw, jig saw, drill, nail set, compass, power miter saw or hand miter box.

Materials: Tongue-and-groove boards, 6d and 4d finish nails, baseboard and cap rail molding, wood-finishing materials.

Tips for Installing Wainscoting

Condition the boards by stacking them in the room where they will be installed. Place spacers between the boards to promote air circulation, and allow the wood to adjust to the room's temperature and humidity for 48 hours. Wait 72 hours before applying any stain or sealer.

With thick boards, you may need to install electrical box extenders to switch and receptacle boxes. Mount the extenders following manufacturer's instructions; make sure the switch or receptacle will be flush with the face of the wainscoting. Make the cutouts with a jig saw.

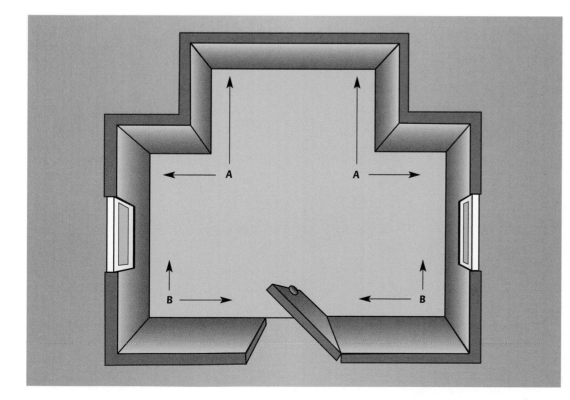

Begin the installation at the corners. Install any outside corners (A) first, working your way toward the inside corners. At outside corners, you can miter the boards for a finished joint or butt them together and cover the joint with corner molding. In sections of a room that have no outside corners, start at the inside corners (B), and work your way toward the door and window casings.

Plan the layout by calculating the number of boards required for each wall, using the reveal dimension (see page 217). Measure the length of the wall and divide that dimension by the reveal, keeping in mind that a side edge may have to be removed from one or more of the corner boards.

If the total number of boards for a wall includes a fraction of less than half a board, plan to trim the first board (and last, if necessary) to avoid ending with a board cut to less than half its original width.

Installing Wainscoting Starting at an Outside Corner

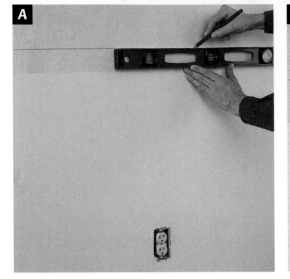
A

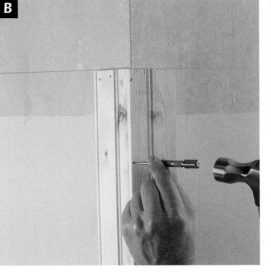
B

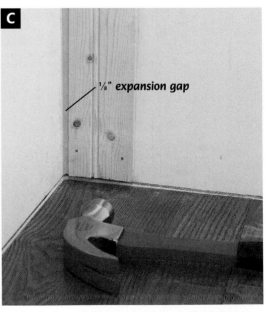
C

Turn off the electricity in the project area, then remove baseboard trim and receptacle coverplates. Mark a level control line along the walls to designate the height of the tongue-and-groove boards. Leave room for a ¼" gap between the boards and the floor, for expansion.

Cut a pair of boards to width, based on your layout. NOTE: If the corner is not plumb, you may have to taper one or both boards so that the uncut edges will be plumb. Face-nail the boards in place, then nail along the joint, using 6d finish nails. Drill pilot holes, if necessary, to prevent splitting the wood. Set the nails with a nail set.

If the corner boards are butted together rather than mitered, nail a piece of corner trim over the corner, using 6d finish nails. Install the remaining boards along both walls (steps E and F, page 215).

Installing Wainscoting Starting at an Inside Corner

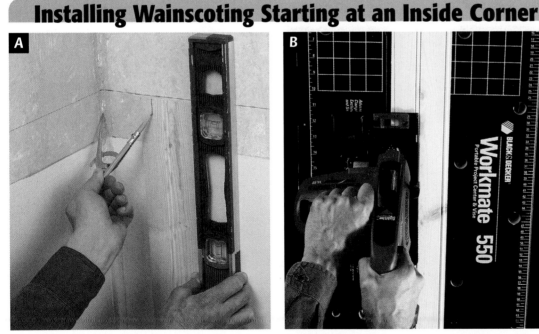
A

B

C

⅛" expansion gap

Check the corner for plumb. If it's not plumb, scribe and trim the first board to compensate: Hold the board plumb, then use a compass to transfer the contours of the wall to the board. Keep in mind the overall width of the board, based on your layout.

Cut along the scribed line with a circular saw. If you found that the corner was plumb in step A, trim the first board to width, following your layout. If you're starting with the tongue edge in the corner, trim off at least the tongue from the first board.

Position the board in the corner, leaving a ⅛" gap for expansion. Make sure the board is plumb, then face-nail it in place with 6d finish nails. Drill pilot holes, if necessary, to prevent splitting. Drive the bottom and top nails where they'll be hidden by the base molding and the cap rail, respectively.

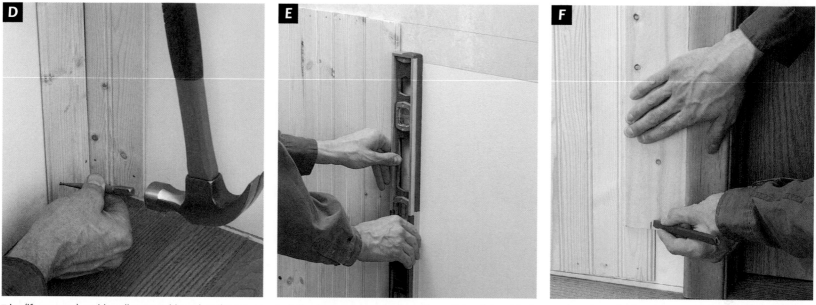

D Trim (if necessary) and install a second board at the corner. Butt the board against the first one and make sure it's plumb; face-nail this second board in place.

E Install subsequent boards along the wall by gluing, blind-nailing, or face-nailing. Leave a 1/16" gap at each joint to allow for expansion. Use a level to check every third board for plumb. If it's out of plumb, adjust the fourth board to compensate.

F Mark and cut the final board to fit. If you're at a door casing, cut the board to fit flush with the casing (trim off at least the tongue). If you're at an inside corner, make sure it's plumb. If not, scribe and trim the board to fit. Set all nails with a nail set.

Finishing Wainscoting

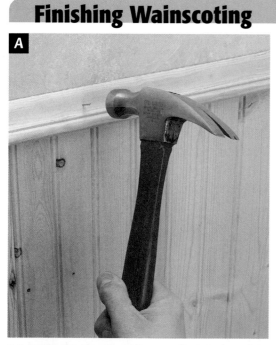

A Cut and fit the cap rail molding over the top edges of the boards (see pages 224 to 227), and fasten it with 4d finish nails driven into the wall studs or backing. Set the nails with a nail set.

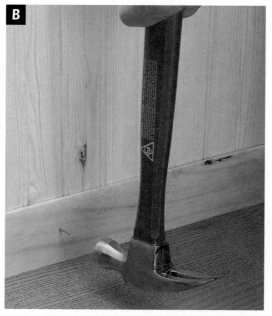

B Cut baseboard molding to fit over the wainscoting, and attach it with 6d finish nails at all wall-stud locations. If you plan to install base shoe, leave a small gap along the floor.

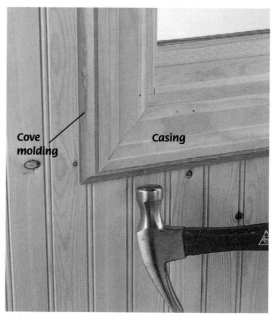

Cove molding   Casing

TIP: On windows with picture-frame casing, install wainscoting up to the casing on the sides and below the window, then hide the joints with cove or another type of molding.

Paneling a Ceiling

Tongue-and-groove paneling offers a warm, attractive finish that's especially suited to vaulted ceilings. Pine is the most common material for tongue-and-groove paneling, but you can choose from many different wood species and panel styles. Panels are typically $3/8$" to $3/4$" thick and are often attached directly to ceiling joists and rafters. Some building codes require the installation of wallboard as a fire stop behind ceiling paneling if it's thinner than $1/4$".

When purchasing paneling, buy enough material to cover about 15% more square footage than the actual ceiling size, to allow for waste. Since the tongue portions of panels slip into the grooves of adjacent pieces, square footage for paneling is based on the *reveal*, or the exposed face of the panels after they are installed.

Tongue-and-groove boards can be attached with flooring nails or finish nails. Flooring nails hold better because they have spiraled shanks, but they tend to have larger heads than finish nails. Whenever possible, drive the nails through the base of the tongue and into the framing. This is called *blind-nailing*, because the groove of the succeeding board covers the nail heads. Add face-nails only at joints and in locations where more support is needed, such as along the first and last boards. To ensure clean cuts, use a compound miter saw (see page 226). These saws are especially useful for ceilings with non-90° angles.

Layout is crucial to the success of a paneling project. Before you start, measure and calculate how many boards will be installed, using the reveal measurement. If the final board will be less than 2" wide, trim the first, or *starter*, board by cutting the long edge that abuts the wall. If the ceiling peak is not parallel to the side (starting) wall, you must compensate for the difference by ripping the starter piece at an angle. The leading edge of the starter piece, and every piece thereafter, must be parallel to the peak.

Tools: *Chalk line, compound miter saw, circular saw, drill, nail set.*

Materials: *Tongue-and-groove paneling, 1$3/4$" spiral flooring nails, trim molding.*

Paneling a Ceiling

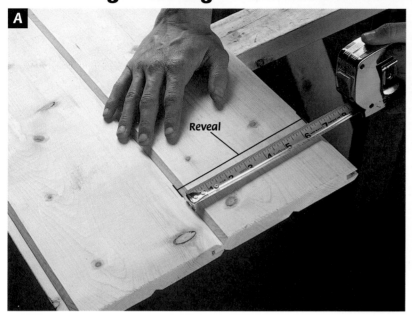

A

Reveal

To plan your layout, first measure the reveal of the boards. Fit two pieces together and measure the exposed surface. Calculate the number of boards needed to cover one side of the ceiling by dividing the reveal dimension into the overall distance between the top of one wall and the peak of the ceiling.

B

Rafters

Side wall

Use the calculation from step A to make a control line indicating the top of the first row of paneling. At both ends of the ceiling, measure down from the peak an equal distance, and make a mark to represent the top (tongue) edges of the starter boards. Snap a chalk line through the marks.

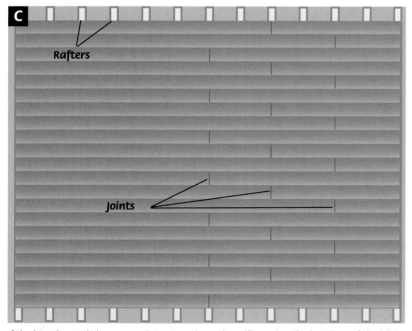

C

Rafters

Joints

If the boards aren't long enough to span the entire ceiling, plan the locations of the joints. Staggering them in a three-step pattern will make the joints less conspicuous. Note that each joint must fall over the middle of a rafter. For best appearance, select boards of similar coloring and grain for each row.

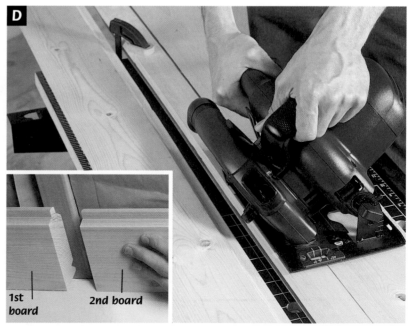

D

1st board

2nd board

Rip the first starter board to width by bevel-cutting the bottom (grooved) edge. If the starter row will have joints, cut the board to length using a 30° bevel cut on the joint-end only. Two beveled ends joined together form a scarf joint (inset), which is less noticeable than a butt joint. If the board spans the ceiling, square-cut both ends.

Continued on next page

Paneling a Ceiling (cont.)

Position the first starter board so the grooved (or cut) edge butts against the side wall and the tongue is aligned with the control line. Leave a ⅛" gap between the square board end and the end wall. Fasten the board by nailing through its face about 1" from the grooved edge and into the rafters. Then, blind-nail through the base of the tongue into each rafter, angling the nail backwards at 45°. Drive the nail heads beneath the wood surface, using a nail set.

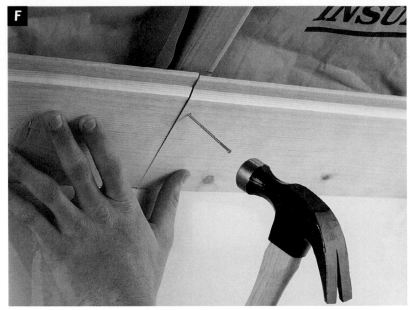

Cut and install any remaining boards in the starter row one at a time, making sure the scarf joints fit together tightly. At each scarf joint, drive two nails through the face of the top board, angling each nail to capture the end of the board behind it. If necessary, drill pilot holes to prevent splitting.

Cut the first board for the next row, then fit its grooved edge over the tongue of the starter board. Use a hammer and a scrap piece of paneling to seat the grooved edge over the tongue of the starter board. Fasten the second row of boards with blind-nails only.

As you install successive rows, measure down from the peak to make sure the rows remain parallel to the peak. Correct any misalignment by adjusting the tongue-and-groove joint slightly with each row. You can also snap additional control lines to help you align the rows.

I Rip the boards for the last row to width, beveling the top edges so they fit flush against the ridge board. Face nail the boards in place. Install paneling on the other side of the ceiling, then cut and install the final row of paneling to form a closed joint under the ridge board (inset).

Ridge board

Panels

J Install trim molding along walls, at joints around obstacles, and along inside and outside corners, if desired. (Select-grade 1 × 2 works well as trim along walls.) Where necessary, bevel the back edges of the trim or miter-cut the ends to accommodate the slope of the ceiling.

Tips for Paneling a Ceiling

Panels

Trim

Use mitered trim to cover joints where panels meet at outside corners. Dormers and other architectural elements create opposing ceiling angles that can be difficult to work around. It may be easier to butt the panels together and hide the joints with custom-cut trim. The trim also makes a nice transition between angles.

Collar tie

Panel material

Wrap collar ties or exposed beams with custom-cut panels. Install the paneling on the ceiling first. Then, rip-cut panels to the desired width. You may want to include a tongue-and-groove joint as part of the trim detail. Angle-cut the ends of the trim pieces so they fit tight to the ceiling paneling.

Installing a Suspended Ceiling

Suspended ceilings have some advantages over standard ceiling finishes, such as wallboard. Because all of the panels can be removed, virtually everything behind a suspended ceiling—plumbing runs, shut-off valves, and wiring—is easily accessible. Suspended ceilings can also compensate for uneven joists.

One notable disadvantage of suspended ceilings is that they take up headroom. Typically, suspended ceilings should hang about 4" below the lowest obstacle to leave enough room for installing or removing the panels. Before you decide on using a suspended system, measure to determine the finished ceiling height, and make sure it will comply with local building codes.

A suspended ceiling is a grid framework made of lightweight metal brackets hung on wires attached to ceiling or floor joists. The frame consists of T-shaped main beams (mains) and cross-tees (tees), and L-shaped wall angles. The grid supports ceiling panels that rest on the flanges of the framing pieces. Ceiling panels come in 2 × 2-ft. or 2 × 4-ft. sections. They're available in a variety of styles, including insulated panels, acoustical tiles that dampen sound, and light-diffuser panels that are used with fluorescent light fixtures. Generally, metal-frame ceiling systems are more durable than those made of plastic.

To begin your ceiling project, determine the ceiling panel layout based on the width and length of the room. Often, some panels must be cut to accommodate the room. Place trimmed panels on opposite sides of your ceiling for a balanced look, as when installing ceramic tile. You'll also want to install your ceiling so it's perfectly level. An inexpensive but effective tool for marking a level line around a room perimeter is a water level. You can make a water level by purchasing two water-level ends (available at hardware stores and home centers) and attaching them to a standard garden hose.

Although suspended ceilings work well for hiding mechanicals, it looks best if you build soffits around low obstacles, such as support beams and large ducts (see pages 327 to 329). Finish the soffits with wallboard, and install the ceiling wall angle to the soffit.

Tools: Water level, chalk line, drill, screw-eye driver, aviation snips, dryline, lock-type clamps, pliers, straightedge, utility knife.

Materials: Suspended ceiling kit (frame), screw eyes, hanger wires, ceiling panels, 1½" wallboard screws or masonry nails.

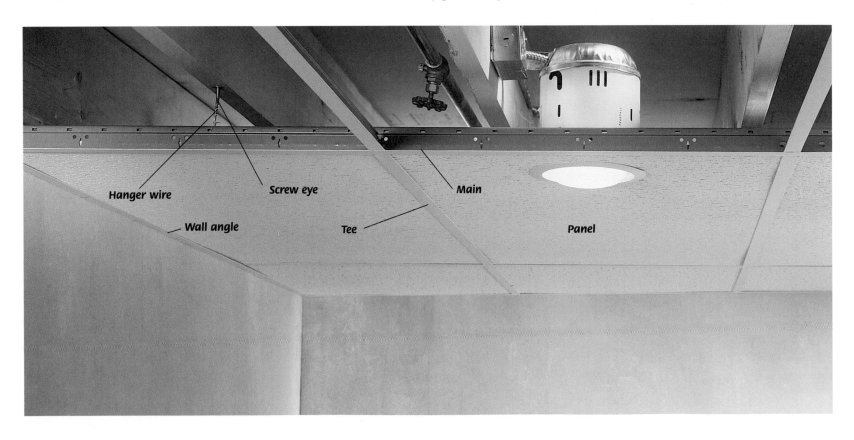

Hanger wire   Screw eye   Main

Wall angle   Tee   Panel

Tips for Installing a Suspended Ceiling

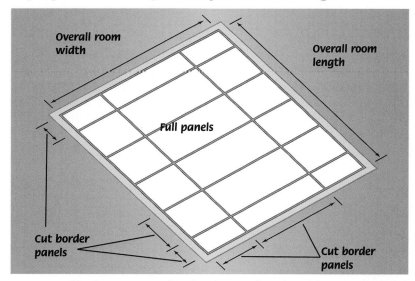

Overall room width

Overall room length

Full panels

Cut border panels

Cut border panels

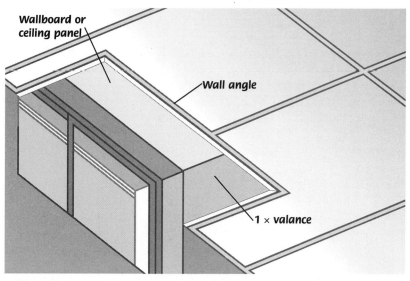

Wallboard or ceiling panel

Wall angle

1 × valance

Draw your ceiling layout on paper, based on the exact dimensions of the room. Plan so that trimmed border panels on opposite sides of the room are of equal width and length (avoid panels smaller than half-size). If you include lighting fixtures in your plan, make sure they follow the grid layout.

Build a valance around basement awning windows so they can be opened fully. Attach 1 × lumber of an appropriate width to joists or blocking. Install wallboard (or a suspended-ceiling panel trimmed to fit) to the joists inside the valance.

Installing a Suspended Ceiling

A

B

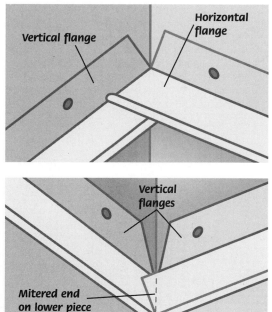

Vertical flange

Horizontal flange

Vertical flanges

Mitered end on lower piece

Make a mark on one wall indicating the ceiling height plus the height of the wall angle. Use a water level to transfer that mark to both ends of each wall, then snap a chalk line to connect the marks. This line indicates the top of the ceiling's wall angle.

Attach wall angle pieces to the studs on all walls, positioning the top of the wall angle flush with the chalk line. Use 1½" wallboard screws (on concrete block walls use short masonry nails driven into mortar joints). Cut angle pieces using aviation snips.

TIP: Trim wall angle pieces to fit around corners. At inside corners (top), back-cut the vertical flanges slightly, then overlap the horizontal flanges. At outside corners (bottom), miter-cut one horizontal flange, and overlap the flanges.

Continued on next page

Installing a Suspended Ceiling (cont.)

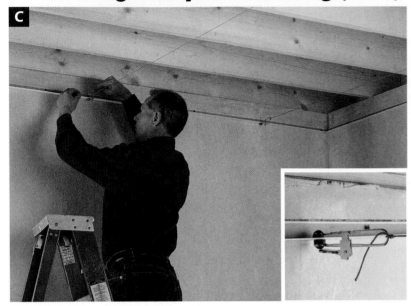

Mark the location of each main on the wall angles at the ends of the room. The mains must be parallel to each other and perpendicular to the ceiling joists. Set up a guide string for each main, using a thin dryline and lock-type clamps (inset). Clamp the strings to the opposing wall angles, stretching them very taut so there's no sagging.

Install screw eyes for hanging the mains, using a drill and screw-eye driver. Drill pilot holes and drive the eyes into the joists every 4 ft., locating them directly above the guide strings. Attach hanger wire to the screw eyes by threading one end through the eye and twisting the wire around itself at least three times. Trim excess wire, leaving a few inches of wire hanging below the level of the guide string.

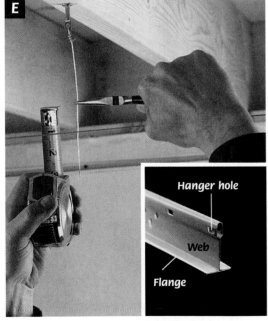

Hanger hole

Web

Flange

Measure the distance from the bottom of a main's flange to the hanger hole in the web (inset). Use this measurement to pre-bend each hanger wire. Measure up from the guide string and make a 90° bend in the wire, using pliers.

Following your ceiling plan, mark the placement of the first tee on opposite wall angles at one end of the room. Set up a guide string for the tee, using a dryline and clamps, as before. This string must be perpendicular to the guide strings for the mains.

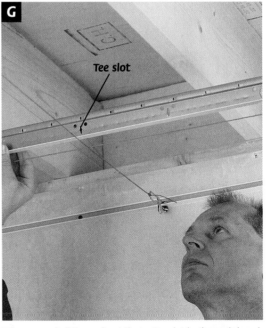

Tee slot

Trim one end of the main so that a tee slot in the main's web is aligned with the tee guide string and the end of the main bears fully on a wall angle. Set the main in place to check the alignment of the tee slot with the string.

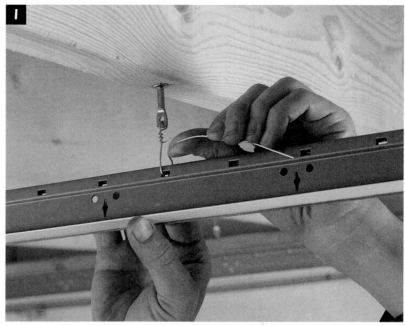

Cut the other end of the main to fit, so that it rests on the opposing wall angle. If a single main cannot span the room, splice two mains together, end-to-end (the ends should be fashioned with male-female connectors). Make sure the tee slots remain aligned when splicing.

Install each main by setting the ends on the wall angle and threading the hanger wires through the hanger holes in the webs. The wires should be as close to vertical as possible. Wrap each wire around itself three times, making sure the main's flange is level with the main guide string. Also install a hanger near each main splice.

Attach tees to the mains, slipping their tabbed ends into the tee slots on the mains. Align the first row of tees with the tee guide string; install the remaining rows at 4-ft. intervals. If you're using 2 × 2-ft. panels, install 2-ft. cross-tees between the midpoints of the 4-ft. tees. Cut and install the border tees, setting the tee ends on the wall angles. Remove all guide strings and clamps.

Place full ceiling panels into the grid first, then install the border panels. Lift the panels in at an angle, and position them so they rest on the frame's flanges. Reach through adjacent openings to adjust the panels, if necessary. To trim the border panels to size, cut them face-up, using a straightedge and a utility knife (inset).

Installing Interior Trim

Interior trim refers to all of the decorative molding and accent pieces that dress up a blank wall or ceiling, hide gaps and joints between surfaces, or cover the edges of a window or door frame. Installing most trim involves the same basic cuts and fastening techniques regardless of the type, material, or style.

Follow the tips on pages 225 to 227 for help with cutting, fastening, and planning the installation of standard types of baseboard and ceiling molding. Pages 228 and 229 show how to install large, polymer crown molding, and the project on pages 230 to 231 demonstrates the techniques for installing door and window casings. Regardless of what type of molding you're installing, it's important to think through the job and devise an installation plan. A good plan will help you minimize the number of tricky cuts required and place them in the least conspicuous areas.

Trim is available in many different wood species, as well as synthetic (polymer) materials. Wood molding still offers the greatest variety of styles, but synthetics, which are lighter than wood and easier to install, are becoming increasingly popular for large or elaborate crown molding. If you plan to install wood molding that will be painted, choose finger-jointed pine. It's less expensive than solid wood, and you can't tell the difference once it's painted.

To avoid problems due to shrinkage after installation, stack the trim in the room where it will be installed and allow it to acclimate for several days. Apply a coat of primer or sealer to all sides of each piece, and let it dry thoroughly before installing it. You may also choose to paint or stain the trim before installing it.

Attach wood trim with finish nails, which have small heads that you drive below the surface using a nail set (see page 227). Nails for most interior trim are size 6d or smaller, depending on the thickness of the trim and the wall surface. At a minimum, nails should be long enough to penetrate the framing by at least ³⁄₄"; heavier trim requires nails with more holding power. Use finish screws for securing trim to steel studs (see page 50). After the trim is installed and all the nails are set, fill the nail holes with wood putty, and touch-up the areas with paint or stain.

Tips for Planning a Baseboard or Ceiling Trim Project

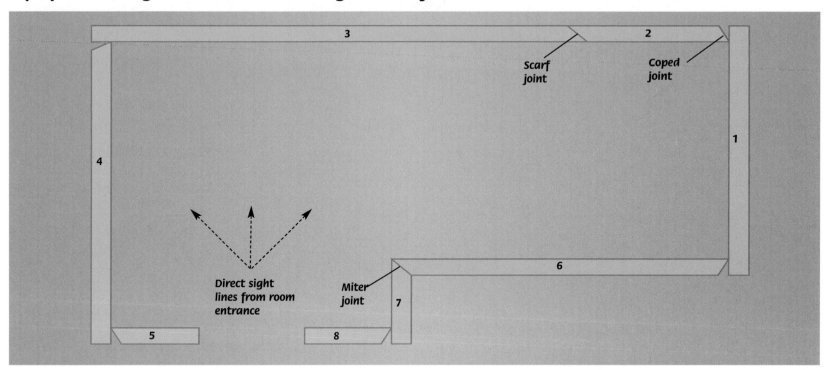

Plan the order of installation for your baseboard or ceiling molding to avoid having to make more than one complex cut on any one piece. Use the longest pieces of molding for the most visible walls, saving the shorter ones for less conspicuous areas. When possible, place the joints so they point away from the direct line of sight from the room's entrance.

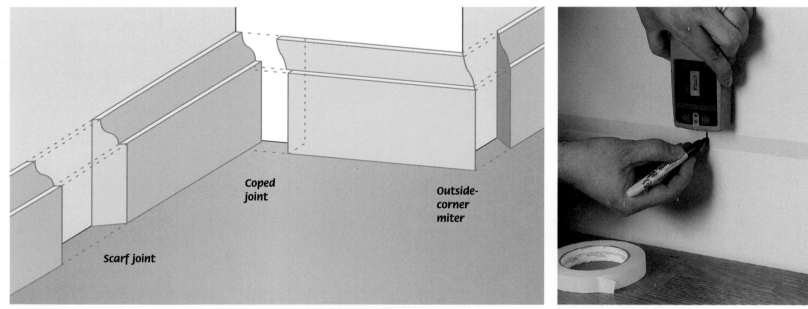

The basic joints for trim are shown here. A scarf joint (see pages 217 to 218) joins two pieces along a length of wall. Coped joints join contoured molding at inside corners. The first piece is butted into the corner; the second piece is cut and fitted against the face of the first (see page 227). Miter joints are made with two 45°-angle cuts. To help with measuring and fitting miter joints, make a pattern by miter-cutting both ends of a scrap piece of trim. Hold the pattern against the wall at outside corners to test-fit and position cut pieces.

Mark stud locations throughout the project area. Mark directly on the wall or ceiling, using light pencil marks, or apply masking tape and mark onto the tape. Make sure the marks will be visible when the trim is in place. Use a stud finder if necessary, to help find the studs.

Tips for Cutting Trim

A basic miter box, made of wood or metal, and a backsaw are the simplest tools for making clean cuts in trim. These typically cut only 90° and 45° angles. A backsaw is a short handsaw with a stiff spine that keeps the blade straight while cutting. To cut crown molding, see below.

Swivel-type miter boxes rotate and lock the blade into position for cutting a wide range of angles. Some types have a special saw used only for the miter box; other types have clamps that accept standard backsaws.

Power miter saws make very accurate cuts. Their bases swivel and lock into position, and their large blades cut cleanly with minimal tearout. Standard miter saws are fixed vertically, while compound miter saws (see below) tilt to make bevel- and miter-cuts in one stroke.

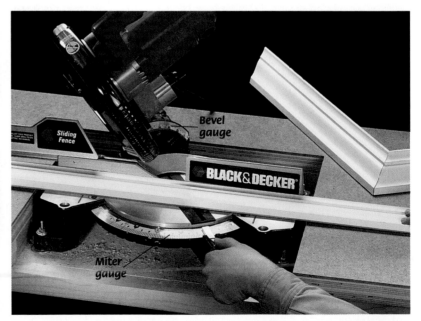

To miter-cut crown molding using a miter box or standard miter saw, flip the molding upside down, and place the flats on the back side of the molding against the table and fence of the saw (think of the table as the ceiling and the fence as the wall).

VARIATION: To cut crown molding using a compound miter saw, lay the molding flat on the saw table and set the miter and bevel angles. For outside-corner miters, the standard settings are 33° (miter) and 31.62° (bevel). These settings on the gauges often are highlighted for easy identification.

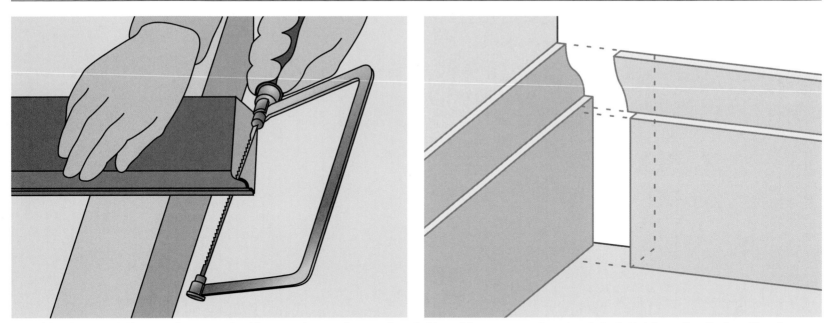

Coped joints form neat inside corners for contoured molding. To make a coped cut, cut the end of the molding at a 45° angle, so that the back side is longer than the front side. Using a coping saw, cut along the front edge of the molding, following the contour exactly. Angle the saw slightly toward the back side to create a sharp edge along the contour. Test-fit the cut using a scrap piece of molding. The coped piece should fit snugly against the profile of the scrap piece. If necessary, make small adjustments to the contoured edge, using sandpaper or a utility knife.

Tips for Nailing Trim

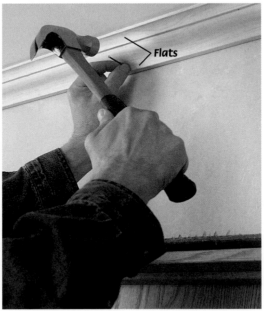

A nail set allows you to recess finish nails in trim. Drill a pilot hole through the molding, drive the nail close to the surface with just the hammer, then set the nail slightly below the surface with the nail set. Nail sets come in different sizes; choose one with a point slightly smaller than the nail head.

Crown molding should be positioned so the flats are flush against the wall and ceiling. Drill pilot holes, and drive finish nails through the flats of the molding at the stud and ceiling-joist locations. Note: To prevent splitting, slightly offset the nails so they are not in line vertically.

Baseboard molding is attached with two nails at each stud location: one driven into the stud; the other into the bottom plate. Drill pilot holes, and keep the nails at least ½" from the edges. Offset the nails slightly so they aren't in line vertically. If you plan to install base shoe, leave a small gap at the floor.

Installing Polymer Crown Molding

Polymer moldings come in a wide variety of single-piece ornate styles, and offer easy installation and maintenance. They are as easy to cut and nail as pine and many can be glued in place. But unlike wood, the polystyrene or polyurethane material won't rot, swell, or shrink, and it can be repaired with vinyl spackling compound.

Polymer moldings can be purchased preprimed for painting, or you can stain them yourself with a non-penetrating heavy-body stain or gel. Most polymers come in 12-ft. lengths, with single-piece design. Special options include corner blocks, which eliminate difficult cuts at inside and outside corners, and bendable profiles, which allow you to mold around curved surfaces.

The cost of simple polymer moldings is similar to that of pine, but ornate polymer moldings generally are less expensive than their multiple-piece wood counterparts.

Tools: Drill with countersink-piloting bit, power miter saw or hand miter box and fine-tooth saw, caulk gun, putty knife.

Materials: Crown molding, finish nails, 150-grit sandpaper, rag, mineral spirits, polymer adhesive, 2" wallboard screws, vinyl spackling compound, paintable latex caulk.

Plan the layout of the molding pieces by measuring the walls of the room and making light pencil marks at the joint locations. For each piece that starts or ends at a corner, add 12" to 24" to compensate for the waste. Avoid pieces less than 36" long, if possible, because short pieces are more difficult to fit.

Hold a section of molding against the wall and ceiling in the finished position. Make light pencil marks on the wall every 12" along the bottom edge of the molding. Remove the molding, and tack a finish nail at each pencil mark. The nails will hold the molding in place while the adhesive dries. If the wall surface is plaster, drill pilot holes for the nails.

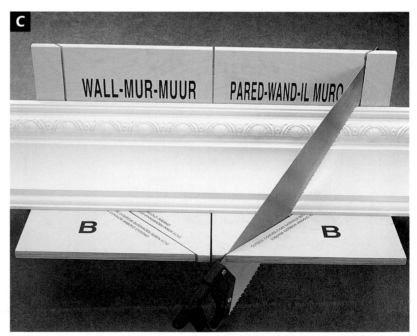

To make the miter cuts for the first corner, position the molding face up in a miter box. Set the ceiling-side flat (see page 226) of the molding against the horizontal table of the miter box, and set the wall-side flat against the vertical back fence. Make the cut at 45°.

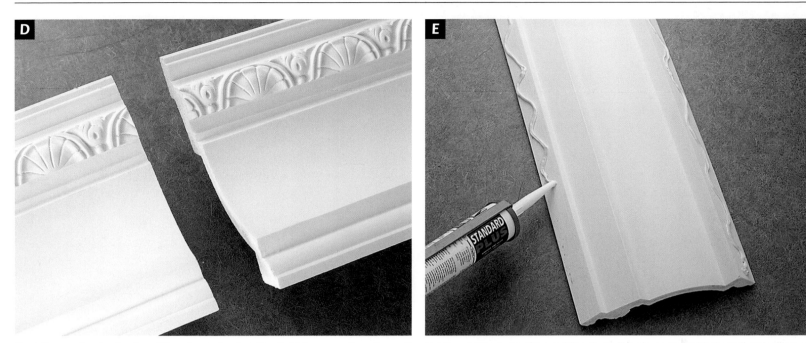

D

Check the uncut ends of each molding piece before installing it. Make sure mating pieces will butt together squarely in a tight joint. Cut all square ends at 90°, using a miter saw or hand miter box.

E

Lightly sand the backs of the molding that will make contact with the wall and ceiling, using 150-grit sandpaper. Slightly dampen a rag with mineral spirits, and wipe away the sanding dust. Run a small bead of polymer adhesive (recommended or supplied by the manufacturer) along both sanded edges.

F

Set the molding in place with the mitered end tight to the corner and the bottom edge resting on the finish nails. Press along the wall and ceiling edges to create a good bond. At each end of the section, drill a countersunk pilot hole through the flats and into the ceiling and wall. Drive 2" wallboard screws through the pilot holes.

G

Cut, sand, and glue the next section of molding. Apply a bead of adhesive to the end where the installed molding will meet the new section. Install the new section, and secure the ends with screws, making sure the joints are aligned properly. Install the remaining molding sections, and allow the adhesive to dry.

H

Carefully remove the finish nails and fill the nail holes with vinyl spackling compound. Fill the screw holes in the molding and any gaps in the joints with paintable latex caulk or filler, and wipe away excess caulk with a damp cloth or a wet finger. Smooth the caulk over the holes so it is flush with the surface.

Installing Door or Window Casing

Casing is the decorative molding that covers the gaps around the edges of door and window jambs. You can find casing in almost any style and in many different materials, including pine, hardwoods, and synthetic materials.

In most situations, it's easiest to paint the walls before you install the casing. You can also save time by pre-painting or staining the casing before cutting and installing it.

For precise miter cuts that make tight joints, use a power miter saw, if you have one; otherwise, make cuts with a hand miter box (see page 226).

> **Tools:** Straightedge, power miter saw or miter box and back-saw, drill, nail set.
>
> **Materials:** Casing, 6d and 4d finish nails, wood putty.

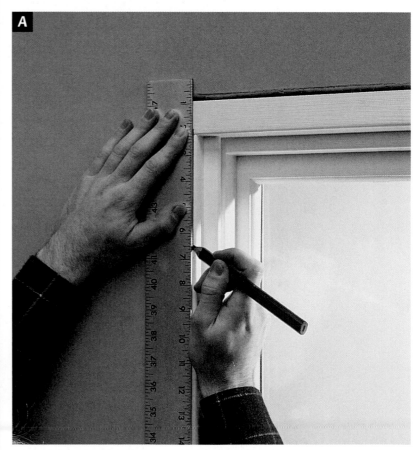

On the front edge of each jamb, mark a setback line to indicate the inside edge of the casing. The typical setback is about ⅛". You can set back your molding as much as you like—just make sure the distance is equal on all jambs. Use a straightedge to mark the lines just at the corners, or extend them along the entire length of the jambs.

Place a length of casing along one side jamb, flush with the setback line. At the top and bottom of the molding, mark the points where the horizontal and vertical setback lines meet. (With doors, mark the top ends only.)

Make 45° miter cuts at the ends of the moldings. Measure and cut the second vertical molding piece, using the same methods.

Tack each vertical piece in place with two 4d finish nails driven through the casing and into the jamb. Drill pilot holes for the nails to prevent splitting. Do not drive the nails flush at this step.

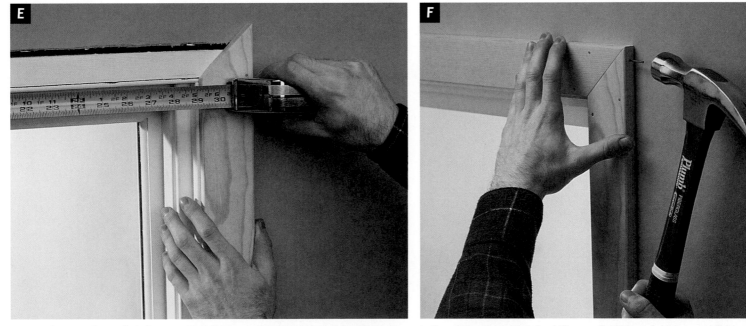

Measure between the vertical pieces, and cut the top and bottom pieces to length, making 45° cuts at the ends. If the joints don't fit well, move the molding pieces slightly, or make new cuts. When all of the pieces fit well, drill pilot holes and attach the casing to the jambs with 4d finish nails, spacing the nails every 12" to 16". Then drive 6d finish nails through the casing near the outer edge and into the wall framing.

Lock-nail the corner joints by drilling a pilot hole and driving a 4d finish nail through each corner, as shown. Drive all nail heads below the wood surface, using a nail set, then fill the nail holes with wood putty.

FLOOR FINISHES

Choosing a Floor Covering

Vinyl Flooring

Vinyl flooring, also known as "resilient flooring," is a versatile, flexible surface that can be used almost anywhere, although it's most often found in kitchens and bathrooms. Vinyl flooring is available in both sheets and tiles, in thicknesses ranging from $1/16$" to $1/8$". Sheets come in 6-ft.-wide or 12-ft.-wide rolls, with either a felt or a PVC backing, depending on the type of installation. Tiles typically come in 12" squares and are available with or without self-adhesive backing.

Installation is easy: Sheet vinyl with felt backing is glued to the floor using the *full-spread* method, meaning the entire project area is covered with adhesive. PVC-backed sheet vinyl is glued only along the edges (*perimeter-bond* method). Tiles are the easiest to install, but because tile floors have a lot of seams, they're less suitable for high-moisture areas. All vinyl flooring must be installed over a smooth underlayment.

Sheet vinyl is priced per square yard; tile is priced per square foot. Cost for either style is comparable to carpet and is less expensive than ceramic tile or hardwood. Prices vary, based on the percentage of vinyl in the material, the thickness of the product, and the complexity of the pattern.

Ceramic Tile

Ceramic tile is a hard, durable, versatile material that's available in a wide variety of sizes, patterns, shapes, and colors. This all-purpose flooring is an excellent choice for high-traffic and high-moisture areas. It's commonly used in bathrooms, entryways, and kitchens.

Common ceramic tiles include unglazed quarry tile, glazed ceramic tile, and porcelain mosaic tile. As an alternative to ceramic, natural-stone tiles are available in several materials, including marble, slate, and granite. Thicknesses for most floor tile range from $3/16$" to $3/4$".

In general, ceramic tile is more expensive than other types of floor coverings, with natural stone tile ranking as the most expensive. And while tile is also more time-consuming to install than other materials, it offers the most flexibility of design.

Floor preparation is critical to the success of a tile installation. In wet areas, such as bathrooms, tile should be laid over a cementboard underlayment that is fastened to the subfloor. All floors that support tile must be stiff and flat to prevent cracking in the tile surface. Tile is installed following a grid-pattern layout and is adhered to the floor with thin-set mortar. The gaps between individual tiles are filled with grout, which should be sealed periodically to prevent staining.

Wood Flooring

Wood floors are resilient and durable, but look warm and elegant. They hold up well in high-traffic areas and are popular in dining rooms, living rooms, and entryways.

Traditional solid-wood planks are the most common type of wood flooring, but there is a growing selection of plywood-backed and synthetic-laminate products (also called *laminated-wood*) that are well suited to do-it-yourself installation. Oak and maple are the most common wood species available, and size options include narrow strips, wide planks, and parquet squares. Most wood flooring has tongue-and-groove construction, which helps to provide a strong, flat surface.

In general, hardwood flooring is slightly less expensive than ceramic tile, and laminated products are typically less expensive than solid hardwood. Most types of wood flooring can be installed directly over a subfloor or sometimes over vinyl flooring. Installation of laminated-wood flooring is easy; it can be glued or nailed down, or "floated" on a foam cushion. Parquet squares typically are glued down. Solid hardwood planks must be nailed—a job for professionals.

Carpet

Carpet is a soft, flexible floor covering that is chosen primarily for comfort rather than durability. It is a popular choice for bedrooms, family rooms, and hallways.

Carpet is made of synthetic or natural fibers bonded to a mesh backing and usually sold in 12-ft.-wide rolls. Some types have a cushioned backing, ready for glue-down installation without pads or strips.

The two basic types of carpeting are *loop-pile*, which is made with uncut loops of yarn to create texture, and *cut-pile*, which has trimmed fibers for a more uniform appearance. Some carpets contain both types. Carpet is similar in price to vinyl flooring, but costs vary depending on density and fiber. Wool is typically more expensive than synthetics.

Installing carpet is not difficult, but it does involve some special tools and techniques. First, tackless strips and padding are installed, then the carpeting is cut and seamed, and secured to the tackless strips.

UNIVERSAL DESIGN

Flooring for Safe & Easy Movement

Choosing the best flooring for everyone usually involves compromise. For example, carpet reduces noise and is safer in case of accidents, but hard flooring is better for wheelchair movement. Here are some tips to consider when weighing your options:

- Floor coverings of different thicknesses can create rough transitions between rooms. Try to keep floor levels consistent, and use low-profile transition strips where necessary.
- Natural-wood floors and solid vinyl flooring with a matte finish may offer the best traction.
- Lightly textured tile is better for wheelchairs than tile with a smooth finish. Avoid wide grout joints with any type of tile.

- Non-slip flooring is best for kitchens and bathrooms. Ask the flooring dealer about the coefficient of friction (should be at least .6).
- Low-pile carpet ($1/4$" to $1/2$") reduces the risk of tripping and provides a better surface for wheelchairs than high-pile carpet.
- Cushion-backed carpet can reduce carpet rippling and drag caused by wheelchairs (see pages 276 to 277).
- Area rugs can be unsafe unless they are secured to the floor.

Preparing for New Flooring

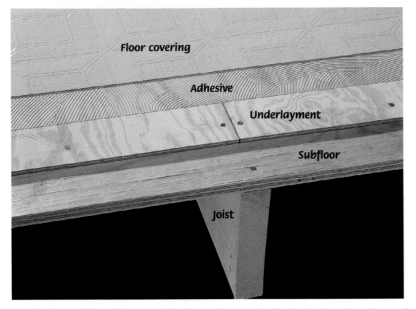

A **typical wood-frame floor** consists of several layers. The floor's structure is made up of *joists*—2 × 10 or larger framing members—and a *subfloor*—plywood or 1 × boards nailed or screwed to the joists. Some floor coverings are installed over an underlayment (see page 246); others are laid directly over the subfloor.

The first step in preparing for a new floor covering is evaluating your old floor. Begin by identifying the existing floor material and the installation method used. Is your sheet vinyl attached using the full-spread method or the perimeter-bond method? Is your carpet glued down or stretched? Next, assess the condition of the floor. Is it securely attached? Is it chipped or cracked? Finally, note the height of the existing floor in relation to adjoining floor surfaces.

Often, a new floor covering or underlayment can be installed on top of existing flooring. If the existing flooring is not sound or smooth, however, you'll have to do some preparation work. Simple modifications to your existing floor may include applying an embossing leveler (see page 246). More complex preparations may involve removing and replacing the underlayment or making spot repairs to the subfloor. Avoid taking shortcuts, as this usually results in an inferior floor.

Warning: Resilient flooring manufactured before 1986 may contain asbestos, which can cause severe lung problems if inhaled. The recommended method for dealing with asbestos-laden flooring is to cover it with an underlayment. If the flooring must be removed, do not do the work yourself. Instead, consult a certified asbestos-abatement contractor.

Tips for Evaluating Floors

Determining the number and type of coverings already on your floor is an important early evaluation step. Too many layers of flooring and underlayment can stress floor joists and ultimately cause a new floor to fail. An easy way to check for old flooring is to remove floor vents.

Measure vertical spaces to make sure enclosed or under-counter appliances will fit once the new underlayment and flooring are installed. Use samples of the new underlayment and floor covering as spacers when measuring.

Check for loose tiles (top), which may indicate widespread failure of the adhesive. If tiles can be pried up easily in several areas of the room, plan on removing all the flooring. Cracks in grout around tile (bottom) indicate movement of the floor covering and possible deterioration of the adhesive.

A Quick Guide for Evaluating Your Existing Floor

Preparing for a new floor can be a simple task or a lengthy, difficult chore, depending on the condition of the existing floor and on your choice of new floor coverings.

The following descriptions summarize the preparation steps for various types of existing floor materials. In some cases, you have several preparation options from which to choose. By carefully considering the options and choosing the most suitable method for your needs, you can avoid wasting time with unnecessary labor. Keep in mind that the goal of any preparation for new flooring is a structurally sound, smooth, and level surface.

Old Resilient (Vinyl) Flooring

Option 1: Your existing resilient floor can serve as the foundation for most new floorings, including resilient flooring, hardwood, or carpet, but only if the existing surface is relatively smooth and sound. Inspect the existing flooring for loose seams, tears, chips, air bubbles, and other areas where the bond has failed. If these loose spots constitute less than 30% of the total area, you can remove the flooring at these spots and fill the voids with floor leveling compound. Then, apply embossing leveler to the entire floor and let it dry before laying new resilient flooring.

Option 2: If the original resilient flooring is suspect, you can install new underlayment over the old surface after repairing obviously loose areas.

Option 3: If you are installing ceramic tile, or if the existing surface is in very poor condition, the old resilient flooring should be removed entirely before you install new flooring. If the old flooring was glued down with full-bond adhesive, it is usually easiest to remove both the flooring and underlayment at the same time. If the old underlayment is removed, you must install new underlayment before laying the new flooring.

Old Ceramic Tile

Option 1: If the existing ceramic tile surface is relatively solid, new flooring usually can be laid directly over the tile. Inspect tiles and joints for cracks and loose pieces. Remove loose material and fill these areas with a floor-leveling compound. If you will be installing resilient flooring, apply an embossing leveler product over the ceramic tile before laying the new flooring. If you will be laying new ceramic tile over the old surface, use an epoxy-based thin-set mortar for better adhesion.

Option 2: If more than 10% of the tiles are loose, remove all the old flooring before installing the new surface. If the tiles don't easily separate from the underlayment, it's best to remove the tile and the underlayment at the same time, then install new underlayment.

Old Hardwood Flooring

Option 1: If you are planning to install carpet, you can usually lay it directly over an existing hardwood floor, provided it is a nailed or glued-down surface. Inspect the flooring and secure any loose areas to the subfloor with spiral-shanked flooring nails, then remove any rotted wood and fill the voids with floor-leveling compound before installing carpet.

Option 2: If you will be installing resilient flooring or ceramic tile over nailed hardwood planks or glued-down wood flooring, you can attach new underlayment over the existing hardwood before installing the new flooring.

Option 3: If the existing floor is a "floating" wood or laminate surface with a foam-pad underlayment, remove it completely before laying any type of new flooring.

Underlayment & Subfloor

Underlayment must be smooth, solid, and level to ensure a long-lasting flooring installation. If the existing underlayment does not meet these standards, remove it and install new underlayment before you lay new flooring.

Before installing new underlayment, inspect the subfloor for chips, open knots, dips, and loose boards. Screw down loose areas, and fill cracks and dips with floor-leveling compound. Remove and replace any water-damaged areas.

Old Carpet

Without exception, carpet must be removed before you install any new flooring. For traditional carpet, simply cut the carpet into pieces, then remove the padding, and the tackless strips if they are damaged. Remove glued-down cushion-back carpet with a floor scraper, using the same techniques as for removing full-bond resilient sheet flooring (see page 239).

Removing Floor Coverings

When old floor coverings must be removed—as is the case with many projects—thorough and careful removal work is essential to the quality of the new flooring installation.

The difficulty of flooring removal depends on the type of floor covering and the method which was used to install it. Carpet and perimeter-bond vinyl are generally quite easy to remove, and vinyl tiles are relatively simple. Full-spread sheet vinyl can be difficult to remove, however, and removing ceramic tile is a lot of work.

With any removal project, be sure to keep your tool blades sharp and avoid damaging the underlayment if you plan to reuse it. If you'll be replacing the underlayment, it may be easier to remove the old underlayment along with the floor covering (see pages 242 to 243).

Tools: Floor scraper, utility knife, spray bottle, wallboard knife, wet/dry vacuum, heat gun, hand maul, masonry chisel, flat pry bar, end-cutting nippers.

Materials: Liquid dishwashing detergent.

Use a floor scraper to remove resilient flooring products and to scrape off leftover adhesives or backings. The long handle provides leverage and force, and it allows you to work in a comfortable standing position. A scraper will remove most flooring, but you may need to use other tools to finish the job.

Removing Sheet Vinyl

A Remove base moldings, if necessary. Use a utility knife to cut old flooring into strips about a foot wide.

B Pull up as much flooring as possible by hand, gripping the strips close to the floor to minimize tearing.

C Cut stubborn sheet vinyl into strips about 5" wide. Starting at a wall, peel up as much of the floor covering as possible. If the felt backing remains, spray a solution of water and liquid dishwashing detergent under the surface layer to help separate the backing. Use a wallboard knife to scrape up particularly stubborn patches.

D Scrape up the remaining sheet vinyl and backing, using a floor scraper. If necessary, spray the backing again with the soap solution to loosen it. Sweep up the debris, then finish the cleanup with a wet/dry vacuum. Tip: Fill the vacuum with about an inch of water to help contain dust.

Removing Vinyl Tiles

Remove base moldings, if necessary. Starting at a loose seam, use a long-handled floor scraper to remove tiles. To remove stubborn tiles, soften the adhesive with a heat gun, then use a wallboard knife to pry up the tile and scrape off the underlying adhesive.

Remove stubborn adhesive or backing by wetting the floor with a water/detergent mixture, then scraping with a floor scraper.

Removing Ceramic Tile

Remove base moldings, if necessary. Knock out tile using a hand maul and masonry chisel. If possible, start in a space between tiles where the grout has loosened. Be careful when working around fragile fixtures, such as drain flanges.

If you plan to reuse the underlayment, use a floor scraper to remove any remaining adhesive. You may have to use a belt sander with a coarse sanding belt to grind off stubborn adhesive.

Removing Carpet

A

Using a utility knife, cut around metal threshold strips to free the carpet. Remove the threshold strips with a flat pry bar.

B

Cut the carpet into pieces small enough to be easily removed. Roll up the carpet and remove it from the room, then remove the padding. NOTE: Padding often is stapled to the floor, and usually will come up in pieces as you roll it up.

C

Using end-cutting nippers or pliers, remove all staples from the floor. TIP: If you plan to lay new carpet, do not remove the tackless strips unless they are damaged.

VARIATION: To remove glued-down carpet, first cut it into strips with a utility knife, then pull up as much material as you can. Scrape up the remaining cushion material and adhesive with a floor scraper.

Remove underlayment and floor covering *as though they were a single layer. This is an effective removal strategy with any floor covering that is bonded to the underlayment.*

Removing Underlayment

Flooring contractors routinely remove the underlayment along with the floor covering before installing new flooring. This saves time and makes it possible to install new underlayment that is ideally suited to the new flooring. Do-it-yourselfers using this technique should make sure they cut flooring into pieces that can be easily handled.

Warning: This floor removal method releases flooring particles into the air. Be sure the flooring you are removing does not contain asbestos (see page 236).

Tools: Goggles, gloves, circular saw with carbide-tipped blade, flat pry bar, reciprocating saw, wood chisel.

TIP: *Examine fasteners to see how the underlayment is attached. Use a screwdriver to expose the heads of the fasteners. If the underlayment has been screwed down, you will need to remove the floor covering and then unscrew the underlayment.*

Removing Underlayment

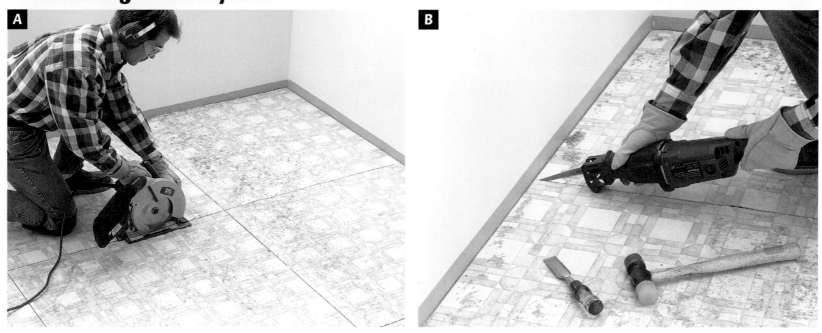

A Remove base moldings, if necessary. Adjust the cutting depth of a circular saw to equal the combined thickness of your floor covering and underlayment (see page 236). Using a carbide-tipped blade, cut the floor covering and underlayment into squares measuring about 3 ft. square. Be sure to wear safety goggles and gloves.

B Use a reciprocating saw to extend cuts close to the edges of walls. Hold the blade at a slight angle to the floor, and try not to damage walls or cabinets. Do not cut deeper than the underlayment. Use a wood chisel to complete cuts near cabinets.

C Separate the underlayment from the subfloor, using a flat pry bar and hammer. Remove and discard the sections of underlayment and floor covering immediately, watching for exposed nails.

VARIATION: If your existing floor is ceramic tile over plywood underlayment, use a hand maul and masonry chisel to chip away the tile along the cutting lines before making the cuts.

Before installing new underlayment and floor covering, refasten any sections of loose subfloor to floor joists using deck screws.

Repairing Subfloors

A solid, securely fastened subfloor minimizes floor movement and squeaks, and it ensures that your new floor covering will last a long time. After removing the old underlayment, inspect the subfloor for loose seams, moisture damage, cracks, and other flaws. If your subfloor is made of dimensional lumber rather than plywood, you can use plywood to patch damaged sections; if the plywood patch does not quite reach the height of the subfloor, use floor leveler to raise its surface to match the surrounding area.

Tools: Trowel, straightedge, framing square, drill, circular saw, cat's paw, wood chisel.

Materials: 2" deck screws, floor leveler, plywood, 2 × 4 lumber, 10d common nails.

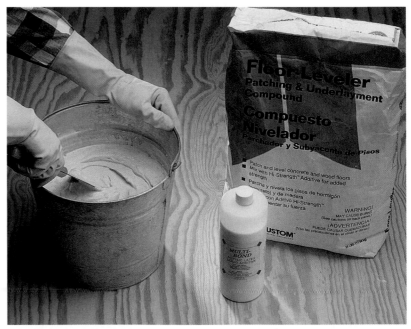

Floor leveler is used to fill in dips and low spots in plywood subfloors. Mix the leveler according to the manufacturer's directions, adding a latex or acrylic additive.

Applying Floor Leveler

A

Mix the leveler according to the manufacturer's directions, then spread it onto the subfloor with a trowel. Build up the leveler in thin layers to avoid overfilling the area.

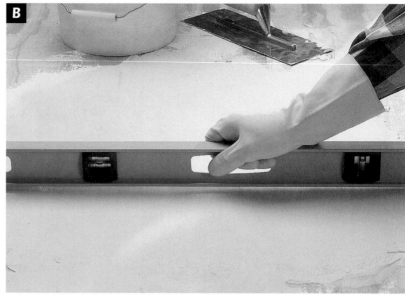

B

Check with a straightedge to make sure the filled area is even with the surrounding area; if necessary, apply more leveler. Allow the leveler to dry, then shave off any ridges with the edge of a trowel, or sand it smooth, if necessary.

Replacing a Section of Subfloor

A

B

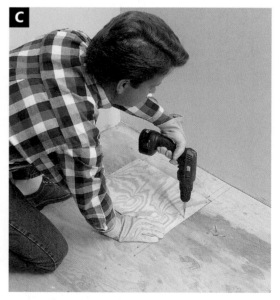

C

Cut out damaged areas of the subfloor. Use a framing square to mark a rectangle around the damage—make sure two sides of the rectangle are centered over floor joists. Remove nails along the lines, using a cat's paw. Make the cut using a circular saw adjusted so the blade cuts through only the subfloor. Use a chisel to complete the cuts near walls.

Remove the damaged section, then nail two 2 × 4 blocks between the joists, centered under the cut edges for added support. If possible, end-nail the blocks from below; otherwise toe-nail them from above, using 10d nails.

Measure the cut-out section, then cut a patch to fit, using material of the same thickness as the original subfloor. Fasten the patch to the joists and blocks, using 2" deck screws spaced about 5" apart.

Installing Underlayment

The type of underlayment you choose depends in part on the type of floor covering you plan to install. For example, ceramic and natural-stone tile floors often require an underlayment that stands up to moisture, such as cementboard. For vinyl flooring, use a quality-grade plywood, since most manufacturers will void their warranties if their flooring is installed over substandard underlayments. Most wood flooring and carpeting do not require underlayment and are often placed directly on a plywood subfloor. If you will use your old flooring as underlayment, apply an embossing leveler to prepare it for the new installation (see below, left).

When installing new underlayment, make sure it is securely attached to the subfloor in all areas, including below all movable appliances. Notch the underlayment to fit room contours. Around door casings and other moldings, you can undercut the moldings and insert the underlayment beneath them.

Plywood is typically used as an underlayment for vinyl flooring and some ceramic tile installations. For vinyl flooring, use ¼" exterior-grade, AC plywood (at least one side perfectly smooth). Wood-based floor coverings, like parquet, can be installed over lower-quality exterior-grade plywood. For ceramic tile, use ½" AC plywood.

Fiber/cementboard is a thin, high-density underlayment used under ceramic tile and vinyl flooring in situations where floor height is a concern. (For installation, follow the steps for cementboard, on page 248.)

Cementboard is used only for ceramic tile (or stone) installations. It remains stable even when exposed to moisture and is therefore the best underlayment to use in areas likely to get wet, such as bathrooms.

Isolation membrane is used to protect ceramic tile installations from movement that may occur on cracked concrete floors. It is used primarily for covering individual cracks with strips of membrane, but it can also be used over an entire floor. Isolation membrane also is available in a liquid form that can be poured over the project area.

Embossing leveler *is a mortar-like substance used for preparing well-adhered resilient flooring or ceramic tile for use as an underlayment. Mix the leveler according to the manufacturer's directions, and spread it thinly over the floor with a flat-edged trowel. Wipe away any excess, making sure all dips and indentations are filled. Work quickly—embossing leveler begins to set in 10 minutes. After the leveler dries, scrape away ridges and high spots with the trowel.*

Tools: Drill, circular saw, wallboard knife, power sander, ¼" notched trowel, straightedge, utility knife, jig saw with carbide blade, ⅛" notched trowel, flooring roller.

Materials: Underlayment, 1" deck screws, floor-patching compound, latex additive, thin-set mortar, 1½" galvanized deck screws, fiberglass-mesh wallboard tape.

Installing Plywood Underlayment

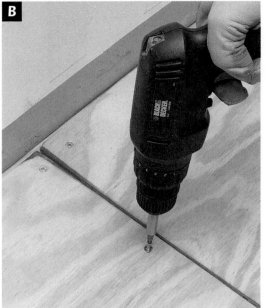

Begin by installing a full sheet of plywood along the longest wall, making sure the underlayment seams will not be aligned with the subfloor seams. Fasten the plywood to the subfloor, using 1" deck screws driven every 6" along the edges and at 8" intervals in the field of the sheet.

Continue fastening sheets of plywood to the subfloor, driving the screw heads slightly below the underlayment surface. Leave ¼" expansion gaps at the walls and between sheets. Offset seams in subsequent rows.

Using a circular saw or jig saw, notch plywood to meet existing flooring in doorways, then fasten the notched sheets to the subfloor.

Mix floor-patching compound and latex or acrylic additive, according to the manufacturer's directions. Then, spread it over seams and screw heads with a wallboard knife.

Let the patching compound dry, then sand the patched areas, using a power sander.

Installing Cementboard

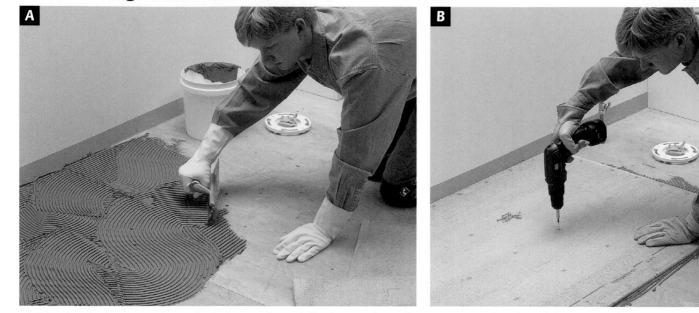

A Mix thin-set mortar (see page 265) according to the manufacturer's directions. Starting at the longest wall, spread the mortar on the subfloor in a figure-eight pattern, using a ¼" notched trowel. Spread only enough mortar for one sheet at a time. Set the cementboard on the mortar with the rough side up, making sure the edges are offset from the subfloor seams.

B Fasten cementboard to subfloor, using 1½" galvanized deck screws driven every 6" along edges and 8" throughout the sheet. Drive the screw heads flush with the surface. Continue spreading mortar and installing sheets along the wall. OPTION: If you are installing fiber/cementboard underlayment, use a ³⁄₁₆" notched trowel to spread the mortar, and drill pilot holes for all screws.

C Cut cementboard pieces as necessary, leaving a ⅛" gap at all joints and a ¼" gap along the room perimeter. For straight cuts, use a utility knife to score a line through the fiber-mesh layer just beneath the surface, then snap the board along the scored line.

D To cut holes, notches, or irregular shapes, use a jig saw with a carbide blade. Continue installing cementboard sheets to cover the entire floor.

E Place fiberglass-mesh wallboard tape over the seams. Use a wallboard knife to apply thin-set mortar to the seams, filling the gaps between sheets and spreading a thin layer of mortar over the tape. Allow the mortar to cure for two days before starting the tile installation.

Installing Isolation Membrane

A Thoroughly clean the subfloor, then apply thin-set mortar (see page 265) with a ⅛" notched trowel. Start spreading the mortar along a wall in a section as wide as the membrane and 8 to 10 ft. long. NOTE: For some membranes, you must use a bonding material other than mortar. Read and follow label directions.

B Roll out the membrane over the mortar. Cut the membrane to fit tightly against the walls, using a straightedge and utility knife.

C Starting in the center of the membrane, use a heavy flooring roller (available at rental centers) to smooth out the surface toward the edges. This frees trapped air and presses out excess bonding material.

D Repeat steps 1 through 3, cutting the membrane as necessary at the walls and obstacles, until the floor is completely covered with membrane. Do not overlap the seams, but make sure they are tight. Allow the mortar to cure for two days before installing the tile.

Installing Vinyl Flooring

Vinyl flooring is available both in sheets and tiles. Sheet vinyl comes in 6- and 12-ft.-wide rolls. Most vinyl tiles are 12" squares, though some manufacturers make 9" square tiles and narrow, 2-ft.-long border strips.

Sheet vinyl is a good choice for bathrooms, kitchens, and other moist locations, since it has few seams for water to seep through; in smaller rooms, you can install sheet vinyl with no seams at all. Vinyl tiles perform best in dry locations, where a floor with many seams is not a liability.

The quality of resilient flooring varies significantly and is based primarily on the amount of vinyl in the material. Solid vinyl is the best and most expensive flooring. The thickness of the flooring also is a good clue to its quality; thicker materials have more vinyl and are therefore more durable.

The most important aspect of a sheet vinyl installation is creating a near-perfect underlayment surface. It's also important to cut the material so it fits perfectly along the contours of a room. Making a cutting template is the best way to ensure that your cuts will be correct (see page 251). When handling sheet vinyl, remember that this product—especially felt-backed—can crease and tear easily if not handled carefully.

Make sure you use the recommended adhesive for the sheet vinyl you are installing. Many manufacturers require that you use their glue to install their flooring products and will void their warranties if you do not follow their directions exactly. Apply adhesive sparingly, using a $1/8$"- or $1/4$"-notched trowel.

To ensure a great-looking vinyl tile installation, carefully position the layout lines. Once those are established, the actual installation of the tile is relatively easy, especially if you are using self-adhesive tile. Before committing to any layout, however, be sure to dry-fit the tiles to identify potential problems.

Tiles with an obvious grain pattern can be laid so the grain of each tile is oriented identically throughout the installation. Or, you can use the quarter-turn method, in which each tile is laid with its pattern grain running perpendicular to that of adjacent tiles (see page 257).

Tools: Utility knife, framing square, compass, scissors, non-permanent felt-tipped pen, linoleum knife, straightedge, $1/4$" V-notched trowel, J-roller, stapler, flooring roller, chalk line, heat gun, $1/16$" V-notched trowel.

Materials: Vinyl flooring, masking tape, heavy butcher's or brown wrapping paper, duct tape, flooring adhesive, $3/8$" staples, metal threshold bars, nails.

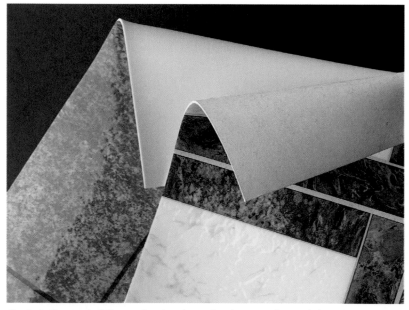

Sheet vinyl comes in full-spread and perimeter-bond types. Full-spread sheet vinyl has a felt-paper backing, and is secured with adhesive that is spread over the floor before installation. Full-spread vinyl flooring bonds tightly to the floor and is unlikely to come loose, but it is more difficult to install and requires a flawlessly smooth and clean underlayment.

Perimeter-bond flooring, identifiable by its smooth, white PVC backing, is laid directly on underlayment and is secured by a special adhesive spread only along the edges and seams. It is easier to install and will tolerate some minor underlayment flaws.

Resilient tile comes in self-adhesive and dry-back styles. Self-adhesive tile has a preapplied adhesive protected by a wax-paper backing that is peeled off as the tiles are installed. Dry-back tile is secured with adhesive spread onto the underlayment before installation.

Self-adhesive tile is easier to install than dry-back tile, but the bond is less reliable. Do not use additional adhesives with self-adhesive tile.

Making a Cutting Template

Place sheets of heavy butcher's or brown wrapping paper along the walls, leaving a ⅛" gap. Cut triangular holes in the paper with a utility knife. Fasten the template to the floor by placing masking tape over the holes.

Follow the outline of the room, working with one sheet of paper at a time. Overlap the edges of adjoining sheets by about 2" and tape the sheets together.

To fit the template around pipes, tape sheets of paper on either side. Measure the distance from the wall to the center of the pipe, and subtract ⅛"

Transfer the measurement to a separate piece of paper. Use a compass to draw the pipe diameter onto the paper, then cut out the hole with scissors or a utility knife. Cut a slit from the edge of the paper to the hole.

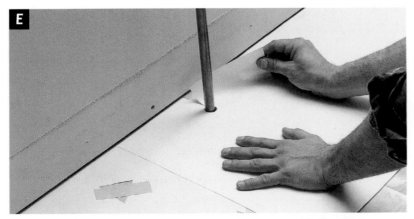

Fit the hole cutout around the pipe. Tape the hole template to the adjoining sheets.

When completed, roll or loosely fold the paper template for carrying.

Installing Perimeter-bond Sheet Vinyl

Unroll the flooring on any large, flat, clean surface. To prevent wrinkles, sheet vinyl comes from the manufacturer rolled with the pattern side out. Unroll the sheet and turn it pattern-side up for marking.

For two-piece installations, overlap the edges of sheets by at least 2". Plan to have the seams fall along the pattern lines or simulated grout joints. Align the sheets so that the pattern matches, then tape the sheets together with duct tape.

Position the paper template over the sheet vinyl, and tape it in place. Trace the outline of the template onto the flooring with a non-permanent felt-tipped pen.

Remove the template. Cut the sheet vinyl with a sharp linoleum knife or a utility knife with a new blade. Use a straightedge as a guide for making longer cuts.

Cut holes for pipes and other permanent obstructions. Then cut a slit from each hole to the nearest edge of the flooring. Whenever possible, make slits along pattern lines.

Roll up flooring loosely and transfer it to the installation area. Do not fold the flooring. Unroll and position the sheet vinyl carefully. Slide the edges beneath undercut door casings.

Cut the seams for two-piece installations, using a straightedge as a guide. Hold the straightedge tightly against the flooring, and cut along the pattern lines through both pieces of vinyl flooring.

Remove both pieces of scrap flooring. The pattern should now run continuously across the adjoining sheets of flooring.

Continued on next page

Installing Perimeter-bond Sheet Vinyl (cont.)

Fold back the edges of both sheets and apply a 3" band of multipurpose flooring adhesive to the underlayment or old flooring, using a ¼" V-notched trowel or wallboard knife.

Lay the seam edges one at a time into the adhesive. Make sure the seam is tight, pressing the gaps together with your fingers, if needed. Roll the seam edges with a J-roller or wallpaper seam roller.

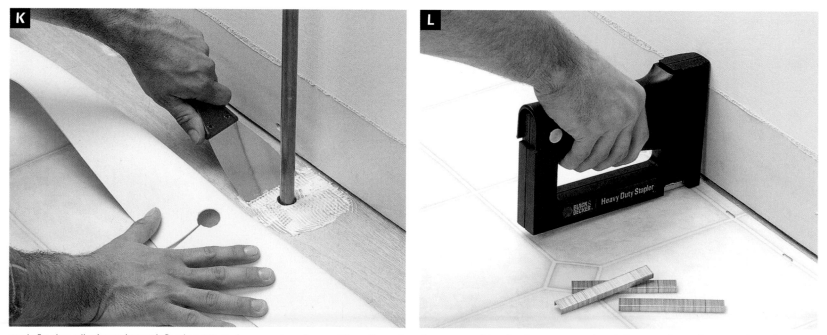

Apply flooring adhesive underneath flooring cuts at pipes or posts and around the entire perimeter of the room. Roll the flooring with the roller to ensure good contact with the adhesive.

If you are applying flooring over a wood underlayment, fasten the outer edges of the sheet with ⅜" staples driven every 3". Make sure the staples will be covered by the base molding.

Installing Full-spread Sheet Vinyl

Cut the sheet vinyl using the techniques described on pages 252 and 253 (steps A through E), then lay the sheet vinyl into position, sliding the edges underneath door casings.

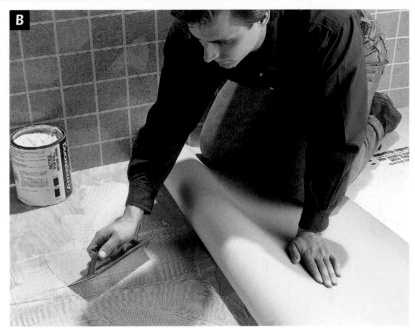

Pull back half of the flooring, then apply a layer of flooring adhesive over the underlayment or old flooring, using a ¼" V-notched trowel. Lay the flooring back onto the adhesive.

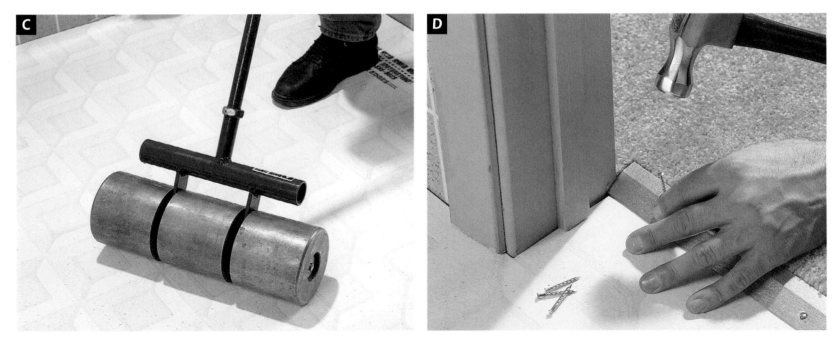

Roll the floor with a heavy flooring roller (available at rental centers), moving toward the edges of the sheet. The roller creates a stronger bond and eliminates air bubbles. Fold over the unbonded section of flooring, apply adhesive, then replace and roll the flooring. Wipe up any adhesive that oozes up around the edges of the vinyl, using a damp rag.

Measure and cut metal threshold bars to fit across doorways, then position each bar over the edge of the vinyl flooring and nail it in place.

Establishing Perpendicular Reference Lines for a Tile Installation

Position a reference line (X) by measuring between opposite sides of the room and marking the center of each side. Snap a chalk line between these marks.

Measure and mark the centerpoint of the chalk line. From this point, use a framing square to establish a second line perpendicular to the first. Snap a second reference line (Y) across the room.

Check for squareness using the "3-4-5 triangle" method. Measure and mark one reference line 3 ft. from the centerpoint on line X. Measure and mark another reference line 4 ft. from the centerpoint on line Y.

Measure the distance between the marks. If the reference lines are perpendicular, the distance will measure exactly 5 ft. If not, adjust the reference lines until they are exactly perpendicular to each other.

Installing Self-adhesive Vinyl Tile

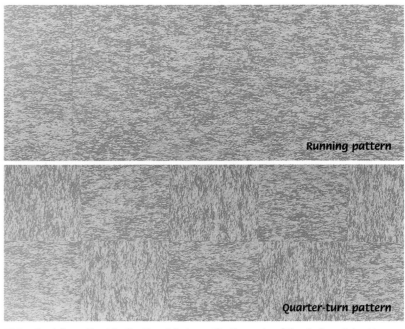

Running pattern

Quarter-turn pattern

Mark perpendicular reference lines (see page 256), and establish the final layout for the tile by dry-fitting full tiles along both reference lines. If you want to adjust the layout to make it visually symmetrical or to reduce tile cutting, create new layout lines parallel to the existing reference lines. Make sure the new lines are perpendicular to each other. To avoid confusion, use chalk of a different color to make the new lines.

TIP: Check for noticeable directional features, like the grain of the vinyl particles. You can choose to set the tile in a running pattern so the directional feature runs in the same direction (top), or you can set the tiles in a checkerboard pattern, called the quarter-turn method (bottom).

Peel off the paper backing and install the first tile in one of the corners formed by the intersecting layout lines. Lay three or more tiles along each layout line in the quadrant. Rub the entire surface of each tile to bond the adhesive to the floor underlayment.

Begin installing tiles in the interior area of the quadrant, keeping the joints tight between tiles. Finish setting full tiles in the first quadrant, then set the full tiles in an adjacent quadrant. Set the tiles along the layout lines first, then fill in the interior tiles.

Continued on next page

Installing Self-adhesive Vinyl Tile (cont.)

D

NOTE: **Cut tiles shown inverted for clarity; tiles should be faceup for marking.**

Cut tiles to fit against the walls. First, lay the tile to be cut (A) faceup on top of the last full tile you installed. Position a ⅛"-thick spacer against the wall, then set a marker tile (B) on top of the tile to be cut. The uncovered portion of the tile to be cut will be the part you install. Trace along the edge of the marker tile to draw a cutting line.

TIP: *To mark tiles for cutting around outside corners, first make a cardboard template to match the space, with a ⅛" gap along the walls. After cutting the template, check to make sure it fits. Place the template on a tile, and trace its outline.*

E

Cut the tile to fit, using a straightedge and a utility knife. Hold the straightedge securely against the cutting lines to ensure a straight cut. You can also use a ceramic-tile cutter (see page 266) to make straight cuts in thick vinyl tiles.

TIP: *Make curved cuts in thick, rigid resilient tile by heating the back of the tile with a heat gun first, then cutting it while it's still warm.*

Install cut tiles next to the walls. Tɪᴘ: For efficiency, you can precut all tiles, but first measure the distance between the wall and installed tiles at various points to make sure the variation does not exceed ½". Continue installing tile in the remaining working quadrants until the room is completely covered. Check the entire floor, and if you find loose areas, press down on the tiles to bond them to the underlayment. Install metal threshold bars at project borders where the new floor joins another floor covering (see page 255).

Installing Dry-back Vinyl Tile

Make perpendicular reference lines (see page 256), and dry-lay tiles to establish the final layout (see step A, page 257). Apply adhesive around the intersection of the layout lines, using a trowel with ¹⁄₁₆" V-shaped notches. Hold the trowel at a 45° angle, and spread adhesive evenly over the surface.

Spread adhesive over most of the installation area, covering three quadrants. Allow the adhesive to set according to the manufacturer's instructions, then begin to install the tile at the intersection of the layout lines. (You can kneel on installed tiles to lay additional tiles.) When one quadrant is completely tiled, spread adhesive over the remaining quadrants, then finish setting the tile.

Installing a Floor–warming System

Ceramic tile is a great floor covering, but it comes with one significant drawback: It can be cold on bare feet. An easy way to remedy this problem is to install a floor-warming system.

A typical floor-warming system consists of one or more thin mats containing electric resistance wires that heat up when energized—like an electric blanket. The mats are installed underneath the floor tile and are hard-wired to a 120-volt GFCI circuit. A thermostat controls the floor temperature, and a timer turns the system on or off automatically. Floor-warming systems require very little energy to run and are designed to heat floors only; they generally are not used as sole heat sources for rooms.

The system shown in this project includes two plastic-mesh mats, each with its own power lead that is wired directly to the thermostat. The mats are laid over a concrete floor and then covered with thin-set adhesive and ceramic tile. If your project involves a wood subfloor, install cementboard (see page 248) before laying the mats.

A crucial part of installing this system is to perform several resistance checks to make sure the heating wires have not been damaged during shipping or during the installation.

Electrical service required for a floor-warming system is based on its size. A smaller system may connect to an existing GFCI circuit, but a larger system will need a dedicated circuit; check with the manufacturer for requirements. The Wiring section of this book can help you with installing electrical boxes, running circuit cable, and making basic connections. If you're installing a new circuit, you'll probably want to hire an electrician to make the connection at the service panel.

To order a floor-warming system, contact the manufacturer or dealer. In most cases, you can send them plans of your project area, and they'll custom-fit a system for your project.

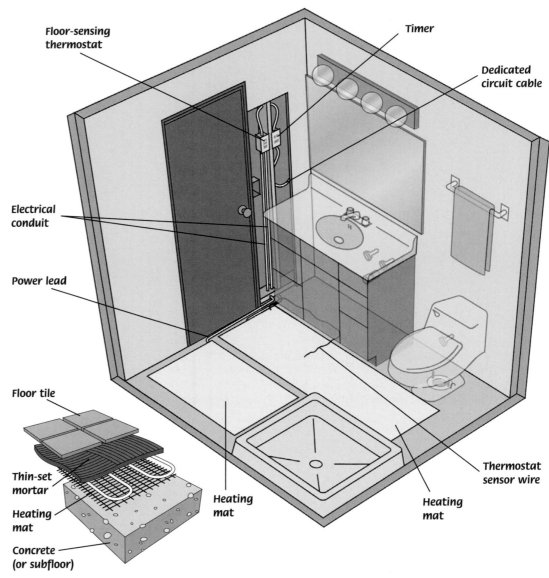

Tools: Multi-tester, drill, plumb bob, chisel, tubing cutter, combination tool, vacuum, chalk line, grinder, glue gun, fish tape, aviation snips, $\frac{3}{8}$" × $\frac{1}{4}$" square-notched trowel, tile tools (see page 265).

Materials: Floor-warming system, $2\frac{1}{2}$ × 4" double-gang electrical box with 4" adapter cover, $2\frac{1}{2}$"-deep single-gang electrical box, $\frac{1}{2}$"dia. thin-wall conduit, setscrew fittings, 12-gauge NM cable, cable clamps, double-sided tape, electrical tape, insulated cable clamps, wire connectors, tile materials (see page 264).

Floor-warming systems *must be installed on a circuit with adequate amperage and a GFCI breaker (some systems have built-in GFCIs). Smaller systems may tie into an existing circuit but larger ones often need a dedicated circuit. Follow all local building and electrical codes that apply to your project.*

Installing a Floor-warming System

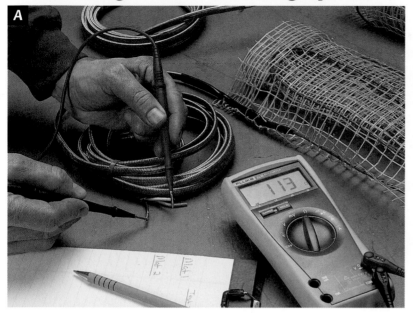

Check the resistance value (OHM) of each heating mat, using a digital multi-tester. Record the reading. Compare your reading to the factory-tested reading noted by the manufacturer. Your reading must fall within the acceptable range determined by the manufacturer. If it does not, the mat has been damaged and should not be installed; contact the manufacturer for assistance.

Install the electrical boxes for the thermostat and timer at an accessible location. Remove the wall surface to expose the framing. Locate the boxes approximately 60" from the floor, making sure the power leads of the heating mats will reach the double-gang electrical box. Mount a 2½"-deep × 4"-wide double-gang electrical box (for the thermostat) to the wall stud closest to the determined location, and a single-gang electrical box (for the timer) on the other side of the stud.

Use a plumb bob or level to mark points on the bottom wall plate, directly below the two knockouts on the thermostat box. At each mark, drill a ½" hole down through the top of the plate. Then, drill two more holes as close as possible to the floor through the side of the plate, intersecting the top holes. The holes will be used for routing the power leads and thermostat sensor wire. Clean up the holes with a chisel to ensure smooth routing.

Cut two lengths of ½" thin-wall electrical conduit to fit between the thermostat box and the bottom plate, using a tube cutter. Place the bottom end of each conduit about ¼" into a hole in the bottom plate, and fasten the top end to the thermostat box, using a setscrew fitting. NOTE: If you are installing three or more mats, use ¾" conduit instead of ½".

Continued on next page

Installing a Floor-warming System (cont.)

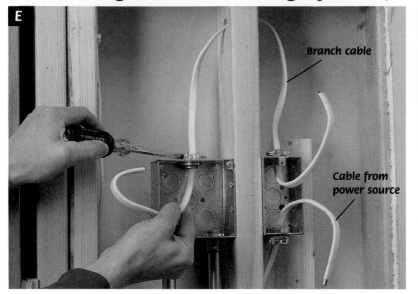

Run 12-gauge NM electrical cable from the service panel (power source) to the timer box. Attach the cable to the box with a cable clamp, leaving 8" of extra cable extending from the box. Drill a ⅝" hole through the center of the stud, about 12" above the boxes. Run a short branch cable from the timer box to the thermostat box, securing both ends with clamps. The branch cable should make a smooth curve where it passes through the stud.

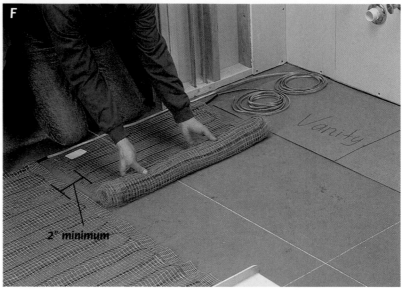

Vacuum the floor thoroughly. Plan the ceramic tile layout and snap reference lines for the tile installation (see pages 256 to 257). Spread the heating mats onto the floor with the power leads closest to the electrical boxes. Position the mats 3" to 6" away from walls, showers, bathtubs, and toilet flanges. You can lay the mats into the kick space of a vanity but not under the vanity cabinet or over expansion joints in the concrete slab. Set the edges of the mats close together, but do not overlap them: The heating wires in one mat must be at least 2" from the wires in the neighboring mat.

Confirm that the power leads still reach the thermostat box. Then, secure the mats to the floor using strips of double-sided tape spaced every 2 ft. Make sure the mats are lying flat with no wrinkles or ripples. Press down firmly to secure the mats to the tape.

Create recesses in the floor for the connections between the power leads and the heating-mat wires, using a grinder or a cold chisel and hammer. These insulated connections are too thick to lay under the tile and must be recessed to within ⅛" of the floor. Clean away any debris, and secure the connections in the recesses with a bead of hot glue.

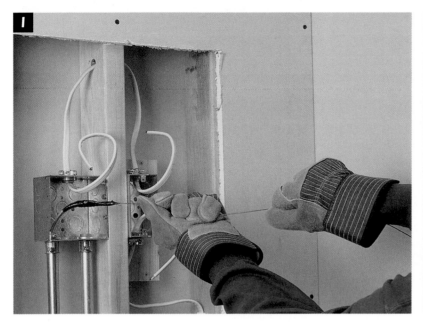

Thread a steel fish tape down one of the conduits, and attach the ends of the power leads to the fish tape, using electrical tape. Pull the fish tape and leads up through the conduit. Disconnect the fish tape, and secure the leads to the box with insulated cable clamps. Use aviation snips or linesman's pliers to cut off excess from the leads, leaving 8" extending from the clamps.

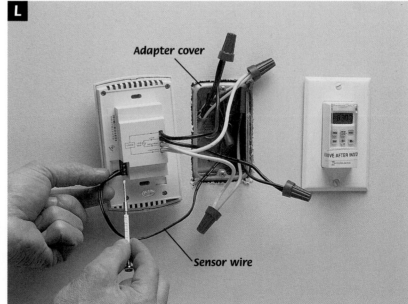

Feed the heat sensor wire down through the remaining conduit and weave it into the mesh of the nearest mat. Use dabs of hot glue to secure the sensor wire directly between two blue resistance wires, extending it 6" to 12" into the mat. Test the resistance of the heating mats with a multi-tester (see step A, page 261) to make sure the resistance wires have not been damaged. Record the reading.

Install the floor tile as directed on pages 264 to 271. Use thin-set mortar as an adhesive, and spread it carefully over the floor and mats with a ⅜" × ¼" square-notched trowel. Check the resistance of the mats periodically during the tile installation. If a mat becomes damaged, clean up any exposed mortar and contact the manufacturer. When the installation is complete, check the resistance of the mats once again and record the reading.

Adapter cover

Sensor wire

Install an adapter cover ("mud ring") to the thermostat box, then patch the wall opening with wallboard (see pages 196 to 202). Complete the wiring connections for the thermostat and timer, following the manufacturer's instructions. Attach the sensor wire to the thermostat setscrew connection. Apply the manufacturer's wiring labels to the thermostat box and service panel. Mount the thermostat and timer. Complete the circuit connection at the service panel or branch connection. After the flooring materials have fully cured, test the system.

Installing Ceramic Floor Tile

Tile flooring should be durable and slip-resistant. Look for *floor* tile that is textured or soft-glazed—for slip resistance—and has a Class or Group rating of 3, 4, or 5—for strength. Floor tile also should be glazed for protection from staining. If you use unglazed tile, be sure to seal it properly after installation. Standard grouts need stain-protection, too. Mix your grout with a latex additive, and apply a grout sealer after the new grout sets, then reapply the sealer once a year thereafter.

Successful tile installation involves careful preparation of the floor and the proper combination of materials. For an underlayment, cementboard (or the thinner fiber/cementboard) is the best for use over wood subfloors, since it is stable and resists moisture (see pages 246 and 248). However, in rooms where moisture isn't a factor, plywood is an adequate underlayment. The most common adhesive for floor tile is called *thin-set*, which comes as a dry powder that is mixed with water. Premixed organic adhesives generally are not recommended for floors.

Ceramic tile installations start with the same steps as vinyl tile projects: snapping perpendicular layout lines and dry-laying tiles for best placement (see pages 256 to 257). If you want to install trim tiles, consider their placement as you plan the layout. Some base-trim tile is set on the floor, with its finished edge flush with the field tile; other types are installed on top of the field tile, after the field tile is laid and grouted (see page 271).

Trim and finishing materials for tile installations include base-trim tiles (A), which fit around the room perimeter, and bull-nose tiles (B), used at doorways and other transition areas. Doorway thresholds (C) are made from synthetic materials as well as natural materials, such as marble, and come in thicknesses ranging from ¼" to ¾" to match different floor levels. The most long-lasting thresholds are made from solid-surface mineral products. If the threshold is too long for the doorway, cut it to fit with a jig saw or circular saw and a tungsten-carbide blade.

Tools: Chalk line, ¼" square-notched trowel, rubber mallet, tile-cutting tools (see pages 266 to 267), needlenose pliers, utility knife, grout float, grout sponge, buff rag, foam brush.

Materials: Tile, thin-set mortar, tile spacers, 2 × 4, threshold material, grout, latex additive (mortar and grout), grout sealer, silicone caulk.

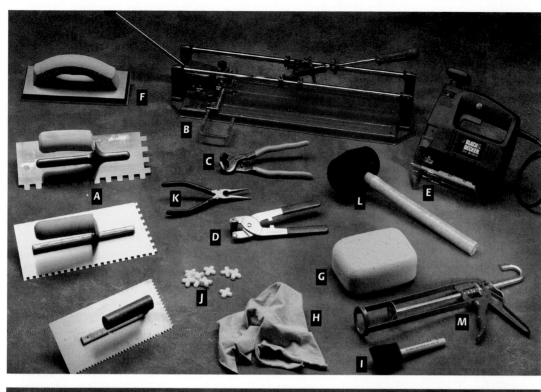

Tile tools include adhesive-spreading tools, cutting tools, and grouting tools. Notched trowels (A) for spreading mortar come with notches of varying sizes and shapes; the size of the notch should be proportional to the size of the tile being installed. Cutting tools include a tile cutter (B), tile nippers (C), hand-held tile cutter (D), and jig saw with carbide blade (E). Grouting tools include a grout float (F); grout sponge (G); buff rag (H); and foam brush (I), for applying grout sealer. Other tile tools include spacers (J), available in different sizes to create grout joints of varying widths; needlenose pliers (K), for removing spacers; rubber mallet (L), for setting tiles into mortar; and caulk gun (M).

Tile materials include adhesives, grouts, and sealers. Thin-set mortar (A), the most common floor-tile adhesive, is often strengthened with latex mortar additive (B). Grout additive (C) can be added to floor grout (D) to make it more resilient and durable. Grout fills the spaces between tiles and is available in pretinted colors to match your tile. Silicone caulk (E) should be used in place of grout where tile meets another surface, like a bathtub. Use wall-tile adhesive (F) for installing base-trim tile. Grout sealer (G) and porous-tile sealer (H) ward off stains and make maintenance easier.

Thin-set mortar is prepared by adding liquid, a little at a time, to the dry powder and stirring the mixture to achieve a creamy consistency. Some mortars include a latex additive in the dry mix, but with others you'll need to add liquid latex additive when you prepare the mortar.

Cutting Tile: Tile Cutter

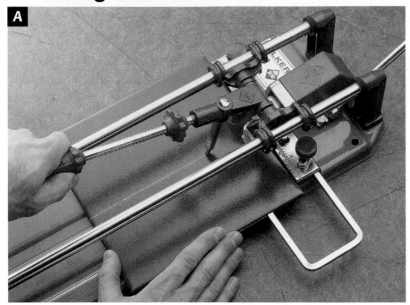

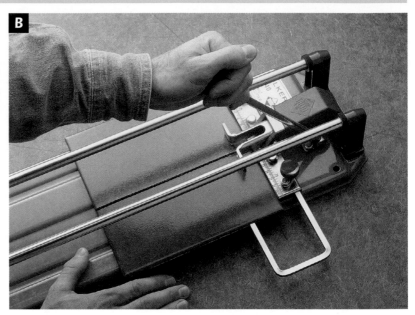

Mark a cutting line on the tile with a pencil, then place the tile in the cutter so the cutting wheel is directly over the line. While pressing down firmly on the wheel handle, run the wheel across the tile to score the surface. For a clean cut, score the tile only once.

Snap the tile along the scored line, as directed by the tool manufacturer. Usually, snapping the tile is accomplished by depressing a lever on the tile cutter.

Cutting Tile: Power Saws

Tile saws (also called "wet saws" because they use water to cool blades and tiles) are used primarily for cutting natural-stone tiles. They are also useful for quickly cutting notches in all kinds of hard tile. Wet saws are available for rent at tile dealers and rental shops.

To make square notches, clamp the tile down on a worktable, then use a jig saw with a tungsten-carbide blade to make the cuts. If you need to cut many notches, a wet saw is more efficient. You can also make square notches using a rod saw (see page 209).

Cutting Tile: Curved Cuts

A

Mark a cutting line on the tile face, then use the scoring wheel of a hand-held tile cutter to score the cut line. Make several parallel scores, no more than ¼" apart, in the waste portion of the tile.

B

Use tile nippers to nibble away the scored portion of the tile. TIP: To cut circular holes in the middle of a tile (step G, page 269), first score and cut the tile so it divides the hole in two, using the straight-cut method, then use the curved-cut method to remove waste material from each half of the circle. To cut a hole through a whole tile, see below.

Cutting Tile: Specialty Cuts

To cut mosaic tiles, use a tile cutter to score tiles in the row where the cut will occur. Cut away excess strips of mosaics from the sheet, using a utility knife, then use a hand-held tile cutter to snap tiles one at a time. NOTE: Use tile nippers to cut narrow portions of tiles after scoring.

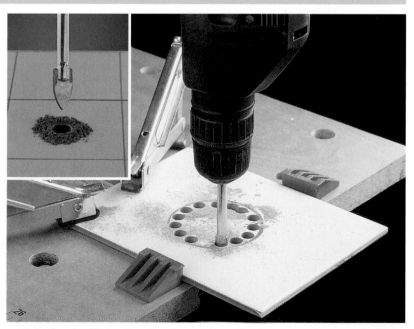

Cut holes for plumbing stub-outs and other obstructions by marking the outline on the tile, then drilling around the edges, using a ceramic tile bit (inset). Gently knock out the waste material with a hammer. The rough edges of the hole will be covered by protective plates on fixtures (called "escutcheons").

Installing Ceramic Floor Tile

A

Draw reference lines and establish the tile layout (see pages 256 to 257). Mix a batch of thin-set mortar, and spread the mortar evenly against both reference lines of one quadrant, using a ¼" square-notched trowel. Use the notched edge of the trowel to create furrows in the mortar bed. NOTE: For large or uneven tiles, you may need a trowel with ⅜" or larger notches.

B

Set the first tile in the corner of the quadrant where the reference lines intersect. TIP: When setting tiles that are 8" square or larger, twist each tile slightly as you set it into position.

C

Using a soft rubber mallet, gently rap the central area of each tile a few times to set it evenly into the mortar.

VARIATION: For mosaic sheets, use a ³⁄₁₆" V-notched trowel to spread the mortar, and use a grout float to press the sheets into the mortar. Apply pressure gently to avoid creating an uneven surface.

D

To ensure consistent spacing between tiles, place plastic tile spacers at corners of the set tile. NOTE: With mosaic sheets, use spacers equal to the gaps between tiles.

Position and set adjacent tiles into the mortar along the reference lines. Make sure the tiles fit neatly against the spacers. To make sure the tiles are level with one another, lay a straight piece of 2 × 4 across several tiles, and rap the board with a mallet. Lay tile in the remaining area covered with mortar. Repeat steps A through E, continuing to work in small sections, until you reach walls or fixtures.

Measure and mark tiles for cutting to fit against walls and into corners (see page 258). Cut the tiles to fit. Apply thin-set mortar directly to the back of the cut tiles, instead of the floor, using the notched edge of the trowel to furrow the mortar. Set the tiles.

Measure, cut, and install tiles requiring notches or curves to fit around obstacles, such as exposed pipes or toilet drains.

Remove the spacers with needlenose pliers before the mortar hardens. TIP: Inspect the tile joints and remove high spots of mortar that could show through the grout, using a utility knife or small screwdriver. Install tile in the remaining quadrants, completing one quadrant at a time.

Install threshold material in doorways. Set the threshold in thin-set mortar so the top is even with the tile. Keep the same space between the threshold as between tiles. Let the mortar cure for at least 24 hours.

Continued on next page

Installing Ceramic Floor Tile (cont.)

Mix a small batch of grout, following the manufacturer's directions. TIP: For unglazed or stone tile, add a release agent to prevent the grout from bonding to the tile surfaces. Starting in a corner, pour the grout over the tile. Use a rubber grout float to spread the grout outward from the corner, pressing firmly on the float to completely fill the joints. For best results, tilt the float at a 60° angle to the floor and use a figure-eight motion.

Use the grout float to remove excess grout from the surface of the tile. Wipe diagonally across the joints, holding the float in a near-vertical position. Continue applying grout and wiping off excess until about 25 sq. ft. of the floor has been grouted.

Remove excess grout by wiping a damp grout sponge diagonally over about 2 sq. ft. of the tile at a time. Rinse the sponge in cool water between wipes. Wipe each area only once; repeated wiping can pull grout from the joints. Repeat steps J through L to apply grout to the rest of the floor. Allow the grout to dry for about 4 hours, then use a soft cloth to buff the tile surface and remove any remaining grout film.

After the grout has cured completely (check the manufacturer's instructions), apply grout sealer to the grout lines, using a small sponge brush or sash brush. Avoid brushing sealer on the tile surfaces. Wipe up any excess sealer immediately.

Installing Base and Trim Tile

Dry-fit the trim tiles to determine the best spacing (grout lines in base tile do not always align with grout lines in the floor tile). Use rounded bullnose tiles at outside corners, and mark tiles for cutting as needed.

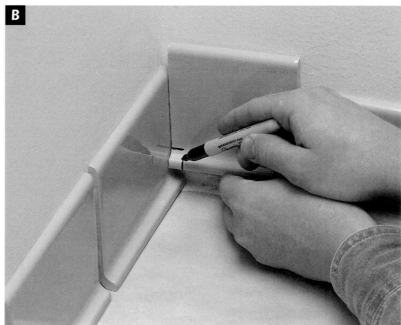

Leaving a ⅛" expansion gap between tiles at corners, mark any contour cuts necessary to allow the coved edges to fit together. Use a jig saw with a tungsten-carbide blade to make curved cuts.

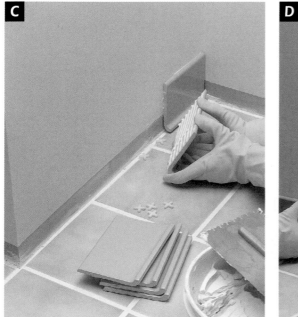

Begin installing base-trim tiles at an inside corner. Use a notched trowel to apply wall-tile adhesive to the back of each tile. Slip ⅛" spacers under the tiles to create an expansion joint. Set the tiles by pressing them firmly onto the wall.

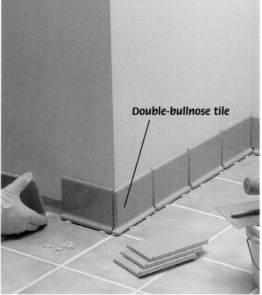

Double-bullnose tile

At outside corners, use a double-bullnose tile on one side, to cover the edge of the adjoining tile.

After the adhesive dries, grout the vertical joints between tiles, and apply grout along the tops of the tiles to make a continuous grout line. After the grout cures, fill the expansion joint at the bottom of the tiles with silicone caulk.

Installing Laminated-wood Flooring

Wood flooring has undeniable appeal, but a traditional solid-hardwood plank floor is expensive and difficult to install. Fortunately, there's a host of laminated-wood products now available that are designed for do-it-yourself installation. These products offer the strength, durability, and attractiveness of traditional wood flooring along with some added benefits.

Laminated-wood flooring is commonly available in two types: *wood laminates* and *plastic laminates*. Both types are designed and prefinished to resist dents, scratches, stains, and fading. They're also easy to clean and should never need sanding or waxing.

Wood laminates are made with layers of solid lumber (similar to plywood) with a top layer of real wood veneer. They're available in 3- and 5-ply tongue-and-groove strips or planks. Wood laminates have a tough polyurethane or acrylic finish, which protects the floor, but many of these products can be

sanded and refinished if necessary.

There are several options for installing laminated-wood flooring. It can be nailed to a wood subfloor, glued down, or "floated" over a subfloor or an existing floor covering. A floating floor starts with a layer of foam backing that is laid over the subfloor. The individual strips or planks are then glued together to form a solid layer that "floats" on top of the foam.

Plastic laminate flooring is made of hardboard or fiberboard topped with a photographic image of wood or stone or a solid color or pattern. These products come in tongue-and-groove tiles, strips, planks, and in specialty trim and transition pieces. Plastic laminates tend to be thinner than wood laminates, which adds less height to a floor. However, be aware that some plastic laminates are not recommended for wet areas.

As for installation, plastic laminate tiles

should be glued down, while panels and strips can be glued down or floated. During installation, strap clamps are often used to bring joints together (check with the manufacturer).

Parquet flooring is another type of laminated-wood flooring. This usually comes in 12" squares made from small strips of solid wood. Parquet flooring is installed with adhesive, using the same installation strategy used for vinyl tile (see pages 256 to 259).

Tools: Chalk line, circular saw, cutting guide, coping saw or jig saw, power miter saw (optional), 1/8" notched trowel, hardwood-flooring tool bar (optional), mallet, flooring roller.

Materials: Flooring, flooring adhesive, wood glue, cardboard, foam backing, scissors, masking tape, 1/2" plywood scraps.

Fiberboard   **Plywood**   **Parquet**

Laminated-wood flooring materials include: fiberboard surfaced with a synthetic laminate layer that mimics the look of wood grain (left), plywood topped with a thin hardwood veneer (center), and parquet tiles made of hardwood strips bonded together in a decorative pattern (right).

Tips for Cutting Wood Flooring

Ripcut wood planks from the back side to avoid splintering the top surface. Measure the distance from the wall to the edge of the last board installed, subtracting ½" to allow for an expansion gap. Transfer the measurement to the back of the flooring, and mark the cut with a chalk line.

Place another piece of flooring next to the piece marked for cutting to provide a stable surface for the foot of the saw. Also, clamp a cutting guide to the planks at the correct distance from the cutting line to ensure a straight cut.

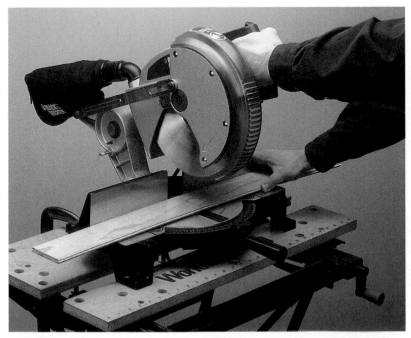

Crosscut wood planks on a power miter box, with the top surface of the planks facing up to prevent splintering. To make crosscuts with a circular saw, cut with the finished side of the planks facing down.

Make notched or curved cuts in wood flooring with a coping saw or jig saw. If you're using a jig saw, the finished surface of the flooring should face down if you have an *up-cutting* blade; up if you have a *down-cutting* blade.

Installing Wood Strip Flooring with Adhesive

Establish a straight layout line by snapping a chalk line parallel to the longest wall, about 30" from the wall. Kneel in this space to begin the flooring installation.

Apply flooring adhesive to the subfloor on the other side of the layout line using a ⅛" notched trowel, following the manufacturer's directions. Cover only a limited area, so that you can install and roll the flooring within 3 hours (see step H).

Apply wood glue to the grooved end of each piece as you install it. The glue will help the end joints stay tight—do not apply glue to the long sides of the boards.

Install the first row of flooring with the edge of the tongues directly over chalk line. Make sure the end joints are tight; wipe up any excess glue immediately. At walls, leave a ½" space to allow for expansion of the wood. This gap will be covered by the baseboard and base shoe.

For succeeding rows, insert the tongue of each strip into the grooves of the strips in the preceding row, and pivot the strip down into the adhesive. Gently slide the tongue-and-groove ends together. Make sure the end-joints are staggered from one row to another. TIP: At walls, you can use a hammer and a hardwood-flooring tool bar to draw together the joints on the last strip (inset).

F

After you've installed three or four rows, use a mallet and a scrap of flooring to tap boards together, closing up the seams. All joints should fit tightly.

G

Use a cardboard template to fit boards in irregular areas. Cut the cardboard to match the space, and allow for a ½" expansion gap next to the walls. Trace the template outline onto a board, then cut it to fit, using a jig saw.

H

Continue laying strips over the glued area, then bond the flooring by rolling it with a heavy flooring roller (available at rental centers). Roll the flooring within 3 hours of applying the adhesive. Install the remaining sections of flooring.

Installing a Floating Plank Floor

A

Roll out the foam backing recommended by the manufacturer. Cut it in strips to fit the room, and arrange the strips with their edges adjoining but not overlapped. Secure all the seams with masking tape.

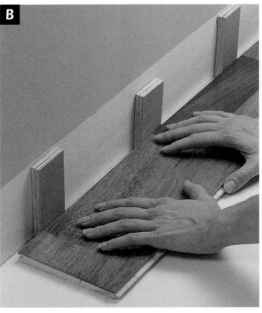

B

Cut spacers from ½"-thick plywood, and place them about every 8" along the longest wall. Lay the first row of flooring, setting the grooved edges of the planks against the spacers. Leave the spacers in place until the job is completed.

C

Join the planks by applying wood glue to the grooved edges and ends of each plank. Complete the installation, using the same method used for glue-down flooring (steps E through G).

Installing Carpet

For beginners, laying carpet can be a time-consuming job, but as you gain confidence using the specialty tools and techniques, the work becomes much easier. For best results, read through this entire project (see pages 276 to 295) before you begin.

Careful planning and layout are critical steps for carpet installation. In large rooms where you might join together several pieces of carpet, a proper layout ensures that the seams will be invisible and fall in low-traffic areas.

Most installations require that you stretch the carpet with specialty tools, using a carefully planned stretching sequence. If you've had little experience laying carpet, practice seaming, stretching, and trimming techniques on scrap pieces before starting the installation.

Have a helper on hand for the initial stages of your project, when you will be moving the heavy rolls of carpet into position and cutting them. Once the carpet is roughly in place, you can easily finish the project on your own.

For a one-piece carpet installation in a room narrower than the carpet roll, it's usually easiest to roll out the carpet in a more spacious area, such as in a basement or on a driveway, then loosely fold it lengthwise to move it into the project area.

Be sure to use the proper pad for your carpeting and application, and secure it as recommended. (The free pad you receive with your carpeting may not be the pad recommended by the carpet manufacturer.) Check the carpet's label for warranty information and pad recommendations.

This carpeting project demonstrates how to install standard wall-to-wall carpet. Installing cushion-backed carpet is somewhat different: It is cut and seamed like standard carpet but is not stretched and does not require tackless strips. Instead, it is laid using the full-bond adhesive method (see page 255).

Installing Carpet: A Step-by-Step Overview

Install carpet transitions at doorways or where the new carpet will meet other floor coverings (see pages 284 to 285).

Install tackless strips around the perimeter of the room for securing the carpet, then roll out the carpet pad, cut it to fit, and staple it to the floor (see pages 286 to 287).

Roll out the carpet and rough-cut it to fit the dimensions of the room. Where necessary, join pieces of carpet with hot-glue seam tape (see pages 288 to 291).

Use a power stretcher and knee kicker to stretch the carpet and attach it to the tackless strips, then trim excess carpet along the edges (see pages 292 to 294).

Buying and Estimating Carpet

When choosing carpet, consider more than just color and pattern. The material used and the construction can affect a carpet's durability: In high-traffic areas, such as hallways, a top-quality fiber will result in longer wear.

Carpet construction—the way in which the fibers are attached to the backing—affects both durability and appearance. The available widths of a certain carpet may also affect your decision, because a roll that's wide enough to cover a room eliminates the need for seaming. When seaming is unavoidable, calculate the total square footage to be covered, then add 20% for trimming and seaming.

The type of carpet you choose will dictate the type of pad you should use; always check carpet-sample labels for the manufacturer's recommendations. Because carpet and padding work together to create a floor-covering system, it makes sense to use the best pad you can afford. In addition to making your carpet feel more plush underfoot, the pad makes your floor quieter and warmer. A high-quality pad also helps reduce carpet wear.

Labels on the back of samples usually tell you the fiber composition, the available widths (usually 12 or 15 ft.), what anti-stain treatments and other finishes were applied, and details of the product warranty.

Carpet padding comes in several varieties, including: bonded urethane foam (A), cellular sponge rubber (B), grafted prime foam (C), and prime urethane (D). Bonded urethane padding is suitable for low-traffic areas, and prime urethane and grafted prime foam are better for high-traffic areas. Generally, cut pile, cut-and-loop, and high-level loop carpets perform best with prime or bonded urethane or rubber pads that are less than 7/16" thick. For berbers or other stiff-backed carpets, use 3/8"-thick bonded urethane foam or cellular sponge rubber. Foam padding is graded by density: the denser the foam, the better the pad. Rubber padding is graded by weight: the heavier, the better.

Tips for Evaluating Carpet

Consider fiber composition when selecting a carpet, and choose materials with characteristics suited for your application.

Fiber Type	Characteristics
Nylon	Easy to clean, very durable, good stain resistance; colors sometimes fade in direct sunlight.
Polyester	Excellent stain resistance, very soft in thick cut-pile constructions; colors don't fade in sunlight.
Olefin	Virtually stain- and fade-proof, resists moisture and static; not as resilient as nylon or as soft as polyester.
Acrylic	Resembles wool in softness and look, good moisture resistance; less durable than other synthetics.
Wool	Luxurious look and feel, good durability and warmth; more costly and less stain-resistant than synthetics.

Carpet Construction

The top surface of a carpet, called the pile, consists of yarn loops pushed up through a backing material. The loops are left intact or cut by the manufacturer, depending on the desired effect. Most carpet sold today is made from synthetic fibers, such as nylon, polyester, and olefin, although natural wool carpet is still popular.

A good rule of thumb for judging the quality of a carpet is to look at the pile density. A carpet with many pile fibers packed into a given area will resist crushing, repel stains and dirt buildup better, and be more durable than carpet with low pile density.

Cushion-backed carpet has a foam backing bonded to it, eliminating the need for additional padding. Cushion-backed carpet is easy to install because it requires no stretching or tackless strips; it is secured to the floor with general-purpose adhesive, much like full-spread sheet vinyl. Cushion-backed carpet usually costs less than conventional carpet, but it is generally a lower-quality product.

Loop-pile carpet has a textured look created by the rounded ends of the uncut yarn loops pushed up through the backing. The loops can be arranged randomly, or they can make a distinct pattern, such as herringbone. Loop pile is ideal for heavy-traffic areas, since loops are virtually impervious to crushing.

Velvet cut-pile carpet has the densest pile of any carpet type. It is cut so that the color remains uniform when the pile is brushed in any direction. Velvets are well suited to formal living spaces.

Saxony cut-pile carpet, also known as plush, is constructed to withstand crushing and matting better than velvets. The pile is trimmed at a bevel, giving it a speckled appearance.

Cushion-backed

Loop-pile

Velvet cut-pile

Saxony cut-pile

Examine the carpet backing, or "foundation." A tighter grid pattern in the backing (left) usually indicates dense-pile carpet that will be more durable and soil-resistant than carpet with looser pile (right).

Buying and Estimating Carpet (cont.)

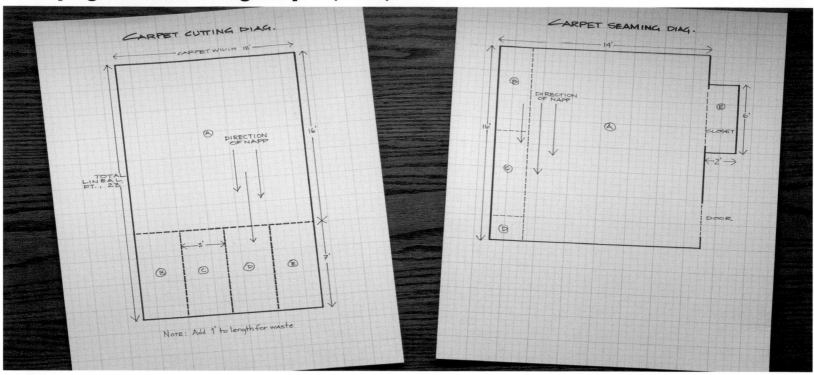

Sketch a scale drawing of the factory carpet roll and another drawing of the room to be carpeted. Use the drawings to plan the cuts and determine how the carpet pieces will be arranged. In most large rooms, the installation will include one large piece of carpet the same width as the factory roll, and several smaller pieces, which are permanently seamed to the larger piece. Consider the information in the following tips when sketching the layout; remember that carpet pieces must be oversized to allow for precise seaming and trimming. Your finished drawings will tell you the length of carpet you need to buy.

Keep pile direction consistent. Carpet pile is usually slanted; this affects how the carpet looks from different angles as light reflects off the surface. Place seamed pieces so the pile faces the same direction.

Maintain patterns when seaming patterned carpet. Because of this necessity, there is always more waste when installing patterned carpet. For a pattern that repeats every 18", for example, each piece must be oversized by 18" to ensure that the pattern is aligned. Pattern repeat measurements are noted on carpet samples.

Add an extra 3" for each seamed edge when estimating the amount of carpet you'll need. The extra material helps when cutting straight edges for seaming.

Add 6" for each edge along a wall. This surplus will be trimmed away when the carpet is cut to the exact size of the room.

Plan to cover closet floors with a separate piece of carpet that is seamed to the carpet in the main room area.

Add together the rise and run of each step when estimating for stairs. Then, measure the width of the stairway to determine how many strips you can cut from the factory roll. For a 3-ft.-wide stairway, for example, you can cut three strips from a 12-ft.-wide roll, allowing for waste. Rather than seaming carpet strips together end to end, plan the installation so the ends of the strips fall in the stair crotches (see page 294). Where practical, however, try to carpet stairs with a single carpet strip.

Tools and Materials for Installing Carpet

Installing carpet requires the use of some specialty tools, most notably the knee kicker and power stretcher. These tools are available at most rental centers and carpet stores.

The knee kicker and power stretcher are used to stretch a carpet smooth and taut before securing it to tackless strips installed around the perimeter of a room.

The power stretcher is the more efficient of the two tools and should be used to stretch and secure as much of the carpet as possible. The knee kicker is used to secure carpet in tight areas where the power stretcher cannot reach, such as closets.

A logical stretching sequence is essential to a good carpet installation. Begin attaching the carpet at a doorway or corner, then use the power stretcher and knee kicker to stretch the carpet away from attached areas and toward the opposite walls.

Carpeting materials include: hot-glue seam tape (A), used to join carpet pieces together; duct tape (B), for seaming carpet pads; double-sided tape (C), used to secure a carpet pad to concrete; staples (D), used to fasten padding to underlayment; and tackless strips (E), for securing the edges of stretched carpet.

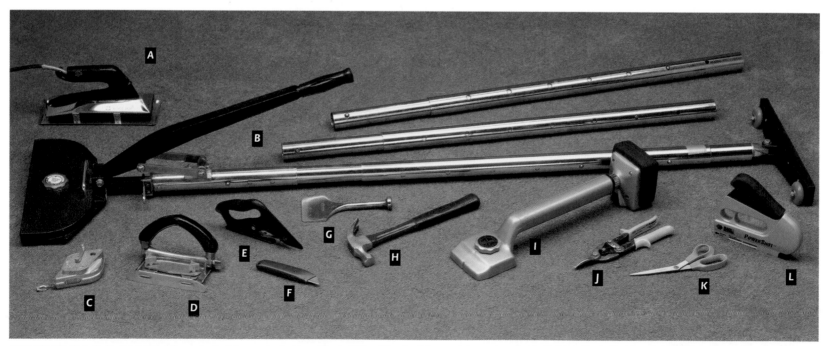

Carpeting tools include: seam iron (A), power stretcher and extensions (B), chalk line (C), edge trimmer (D), row-running knife (E), utility knife (F), stair tool (G), hammer (H), knee kicker (I), aviation snips (J), scissors (K), and stapler (L).

Using a Knee Kicker

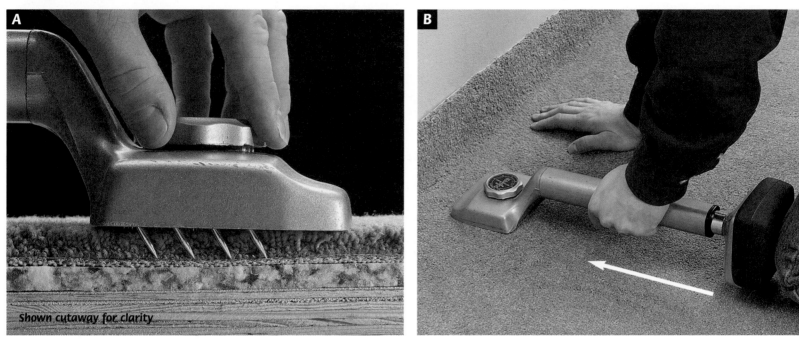

A — Shown cutaway for clarity

A knee kicker (and power stretcher) has teeth that grab the carpet foundation for stretching. Adjust the depth of the teeth by turning the knob on the knee kicker head. The teeth should be set deeply enough to grab the carpet foundation without penetrating to the padding.

B

Place the kicker head a few inches away from the wall to avoid dislodging the tackless strips, then strike the kicker cushion sharply with your knee, stretching the carpet taut. Tack the carpet to the pins on the tackless strips to hold it in place.

Using a Power Stretcher

A

Tail   Extension poles   Head

Align the pieces of the power stretcher along the floor, with the tail positioned at a point where the carpet is already secured and the head positioned just short of the opposite wall. Fit the ends of the sections together. Telescope one or more of the extension poles until the tail rests against the starting wall or block and the head is about 5" from the opposite wall.

B

Adjust the teeth on the head so they grip the carpet (see step A, above). Depress the lever on the head to stretch the carpet. The stretcher head should move the carpet about 2".

Installing Carpet Transitions

Doorways and other transitional areas require special treatment when you are installing carpet. Transition materials and techniques vary, depending on the level and type of the adjoining flooring (see photos, right).

For a transition to a floor that is either at the same height or lower than the bottom of the carpet, attach a metal carpet bar to the floor, and secure the carpet inside the bar. This transition is often used where carpet meets a vinyl or tile floor. Carpet bars are sold in standard door-width lengths and in longer strips.

For a transition to a floor that is higher than the carpet bottom, use tackless strips, as if the adjoining floor surface were a wall. This transition is common where carpet meets a hardwood floor.

For a transition to another carpet of the same height, join the two carpet sections with hot-glue seam tape (see pages 290 to 291).

For a transition in a doorway between carpets of different heights or textures, install tackless strips and a hardwood threshold. Thresholds are available predrilled and ready to install with screws.

Tools: *Hacksaw, marker, utility knife, knee kicker, stair tool, straightedge.*

Materials: *Transition materials, wood block.*

Metal Carpet bar

Tackless strip tuck-under

Hot-glue seam tape

Hardwood threshold

Making Transitions with Metal Carpet Bars

Measure and cut a carpet bar to fit the space, then nail it in place. In doorways, the upturned metal flange should lie directly below the center of the door when closed. To install a carpet bar on concrete, see page 286.

Roll out, cut, and seam the carpet. Fold the carpet back in the transition area, then mark it for trimming—the edge of the carpet should fall ⅛" to ¼" short of the corner of the carpet bar so it can be stretched into the bar.

Use a knee kicker to stretch the carpet snugly into the corner of the carpet bar. Press the carpet down onto the pins with a stair tool. Then, bend the carpet bar flange down over the carpet by striking with a hammer and a block of wood.

Making Transitions with Tackless Strips

Install a tackless strip, leaving a gap equal to ⅔ the thickness of the carpet for trimming. Roll out, cut, and seam the carpet. Mark the edges of the carpet between the strip and the adjoining floor surface about ⅛" past the point where it meets the adjacent floor.

Use a straightedge and a utility knife to trim off the excess carpet. Stretch the carpet toward the strip with a knee kicker, then press it onto the pins of the strip.

Tuck the edge of the carpet into the gap between the tackless strip and the existing floor, using a stair tool.

Installing Padding and Tackless Strips

The easiest way to secure carpeting is to install tackless strips around the perimeter of the room. Once the strips are installed, carpet padding is rolled out as a foundation for the carpet.

Standard ¾"-wide tackless strips are adequate for securing most carpet. For carpets laid on concrete, use wider tackless strips that are attached with masonry nails. Be careful when handling tackless strips, as the sharp pins can be dangerous. Where the carpet will meet a doorway or another type of flooring, install the appropriate transitions (see pages 284 to 285).

Tools: Aviation snips, utility knife, stapler.

Materials: Tackless strips, nails, carpet pad, duct tape.

Install tackless strips next to walls, leaving a gap equal to about ⅔ the thickness of the carpet. Make sure the angled pins on the tackless strips point toward the walls. Cut and install the padding so it fits snugly against the strips. Many carpet pads have one side that is covered with a smooth coating. For information on selecting carpet padding, see page 278.

Installing Tackless Strips

A Starting in a corner, nail tackless strips to the floor, maintaining a slight gap between the strips and the walls (see photo, top of page). Use a scrap of plywood or cardboard as a spacing aid.

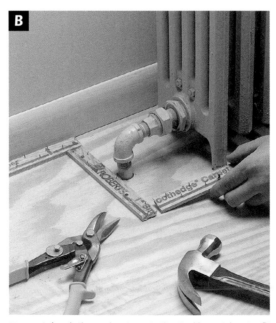

B Use metal aviation snips to cut the tackless strips to fit around radiators, door moldings, and other obstacles.

VARIATION: On concrete, use wider tackless strips. Drill pilot holes through the strips and into the floor, using a masonry bit, then fasten the strips by driving 1½" fluted masonry nails.

Installing Carpet Padding

A

Roll out enough padding to cover the entire floor. Make sure the seams between the strips are tight. If one face of the padding has a slicker surface, make sure the slick face is up. This makes it easier to slide the carpet over the pad during installation.

B

Use a utility knife to cut away any excess padding along the edges. The padding should touch, but not overlap, the tackless strips.

C

Tape the seams together with duct tape, then staple the padding to the floor every 12".

VARIATION: To fasten carpet padding to a concrete floor, apply double-sided tape next to the tackless strips, along the seams, and in an "X" pattern across the floor.

Cutting and Seaming Carpet

Position the carpet roll against one wall, with its loose end extending up the wall by about 6", then roll out the carpet until it reaches the opposite wall.

At the opposite wall, mark the back of the carpet at each edge, about 6" beyond the point where the carpet touches the wall. Pull the carpet back away from the wall, so the marks are visible.

Snap a chalk line across the back of the carpet between the marks. Place a piece of scrap plywood under the cutting area to protect the carpet and padding from the knife. Cut along the line, using a straightedge and utility knife.

VARIATION: When cutting loop-pile carpet, avoid severing the loops by cutting from the top side, using a row-running knife (see page 282). First fold the carpet back along the cut line to part the pile (left) and make a crease along the part line. Then, lay the carpet flat and cut along the part in the pile (right). Cut slowly to ensure a smooth, straight cut.

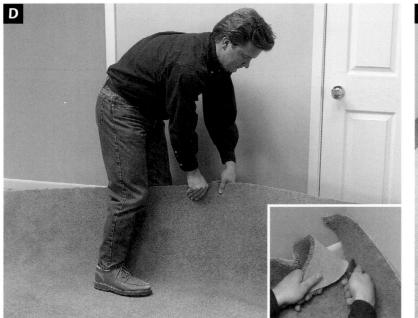

Next to walls, straddle the edge of the carpet and nudge it with your foot until it extends up the wall by about 6" and is parallel to the wall. At the corners, relieve buckling by slitting the carpet with a utility knife, allowing the carpet to lie somewhat flat (inset). Be careful to make the corner cuts only a few inches long to prevent cutting into usable carpet.

Using your seaming plan (see pages 280 to 281) as a guide, measure and cut fill-in pieces of carpet to complete the installation. Be sure to include a 6" surplus at each wall and a 3" surplus on each edge that will be seamed to another piece of carpet. Set the cut pieces in place, making sure the pile faces in the same direction on all pieces.

Roll back the large piece of carpet on the side to be seamed, then use a chalk line to snap a straight seam edge, about 2" in from the factory edge. Keep the ends of the line about 1½ ft. in from the ends of the carpet, where the overlap at the walls causes the carpet to buckle.

Place scrap wood under the cutting area to protect the carpet while cutting. Using a straightedge and utility knife, carefully cut the carpet along the chalk line. To extend the cutting lines to the edges of the carpet, pull the corners back at an angle so they lie flat, then cut with the straightedge and utility knife.

Continued on next page

Cutting and Seaming Carpet (cont.)

On the smaller carpet pieces, cut straight seam edges where the small pieces will be joined to one another. Do not cut the edges that will be seamed to the large carpet piece until after the small pieces are joined together.

OPTION: Apply a continuous bead of seam glue along the cut edges of the backing at seams to ensure that the carpet will not fray.

Plug in the seam iron and set it aside to heat up, then measure and cut hot-glue seam tape for all seams. Begin by joining the small fill-in pieces to form one large piece. Center the tape under a seam, with the adhesive side facing up.

Set the iron under the carpet at one end of the tape until the adhesive liquifies—usually about 30 seconds. Working in 12" sections, slowly move the iron along the tape, letting the carpet fall onto the hot adhesive behind it. Set weights at the end of the seam to hold the pieces in place.

Press the edges of the carpet together into the melted adhesive behind the iron. Separate the pile with your fingers to make sure no fibers are stuck in the glue and that the seam is tight, then place a weighted board over the seam to keep it flat while the glue sets.

VARIATION: To close any gaps in loop-pile carpet seams, use a knee kicker, and gently push the seam edges together while the adhesive is still hot.

Continue seaming the fill-in pieces together. When the tape adhesive has dried, turn the seamed piece over, and cut a fresh seam edge as done in steps F and G (see page 289). Reheat and remove about 1½" of tape from the end of each seam to keep it from overlapping the tape on the large piece.

Use hot-glue seam tape to join the seamed pieces to the large piece of carpet, repeating steps I through K.

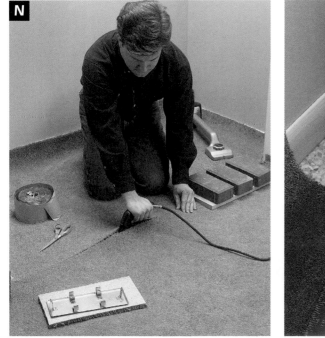

If you're laying carpet in a closet, cut a fill-in piece, and join it to the main carpet with hot-glue seam tape, using the same technique.

TIP: At radiators, pipes, and other obstructions, cut slits in the carpet. First, cut long slits from the edge of the carpet to the obstruction, then cut short cross-slits where the carpet will fit around the obstruction.

TIP: To fit carpet around partition walls where the edges of the wall or door jamb meet the floor, make diagonal cuts from the edge of the carpet at the center of the wall to the points where the edges of the wall meet the floor.

Stretching and Securing Carpet

Before you start to stretch the seamed carpet, read through this entire section and create a stretching sequence similar to the one shown here. Start the process by fastening the carpet at a doorway threshold, using carpet transitions (see pages 284 to 285).

If the doorway is close to a corner, use the knee kicker to secure the carpet to the tackless strips between the door and the corner. Also secure a few feet of carpet along the adjacent wall, again working toward the corner.

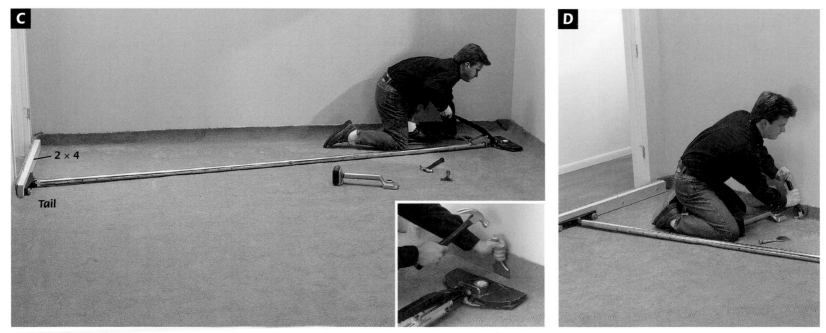

Use a power stretcher to stretch the carpet toward the wall opposite the door, bracing the tail with a length of 2 × 4 placed across the doorway. Secure the carpet onto the tackless strips with a stair tool or the head of a hammer (inset). Leaving the tail in place and moving only the stretcher head, continue stretching and securing carpet along the wall, working toward the nearest corner in 12" to 24" increments.

With the power stretcher still extended from the doorway to the opposite side of the room, knee-kick the carpet onto the tackless strips along the closest wall, starting near the corner closest to the stretcher tail. Disengage and move the stretcher only if it's in the way.

Reposition the stretcher so its tail is against the center of the wall you just secured (step D). Stretch and secure the carpet along the opposite wall, working from the center toward a corner. NOTE: If there is a closet in an adjacent wall, work toward that wall, not the closet.

Use the knee kicker to stretch and secure the carpet inside the closet (if any). Stretch and fasten the carpet against the back wall first, then do the side walls. After the carpet in the closet is stretched and secured, use the knee kicker to secure the carpet along the walls next to the closet. Disengage the power stretcher only if it's in the way.

Return the head of the power stretcher to the center of the wall, then finish securing carpet along this wall, working toward the other corner of the room.

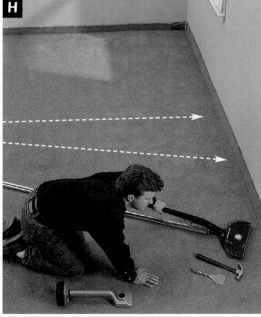

Reposition the stretcher to secure the carpet along the last wall of the room, working from the center toward the corners. The tail block should be braced against the opposite wall.

TIP: Locate any floor vents under the stretched carpet, then use a utility knife to cut away the carpet, starting at the center. It is important that this be done after the stretching is completed.

Continued on next page

Stretching and Securing Carpet (cont.)

Use a carpet edge trimmer to trim surplus carpet away from the walls. At corners, use a utility knife to finish the cuts.

Tuck the trimmed edges of the carpet neatly into the gaps between the tackless strips and the walls, using a stair tool and hammer.

Carpeting Stairs

Where practical, try to carpet stairs with a single strip of carpet. If you must use two or more pieces, plan the layout so the pieces meet where a riser meets a tread. Do not seam together carpet pieces in the middle of a tread or riser.

The project shown here involves a staircase that is enclosed on both sides. For open staircases, turn down the edges of the carpet and secure them with carpet tacks.

Measure the carpet to fit your stairway (see page 281), then cut the carpet to the correct dimensions (see page 288).

Tools: Straightedge, utility knife, aviation snips, stapler, stair tool, knee kicker.

Materials: Carpet, carpet padding, tackless strips, nails.

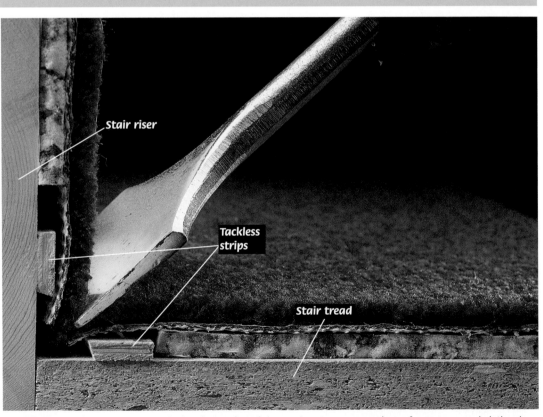

On stairways, tackless strips are attached to the treads and risers. Where two or more pieces of carpet are needed, the pieces should meet at the "crotch" of the step (where the riser and tread meet).

Fasten tackless strips to the risers and treads. On the risers, place the strips about 1" above the treads; on the treads, place the strips about ¾" from the risers. Make sure the pins point toward the crotch of the step. On the bottom riser, leave a gap equal to ⅔ the carpet thickness.

For each step, cut a piece of carpet padding the width of the step and long enough to cover the tread and a few inches of the riser below it. Staple the padding in place.

Position the carpet on the stairs with the pile direction pointing down. Secure the bottom edge, using a stair tool to tuck the end of the carpet between the tackless strip and the floor.

Use a knee kicker and stair tool to stretch the carpet onto the tackless strip on the first tread. Start in the center of the step, then alternate kicks on either side until the carpet is completely secured on the step.

Use a hammer and the stair tool to wedge the carpet firmly into the back corner of the step. Repeat this process for each step.

Where two carpet pieces meet, secure the edge of the upper piece first, then stretch and secure the lower piece.

CONVERTING
ℬASEMENTS & ATTICS

Planning the Project

Although many attics and basements are good candidates for finishing, not all are suitable. Some spaces are simply too small or have very low ceilings or problems like flooding that make the investment too risky. Other spaces may require expensive preparation before they can be finished. So before you make any serious plans, it's a good idea to evaluate the space to find out what you have to work with and what changes are necessary.

The primary gauge by which to measure your attic or basement is the local building code. This describes all the requirements for livable spaces in your area, and it will govern every aspect of your project. There are code specifications for everything from minimum headroom to how many electrical receptacles you'll need. You can probably find a copy of the building code at a local library, but for the most part, it's best to learn about the requirements from the officials at the building department.

This section will help you evaluate your basement or attic and begin planning the remodeling project. Much of this you can do yourself, while other matters may require professional help. If your attic or basement passes your evaluation, hire an architect, engineer, or building contractor to have a look at the space and the elements that will be affected by the project.

You can use your home's original blueprints to learn about the basic structure of your house and locate mechanical rough-ins. If you don't have blueprints, contact your home's builder or the city office to get a copy of them.

Evaluating Your Basement

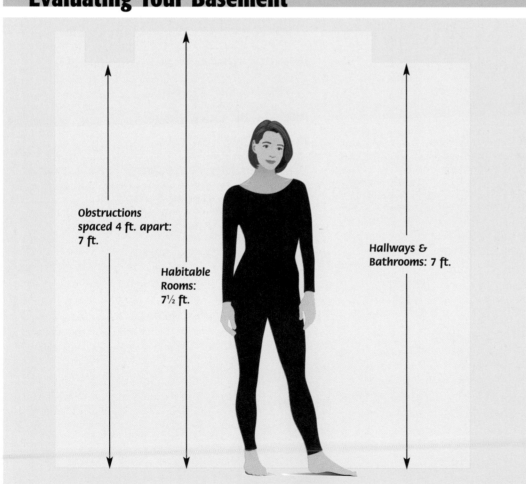

Obstructions spaced 4 ft. apart: 7 ft.

Habitable Rooms: 7½ ft.

Hallways & Bathrooms: 7 ft.

Basement headroom is often limited by beams, ducts, pipes, and other elements. Typical minimums for ceiling height are shown here: 7½ ft. for habitable rooms; 7 ft. for bathrooms and hallways; 7 ft. for obstructions spaced no less than 4 ft. apart.

Two things that put an end to the most basement finishing plans: inadequate headroom and moisture. Begin your evaluation by measuring from the basement floor to the bottom of the floor joists above. Most building codes require habitable rooms to have a finished ceiling height of 7½ ft., measured from the finished floor to the lowest part of the finished ceiling. However, obstructions, such as beams, soffits, and pipes, (spaced at least 4 ft. on center) usually can hang down 6" below that height. Hallways and bathrooms typically need at least 7-ft. ceilings.

While it's impractical to add headroom in a basement, there are some ways of working around the requirements. Ducts and pipes often can be moved, and beams and other obstructions can be incorporated into walls or hidden in closets or other uninhabitable spaces. Also, some codes permit lower ceiling heights in rooms with specific purposes, such as recreation rooms. If headroom is a problem, talk to the local building department before you dash your dreams.

If your basement passes the headroom test, you can move on to the next issue: moisture. For a full discussion on this critical matter, see *Dealing with Basement Moisture*, on pages 303 to 305. Be aware that moisture problems must be corrected before you start the finishing process.

Rerouting service lines *and mechanicals adds quickly to the expense of a project, so consider your options carefully.*

Weakened or undersized joists *and other framing members must be reinforced or replaced.*

Minor cracks *such as these in masonry walls and floors usually can be sealed and forgotten, while severe cracking may indicate serious structural problems.*

A well-built basement provides plenty of structural support for finished space, but before you cover up the walls, floor, and ceiling, check for potential problems. Inspect the masonry carefully. Large cracks may indicate shifting of the soil around the foundation; severely bowed or out-of-plumb walls may be structurally unsound. Small cracks usually cause moisture problems rather than structural woes, but they should be sealed to prevent further cracking. Contact an engineer or foundation contractor for help with foundation problems. If you have an older home, you may find sagging floor joists overhead or rotted wood posts or beams; any defective wood framing will have to be reinforced or replaced.

Your basement's mechanicals are another important consideration. The locations of water heaters, pipes, wiring, circuit boxes, furnaces, and ductwork can have a significant impact on the cost and difficulty of your project. Can you plan around components, or will they have to be moved? Is there enough headroom to install a suspended ceiling so mechanicals can remain accessible? Or, will

you have to reroute pipes and ducts to increase headroom? Electricians and HVAC contractors can help you assess your systems and suggest modifications.

Aside from being dark and scary places, unfinished basements often harbor toxic elements. One of the most common is *radon*, a naturally occurring radioactive gas that is odorless and colorless. It's believed that prolonged exposure to high levels of radon can cause lung cancer. The Environmental Protection Agency (see page 503) has free publications to help you test for radon and take steps to reduce the levels in your house. For starters, you can perform a "short-term" test using a kit from a hardware store or home center. Look for the phrase "Meets EPA requirements" to ensure the test kit is accurate. Keep in mind that short-term tests are not as conclusive as professional, long-term tests. If your test reveals high levels of radon, contact a radon specialist.

Another basement hazard is insulation containing asbestos, which was commonly used in older homes for insulating ductwork and heat-

ing pipes. In most cases, this insulation can be left alone if it's in good condition and is protected from damage. If you fear the insulation in your basement poses a hazard, contact an asbestos abatement contractor to have it evaluated or safely removed.

Check the local codes regarding exits from finished basements—most codes require two. The stairway commonly serves as one exit, while the other exit can be a door to the outside, an egress window (see page 15), or a code-compliant *bulkhead* (an exterior stairway with cellar doors). Each bedroom will also need an egress window or door for escape.

Stairways must also meet local code specifications. If yours doesn't, you'll probably have to hire someone to rebuild it. See page 302 for an overview of typical staircase requirements.

Finally, if you're planning to finish the basement in a new house, ask the builder how long you should wait before starting the project. Poured concrete walls and floors need time to dry out before they can be covered. Depending on where you live, you may be advised to wait up to two years, just to be safe.

Evaluating Your Attic

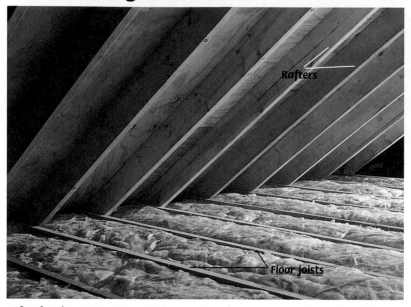

Rafter framing *creates open space because the rafters carry most of the roof's weight.*

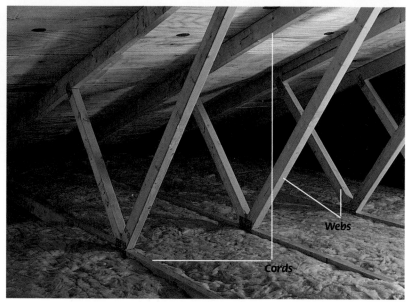

Trusses *are made of interconnected cords and webs, which close off most of the attic space.*

Start your attic evaluation with a quick framing inspection. If the roof is framed with rafters, you can continue to the next test. If it's built with trusses, however, consider other ways to add space to your home. Internal supports in trusses leave too little space to work with, and trusses cannot be altered.

The next step is to check for headroom and overall floor space. Most building codes call for 7½ ft. of headroom over 50% of the "usable" floor space. Usable floor space is defined as any space with a ceiling height of at least 5 ft. Remember that these minimums apply to the

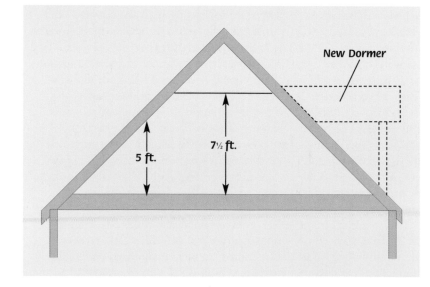

finished space—after the flooring and ceiling surfaces are installed. Other things can affect headroom, as well, such as reinforcing the floor frame, and increasing rafter depth for strength or insulation.

You may also find that various supports in your attic strengthen your roof but limit your space. *Collar ties* (see page 301) are horizontal boards that join two rafters together in the upper third of the rafter span. They prevent rafter uplift in high winds. Collar ties often can be moved up a few inches but cannot be removed. *Rafter ties* join rafters in the lower third of their span to prevent spreading. In most attics, the ceiling or floor joists serve as rafter ties. *Purlins* are horizontal boards that run at right angles to the rafters and are supported by struts. These systems shorten the rafter span, allowing the use of smaller lumber for the rafters. You may be allowed to substitute kneewalls for purlins and struts. If you think you need to have any support system altered or moved, consult an architect or engineer.

The rafters themselves also need careful examination. Inspect them for signs of stress or damage, such as cracks, sagging, and insect infestation. Look for dark areas indicating roof leaks. If you find leaks or you know your roofing is past its useful life, have it repaired or replaced before you start the finishing process. And even if the rafters appear healthy, they may be too small to support the added weight of finish

Habitable rooms *must be at least 70 sq. ft. total and measure at least 7 ft. in any one direction. To meet headroom requirements, 50% of the usable floor space must have a ceiling height of 7½ ft. You can increase your floor space and headroom by adding protruding windows called dormers. In addition to space, dormers add light and ventilation to your attic.*

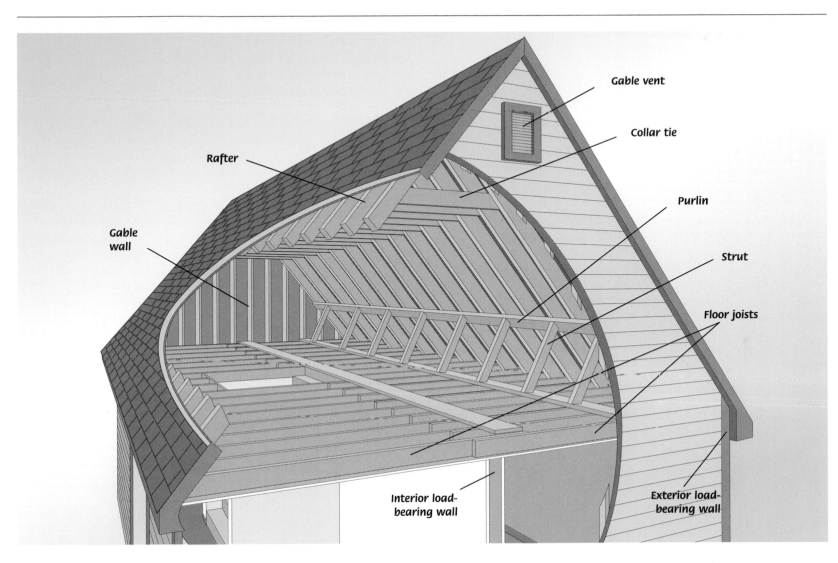

Rafter

Gable vent

Collar tie

Purlin

Strut

Floor joists

Gable wall

Interior load-bearing wall

Exterior load-bearing wall

materials. Small rafters can also be a problem if they don't provide enough room for adequate insulation.

At this point, it's a good idea to have a professional check the structure of your attic, including the rafters and everything from the floor down. In some cases, finishing an attic is like adding a story to your home, which means that the structure must have adequate support for the new space. Attic floors are often built as ceiling frames for the level below and are not intended to support living space. Floors can be strengthened with additional joists, known as *sister* joists, or with new joists installed between the existing ones.

Support for the attic floor is provided by the load-bearing walls below and, ultimately, by the foundation. If these elements can't support the finished attic, they'll need to be reinforced. This may be as simple as strengthening the walls with plywood panels or as complicated as adding support posts and beams or reinforcing the foundation.

In addition to these structural matters, there are a few general code

requirements you should keep in mind as you inspect your attic. If you plan to add a bedroom, it will need at least one exit to the outside. This can be a door leading to an outside stairwell or an egress window (see page 15). Most codes also have minimum requirements for ventilation and natural light, which means you may have to add windows or skylights.

One of the largest expenses of finishing an attic is in providing access: You'll need a permanent stairway at least 36" wide, with room for a 36" landing at the top and bottom. This is an important planning issue because adding a stairway affects the layout and traffic patterns of the attic, as well the rooms on the floor below. See page 302 for more information on stairway requirements.

Finally, take an inventory of existing mechanicals in your attic. While plumbing and wiring runs can be moved relatively easily, other features, such as chimneys, must be incorporated into your plans. This is a good time to have your chimney inspected by a fire official and to obtain the building code specifications for framing around chimneys.

Stairways

A finished attic or basement requires safe access, and while you may have an existing stairway that's seen plenty of use, it may not meet building code requirements for finished spaces. If there is no stairway, you'll need to plan carefully to find the best location for a new one.

According to most building codes, stairways must be at least 36" wide, with a minimum of 6 ft., 8" of headroom. Each step may have a maximum riser height of $7\frac{3}{4}$" and a minimum tread depth of 10". The top and bottom of the stairs must have a landing at least 36" deep. All stairways must be illuminated, preferably by a light fixture controlled by three-way switches.

The handrail is another important element. All stairways with two or more steps must have at least one handrail mounted 34" to 38" above the treads. The railing itself should have a diameter between $1\frac{1}{2}$" and 2" and must be mounted at least $1\frac{1}{2}$" from the wall. Handrail ends must terminate into the wall or have a turnout or easing at the bottom end of the stairs. As a minimum, handrails must extend from a point directly above the bottom riser to a point directly above the top riser.

For increased accessibility, include two handrails—one on each side—and extend them to include horizontal sections at both ends: 12"

beyond the top riser and 12" plus the width of one tread beyond the bottom riser. If you have enough space, you can also plan the stairway with deeper treads and shorter risers, making the stairs easier to use for those with physical challenges.

When evaluating your stairway, take into account your finishing plans. Steps must be as uniform as possible, with no more than a $\frac{3}{8}$" variance in riser height. Thick tile or a basement subfloor that runs up to the first step will shorten the height of the first riser, creating an unsafe situation that doesn't meet code. You can adjust a new staircase to compensate for this, but an existing one doesn't offer such flexibility.

When planning a new staircase, consider how it will affect the surrounding spaces, as well as the traffic patterns on both floors. The type of staircase you choose and where you put it will largely be determined by the available floor space. A standard straight-run stairway will occupy almost 50 sq. ft. of floor space on the lower level and 35 to 40 sq. ft. on the upper level. L- and U-shape stairways make 90° and 180° turns, respectively, allowing them to fit into smaller areas. *Winders* are L-shape stairs that make the turn with wedge-shape steps rather than a square platform. These allow a steeper rise in a confined area.

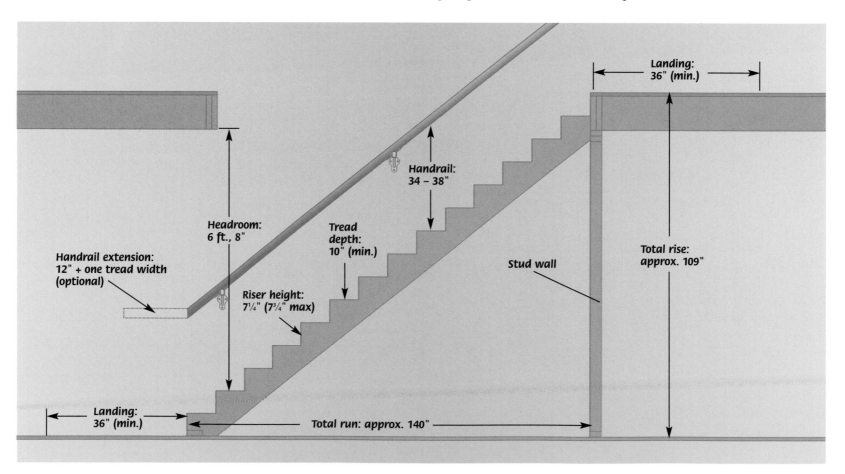

Dealing with Basement Moisture

Basement moisture can destroy your efforts to create functional living space. Over time, even small amounts of moisture can rot framing, turn wallboard to mush, and promote the growth of mold and mildew. Fortunately, most moisture problems can be resolved, but any measures you take must prove effective before you proceed with your project. Ensuring your basement will stay dry throughout the seasons may require waiting a year or more after the home is constructed, but considering the time and money involved, it will be worth the delay.

Basement moisture appears in two forms: condensation and seepage. Condensation comes from airborne water vapor that turns to water when it contacts cold surfaces. Common sources of vapor include humid outdoor air, poorly ventilated appliances, damp walls, and traces of water released from concrete. Seepage is water that enters the basement by infiltrating cracks in the foundation or by leeching through the masonry. Typically caused by ineffective exterior drainage, seepage comes from rain or groundwater collected around the foundation or from a rising water table.

If you've had a wet basement in the past, you may know when to expect moisture but not where it's coming from. Even if your basement has been dry for a long time, look for evidence of moisture problems. Typical signs include peeling paint, white residue on masonry, mildew stains, sweaty windows and pipes, rusted appliance feet, rotted wood near the floor, buckled floor tile, and the odor of mildew.

Once you determine that a moisture problem exists, locate the source. The first step is to test for condensation and seepage: Lay a square of plastic or aluminum foil on the floor and another on an exterior foundation wall. Tape down all four sides of each. Check the squares after two days. If moisture has formed on top of a square, you probably have a condensation problem; moisture on the underside indicates seepage.

To reduce condensation, run a dehumidifier in the dampest area of the basement. Insulate cold-water pipes to prevent condensate drippage, and make sure your dryer and other appliances are vented to the outside. Central A/C service in the basement can help reduce vapor during warm, humid months.

Crawlspaces also can promote condensation, as warm, moist air enters through crawlspace vents and meets the cooler interior air. Crawlspace ventilation is a source of ongoing debate, and there's no universal method that applies to all climates. It's best to ask the local building department or an experienced local contractor for advice on this matter.

Solutions for preventing seepage range from simple do-it-yourself projects to expensive professional jobs requiring excavation and foundation work. Since it's often difficult to determine the source of seeping water, try some common cures before calling in professional help. Begin by checking your yard's grade. The first 6 ft. of ground around the foundation should slope away at a rate of 1" per foot and at least

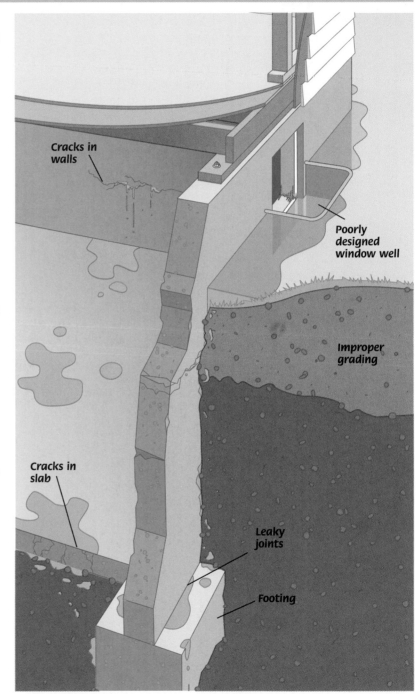

Common causes of basement moisture *include improper grading around the foundation, inadequate or faulty gutter systems, humidity and condensation, cracks in foundation walls, leaky joints between structural elements, and poorly designed window wells. More extensive problems include large cracks in the foundation, damaged or missing drain tiles, a high water table, or the presence of underground streams. Often, a combination of factors is at fault.*

Cracks in walls

Poorly designed window well

Improper grading

Cracks in slab

Leaky joints

Footing

Continued on next page

Dealing with Basement Moisture (cont.)

¾" per foot beyond that. Use a level, a long board, and a tape measure to check the grade. If the slope is inadequate, build up the ground around the foundation to improve drainage.

Next, inspect your downspouts and gutters. Give the gutters a thorough cleaning, and patch any holes. Make sure the gutters slope toward the downspouts at about ¹⁄₁₆" per foot. And most important, add downspout extensions and splashblocks to keep roof runoff at least 8 ft. away from the foundation.

Window wells allow water into a basement, and covering them with removable plastic covers is the easiest way to keep them dry. If you prefer to leave wells uncovered, add a gravel layer and a drain to the bottom of the well. Clean the well regularly to remove moisture-heavy debris. See page 308 for more information on window wells.

To help stop seepage from inside the basement, patch cracks in the foundation walls and floors. Use waterproof masonry sealant for cracks under ¼" wide, and use hydraulic cement for larger cracks. Whole-wall interior coatings, such as masonry waterproofer, may also help reduce basement moisture. However, be aware that while sealing the foundation from the inside can help block occasional light moisture, it will not solve serious moisture problems, regardless of the manufacturer's claims.

If these simple measures don't correct your basement's moisture problems, consider more extensive action. Serious water problems are

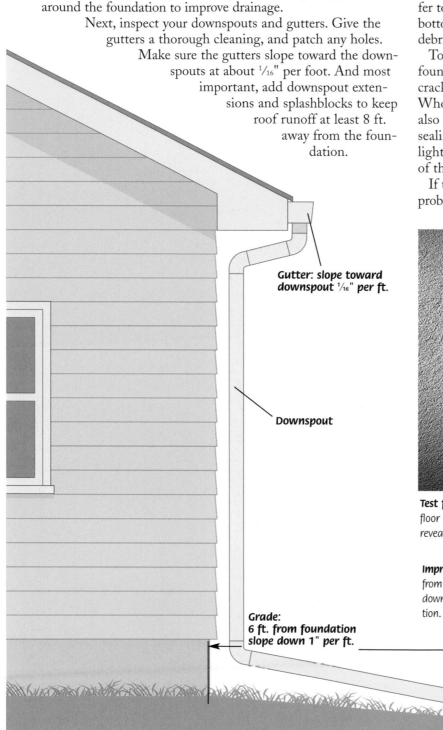

Gutter: slope toward downspout ¹⁄₁₆" per ft.

Downspout

**Grade:
6 ft. from foundation slope down 1" per ft.**

Downspout extension

Splashblock

Test for condensation and seepage (above) by taping a square of aluminum foil to the floor and a wall. Moisture on top of the foil indicates condensation; moisture underneath reveals seepage.

Improve your gutter system and foundation grade (left) to prevent rainwater and snow-melt from flooding your basement. Keep gutters clean and in good condition. Make sure there's a downspout for every 50 ft. of roof eave, and extend downspout piping 8 ft. from the foundation. Build up the grade around the foundation so it carries water away from the house.

typically handled by footing drains or sump systems. Footing drains, which are installed around the foundation's perimeter near the footing, drain out to a distant area of the yard. They usually work in conjunction with waterproof coatings on the foundation walls. Sump systems use an interior under-slab drain pipe to collect water in a pit. From there, the water is sent outside by an electric sump pump. In cases where a basement is affected only by excess surface water, a landscape drain may solve the problem.

Find out if your house has one of these systems in place. It may be that your footing drain pipes are clogged with silt or have been damaged by tree roots. If you have a sump pit in your basement floor but no pump or discharge pipe in place, you may need to install a pump and drain lines. (Be aware that there may be regulations about where the sump pump can drain.)

Installing a new drainage system is expensive and must be done properly. Adding a sump system involves breaking up the concrete floor along the basement's perimeter, digging a trench, and laying a perforated drain pipe in a bed of gravel. After the sump pit is installed, the floor is patched with new concrete. Installing a footing drain is far more complicated. This involves digging out the foundation, installing gravel and drain pipe, and waterproofing the foundation walls.

Thus, a footing drain is typically considered a last-resort measure.

Before you hire someone to install a drainage system, do some homework. Learn about the procedure the contractor has planned, and find out if it has been successful with other homes in your area. Check the contractor's references, and don't be afraid to get a second or third opinion before making a commitment.

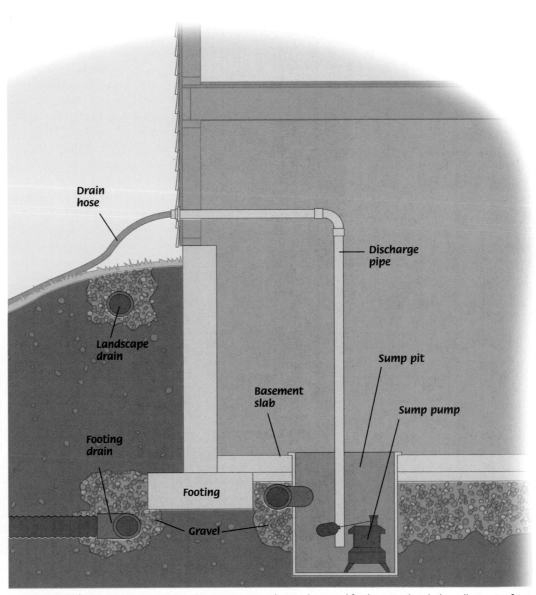

Fill cracks in the foundation with masonry waterproofer or hydraulic cement. This can help reduce minor seepage and prevent further cracking.

Foundation drainage systems are designed to remove water that pools around footings. Footing drains collect water from outside the footing and carry it out to daylight. Sump systems collect water underneath the basement floor and divert it into a pit. As the pit fills, a sump pump sends the water outside. Landscape drains remove water near the surface.

Planning the Framing

To determine where your new walls should go, start with an investigation of the unfinished space. All obstacles, such as mechanical equipment and service lines, support columns, chimneys, and roof framing, must be considered. Think about which of these elements can be enclosed by walls, which can be hidden within a wall or concealed by a soffit or chase, and which, if any, can be moved.

One technique to help you get started is to draw full-scale "walls" onto your basement floor, using children's sidewalk chalk (on wood attic floors, use wide masking tape instead of chalk). This helps you visualize the planned spaces and gives you a better sense of room sizes. Complete the layout in chalk, then walk through the rooms to test traffic patterns.

As you plan your rooms, keep in mind that most building codes require habitable rooms to have at least 70 sq. ft. of floor space and measure a minimum of 7 ft. in any direction. See page 15 for more code minimums regarding room sizes. And don't forget to include any new or enlarged windows in your plans.

This is especially important in basements, where adding or enlarging a window can be a major project (see page 308).

The next step is to draw floor plans (see pages 18 to 19). Simply measure your basement or attic floor space, then scale down the dimensions and transfer them to graph paper. Add all obstacles, windows, doors, and other permanent fixtures. When everything is in place, start experimenting with different layouts. If you have your home's original blueprints, trace the floor plans onto tracing paper and work on new layouts from there.

Creating a successful layout takes time and often requires creative problem-solving. To help generate ideas for your remodel, study the before-and-after drawings on page 307. While these floor plans may not look like your basement, they include many of the common elements and obstacles involved in a finishing project. They also show how carefully placed walls can transform an unfinished space into several livable areas that still leave room for storage and mechanical elements.

Draw layouts *onto your basement floor with sidewalk chalk. Use different colors to represent elements such as doors, windows, and ceiling soffits.*

Enclosing Mechanicals

Gas-burning appliances—like furnaces, hot-water heaters, and boilers, require air for combustion and space for servicing. When planning walls that enclose mechanicals, follow local building codes and manufacturer's recommendations for each appliance.

Standard minimum clearances are shown here. A furnace must have a minimum of 3" at the sides and back of the unit with a total clear space that is at least 12" wider than the unit width. The front of the unit (where the combustion chamber is located) must be 6" from any obstruction, such as a closed door. There also must be a 30"-deep work space directly in front of the unit. Door openings for mechanical rooms must be at least 24" wide.

Water heaters typically need 1" to 3" of clearance along the sides and back, and a 30"-deep work space in front.

Depending on the room size and the appliances contained within, air vents may be required to ensure safe combustion and ventilation. Combustion air is often provided by louvered doors, wall vents, or ducts that draw outdoor air: Consult the local building codes and appliance manufacturers for recommendations.

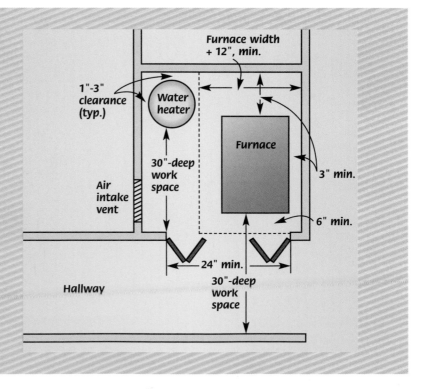

Basement Layouts: Before and After

Before: This standard basement had three utility windows along the end walls and structural columns running parallel to the long side wall. A furnace and water heater broke up the central space, and there was a sump pit in one corner. The goal for this space was to create a large family room, a home office, a bathroom, a pool room, and a storage area.

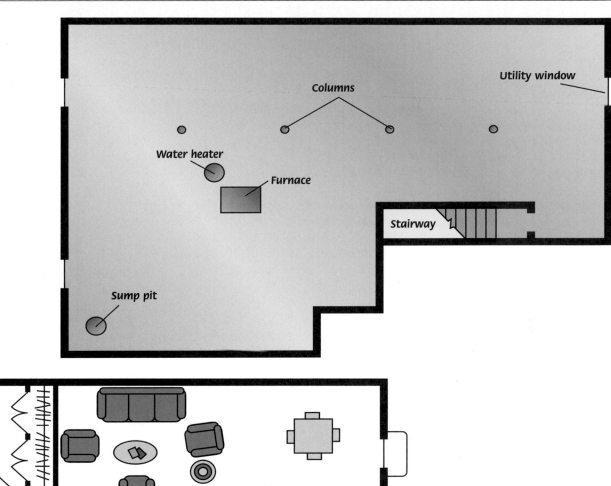

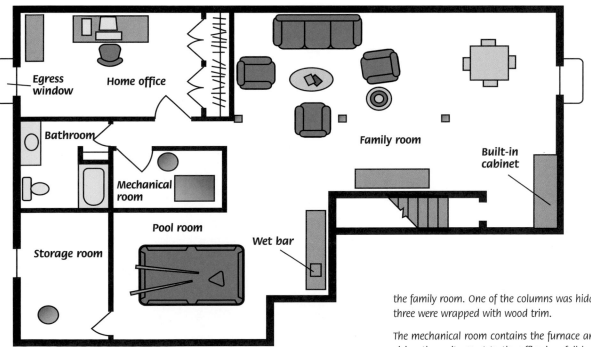

the family room. One of the columns was hidden within the office wall, and the remaining three were wrapped with wood trim.

The mechanical room contains the furnace and water heater, with plenty of space for servicing the units. Next to the office is a full bathroom, designed with a square layout that leaves a comfortable amount of space between the fixtures. The pool room occupies a well-defined space, where games won't disrupt activity in the family room. A wet bar can easily be accessed from both the pool room and family room. The stairway needed only a new handrail to become code-compliant. At the bottom of the stairs, a built-in cabinet provides storage and adds a decorative touch to the basement entrance.

After: A few walls at one end of the basement define several of the new rooms. To add light to the home office, the existing window opening was expanded, and an egress window was installed, which allows the room to be used as a bedroom, as well. A larger window and well were also installed at the other end of the basement to provide light and a better view from

Adding or Enlarging Basement Windows

Whether the goal is to add natural light or provide emergency egress, adding or enlarging windows is a common project for basement remodels. However, considering the structural aspects involved (not to mention labor), it's not always a do-it-yourself job.

Cutting into a foundation or load-bearing stud-wall in walkout basements requires adding a new header or steel lintel above the opening to carry the house's weight. In standard basements, adding or enlarging a window also requires digging and installing a window well. All of this work must be approved by a building inspector to ensure that the strength of the wall isn't compromised.

Creating a new opening in a wood-frame basement wall is similar to framing for any other load-bearing wall. With poured concrete or block foundations, the wall opening must be cut and broken out. The inside edges of masonry are then wrapped with pressure-treated lumber to provide a rough frame for the new window.

Window wells require important consideration. Some must be designed to allow easy emergency escape, while all wells should let in plenty of light to make the most of the new windows. As general minimums, a window well should be about 6" wider than the window opening and should extend at least 18" from the foundation wall. And all wells should extend 8" below the window sill and 4" above grade.

The minimum dimensions for an egress window well are determined by your local building code. Typically, wells for egress windows must be at least 9 sq. ft. overall, measure at least 36" in width, and extend 36" from the foundation wall. Any egress well more than 44" deep must have a permanently attached ladder or a step system that doesn't interfere with the window's operation.

Drainage for window wells is another important issue, particularly if they are uncovered. All wells should have a layer of gravel that is at least 6" deep and stops 3" below the window frame. Uncovered wells may need a drain pipe or a continuous layer of gravel that leads to footing drain or other perimeter drain system. Covering wells with clear, plastic covers keeps out the weather and prevents children or animals from falling into the well. Covers on egress window wells must be hinged or easily removable from inside the well.

Egress windows *in basements require large wells that meet code specifications. The prefabricated window well shown here has a stepped side that serves as stairs for emergency escape.*

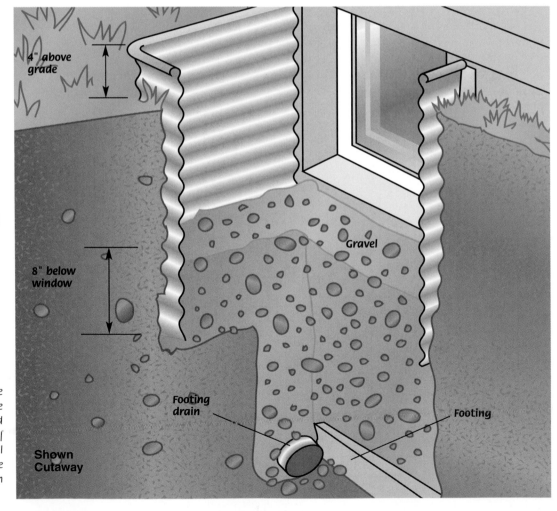

Window wells *should extend 8" below the window frame and 4" above the ground. Wells for egress windows must be at least 36" wide and project 36" from the foundation, and those deeper than 44" must have a ladder or other means of escape. To keep water from pooling near the window, well bases should have a 6" layer of gravel. More drainage can be provided by gravel that passes water down to a footing drain or by a well drain leading to daylight.*

4" above grade

8" below window

Gravel

Footing drain

Footing

Shown Cutaway

Photo courtesy of The Bilco Company

Planning the Systems

Adding the plumbing, wiring, and HVAC (heating, ventilation, and air conditioning) elements is one of the more challenging aspects of a basement or attic conversion. If your current systems can accommodate the added loads, you can expand them by adding new lines to provide service to the space, but making the connections and finding room for everything can be difficult.

To find out what's needed for the converted space, start by planning the fixtures and outlets for each proposed room and making rough plans of the overall room layout. Then consult the local building codes to determine what systems are required (such as a hard-wired vent fan in a bathroom), minimum room dimensions, and required clearances around fixtures.

When you have a general systems plan for all of the new rooms, hire the appropriate contractors to assess the plans based on the existing systems in your house. They will check the capacity of each system to determine if it can handle the additional load. For example, if your electrical service panel is nearly full, you may need to install a new sub-panel to supply electricity to the new rooms.

The contractors should also help you with the next step: figuring out how to route all the pipes, wires, ducts, etc. to the new rooms. This can be tricky, and you may find it's easier to change the room plans than to move the needed systems lines.

Routing the lines themselves often requires creative solutions. Think about the major issues first—ducts and drain pipes are more difficult to route than supply pipes and wiring. You can run many of the lines through and between the framing members of floors, ceilings, and walls. Be sure to follow code restrictions for notching and boring joists and studs, to maintain their structural integrity. When lines can't be hidden within framing, try to group them together so they can be enclosed in a soffit or vertical chase.

Wiring

To avoid long wiring runs or crowding the main service panel, consider installing a circuit breaker subpanel in or near the finished space. Powered by a single cable leading from the main panel, a subpanel is like a satellite service panel, allowing you to run new circuits from a convenient location.

The following are some of the basic electrical elements to consider when creating your wiring plan. (For more information on planning and installing wiring, see pages 94 to 139.)

Receptacles: The National Electrical Code requires that receptacles be spaced no more than 12 ft. apart, but for convenience you can space them as close as 6 ft. You may also need some non-standard receptacles, such as a GFCI for bathrooms and wet areas and a 20-amp or 240-volt receptacle for large appliances.

Lighting: Lighting is an important consideration for every room, particularly those with limited sources of ambient light. Most codes require that each room have at least one switch-controlled light fixture, and a switch near the entrance. Stairways must have a fixture that illuminates each step and is controlled by three-way switches at the top and bottom landings. Hallways and closets also need switch-controlled lights. Your general lighting plan should provide versatility for everyday tasks as well as visual warmth. This is especially true in basements, which generally need more artificial light than upper floors.

HVAC: Your new space probably will need additional wiring to supply auxiliary HVAC equipment. A typical bathroom vent fan or a ceiling fan runs on a standard 120-volt circuit, while most window air conditioners and baseboard heaters require 240-volt circuits. For an electric radiant heating system, check the manufacturer's requirements.

Network Wiring: A remodeling project is a good opportunity to prepare your house for the future. As with conventional wiring, it's easier and cheaper to install specialty cables for telephones, computers, and entertainment systems while you're building new walls and floors. And the minor expense you incur now will be more than offset by the convenience of having the wiring in place if you need it in the future.

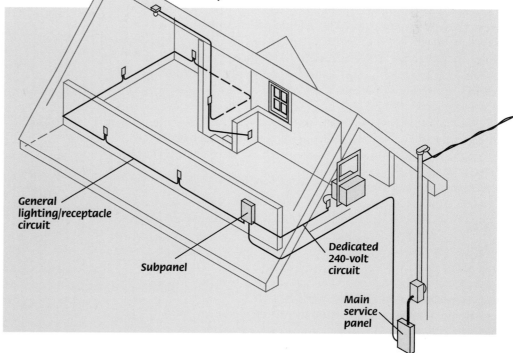

General lighting/receptacle circuit

Subpanel

Dedicated 240-volt circuit

Main service panel

Plumbing

Installing new plumbing in a basement or attic is made much easier and less expensive if you locate the fixtures near existing plumbing

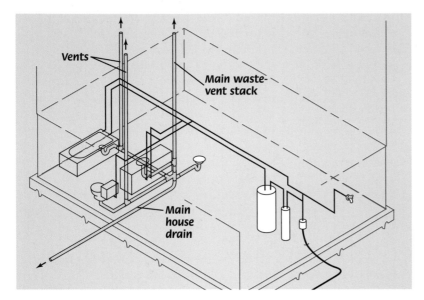

lines. This usually means placing attic bathrooms directly above another bathroom or the kitchen and locating basement baths or laundry centers close to the main waste-vent stack and house drain.

Drain rough-ins for basement bathrooms are installed during initial construction of many newer homes. Without the rough-ins in place, adding a basement bath usually requires cutting into the slab floor to make the drain connections. In some basements, however, the main house drain does not extend through the basement floor but instead makes a turn above the floor and begins its run out to the city sewer. In this situation, a bathroom requires a sewage ejector to collect the waste from each fixture and pump it up to the main drain. Ejectors are available from plumbing dealers, in both under-floor and above-floor models.

Building codes typically allow 7-ft. ceilings in bathrooms, which makes it easier to fit them into small attic spaces. If you plan to install a bathtub in an attic bath, make sure the floor is strong enough the support it.

See pages 62 to 93 for more information on planning and installing new plumbing.

HVAC

To supply heat and air conditioning to your basement or attic you may need to expand your home's central system, add a new system, or simply install auxiliary heating or cooling appliances.

Expanding a forced-air system in a basement usually requires only a few added ducts (see page 311). Running ducts to the attic is more challenging: It's often easiest to extend a duct straight up through the intermediate floors. You can conceal the ducts in closets and other inconspicuous areas or build a small wall around it. A hydronic (water or steam) heating system can be expanded by adding new pipes and fixtures; this is a job for a plumber or mechanical contractor.

The main concern is whether your central HVAC system can handle the additional load. If not, and upgrading the furnace or boiler isn't realistic, consider supplemental units, such as electric baseboard heaters and room air conditioners.

Room A/C units typically plug into a 240-volt receptacle, while heaters either plug into a standard 120-volt receptacle or are hard-wired to a 240-volt circuit (see page 113). Either may require a new circuit in your electrical panel.

A gas fireplace (see pages 336 to 342) is another good source of supplemental heat, and today's direct-vent fireplaces can be installed in almost any room. *Heater* models reach higher temperatures than standard models, and units with electric fans circulate warm air efficiently.

Radiant heating systems are an increasingly popular option. These systems provide heat via electrical wires or hot-water tubing laid out

behind the finish surfaces of walls, ceilings, and floors. Radiant systems can supply dry, consistent heat to warm anything from a tiled floor (see pages 260 to 263) in a half-bath to an entire basement slab. Large-scale installations, however, are not for do-it-yourselfers.

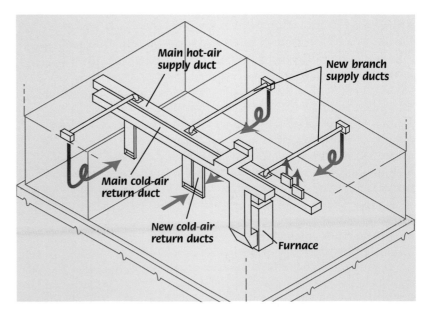

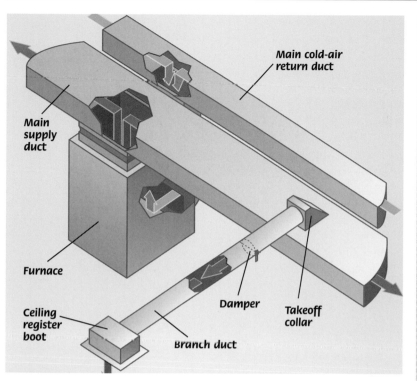

Expanding a forced-air system typically involves tapping into a main duct, using a takeoff collar that directs air into a new branch duct. All branch ducts need dampers to control flow.

Forced-Air Systems

A typical gas-furnace forced-air system (see above) has a main *supply* duct that supplies the warm air to the entire house via a network of *branch* ducts. The *return* ducts are just the reverse. They bring cool air from the rooms back to the furnace, providing air circulation throughout the house. To find out which is which, turn on the furnace and feel the ducts. Supply ducts will be warm, return ducts cool. The whole system is balanced by adjustable *dampers* located inside the branch ducts and controlled by the home's thermostat.

Some systems—called *zone systems*—are balanced by several automatic dampers. Each damper is controlled by its own thermostat, thus maintaining a consistent temperature within a specific zone. Zone systems are complicated, and you'll need the help of an HVAC specialist to expand the system.

With standard systems, providing heat and air conditioning to remodeled spaces is fairly straightforward. While you're planning the walls and thinking about which rooms are going where, have an HVAC specialist take a look at your system. He or she can help you find the best way to distribute air to the new space without compromising service to the rest of the house.

In most cases, you can run new branch ducts directly from the main supply duct or from another branch duct and use empty wall-stud cavities to serve as branch cold-air return ducts. Here are a few tips to help

Ventilating Attics

Windows and skylights provide effective passive ventilation for attics. Opening the widows in the house encourages natural circulation of cool air up through the floors. Whenever possible, install windows on opposing walls to create a cross-breeze when both windows are open. Room air conditioners also can help ventilate an attic by replacing stale indoor air with outdoor air. However, a single unit many not provide adequate ventilation for an entire attic. Check with the local building department for ventilation requirements in your area.

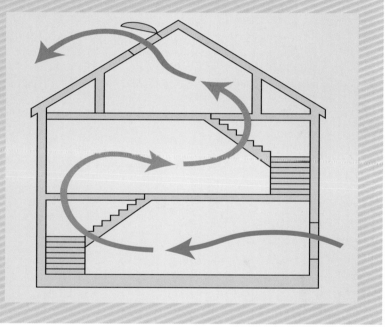

you with the planning:
- Plan branch ducts with as few turns as possible; air moves most efficiently through short, straight runs of duct.
- Use round, galvanized metal duct wherever possible; it's the most efficient for moving air. Use flexible duct only where metal isn't practical. To save space, you may be able to use shallow rectangular metal duct that fits between studs and joists.
- Locate supply registers near exterior walls, below or above windows, if possible. Include at least one in each room. Place return air inlets on walls opposite the supply registers, to draw heated or cooled air across the space. Do not place return inlets in bathrooms or kitchens or within 10 ft. of a gas-burning appliance.
- Run ducts inside joist cavities, where possible. Otherwise, route them through closets or behind kneewalls in attics to help conceal them.
- Use existing ductwork to help size the new branch ducts. Note the sizes and lengths of the old ducts and the sizes of the rooms they serve.

Designing a Guest Suite

Converting a basement into a guest suite has become an increasingly popular remodeling project. Set apart from the main areas of the house, a basement suite offers guests privacy and independence. And, because many families today have three or more generations living under one roof, a guest suite can be the perfect solution. Incorporating universal design into your guest suite will make the space more versatile for your family and visitors and more attractive to potential buyers in the future.

More than a convenience for visitors, guest suites are often semi-permanent living quarters for adult children and their children, live-in caretakers, aging parents, or teens who want private space. Designs can range from a simple plan with a single bedroom and adjoining bathroom to an apartment-style layout with a kitchenette, dining area, reading room or playroom, home office, and laundry facilities. When planning a guest suite, the key is to evaluate all potential uses for the space to make sure that it will accommodate your family's needs as they change over time.

An important consideration for a basement guest suite is providing safe and easy access for everyone. Because stairs can be difficult for some, it's a good idea to plan for stepless access, either now or in the future. A stair lift is a good option. Or you may want to plan for the future installation of a residential elevator by building two large closets—one above the other—that can be converted to an elevator shaft.

In addition to the ideas given here, you may want to incorporate many of the universal design topics discussed in this book (see page 17).

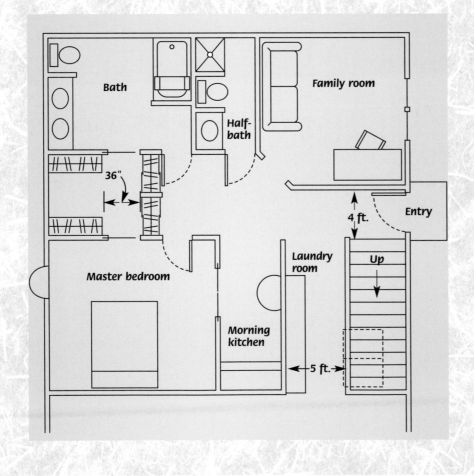

General Design
Simplicity should guide your design. Ample space and open floor plans make it easier for people with walkers or in wheelchairs to move around. Plan for a range of sleeping habits and schedules by separating playrooms, kitchens, and laundry facilities from bedrooms and reading rooms. Include two bathrooms if possible—one attached to the master bedroom and one for visitors.

- Provide or plan for stepless access to the suite.
- Frame doorways 36" wide and hallways 42" wide.
- Eliminate thresholds and changes in floor heights; install smooth transition devices between floor coverings.
- Include wiring that can accommodate a range of needs over time. Overnight guests may not require modem capabilities, for example, but long-term residents will. Install as many electrical receptacles as is practical, so appliances and fixtures can remain in place.
- Maximize natural and non-glare lighting— visitors of all ages will appreciate this,

Stair lifts are available in a variety of styles. Most are mounted to the stair treads or the stairway walls.

especially if your home is unfamiliar to them.

• Place telephones in each room of the suite, including the bathroom.
• Consider installing an intercom system for communication within the suite and between the suite and the main house.
• Ensure that people of different heights will be able to reach windows, cabinets, closet rods, appliances, fixtures, switches, and electrical receptacles.

Guest Suite Bedrooms

The guest suite bedroom should feel like a home away from home, and its location should provide privacy without being inconvenient. Laundry rooms also are nice luxuries; be sure to place them where noise won't be a problem. Allow plenty of space within the bedroom for maneuvering and provide clear pathways between the bed, bathroom, and closets.

Guest Suite Kitchens

A kitchen can be a great convenience for your guests. It provides independence for guests; a suite kitchen can range from very simple to full-sized. A popular feature in many homes today is the *morning kitchen*. Usually small and simple, a typical morning kitchen might include a coffee maker, small sink with an instant-hot-water tap, and an under-counter refrigerator. Larger morning kitchens might include a toaster, microwave, small dishwasher, or even a small cooktop and oven.

Your suite kitchen should include at least one section of countertop at a lower height and with knee space underneath to provide a work space for a seated user. Make sure shelving and appliances are reachable by small or seated users. If space is a concern, consider alternatives to standard cabinetry and appliances, like drawer-type refrigerators and dishwashers or narrow pull-out pantries.

See pages 368 to 371, for more advice on universal kitchen design.

Guest Suite Bathrooms

Your suite should include at least one full bathroom designed for universal use. An additional half bath can make a suite more livable, but if space limits you to one bathroom, be sure it has two entrances—one from the main

An under-counter refrigerator with an ice maker is perfect for a guest suite morning kitchen.

bedroom and one from the living area.

Plan for sufficient space and good lighting; older adults require more light—especially in bathrooms, where accidents are most likely to occur. Varied countertop and low mirror heights, non-slip flooring, and reachable shelving are also important considerations.

People of all sizes and abilities use the fixtures in a guest bathroom, so explore a variety of options before buying. Several manufacturers offer tubs and whirlpool baths that have doors that open for easier entry and exit. Barrier-free showers are also available.

Include standard safety features in your guest bathroom. Install grab bars or add blocking so they can be installed in the future (pages 494 to 495). Anti-scald faucets are required in showers, but it's a good idea to install them on sinks, as well. Features like lower sinks and vanities with fold-away doors, maintain the appearance of standard fixtures while providing greater accessibility for those who need it.

See pages 448 to 451 for more bathroom guidelines and universal design tips.

Any guest or resident will appreciate the luxury of a barrier-free whirlpool tub.

Preparing Basement Floors

The way you prepare a concrete basement floor largely depends upon the condition of the floor, the type of floor covering you plan to use, and how you want the floor to feel underfoot. Flooring manufacturers have specifications for installing their products over concrete; follow these carefully, as they may affect the products' warranties. It's best to decide on a floor covering before preparing the floor. Also, it's imperative that you solve any moisture problems with a concrete floor before covering it (see pages 303 to 305).

To lay flooring directly over concrete, prepare the floor so that it's smooth and flat. Fill cracks, holes, and expansion joints with a vinyl or cement-based floor patching compound. If the concrete is especially rough or uneven, apply a *floor leveler*—a self-leveling, cement-based liquid that fills deviations in the floor and dries to form a hard, smooth surface.

For a more resilient basement floor, you can build a wood subfloor. A basement subfloor starts with a plastic moisture barrier and uses pressure-treated 2 × 4s laid flat—called *sleepers*—to act as floor joists. The sleepers are anchored to the concrete and topped with a layer of ¾" tongue-and-groove plywood.

A basement subfloor provides a flat, level surface that's more com-

fortable underfoot than concrete, and it serves as a nailing surface for certain types of flooring. A subfloor does take up valuable headroom, however, so you may want to save space by using 1 × 4 sleepers instead of 2 × 4s. Also consider how the added floor height will affect room transitions, as well as the bottom step of the basement stairs (see page 302).

Before laying out the sleepers, determine where the partition walls will go. If a wall will fall between parallel sleepers, add an extra sleeper to support the planned wall.

Tools: *Vacuum, masonry chisel, trowel, floor scraper, long-nap paint roller, wheelbarrow, gage rake, 4-ft. level, circular saw, caulk gun, powder-actuated nailer, chalk line, drill, sledgehammer.*

Materials: *Vinyl floor patching compound, concrete primer, floor leveler, pressure-treated 2 × 4s, 6-mil polyethylene sheeting, packing tape, cedar shims, construction adhesive, concrete fasteners, ¾" T&G plywood, 2" wallboard screws.*

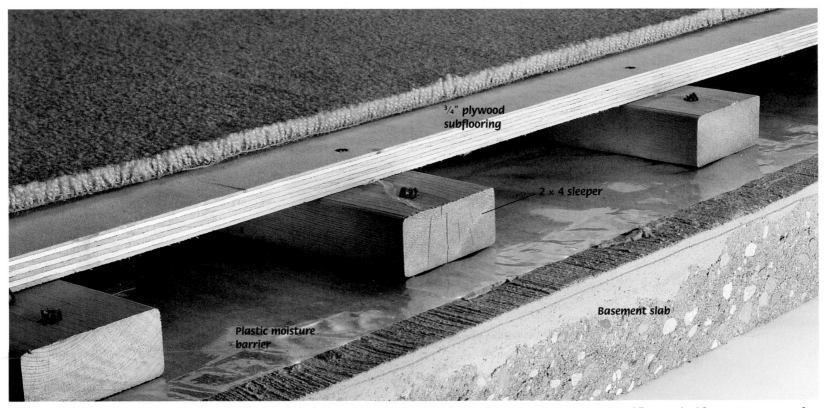

¾" plywood subflooring

2 × 4 sleeper

Basement slab

Plastic moisture barrier

Most basement floors *need some preparation before flooring can be laid. Patching compound and floor leveler can smooth rough concrete, while a wood subfloor creates a new surface that feels like a framed wood floor.*

Patching Concrete Floors

Clean the floor with a vacuum, and remove any loose or flaking concrete with a masonry chisel and hammer. Mix a batch of vinyl floor patching compound following the manufacturer's directions. Apply the compound using a smooth trowel, slightly overfilling the cavity. Smooth the patch flush with the surface.

After the compound has cured fully, use a floor scraper to scrape the patched areas smooth.

Applying Floor Leveler

Remove any loose material and clean the concrete thoroughly; the surface must be free of dust, dirt, oils, and paint. Apply an even layer of concrete primer to the entire surface, using a long-nap paint roller. Let the primer dry completely.

Following the manufacturer's instructions, mix the floor leveler with water. The batch should be large enough to cover the entire floor area to the desired thickness (up to 1"). Pour the leveler over the floor.

Distribute the leveler evenly, using a gage rake or spreader. Work quickly—the leveler begins to harden in 15 minutes. You can use a trowel to feather the edges and create smooth transitions with uncovered areas. Let the leveler dry for 24 hours.

Installing a Basement Subfloor

Chip away loose or protruding concrete with a masonry chisel and hammer, then clean the floor thoroughly with a vacuum. Roll out strips of 6-mil polyethylene sheeting, extending them 3" up each wall. Overlap the strips by 6", then seal the seams with packing tape. Temporarily tape the edges along the walls. Be careful not to damage the sheeting.

Lay out pressure-treated 2 × 4s along the perimeter of the room. Position the boards ½" in from all walls (inset).

Cut the sleepers to fit between the perimeter boards, leaving a ¼" gap at each end. Position the first sleeper so its center is 16" from the outside edge of the perimeter board. This ensures that one edge of the subflooring sheets will cover the perimeter board and the other edge will fall on the middle of a sleeper. Lay out the remaining sleepers using 16"-on-center spacing.

Where necessary, use tapered cedar shims to compensate for dips and variations in the floor. Set a 4-ft. level across the neighboring sleepers. Apply a small amount of construction adhesive to two shims of equal size. Slide the shims underneath the board from opposite sides until the board is level with the neighboring sleepers.

Fasten the perimeter boards and sleepers to the floor, using a powder-actuated nailer or masonry screws (see pages 323 to 324). Drive a single fastener through the center of each board at 16" intervals. The fastener heads should not protrude above the surface of the board. Place a fastener at each shim location, making sure the fastener captures both shims.

Create a control line for the first row of plywood sheets by measuring out 49" from the wall and marking the outside sleeper at each end of the room. Snap a chalk line across the sleepers at the marks, perpendicular to the sleepers. Run a ¼"-wide bead of adhesive along the first six sleepers, stopping just short of the control line.

Position the first sheet of plywood, making sure the end is ½" away from the wall and the grooved edge is aligned with the control line. Fasten the sheet with 2" wallboard screws. Drive a screw every 6" along the edges and every 8" in the field of the sheet. Don't drive screws along the grooved edge until the next row of sheets is in place.

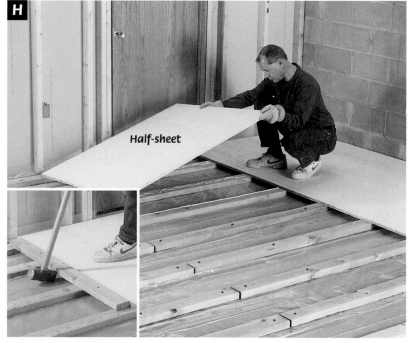

Install the remaining sheets in the first row, maintaining a ⅛" gap between the ends. Begin the second row with a half-sheet (4 ft.-long) so that the end joints between rows are staggered. Fit the tongue of the half sheet into the groove of the sheet behind it. If necessary, use a sledgehammer and a wood block to help close the joint (inset). After completing the second row, begin the third row with a full sheet, and so on, until the subfloor is complete.

Building Attic Floors

Before you build the walls that will define the rooms in your attic, you'll need a sturdy floor. Existing floors in most unfinished attics are merely ceiling joists for the floor below and are too small to support living spaces.

There are several options for strengthening your attic's floor structure. The simplest method is to install an additional, identically sized joist next to each existing joist, connecting the two with nails. This process is known as *sistering*.

Sistering doesn't work when joists are smaller than 2 × 6s, where joists are spaced too far apart, or where there are obstructions, such as plaster keys from the ceiling below. An alternative is to build a new floor by placing larger joists between the existing ones. By resting the joists on 2 × 4 spacers, you avoid obstructions and minimize damage to the ceiling surfaces below. However, be aware that the spacers will reduce your headroom by 1½" inches, plus the added joist depth.

To determine the best option for your attic, consult an architect, engineer, or building contractor, as well as a local building inspector. Ask what size of joists you'll need and which options are allowed in your area. Joist sizing is based on the *span* (the distance between support points), the joist spacing (typically 16" or 24" on-center), and the type of lumber used. In most cases, an attic floor must be able to support 40 pounds per sq. ft. of *live load* (occupants, furniture) and 10 psf of *dead load* (wallboard, floor covering).

The floor joist cavities offer space for concealing the plumbing, wiring, and ductwork servicing your attic, so consider these systems as you plan. You'll also need to plan the locations of partition walls to determine if any additional blocking between joists is necessary (see pages 46 to 47).

When the framing is done, the mechanical elements and insulation are in place, and everything has been inspected and approved, complete the floor by installing ¾" tongue-and-groove plywood. If your remodel will include kneewalls, you can omit the subflooring behind the kneewalls, but there are good reasons not to: A complete subfloor will add strength to the floor and will provide a sturdy surface for storage.

> **Tools:** Circular saw, rafter square, drill, caulk gun.
>
> **Materials:** 2 × joist lumber; 16d, 10d, and 8d common nails; 2 × 4 lumber; ¾" T&G plywood; construction adhesive; 2¼" wallboard screws.

Attic joists typically rest on top of exterior walls and on an interior load-bearing wall, where they overlap from side to side and are nailed together. Always use a sheet of plywood as a platform while working over open joists.

Adding Sister Joists

A

Remove all insulation from the joist cavities and carefully remove any blocking or bridging between the joists. Determine the lengths for the sister joists by measuring the existing joists. Also measure at the outside end of each joist to determine how much of the top corner was cut away to fit the joist beneath the roof sheathing. NOTE: Joists that rest on a bearing wall should overlap each other by at least 3".

B

Before cutting, sight down both narrow edges of each board to check for *crowning*—upward arching along the length of the board. Draw an arrow that points in the direction of the arch. Joists must be installed "crown-up;" this arrow designates the top edge. Cut the board to length, then clip the top, outside corner to match the existing joists.

C

Set the sister joists in place, flush against the existing joists and with their ends aligned. Toenail each sister joist to the top plates of both supporting walls, using two 16d common nails.

D

Nail the joists together using 10d common nails. Drive three nails in a row, spacing the rows 12" to 16" apart. To minimize damage (such as cracking and nail popping) to the ceiling surface below caused by the hammering, you can use an air-powered nail gun (available at rental stores), or 3" lag screws instead of nails. Install new blocking between the sistered joists, as required by the local building code.

Building a New Attic Floor

Remove any blocking or bridging from between the existing joists, being careful not to disturb the ceiling below. Cut 2 × 4 spacers to fit snugly between each pair of joists. Lay the spacers flat against the top plate of all supporting walls, and nail them in place with 16d common nails.

Create a layout for the new joists by measuring across the tops of the existing joists and using a rafter square to transfer the measurements down to the spacers. Following 16"-on-center spacing, mark the layout along one exterior wall, then mark an identical layout onto the interior bearing wall. Note that the layout on the opposing exterior wall will be offset 1½", to account for the joist overlap at the interior wall.

To determine joist length, measure from the outer edge of the exterior wall to the far edge of the interior bearing wall. The joists must overlap each other above the interior wall by 3". Before cutting, mark the top edge of each joist (see step B, page 319). Cut the joists to length, then clip the top, outside corners so the ends can fit under the roof sheathing.

Set the joists in place on their layout marks. Toenail the outside end of each joist to the spacer on the exterior wall, using three 8d common nails.

Nail the joists together where they overlap atop the interior bearing wall, using three 10d nails for each. Toenail the joists to the spacers on the interior bearing wall, using 8d nails.

Install blocking or bridging between the joists, as required by the local building code. As a suggested minimum, the new joists should be blocked as close as possible to the outside ends and at the points where they overlap at the interior wall.

Installing Subflooring

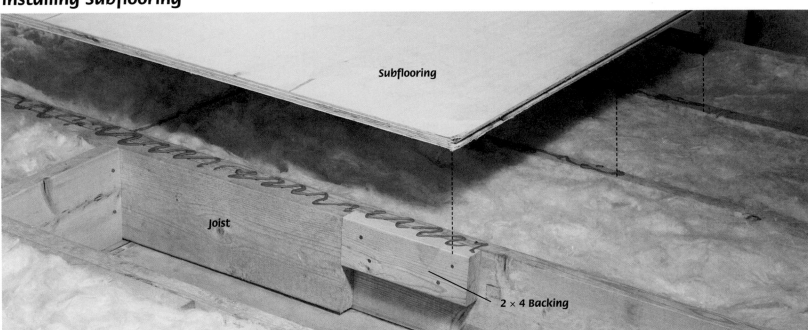

Subflooring

Joist

2 × 4 Backing

Install the subflooring only after all framing, plumbing, wiring, and ductwork is completed and has received the required building inspections. Also install any insulation and complete any caulking necessary for soundproofing (see pages 194 to 195). Follow steps F-H on page 317 for the general subflooring procedure. Fasten the sheets with construction adhesive and 2¼" wallboard or deck screws, making sure the sheets are perpendicular to the joists and the end joints are staggered between rows. Where joists overlap at an interior bearing wall, add backing as needed to compensate for the offset in the layout. Nail a 2 × 4 (or wider) board to the face of each joist to support the edges of the intervening sheets.

Covering Foundation Walls

There are two common methods for covering foundation walls. Because it saves space, the more popular method is to attach 2 × 2 furring strips directly to masonry walls. These strips provide a 1½"-deep cavity between strips for insulation and service lines, as well as a framework for attaching wallboard. The other method is to build complete 2 × 4 stud walls just in front of the foundation walls. This method offers a full 3½" for insulation and lines, and it provides a flat, plumb wall surface, regardless of the foundation wall's condition.

To determine the best method for your project, examine the foundation walls. If they're fairly plumb and flat, you can consider furring them. If the walls are wavy or out of plumb, however, it may be easier to build stud walls. Also check with the local building department before you decide on a framing method. There may be codes regarding insulation minimums and methods of running service lines along foundation walls.

A local building official can also tell you what's recommended—or required—in your area for sealing foundation walls against moisture.

Common types of moisture barriers include masonry waterproofers that are applied like paint and plastic sheeting installed between masonry walls and wood framing. The local building code will also specify whether you need a vapor barrier between the framing and the wallboard (see pages 192 to 193).

Before you shop for materials, decide how you'll fasten the wood framing to your foundation walls and floor. The three most common methods are shown on pages 323 to 325. For covering a large wall area, it will be worth it to buy or rent a powder-actuated nailer for the job.

Tools: Caulk gun, trowel, paint roller, circular saw, drill, powder-actuated nailer, plumb bob.

Materials: Paper-faced insulation, silicone caulk, hydraulic cement, masonry waterproofer, 2 × 2 and 2 × 4 lumber, 2½" wallboard screws, construction adhesive, concrete fasteners, insulation.

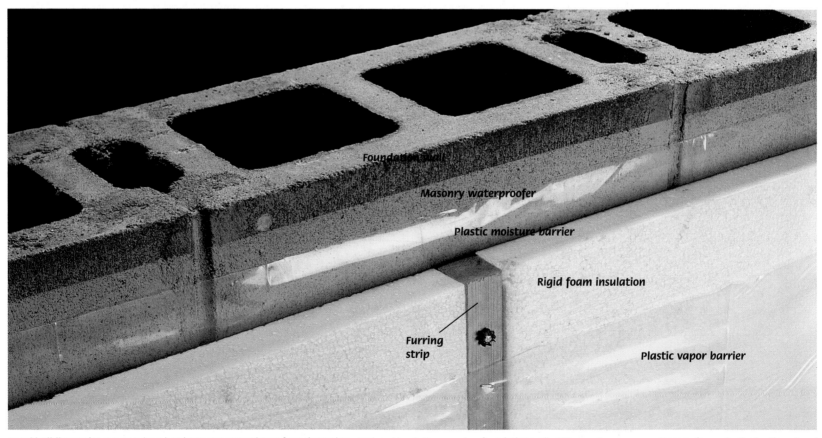

Foundation wall

Masonry waterproofer

Plastic moisture barrier

Rigid foam insulation

Furring strip

Plastic vapor barrier

Local building codes may require a barrier to prevent moisture from damaging wood and insulation covering foundation walls. This may be masonry waterproofer or plastic sheeting placed behind or in front of the framing.

Sealing and Preparing Masonry Walls

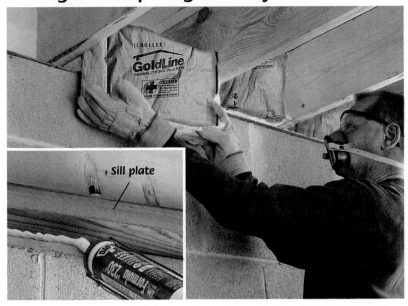

Insulate the rim-joist cavities (above the foundation walls) with solid pieces of paper-faced fiberglass insulation. Make sure the paper, which serves as a vapor barrier, faces the room. Also apply silicone caulk to the joints between the sill plates and the foundation walls (inset).

Fill small cracks with hydraulic cement or masonry caulk, and smooth the excess with a trowel. Ask the building department whether masonry waterproofer or a plastic moisture barrier is required in your area. Apply waterproofer as directed by the manufacturer, or install plastic sheeting following code specifications.

Options for Attaching Wood to Masonry Walls

Masonry nails offer the cheapest way to attach wood to concrete block walls. Drive the nails into the mortar joints for maximum holding power and to avoid cracking the blocks. Drill pilot holes through the strips if the nails cause the wood to split. If the walls are poured concrete, consider another method—it's difficult to drive masonry nails into poured concrete.

Self-tapping masonry screws hold well in block or poured concrete, but they must be driven into predrilled holes. Position the wood, then use a hammer drill to drill holes of the same size in both the wood and the concrete. Drive the screws into the web portion of the blocks (see page 324).

Continued on next page

Options for Attaching Wood to Masonry Walls (cont.)

Webs

Powder-actuated nailers offer the quickest and easiest method for fastening framing to block, poured concrete, and steel. They use individual caps of gunpowder—called *loads*—to propel a piston that drives a hardened-steel nail (*pin*) through the wood and into the masonry. The loads are color-coded for the charge they produce, and the pins come in various lengths. NOTE: Always drive pins into the solid web portions of concrete blocks, not into the voids.

Trigger-type nailers, like the one shown here, are easiest to use, but hammer-activated types are also available. You can buy nailers at home centers and hardware stores or rent them from rental centers. (Ask for a demonstration at the rental center.) Always wear hearing and eye protection when using these extremely loud tools.

Installing Furring Strips

A

Joist

Backer

Sill plate   Top plate

Cut a 2 × 2 top plate to span the length of the wall. Mark the furring-strip layout onto the bottom edge of the plate, using 16"-on-center spacing (see step B, page 47). If the joists are perpendicular to the wall, align the back edge of the plate with the faces of the blocks, and attach the plate to the joists with 2½" wallboard screws. If the joists are parallel with the wall, attach the top plate to the foundation wall so its top edge is flush with the top of the blocks.

TIP: If the joists run parallel to the wall, you'll need to install backers between the outer joist and the sill plate to provide support for ceiling wallboard. Make T-shaped backers from short 2 × 4s and 2 × 2s. Install each so the bottom face of the 2 × 4 is flush with the bottom edge of the joist.

Install a bottom plate cut from pressure-treated 2 × 2 lumber so the plate spans the length of the wall. Apply construction adhesive to the back and bottom of the plate, then attach it to the floor with a nailer. Use a plumb bob to transfer the furring-strip layout marks from the top plate to the bottom plate.

Cut 2 × 2 furring strips to fit between the top and bottom plates. Apply construction adhesive to the back of each furring strip, and position the strips on the layout marks on the plates. Nail along the length of each strip at 16" intervals.

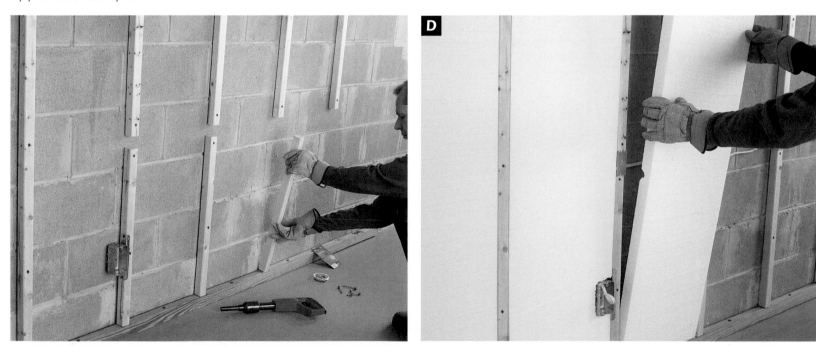

VARIATION: Leave a channel for the installation of wires or pipes by installing pairs of vertically aligned furring strips with a 2" gap between each pair. Note: Consult local codes to ensure proper installation of electrical or plumbing materials.

Fill the cavities between furring strips with rigid insulation board. Cut the pieces so they fit snugly within the framing. If necessary, make cutouts in the insulation to fit around mechanical elements, and cover any channels with metal protective plates before attaching the wall surface. Add a vapor barrier if required by local building code.

Tips for Covering Foundation Walls with Stud Walls

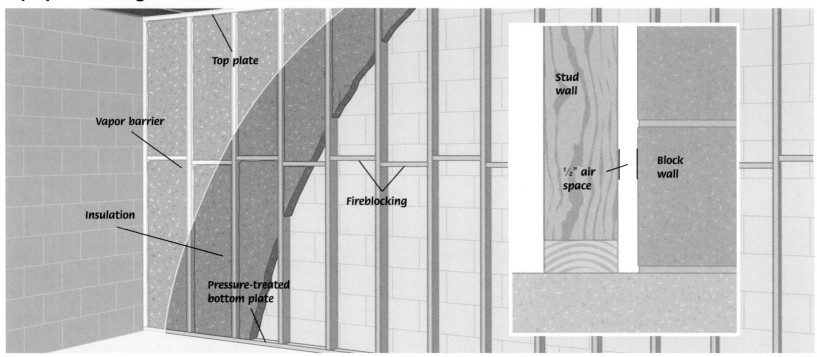

Build a standard 2 × 4 partition wall, following the basic steps on pages 46 to 49. Use pressure-treated lumber for bottom plates that rest on concrete. To minimize moisture problems and avoid unevenness in foundation walls, leave a ½" air space between the stud walls and the masonry walls (inset). Insulate the stud walls with fiberglass blankets, and install a vapor barrier if required by local code. Also install all fireblocking required by local code. As an alternative, you can build the walls using full-width (3⅝") steel studs (see pages 50 to 51).

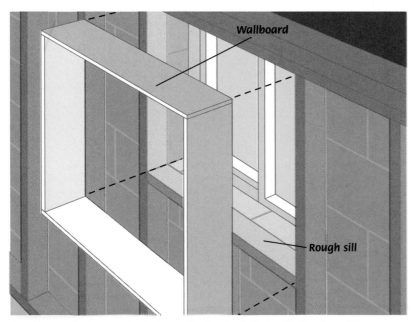

Frame around a basement window so the framing is flush with the edges of the masonry on all sides. Install a rough sill at the base of the window opening and add a header, if necessary. Fill the space between the framing members and the masonry with fiberglass insulation or non-expanding foam insulation. Install wallboard so it butts against the window frame.

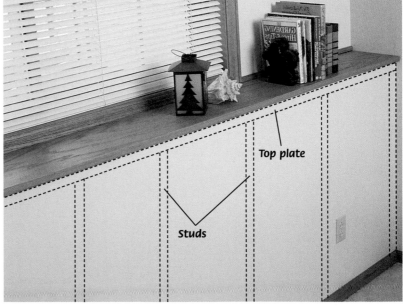

Build a short stud wall to cover a low foundation wall in a walkout or "daylight" basement. Install the top plate flush with the top of the foundation wall. Finish the wall surface with wallboard or other finish, then cap the walls with finish-grade lumber or plywood to create a decorative shelf.

Framing Soffits and Chases

Your unfinished basement or attic is sure to have beams, pipes, posts, ductwork, and other elements that are vital to your house but become big obstacles to finishing the space. When you can't conceal the obstructions within walls and you've determined it's too costly to move them, hide them inside a framed soffit or chase. This can also provide a place to run smaller mechanicals, like wiring and water supply lines.

Soffits and chases are easy to build. A soffit is usually constructed with 2 × 2 lumber or 1⅝" steel studs (see pages 50 to 51), both of which are easy to work with and inexpensive. You can use 2 × 4s for large soffits that will house other elements, such as lighting fixtures. Chases should be framed with 2 × 4s or steel studs.

This section shows you some basic techniques for building soffits and chases, but the design of your framing is up to you. For example, you may want to shape your soffits for a decorative effect, or build an over-size chase that holds bookshelves. Just make sure the framing conforms to local building codes. There may be code restrictions about the types of mechanicals that can be grouped together, as well as minimum clearances between the framing and the elements it encloses. And most codes specify that soffits, chases, and other framed structures have fire-blocking every 10 ft. and at the intersections between soffits and neighboring walls. Remember, too, that drain cleanouts and shutoff valves must be accessible, so you'll need to install access panels at these locations.

> **Tools:** Circular saw, drill, powder-actuated nailer.
>
> **Materials:** Standard lumber (2 × 2, 2 × 4), pressure-treated 2 × 4s, construction adhesive, wallboard, unfaced fiberglass insulation, nails, wood trim, plywood, wallboard screws, decorative screws.

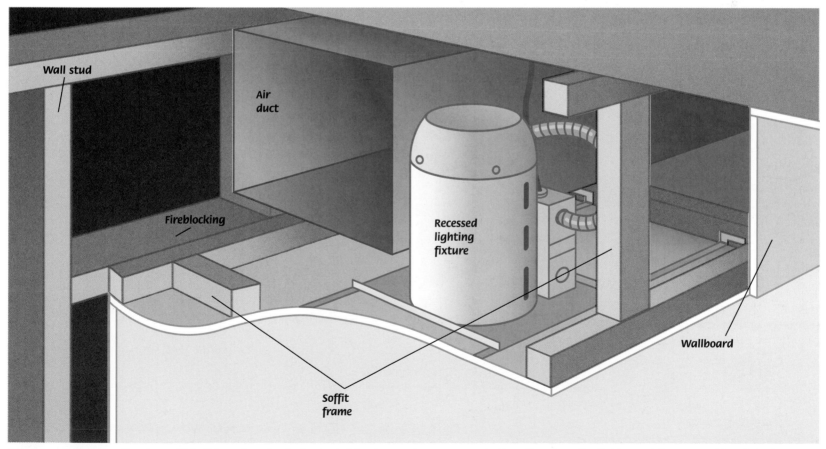

Hide immovable obstructions in a soffit built from dimension lumber or steel framing members and covered with wallboard or other finish material. An extra-wide soffit is also a great place to install recessed lighting fixtures.

Building Soffits

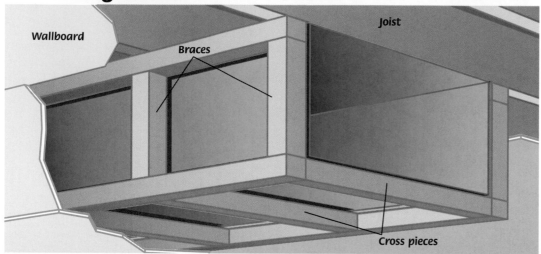

Wallboard

Braces

Joist

Cross pieces

Obstructions perpendicular to joists. Build two ladder-like frames for the soffit sides, using standard 2 × 2s. Install 2 × 2 braces (or "rungs") every 16" or 24" to provide nailing support for the edges of the wallboard or other finish material. Attach the side frames to the joists on either side of the obstruction, using nails or screws. Then, install cross pieces beneath the obstacle, tying the two sides together. Cover the soffit with wallboard, plywood, or other finish material.

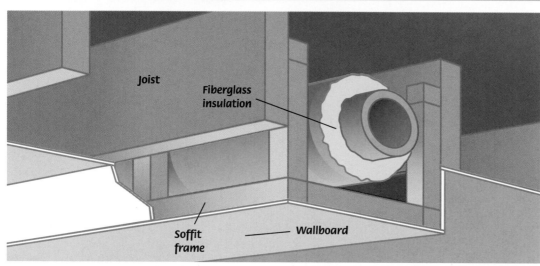

Joist

Fiberglass insulation

Soffit frame

Wallboard

Obstructions parallel to joists. Build side frames as with perpendicular obstructions, but size them to fit in between two joists. This provides nailing surfaces for both the soffit and ceiling finish materials. Attach the frames to the joists with screws, then install cross pieces. NOTE: If you are enclosing a drain pipe, wrap the pipe in unfaced fiberglass insulation to muffle the sound of draining water.

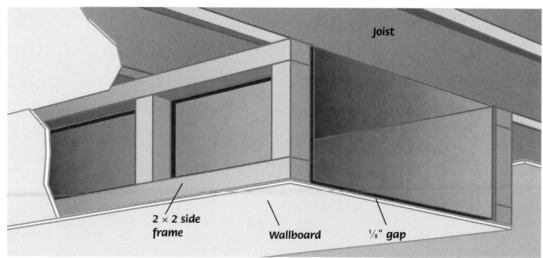

Joist

2 × 2 side frame

Wallboard

⅛" gap

Maximize headroom. In rooms with low ceilings, and where an obstruction is less than 12" wide and the finish material will be wallboard or plywood, build side frames (see above) so that the bottom edges are ⅛" lower than the lowest point of the obstruction. For this type of soffit, the bottom piece of wallboard or plywood stabilizes the structure, so cross pieces between side frames aren't necessary. Use this construction method if you are framing with steel (see pages 50 to 51). Soffits framed with steel often are easier to build in-place.

Framing a Chase

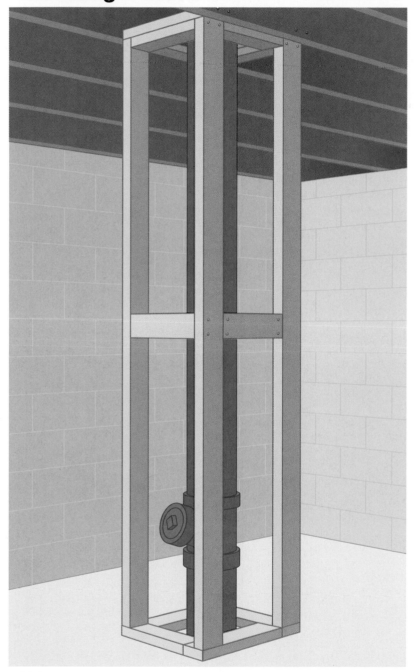

Build chases with 2 × 4s or steel studs. For wood frames, use pressure-treated lumber for bottom plates on concrete floors, attaching them with construction adhesive and powder-actuated nailer fasteners (see page 324). Cut top plates from standard lumber and nail or screw them in place. Install studs to form the corners of the chase, and block in between them for stability. To make the chase smaller, notch the top and bottom plates around the obstruction, and install the studs flat. If you're framing around a vertical drain pipe (especially the main DWV stack), leave room around the pipe for soundproofing insulation; plastic pipes can be especially noisy.

Making Access Panels

Make access panels after installing wallboard. In a horizontal surface, cut out a square piece of wallboard at the access location; set it inside the soffit. Glue mitered trim around the opening so it overlaps the edges by ½". Position the cutout over the trim to cover the opening. In a vertical surface, glue the trim to the cutout to create the panel. Install plywood strips to the back of the wallboard at two sides of the opening. Secure the panel to the strips with screws.

Attaching Framing to Steel

Steel beam

Joists

Minimum
fastening
distance:
1½" from
edge

2 × 8"
top plate

Support column

SHOWN
CUTAWAY

Use a powder-actuated nailer (see page 324) to attach wood and steel framing to steel I-beams and columns. Hold the nailer at a right angle to the surface and drive the fastener at least 1½" from the edge of the steel. Use a fastener and power load appropriate to the tool and each application. The tool manufacturer should supply a manual, fastener charts, and load charts with the tool. Always wear eye and ear protection when working with these tools.

Building Attic Kneewalls

Attic kneewalls are just the right height to be backdrops for furniture, and they make a perfect foundation for built-in storage units (see pages 350 to 353).

Attic kneewalls are short walls that extend from the attic floor to the rafters. They provide a vertical dimension to attic rooms and without them, attics tend to feel cramped. Kneewalls are typically 5 ft. tall, for a couple of reasons: That's the minimum ceiling height for usable floor space according to most building codes, and it defines a comfortable room without wasting too much floor space. The unfinished space behind kneewalls doesn't have to go to waste. It's great for storage and for concealing service lines. To provide access to this space, create a framed opening in the wall during the framing process much like framing an opening for a door or window (see pages 52 to 54).

Kneewalls are similar to partition walls, except they have beveled top plates and angle-cut studs that follow the slope of the rafters. The added stud depth created by the angled cut requires a 2 × 6 top plate. Before starting on your kneewall project, review the techniques for building a partition wall (pages 46 to 49).

> **Tools:** Circular saw, level, chalk line, T-bevel.
>
> **Materials:** 2 × 4 and 2 × 6 lumber, 16d and 8d common nails.

Building an Attic Kneewall

A

Create a storyboard using a straight 2 × 4. Cut the board a few inches longer than the planned height of the wall. Measure from one end and draw a line across the front edge of the board at the exact wall height.

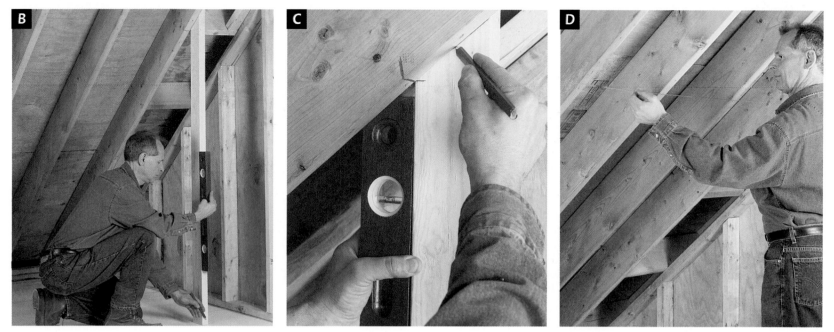

B At one end of the room, set the storyboard flat against the outer rafter. Plumb the storyboard with a level while aligning the height mark with the bottom edge of the rafter. Transfer the height mark onto the rafter edge, then make a mark along the front edge of the storyboard onto the subfloor. These marks indicate the top and bottom wall plates.

C Holding the storyboard perfectly plumb, trace along the bottom edge of the rafter to transfer the rafter slope onto the face of the storyboard.

D Repeat the wall-plate marking process on the other end of the room. Snap a chalk line through the marks—across the rafters and along the subfloor. If necessary, add backing for fastening the top plate to the gable wall.

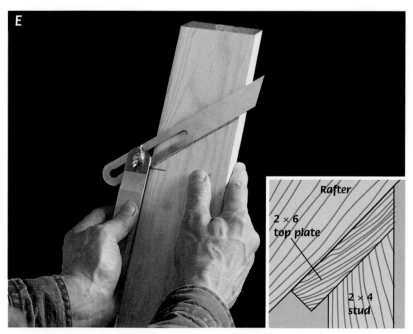

E To cut a beveled edge on the top wall plate, set a T-bevel to match the rafter-slope line on the storyboard. Use the T-bevel to adjust the blade of a circular saw or table saw to the proper angle. Then, bevel-cut one edge of the 2 × 6 top plate. NOTE: When the top plate is laid flat across the rafters, the front edge should be perpendicular to the floor (inset).

Inset labels: *Rafter*, *2 × 6 top plate*, *2 × 4 stud*

F Mark the stud locations on the wall plates (see pages 47 to 48). Install the plates along the chalk lines, fastening them to the rafters and floor joists, respectively, using 16d nails. Measure and cut each stud to fit, angle-cutting the top end so that it meets flush with the top plate. Toenail each stud in place with three 8d nails.

Framing an Attic Ceiling

Flat attic ceilings provide space for recessed light fixtures, vents, and speakers.

By virtue of sloping roofs, most attics naturally have "cathedral" ceilings. It's up to you whether to leave the peaks intact—and apply a finish surface all the way up to the ridge—or to frame-in a horizontal ceiling, creating a flat surface that's more like a standard ceiling. Before deciding, consider the advantages and disadvantages of each treatment.

If your attic has collar ties—horizontal braces installed between opposing rafters (see page 301)—your planning should start with those. Are the ties high enough to meet the code requirements for attic headroom? If not, consult an architect or engineer to see if you can move them up a few inches (do not move or remove them without professional guidance). If the ties are high enough, you can incorporate them into a new ceiling or leave them exposed and wrap them with a finish material, such as wallboard or finish-grade lumber. Do not use collar ties as part of your ceiling frame.

A peaked ceiling is primarily an aesthetic option. Its height expands the visual space of the room, and its rising angles provide a dramatic look that's unique in most homes. Because a peaked ceiling encloses the rafter bays all the way up to the ridge, this treatment may require additional roof vents to maintain proper ventilation (see pages 334 to 335).

By contrast, a flat ceiling typically offers a cleaner, more finished appearance closer to that of a conventional room, and flat ceilings offer some practical advantages over peaked styles. First, they provide a concealed space above the ceiling, great for running service lines. If there are vents high on the gable walls, this open space can help ventilate the roof (make sure to insulate above the ceiling). The ceiling itself can hold recessed lighting fixtures or support a ceiling fan. And if your plans call for full-height partition walls, you may want a ceiling frame to enclose the top of the walls.

When determining the height of flat-ceiling framing, be sure to account for the floor and ceiling finishes. And remember that most building codes require a finished ceiling height of at least $7\frac{1}{2}$ ft.

Exposed collar ties can add an interesting architectural element to a peaked ceiling. By adding trim boards to the existing ties, you can create a channel for holding small light fixtures (inset).

Tools: 4-ft. level, chalk line, circular saw.

Materials: 2 × 4 and 2 × 6 lumber, 10d common nails.

Framing a Flat Attic Ceiling

A

Make a storyboard for the planned height of the ceiling frame (see step A, page 330). At one end of the attic, hold the storyboard plumb and align the height mark with the bottom edge of a rafter. Transfer the mark to the rafter. Repeat at the other end of the attic, then snap a chalk line through the marks. This line indicates the bottom edge of the ceiling frame.

B

Using a level and the storyboard, level over from the chalk line and mark two outside rafters on the other side of the attic. Snap a chalk line through the marks. NOTE: The storyboard is used merely as a straightedge for this step.

C

Cut 2 × 6 joists to span across the rafters, angle-cutting the ends to follow the roof pitch. Check each joist for crowning to make sure you're cutting it to be installed with the crowned edge up (see step B, page 319). Make the overall length about ½" short so the ends of the joists won't touch the roof sheathing.

D

Nail each joist to the rafters with three 10d common nails at each end. Be sure to maintain 16"- or 24"- on-center spacing between joists to provide support for attaching wallboard or other finish material.

Insulating & Ventilating Roofs

Ventilation works in concert with insulation to keep your roof deck healthy. Roofs need ventilation for a number of reasons. During hot weather, direct sunlight can heat a roof considerably, and air flow underneath the roof deck helps reduce temperatures, keeping your attic cooler. In cold climates, and particularly in areas with heavy snowfall, roofs need ventilation to prevent ice dams and other moisture problems. As you insulate your attic ceiling, you need to make sure the roof will remain properly ventilated.

Here's how roof ventilation works: Air intake vents installed in the soffits—called *soffit vents*—allow outdoor air to pass under the roof sheathing and flow up toward the ridge, where it exits through one or more exhaust vents. In unfinished attics, with insulation only along the floor, air is allowed to flow from open rafter bays into a common air space under the roof. It can then be exhausted through any of the roof or gable vents. When you finish your attic, however, you enclose part or all of each rafter bay with insulation and a ceiling finish. A flat attic ceiling will provide some open air space above the ceiling, but air flow still may be limited. With a peaked ceiling, the rafter bays are enclosed up to the ridge, and a single roof vent can serve only one rafter bay. To improve ventilation, you can install additional roof and soffit vents or a continuous ridge vent, which provides ventilation to all of the rafter bays.

A roof ventilation system must have a clear air path between the intake and exhaust vents. For this reason, most building codes call for 1" of air space between the insulation and the roof sheathing. To ensure this air space remains unobstructed, install insulation baffles in the rafter bays. Also be sure to install enough insulation to meet the recommended R-value for your area. This may require increasing the depth of your attic rafters to accommodate the insulation and baffles. For more information on insulation R-values and installation, see pages 192 to 193.

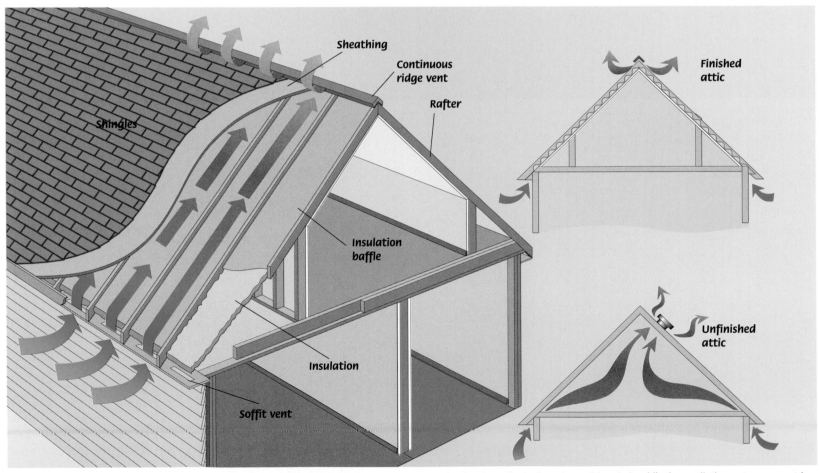

Labels: Sheathing, Continuous ridge vent, Rafter, Finished attic, Shingles, Insulation baffle, Insulation, Soffit vent, Unfinished attic

A roof ventilation system works *in conjunction with attic insulation: Insulation forms a thermal barrier that keeps in the home's conditioned air, while the ventilation system uses outdoor air to keep the roof deck cool and dry. In most unfinished attics, the entire attic space is ventilated, and proper air flow can be achieved with roof vents or gable-wall vents.*

Tips for Insulating Roofs

Increase the rafter depth to make room for thicker insulation by attaching 2 × 2s to the rafter edges. Fasten the 2 × 2s with 3"-long, countersunk screws. You can also save space by using high-density insulation.

Use insulation baffles to provide a continuous air channel behind the insulation. The baffles should start just in front of the exterior walls' top plates and extend up to the exhaust vents. Attach the baffles to the roof sheathing with staples.

Lay fiberglass insulation, stopping short of the baffle opening to avoid restricting air flow. Insulation in the attic floor should cover the exterior walls' top plates but not extend into the soffit cavities.

Options for Ventilating Roofs

Roof vents (box- or mushroom-type) are commonly used to ventilate unfinished attics. You can improve ventilation by adding more roof vents and soffit vents (inset). If your rafter bays are enclosed all the way to the ridge, be sure the soffit vents and roof vents are installed along the same rafter bays.

Continuous ridge vents are the most effective roof vents, because they ventilate along the entire ridge. It costs less to have one installed during a re-roofing project, but they can be installed onto an existing roof that's in good condition. This type of vent works best when used in conjunction with continuous soffit vents (inset).

Installing a Gas Fireplace

A new gas fireplace with direct venting can be the perfect addition to an attic or basement. Direct venting is a ventilation system that uses a special 2-in-1 vent pipe: The inner pipe carries exhaust fumes outside, while the outer pipe draws in fresh air for combustion. The vent pipe can be routed in many different ways, which means you can install a gas fireplace in almost any room.

Gas fireplaces are commonly available as standard (*decorative*) or *heater* types. They are similar in appearance, but heater models are designed to provide much more heat. This heat can enter the room passively or be blown out by an optional electric fan. Other options for both types include remote starting and electronic ignition.

Installing a gas fireplace is a great do-it-yourself project because you can design and build the fireplace frame to suit your needs and add your own finish treatments. It all starts with some careful planning. Once you decide on a fireplace model and determine where to place it, order all of the vent pipes and fittings needed to complete the vent run.

The project shown here demonstrates the installation of a decorative fireplace in a basement. The unit is top-vented upward and out through a concrete block wall. The frame is a rectangular box that extends from floor to ceiling and is finished with wallboard. A factory-made oak mantel sits above the fireplace, and a row of ceramic floor tile surrounds the fireplace opening.

Your fireplace project can match this one, or you can adapt the basic steps to suit your own design. The main difference among fireplace installations is the venting. Regardless of your project plans, make sure to use all the required parts and follow the installation methods specified by the manufacturer and local building codes.

Planning the Project

NOTE: Consult the manufacturer's instructions for the specifications regarding placement, clearances, and venting methods for your fireplace.

Start your planning by determining the best location for the fireplace. Placing the unit next to an exterior wall simplifies the venting required. One important specification for a basement fireplace is that the *termination cap* (on the outside end of the vent) must be 12" above the ground. In the project shown, the vent runs up 3 ft. before it turns at an elbow and passes through a masonry wall. Because the wall is non-combustible, no heat shield is needed around the vent penetration.

Next, design the frame. As long as it meets the clearance requirements for your fireplace, the frame can be any size and shape you'd like. Typical clearance minimums include a ½" space between the framing and the sides and back of the unit and a ¼" space (for positioning and adjusting the unit) above the *standoffs*. The easiest way to build a frame is to use 2 × 4s and wallboard.

Finally, plan the rough-ins. Most fireplaces use a ½" gas supply line that connects directly to the unit. Check with the local gas utility or building department to determine what piping you'll need and the gas output required for your model. You may also need electrical wiring installed if your fireplace includes optional equipment, such as a blower or remote ignition. Complete the rough-ins after the frame is built. If you're not qualified to do the job yourself, hire professionals.

For help with any of these planning issues, talk with knowledgeable dealers in your area. They can help you choose the best fireplace model for your situation and help you with venting and other considerations. And remember, all installation specifications are governed by local building codes: Check with the building department to make sure your plans conform to regulations.

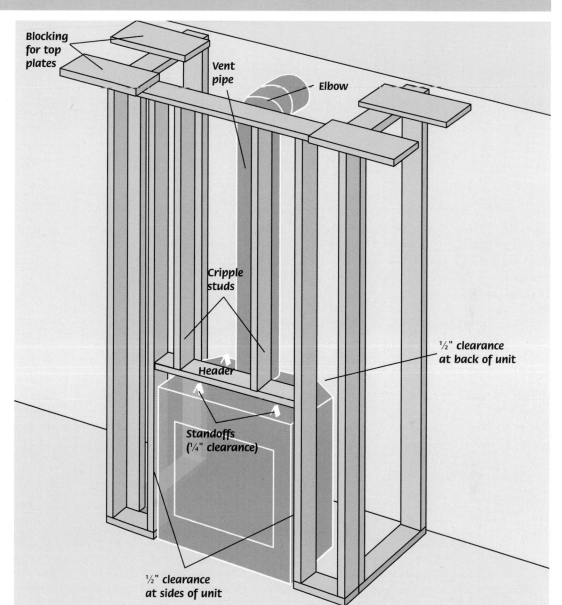

Tools: Framing square, chalk line, plumb bob, circular saw, drill, 2-ft. level, hammer drill, masonry bit, masonry chisel, hand maul, adjustable wrenches, brush, nail set, V-notched trowel, screwdriver, grout float, sponge.

Materials: Fireplace unit, vent sections, termination cap, ½" copper tubing, 2 × blocking lumber, 2 × 4 lumber, construction adhesive, masonry fasteners, 3" wallboard screws, sheet metal plates, plastic sheet, scrap plywood, sheet metal screws, caulk, ⅝" wallboard, wallboard finishing materials, high-temperature sealant, primer, paint, mantle, wood-finishing materials, 6d and 4d finish nails, wood putty, ceramic tile, tile spacers, latex tile adhesive, masking tape, grout, cap rail trim, buildup strips.

Installing a Gas Fireplace

A

2 × blocking

B

Header

Mark the frame's outer edges onto the floor. Use a framing square to draw perpendicular lines for the side walls. Measure and mark the front of the frame with a chalk line. Measure diagonally from corner to corner to ensure the layout lines are square; adjust the lines, if necessary. Transfer the lines from the floor to the ceiling joists with a plumb bob. If any top plates fall between parallel joists, install 2 × blocking between the joists. Snap a line through the marks to complete the top-plate layout.

Cut the bottom plates to size from pressure-treated 2 × 4s. Position the plates inside the layout lines, and fasten them to the floor with construction adhesive and masonry screws, or a powder-actuated nailer (see pages 323 to 324). Cut the top plates from standard 2 × 4s. Attach them to joists or blocking with 3" screws or 16d nails (drill pilot holes for screws). If the plates are attached directly to parallel joists, add backing for attaching the ceiling wallboard.

Mark the stud layout on the bottom plates, then transfer the layout to the top plates, using a plumb bob. Measure and cut studs to length. Attach two studs along the back wall with construction adhesive and masonry screws, or a powder-actuated nailer. Attach the remaining studs to the top and bottom plates with 3" screws or 8d nails.

Measure up from the floor and mark the height of the header onto each stud at the side of the front opening. Cut and install the header. Cut the cripple studs to fit between the header and the top plate. To allow easy access for running the vent pipe, do not install the cripple studs until after the vent is in place. Add any blocking needed to provide nailing surfaces for the tile trim.

Bend out the nailing tabs at the sides of the fireplace unit. Slide the unit into the frame until the tabs meet the framing, then center the unit within the opening. Level the unit from side to side and front to back. Use thin sheet metal shims to make any adjustments. Add a little construction adhesive to the shims to keep them in place. Measure at the sides and back of the unit to be sure the clearance requirements are met.

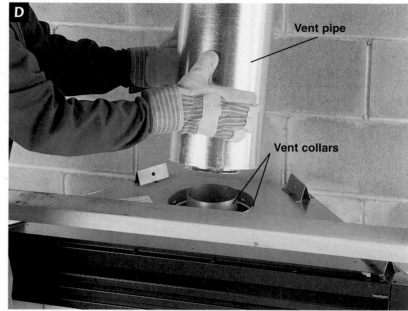

Dry-fit the vent pieces. Fit the flared end of the first vent section over the vent collars on top of the unit, aligning the inner and outer pipes of the vent with the matching collars. Push straight down on the vent until it snaps into place over the lugs on the outside of the collar. Pull up on the vent slightly to make sure it's locked into place.

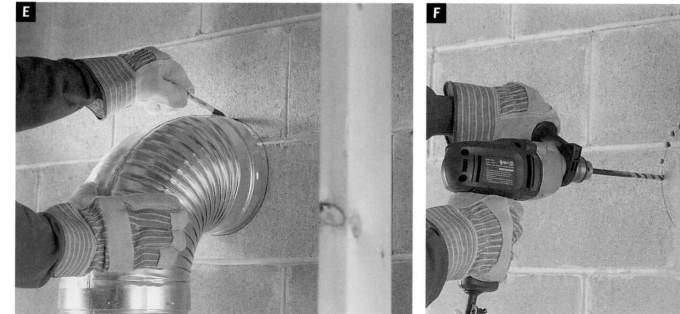

Attach the 90° elbow so that the free end points toward the exterior wall. NOTE: Horizontal vent runs must slope upward ¼" per foot. If your vent includes additional horizontal sections leading from the elbow, adjust the vent pieces and elbow to follow the required slope. Trace the circumference of the elbow end onto the wall.

Remove the vent from the unit, and set it aside. Cover the fireplace with plastic and scrap plywood to protect it from debris. Using a long masonry bit and hammer drill, drill a series of holes just outside the marked circle, spacing them as close together as possible. Drill the holes all the way through the block. Be patient; the block cavities may be filled with concrete.

Continued on next page

Installing a Gas Fireplace (cont.)

G

Carefully knock out the hole, using a masonry chisel and a hand maul. Work inward from both sides of the wall to ensure a clean cutout on the wall surfaces. Smooth the hole edges, test-fit the horizontal vent piece, and make any necessary adjustments. Uncover the fireplace, and clean up around the unit.

H

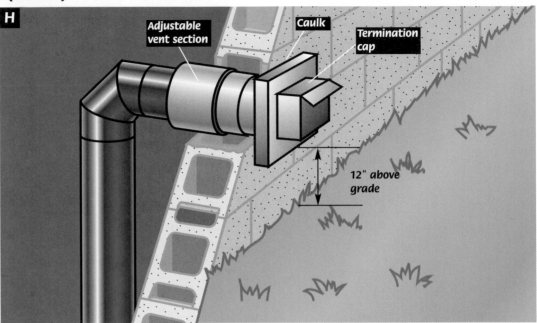

Adjustable vent section

Caulk

Termination cap

12" above grade

Reinstall the vertical vent section and elbow, locking the pieces together. Prepare the adjustable horizontal vent section by measuring from the elbow to the termination cap. Adjust the section to length, and secure the sliding pieces together with two sheet metal screws. Install the horizontal vent section and termination cap, following the manufacturer's instructions. Seal around the cap perimeter with an approved caulk. When the vent run is complete, fasten the fireplace unit to the framing by driving screws through the nailing tabs. Install the cripple studs between the header and top plate.

I

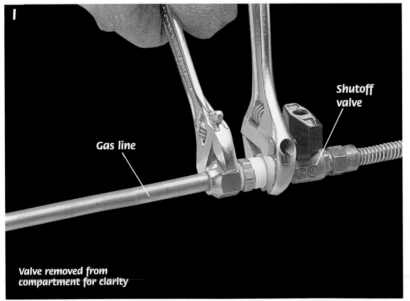

Gas line

Shutoff valve

Valve removed from compartment for clarity

To make the gas connection, remove the lower grill from the front of the unit. Feed the gas supply pipe into the access hole on the side of the unit, and connect it to the manual shutoff valve. Tighten the connection with adjustable wrenches.

J

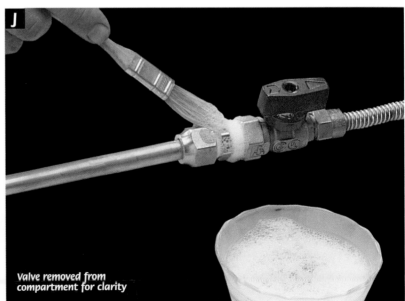

Valve removed from compartment for clarity

Turn on the gas supply, and check for leaks by brushing on a solution of soapy water. If you see bubbles, you have a leak. Turn off the gas, tighten the connection, then retest before proceeding.

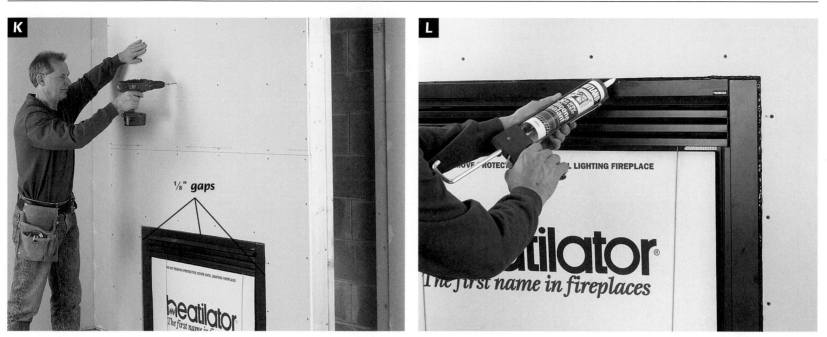

Before installing the wallboard, test the unit. Prepare the firebox and light a fire, following the manufacturer's instructions. Let it run for 15-20 minutes while you inspect the flame and vent. Report any problems to the manufacturer. Turn off the fireplace and let it cool down. Install ⅝" wallboard over the framing (see pages 196 to 200). To provide a space for sealant, leave a ⅛" gap between the wallboard and the top and sides of the front face of the unit.

Fill the gap around the front face with a high-temperature sealant supplied (or recommended) by the manufacturer. Tape and finish the wallboard (see pages 201 to 202).

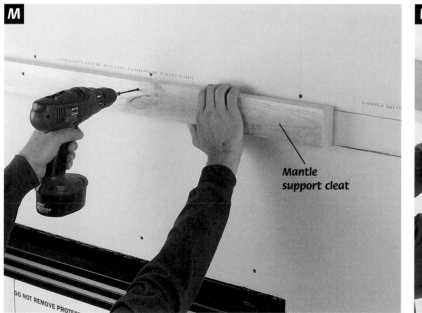

To install the mantle, measure up from the floor and mark the height of the support cleat. Use a level to draw a level line through the mark. Mark the stud locations just above the level line. Position the cleat on the line, centered between the frame sides, and drill a pilot hole at each stud location. Fasten the cleat to the studs with screws provided by the manufacturer.

Paint the areas of wallboard that won't be tiled. Finish the mantle as desired, then fit it over the support cleat and center it. Drill pilot holes for 6d finish nails through the top of the mantle, about ¾" from the back edge. Secure the mantle to the cleat with four nails. Set the nails with a nail set, fill the holes with wood putty, then touch-up the finish.

Continued on next page

Installing a Gas Fireplace (cont.)

Dry-fit the tile around the front of the fireplace. You can lay tile over the black front face, but do not cover the glass or any portion of the grills. If you're using floor tile without spacer lugs on the side edges, use plastic tile spacers to set the grout gaps between tiles (at least ⅛" for floor tile). Mark the perimeter of the tile area and make any other layout marks that will help with the installation. Pre-cut tiles, if possible.

Mask off around the tile, then use a V-notched trowel to apply latex mastic tile adhesive to the wall, spreading it evenly just inside the perimeter lines. Set the tiles into the adhesive, aligning them with the layout marks, and press firmly to create a good bond. Install spacers between tiles as you work, and scrape out excess adhesive from the grout joints, using a small screwdriver. Install all of the tile, then let the adhesive dry completely.

Mix a batch of grout, following the manufacturer's instructions. Spread the grout over the tiles with a rubber grout float, forcing the grout into the joints. Then, drag the float across the joints diagonally, tilting the float at a 45° angle. Make another diagonal pass to remove excess grout. Wait 10-15 minutes, then wipe smeared grout from the tile with a damp sponge, rinsing frequently. Let the grout dry for one hour, then polish the tiles with a dry cloth. Let the grout dry completely.

Cap rail trim

Buildup strip

Cut pieces of cap rail trim to fit around the tile, mitering the ends. If the tile is thicker than the trim recesses, install buildup strips behind the trim, using finish nails. Finish the trim to match the mantle. Drill pilot holes and nail the trim in place with 4d finish nails. Set the nails with a nail set. Fill the holes with wood putty and touch up the finish.

Building a Wet Bar

A wet bar typically consists of a small set of cabinets, a countertop, and a sink—a convenient setup for serving drinks or snacks. But by expanding on this basic theme, you can build a bar that brings several amenities of a kitchen right into a family room or home theater. In addition to providing a place to serve drinks, the new bar will be great for microwaving popcorn or grabbing a cold soda during halftime or movie intermissions.

This project shows you how to build a wet bar that includes a countertop with plenty of room for appliances (and a nearby GFCI receptacle), an under-counter refrigerator/freezer, four full-size cabinets, and a set of elegant glass shelves. At 2 × 6½ ft., the bar can fit easily into a corner or along a wall. Low-voltage halogen lights placed under the cabinets provide task lighting while additional lights above accent the bar without brightening the room too much.

To begin planning the project, review Making Preparations for a Wet Bar, on pages 344 to 345. This gives you an overview of the framing requirements and the plumbing and wiring rough-ins needed for the bar. Consult the Basic Techniques section of this book for help with planning and installing the frame and mechanical rough-ins. Also, the Kitchens section has plenty of information about buying cabinets, countertops, and sinks.

After you've built the frame and completed the rough-ins, follow the step-by-step instructions to install the cabinets, shelves, countertop, and sink, then complete the plumbing and wiring connections, and install the cabinet lights.

Careful placement of the bar will help the project go more smoothly. Wiring can go almost anywhere, but plumbing requires more consideration: To save time and money, locate the bar as close as possible to existing plumbing lines.

Be aware that the fixtures and configurations in this project may not meet code requirements in your area, so have your project plans reviewed by a local building inspector before you start.

Making Preparations for a Wet Bar

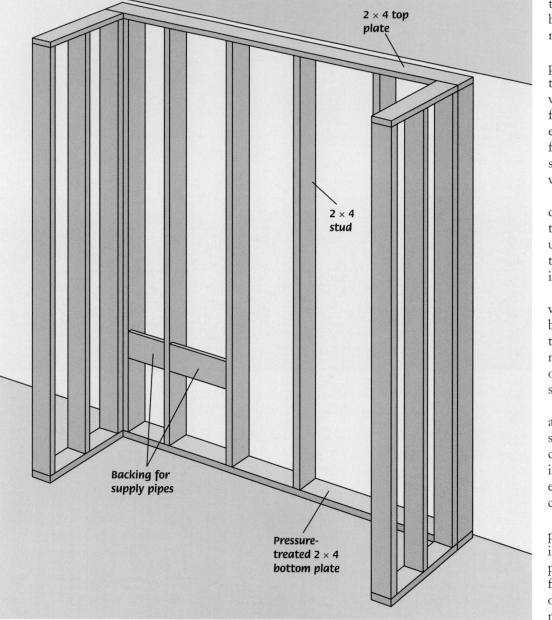

2 × 4 top plate

2 × 4 stud

Backing for supply pipes

Pressure-treated 2 × 4 bottom plate

through that framing. If the wall is load-bearing, be sure to follow local code requirements for notching and boring into framing.

Before you start the framing, you'll need to plan the rough-ins. You'll also need to know the dimensions of the fixtures going into the wet bar so you can determine the size of the frame. Confirm with the manufacturers the exact dimensions of the cabinets, appliances, fixtures, and countertop you've chosen. Be sure to add the thickness of the wallboard when sizing the frame.

Building the frame itself is simple (see drawing, left). Construct standard 2 × 4 partition walls, with single bottom and top plates, using 16"-on-center spacing. Use pressure-treated lumber for the bottom plates if the bar is in the basement.

It's very important that the framing of the wet bar walls be square: The side walls must be perpendicular to the back wall and parallel to each other. This affects how well the cabinets and countertop fit. Since the side walls of the bar are short, you can use a framing square to check them.

The wet bar in this project has a 12" space above the wall cabinets, which is typical of standard cabinets installed under 8-ft.-high ceilings. You can leave this space open and use it for accent lighting or as a display shelf, or enclose the space with a framed soffit, as is common in many kitchens.

After the frame is built, complete the plumbing and electrical rough-ins (see drawing, page 345). First, install the drain and vent pipes for the bar sink. Run 1½" drain pipe from the sink location to the main stack or other waste/vent pipe. In a basement, this may require cutting into and breaking up a section of the concrete floor (see pages 462 to

NOTE: Always shut off the water supply before working with plumbing. Shut off electrical power at the main service panel and test for power with a circuit tester before doing any electrical work.

The frame requirements for your wet bar depend upon its location. If the back of the bar is set against a masonry wall, the bar will need a framed back wall for holding plumbing and wiring. If the bar is set against an existing framed wall, you may be able to run the service lines

467). Set the height of the drain stub-out as required by local code (typically 19" above the floor). Remember that most horizontal drain runs must have a downward slope of ¼" per foot.

According to most codes, sinks must be ventilated within 3½ ft. of the fixture's drain trap. If the waste/vent pipe is within this limit, it can serve as both drain and vent for the sink. Otherwise, you'll need a 1½" vent pipe that extends up and over to the nearest acceptable vent. The new vent pipe must extend upward a minimum of 6" above the flood level of the sink before turning to begin a horizontal run.

To provide hot and cold water to the sink, tap into the nearest water distribution lines with ¾ × ½" reducing T-fittings. Run ½" supply pipes from the fittings to the sink location. Complete the supply stub-outs with an angle stop shutoff valve on each supply pipe. The stub-outs should be spaced about 8" apart.

Install five electrical boxes: one for a single-pole switch, centered 45" above the floor; one for the refrigerator receptacle, centered 12" above the floor; one for the over-counter GFCI receptacle; and one for each cable leading to the low-voltage lighting transformers, located just above the wall cabinets.

Next, run cable to the boxes. Lighting for the bar is supplied by one 14/2 cable that can be branched from an existing 15-amp lighting circuit. Run the cable to the box for the switch, then run a branch cable from the switch box to the box for the first transformer. Run another cable between the transformer boxes.

To prevent circuit trippings that would shut off the refrigerator, wire the two receptacles on a dedicated 20-amp circuit. Run 12/2 cable from the service panel to the GFCI receptacle box, then add a branch cable leading to the box for the standard 20-amp receptacle.

Install metal protector plates at locations where pipes and cables pass through framing. After the framing and rough-ins have been inspected and approved, cover the walls and ceiling of the bar with ½" wallboard. Tape and finish the wallboard so the surfaces are completely smooth and flat (see pages 196 to 202). Apply primer, then paint the walls and ceiling the color of your choice.

Complete the wiring connections for all devices except the low-voltage lights (see page 349). Install each device in its electrical box, and attach the coverplate.

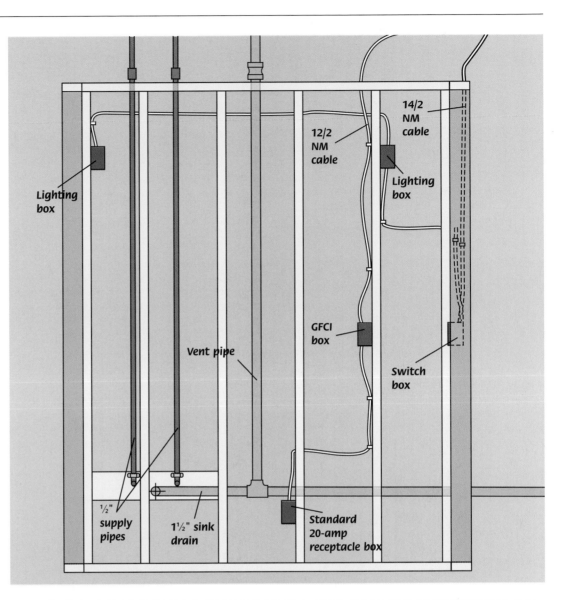

Tools: 4-ft. and 2-ft. level, chisel, drill, hole saw, utility knife, nail set, circular saw, compass, belt sander, jig saw and laminate blade, caulk gun, channel-type pliers, framing square, wallboard finishing tools, combination tool (for wiring).

Materials: 2 × 4 lumber, 16d common nails, 1½" drain pipe and fittings, ¾ × ½" reducing T-fittings, ½" copper pipe, shutoff valves, escutcheons, electrical boxes, 12/2 and 14/2 NM cable, 20-amp GFCI receptacle, 20-amp receptacle, 15-amp single-pole switch, low-voltage lighting kit, wire connectors, coverplates w/knockouts, cable clamps, ½" wallboard, wallboard finishing materials, primer, paint, cabinets, duct tape, 2½" sheet metal screws, shelf brackets, glass shelves, cedar shims, construction adhesive, toe-kick molding, finish nails, ¾" plywood, wallboard screws, masking tape, silicone caulk, bar sink, faucet, sink-drain assembly, supply tubes.

Building a Wet Bar

A

Draw layout lines for both sets of cabinets. Use a level to determine if the floor is even. If not, make a mark on the wall near the high point of the floor. Measure straight up from the high point and make a mark for the base cabinets at 34½". Make a mark for the wall cabinets at 84". Use the level to draw level lines through each of these marks to indicate the top edges of all four cabinets. Also mark the stud locations just above each level line.

B

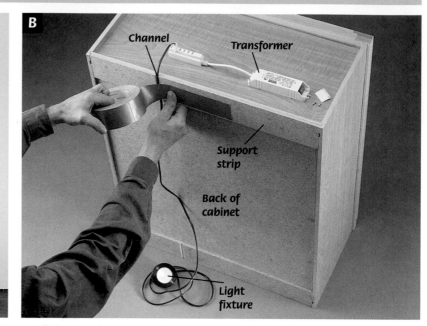

Install the coverplates onto the lighting-cable boxes, feeding the cable ends through the clamps in the coverplates and clamping them in place. Prepare the wall cabinets by installing the transformers and fixture wires. Mount one transformer on the top of each wall cabinet with screws. Create a recess for the fixture wires by chiseling a small channel into the back of the support strips at the top and bottom of each wall cabinet. Connect the fixture wires to the transformers, lay them in the channels, and hold them in place with tape.

C

Have a helper position one wall cabinet against the back and side walls, aligning its top edge with the upper layout line. Drill pilot holes through the hanging strips inside the cabinet and into the wall studs. Fasten the cabinet to the wall with 2½" sheet metal screws. Install the remaining wall cabinet against the opposite side wall.

D

Measure up from the bottom edge on the inside face of each wall cabinet, and lightly mark the height of each shelf bracket. Make sure the marks are level. Drill holes for the bracket posts and install the brackets. Measure between the brackets to determine the length of the glass shelves, then order the shelves from a glass dealer.

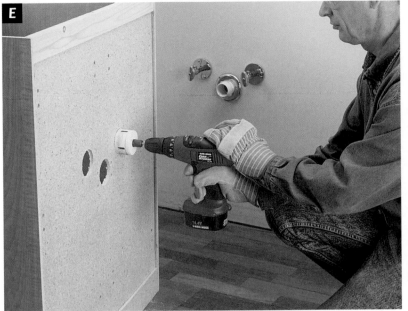

To set the sink base cabinet, measure the locations of the plumbing stub-outs and transfer the measurements to the back panel of the cabinet. Cut the holes for the stub-outs, using a drill and hole saw. If necessary, use a jig saw to cut the hole for the drain stub-out.

Set the sink base cabinet in place. Where necessary, slide tapered cedar shims under the cabinet's bottom edges until the cabinet is aligned with the layout line and is perfectly plumb from front to back. Apply a small amount of construction adhesive to the shims to hold them in place. Fasten the cabinet to the wall studs, in the same manner as the wall cabinets. Install the remaining cabinet against the opposite side wall.

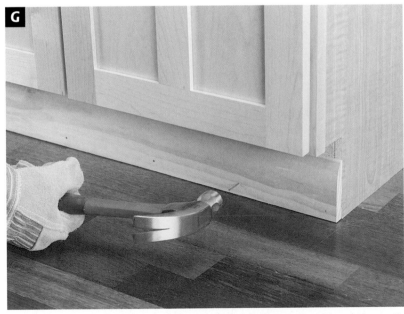

After the adhesive on the shims has dried, cut the shims flush with the cabinets, using a utility knife. Install the toe-kick molding supplied by the manufacturer. Position the molding flush along the floor, with the ends flush with the cabinet sides. Drill pilot holes through the toe-kicks, and fasten them to cabinets with finish nails. Set the nails with a nail set.

Install a ¾"-thick × 2"-wide plywood support cleat to the back wall between the base cabinets, keeping the cleat ¾" above the layout line. Attach ¾"-thick × 2"-wide plywood buildup strips to the front and back edges of the cabinets (these raise the countertop so that its front edge doesn't overhang the drawer fronts). Drill pilot holes and fasten the strips flush with the outside edges of the cabinet, using wallboard screws.

Continued on next page

Building a Wet Bar (cont.)

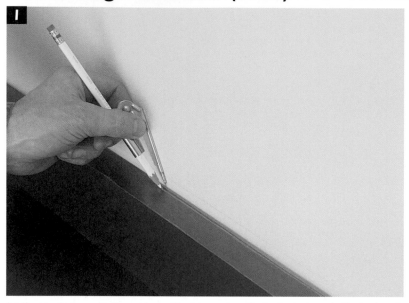

Set the countertop onto the cabinets. Check to see how the backsplash meets the back wall: If there are any gaps over ¹⁄₁₆", scribe the backsplash with a compass. Set the compass to the width of the widest gap, then run it along the wall to transfer the wall contours onto the backsplash.

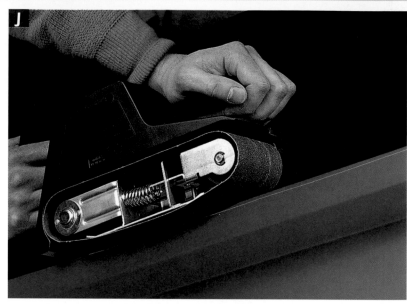

Remove the countertop and sand the edge of the backsplash down to the scribed line. Use a belt sander, holding it parallel to the backsplash to prevent chipping.

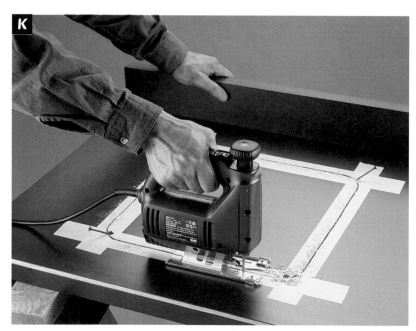

Using the sink template, trace the sink cutout onto strips of masking tape on the countertop. Apply tape to the foot of a jig saw to prevent scratching. Drill a starter hole just inside the cutting line, then complete the cutout with the saw. Use a laminate blade or a down-cutting blade, and cut from the finished side of the countertop. After cutting around each corner, drive an angled screw into the edge of the cutout piece, to keep the piece from falling before the cut is complete, which could chip the laminate.

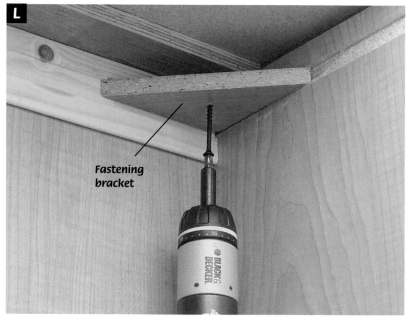

Fastening bracket

Reset the countertop, and secure it in place by driving wallboard screws up through the fastening brackets in the cabinet corners (and the buildup strips) and into the particleboard core of the countertop. Be careful not to puncture the laminate surface. Complete the countertop installation by sealing all joints along the walls with a thin bead of silicone caulk.

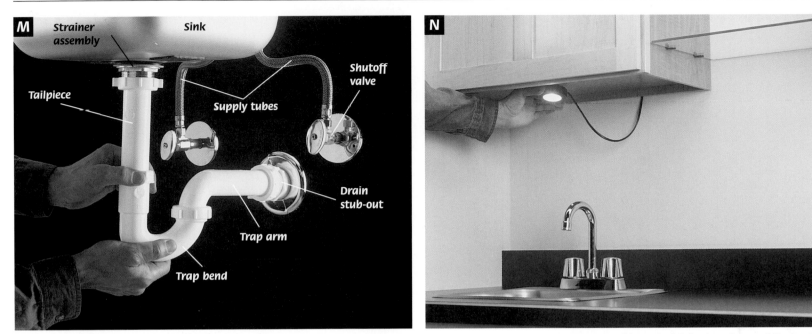

Install the faucet, attach the sink strainer assembly, and install the sink in the countertop, following the manufacturer's instructions (also see page 432). Connect flexible supply tubes to the shutoff valves, and tighten the connecting nuts. Assemble the sink drain (see page 434).

Install the glass shelves. Connect the circuit cables to the lighting transformers, following the manufacturer's instructions. Turn on the lights and position fixtures as desired. Turn off the lights, and screw them to the cabinets. Staple the fixture wires to the bottoms of the cabinets.

Making the Electrical Connections

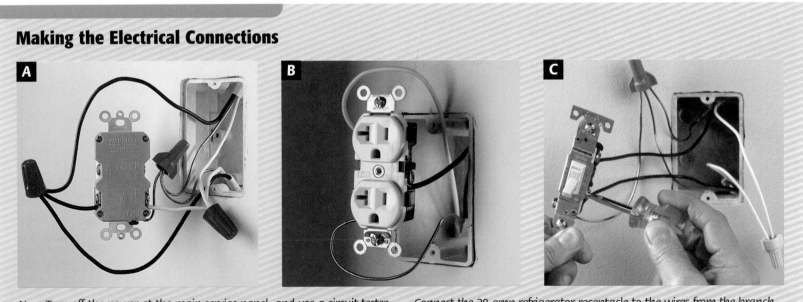

NOTE: Turn off the power at the main service panel, and use a circuit tester to confirm the power is off before working with electrical cables.

Connect the GFCI receptacle so that it protects itself but not the receptacle for the refrigerator. Pigtail the hot wires to the HOT LINE terminal, and pigtail the neutral wires to the WHITE LINE terminal. Pigtail the grounding wires to the GFCI's grounding screw **(photo A)**.

Connect the 20-amp refrigerator receptacle to the wires from the branch cable **(photo B)**.

Install the single-pole switch with middle-of-run wiring configuration. Attach one hot wire to each screw terminal, and join the neutral wires together with a wire connector. Pigtail the ground wires to the switch grounding screw **(photo C)**.

Adding Recessed Kneewall Shelves

One way to utilize the space behind an attic kneewall is to install custom-made storage units. This recessed shelf cabinet provides over nine sq. ft. of storage area without taking up floor space. And it's a simple project to build using standard materials and basic hand and power tools.

Support for the shelving cabinet is provided by a framed rough opening (similar to a window frame) and two pedestals made from 2 × 4s that sit below the cabinet behind the wall framing. It's best to build the rough opening and pedestals when you frame the kneewall (see pages 330 to 331). The main part of the cabinet is made of plywood. A face frame made of solid lumber dresses up the front edges of the cabinet and hides gaps around the wall

opening. The drawings on page 351 show you all of the parts needed for the project, and the cutting list includes the materials and dimensions of each part of the project shown.

The type of lumber you use for your shelves depends on how you want to finish them. If you'll be painting the unit, build the cabinet with A/B plywood, which has one side that's smooth and free of defects. For the face frame, use a quality-grade softwood, such as pine or aspen, without knots or saw marks.

If you want to stain the wood or apply a clear topcoat to retain the natural color, use finish-grade veneer plywood for the cabinet. Veneer plywoods are commonly available in pine, birch, and oak. Specialty lumber yards also offer veneers in maple, cherry, and other

species. You can build the face frame from solid lumber that's the same species as the veneer, or choose a different wood that complements the color and grain of the cabinet material.

Tools: Circular saw, 2-ft. level, drill, framing square, bar clamps, nail set.

Materials: 2 × 4 lumber; ¾" and ¼" plywood; 1 × 4 and 1 × 2 lumber; shims; 3", 2", and 1" wallboard screws; wood glue; 3" and 1½" finish nails; fine-grit sandpaper; wood putty; finishing materials.

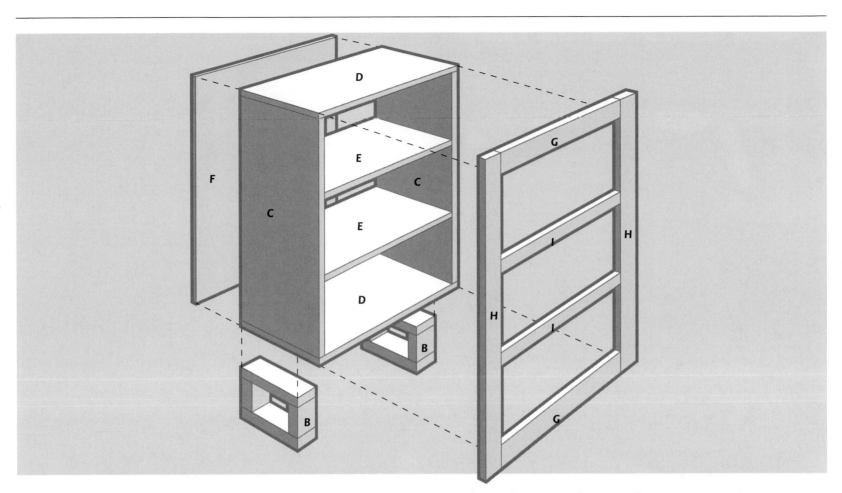

Cutting List

Key	Part	Material	Pieces	Size
A	Header and sill	2 × 4s	1 each	30½"
B	Pedestals	2 × 4s	2	14 × 15"
C	Sides	¾" plywood	2	19 × 28½"
D	Top and bottom	¾" plywood	2	19 × 30"
E	Shelves	¾" plywood	2	19 × 28½"
F	Back panel	¼" plywood	1	30 × 30"
G	Rails	1 × 4	2	28½"
H	Stiles	1 × 4	2	35½"
I	Shelf rails	1 × 2	2	28½"

Framing the Rough Opening

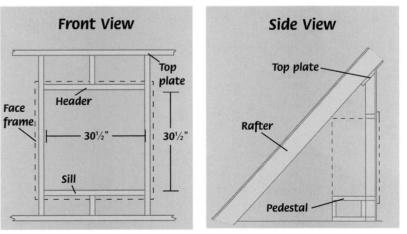

Front View

Side View

Make the rough opening ½" wider and taller than the outer dimensions of the cabinet. For the project shown, the rough opening is 30½" wide × 30½" tall. (Be sure to leave a few inches of space between the back of the cabinet and the rafters.) Attach the side studs to the plates of the kneewall, then install the sill and header, and cripple studs centered between the side studs. Make sure the sill and header are level. Install the wallboard after the frame is completed.

Adding Recessed Kneewall Shelves

Measure from the subfloor to the top of the sill to determine the height of the pedestals. The length of the pedestals should equal the depth of the cabinet minus 4". Build the pedestals with 2 × 4s, then set them on the floor behind the wall so their outside edges are flush with the sides of the rough opening and their tops are flush with the sill. Make sure the pedestals are level, and shim underneath them, if necessary. Attach the pedestals to the subfloor with 3" wallboard screws.

Cut the top, bottom, and side panels and the shelves, using the dimensions from the cutting list on page 351. If you're building your cabinets to fit an existing opening, measure the width and height of the rough opening, and cut the side panels 2" shorter than the height of the rough opening. Cut the top and bottom panels ½" shorter than the width of the rough opening, and cut the shelves 1½" shorter than the length of the top and bottom panels. Use a framing square to ensure the shelf and panel edges are straight and square.

Make marks on the inside faces of the side panels to indicate the top faces of the shelves. Then, draw lines on the outside faces of the panels, ⅜" below the inside marks, to indicate the centers of the shelves for fastening. Apply wood glue to the end of each shelf. Position the shelves on the layout lines, and clamp together the assembly with bar clamps. Drill pilot holes through the side panels and into the shelves, and fasten the pieces with 2" wallboard screws.

Apply wood glue to the ends of the side panels. Position the top and bottom panels over the ends of the sides, and clamp them in place. Drill pilot holes through the top and bottom panels and into the side panels, then fasten the pieces together with screws.

Cut the back panel to size from ¼" plywood. The back panel should match the outer dimensions of the cabinet. Set the back panel over the cabinet so its edges are flush with the outsides of the cabinet. To ensure that the unit is square, adjust the cabinet to keep it flush with the edges of the back panel as you fasten. Drill pilot holes, and fasten the back panel to the top and bottom panels and the shelves with 1" wallboard screws (do not use glue).

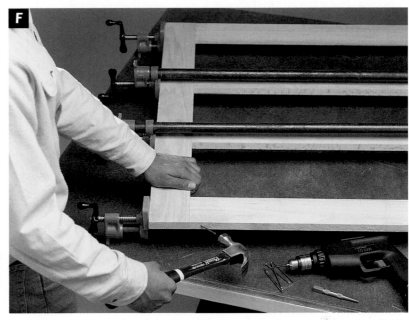

Cut the stiles and rails to length from 1 × 4 lumber. Apply glue to the rails and shelf rails, then assemble the frame as shown on page 351 (position the top edges of the shelf rails so they will be flush with the top faces of the shelves). Clamp the frame, and measure diagonally from corner to corner. If the frame is not square, apply pressure to one side until the measurements are equal. Drill pilot holes, and toenail 3" finish nails through the ends of the rails and into the stiles. Let the glue dry.

Apply glue to the front edges of the cabinet. Position the face frame over the cabinet so the inside edges of the frame are flush with the side, top, and bottom panels. Drill pilot holes and fasten the frame to the cabinet with 1½" finish nails, driven every 8". Set the nails with a nail set. After the glue dries, sand the exposed surfaces with fine-grit sandpaper, and finish the unit as desired.

Set the unit into the wall and center it within the rough opening. Anchor the unit by drilling pilot holes and driving 3" finish nails through the face frame and into the wall studs, header, and sill. Space the nails evenly, and set the nail heads with a nail set. Fill the nail holes with wood putty and touch up the finish as needed.

Building Custom Light Boxes

These light boxes can supply plenty of light to a finished space without taking up valuable headroom or floor area. An even greater feature is that the boxes are custom-made: You can build them with 2-, 4-, or 6-ft. light fixtures, and you can add one anywhere there's an open area between joists.

Here's how a light box is made: Two pieces of blocking are installed between two floor joists to form the box (see page 355). The wiring is run from a wall switch into the box, then the inside of the box is wrapped with ¼" wallboard. After the wallboard is finished and painted, one fluorescent light fixture is installed on each long side of the box, and the wiring connections are made. Then, a piece of crown molding and a spacer are cut to length to fit under each fixture. Reflective tape is applied to the back of the molding, and the molding and spacers are painted and fastened to the box sides.

Part of building a light box is finding an effective combination of molding and spacer pieces. The molding must project far enough from the side of the box that it conceals the fixture and allows enough room for changing the lamp. A spacer cut from standard 2 × lumber combined with a 5" or 6" crown molding should provide the desired effect. Another option is to make boxes without using spacers (see page 357).

The wiring diagrams on page 355 show you a fixture connection and the basic wiring layout for multiple light boxes. Refer to the wiring section of this book (see pages 94 to 139) for help with running the cables and making the electrical connections. Be sure to have all of the electrical work approved by a building inspector.

> **Tools:** *Combination square, circular saw, drill, wallboard knives, paintbrush, nail set, caulk gun.*
>
> **Materials:** *2 × lumber, 3" wallboard screws, 14/2 NM cable, cable staples, single-pole light switch, electrical box, wire connectors, fluorescent light fixtures, ¼" wallboard, corner bead, wallboard tape & compound, paint, crown molding, foil duct tape, finish nails, caulk, wood putty.*

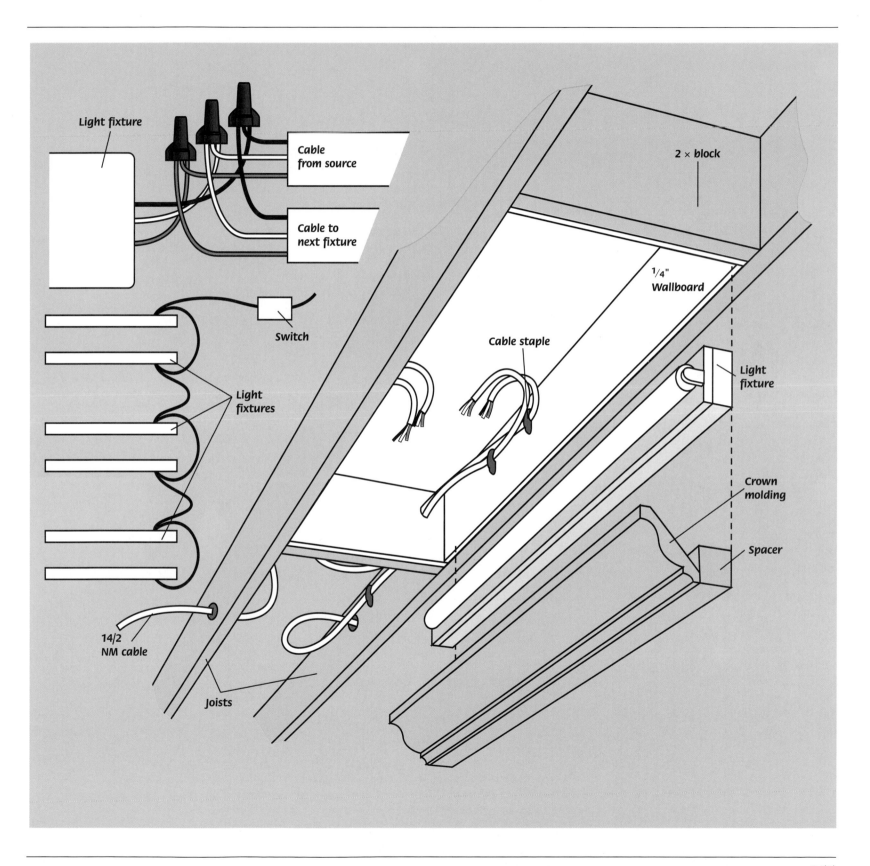

Light fixture

Cable from source

Cable to next fixture

Switch

Light fixtures

14/2 NM cable

Joists

2 × block

1/4" Wallboard

Cable staple

Light fixture

Crown molding

Spacer

Building Custom Light Boxes

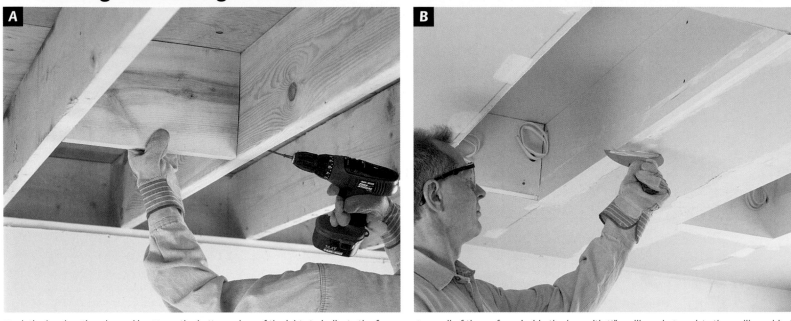

Mark the box locations by making Xs on the bottom edges of the joists to indicate the frame blocks. The inside of the frames should be about 2" longer than the light fixtures. Use a combination square to extend the layout lines onto the faces of the joists. Cut each block to fit, using the same size lumber as the joists. Set the blocks along the layout lines, and attach them with 3" wallboard screws. Drill ⅝" holes through the end blocks and run wiring for the boxes (see diagram, page 355).

Cover all of the surfaces inside the box with ¼" wallboard. Complete the wallboard installation over the main ceiling surface, using ½" or ⅝" wallboard, then finish the outside corners of the box with corner bead (see pages 196 to 202). Tape and finish the inside corners of the boxes. Paint the entire surface inside each box with a light-colored, semi-gloss latex paint.

Install the fixtures in each box, positioning them so that the lamp will face the center of the box. Center the fixtures from side to side, and fasten them to the joists with screws. Connect the fixture wiring to the circuit cables, following the manufacturer's instructions.

Cut the crown molding to fit snugly between the ends of the boxes. Paint the front faces of the molding, using the same paint used inside the boxes. Line the inside surfaces of each piece of molding with reflective foil duct tape.

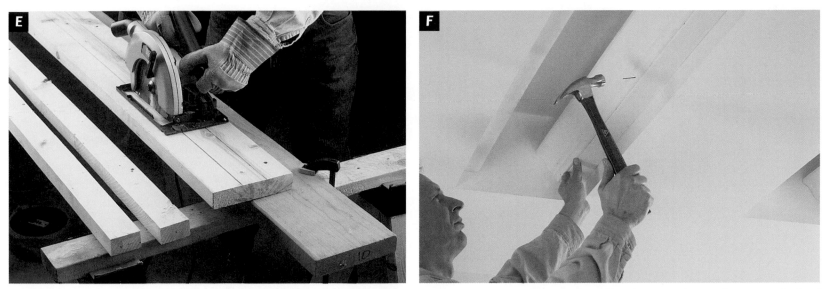

Determine the size of the spacers by positioning a piece of molding under a fixture with a lamp installed. Hold the molding away from the box side until you find the desired position. Then, measure between the molding and the box side to find the width of the spacer. Cut the spacers to width from 2 × lumber. Drill pilot holes for screws through the front edge of each spacer, then sand and paint spacers to match the molding.

Attach the spacers inside the boxes with wallboard screws. Make sure all spacers are level and at the same height. Attach the crown molding pieces to the front edges of the spaces with finish nails driven through pilot holes. Set the nails with a nail set, and fill the holes with wood putty. Seal any gaps at the ends of the molding with paintable caulk, then touch-up the paint on the joints and nail holes.

Molding Variations

With molding that's wide enough to cover the fixtures, you can omit the spacers and attach the molding directly to the box sides **(A).** You can also add molding on the ends of the boxes, fitting the pieces together with coped joints **(B).**

For a look that's more linear, use 1 × trim pieces instead of crown molding. Install nailers to the boxes, and attach the trim pieces to the nailers **(C).** This trim style looks best when the ends of the boxes are left open **(D).**

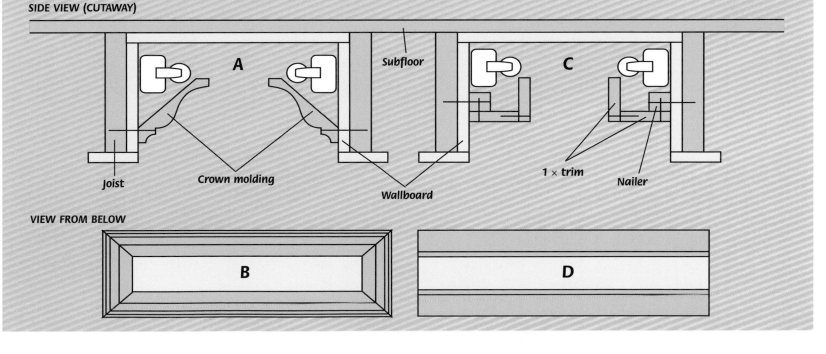

SIDE VIEW (CUTAWAY)

Subfloor

A

Joist

Crown molding

Wallboard

C

1 × trim

Nailer

VIEW FROM BELOW

B

D

REMODELING KITCHENS

Planning the Project

A successful kitchen remodeling project combines form and function. You want your new kitchen to look beautiful, but you also want it to serve your needs well.

Begin by identifying what you hope to accomplish. Do you simply want to make cosmetic changes, such as adding new wallpaper, paint, countertops, appliances, or flooring? Or do you want to reconfigure or add to the current kitchen space?

Consider how you use your kitchen. Do you cook often? Do you entertain frequently? Do other activities take place in the kitchen, such as homework, laundry, or eating?

Give yourself time to determine your needs. As you work in your kitchen, make a list of things that are inconvenient. Write down what would make your life easier. Think about where you set down grocery bags as you come through the door, where you stack dirty dishes, whether you can converse with family and friends while you prepare dinner and clean up after meals.

This also is a good time to consider traffic flow through the kitchen and surrounding rooms. Would moving a doorway allow better access to the dining room? Would removing a wall provide better lighting or make it easier to communicate with someone in the family room?

After you've made your wish list, make a realistic budget, then prioritize. Put your most important issues at the top of the list. If you absolutely must have more storage or a place for the kids to do homework, don't compromise; there will be other places where you can cut back.

Next, consider the style of your home. Your new kitchen should enhance that overall style. Pay special attention to the cabinets—they play a large part in setting the style of kitchen.

After you've compiled your lists, consider consulting a kitchen designer. These professionals can help you plan new cabinets, enhance the kitchen space, and suggest add-ons that can make your life easier.

Be realistic about how much of the work you are able or willing to do. You can save money by doing some or all of the work yourself, but remember that during construction, your kitchen will be unusable; plan alternative space during remodeling.

Determining Your Needs

Your kitchen remodel will probably fall into one of five categories, based upon your overall objective. A remodel can be as simple or as complex as you desire, ranging from a cosmetic makeover to a project that involves removal and construction of both interior and exterior walls.

Category 1: Cosmetic Makeover

The most basic level of remodeling is the cosmetic makeover, in which you leave the layout unchanged and simply replace the surfaces. Typically this involves renewing the walls, floors, cabinets, and countertops, while retaining many of the existing appliances and fixtures.

At first glance, the kitchen shown here looks completely new—but looks are deceiving. The only layout change is the small base cabinet added in the corner next to the range. The kitchen was updated by refinishing the appliances, repainting the cabinets, replacing the countertop and cabinet hardware, adding new wallpaper, and retrimming the windows.

After

Before

©Malebee M. Miller for Geraldine Kaupp Interiors

Categories 2-5: Changing Your Kitchen's Layout

Building your dream kitchen may involve more than simple cosmetic changes, and there is a variety of ways to address a kitchen's flaws. You can simply reposition appliances and eating areas, or change doorways and add islands to redirect traffic. More extensive layout remodeling usually involves expanding the kitchen area to other rooms of the home or adding space by building an addition.

At left is a typical kitchen before layout remodeling. Counter space is lacking, traffic flow is poor, and the kitchen work areas are poorly organized. The layout options that follow show various ideas for addressing these problems.

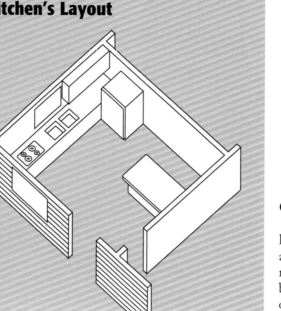

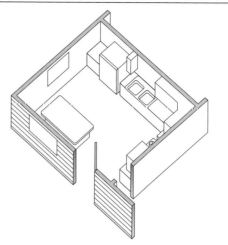

Category 2: Reconfiguring the Basic Layout

In this remodel, the basic footprint of the kitchen is retained, but the appliances, fixtures, and eating areas are repositioned to create a more efficient layout. (Counter space is gained by creating an L-shaped grouping.) This type of project may require carpentry, electrical, or plumbing work. The result is a more efficient kitchen with relatively minor layout changes.

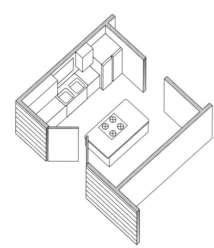

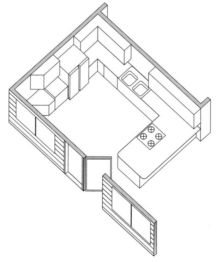

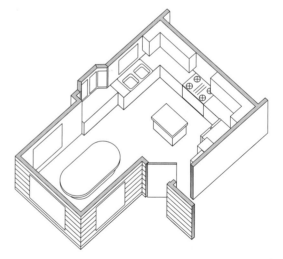

Category 3: Redirecting Traffic

A more extensive layout change can help to redirect traffic moving through the kitchen. Often this involves adding or moving a doorway in a partition wall, as well as redesigning the basic kitchen footprint. The result is a kitchen that feels bigger, works more efficiently with surrounding rooms, and perhaps offers extra island storage and counter space.

Category 4: Expanding Within

If your kitchen is just too small, you can enlarge it by borrowing space from adjacent rooms. This project involves moving or removing partition walls, in addition to re-arranging appliances and cabinets. The result is a larger kitchen, a countertop eating area, significantly more in storage, and open access to the adjoining room.

Category 5: Expanding Outward

The most extensive kitchen remodel includes a new addition. This is a big job that usually requires the help of many professionals, including a general contractor. The result can be anything you desire, and may involve both exterior and interior changes to your home. This type of project can completely change the function and flow of your kitchen.

Selecting Kitchen Elements

©Roger Turk

Countertops

Most homeowners choose plastic laminate, ceramic tile, or solid-surface countertops for their kitchen, but there are many other materials from which to choose, including wood, natural stone, and stainless steel.

Consider the advantages and disadvantages of each countertop material, and remember that you aren't limited to one type. You may use a plastic laminate surface for most of your counters, for example, then splurge for a small section of butcher block or marble.

Also consider the cost and ease of working with each type of material. In general, plastic laminates offer the most versatility at the lowest cost, and solid-surface materials offer fewer design options at higher prices.

The countertop material you choose will impact the style of your kitchen. Color, texture, and form all set a tone. If you are remodeling with a particular style in mind, choose countertops consistent with that style. Remember that countertops can be enhanced with molded edges, color accents, and wood overlays.

Last, choose a countertop that is both durable and beautiful, because your kitchen is central to the appearance as well as the function of your home.

©Karen Melvin/Knapp Cabinetry & Woodworking

Cabinets

The choice to replace cabinets usually defines the choice between a cosmetic makeover and a major kitchen remodel. Cabinets typically reflect one of the most significant investments in a kitchen remodeling project.

If your current cabinets provide adequate storage, you may consider refacing or painting them rather than replacing them. However, if your current cabinet layout is insufficient, new cabinets may be your best option.

New cabinets will quickly change the look of your kitchen. There are many styles to match your design ideas and many options to match your storage needs. Door styles, woods, and finishes will play a large part in setting the style of your kitchen. Remember to choose a style compatible with the rest of your home, especially if your kitchen is open to surrounding rooms.

Investigate storage options. It's not necessary to fill every inch of wall space with cabinetry to gain storage. Other options include island and pantry storage, as well as slide outs, partitions, and open racks.

The layout of your cabinets will be as important as the cabinets themselves. Pay attention to door and drawer clearances, shelf height, and appliance placement to ensure that your finished kitchen will function as beautifully as you have planned.

Lighting

An effective lighting plan incorporates both electrical and natural sources. Each should be an integral element in your kitchen design.

A comfortable and efficient kitchen requires a combination of natural and artificial light sources to provide well-lighted work areas, as well as inviting spaces for your family and friends to gather.

Good lighting ensures your safety when handling hot pans, sharp knives, and wet utensils, and it helps make cooking and cleanup easier.

Windows and skylights are a kitchen's main source of natural light, but they also serve other functions. A window's design and treatment can add personality and charm to a room, while its shape and placement allow you to direct light where it's needed. When choosing windows, consider their effect on your home's interior as well as its exterior.

For help with designing your lighting plan, visit a showroom or contact the American Lighting Association (see page 503) for a list of qualified dealers and designers in your area.

©David Livingston

Fixtures & Appliances

©David Livingston

If your major appliances and plumbing fixtures are more than fifteen years old, they are probably at the end of their useful lives and should be replaced during your remodeling project.

Common plumbing and appliance improvements include upgrading faucets, adding a water filtration system, and replacing a countertop microwave with a model that fits into a custom cabinet.

In addition to upgrading your major appliances, consider adding some of the many useful small appliances that are available, such as trash compactors, warming drawers, instant hot-water taps, cabinet-mounted can openers,

and built-in stereo and television units.

Even if your appliances aren't old, it may still be worthwhile to upgrade them. During your planning process, research current models to determine if an investment in more energy-efficient appliances will save you money in the long run.

Many homeowners replace plumbing fixtures and appliances simply for cosmetic reasons. However, if you have an energy-efficient, high-quality appliance that's only a few years old, you might consider simply refinishing it or adding a decorative panel to update its look.

Flooring

Your kitchen floor provides the base for all other elements in your kitchen. If you plan to add new appliances, counters, or cabinets, you may want to consider upgrading your floor at the same time to maintain a consistent tone throughout your kitchen.

You can either replace an old floor or renew it. Either way, the investment will have a positive impact on your remodeled kitchen.

Installing new kitchen flooring is an excellent way to transform a kitchen, since the floor is usually the largest surface in the room. From a design standpoint, flooring is far more

than the surface you walk on and mop up. Designers and remodelers routinely use flooring to alter the way a room looks. A custom-designed floor creates a focal point. With a little planning, you can do the same.

Finally, consider the advantages and disadvantages of each type of flooring material. In most homes, the kitchen floor gets used—and cleaned—more than any other floor in the house. It makes sense to choose a floor covering that is durable and easy to clean. Also, consider the ease of installation if you will be installing the flooring yourself.

Photo courtesy of Florida Tile Industries, Inc.

Designing Your Kitchen

Design Standards

The goal of any kitchen layout is to make the cook's work easier and, where possible, to allow other people to enjoy the same space without getting in the way. Understanding accepted kitchen design standards can help you determine whether your present layout is sufficient or if your kitchen needs a radical layout change or expansion. The most important standards are those that deal with the arrangement of the major work areas and the sizes and placement of the countertops, appliances, and cabinets.

The Work Triangle

The *work triangle* describes the arrangement of the three main work areas of a kitchen—storage (refrigerator), food prep (oven and cooktop) and cleanup (sink and dishwasher). Each work area represents a *point* on the triangle, and the distance between any two points is called a *leg*. Although many sources offer what may sound like rules for the work triangle, the concept is merely a planning tool for balancing the relationship of the points to one another.

Guidelines offered by the National Kitchen and Bath Association (NKBA) indicate that each leg of the triangle should be between 4 and 9 ft., and the total length of all the legs should be less than 26 ft. The arrangement of the points should discourage foot traffic through the triangle. Whenever possible, there should be a 4-ft. corridor between stationary elements, such as a perimeter counter and an island; anything less than 3 ft. results in reduced efficiency.

Of course, not all kitchens can accommodate what might be described as an ideal work triangle, or even a triangle at all. Some kitchens have four work stations rather than three, while others, such as galley kitchens, position all the work areas along one wall.

The illustrations below show four of the most common kitchen layouts. The important thing is not to religiously follow a set of guidelines, but to create a plan that lets you work efficiently in your kitchen. For more information regarding the work triangle, contact the NKBA (see page 503).

Countertops

Lack of countertop space is one of the most common complaints people have about their kitchens. But having adequate space is more than just a matter of surface area. The most useful counter spaces are those next to the main work areas and appliances. Table 1 (see page 365) lists the principle kitchen appliances and the minimum recommended countertop space next to each appliance. Although standard dimensions are given for each appliance, the actual sizes of your appliances won't necessarily affect the amount of countertop space needed.

In addition to the allowances given in the table, a kitchen should have at least one uninterrupted counter surface that's a minimum of 3 ft. long, for a food preparation area. As for overall countertop space, follow these recommendations: if your kitchen is less than 150 sq. ft., you should have at least 11 linear ft. of countertop space; if your kitchen is over 150 sq. ft., try to include at least 16½ ft. of counter space.

Use Table 2 (see page 365) to calculate the amount of space you'll need for eating areas. Most eating surfaces are 30", 36", or 42" above the floor. The horizontal space you need to allow for each diner varies according to the height of the surface and the type of dining.

Common Kitchen Shapes

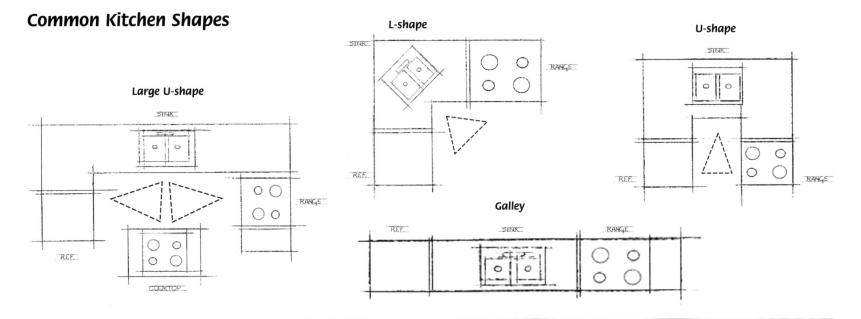

Large U-shape

L-shape

U-shape

Galley

Appliances

Your kitchen plan should allow space for all of the major appliances, as well as for the safe and comfortable use of each unit. If you're buying a new appliance and don't know its size, you can use the standard dimensions given in Table 1, below. Keep in mind that most appliances come in many different sizes, so you're not necessarily limited to the dimensions shown.

When placing the appliances in your kitchen layout, be sure to leave a clear access space of at least 30 × 48" in front of each appliance. Also, position each appliance so that its doors open away from traffic areas and from other appliances. The *Comments* column in Table 1 contains additional recommendations for the placement of each appliance.

Cabinets

Most people would like to have unlimited room for cabinets, but working them into limited kitchen space can be tricky. For kitchens with less than 150 sq. ft., designate a minimum of 13 linear ft. for base cabinets, 12 linear ft. for wall cabinets, and 10 linear ft. of drawers or roll-out shelving. For kitchens of 150 sq. ft. or more, plan a minimum of 16 linear ft. of base cabinets, 15½ ft. of wall cabinets, and 13¾ ft. of drawers or roll-out shelving. When calculating cabinet spaces, exclude any unusable corner space.

The sizes of base and wall cabinets are fairly uniform among manufacturers, and unless you have your cabinets custom-built, they'll probably follow the standards shown in the chart on page 366. (If you've already selected new cabinets, refer to the product literature for the actual dimensions.) Figure 1 on page 366 shows some general measurements for drawing or selecting standard base and wall cabinets.

Table 1: Standard Appliance Dimensions

Appliance	Standard Dimensions (width)	Minimum Countertop Space	Comments
Refrigerator	30" to 36"	15" on latch side	12 cu. ft. for family of four; 2 cu. ft. for each additional person
Sink	27" single 36" double	24" on one side 18" on other side	Minimum of 3" of countertop space between sink and edge of base cabinet
Range	30", 36"	15" on one side 9" on other side	If a window is positioned above a cooking appliance, the bottom edge of the window casing must be at least 24" above the cooking surface
Cooktop	30", 36", 42", 48"	15" on one side 9" on other side	
Wall oven	24", 27", 30"	15" on either side	Oven bottom should be between 24" and 48" above the floor
Microwave	19", 24", 30"	15" on either side	When built in, place low in wall cabinets or just under counter

Table 2: Eating-surface Standards

	Height of Eating Surface		
	30"	36"	42"
Min. width for each seated diner	30"	24"	24"
Min. depth for each seated diner	19"	15"	12"
Minimum knee space	19"	15"	12"

Continued on next page

Designing Your Kitchen (cont.)

Standard Cabinet Sizes

Base Cabinets (without countertop)

    height: 34½"

    depth: 23" to 24"

    width: 9" to 48", in 3" increments

Wall Cabinets

    height: 12", 15", 18", 24", 30", 33", 42"

    depth: 12"

    width: 9" to 48", in 3" increments

Oven Cabinets

    height: 84", 96"

    depth: 24"

    width: 27", 30", 33"

Utility Cabinets

    height: 84"

    depth: 12", 24"

    width: 18", 24", 36"

Figure 1

Maximum height 80"

12-15"

Minimum 18"

80"

Sink

36"

3½" min.

36" min.

3" min.

24"

Shown cutaway for clarity

Building Codes

If your kitchen remodel involves anything more than redoing the surfaces, chances are there are codes you'll need to follow. Knowing a few of the basic guidelines can help you understand and plan for the various utilities that make a kitchen work. Be aware that the regulations listed here are merely general guidelines. Consult your local building department for a complete and current list of codes and regulations for your area.

Basic Construction

Most building codes require that a kitchen have at least one window that provides a minimum of 10 sq. ft. of glass surface. Some localities allow windowless kitchens as long as the kitchen is properly vented. However, a windowless kitchen is less appealing than one that has windows or other openings to the outdoors. Kitchen designers recommend that kitchens have windows, doors, or skylights that together have a total glass surface equal to at least 25% of the total floor area.

Kitchens may be required to have at least two points of entry (keep in mind that the traffic flow between them should not intrude on the work triangle). As a rule, exterior entry doors leading into a kitchen must be at least 3 ft. wide (called a *three-o* door) and interior passage doors between kitchens and other rooms must be at least 2½ ft. wide (called *two-six* doors).

Electrical Service & Lighting

Nearly any kitchen remodeling project will require some upgrading of the electrical service. While your current kitchen may be served by a single 120-volt circuit, it's not uncommon today for a large kitchen to use as many as seven individual circuits. In some cases, the additional load may mean you have to upgrade the main electrical service for the entire house.

To get an idea of how extensive your electrical improvements need to be, compare your current service with the code guidelines in Estimating Electrical Needs (right). Depending on the size of your project, you may want to call in an electrician to assess your current service and review your planned changes.

In regard to lighting, the National Electrical Code requires that a kitchen have a wall-switch controlled general lighting circuit (120-volt, 15-amp) that operates independently from circuits that control appliances or counter receptacles. For reasons of safety, comfort, and aesthetics, you may also want to include plentiful task lighting, including hanging lights, under-cabinet fixtures or recessed lighting to illuminate each work area as well as decorative lighting fixtures for highlighting attractive cabinets or other features.

Plumbing

If your new layout calls for relocating the sink, or if you're adding an additional sink or dishwasher, you'll need to extend your water supply and drain and vent piping.

Extending plumbing lines for a new kitchen generally is easy and inexpensive, but there are some exceptions. For example, if you're putting in an island sink, the pipes will have to be run under the floor, which is more expensive than plumbing a wall sink.

If your plumbing is more than 25 years old, your costs may go up, depending on the type and condition of your existing pipes. It's a good idea to check out your old plumbing. Even if the new kitchen requires expensive replacement plumbing, it makes sense to have it done during a remodel, and it may prevent a disaster down the road. (Older plumbing may also have drain traps and vents that don't conform to current codes, and your plumber may recommend new runs.)

Heating, Ventilation & Air Conditioning (HVAC)

If you're planning a cosmetic makeover or simple layout changes, you can probably continue to use your existing registers or radiators. But if the new kitchen will be substantially larger or if the ratio of glass surfaces will be greater, you may need to expand the heating/cooling system. This can be as simple as extending the ducts a few feet or as complicated as installing a new furnace to handle the additional space.

To determine your kitchen's HVAC needs, consult a professional. Although the code requirements are quite simple, HVAC contractors use a complicated formula to determine the equipment necessary to meet the code requirements.

For proper ventilation, your cooktop should be equipped with an electric vent hood to exhaust cooking fumes and moisture from the kitchen. Since the capacity of the vent is governed by code, check with a building inspector before selecting a vent hood. Many island cooktops use downdraft fans and ducts that are routed through the floor, which is a more costly and complicated job.

Estimating Electrical Needs

The National Electrical Code requires that all kitchens meet the following electrical guidelines:

- Wall outlets spaced no more than 12 ft. apart.
- Countertop outlets spaced no more than 4 ft. apart.
- GFCI (Ground-fault circuit-interrupter) protection for all countertop receptacles.
- At least two 120-volt, 20-amp circuits; one to supply power for the refrigerator and the other for plug-in countertop appliances.
- Dedicated circuits for each major appliance. Install a 120-volt, 20-amp circuit for a built-in microwave, a 15-amp circuit for the dishwasher and food disposer. An electric range, cooktop, or wall oven requires a dedicated 240-volt, 50-amp circuit.

After you estimate how much electrical service your new kitchen will need, compare it to your existing service by examining your service panel. If the panel has a number of open slots, your electrician should be able to add additional circuits easily. If it doesn't, your new kitchen may require an upgraded service panel.

Cooktops must have vents to remove moisture and smoke created by cooking. Better ventilation systems exhaust air to the outdoors rather than recirculate it through the kitchen.

The Universal Kitchen

In most homes, the kitchen is the center of activity, so remodeling your kitchen for universal use does more than just prepare your home for the future; universal design can improve circulation in your kitchen, enable family members to be more independent, and minimize the effort required for everyday tasks.

Much of universal kitchen design comes from common-sense ideas. For example, a cook need not stand for every stage of meal preparation; a lowered section of countertop with open space underneath enables a person to sit while mixing, chopping, or stirring. A side-by-side refrigerator has low shelving that allows children to serve themselves, whereas a freezer-below model might require them to rely on parents for a snack or a glass of juice.

As universal design becomes more mainstream, kitchen planners and manufacturers are responding with improved product design and with an emphasis on universal use. This translates into better ideas and more options for the consumer. The following guidelines and suggestions will help you make your new kitchen a lifespan kitchen.

Layout & Space Planning
The layout of your kitchen should follow basic kitchen design standards and code requirements (see pages 364 to 367), but providing additional floor area and work surfaces are key to creating a universal space.

A kitchen should have enough room that two or more people can use it at once and through-traffic doesn't interrupt workflow. Designing your kitchen around a clear, circular space at least 5 ft. in diameter will provide room for a wheelchair to maneuver and for people to walk through the kitchen while others are cooking.

To provide work spaces for a variety of users, include an island or peninsula in your plan, as well as countertop surfaces at various heights. A window or pass-through between the kitchen and dining area shortens the distance that food and dishes have to be carried during meal times.

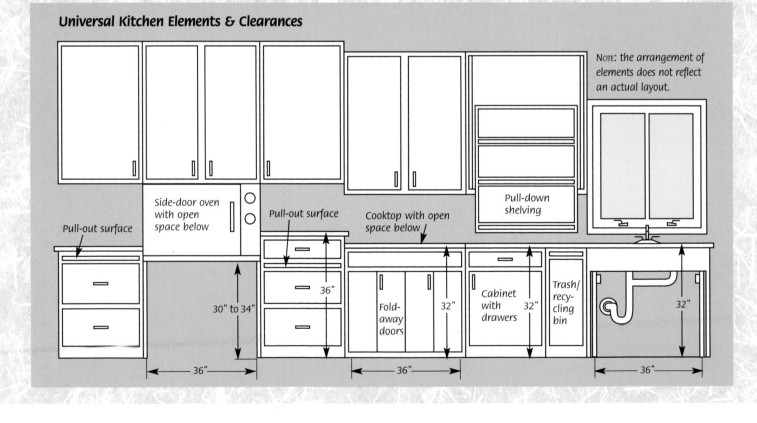

Universal Kitchen Elements & Clearances

NOTE: the arrangement of elements does not reflect an actual layout.

Pull-out surface

Side-door oven with open space below

Pull-out surface

Cooktop with open space below

Pull-down shelving

Fold-away doors

Cabinet with drawers

Trash/recycling bin

30" to 34" 36" 36" 32" 32" 32" 36"

Cabinets

A universal kitchen should have ample storage space in a variety of forms and places so that some storage is within the reach of each user. When planning for cabinets, keep in mind that countertop heights are determined by the cabinet heights. Following are some considerations for wall and base cabinets and for pantries.

- Select base cabinets with pull-out drawers for better access to items in the back.
- Choose a sink-base cabinet that is open underneath, with fold-away doors to accommodate a seated user.
- Consider base cabinets with high toe-kick spaces for wheelchair footrests.
- Choose loop handles for new cabinetry and replace existing knobs with loops.
- Include at least one rolling-cart cabinet that can be pulled away to open up space under a low countertop for a seated cook.
- Equip corner cabinets and/or pantries with lazy Susans.
- Include a tall, narrow space with slots that provide space to store cookie sheets and trays vertically.
- Purchase wall cabinets with pull-down shelf systems.
- Consider installing wall cabinets at a height of 12" to 15" above the countertop, rather than the standard 18". (Make sure appliances will fit under lower cabinets.)
- Choose pantries with door-shelving, as well as shallow, adjustable shelving inside.

Countertops

Plan countertop space carefully to include ample surface area at varied heights to accommodate everyone in your home.

Supplement countertop space with work surfaces that pull out of cabinets.

- Install countertops at varied heights: 36" high for standing users, 30" or 32" high for seated users, and 42" high for taller users; also consider adjustable countertops.
- Include at least one 32" countertop workspace, open underneath, for seated users.
- Finish the floor underneath countertops with open space below, to ease wheelchair movement.
- Include heat-resistant fixed or pull-out surfaces next to the oven, microwave, cooktop, sink, and refrigerator.
- Consider countertop features: a color-contrasted edge makes it easier for people with vision limitations to see countertop boundaries; a lipped edge contains spills; and rounded edges are safer than sharp ones.

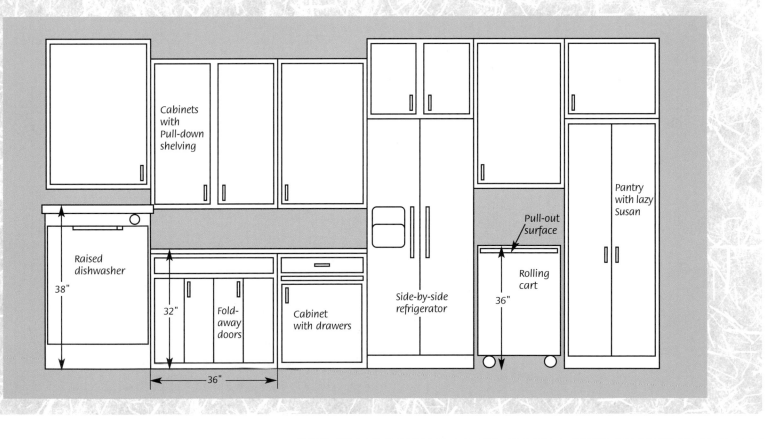

Cabinets with Pull-down shelving

Raised dishwasher

38"

32"

Fold-away doors

36"

Cabinet with drawers

Side-by-side refrigerator

Pull-out surface

36"

Rolling cart

Pantry with lazy Susan

The Universal Kitchen

Lighting and Electrical

While all well-designed kitchens combine natural, overhead, and task lighting to create safe, welcoming space, specific lighting needs vary, depending on the kitchen's size, color, and surfaces. A kitchen with light-colored walls and cabinets, for example, requires less lighting than one with dark surfaces. Glossy surfaces reflect light well but can often cause glare. Contrasting colors help define boundaries, but stark patterns can be confusing to the eye; finding a balance is important.

Install task lighting at all work centers, and avoid creating shadowed areas. Under-cabinet lights are helpful for countertop tasks and can offset shadows.

Having plenty of electrical receptacles in easy-to-reach places makes a kitchen versatile and safe. Having extra countertop (backsplash) receptacles means you don't have to shuffle small appliances each time they're used. But backsplash receptacles can be hard to reach for seated users, so consider alternative locations, as well: the end of an island or peninsula, behind a false drawer front, or underneath wall cabinets. Check the local building code regarding receptacle placement, and keep in mind that some locations may give children access to receptacles.

Sink and Garbage Disposal

There are many sinks and faucets available that are well-suited for universal kitchens. A shallow sink, for example, enables a user to wash lettuce or dishes while sitting down. A lever-handled faucet is easier for everyone to use and allows a cook with dirty hands to turn on the water using an elbow.

- Mount the sink at a height of 32" or install a height-adjustable sink.
- Install a removable cabinet or slide-away doors under the sink to create an open space for seated users that is at least 32" wide (36" preferred). Insulate hot water pipes and install a protective panel to protect legs and knees from scalding.
- Consider a shallow sink (5" to 6 ½" deep instead of the standard 7" to 8"), which will leave room for knee space and will make reaching dishes easier.
- Choose a sink that drains at the rear, to maximize knee space (check whether it requires specific plumbing).
- Install a long spray hose that allows a person to fill a pot with water while the pot is on the cooktop.
- Select a single-lever or hands-free faucet.
- Place a faucet and a disposal switch no more than 21" from the countertop edge.
- Position the sink near the dishwasher and cooktop to make it easier to transfer dishes and pots filled with hot water.

Photos courtesy of Dura Supreme, Inc.

This compact kitchen has open spaces beneath the sink and cooktop hidden by fold-away doors.

Photo courtesy of KraftMaid Cabinetry, Inc.

Pull-out surfaces provide temporary work spaces that are lower than countertops and perfect for seated users.

Photo courtesy of Frigidaire

An oven door that opens to the side provides safe and easy access for a variety of cooks.

Oven and Cooktop

For reasons of safety and convenience, take careful consideration when choosing an oven and cooktop. It is important that the oven can be opened safely and that heavy pots can be removed from the cooktop easily. All users must be able to reach the controls on both appliances.

- Install a wall-mounted oven with its base at a height of 30" to 34".
- Choose an oven with a side-opening door to eliminate reaching over a hot door to remove dishes.
- Plan for a 30 × 48" clear approach space in front of the oven.
- Install pull-out work surfaces next to the oven and cooktop for placing hot dishes.
- Choose an oven and cooktop with controls on the front or side of the unit, with a maximum reach of 21" to those dials. If your family includes young children, side controls might be better. All dials should be clearly marked and easy to grasp and read.
- Consider smooth cooktops, which make it easier to place and remove pots and pans.

- Look for cooktops with staggered burners, so a cook needn't reach across one to use another.
- Install a tilted mirror above the cooktop so shorter cooks can see food as it cooks.

Other Appliances

Appliances such as refrigerators, dishwashers, and microwaves can be very convenient, but only if they are well-designed and in good locations. Both tall and short people should be able to reach refrigerated items, and everyone in the home should be able to empty the dishwasher without a struggle.

- Consider a side-by-side refrigerator unit, which allows shorter people to use the bottom portions and taller people to use the top portions.
- Look for refrigerator models that have pull-out shelves or lazy Susans and ice and water dispensers on the outside.
- Consider adding refrigerated drawers so fresh foods can be placed near work areas.
- Select a countertop-type microwave oven with a side-opening door and controls that are clearly marked and easy to operate; models that mount in wall cabinets place the

Photo courtesy of Frigidaire

Front-mounted controls make this cooktop easy and safe to operate, and its smooth cooking surface simplifies cleanup.

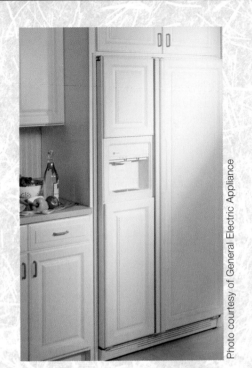

Photo courtesy of General Electric Appliance

Side-by-side refrigerator/freezers provide storage space at a wide range of heights.

food above a user's head, which is awkward and can be dangerous.
- Place the microwave on a 32"-high countertop to make it accessible to everyone, including children and seated users.
- Put your microwave next to a pull-out surface or countertop, where heavy or hot dishes can be placed.
- Install the dishwasher between the sink and a countertop that is open underneath, so a seated person can load the dishwasher from the sink and unload dishes directly into their cabinets.
- Consider installing the dishwasher 6" higher than standard height to minimize bending and to allow ample toe-kick space; this works best in a kitchen with sufficient countertop space at the 32" and 36" heights.

Plumbing a Kitchen

Plumbing a remodeled kitchen is a relatively easy job if your kitchen includes only a wall sink. If your project includes an island sink, the work becomes more complicated.

An island sink poses problems because there is no adjacent wall in which to run a vent pipe. For an island sink, you will need to use a special plumbing configuration known as a *loop vent*.

Each loop vent situation is different; your configuration will depend on the location of existing waste-vent stacks, the direction of the floor joists, and the size and location of your sink base cabinet.

Consult your local plumbing inspector for help in laying out the loop vent. And create a detailed plumbing plan to guide your work and help you obtain the permit that will be required.

The project overview presented here includes a double wall sink and an island sink. The 1½" drain for the wall sink connects to an existing

2" galvanized iron auxiliary waste-vent stack; since the trap is within 3½ ft. of the stack, no vent pipe is required. The drain for the island sink uses a loop vent configuration connected to an auxiliary waste-vent stack in the basement. Keep in mind that your pipe and fitting sizes, fixture layout, and pipe routing will vary according to your circumstances.

This project overview is divided into three phases:
- Installing DWV pipes for a wall sink (pages 375 to 377)
- Installing DWV pipes for an island sink (pages 377 to 381)
- Installing new supply pipes (pages 382 to 383)

The tips presented on pages 373 and 374 provide general considerations to help you plan your kitchen plumbing project. Refer to pages 62 to 93 for more information on basic plumbing materials, installation techniques, and plumbing code requirements.

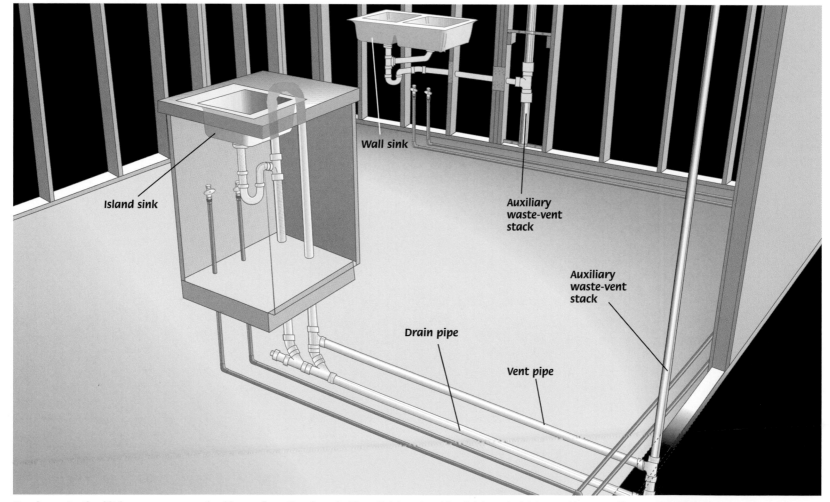

Wall sink

Island sink

Auxiliary waste-vent stack

Auxiliary waste-vent stack

Drain pipe

Vent pipe

Our demonstration kitchen *uses common plumbing configurations for a double wall sink and an island sink. Each sink is served by an auxiliary waste-vent stack.*

Tips for Plumbing a Kitchen

Insulate exterior walls if you live in a region with freezing temperatures in winter. Where possible, run water supply pipes through the floor or interior partition walls, rather than exterior walls.

Use existing waste-vent stacks to connect the new DWV pipes. In addition to a main waste-vent stack, most homes have one or more auxiliary waste-vent stacks in the kitchen that can be used to connect new DWV pipes.

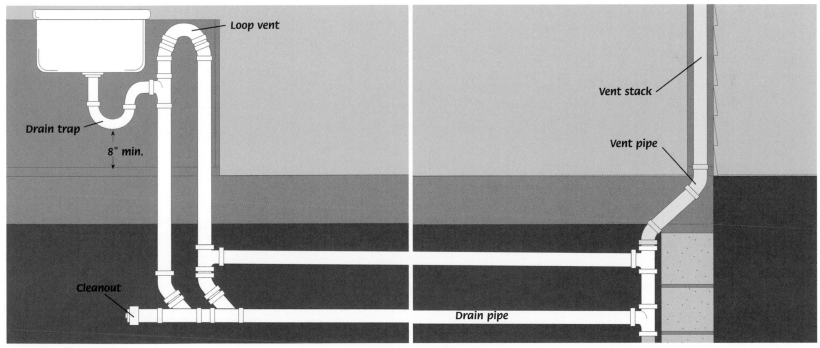

Use a loop vent to vent a sink when there is no adjacent wall to house the vent pipe. The drain is vented with a loop of pipe that arches up against the countertop and away from the drain before dropping through the floor. The vent pipe then runs horizontally to an existing vent pipe. In our project, we have tied the island vent to a vent pipe extending up from a basement utility sink. NOTE: Loop vents are subject to local code restrictions. Always consult your building inspector for guidelines on venting an island sink.

Tips for Plumbing a Kitchen (cont.)

Use 2 × 6 studs to frame "wet walls" when constructing a new kitchen. The extra dimension provides more room to run drain pipes and main waste-vent stacks, making installation much easier.

Install control valves at the points where the new branch supply lines meet the main distribution pipes. By installing valves, you can continue to supply the rest of the house with water while you are working on the new branches.

Consider the location of cabinets when roughing in the water supply and drain stub-outs. Read the layout specifications that come with each fixture or appliance, then mark the drain and supply lines accordingly.

Create access panels so that in the future you will be able to service fixture fittings and shut-off valves located inside the walls. Frame an opening between studs, then trim the opening with wood moldings. Cover the opening with a removable plywood panel the same thickness as the wall surface; finish the panel to match the surrounding walls.

Determine the location of the sink drain by marking the position of the sink and base cabinet on the floor. Mark a point on the floor indicating the position of the sink drain opening. This point will serve as a reference for aligning the sink drain stub-out.

Mark a route for the new drain pipe through the studs behind the wall sink cabinet. The drain pipe should angle ¼" per foot down toward the waste-vent stack.

Use a right-angle drill and hole saw to bore holes for the drain pipe (see page 90 for hole sizes). On non-load-bearing studs, such as the cripple studs beneath a window, you can notch the studs with a reciprocating saw to simplify the installation of the drain pipe. If the studs are load-bearing, however, you must thread the pipe though the bored holes, using couplings to join short lengths of pipe as you create the run.

Measure, cut, and dry-fit a horizontal drain pipe to run from the waste-vent stack to the sink drain stub-out. Create the stub-out with a 45° elbow and 6" length of 1½" pipe. NOTE: If the sink trap in your installation will be more than 3½ ft. from the waste-vent pipe, you will need to install a waste T and run a vent pipe up the wall, connecting it to the vent stack at a point at least 6" above the lip of the sink.

Continued on next page

Installing DWV Pipes for a Wall Sink (cont.)

Remove the neoprene sleeve from a banded coupling, then roll the lip back and measure the thickness of the separator ring.

Attach two lengths of 2" pipe, at least 4" long, to the top and bottom openings on a 2" × 2" × 1½" waste T. Hold the fitting alongside the waste-vent stack, then mark the stack for cutting, allowing space for the separator rings on the banded couplings.

Use riser clamps and 2 × 4 blocking to support the waste-vent stack above and below the new drain pipe, then cut out the waste-vent stack along the marked lines, using a reciprocating saw and metal-cutting blade.

Slide banded couplings onto the cut ends of the waste-vent stack, and roll back the lips of the neoprene sleeves. Position the waste T assembly, then roll the sleeves into place over the plastic pipes.

Slide the metal bands into place over the neoprene sleeves, and tighten the clamps with a ratchet wrench or screwdriver.

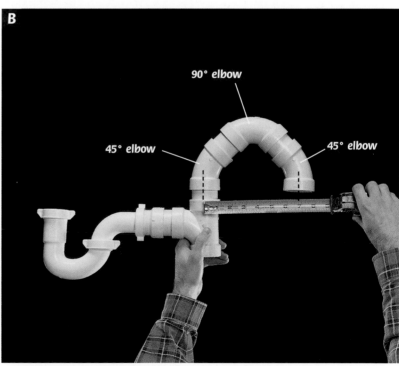

Solvent-glue the drain pipe, beginning at the waste-vent stack. Use a 90° elbow and a short length of pipe to create a drain stub-out extending about 4" out from the wall.

Installing DWV Pipes for an Island Sink

Position the base cabinet for the island sink, according to your kitchen plans. Mark the cabinet position on the floor with tape, then move the cabinet out of the way.

45° elbow

90° elbow

45° elbow

Create the beginning of the drain and loop vent by test-fitting a drain trap, waste T, two 45° elbows, and a 90° elbow, linking them with 2" lengths of pipe. Measure the width of the loop between the centerpoints of the fittings.

Continued on next page

Installing DWV Pipes for an Island Sink (cont.)

Reference line

Draw a reference line perpendicular to the wall to use as a guide when positioning the drain pipes. A cardboard template of the sink can help you position the loop vent inside the outline of the cabinet.

Position the loop assembly on the floor, and use it as a guide for marking the hole locations. Make sure to position the vent loop so the holes are not over joists.

Use a hole saw with a diameter slightly larger than the vent pipes to bore holes in the sub-floor at the marked locations. Note the positions of the holes by carefully measuring from the edges of the taped cabinet outline; these measurements will make it easier to position matching holes in the floor of the base cabinet.

Reposition the base cabinet, and mark the floor of the cabinet where the drain and vent pipes will run. (Make sure to allow for the thickness of the cabinet sides when measuring.) Use the hole saw to bore holes in the floor of the cabinet, directly above the holes in the subfloor.

Measure, cut, and assemble the drain and loop vent assembly. Tape the top of the loop in place against a brace laid across the top of the cabinet, then extend the drain and vent pipes through the holes in the floor of the cabinet. The waste T should be about 18" above the floor, and the drain and vent pipes should extend about 2 ft. through the floor.

In the basement, establish a route from the island vent pipe to an existing vent pipe. (In our project, we are using the auxiliary waste-vent stack near a utility sink.) Hold a long length of pipe between the pipes, and mark for T-fittings. Cut off the plastic vent pipe at the mark, then dry-fit a waste T-fitting to the end of the pipe.

Hold a waste T against the waste-vent stack, and mark the horizontal vent pipe at the correct length. Fit the horizontal pipe into the waste T, then tape the assembly in place against the waste-vent stack. The vent pipe should angle ¼" per foot down toward the drain.

Fit a 3" length of pipe in the bottom opening on the T-fitting dry-fitted to the vent pipe, then mark both the vent pipe and the drain pipe for 45° elbows. Cut off the drain and vent pipes at the marks, then dry-fit the elbows onto the pipes.

Continued on next page

Installing DWV Pipes for an Island Sink (cont.)

Extend both the vent pipe and drain pipe by dry-fitting 3" lengths of pipe and Y-fittings to the elbows. Using a level, make sure the horizontal drain pipe will slope toward the waste-vent at a pitch of ¼" per ft. Measure and cut a short length of pipe to fit between the Y-fittings.

Cut a horizontal drain pipe to reach from the vent Y-fitting to the auxiliary waste-vent stack. Attach a waste T to the end of the drain pipe, then position it against the waste-vent stack, maintaining a downward slope of ¼" per ft. Mark the waste-vent stack for cutting, above and below the fittings.

Cut out the waste-vent stack at the marks. Use the T-fittings and short lengths of pipe to assemble an insert piece to fit between the cutoff ends of the waste-vent stack. The insert assembly should be about ½" shorter than the removed section of stack.

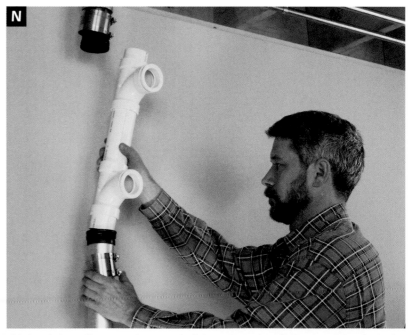

Slide banded couplings onto the cut ends of the waste-vent stack, then insert the plastic pipe assembly, and fit the coupling sleeves and bands over the pipe ends. Gently tighten the coupling clamps.

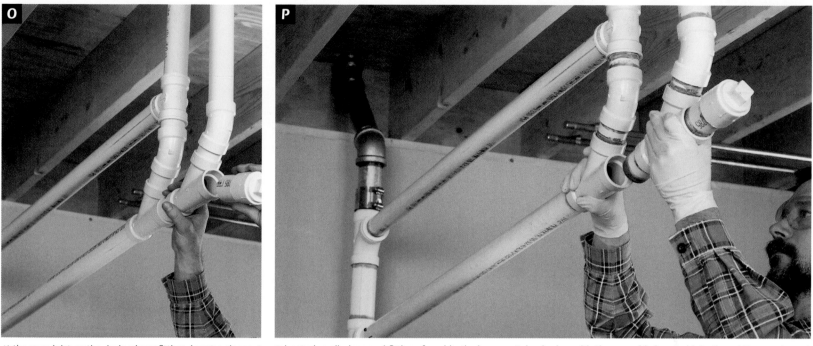

At the open inlet on the drain pipe Y-fitting, insert a cleanout fitting.

Solvent-glue all pipes and fittings found in the basement, beginning with the assembly inserted into the existing waste-vent stack, but do not glue the vertical drain and vent pipes running up into the cabinet. Tighten the banded couplings at the waste-vent stack. Support the horizontal pipes every 4 ft. with strapping nailed to the joists, then detach the vertical pipes extending up into the island cabinet. The final connection for the drain and vent loop will be completed as other phases of the kitchen remodeling project are finished.

After installing flooring and attaching cleats for the island base cabinet, cut away the flooring covering the holes for the drain and vent pipes.

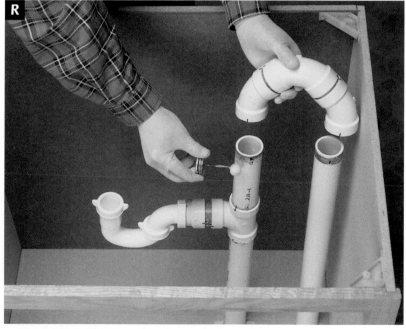

Install the base cabinet, then insert the drain and vent pipes through the holes in the cabinet floor and solvent-glue the pieces together.

Installing New Supply Pipes

A

Drill two 1"-diameter holes, spaced about 6" apart, through the floor of the island base cabinet and the underlying subfloor. Position the holes so they are not over floor joists. Drill similar holes in the floor of the base cabinet for a wall sink.

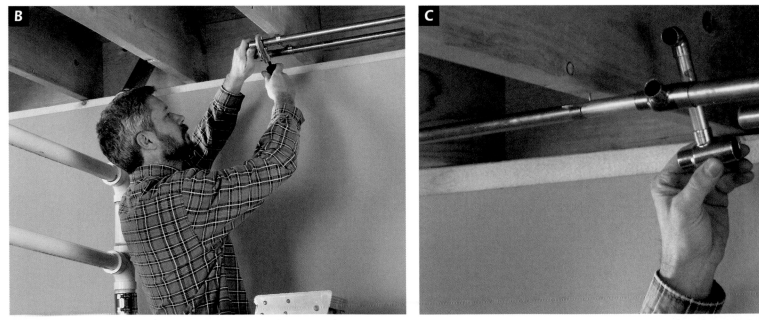

B

Turn off the water at the main shutoff, and drain the pipes. Cut out any old water supply pipes that obstruct the new pipe runs, using a tubing cutter or hacksaw. In our project, we are removing the old pipe back to a point where it is convenient to begin the new branch lines.

C

Dry-fit T-fittings on each supply pipe (we used ¾" × ½" × ½" reducing T-fittings). Use elbows and lengths of copper pipe to begin the new branch lines running to the island sink and the wall sink. The parallel pipes should be routed so they are between 3" and 6" apart.

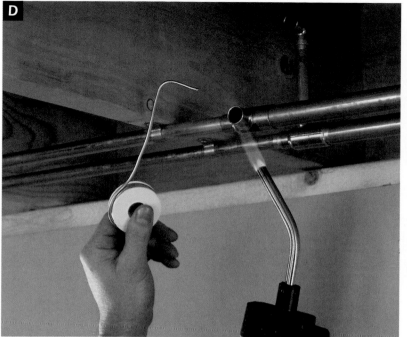

D

Solder the pipes and fittings together, beginning at the T-fittings. Support the horizontal pipe runs every 6 ft. with strapping attached to joists.

E

Extend the branch lines to points directly below the holes leading up into the base cabinets. Use elbows and lengths of pipe to form vertical risers extending at least 12" into the base cabinets. Use a small level to position the risers so they are plumb, then mark the pipes for cutting.

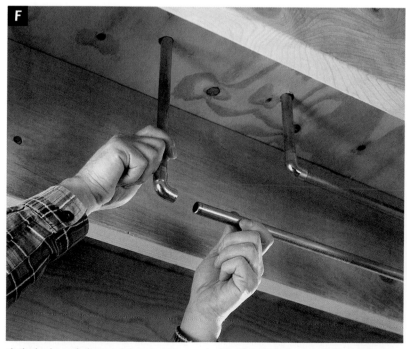

F

Fit the horizontal pipes and risers together, and solder them in place. Install blocking between joists, and anchor the risers to the blocking with pipe straps.

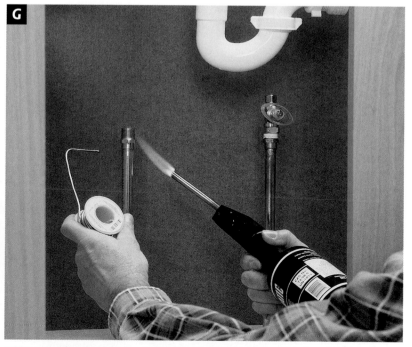

G

Solder male threaded adapters to the tops of the risers, then screw threaded shutoff valves onto the fittings.

Wiring a Remodeled Kitchen

In most cases, adding new circuits during a remodeling project will help your kitchen better serve your needs. In this project overview, you'll learn how to plan for the many power requirements of the modern kitchen, and how to install circuits and fixtures for recessed lights, under-cabinet lights, and a ceiling light controlled by three-way switches. You'll also learn how to install circuits and receptacles for a range, microwave, dishwasher, and food disposer. Methods for installing two small-appliance circuits are also shown. While your kitchen remodeling project will differ from this one, the methods and concepts shown apply to any kitchen wiring project containing any combination of circuits.

This illustration (right) shows the layout of seven circuits, in addition to the location of switches, receptacles, and lights. The size and number of circuits and the specific features included in this project are based on the particular needs of this 170-sq.-ft. kitchen.

Four of these circuits are dedicated circuits: a 50-amp circuit supplying the range, a 20-amp circuit powering the microwave, and two 15-amp circuits supplying the dishwasher and food disposer. In addition, two 20-amp circuits for small appliances supply power to all receptacles above the countertops and in the eating area. Finally, a 15-amp basic lighting circuit controls the ceiling fixture, all of the recessed fixtures, and the under-cabinet task lights. The final connections for these circuits are shown on pages 390 to 395.

Because no two kitchens are exactly alike, you'll need to create a wiring diagram for your own wiring project. Keep in mind that all rough construction and plumbing work should be finished and inspected before beginning the electrical work. It also helps to divide the project into steps and complete each step before beginning the next. For more information on basic wiring methods and techniques, refer to pages 94 to 139.

Circuit #7
14/2 cable

Circuits
#1 & #2:
12/3 cable

Circuit #4:
12/2 cable

Circuit #3:
6/3 cable

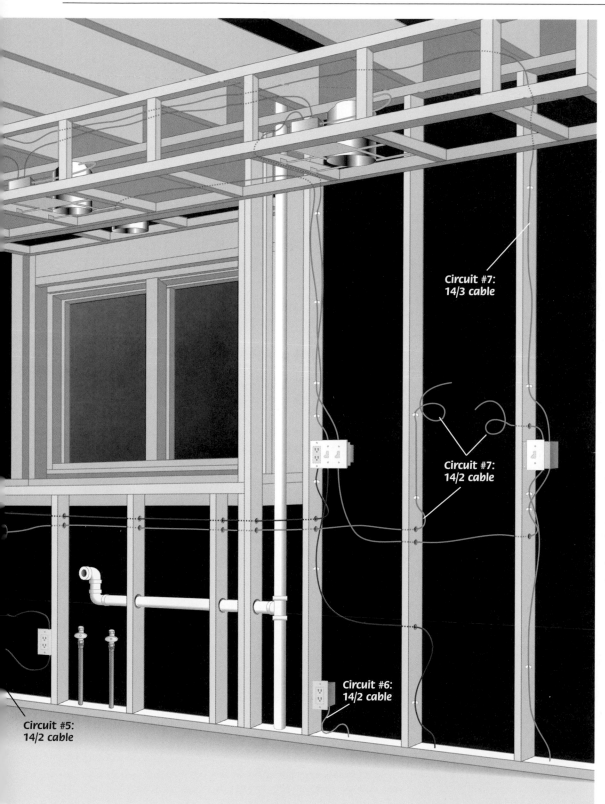

Circuit #7:
14/3 cable

Circuit #7:
14/2 cable

Circuit #6:
14/2 cable

Circuit #5:
14/2 cable

■ **#1 & #2: Small-appliance circuits.** Two 20-amp, 120-volt circuits supply power to countertop and eating areas for small appliances. All general-use receptacles must be on these circuits. One 12/3 cable, fed by a 20-amp double-pole breaker, wires both circuits. These circuits share one electrical box with the disposer circuit (#5), and another with the basic lighting circuit (#7).

■ **#3: Range circuit.** A 50-amp, 120/240-volt dedicated circuit supplies power to the range/oven appliance. It is wired with 6/3 cable.

■ **#4: Microwave circuit.** A dedicated 20-amp, 120-volt circuit supplies power to the microwave. It is wired with 12/2 cable. Microwaves that use less than 300 watts can be installed on a 15-amp circuit or plugged into the small-appliance circuits.

■ **#5: Food disposer circuit.** A dedicated 15-amp, 120-volt circuit supplies power to the disposer. It is wired with 14/2 cable. Some local codes allow the disposer to be on the same circuit as the dishwasher.

■ **#6: Dishwasher circuit.** A dedicated 15-amp, 120-volt circuit supplies power to the dishwasher. It is wired with 14/2 cable. Some local codes allow the dishwasher to be on the same circuit as the disposer.

■ **#7: Basic lighting circuit.** A dedicated 15-amp, 120-volt circuit powers the ceiling fixture, recessed fixtures, and under-cabinet task lights. 14/2 and 14/3 cables connect the fixtures and switches in the circuit. Each task light has a self-contained switch.

Planning the Circuits

A kitchen generally uses more power than other rooms because it contains many fixtures and appliances. Where you locate these items depends upon your needs. Make sure the main work areas of your kitchen have plenty of light and enough receptacles. Try to anticipate future needs: for example, you may want to install a range receptacle when remodeling, even if you currently have a gas range. It is difficult and expensive to make those changes later.

Contact the local building department before you begin planning. They may have requirements that differ from the National Electrical Code. Remember that the code contains minimum requirements primarily concerning safety, not convenience or need. Work with the inspectors to create a safe plan that also meets your needs.

To help locate receptacles, plan carefully where cabinets and appliances will be in the finished project. Appliances installed within cabinets, such as microwaves or food disposers, must have their receptacles positioned according to manufacturer's instructions. Putting at least one receptacle at table height in dining areas will make it more convenient to operate small appliances.

The primary ceiling fixture should be centered in the kitchen ceiling. Or, if your kitchen contains a dining area or breakfast nook, you may want to center the light fixture over the table. Locate recessed light fixtures and under-cabinet task lights where they will efficiently illuminate the main work areas.

Before drawing diagrams and applying for a permit, evaluate your existing service and make sure it provides enough power to supply the new circuits you are planning to add. If you find that it will not, contact a licensed electrician to upgrade your service before beginning your work.

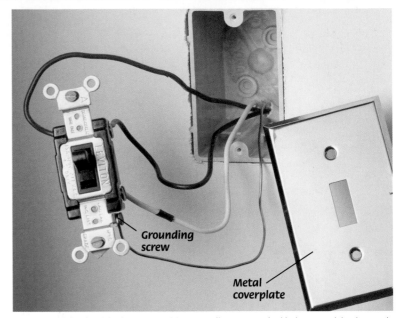

Inspectors may require switches with grounding screws in kitchens and baths. Code requires them when metal coverplates are used with plastic boxes.

Bring the wiring plan and materials list to the inspector's office when applying for the permit. Follow any suggestions made by your inspector. These tips can save you time and money.

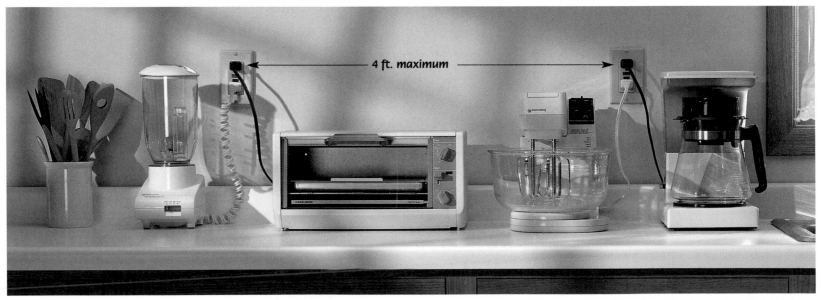

Code requires receptacles above countertops to be no more than 4 ft. apart. Put receptacles closer together in areas where many appliances will be used. Any section of countertop that is wider than 12" must have a receptacle located above it. (Countertop spaces separated by items such as range tops, sinks, and refrigerators are considered separate sections.) All accessible receptacles in kitchens and bathrooms must be a GFCI. On walls without countertops, receptacles should be no more than 12 ft. apart.

Tips for Planning Kitchen Circuits

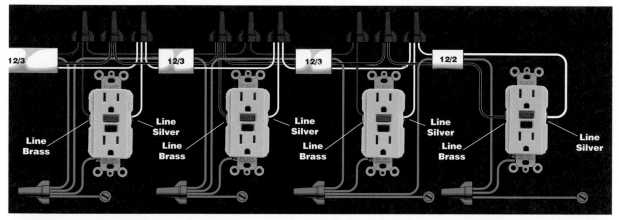

Two circuits supplied by one 3-wire cable.

Two 20-amp small-appliance circuits can be wired with one 12/3 cable supplying power to both circuits (top, right), rather than using separate 12/2 cables for each circuit (bottom, right), to save time and money. In 12/3 cable, the black wire supplies power to one circuit for alternate receptacles (the first, third, etc.), the red wire supplies power for the second circuit to the remaining receptacles. The white wire is the neutral for both circuits. For safety, the neutral must be attached with a pigtail to each receptacle, instead of being connected directly to the terminal. These circuits must contain all general-use receptacles in the kitchen, pantry, breakfast area, or dining room. No lighting outlets or receptacles from any other rooms can be connected to them.

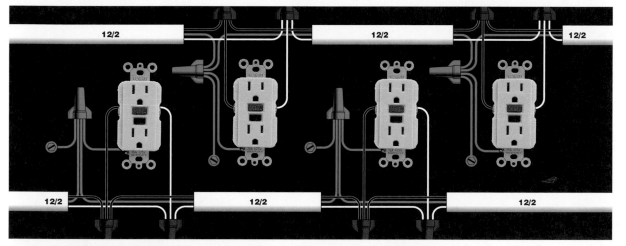

Two circuits supplied by two 2-wire cables.

Work areas at the sink and range should be well-lighted for convenience and safety. Install switch-controlled lights over these areas.

Ranges require a dedicated 40- or 50-amp 120/240-volt circuit (or two circuits for separate oven and countertop units). Even if you do not have an electric range, it's a good idea to install the circuit when remodeling.

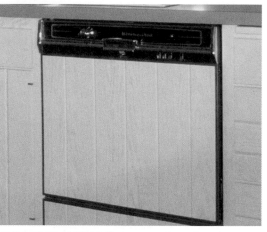

Dishwashers and food disposers require dedicated 15-amp, 120-volt circuits according to most local codes. Some inspectors will allow these appliances to share one circuit.

Completing the Rough-ins

After the inspector issues you a work permit, you can begin installing electrical boxes for switches, receptacles, and fixtures. Install all boxes and frames for recessed fixtures, such as vent fans and recessed lights, before cutting and installing any cable. However, some surface-mounted fixtures, such as under-cabinet task lights, have self-contained wire connection boxes. These fixtures are installed after the walls are finished and the cabinets are in place.

First determine locations for the boxes above the countertops (see page 389). After establishing the height for these boxes, install all of the other visible wall boxes at this height. Boxes that will be behind appliances or inside cabinets should be located according to the appliance manufacturer's instructions. For example, the receptacle for the dishwasher cannot be installed directly behind that appliance; it is often located in the sink cabinet for easy access.

Always use the largest electrical boxes that are practical for your installation. Using large boxes ensures that you will meet code regulations concerning box volume, and simplifies making the connections.

After all the boxes and recessed fixtures are installed, you are ready to measure and cut the cables. First install the feeder cables that run from the circuit breaker panel to the first electrical box in each circuit. Then cut and install the remaining cables to complete the circuits.

Heights of electrical boxes in a kitchen vary depending upon their use. In the kitchen project shown here, the centers of the boxes above the countertop are 45" above the floor, centered within 18" backsplashes extending from the countertop to the cabinets. All boxes for wall switches also are installed at this height. The center of the box for the microwave receptacle is 72" above the floor, where it will fit between the cabinets. The centers of the boxes for the range and food disposer receptacles are 12" above the floor, but the center of the box for the dishwasher receptacle is 6" above the floor, next to the space that the appliance will occupy.

Tips for Roughing-In Kitchen Wiring

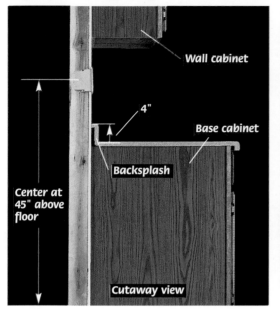

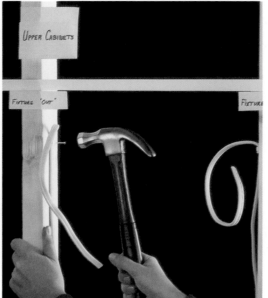

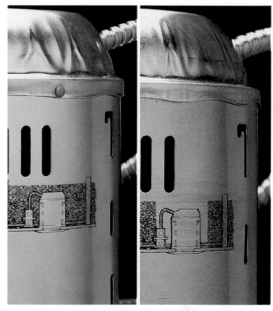

Mount electrical boxes above countertops centered 45" above the floor. However, if the backsplash is more than 4" high (standard) or the distance between the countertop and the bottom of the cabinet is less than 18", center the box in the space between the countertop and the bottom of the wall cabinet.

Install cables for an under-cabinet light at positions that will line up with the knockouts on the fixture box (which is installed after the walls and cabinets are in place). Cables will be retrieved through ⅝" drilled holes (see page 395), so it is important to position the cables accurately.

Choose the proper type of recessed light fixture for your project. There are two types of fixtures: those rated for installation within insulation (left), and those that must be kept at least 3" from insulation (right). Self-contained thermal switches shut off power if the unit gets too hot for its rating. A recessed light fixture must be installed at least ½" from combustible materials.

Mounting a Recessed Light Fixture

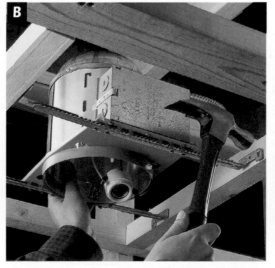

Extend the mounting bars on the recessed fixture to reach the framing members. Adjust the position of the light unit on the mounting bars to locate it properly.

Align the bottom edges of the mounting bars with the bottom edges of the framing members, then nail or screw the mounting bars to the framing members.

Remove the wire connection box cover and open one knockout for each cable entering the box. Install a cable clamp for each open knockout, and tighten the locknut, using a screwdriver to drive the lugs.

Making the Final Connections

Make the final connections for switches, receptacles, and fixtures after the rough-in inspection. First, make final connections on recessed fixtures (it is easier to do this before wallboard is installed). Then, finish the work on walls and ceiling, install the cabinets, and make the remaining final connections. Use the photos on the following pages as a guide for making the final connections. The last step is to connect the circuits at the main service panel (you'll probably want to hire an electrician for this). After all connections are made, your work is ready for the final inspection.

■ Circuits #1 & #2

Two 20-amp, 120-volt small-appliance circuits.

• 7 GFCI receptacles
• 20-amp double-pole circuit breaker

NOTE: In this project, two of the GFCI receptacles are installed in boxes that also contain switches from other circuits (see page 391).

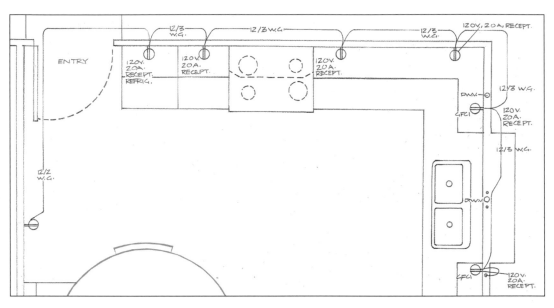

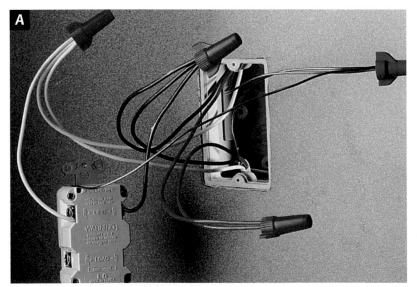

Connecting small-appliance receptacles (two alternating 20-amp circuits in one 12/3 cable): At alternate receptacles in the cable run (first, third, etc.), attach a black pigtail to a brass screw terminal marked LINE on the receptacle and to the black wire from both cables. Connect a white pigtail to a silver screw (LINE) and to both white wires. Connect a grounding pigtail to the grounding screw and to both grounding wires. Connect both red wires together. Tuck the wires into the box, then attach the receptacle and coverplate.

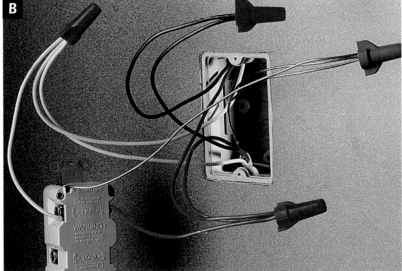

At the remaining receptacles in the run, attach a red pigtail to a brass screw terminal (LINE) and to the red wires from the cables. Attach a white pigtail to a silver screw terminal (LINE) and to both white wires. Connect a grounding pigtail to the grounding screw and to both grounding wires. Connect both black wires together. Tuck the wires into the box and attach the receptacle and coverplate. (See page 387 for an optional wiring method using two separate 12/2 cables, one for each circuit.)

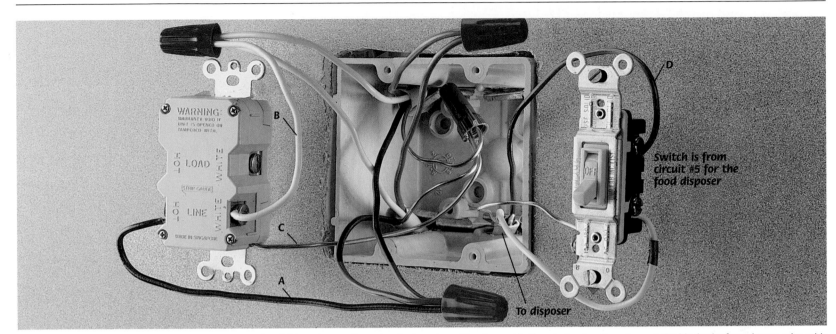

Installing a GFCI & disposer switch: Connect a black pigtail (A) to the GFCI brass terminal marked LINE, and to the black wires from three-wire cables. Attach a white pigtail (B) to the silver terminal marked LINE, and to the white wires from the three-wire cables. Attach a grounding pigtail (C) to the GFCI grounding screw and to the grounding wires from the three-wire cables. Connect both red wires together. Connect the black wire from the two-wire cable (D) to one switch terminal. Attach the white wire to the other terminal and tag it black to indicate it is hot. Attach the grounding wire to the switch grounding screw. Tuck the wires into the box and attach the switch, receptacle, and coverplate.

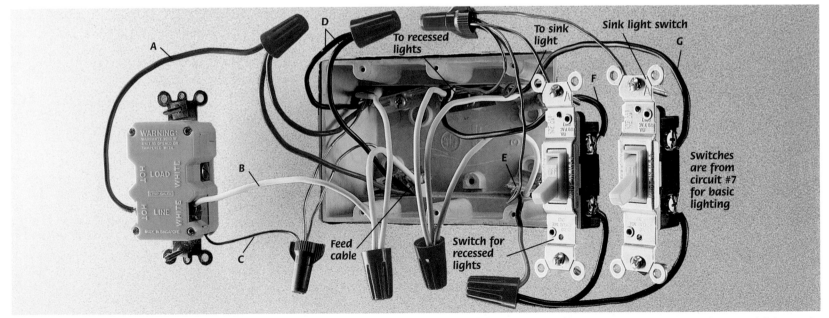

Installing a GFCI & two switches for recessed lights: Connect a red pigtail (A) to the GFCI brass terminal labeled LINE and to the red wires from the three-wire cables. Connect a white pigtail (B) to the silver LINE terminal and to the white wires from the three-wire cables. Attach a grounding pigtail (C) to the grounding screw and to the grounding wires from the three-wire cables. Connect the black wires from the three-wire cables (D) together. Attach a black pigtail to one screw on each switch and to the black wire from the two-wire feed cable (E). Connect the black wire (F) from the two-wire cable leading to the recessed lights, to the remaining screw on the switch for the recessed lights. Connect the black wire (G) from the two-wire cable leading to sink light, to the remaining screw on the sink light switch. Connect the white wires from all the two-wire cables together. Connect pigtails to the switch grounding screws, and to all the grounding wires from the two-wire cables. Tuck the wires into the box and attach the switches, receptacle, and coverplate.

Continued on next page

Making the Final Connections (cont.)

Circuit #3

A 50-amp, 120/240-volt circuit serving the range.

• 50-amp receptacle for range
• 50-amp double-pole circuit breaker

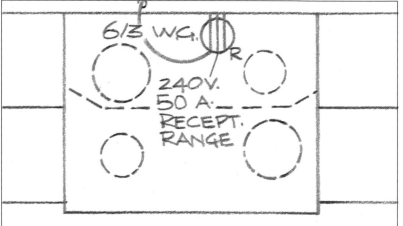

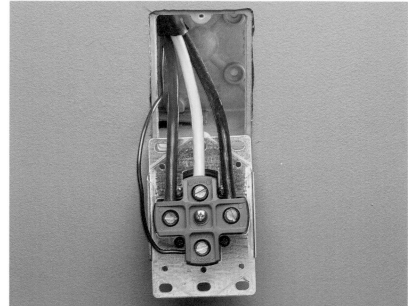

Installing a 120/240 Range Receptacle: *Attach the white wire to the neutral terminal, and the black and red wires to the remaining terminals. The neutral white wire acts as the grounding wire for this circuit, so push the bare copper ground wire from the cable to the back of the box. Tuck the rest of the wires into the box. Attach the receptacle and coverplate.*

Circuit #4

A 20-amp, 120-volt circuit for the microwave.

• 20-amp duplex receptacle
• 20-amp single-pole circuit breaker

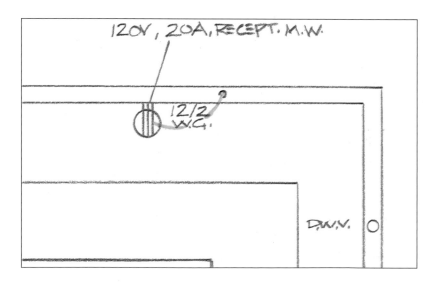

Connecting a Microwave Receptacle: *Connect the black wire from the cable to a brass screw terminal on the receptacle. Attach the white wire to a silver screw terminal, and connect the grounding wire to the receptacle's grounding screw. Tuck the wires into the box and attach the receptacle and coverplate.*

Circuit #5

A 15-amp, 120-volt circuit for the food disposer.

- 15-amp duplex receptacle
- Single-pole switch
- 15-amp single-pole circuit breaker

NOTE: Final connection of the single-pole switch controlling the disposer is shown on page 391.

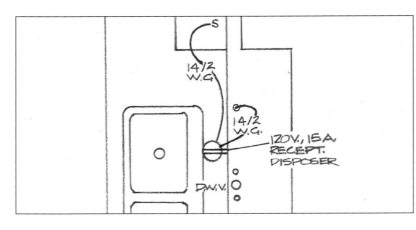

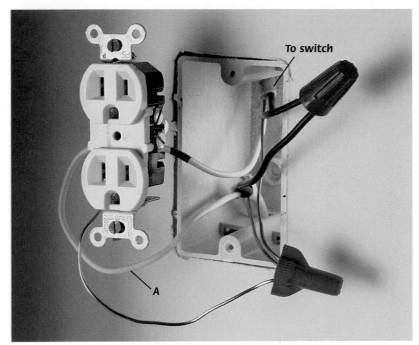

Connecting a Disposer Receptacle: *Connect the black wires together. Connect the white wire from the feed cable (A) to a silver screw on the receptacle. Connect the white wire from the cable going to the switch to a brass screw terminal on the receptacle, and tag the wire with black to indicate it is hot. Attach a grounding pigtail to the grounding screw and to both cable grounding wires. Tuck the wires into the box and attach the receptacle and coverplate.*

Circuit #6

A 15-amp, 120-volt circuit for the dishwasher.

- 15-amp duplex receptacle
- 15-amp single-pole circuit breaker

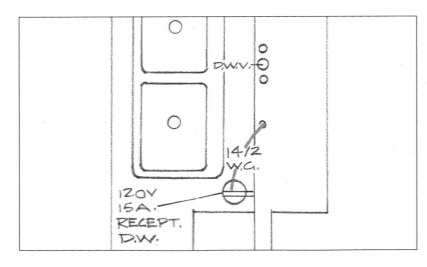

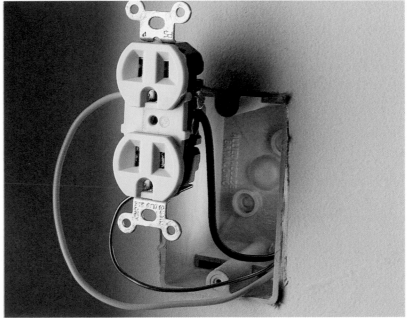

Connecting a Dishwasher Receptacle: *Connect the black wire to a brass screw terminal. Attach the white wire to a silver screw terminal. Connect the grounding wire to the grounding screw. Tuck the wires into the box, then attach the receptacle and coverplate.*

Continued on next page

Making the Final Connections (cont.)

Circuit #7

A 15-amp basic lighting circuit serving the kitchen.

- 2 three-way switches with grounding screws
- 2 single-pole switches with grounding screws
- Ceiling light fixture
- 6 recessed light fixtures
- 4 fluorescent under-cabinet fixtures
- 15-amp single-pole circuit breaker

NOTE: Final connections for the single-pole switches are shown on page 391.

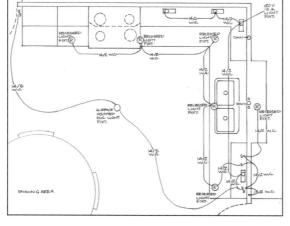

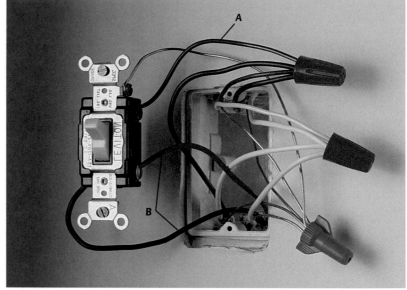

Connecting the First Three-way Switch: Connect a black pigtail to the COMMON screw on the switch (A) and to the black wires from the two-wire cables. Connect the black and red wires from the three-wire cable to the TRAVELER terminals (B) on the switch. Connect the white wires from all cables entering box together. Attach a grounding pigtail to the switch grounding screw and to all the grounding wires in the box. Tuck the wires into the box, then attach the switch and coverplate.

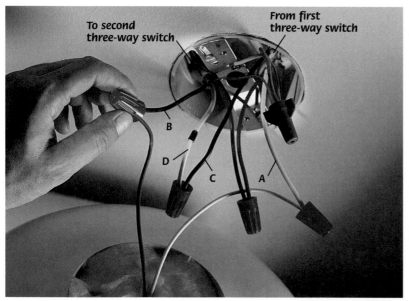

Connecting a Surface-mounted Ceiling Fixture: Connect the white fixture lead to the white wire (A) from the first three-way switch. Connect the black fixture lead to the black wire (B) from the second three-way switch. Connect the black wire (C) from the first switch to the white wire (D) from the second switch, and tag this white wire with black to indicate that it is hot. Connect the red wires from both switches together. Connect all the grounding wires together. Mount the fixture following manufacturer's instructions.

Connecting the Second Three-way Switch: Connect the black wire from the cable to the COMMON screw terminal (A). Connect the red wire to a TRAVELER screw terminal. Attach the white wire to the other TRAVELER screw terminal and tag it with black to indicate it is hot. Attach the grounding wire to the grounding screw on the switch. Tuck the wires in the box, then attach the switch and coverplate.

Connecting Recessed Light Fixtures

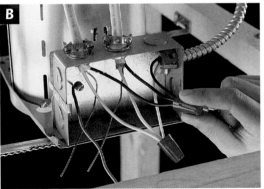

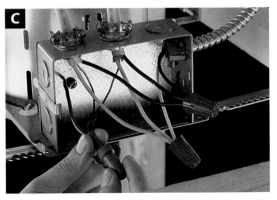

Make the connections before installing the wallboard (the work also must be inspected first). For each fixture, connect the white cable wires to the white fixture lead.

Connect the black wires to the black lead from the fixture.

Attach a grounding pigtail to the grounding screw on the fixtures, then connect all the grounding wires. Tuck the wires into the junction box, and replace the cover.

Connecting Under-cabinet Fluorescent Task Light Fixtures

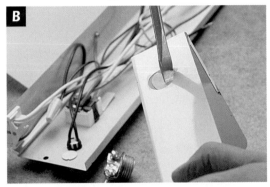

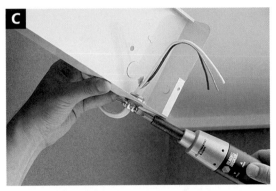

Drill ⅝" holes through the wall and cabinet at locations that line up with knockouts on the fixture, and retrieve the cable ends (see page 389).

Remove the access cover on the fixture. Open one knockout for each cable that enters the fixture box, and install cable clamps.

Strip 8" of sheathing from each cable end. Insert each end through a cable clamp, leaving ¼" of sheathing in the fixture box.

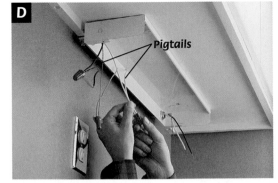

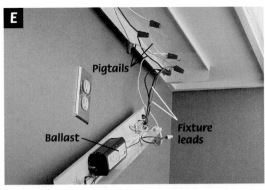

Screw the fixture box to the cabinet. Attach the black, white, and green pigtails of the THHN/THWN wire (see page 102) to the wires from one cable entering the box. The pigtails must be long enough to reach the cable at other end of the box.

Connect a black pigtail and circuit wire to the black lead from the fixture. Connect a white pigtail and circuit wire to the white lead from the fixture. Attach a green pigtail and copper circuit wire to the green grounding wire attached to the fixture box.

Tuck the wires into the box, and route the THHN/THWN pigtails along one side of the ballast. Replace the access cover and fixture lens.

Painting Cabinets

Painting your cabinets is a quick, inexpensive way to renew your kitchen's appearance. Cabinets receive heavy use and are frequently scrubbed, so paint them with heavy-duty gloss enamel, which is more durable than flat wall paint. Most jobs will require two coats of paint. Sand the surfaces lightly between coats.

Use natural bristle paint brushes with alkyd (oil-based) paints; use synthetic bristle brushes with latex (water-based) paints.

Varnished cabinets can be painted if the surface is properly prepared. Use liquid deglosser to dull the shine, then prime all surfaces. Alkyd paints work best for painting varnished cabinets. Cabinets covered with plastic laminate should not be painted.

If you decide to varnish your cabinets, prepare them by stripping the wood, filling any holes or scratches, and sealing the wood. Then apply varnish, sanding lightly between coats. Heat guns can speed up the stripping process, but be careful not to damage or blister surfaces around cabinets. Use chemical strippers for spot-stripping.

Tools: Screwdriver, work light, paint pan, tapered sash brush, trim brush, scraper, sandpaper, short-nap paint rollers.

Materials: Paint remover, mild detergent, wood-patching compound, primer/sealer, gloss enamel paint.

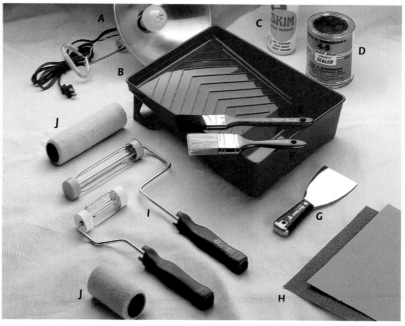

Specialty tools & supplies for painting cabinets include: work light (A), paint pan (B), paint remover (C), primer/sealer (D), tapered sash brush (E), trim brush (F), scraper (G), sandpaper (H), paint rollers (I), roller covers (J).

Painting Cabinets

Empty the cabinets. Remove the doors, drawers, removable shelves, and all hardware. If the hardware is to be repainted, strip the old paint by soaking the hardware in paint remover.

Wash the cabinets with a mild detergent. Scrape any loose paint. Fill any deep scratches and dents with a wood-patching compound. Sand all the surfaces. Wipe away the sanding dust, and prime all the bare wood with a sealer.

Paint the cabinet interiors first, in this order: 1) back walls, 2) tops, 3) sides, 4) bottoms. Paint the bottoms, tops, and edges of the shelves last.

Paint the large outside surfaces using a short-nap paint roller. Work from the top down.

Paint both sides of the doors, beginning with the inner surfaces. With panel doors, paint in this order: 1) recessed panels, 2) horizontal rails, 3) vertical stiles.

Paint the drawer fronts last. Let the doors and drawers dry for several days, then install the hardware and rehang the doors.

Refacing Cabinets

Refacing existing kitchen cabinets produces a dramatic change in style. Refacing kits allow you to change the style, color, and decor of your kitchen for significantly less than cabinet replacement.

Standard refacing kits include new doors, drawer fronts, and natural-wood veneer for resurfacing cabinet face frames and sides. Additional options include replacement and storage hardware, hinges, drawer boxes, lazy Susans, molding, and valances.

Tools: Drill, utility knife, straightedge, wallcovering roller, handsaw.

Materials: Latex wood patch, paint scraper, 150-grit sandpaper, refacing kit, stain and polyurethane (if needed), wood blocks, cabinet hardware.

Remove the old doors, hinges, catches, and other hardware. Paint the interior of the cabinets, if desired (see pages 396 to 397). Scrape off any loose or peeling finish. Fill any holes or chips with latex wood patch. Let the patch dry, then lightly sand the cabinet sides, faces, and edges with 150-grit sandpaper.

Remove the veneer from the package and lay it flat on a smooth surface. Measure each surface to be covered, and add ¼" for overlap. Cut the veneer pieces with a utility knife and a straightedge.

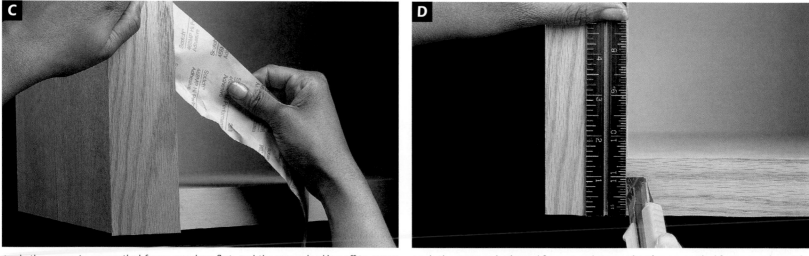

Apply the veneer to any vertical frame members first. Peel the veneer backing off to expose one corner of the adhesive. Align the veneer and press lightly to adhere it to the corner. Gradually remove the backing, and smooth out any air bubbles with your fingertips. Trim the excess veneer with a utility knife.

Apply the veneer to horizontal frame members, overlapping any vertical frame members. Trim the excess with a utility knife, using a straightedge as a guide. Apply veneer to the cabinet sides, and trim away the excess with a utility knife.

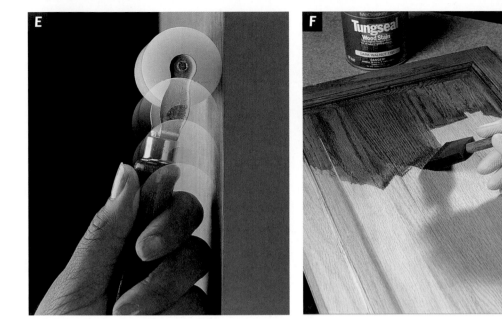

Bond the veneer by rolling the entire surface with a wallcovering roller.

Stain the new doors and drawer fronts, if they are unfinished. Stain any unfinished veneer to match. Apply three coats of polyurethane finish, sanding lightly between coats with 150-grit sandpaper.

Mount the hinges to the cabinet doors, following the kit manufacturer's instructions. Attach the doors to the cabinet frames, aligning them carefully so they overlap the frames equally on all sides and the gaps between doors are even. Install all door hardware.

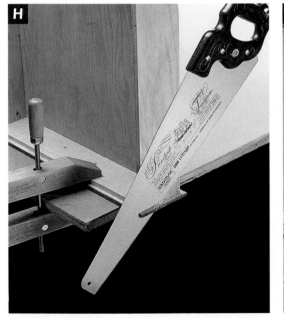

Saw off all the overhanging edges of the existing solid (one-piece) drawer fronts. If the drawer fronts are two-piece, remove the screws and discard the decorative face panels.

Attach the new fronts by drilling pilot holes and driving screws through the insides of the drawers into the new drawer fronts. Make sure the drawer fronts overlap the drawers by an equal margin on all sides. Install all hardware.

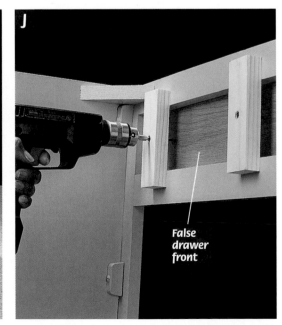

False drawer front

Attach the false drawer fronts on the sink and cooktop cabinets by cutting wood blocks to span the drawer openings. Place the blocks across the openings on the insides of the cabinets. Fasten the false fronts by driving screws through wood blocks into the fronts.

Installing New Cabinets

Cabinets determine the style and function of a kitchen more than any other element. They also represent a significant portion of the expense of kitchen remodeling. For these reasons and because new cabinets may be in place for decades, buying new cabinets is perhaps the most important decision you'll make in the remodeling process. The result can be the most satisfying.

Installing cabinets is fairly simple; with one or two helpers, most do-it-yourselfers can do a fine job of installing them. The most important factors in an installation are preparing the walls so they are perfectly smooth and flat, and marking the cabinet layout using perfectly level and plumb reference lines.

©Karen Melvin/Knapp Cabinetry & Woodworking

Selecting Cabinets

Kitchen cabinets are generally divided into three grades, based on how they are constructed. To some extent, the grades indicate quality, but not very accurately. The best test of quality is a thorough physical inspection.

• *Stock cabinets* are factory-made to standard sizes and typically are sold off-the-shelf in home centers. Widths range from 9" to 48", in 3" increments. Stock cabinets are the least expensive of the three grades, but they offer the fewest design options. While the quality is generally lower, a well-made stock cabinet can be a very good value. If your stock cabinets have to be ordered, it may be a couple of days to a couple of weeks before they arrive.

• *Semi-custom cabinets* are also factory-made to standard sizes, but they offer many more options of finish, size, features, and materials than stock cabinets. These are typically sold in showrooms, and are priced between stock and custom cabinets. Semi-custom cabinets are the best choice for homeowners who want better-quality with some special features but don't want to pay the high prices for a custom prod-

uct. You should allow 3 to 8 weeks lead time when ordering semi-custom cabinets.

• *Custom cabinets* offer the most in both quality and available options. Each unit is custom-built to fit your kitchen. It's wise to shop around before settling on a custom cabinetmaker, as prices can vary widely. If you choose to have your cabinets custom-made, expect a lead time of about 6 to 10 weeks.

Cabinets are available in two types: *face-frame* and *frameless,* or *Euro-style.* Face-frame cabinets have frames around the front of the cabinet box, or *carcase,* made of solid hardwood. The doors on face-frame cabinets mount over the frame, and the hinges are exposed. Face-frame cabinets typically have a more traditional look.

Frameless cabinets have no face-frame and the doors span the entire width of the carcase. The doors are mounted using *cup* hinges, which are invisible when the doors are closed. The plainer, cleaner styling of frameless cabinets gives them a contemporary look.

Both types of cabinets are available in

Specification booklets list all the dimensions of cabinets and trim pieces. Draw a kitchen floor plan on graph paper, and use the booklets when sketching your cabinet layout.

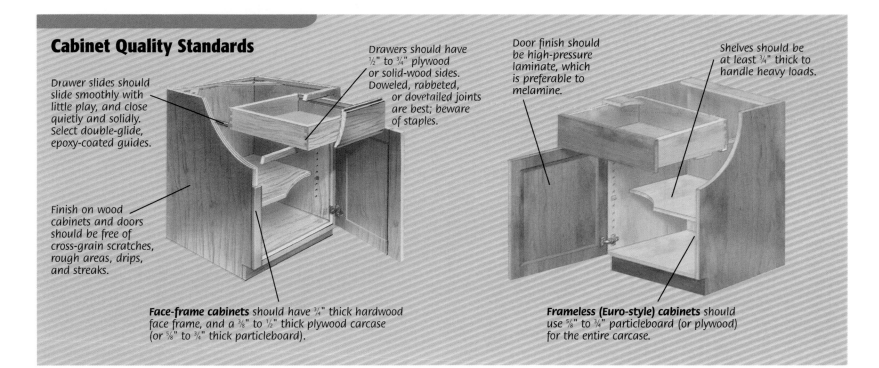

Cabinet Quality Standards

Drawer slides should slide smoothly with little play, and close quietly and solidly. Select double-glide, epoxy-coated guides.

Drawers should have ½" to ¾" plywood or solid-wood sides. Doweled, rabbeted, or dovetailed joints are best; beware of staples.

Door finish should be high-pressure laminate, which is preferable to melamine.

Shelves should be at least ¾" thick to handle heavy loads.

Finish on wood cabinets and doors should be free of cross-grain scratches, rough areas, drips, and streaks.

Face-frame cabinets should have ¾" thick hardwood face frame, and a ⅜" to ½" thick plywood carcase (or ⅝" to ¾" thick particleboard).

Frameless (Euro-style) cabinets should use ⅝" to ¾" particleboard (or plywood) for the entire carcase.

modular units, which have finished panels on both sides and can be arranged in a variety of ways to fit any kitchen layout. Modular cabinet doors can be reversed to open from either the left or right. They are especially suited to do-it-yourself installations.

There are no distinct advantages or disadvantages between the two cabinet types. However, by virtue of not having a face frame, frameless cabinets offer slightly more storage space than framed types, and their drawers are a bit wider, for the same reason.

To be sure you're getting your money's worth with your cabinet purchase, inspect all major components.

Basic Materials

Most cabinet carcases are made with plywood or particle board. Plywood is stronger than particle board of the same thickness, but that doesn't mean you should avoid the latter. If the cabinet is made with particle board, make sure the board used is ⅝" to ¾" thick. It should also have a vinyl or melamine coating on the inside surfaces, to protect it from water damage. Most frameless cabinets (including the doors) are made with particle board.

On cabinets with natural wood surfaces, pay close attention to how well the grain and colors of the different pieces match.

Drawers

A drawer is a good indicator of a cabinet's quality. Better drawers are made with plywood or solid wood, and their pieces are assembled with strong joints, such as dovetail, dowel, or rabbet joints. Avoid drawers that were put together with staples. Also, four-sided drawers, with the drawer front attached to the front side, are stronger and more durable than those with three sides that use the drawer front as the fourth side.

Drawer slides should be smooth and sound and allow little play from side to side. You can also check the slide's load rating, which should be at least 75 pounds.

Doors

If the rest of the cabinet is of a suitable quality, the doors should be fine, and your decision will be based largely on appearance. But cabinet doors receive a lot of use, and they need a durable finish to protect them over the years. Flat particleboard doors, which are

commonly found on frameless cabinets, may be faced with a plastic laminate similar to the material used on countertops. This is a durable, washable material that should last a very long time; just make sure the facing is laminate and not just a coating of melamine—a much less durable finish.

If you're looking for wood doors with a stain or a clear finish, make sure the outer wood veneers look good and the blending of the grain and color variations is attractive. Examine the finish for common flaws, such as inconsistency, rough areas, drips or cross-grain sanding marks. You may have specific reasons for choosing pine or another softwood, but remember that hardwoods, such as maple, oak, and cherry, are more durable.

An alternative to the traditional raised-panel wood door is the vinyl-clad door. Made from medium-density fiberboard (MDF) with a tough vinyl foil, vinyl-clad doors look like painted wood doors, but have a more durable finish. Another advantage is that vinyl-clad doors expand and contract less than wood doors, so there's less risk of the paint cracking along the edges of the panel.

Preparing the Walls

Installing new cabinets is easiest if the kitchen is completely empty. Remove the old cabinets, disconnect the plumbing and wiring, and temporarily remove the appliances. If the new kitchen requires plumbing or electrical changes, now is the time to get this work done. If the kitchen flooring is to be replaced, finish it before beginning layout and installation of the cabinets.

Cabinets must be installed plumb and level. Using a level as a guide, draw reference lines on the walls to indicate cabinet location. If the kitchen floor is uneven, find the highest point of the floor in the area that will be covered by base cabinets. Measure up from this point to draw reference lines.

Tools: *Level, trowel, stud finder, drill.*

Materials: *Straight 6- to 8-ft.-long 2 × 4, wallboard compound, sandpaper, 1 × 3 boards, 2½" wallboard screws.*

Find the high and low spots on the wall surfaces using a long, straight 2 × 4. Sand down any high spots.

Fill in the low spots of the wall. Apply wallboard taping compound with a trowel. Let the compound dry, then sand it lightly.

Locate and mark all wall studs in the project area, using an electronic stud finder. The cabinets will be hung by driving screws into the studs through the backs of the cabinets.

High point

Find the high point along the floor in the area that will be covered by the base cabinets. Place a level on a long, straight 2 × 4, and move the board across the floor to determine if the floor is uneven. If so, mark the wall at the high point.

E

Measure up 34½" from the high-point mark. Use a level to mark a reference line on the walls. The base cabinets will be installed with their top edges flush against this line.

High point

34½"

F

Measure up 84" from the high-point mark and draw a second reference line. The wall cabinets will be installed with their top edges flush against this line.

High point

84"

G

Measure down 30" from the wall-cabinet reference line and draw another level line where the bottom of the cabinets will be. Temporary ledgers will be installed against this line.

30"

H

Install 1 × 3 temporary ledgers with the top edges flush against the reference line. Attach the ledgers with 2½" wallboard screws driven into every other wall stud. Mark the stud locations on the ledgers. The cabinets will rest temporarily on the ledgers during installation.

Installing Cabinets

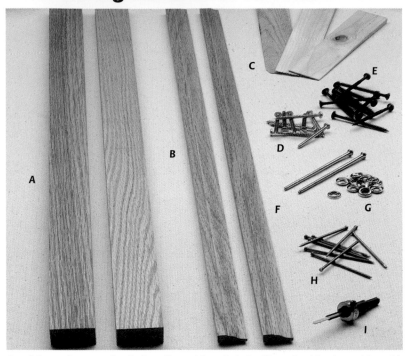

Specialty tools & supplies for installing cabinets include: filler strips (A), trim moldings (B), wood shims (C), No. 8 gauge 2½" sheetmetal screws (D), 3" wallboard screws (E), No. 10 gauge 4" wood screws (F), finish washers (G), 6d finish nails (H), No. 9 counterbore drill bit (I).

Cabinets must be firmly anchored with screws to wall studs, and must be exactly plumb and level, so that doors and drawers operate smoothly. In older homes, where walls and floors may be out of square, hanging cabinets often involves shimming cabinets up and out.

To protect the finish of your new cabinets, keep the protective wrapping on the units until you are ready to install them. Number each cabinet and mark its position on the wall. Just before installation, remove the cabinet doors and drawers, and number them so they can be easily replaced after the cabinets are installed.

Before you begin screwing cabinets to the wall, make sure the electricity to the area is off. If you are installing both wall and base cabinets, begin with the wall cabinets. Where cabinets run along two walls, start at a corner; otherwise, begin at either end. Correct placement of corner cabinets is essential to making adjacent cabinets plumb.

Tools: Circular saw or miter saw, handscrew clamps, level, utility knife, drill with ³⁄₁₆" twist bit, nail set, jig saw with wood-cutting blade, No. 9 counterbore drill bit, screwdriver, stud finder.

Materials: Cabinets, valance, finish nails, 1 × 3 lumber, cardboard, 2 × 4 lumber.

Specialty Materials: see photo, left.

Fitting Blind Corner Cabinets

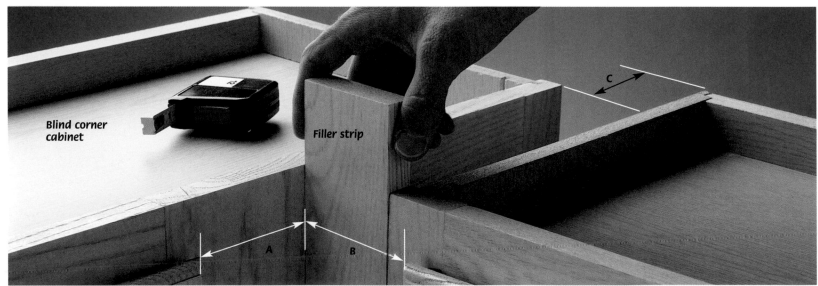

Blind corner cabinet

Filler strip

Before installation, test-fit the corner and adjoining cabinets to make sure the doors and handles do not interfere with each other. If necessary, increase the clearance by pulling the blind cabinet away from the side wall by no more than 4". To maintain even spacing between the edges of the doors and the cabinet corner (A, B), cut a filler strip and attach it to the adjoining cabinet. Measure distance (C) as a reference when positioning the blind cabinet against the wall.

Installing Wall Cabinets

Position the corner cabinet on the ledger. Drill ³⁄₁₆" pilot holes into the studs through the hanging strips at the rear of the cabinet. Attach the cabinet to the wall with 2½" sheetmetal screws. Do not tighten the screws fully until all the cabinets are hung.

Attach a filler strip to the adjoining cabinet, if needed (see page 404). Clamp the filler in place, using handscrew clamps. Drill pilot holes through the cabinet face frame near the hinge locations, using a counterbore bit. Attach the filler to the cabinet with 2½" sheetmetal screws. NOTE: Handscrew clamps will not damage the wood face frames.

Position the adjoining cabinet on the ledger, tight against the blind corner cabinet. Check the face frame for plumb. Drill ³⁄₁₆" pilot holes into the wall studs through hanging strips in the rear of the cabinet. Attach the cabinet with sheetmetal screws. Do not tighten the screws fully until all cabinets are hung.

Clamp the corner cabinet and the adjoining cabinet together at the top and bottom.

Continued on next page

Installing Wall Cabinets (cont.)

Attach the blind corner cabinet to the adjoining cabinet. From inside the corner cabinet, drill pilot holes through the face frame. Join the cabinets with sheetmetal screws.

Position and attach each additional cabinet. Clamp the frames together, and drill counterbored pilot holes through the sides of the face frames. Join the cabinets with sheetmetal screws. Drill ³⁄₁₆" pilot holes in the hanging strips, and attach the cabinets to the studs with sheetmetal screws.

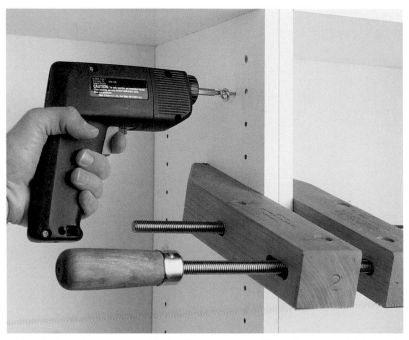

VARIATION: Join frameless cabinets with No. 8 gauge 1¼" wood screws and finish washers. Each pair of cabinets should be joined by at least four screws.

Fill small spaces between a cabinet and a wall or appliance with a filler strip. Cut the filler strip to fit the space, then wedge the filler into place with wood shims. Drill counterbored pilot holes through side of the cabinet face frame, and attach the filler with sheetmetal screws.

Remove the temporary ledger below the cabinets. Check the cabinet run for plumb, and adjust if necessary by placing wood shims behind the cabinets, near the stud locations. Tighten the wall screws completely. Cut off the shims, using a utility knife.

Use trim moldings to cover any gaps between cabinets and walls. Stain or paint the moldings to match the cabinet finish, and attach them to the cabinet sides with finish nails.

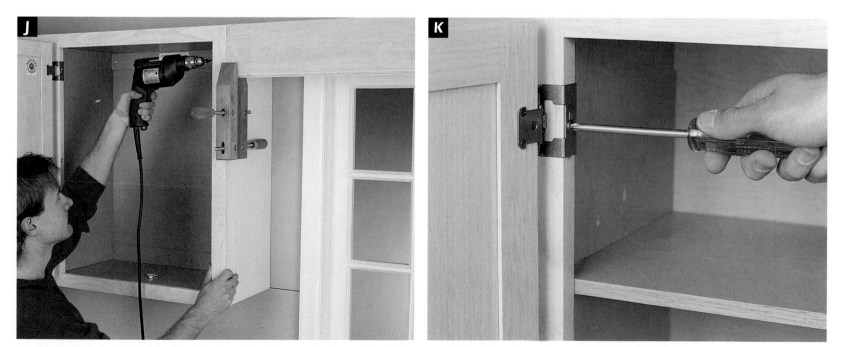

Attach a decorative valance above the sink. Clamp the valance to the edges of the cabinet frames, and drill counterbored pilot holes through the cabinet frames into the ends of the valance. Attach the valance with sheetmetal screws.

Install the cabinet doors, following the cabinet manufacturer's instructions. If necessary, adjust the hinges so that the doors are straight and plumb.

Installing Base Cabinets

Begin the installation with a corner cabinet. Position the cabinet so that the top is flush with the reference line. Make sure the cabinet is plumb and level. If necessary, adjust the cabinet by driving wood shims under the base. (Be careful not to damage the flooring.) Drill ³⁄₁₆" pilot holes through the cabinet hanging strip into the wall studs. Attach the cabinets loosely to the wall with sheetmetal screws.

Attach a filler strip to the adjoining cabinet, if necessary (see pages 404 to 405). Clamp the filler in place, and drill counterbored pilot holes through side of the face frame. Attach the filler with sheetmetal screws.

Clamp the adjoining cabinet to the corner cabinet. Make sure the cabinet is plumb, then drill counterbored pilot holes through the corner-cabinet face frame into the filler strip (see page 406, step E). Join the cabinets with sheetmetal screws. Drill ³⁄₁₆" pilot holes through the hanging strips into the wall studs. Attach the cabinets loosely with sheetmetal screws.

Use a jig saw to cut any openings needed for plumbing, wiring, or heating ducts.

Position and attach any additional cabinets, making sure the frames are aligned. Clamp the cabinets together, then drill counterbored pilot holes through the sides of the face frames. Join the cabinets with sheetmetal screws. Frameless cabinets are joined with No. 8 gauge 1¼" wood screws and finish washers (see page 406).

Make sure all the cabinets are level. If necessary, adjust by driving wood shims underneath the cabinets. Place wood shims behind the cabinets near stud locations wherever there is a gap. Tighten the wall screws. Cut off the shims with a utility knife.

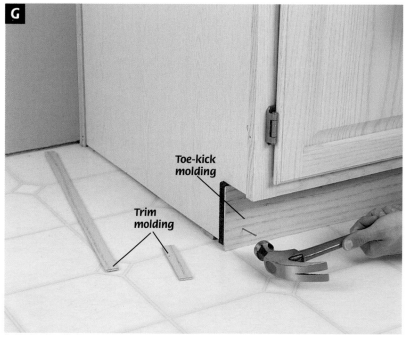

Toe-kick molding

Trim molding

Use trim moldings to cover any gaps between the cabinets and the wall or floor. The toe-kick area is often covered with a strip of hardwood finished to match the cabinets.

If the corner has a void area not covered by cabinets, screw 1 × 3 cleats to the wall, flush with the reference line. The cleats will help support the countertop.

Installing a Ceiling-hung Cabinet to Joists

Cut a cardboard template to the same size as the top of the wall cabinet. Use a template to outline the position of the cabinet on the ceiling. Mark the position of the cabinet face frame on the outline.

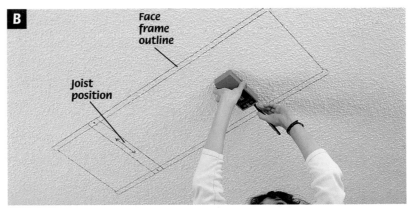

Locate the joists with a stud finder. If the joists run parallel to the cabinet, install blocking between the joists to hang the cabinet (below). Measure the joist positions and mark the cabinet frame to indicate where to drive the screws.

Have one or more helpers position the cabinet against the ceiling. Drill ³⁄₁₆" pilot holes through the top rails into the ceiling joists. Attach the cabinets with 4" wood screws and finish washers.

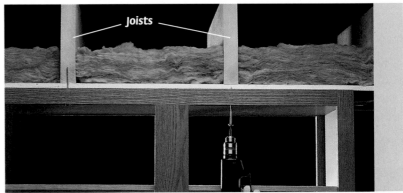

Shown in cutaway: The cabinet is attached to joists with wood screws and finish washers.

Installing a Ceiling-hung Cabinet to Blocking (joists must be accessible)

Complete step A at the top of this page. Drill reference holes through the ceiling at each corner of the cabinet outline. From above the ceiling, install 2 × 4 blocks between the joists. Blocking can be toenailed or end-nailed through the joists.

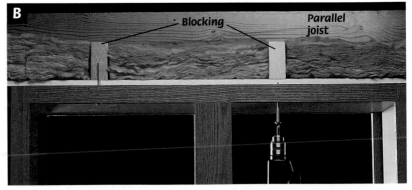

Measure the distance between each block and the drilled reference holes. Mark the cabinet frame to indicate where to drive the anchoring screws. Drill pilot holes and attach cabinet to the blocking with 4" wood screws and finish washers, as shown in cutaway above.

Installing a Base Island Cabinet

Set the base cabinet in the correct position, and lightly trace the cabinet outline onto the flooring. Remove the cabinet.

Attach L-shaped 2 × 4 cleats to the floor at opposite corners of the cabinet outline. Allow for thickness of the cabinet walls by positioning cleats ¾" inside the cabinet outline. Attach the cleats to the floor with 3" wallboard screws.

Lower the base cabinet over the cleats. Check the cabinet for level, and shim under the base if necessary.

Attach the cabinet to the floor cleats using 6d finish nails. Drill pilot holes for nails, and recess the nail heads with a nail set.

Installing a Post-form Countertop

A post-form laminate countertop is created by heating and bending laminate over curved particleboard to create a seamless counter-and-backsplash unit. Countertop manufacturers and suppliers offer countertop sections in a wide range of colors and finishes, as well as several types of edges. Most home centers carry only a few styles in stock.

Countertops are manufactured in stock widths of 25½", and in lengths from 6 to 12 ft. Premitered sections are available for two- or three-piece countertops that continue around corners. Manufacturers also supply end caps and end splashes to match countertops. If your countertop has an exposed end, you'll need an endcap kit that contains a preshaped strip of matching laminate.

If your project requires joining two countertop pieces at either a straight or mitered joint, have those end cuts made by the manufacturer or supplier to ensure a clean joint. To prevent water damage, plan so that joints fall well away from sinks and other wet areas.

The front edge of most post-form countertops have a lip along the bottom edge. If the countertop is installed directly on top of the cabinets, this lip may overhang the cabinet drawer fronts, interfering with the drawer operation. To prevent this, install buildup strips on the tops of the cabinets.

For a precise fit, the backsplash of your countertop must be shaped to follow any unevenness in the back wall—a process known as *scribing*. Always use caution when cutting or attaching laminate, as breaks, chips, and deep scratches cannot be repaired.

Tools: Circular saw, drill, framing square, straightedge, C-clamps, level, belt sander, caulk gun, jig saw.

Materials: Post-form countertop sections, 1¼" wallboard screws,

Specialty Tools & Materials: see photo, right.

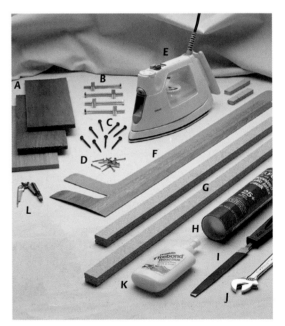

Specialty tools & materials *for installing a post-form countertop include: wood shims (A), take-up bolts (B), wallboard screws (C), 1¼" brads (D), household iron (E), endcap laminate (F), endcap battens (G), silicone caulk (H), file (I), adjustable wrench (J), wood glue (K), scribing compass (L).*

Installing a Post-form Countertop

A

Measure the cabinets to determine the length of the countertop. Because the walls may not be square, measure along the back wall and along the fronts of the cabinets. Add 1" for overhang if the end will be exposed. If an end will butt against an appliance, subtract ¹⁄₁₆" to prevent scratches.

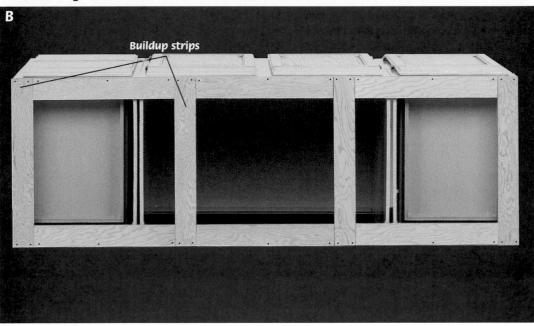

B

Buildup strips

Cut 3"-wide buildup strips from ¾" plywood or particleboard. Use 1¼" wallboard screws to attach the strips every 24" across the cabinets, around the perimeter, and next to any cutout locations. If an exposed end of the counter will receive a batten (see step D), you may not need a buildup strip on the end of the cabinet.

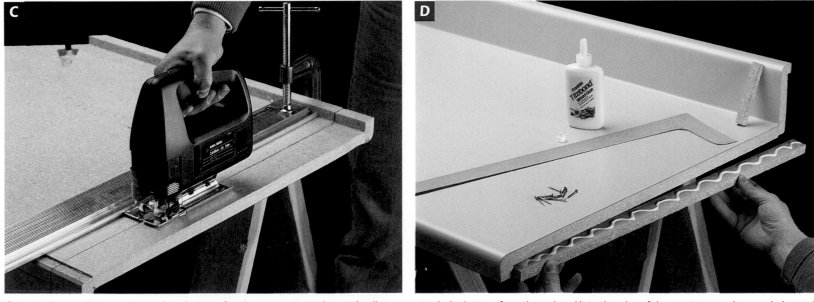

C

If you need to cut the countertop to length, use a framing square to mark a cutting line on the bottom surface of the countertop. Cut off the countertop with a jig saw, using a clamped straightedge as a guide. Cut from the bottom side of the countertop if you're using an up-cutting blade; cut from the top side with a down-cutting blade.

D

Attach the battens from the endcap kit to the edge of the countertop, using wood glue and 1¼" brads. Sand out any unevenness with a belt sander.

Continued on next page

Installing a Post-form Countertop (cont.)

Hold the endcap laminate against the end, slightly overlapping the edges. Activate the adhesive by pressing an iron set at medium heat against the endcap. Cool the endcap with a wet cloth, then file it flush with the edge of the countertop.

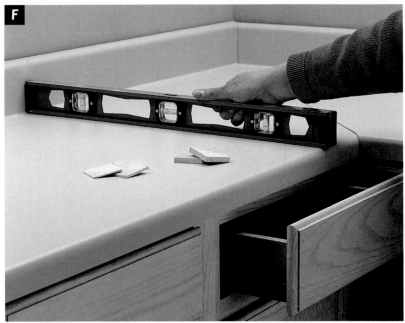

Position the countertop on the base cabinets. Make sure the front edge of the countertop is parallel to the cabinet face. Check the countertop for level. Make sure that the drawers and doors can open and close freely. If necessary, adjust the countertop with wood shims.

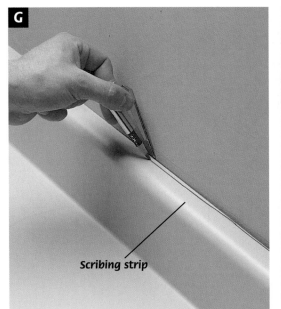

Scribing strip

Use a compass to transfer the wall contours onto the back-splash scribing strip. Set the compass arms to match the widest gap, then move it along the wall, marking the strip. If the laminate is too dark to show the pencil line, scribe onto a strip of masking tape applied to the scribing strip.

Remove the countertop. Use a belt sander with a coarse-grit belt to grind the backsplash to the scribe line. To avoid chipping the laminate, hold the sander parallel to the top of the backsplash. Bevel the strip inward slightly. Test-fit the countertop.

To mark a cutout for a self-rimming sink, position the sink upside down on the countertop and trace an outline. Remove the sink and draw a cutting line ⅝" inside the sink outline.

To mark a cutout for a cooktop or sink with a frame, position the metal frame on the countertop and trace an outline around the edge of the vertical flange of the frame.

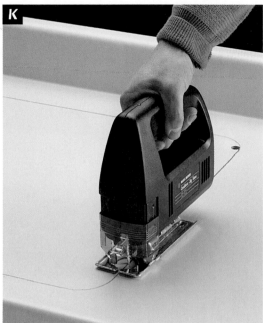

Drill a pilot hole just inside the cutting lines. Make the cutouts with a jig saw using a down-cutting blade. Support each cutout area from below to keep the cutout piece from falling before the cut is complete, which could chip the laminate.

Complete the miter joint by applying a bead of silicone caulk along the edges of the mitered countertop sections. Force the countertop pieces tightly together.

From underneath the cabinet, install and tighten the miter take-up bolts. Position the countertop tightly against the wall and fasten it to the cabinets by driving wallboard screws up through corner brackets into the countertop (see page 428). The screws should be long enough to provide maximum holding power, but not long enough to puncture the laminate.

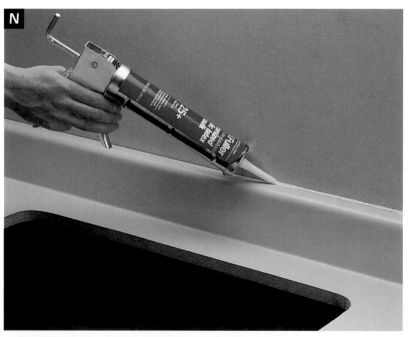

Seal the seam between the backsplash and the wall with a fine bead of silicone caulk. Smooth the bead with a wet fingertip. Wipe away any excess caulk.

Building a Custom Laminate Countertop

Build your own durable, beautiful countertop with plastic sheet laminates. Laminates are available in hundreds of colors, styles, and textures. A countertop made with laminates can be tailored to fit any space.

Laminate sheets are sold in 6-, 8-, 10-, or 12-foot lengths and in various thicknesses. Widths range from 30" to 48". For greatest impact resistance and resilience, choose thicker sheets for countertops.

Most laminates are made by bonding a thin surface layer of colored plastic to a core of hardened resins. Another type of laminate, known as *solid-color*, has consistent color through the sheet. Solid-core laminates don't show dark lines at the trimmed edges like traditional laminates, but they chip more easily and are available in fewer colors.

A popular way to dress up a laminate countertop is to add hardwood edges (see pages 424 to 425). This requires some pre-planning: Some edge treatments are installed before the laminate; others are installed after the laminate is glued down. Wood edges must be shaped with a router before the backsplash can be installed. Also, the backsplash must be built shorter so that it doesn't cover the exposed edging (see photo, page 417).

Choose nonflammable contact cement when building a countertop, thoroughly ventilate your work area, and take care with sharp, unfiled edges.

Tools: *Framing square, circular saw, drill, straightedge, clamps, router, belt sander, caulk gun, bar clamps.*

Materials: *¾" particleboard, sheet laminate, 2" and 1¼" wallboard screws, ¼"-thick scrap wood, ¼" plywood.*

Specialty Tools & Materials: *See photo, page 417.*

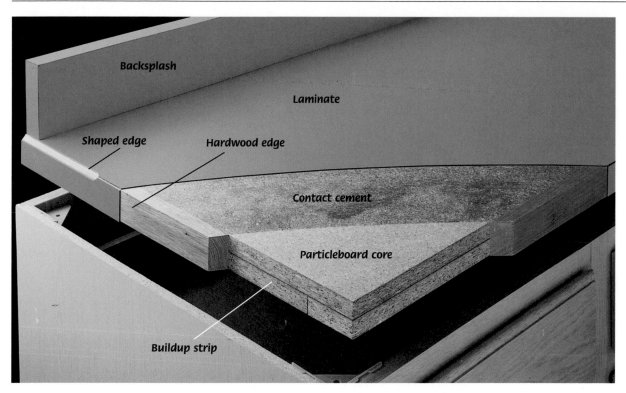

A custom laminate countertop has a core of ¾" particleboard. The perimeter is built up with strips of particleboard screwed to the bottom of the core. For decorative edge treatments, hardwood strips can be attached to the core. Laminate pieces are bonded to the countertop with contact cement. The edges are trimmed or shaped with a router.

Labels on image: Backsplash, Laminate, Shaped edge, Hardwood edge, Contact cement, Particleboard core, Buildup strip

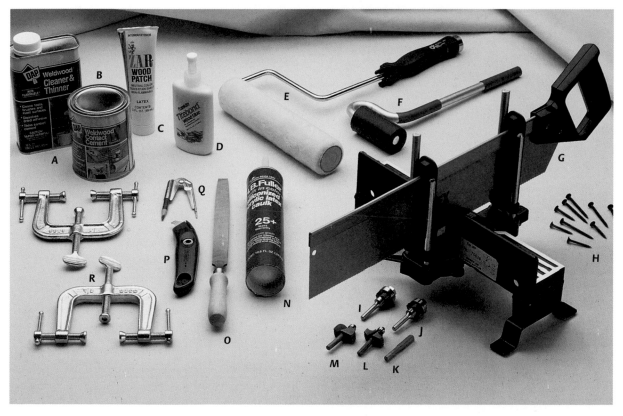

Specialty tools & supplies for building a custom laminate countertop include: contact cement thinner (A), contact cement (B), latex wood patch (C), wood glue (D), paint roller (E), J-roller (F), miter box (G), wallboard screws (H), flush-cutting router bit (I), 15° bevel-cutting router bit (J), straight router bit (K), roundover router bit (L), cove router bit (M), silicone caulk (N), file (O), scoring tool (P), scribing compass (Q), 3-way clamps—for installing hardwood edging (R).

Building a Custom Laminate Countertop

A

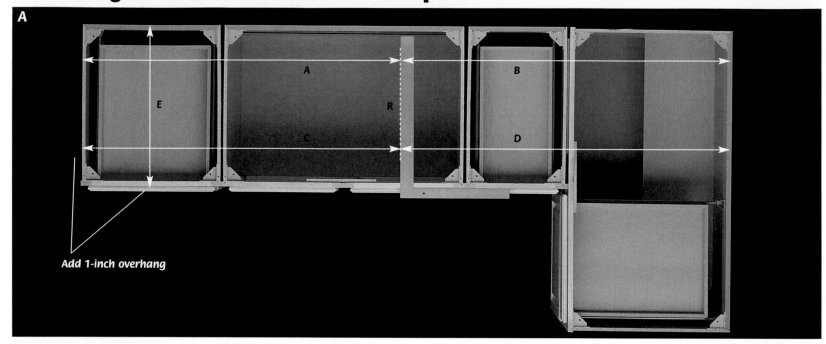

Add 1-inch overhang

Measure along the tops of the base cabinets to determine the size of the countertop. If the wall corners are not square, use a framing square to establish a reference line (R) near the middle of the base cabinets, perpendicular to the front of the cabinets. Take four measure-ments (A, B, C, D) from the reference line to the cabinet ends. Allow for overhangs by adding 1" to the length for each exposed end, and 1" to the width (E). If an end butts against an appliance, subtract ¹⁄₁₆" from the length to prevent scratching the appliance.

B

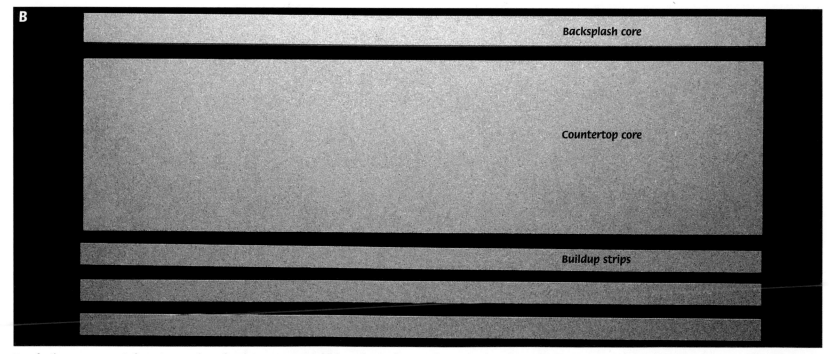

Backsplash core

Countertop core

Buildup strips

Transfer the measurements from step A, using a framing square to establish a reference line. Cut the core to size using a circular saw with a clamped straightedge as a guide. Cut 4" strips of particleboard for the backsplash, and for joint supports where sections of the countertop core are butted together. Cut 3"-wide strips for edge buildups.

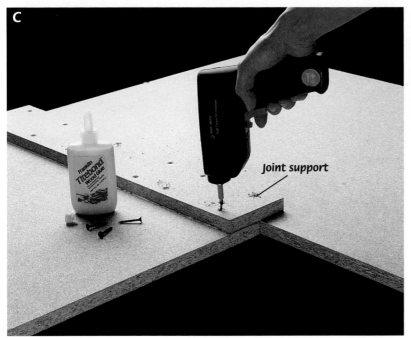

C

Joint support

Join the countertop core pieces on the bottom side. Attach a 4"-wide particleboard joint support across the seam, using wood glue and 1¼" wallboard screws.

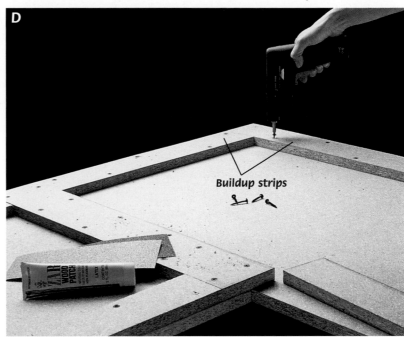

D

Buildup strips

Attach 3" edge buildup strips to the bottom of the countertop, using glue and 1¼" wallboard screws. Fill any gaps on the outside edges with latex wood patch, then sand the edges with a belt sander. (For decorative edge treatments, see page 424.)

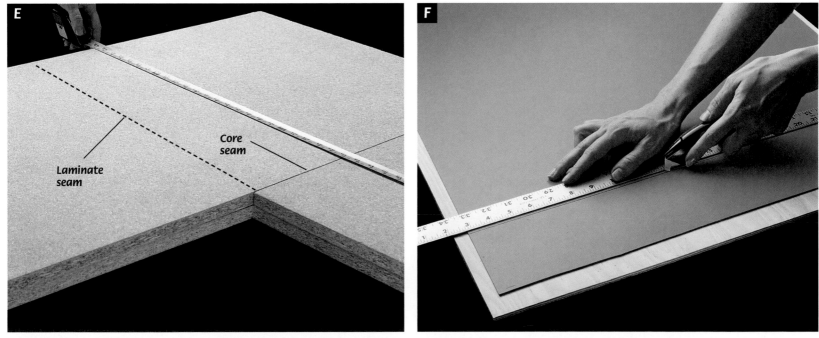

E

Laminate seam

Core seam

To determine the size of the laminate top, measure the countertop core. For strength, laminate seams should run opposite to core seams. Add ½" trimming margin to both the length and width of each piece. Measure the laminate needed for the face and edges of the backsplash, and for any exposed edges of countertop core. Add ½" to each measurement.

F

Cut the laminate by scoring and breaking it. Draw a cutting line, then etch along the line with a scoring tool, using a straightedge as a guide. Make two passes with the scoring tool.

Continued on next page

Building a Custom Laminate Countertop (cont.)

Bend the laminate toward the scored line until the sheet breaks cleanly. For better control on narrow pieces, clamp a straightedge along the scored line before bending the laminate. Wear gloves to avoid being cut by any sharp edges.

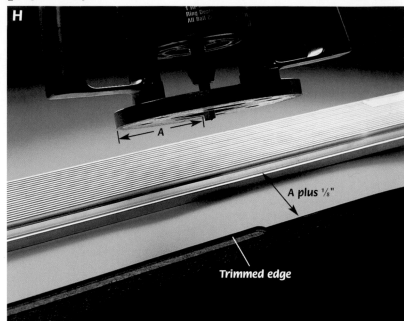

Trim edges that will butt together, using a router and a straightedge. Measure from the cutting edge of the bit to the edge of the router baseplate (A). Place the laminate on scrap wood and align the edges. To guide the router, clamp a straightedge on the laminate at distance A plus ⅛", parallel to laminate edge. Trim the laminate.

Apply laminate to the sides of the countertop first. Using a paint roller, apply two coats of contact cement to the edge of the countertop and one coat to the back of the laminate. Let the cement dry according to the manufacturer's directions. Position the laminate carefully, then press it against the edge of the countertop. Bond the laminate with a J-roller.

Use a router and flush-cutting bit to trim the edge strip flush with top and bottom surfaces of the countertop core. At the edges where the router cannot reach, trim the excess laminate with a file. Apply laminate to the remaining edges, and trim them with a router.

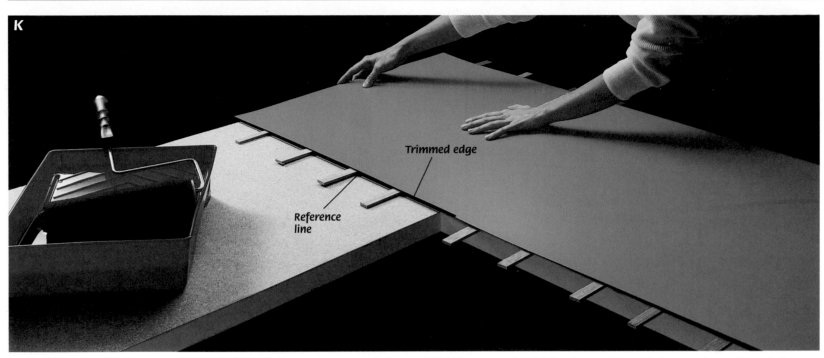

Test-fit the laminate top on the countertop core. Check that the laminate overhangs all edges. At the seam locations, draw a reference line on the core where the laminate edges will butt together. Remove the laminate. Make sure all the surfaces are free of dust, then apply one coat of contact cement to back of the laminate and two coats to the core. Place spacers made of ¼"-thick scrap wood at 6" intervals across the countertop core. Because the contact cement bonds instantly, spacers allow the laminate to be positioned accurately over the core without bonding. Align the laminate with the seam reference line. Beginning at one end, remove the spacers and press the laminate to countertop core.

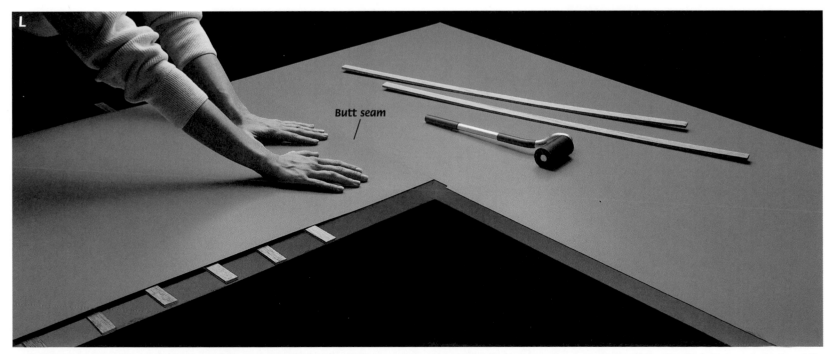

Apply contact cement to the remaining core and the next piece of laminate. Let the cement dry, then position the laminate on spacers, and carefully align the butt seam. Beginning at the seam edge, remove the spacers and press the laminate to the counter-top core.

Continued on next page

Building a Custom Laminate Countertop (cont.)

Roll the entire surface with a J-roller to bond the laminate to the core. Clean off any excess contact cement with a soft cloth and contact cement thinner.

Remove any excess laminate with a router and flush-cutting bit. At the edges where the router cannot reach, trim the excess laminate with a file. The countertop is now ready for a final trimming with a bevel-cutting bit.

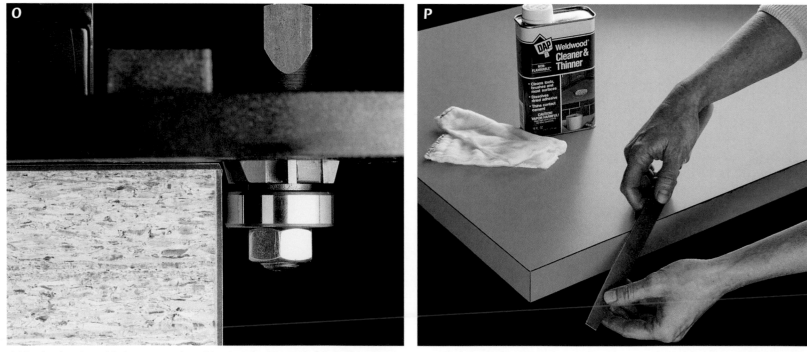

Finish-trim the edges with the router and a 15° bevel-cutting bit. Set the bit depth so that the bevel edge is cut only on the top laminate layer. The bit should not cut into the surface of the vertical edge.

File all edges smooth. Use downward file strokes to avoid chipping the laminate. Remove excess contact cement with contact cement thinner.

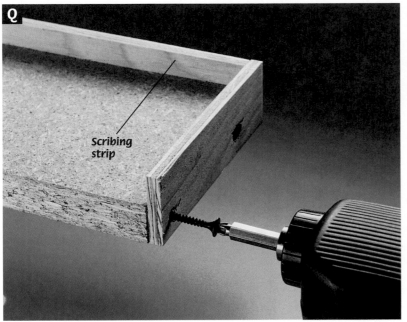

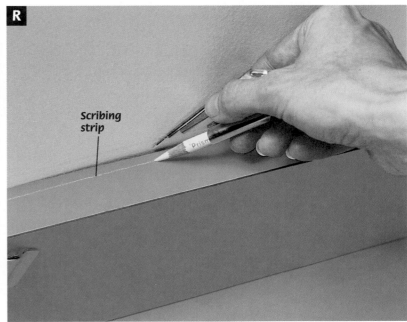

Cut 1¼"-wide strips of ¼" plywood to form an overhanging scribing strip for the backsplash. Attach it to the top and sides of the backsplash core with glue and 1¼" wallboard screws. Cut the laminate pieces to size and apply them to exposed sides, top, and front of the backsplash. Trim each piece after it is applied.

Test-fit the countertop and the backsplash. Because the walls may be uneven, use a compass to trace the wall outline onto the backsplash scribing strip. Use a belt sander to grind backsplash to the scribe line (see page 414).

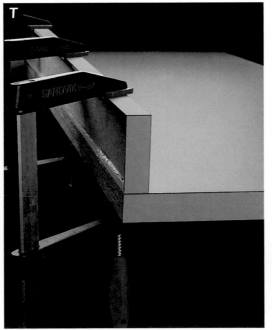

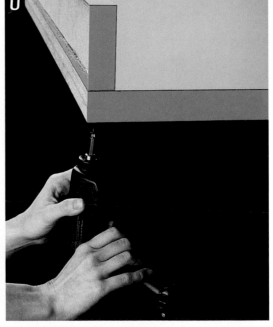

Apply a bead of silicone caulk to the bottom edge of the backsplash.

Position the backsplash on the countertop, and clamp it into place with bar clamps. Wipe away any excess caulk, and let the seam dry completely.

Screw 2" wallboard screws through the countertop into the backsplash core. Make sure the screwheads are countersunk completely for a tight fit against the base cabinet. See pages 414 to 415 to install the countertop.

Making Custom Wood Countertop Edges

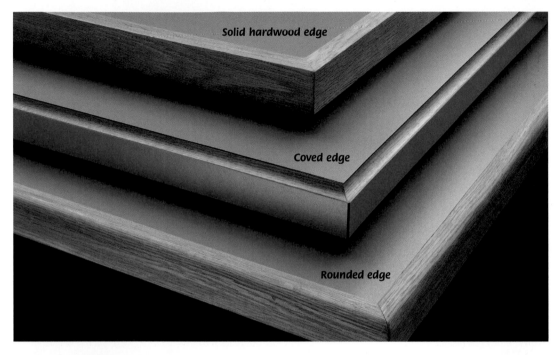

Solid hardwood edge

Coved edge

Rounded edge

For an elegant touch, add hardwood edges to your laminate countertops. Choose edging of solid hardwood, such as oak, maple, hickory, or cherry. Shape the edges with a router before attaching the backsplash to the countertop.

Secure the edging to the countertop core with wood glue and finish nails. You can stain the exposed wood if desired. To prevent water damage, finish all exposed edging with several coats of durable varnish, such as polyurethane.

Tools: Drill, nail set, 3-way clamps, finish nails, belt sander with 120-grit sanding belt, router, router bits.

Materials: 1 × 2 hardwood strips, wood glue, 220-grit sandpaper, stain (if desired), wood finishing materials.

Building Solid Hardwood Edges

A

Particleboard core

Hardwood edge

B

Roundover bit

Laminate the top of the countertop (see pages 416 to 423), then attach the edge strip flush with the surface of the laminate, using wood glue and finish nails (see steps A and B, page 425).

Mold the top and bottom edges of the strip with a router and edging bit, if desired. Stain and finish the wood as desired.

Building Covered Hardwood Edges

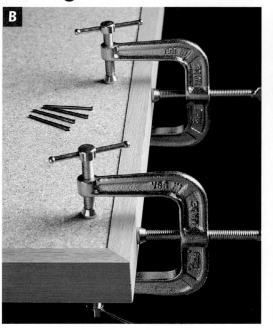

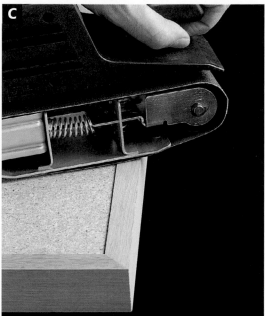

Cut 1 × 2 hardwood strips to fit the edges of the countertop. Sand the strips smooth. Miter-cut inside and outside corners.

Attach the edge strips to the countertop with wood glue and 3-way clamps. Drill pilot holes, then attach the strips with finish nails. Recess nail heads with a nail set.

Sand the edge strips flush with the top surface of the countertop, using a belt sander and 120-grit sanding belt.

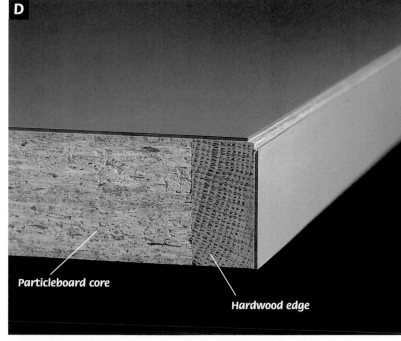

Particleboard core

Hardwood edge

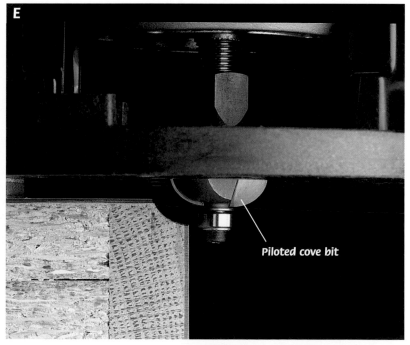

Piloted cove bit

Apply laminate to the edge and top of the countertop (see pages 416 to 423).

Cut a coved edge, using a router and cove bit with a ball-bearing pilot. Smooth the cove with 220-grit sandpaper. File the outer edges of the laminate to remove any sharpness. Stain and finish exposed wood as desired.

Building a Ceramic Tile Countertop

Ceramic tile is a popular choice for countertops and backsplashes for a few good reasons. It's available in a vast range of sizes, styles, and colors; it's durable and can be repaired; and some tile—not all—is reasonably priced. With careful planning, tile is also easy to install, and building a custom countertop with tile is a good do-it-yourself project.

The best tile for most countertops is glazed ceramic floor tile. Glazed tile is better than unglazed because of its stain resistance, and floor tile is better than wall tile because it's harder and more durable. Most residential floor tile is rated for light commercial or commercial use, with a hardness rating of Class 3 or better. Porcelain tile also is suitable for countertops; it's very hard and durable, but typically much more expensive than ceramic tile.

While glazing protects tile from stains, the grout between tiles is still vulnerable because it's so porous. To minimize future staining, use a grout that contains a latex additive, or mix the grout powder with a liquid latex additive instead of water. After the grout cures fully, apply a quality grout sealer (be sure it's safe for food contact), and reapply the sealer once a year thereafter.

The countertop in this project has a core of ³/₄" exterior-grade plywood that's cut to fit and fastened to the cabinets. The plywood is covered with a layer of plastic (for a moisture barrier) and a layer of ¹/₂"-thick cementboard. Cementboard is an effective backer for tile

because it won't break down if water gets through the tile layer. The tile is adhered to the cementboard with thin-set adhesive (see page 265), which also can survive prolonged water contact. The overall thickness of the finished countertop is about 1¹/₂". If you want a thicker countertop, you can fasten an additional layer of plywood (of any thickness) to the core.

When laying-out the tile for your countertop, account for the placement of any fixtures, like a sink or cooktop. The tile should break evenly where it meets fixtures and along the counter's perimeter. If you'll be installing a tile-in sink, make sure the tile thickness matches the rim of the sink to create a smooth transition.

Tools: *Circular saw, drill, utility knife, stapler, wallboard knife, framing square, notched trowel, tile cutter, carpeted 2 × 4, rubber grout float, sponge, foam brush, caulk gun.*

Basic Materials: *Ceramic tile, ³/₄" exterior-grade (CDX) plywood, 4-mil polyethylene sheeting, packing tape, ¹/₂" cementboard, 1¹/₄" galvanized deck screws, fiberglass mesh wallboard tape, thin-set mortar, grout, silicone caulk, silicone grout sealer.*

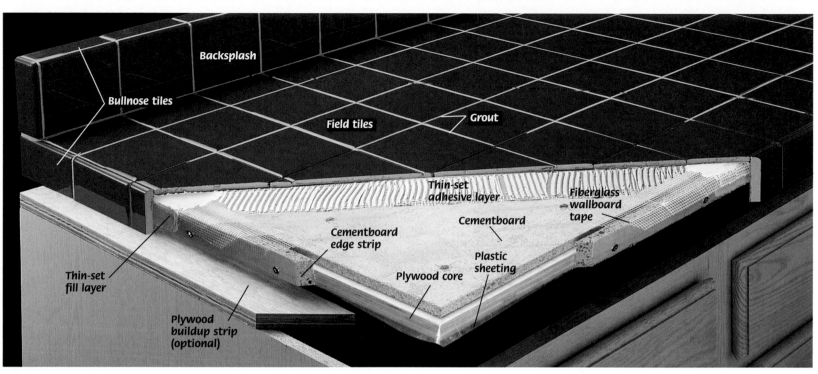

A **ceramic tile countertop** *starts with a core of ¾" exterior-grade plywood that's covered with a waterproofing membrane of 4-mil polyethylene sheeting. ½" cementboard is screwed to the plywood, and the edges are capped with cementboard and finished with fiberglass mesh tape and thin-set mortar. Tiles for edging and backsplashes may be bullnose or other type of specialty tile (see below).*

Options for Backsplashes & Countertop Edges

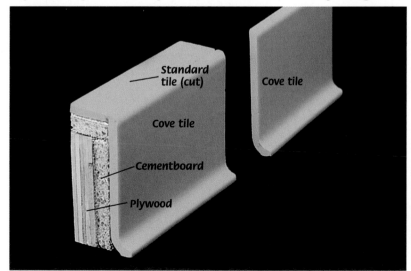

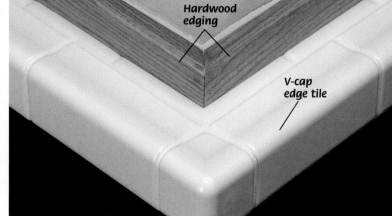

Backsplashes *can be made from cove tile (right) attached to the wall at the back of the countertop. You can use the tile alone or build a shelf-type backsplash (left), using the same construction used for the countertop. Attach the plywood backsplash to the plywood core of countertop. Wrap the front face and all edges of the plywood backsplash with cementboard before laying the tile.*

Edge options *include V-cap edge tile and hardwood strip edging. V-cap tiles have raised and rounded corners that create a ridge around the countertop perimeter—good for containing spills and water. V-cap tiles must be cut with a tile saw. Hardwood strips should be prefinished with at least three coats of polyurethane. Attach the strips to the plywood core so the top of the wood will be flush with the faces of the tiles.*

Building a Ceramic Tile Countertop

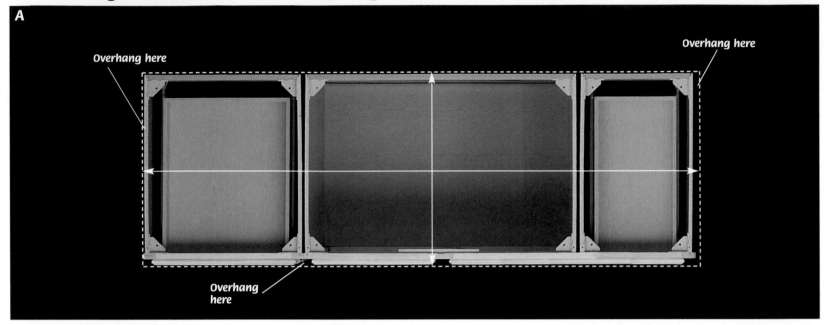

A

Overhang here

Overhang here

Overhang here

Determine the size of the plywood core by measuring across the top of the cabinets. The finished top should overhang the drawer fronts by at least ¼". Be sure to account for the thickness of the cementboard, adhesive, and tile when deciding how large to make the overhang. Cut the core to size from ¾" plywood, using a circular saw. Also make any cutouts for sinks and other fixtures.

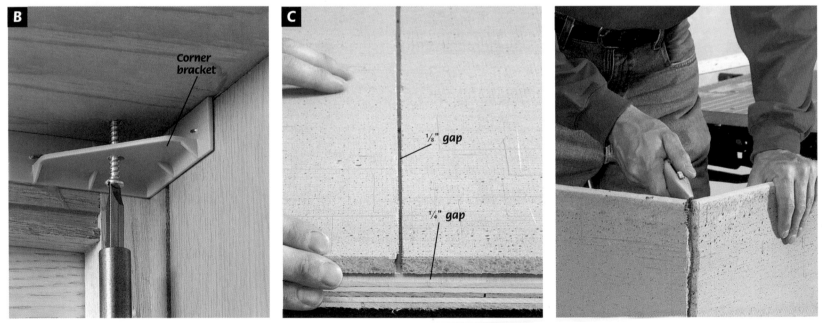

B

Corner bracket

C

⅛" gap

¼" gap

Set the core on top of the cabinets, and attach it with screws driven through the cabinet corner brackets. The screws should not be long enough to go through the top of the plywood core.

Cut pieces of cementboard and dry-fit them on the plywood core with the rough sides of the panels facing up. Leave a ⅛" gap between the cementboard sheets and a ¼" gap along the perimeter.

TIP: Cut cementboard using a straightedge and utility knife or a cementboard cutter with a carbide tip. Hold the straightedge along the cutting line, and score the board several times with the knife. Bend the piece backwards to break it along the scored line. Back-cut to finish.

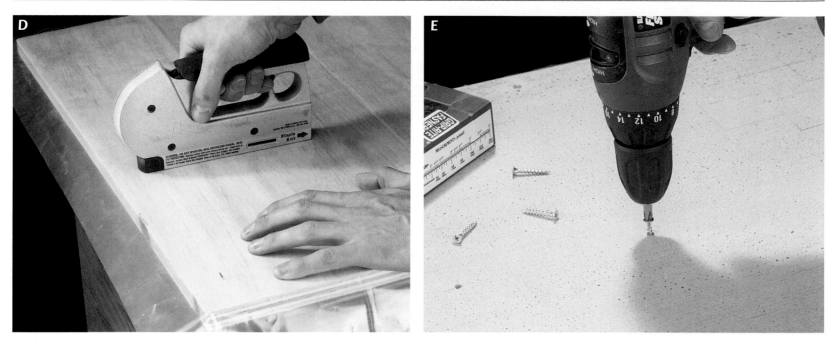

D Lay the plastic moisture barrier over the plywood core, draping it over the edges. Tack it in place with a few staples. Overlap the seams in plastic by 6", and seal them with packing tape.

E Lay the cementboard pieces rough-side-up on the plywood and attach them with 1¼" galvanized deck screws driven every 6". If needed, predrill holes through the cementboard, using a masonry bit. Make sure all screw heads are flush with the surface. Wrap the countertop edges with 1¼"-wide cementboard strips, and attach them to the core with deck screws.

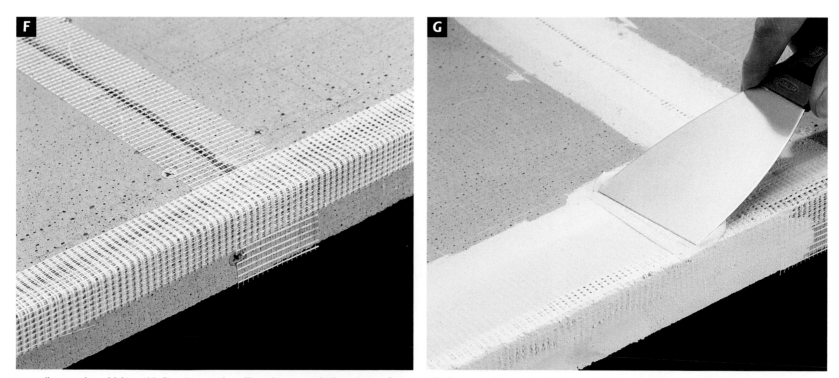

F Tape all cementboard joints with fiberglass mesh wallboard tape. Apply three layers of tape along the front edge where the horizontal cementboard sheets meet the cementboard edging.

G Fill all gaps and cover all of the tape with a layer of thin-set mortar. Feather out the mortar to create a smooth, flat surface, using a wallboard knife.

Continued on next page

Building a Ceramic Tile Countertop (cont.)

Dry-fit tiles on the countertop to find the layout that works best. If the tiles do not have spacing lugs on their edges, use plastic spacers to set the grout-joint gaps between tiles. Once the layout is established, make marks along the vertical and horizontal rows. Draw reference lines through the marks, and use a framing square to make sure the lines are perpendicular.

Install the edge tiles by applying a layer of thin-set mortar to the back of the tile and the edges of the countertop, using a notched trowel. Place the tiles with a slight twisting motion. Add plastic spacers, if needed. Use a dry tile set on top of the countertop to determine the height of the edge tiles.

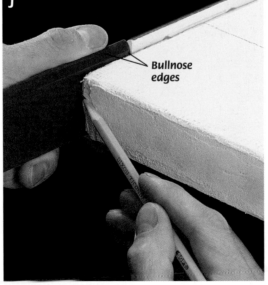

Use bullnose corner tile (with adjacent bullnose edges) to finish corner edges of the countertop. Place dry tile glazed-side down on the edge face. Mark and cut the tile so the bullnose edge will sit directly on the corner. Install the piece with thin-set mortar. See pages 266 to 267 for help with cutting tile.

Install the field tile after the edge tiles have set. Spread a layer of thin-set on the cementboard along the layout lines, and install perpendicular rows of tile. Make sure the spacing is correct, and use a framing square to check your work as you go.

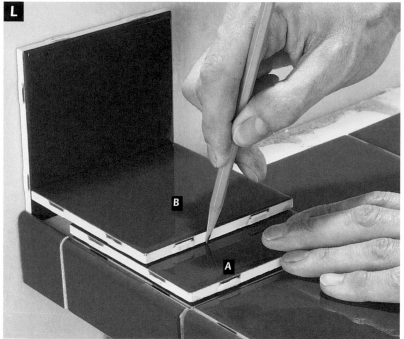

To mark border tiles for cutting, allow space for backsplash tiles or grout by placing a tile against the back wall. Set another tile (A) on top of the last full tile in the field, then place a third tile (B) over tile A and hold it against the upright tile. Mark tile A where the cut will be. Cut tile A on the marked line, and install it with the cut edge toward the wall.

As you install small sections of tile, lay a carpeted 2 × 4 block over the tile and tap the block lightly with a mallet or hammer. Run your hand over the tiles to make sure they are flush with one another. Remove any plastic spacers with a toothpick, and carefully scrape any excess adhesive from the grout joints. Let the adhesive dry completely.

Mix a batch of grout with a latex additive and apply it with a rubber float, forcing the grout into the joints with a sweeping motion (see page 270). Wipe away excess grout with a damp sponge. Wait one hour and wipe away the powdery haze. Let the grout cure fully.

Caulk along the backsplash and around penetrations with a fine bead of silicone caulk. Smooth the bead with a wet finger. After the grout cures completely, apply silicone sealer to the grout with a foam brush. Let the sealer dry, and apply a second coat.

Installing a Kitchen Sink

Kitchen sinks for do-it-yourself installation are made from stainless steel, enameled steel, or cast iron coated with enamel.

Cast-iron sinks are heavy, durable, and relatively easy to install. Most cast-iron sinks are frameless, requiring no mounting hardware.

Stainless steel and enameled steel sinks weigh less than cast iron. They may require a metal frame and mounting brackets. A good

stainless steel sink is made of heavy 18- or 20-gauge nickel steel, which holds up well under daily use. Lighter steel (designated by numbers higher than 20) dents easily.

Some premium-quality sinks are made from solid-surface material or porcelain and are usually installed by professionals.

When choosing a sink, make sure the pre-drilled openings will fit your faucet. To make

the countertop cutout for a kitchen sink installation, see pages 414 to 415.

Tools: Caulk gun, screwdrivers.

Materials: Sink, sink frame, mounting clips, plumber's putty, silicone caulk.

Installing a Frameless Sink

After making the countertop cutout, lay the sink upside down. Apply a ¼" bead of silicone caulk or plumber's putty around the underside of the sink flange.

Position the front of the sink in the countertop cutout, by holding it from the drain openings. Carefully lower the sink into position. Press down to create a tight seal, then wipe away any excess caulk. Let the caulk dry completely.

Installing a Framed Sink

Turn the sink frame upside down. Apply a ¼" bead of silicone caulk or plumber's putty around both sides of the vertical flange.

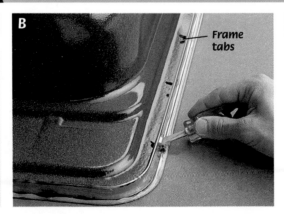

Set the sink upside down inside the frame. Bend the frame tabs to hold the sink. Carefully set the sink into the cutout opening, and press down to create a tight seal.

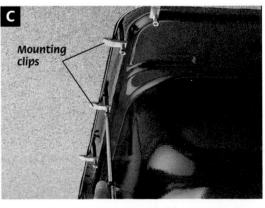

Hook the mounting clips every 6" to 8" around the frame from underneath the countertop. Tighten the mounting screws. Wipe away any excess caulk from the frame.

Installing a Kitchen Faucet & Drain

Most new kitchen faucets feature single-handle control levers and washerless designs. They rarely require maintenance. More expensive designer styles offer added features, like colorful enameled finishes, detachable spray nozzles, or even digital temperature readouts.

Connect the faucet to hot and cold water lines with easy-to-install flexible supply tubes made from vinyl or braided steel.

Where local codes allow, use plastic piping for drain hookups. Plastic is inexpensive and easy to install.

A wide selection of extensions and angle fittings let you easily plumb any sink configuration. Manufacturers offer kits that contain all the fittings needed for attaching a food disposer or dishwasher to the sink drain system. See page 77 to install shutoff valves.

Tools: *Channel-type pliers, basin wrench (if needed), hacksaw.*

Materials: *Faucet, flexible vinyl or braided steel supply tubes, drain components, plumber's putty, silicone caulk.*

Installing a Kitchen Faucet

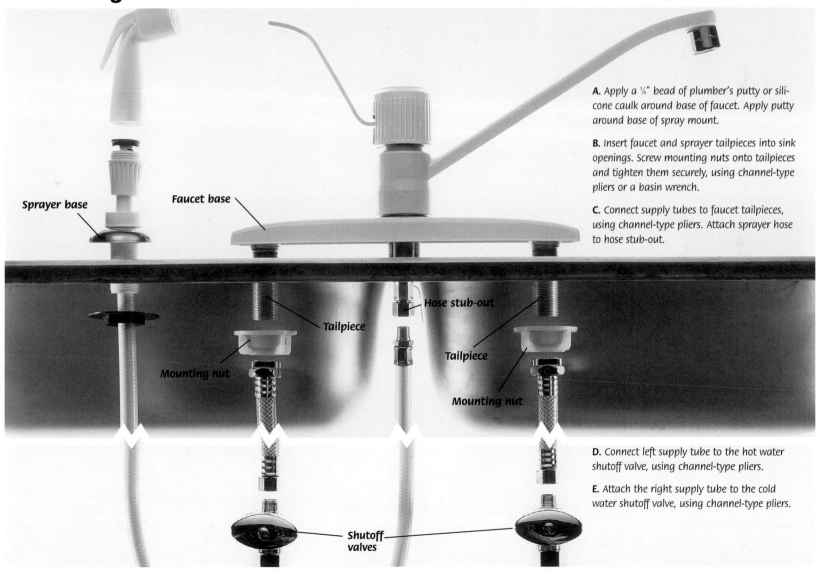

Sprayer base

Faucet base

Hose stub-out

Tailpiece

Mounting nut

Tailpiece

Mounting nut

Shutoff valves

A. *Apply a ¼" bead of plumber's putty or silicone caulk around base of faucet. Apply putty around base of spray mount.*

B. *Insert faucet and sprayer tailpieces into sink openings. Screw mounting nuts onto tailpieces and tighten them securely, using channel-type pliers or a basin wrench.*

C. *Connect supply tubes to faucet tailpieces, using channel-type pliers. Attach sprayer hose to hose stub-out.*

D. *Connect left supply tube to the hot water shutoff valve, using channel-type pliers.*

E. *Attach the right supply tube to the cold water shutoff valve, using channel-type pliers.*

Attaching Drain Lines

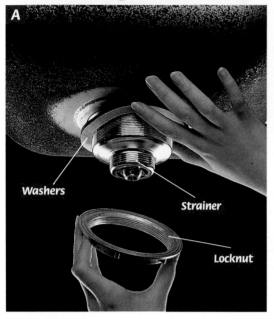

A

Washers

Strainer

Locknut

Install a sink strainer in each sink drain opening. Apply a ¼" bead of plumber's putty around the bottom of the flange. Insert a strainer into the drain opening. Place the rubber and fiber washers over the neck of the strainer. Screw a locknut onto the neck and tighten it with channel-type pliers.

B

Insert washer

Slip nut

Attach the drain tailpiece to the strainer. Place an insert washer in the flared end of the tailpiece, then attach the tailpiece by screwing a slip nut onto the sink strainer. If necessary, cut the tailpiece to fit with a hacksaw.

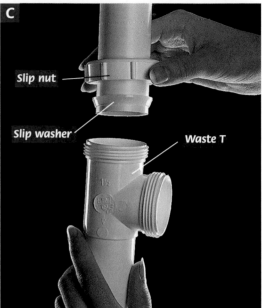

C

Slip nut

Slip washer

Waste T

On sinks with two basins, use a continuous waste T-fitting to join the tailpieces. Attach the fitting with slip washers and nuts. The beveled sides of the washers should face the threaded portions of the pipes.

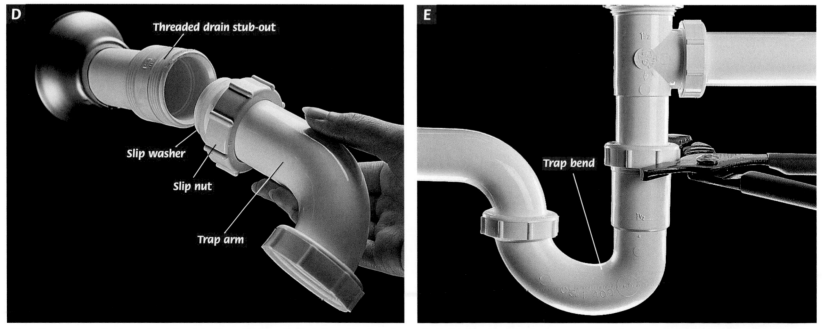

D

Threaded drain stub-out

Slip washer

Slip nut

Trap arm

Attach the trap arm to the drain stub-out in the wall, using a slip nut and washer. The beveled side of the washer should face the threaded drain stub-out. If necessary, cut the trap arm to fit with a hacksaw.

E

Trap bend

Attach the trap bend to the trap arm using slip nuts and washers. The beveled side of the washers should face the trap bend. Tighten all the nuts with channel-type pliers.

Installing a
Water Filtration System

Water filtration systems are available for *whole-house* and for *point-of-use* applications. Whole-house systems are effective for reducing amounts of sediment and chlorine. Point-of-use systems are very effective at reducing lead, chlorine, bacteria, rust, and other contaminants and typically are used to improve the taste of drinking water. Installing both provides the best-tasting and safest water.

A point-of-use water filtration system is easily installed underneath the kitchen sink. Though most systems are installed in much the same way, always follow the manufacturer's instructions. Our installation includes a secondary filter and water line that supplies a refrigerator icemaker; both are optional. If you choose not to install the additional filter or line, connect the drinking faucet line directly to the main filter unit.

Tools: Drill (for faucet), channel-type pliers.

Materials: ¼" flexible vinyl mesh tubing, saddle valve, brass compression fittings, T-coupling, point-of-use filtration unit, refrigerator icemaker filter (optional).

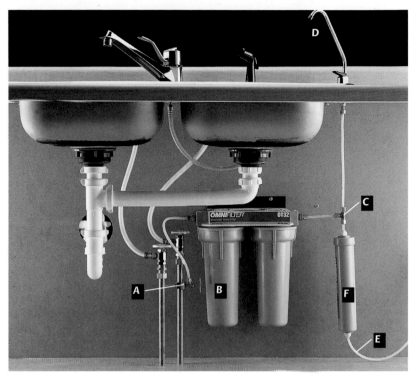

*A **point-of-use water filtration system** includes a saddle valve (A), filtration unit (B), T-coupling (C), drinking water faucet (D), refrigerator icemaker line (E), and an additional filter for the icemaker line (F).*

Installing a Point-of-use Filtration System

Mount the filter unit under the sink according to the manufacturer's directions. Shut off the main water supply, then install a saddle valve on the cold water line (see page 67)—make sure the valve is closed. Connect vinyl mesh tubing from the intake side of the filtration unit to the saddle valve. Attach another tube to the outtake side of the filtration unit. If you're installing an icemaker filter, attach a T-coupling to the free end of this tube.

Install a drinking water faucet on the countertop or sink, following the manufacturer's directions. Install a vinyl tube between the faucet tailpiece and the top of the T-coupling (or directly to the water filter, if you're not installing an icemaker line). Attach the icemaker filter to the other outlet on the T-coupling, then run vinyl tubing to the icemaker. Turn on the water and open the saddle valve. Inspect all connections for leaks.

Installing a Food Disposer

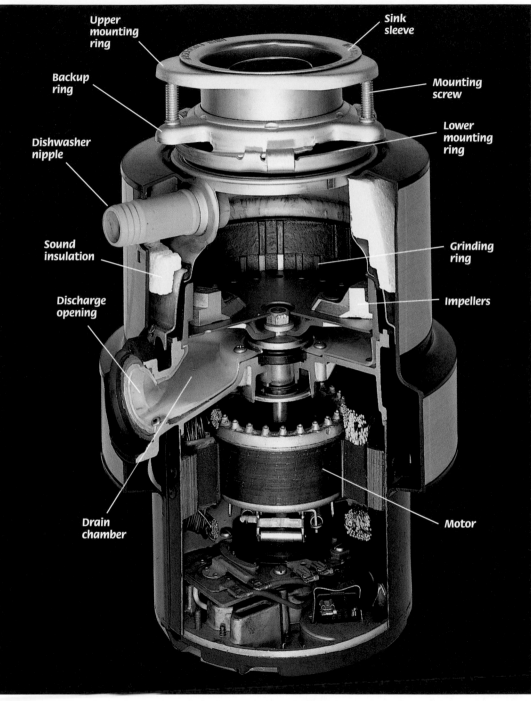

Upper mounting ring

Sink sleeve

Backup ring

Mounting screw

Dishwasher nipple

Lower mounting ring

Sound insulation

Grinding ring

Discharge opening

Impellers

Drain chamber

Motor

Food disposers *grind food waste into a mostly liquid form, so it can be flushed away through the sink drain system. A quality disposer has a ½-horsepower or larger motor and a self-reversing feature. Also look for added features, such as foam sound insulation, a cast-iron grinding ring, corrosion-resistant parts, and overload protection that allows the motor to be reset if it overheats. Better food disposers also have 5-year manufacturers' warranties.*

Choose a food disposer with a motor rated at ½ horsepower or more. These disposers can handle heavier loads with less chance of jamming. Better models also have a self-reversing feature to prevent jams and extend the life of the motor.

Local plumbing codes may require that a disposer be plugged into a grounded outlet controlled by a switch above the sink.

Tools: *Screwdriver, combination tool, hacksaw, channel-type pliers, hose clamps.*

Materials: *12-gauge appliance cord with grounded plug, wire connectors, plumber's putty, hose clamp, continuous waste pipe, silicone caulk.*

Installing a Food Disposer

A

Remove the plate on the bottom of the disposer. Use a combination tool to strip about ½" of insulation from each wire in the appliance cord. Connect the white wires, using a wire connector. Connect the black wires. Attach the green insulated wire to the green ground screw. Gently push the wires into the opening. Replace the bottom plate.

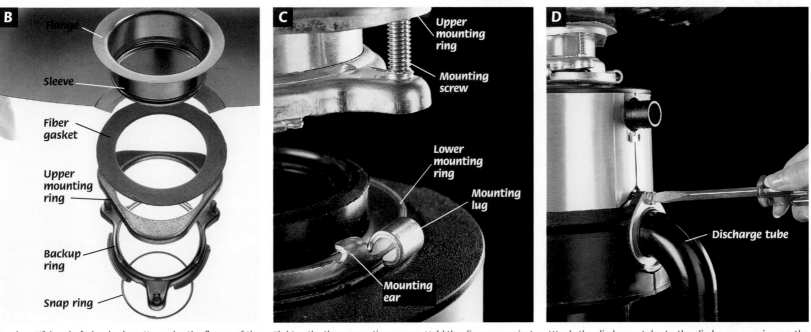

B Flange · Sleeve · Fiber gasket · Upper mounting ring · Backup ring · Snap ring

C Upper mounting ring · Mounting screw · Lower mounting ring · Mounting lug · Mounting ear

D Discharge tube

Apply a ¼" bead of plumber's putty under the flange of the disposer sink sleeve. Insert the sleeve in the drain opening, and slip the fiber gasket and the upper mounting ring onto the sleeve. Place the backup ring on the sleeve and slide the snap ring into the groove on the sleeve.

Tighten the three mounting screws. Hold the disposer against the backup ring so that the mounting lugs on the lower mounting ring are directly under the mounting screws. Turn the lower mounting ring clockwise until the disposer is supported by the mounting assembly.

Attach the discharge tube to the discharge opening on the side of the disposer, using the rubber washer and metal flange.

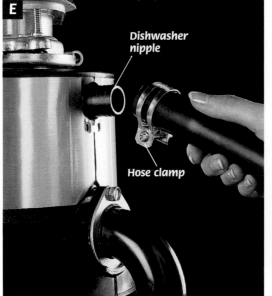

E Dishwasher nipple · Hose clamp

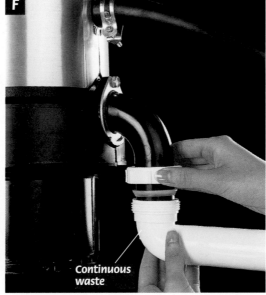

F Continuous waste

G Mounting lug · Lower mounting ring

If a dishwasher will be attached to the disposer, knock out the plug in the dishwasher nipple, using a screwdriver. Attach the dishwasher drain hose to the nipple with a hose clamp.

Attach the discharge tube to the continuous waste pipe with a slip washer and nut. If necessary, cut the discharge tube to fit with a hacksaw or tubing cutter. The washer's beveled side should face the waste tube threads. Connect the waste pipe to the waste T of the sink drain assembly (see page 434).

Lock the disposer into place by inserting a screwdriver or disposer wrench into a mounting lug on the lower mounting ring and turning it clockwise until the mounting ears are locked. Tighten all drain slip nuts with a channel-type pliers.

Installing a Vent Hood

A vent hood removes heat, moisture, and cooking vapors from your kitchen. It has an electric fan unit with one or more filters, and a system of metal ducts to vent air to the outdoors. A ducted vent hood is far more effective than a ductless model, which filters and recirculates air without removing it. The National Kitchen and Bath Association (NKBA) recommends that kitchen ventilation systems have a minimum rating of 150 cubic feet per minute (CFM).

Metal ducts for a vent hood can be round or rectangular. Elbows and transition fittings are available for both types of ducts. These fittings let you vent around corners or join duct components that differ in shape or size.

Tools: Drill, stud finder, compass, screwdrivers.

Materials: 1 × 4 lumber, 1¼" wallboard screws, duct sections, adjustable duct elbow, duct cap, 1½" sheet-metal screws.

Specialty Tools & Materials: See photo, below

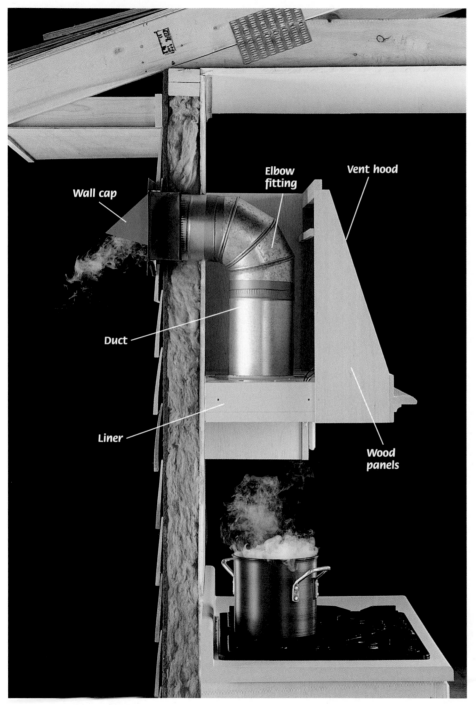

A wall-mounted vent hood (shown here cutaway) is installed between the wall cabinets. A fan unit is fastened to a metal liner that is anchored to the cabinets. Duct and elbow fittings exhaust cooking vapors to the outdoors through a wall cap. The vent fan and duct are covered by wood or laminate panels that match the cabinet finish.

Labels on photo: Wall cap, Elbow fitting, Vent hood, Duct, Liner, Wood panels

Specialty tools & materials for installing a vent hood include: reciprocating saw with coarse wood-cutting blade (A), silicone caulk (B), foil duct tape (C), wire connectors (D), ⅛" twist bit (E), No. 9 counterbore drill bit (F), ¾" sheetmetal screws (G), 2½" sheetmetal screws (H), combination tool (I), masonry chisel (J), 2" masonry nails (K), aviation snips (L), masonry drill bit (M), ball peen hammer (N).

Installing a Vent Hood

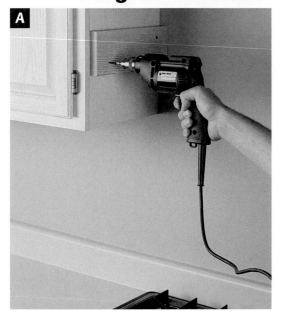

A

Attach ¾" × 4" × 12" wooden cleats to the sides of the cabinets with 1¼" wallboard screws. Make sure the screws aren't long enough to penetrate the interior side of the cabinets. Follow the manufacturer's directions for the proper distance from the cooking surface.

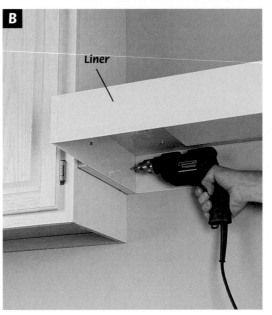

B

Liner

Position the hood liner between the cleats and attach it with ¾" sheetmetal screws.

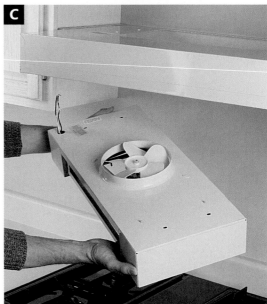

C

Remove the cover panels for the light, fan, and electrical compartments on fan unit, as directed by manufacturer. Position the fan unit inside the liner and fasten it by attaching nuts to the mounting bolts inside the light compartments.

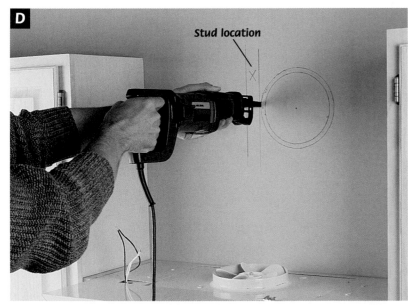

D

Stud location

Locate the studs in the wall where the duct will pass, using a stud finder. Mark the hole location, using a compass to draw the circular cutout. The hole should be ½" larger than the diameter of the duct. Shut off the electrical power to the area, and make sure there are no pipes or wires in the wall. Complete the cutout with a reciprocating saw or jig saw. Remove any wall insulation. Drill a pilot hole through the outside wall (see step F, page 440).

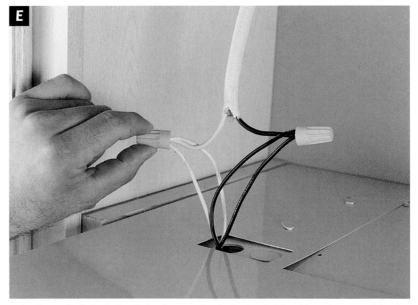

E

Strip about ½" of plastic insulation from each wire in the circuit cable, using a combination tool. Connect the black wires, using a wire connector. Connect the white wires. Gently push the wires into the electrical box. Replace the cover panels on the light and fan compartments.

Continued on next page

Installing a Vent Hood (cont.)

Make a duct cutout on the exterior wall. On masonry walls, drill a series of holes around the outline of the cutout, using a masonry bit. Remove the waste with a masonry chisel and a ball peen or masonry hammer. On wood siding, make the cutout with a reciprocating saw.

Attach the first duct section by sliding the smooth end over the outlet flange on the vent hood. Cut the duct sections to length with aviation snips.

Outlet flange

Drill three or four pilot holes around the joint, through both layers of metal, using a ⅛" twist bit. Attach the duct with ¾" sheetmetal screws. Seal the joint with foil duct tape.

Join additional duct sections by sliding the smooth end over the corrugated end of each preceding section. Use an adjustable elbow to change directions in the duct run. Secure all joints with sheetmetal screws and foil duct tape.

Install a duct cap on the exterior wall. Apply a thick bead of silicone caulk to the cap flange. Slide the cap over end of the duct.

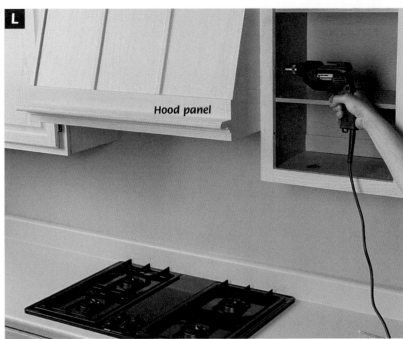

Attach the cap to the wall with 2" masonry nails (or 1½" sheetmetal screws on wood siding). Wipe away any excess caulk.

Slide the decorative hood panel into place between the wall cabinets. Drill pilot holes through the cabinet face frame with a counterbore bit. Attach the hood panel to the cabinets with 2½" sheetmetal screws.

Vent Hood Variations

A downdraft cooktop has a built-in blower unit that vents through the back or the bottom of a base cabinet. A downdraft cooktop is a good choice for a kitchen island or peninsula.

A cabinet-mounted vent hood is attached to the bottom of a 12"- to 18"-tall wall cabinet. A metal duct runs inside the wall cabinet.

REMODELING

*B*ATHROOMS

Planning the Project

Bathroom remodeling projects are high on many homeowners' wish lists. Whether you repair a leaky faucet, redesign the layout of fixtures, or tear out and start over, a bathroom remodeling project should make your bathroom more efficient and comfortable. Before you rush out to buy new fixtures or flooring, however, consider three elements of your new bath: type, style, and color.

What type of bathroom are you remodeling or building? The three basic types are *family* baths (both large and small), *master* (or luxury) baths, and *half* (or guest) baths. Each has its own requirements for space, fixtures, layout, and color. To help you determine what type of bath you want, consider who uses the bathroom and how often, where the bathroom will be located, what features you want most, and whether the bathroom must be accessible to someone with physical limitations.

Next, think about your bathroom's style. Since the bathroom is one of your home's most-used spaces, it should blend in with the overall style of your home. Look through magazines for style ideas. Attend home shows. Visit open houses. You will find design ideas that range from American, English, and French Country to Contemporary, Southwest, and Colonial.

Then, think about color. Your choices of bathroom type and style often will influence your choice of color. But consider the overall style of your home when choosing colors for fixtures, flooring, and lighting. Remember that children grow up, and that you can grow tired of trends. Try to think about how the bathroom will function in years to come. The best option may be to choose neutral-colored fixtures and tile, and then add color accents with wallpaper, paint, or towels.

Keep a notebook of ideas. A bathroom remodeling project involves lots of planning; thinking about what you want is the first big step. However, for most people, a bathroom remodeling project is determined not only by wants, but also by budget and space.

You may want to build a grand master bathroom with whirlpool and sauna, but think you can afford only to update your large master bath in its current location. Before you give up on your dream of an ideal bath, consider your options. It is often possible to borrow space from adjacent rooms and closets. And you can save money by reusing functional fixtures, shelving, storage, and lighting from your current bathroom. You also can create the feel of a new bathroom by rearranging fixtures and improving the room's traffic flow. A bathroom designer (see page 22) may be able to help you consider your space in new ways.

Determining Your Needs

Before you can put your plans on paper, you must determine your needs. A bathroom is divided into three activity areas: the toilet, the sink, and the shower/tub. Successful bath design considers the relationship of these areas, allowing for accessibility and safety. The type of bathroom you want will influence your decisions on layout, fixtures, and space.

Half Baths

Also called *powder rooms* or *guest baths*, half baths are small rooms designed for visitors to use. They can be as small as 20 sq. ft. and typically feature only a toilet and vanity. When designed as a guest bath, they sometimes also feature a shower and are located near the guest bedroom. When a shower is included, these rooms require more space and are called *three-quarter baths*.

Half baths often are located near entrances or entertainment areas in a home. It's often best to have their doorways open into hallways, rather than dining rooms, living rooms, or

©Karen Melvin

other public areas.

Since these rooms are small, they can be finished with smaller fixtures and finer materials. They typically have little storage space and may have pedestal sinks and wall mirrors.

Family Bath

The family bath is a busy place, often located near the sleeping areas in a home. It is used by more than one family member, and it often must provide storage for toiletries, towels, and cleaning supplies. It features at least one sink, one toilet, and a shower and tub.

The typical family bath can fit in a 5 × 7-ft. area. A larger bath may allow room for extra features, such as a double-bowl sink or separate shower and tub area, to accommodate several users at a time. A small family bath may conserve space by combining the tub and shower, incorporating recessed shelving, and featuring space-efficient fixtures and storage cabinets. Fixtures and finishes should be low-maintenance, highly durable items, such as ceramic tile and enameled fixtures.

Bathrooms for children have specific considerations: they must be safe for children to use unsupervised and should be easy to adapt as the children grow. Features that make daily hygiene easier and safer for children include single-handle faucets with anti-scald guards, adjustable shower heads, safety plugs, grab bars, smaller toilets, lowered sinks, and vanities with built-in step stools.

Master Bath

A master bath, or *luxury bath*, is a sanctuary for the owners of the house. It is a separate bath, usually connected to the master bedroom. A master bath may have separate activity centers containing features such as a whirlpool tub, shower, partitioned toilet, and multiple sinks and vanities.

These bathrooms are usually quite large. They often feature luxuries, such as saunas and steam rooms. The fixtures and finishing materials generally feature ceramic tiles, custom cabinets, and upscale accessories.

©Christian Korab

©Karen Melvin

Designing Your Bathroom

Because so many activities occur in such a relatively small space, remodeling a bathroom requires careful planning and design. The National Kitchen and Bath Association (NKBA) publishes a list of bathroom design standards to help people plan rooms that are safe and accessible to all users. Some of the basic standards are listed in the chart at the right. More standards specific to universal design can be found on pages 448 to 451.

Your bathroom probably won't conform to all of the recommended standards, but they can help guide your overall plan. What your plan must include is everything prescribed by the local building codes. Page 447 lists many of the common code issues for bathrooms.

The following steps outline the next phase of your project—drawing plans and obtaining permits.

Sketch a plan.
Draw your bathroom's floor plan and wall dimensions to scale (see pages 18 to 19). Buy or make your own templates for the existing and new fixtures, and experiment with different layouts for the room. Remember to plan for both fixtures and plumbing lines.

Keep in mind that moving existing fixture drains can add significantly to the cost and difficulty of the project. You can keep down costs by locating new plumbing near existing waste-vent lines.

Check the building codes.
Consult the local building codes regarding all aspects of the project, particularly the minimum clearances required around fixtures. If you find you're short on space, consider compact fixtures and built-ins to gain room. The floor space needed for the room will largely depend on the types and number of fixtures included.

Create a scale drawing and materials list.
Detail your initial plans, adding all dimensions and fixtures for your new bathroom. Include all plumbing, wiring, and HVAC connections. When you have completed your drawing, make a materials list, set a timetable, and decide what work you will complete yourself and what work you will hire out.

Have your plans reviewed.
Take your completed drawings to the local building department for review. Getting input early in the process will save you time and expense later. The building inspector will check your plans and materials list and recommended changes. You also will need to obtain one or more building permits, which include scheduled inspections. Typically, the building inspector will review your work after the framing and rough-in plumbing and wiring are completed and again when the job is done.

Bathroom Design Standards

For more information regarding bathroom design, contact the NKBA (see page 503).

- Plan doorways with a clear floor space equal to the door's width on the push side and greater than the door's width on the pull side.
  NOTE: Clear floor spaces within the bathroom can overlap.

- Design toilet enclosures with at least 36 × 66" of space; include a pocket door or a door that swings out toward the rest of the bathroom.

- Install toilet-paper holders approximately 26" above the floor, toward the front of the toilet bowl.

- Place fixtures so faucets are accessible from outside the tub or shower. Add anti-scald devices to tub and sink faucets (they are required for shower faucets).

- Avoid steps around showers and tubs, if possible.

- Fit showers and tubs with safety rails and grab bars.

- Install shower doors so they swing open into the bathroom, not the shower.

- Use tempered glass or another type of safety glass for all glass doors and partitions.

- Include storage for soap, towels, and other items already mentioned near the shower, located within 15" to 48" above the floor. These should be accessible to a person in the shower or tub.

- Provide natural light equal to at least 10% of the floor area in the room.

- Illuminate all activity centers in the bathroom with task and ambient lighting.

- Provide a minimum clearance of 15" from the centerline of sinks to any sidewalls. Double-bowl sinks should have 30" clearance between bowls, from centerline to centerline.

- Provide access panels for all electrical, plumbing, and HVAC systems connections.

- Include a ventilation fan that exchanges air at a rate of 8 air changes per hour.

- Choose countertops and other surfaces with edges that are smoothed, clipped, or radiused.

Building Codes

The following are some of the most common building codes for bathrooms. Contact your local building department for a list of all codes enforced in your area.

• The minimum ceiling height in bathrooms is 7 ft. (Minimum floor area is determined by clearances around fixtures.)

• Sinks must be at least 4" from side walls and have 21" of clearance in front.

• Sinks must be spaced 4" away from neighboring sinks and toilets, and 2" away from bathtubs.

• Toilets must be centered 15" from side walls and tubs, with 21" clearance in front.

• New and replacement toilets must be low-flow models.

• Shower stalls must be at least 30 × 30", with 24" of clearance in front of shower openings.

• Steps must be at least 10" deep and no higher than 7¼".

• Faucets for showers and combination tub-showers must be equipped with anti-scald devices.

• Supply lines that are ½" in diameter can supply a single fixture, or one sink and one toilet. A ¾" diameter supply line must be used to supply 2 or more fixtures.

• Waste and drain lines must slope ¼" per foot toward the main DWV stack to aid flow and prevent blockage.

• Each bathroom must be wired with at least one dedicated 15-amp circuit. Only light fixtures, receptacles, and vent fans without heating elements can be powered by this circuit.

• All receptacles must be GFCI-protected.

• There must be at least one permanent light fixture controlled by a wall switch.

• Wall switches must be at least 60" away from bathtubs and showers.

• Toilet, shower, vanity, or other bathroom compartments must have adequate lighting.

• Light fixtures over bathtubs and showers must be vapor-proof, with a U.L. rating for wet areas.

• Vanity light fixtures with built-in electrical receptacles are prohibited.

• Whirlpool motors must be powered by dedicated GFCI-protected circuits.

• Bathroom vent ducts must terminate no less than 10 ft. horizontally or 3 ft. vertically above skylights.

Follow minimum clearance and size guidelines when planning locations of bathroom fixtures. Easy access to fixtures is fundamental to creating a bathroom that is comfortable, safe, and easy to use.

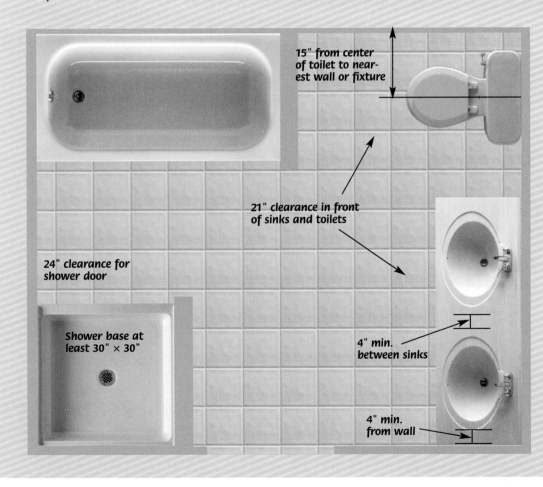

15" from center of toilet to nearest wall or fixture

21" clearance in front of sinks and toilets

24" clearance for shower door

Shower base at least 30" × 30"

4" min. between sinks

4" min. from wall

The Universal Bathroom

Maximizing safety and space is a goal for anyone remodeling a bathroom, but these are critical elements in a universally designed bathroom. Sufficient space, proper lighting and flooring, and, of course, safe and accessible fixtures all are essential features. Additional considerations, such as a second sink and a section of countertop that is open underneath, can make your bathroom accessible to a wide range of users.

The universally designed bathroom has a few basic characteristics. The layout provides room for maneuvering and, if possible, enough space for two people to use the bathroom at once; there's non-slip flooring and plenty of lighting; fixtures have sufficient approach space—from either side, if possible; and seated users have easy access to all fixtures and amenities, such as cabinets, mirrors,

switches, and electrical receptacles.

While many fixtures on the market today are designed for universal use, they are not yet standard, so discuss your project with dealers and salespeople to find the best products to meet your needs.

Grab bars are important safety features for universal bathrooms. If the wall framing in your bathroom will be exposed during the remodel, add backing or blocking for installing grab bars now and in the future. See pages 494 to 495 for more information on installing grab bars. Additional safety features include anti-scald faucets for the shower and sink, and a telephone for making distress calls.

As you plan, keep in mind that a lifespan home should have at least one centrally located full bathroom on every floor; this is a necessity for those with limited mobility.

Bathroom Layout

Approach spaces (patterned areas) and clearances shown here include some ADA guidelines and recommendations from universal design specialists.

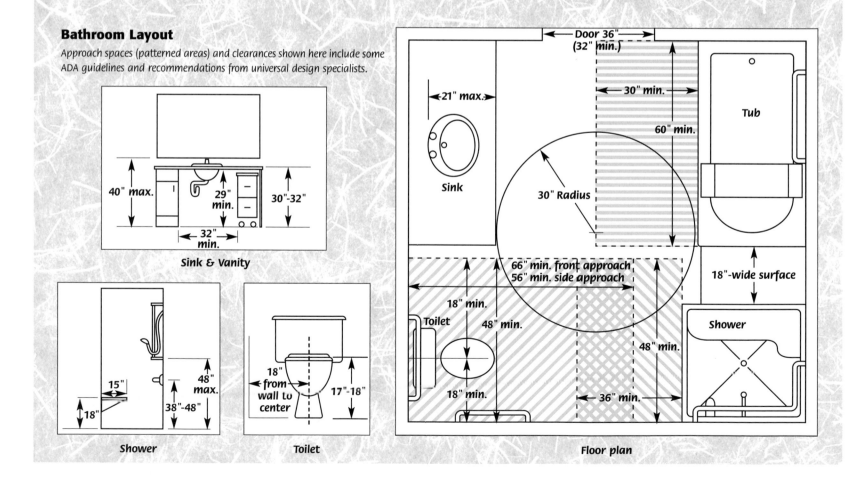

Sink & Vanity

Shower

Toilet

Floor plan

Space Planning

Plan your bathroom around a clear space that's 5 ft. in diameter—the minimum area needed for a wheelchair to turn around. If this is impossible, plan for a minimum space of 30 × 48" beyond the door; although this space is not enough for a wheelchair to turn around in, it provides easy passage for a wheelchair. To help make bathroom fixtures accessible to everyone, plan the following approach spaces, keeping in mind that the spaces for individual fixtures may overlap:

- Sink: 30"-wide × 48"-deep space in front.
- Toilet: 48"-wide × 66"-deep space for front approach; 48"-wide × 56"-deep space for side approach. Position the toilet so that its center is 18" from walls, fixtures, or vanities, on either side.
- Tub: 30 × 60" space along the side of the tub. Include an 18"-wide surface on at least one end of the tub, but preferably at both ends. This surface enables a bather to sit and swing his or her legs into the tub.
- Shower: 48"-wide × 36"-deep space in front of shower opening.

Lighting and Electrical

- Design your bathroom with a combination of natural and artificial light, keeping in mind that short and seated users must be able to open windows.
- Install plenty of task lighting in addition to diffused overhead lighting. Include task lighting above and beside the sink and mirror, and in and around the bath and shower; these are areas where accidents can occur easily. Avoid large shadowed areas, which can be visually confusing.
- Consider motion- or voice-activated light fixtures.
- Install electrical receptacles in walls at a

minimum height of 18". Install countertop receptacles at a maximum distance of 21" from the front edge of the countertop.
- Install as many receptacles as is practical, to prevent clutter and the need to move small appliances.

Flooring

- Consider all available non-slip options before choosing a floor covering for your bathroom. Some good options are textured ceramic tiles, indoor/outdoor carpeting, and non-slip vinyl.
- Ask your flooring dealer about the coefficient of friction for each type of flooring (it should be at least .6).
- Avoid shiny tile and other polished flooring.

Doors

- Ensure that bathroom doors have a clear opening at least 32" wide; 36" is preferred.
- Install hinged doors so they open into the hallway; this will ensure access to someone in the bathroom who needs assistance.
- Consider a pocket door for your bathroom: with appropriate hardware, pocket doors are easy to use, and they save a lot of space.

Photo courtesy of Kohler, Co.

Features in this sleek tub-shower unit include built-in grab bars, a seat, an adjustable shower head, and offset controls.

The Universal Bathroom

Bathtub and Shower

Perhaps the most important aspect of a universally designed bathroom is a safe bathing environment. Tubs and showers must be easy to get in and out of, and sitting should be an option in a shower. All controls and hardware should be within easy reach. Many tubs and showers available today are designed for universal use, so check out several options before choosing a unit.

• Include handholds or grab bars in and around your tub and shower.

• Offset water controls toward the room so they are reachable from outside the tub or shower as well as from inside.

• Choose a tub with a seat at least 15" deep, whether built-in or pull-down type. Consider ease of use for a person transferring from a wheelchair to and from the tub.

• Consider special options for tubs, including a door that enables users to enter and exit safely, or a built-in seat that adjusts hydraulically.

• Look for tubs with soft edges and surfaces.

• Install rod-mounted curtains.

Photo courtesy of Kohler Co.

This universally designed sink has a hands-free faucet and a square front that makes the basin more accessible.

The Swan Corporation, photo courtesy of Access One, Inc.

• Consider a stand-alone shower with no threshold or a removable one. This shower, with a pull-down seat, can accommodate most users and a wide range of abilities. A slightly sloping floor will direct water to the drain.

• Install a pull-down or permanent seat in a stand-alone shower at a height of 18". The seat should be at least 15" deep.

• Choose a shower that has a minimum 36"-wide opening and 36 × 36" base.

• Mount shower controls at a height of 38" to 48"; offset them toward the room.

• Install a hand-held shower head mounted on a vertical slide bar, so its height is adjustable. The bottom end of the bar should be no higher than 48" from the floor.

A barrier-free shower with a fold-down seat can accommodate almost any user. Some shower units fit in the space needed for a standard 30 × 60" bathtub.

Sink and Vanity

Adding varied countertop heights and removable base cabinets can greatly improve the functionality of your bathroom. Keep in mind that seated users will need access to mirrors and medicine chests.

• Install countertops at varied heights: 34" to 36" for standing users and 30" to 32" for seated users. Lower countertops should be open underneath or have removable base cabinets that can be rolled out of the way.

• Provide a clear space that is 29" high and 32" to 36" wide under sinks and sections of lowered countertops designed for seated users.

Photo courtesy of Kohler Co.

Photo courtesy of Access One, Inc.

Height-adjustable countertops and movable base cabinets make this vanity area a versatile workspace. Grab-railings provide support and convenient places for hand towels.

This 17"-high toilet is flanked by adjustable grab bars that can be flipped up and out of the way when not in use.

- Install one sink at 30" to 32" high for a seated user, if possible.
- Finish the floor under removable base cabinets.
- Select sinks that are shallow at the front and deepen toward the drain. These provide space for the legs of a seated user, yet are deep enough for rinsing clothes.
- Insulate exposed pipes underneath sinks.
- Choose anti-scald faucets with hands-free, single-lever, or push-button type controls. Be sure that the sink drain plug is accessible and easy to operate.
- Install faucets within 21" of the front edge of the countertop.
- Position mirrors so their bottom edges are no more than 40" above the floor. Also, consider a tilting or adjustable mirror.
- Replace drawer and cabinet knobs with loop handles.
- Consider pull-down shelves for your vanity and ensure that there is sufficient storage within the reach of short or seated users.

Toilet

Generally, there are fewer choices for universally designed toilets than for other fixtures, but toilet design is important. Safety and ease of use are the two main factors to consider. The toilet should be an appropriate height for all users, including those who may be transfering from a wheelchair. Be sure to install grab bars around each toilet.

- Standard toilets with 15"-high seats may be too low for a person with limited leg strength or for transferring from a wheelchair, while a 19" toilet may be too high for a short person. For most users, a height of 17" to 18" is best.
- Height adjustable toilets also are available, as well as height-adjustment adapters for standard toilets.
- Wall-mounted toilets are another option. These can be installed at any height, provide additional clear floor space, and are easy to clean.

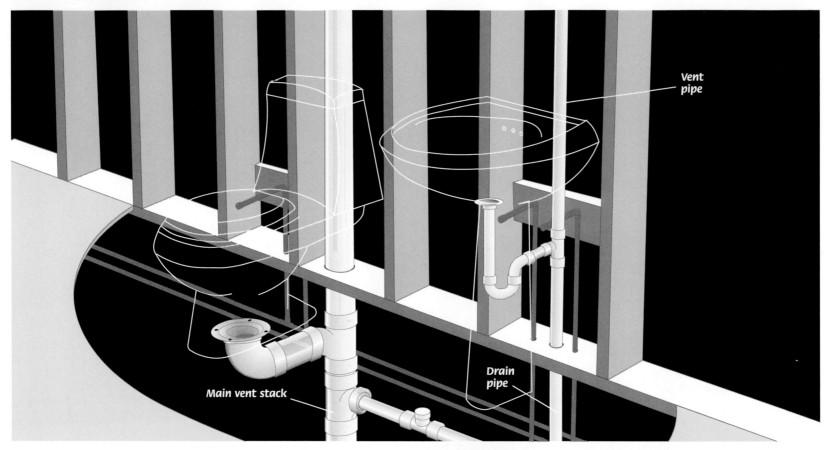

Vent
pipe

Main vent stack

Drain
pipe

Plumbing a Half Bath

A first-story half bath is easy to install when located behind a kitchen or existing bathroom, because you can take advantage of accessible supply and DWV lines. It is possible to add a half bath in an upper story or in a location distant from existing plumbing, but the complexity and cost of the project may be increased considerably.

Be sure that the new fixtures are adequately vented. In the project overview shown here, the pedestal sink is vented with a pipe that runs up the wall a few feet before turning to join the main stack. However, if there are higher fixtures draining into the main stack, you would be required to run the vent up to a point at least 6" above the highest fixture before splicing it into the main stack or an existing vent pipe. When the toilet is located within 6 ft. of the stack, as in this design, it requires no additional vent pipe.

The techniques for plumbing a half bath are similar to those used for a master bathroom. Refer to pages 454 to 461 for more detailed information.

In our demonstration half bath, *the toilet and sink are close to the main stack for ease of installation but are spaced far enough apart to meet minimum allowed distances between fixtures. Check the local code for any restrictions in your area. Generally, there should be at least 15" from the center of the toilet drain to a side wall or fixture, and a minimum of 21" of space between the front edge of the toilet and the wall.*

Plumbing a Half Bath

Locate the main waste-vent stack in the wet wall, and remove the wall surface behind the planned location for the toilet and sink. Cut a 4½"-dia. hole for the toilet flange (centered 12" from the wall, for most toilets). Drill two ¾" holes through the bottom plate for the sink supply lines and one hole for the toilet supply line. Drill a 2" hole for the sink drain.

In the basement, cut away a section of the stack and insert two waste T-fittings. The top fitting should have a 3" side inlet for the toilet drain; the bottom fitting requires a 1½" reducing bushing for the sink drain. Install a toilet bend and 3" drain pipe for the toilet, and install a 1½" drain pipe with a sweep elbow for the sink.

Tap into the water distribution pipes with ¾" × ½" reducing T-fittings, then run ½" copper supply pipes through the holes in the bottom plate to the sink and toilet. Support all pipes at 4-ft. intervals with strapping attached to the joists.

Attach drop ear elbows to the ends of the supply pipes, and anchor them to blocking installed between studs. Anchor the drain pipe to the blocking, then run a vertical vent pipe from the waste T-fitting up the wall to a point at least 6" above the highest fixture on the main stack. Then, route the vent pipe horizontally and splice it into the vent stack with a vent T.

Plumbing a Master Bath

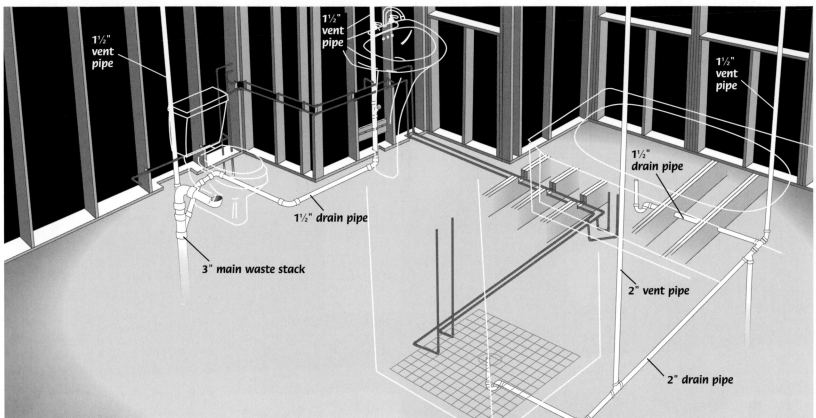

1½" vent pipe

1½" vent pipe

1½" vent pipe

1½" drain pipe

1½" drain pipe

3" main waste stack

2" vent pipe

2" drain pipe

A large bathroom has more plumbing fixtures and consumes more water than any other room in your house. For this reason, a master bath has special plumbing needs.

Frame bathroom wet walls with 2 × 6 studs, to provide plenty of room for running 3" pipes and fittings. If your bathroom includes a heavy whirlpool tub, you will need to reinforce the floor by installing sister joists alongside the existing floor joists underneath the tub.

When making any alterations to floors or load-bearing walls, including adding sister joists, installing joist headers, and notching and boring framing members, be sure to follow all requirements prescribed by the local building code. The chart on page 90 lists some typical allowable sizes for holes and notches cut into framing members.

For convenience, this project overview is divided into the following sequences:

- Installing DWV Pipes for the Toilet & Sink (pages 455 to 457).
- Installing DWV Pipes for the Tub & Shower (pages 458 to 459).
- Connecting the Drain Pipes & Vent Pipes to the Main Waste-vent Stack (page 460).
- Installing the Water Supply Pipes (page 461) .

Our demonstration bathroom is a second-story master bath. We are installing a 3" vertical drain pipe to service the toilet and the pedestal sink, and a 2" vertical pipe to handle the tub and shower drains. The branch drains for the sink and bathtub are 1½" pipes; for the shower, 2" pipe. Each fixture has its own vent pipe extending up into the attic, where they are joined together and connected to the main stack.

Installing DWV Pipes for the Toilet & Sink

Use masking tape to outline the locations of the fixtures and pipe runs on the subfloor and walls. Mark the location for a 3" vertical drain pipe on the bottom plate in the wall behind the toilet. Mark a 4½"-dia. circle for the toilet drain on the subfloor.

Cut out the drain opening for the toilet, using a jig saw. Mark and remove a section of subfloor around the toilet area, large enough to provide access for installing the toilet drain and for running drain pipe from the sink. Make the cuts using a circular saw with the blade set to the thickness of the subfloor.

If a floor joist interferes with the toilet drain, cut away a short section of the joist and box-frame the area with double headers. (Check the local building code regarding the construction and fastening requirements for double headers.) The framed opening should be just large enough to install the toilet and sink drains.

To create a path for the vertical 3" drain pipe, cut a 4½" × 12" notch in the bottom plate of the wall behind the toilet. Make a similar cutout in the double wall plate at the bottom of the joist cavity. From the basement, locate the point directly below the cutout by measuring from a reference point, such as the main waste-vent stack.

Mark the location for the 3" drain pipe on the basement ceiling, then drill a small test hole up through the center of the marked area. Direct the beam of a bright flashlight up into the hole, then return to the bathroom and look down into the wall cavity. If you can see light, return to the basement and cut a 4½"-dia. hole centered over the test hole.

Continued on next page

Installing DWV Pipes for the Toilet and Sink (cont.)

F

Low-heel vent 90° fitting

Y-fitting

Measure and cut a length of 3" drain pipe to reach from the bathroom floor cavity to a point flush with the bottom of the ceiling joists in the basement. Solvent-glue a 3" × 3" × 1½" Y-fitting to the top of the pipe, and a low-heel vent 90° fitting above the Y. The branch inlet on the Y should face toward the sink location; the front inlet on the low-heel should face forward. Carefully lower the pipe into the wall cavity.

G

Lower the pipe so the bottom end slides through the opening in the basement ceiling. Support the pipe with vinyl pipe strap wrapped around the low-heel vent 90° fitting and screwed to framing members.

H

Use a length of 3" pipe and a 4" × 3" reducing elbow to extend the drain out to the toilet location. Make sure the drain slopes at least ⅛" per ft. toward the wall, then support it with pipe strap attached to the joists. Insert a short length of pipe into the elbow, so it extends at least 2" above the subfloor. After the new drains are pressure tested, this stub-out will be cut flush with the subfloor and fitted with a toilet flange.

Waste T

Sweep 90° elbow

Notch out the bottom plate and subfloor below the sink location. Cut a length of 1½" plastic drain pipe, then solvent-glue a waste T to the top of the pipe and a sweep 90° elbow to the bottom. NOTE: The distance from the subfloor to the center of the waste T should be 14" to 18". The branch of the T should face out, and the discharge on the elbow should face toward the toilet. Adjust the pipe so the top edge of the elbow nearly touches the bottom of the bottom plate. Anchor it with pipe strap and a ¾"-thick backing board nailed between studs.

Dry-fit lengths of 1½" drain pipe and elbows to extend the sink drain to the 3" drain pipe behind the toilet. Use a right-angle drill to bore holes in the joists, if needed. Make sure the horizontal drain pipe slopes at least ¼" per ft. toward the vertical drain. When satisfied with the layout, solvent-glue the pieces together and support the drain pipe with vinyl pipe straps attached to the joists.

Toilet vent pipe

In the top plates of the walls behind the sink and toilet, bore ½"-dia. holes up into the attic. Insert pencils or dowels into the holes, and tape them in place. Enter the attic and locate the pencils, then clear away any insulation and cut 2"-dia. holes for the vertical vent pipes. Cut and install 1½" vent pipes running from the toilet and sink drains and extending at least 1 ft. up into the attic.

Installing DWV Pipes for the Tub & Shower

On the subfloor, use masking tape to mark the locations of the tub and shower, the water supply pipes, and the tub and shower drains, according to your plumbing plan. Use a jig saw to cut out a 12"-square opening for each drain, and drill 1"-dia. holes in the subfloor for each water supply riser.

When installing a large whirlpool tub, cut away the subfloor to expose the full length of the joists under the tub, then nail, screw, or bolt a second joist, called a *sister*, against each existing joist. Make sure both ends of each joist are supported by load-bearing walls. (See pages 318 to 319 for more information on adding sister joists.)

In a wall adjacent to the tub, establish a route for a 2" vertical waste-vent pipe running from the basement. This pipe should be no more than 3½ ft. from the bathtub trap. Then, mark a route for the horizontal drain pipe running from the bathtub drain to the waste-vent pipe location. Cut 3"-diameter holes through the centers of the joists for the bathtub drain.

2" inlet for shower drain

1½" inlet for tub drain

Cut and install a vertical 2" drain pipe running from the basement to the joist cavity adjoining the tub location, using the same technique as for the toilet drain (steps D through F, pages 455 to 456). At the top of the drain pipe, use assorted fittings to create three inlets: branch inlets for the bathtub and shower drains, and a 1½" top inlet for a vent pipe running to the attic.

Dry-fit a 1½" drain pipe running from the bathtub drain location to the vertical waste-vent pipe in the wall. Make sure the pipe slopes ¼" per ft. toward the wall. When satisfied with the layout, solvent-glue the pieces together and support the pipe with vinyl pipe straps attached to the joists.

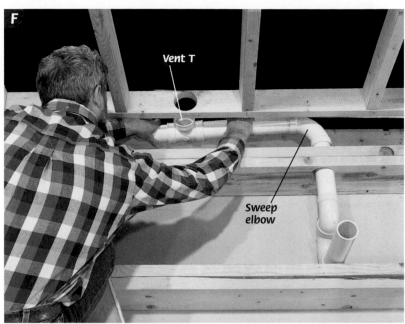

Dry-fit a 2" drain pipe from the shower drain to the vertical waste-vent pipe near the tub. Install a solvent-glued trap at the drain location, and cut a hole in the bottom plate and insert a 2" × 2" × 1½" vent T within 5 ft. of the trap. Make sure the drain is sloped ¼" per ft. downward, away from the shower drain. When satisfied with the layout, solvent-glue the pipes together.

Cut and install vertical vent pipes for the bathtub and shower, extending them up through the wall plates and at least 1 ft. into the attic. These vent pipes will be connected in the attic to the main waste-vent stack. In our project, the shower vent is a 2" pipe, while the bathtub vent is a 1½" pipe.

Connecting the Drain Pipes to the Main Waste-vent Stack

In the basement, cut into the main waste-vent stack and install the fittings necessary to connect the 3" toilet-sink drain and the 2" bathtub-shower drain. In our project, we created an assembly made of a waste T-fitting with an extra side inlet and two short lengths of pipe, then inserted it into the existing waste-vent stack using banded couplings (see pages 84 to 85). Position the T-fittings so the drain pipes will have the proper downward slope toward the stack. NOTE: If your stack is cast iron, install supports before cutting into the pipe (see page 84).

Dry-fit Y-fittings with 45° elbows onto the vertical 3" and 2" drain pipes. Position the horizontal drain pipes against the fittings, and mark them for cutting. When satisfied with the layout, solvent-glue the pipes together, then support the pipes every 4 ft. with vinyl pipe straps. Solvent-glue cleanout plugs on the open inlets on the Y-fittings.

Connecting the Vent Pipes to the Main Waste-vent Stack

In the attic, cut into the main waste-vent stack and install a vent T-fitting, using banded couplings. The side outlet on the vent T should face the new 2" vent pipe running down to the bathroom. Attach a test T-fitting to the vent T. NOTE: If your stack is cast iron, make sure to adequately support it before cutting into it (see page 84).

Use elbows, vent T-fittings, reducers, and lengths of pipe as needed to link the new vent pipes to the test T-fitting on the main waste-vent stack. Vent pipes can be routed in many ways, but you should make sure the pipes have a slight downward angle to prevent moisture from collecting in the pipes. Support the pipes every 4 ft.

Installing the Water Supply Pipes

After shutting off the water, cut into the existing supply pipes and install T-fittings for new branch lines. Notch out the studs and run copper pipes to the toilet and sink locations. Use an elbow and threaded female fitting to form the toilet stub-out. When satisfied with the layout, solder the pipes in place.

Cut 1" × 1"-tall notches around the wall, and extend the supply pipes to the sink location. Install reducing T-fittings and female threaded fittings for the sink faucet stub-outs. Position the stub-outs about 18" above the floor, spaced 8" apart. When satisfied with the layout, solder the joints, then insert ¾" blocking behind the stub-outs and strap them in place.

Extend the water supply pipes to the bathtub and shower. In our project, we removed the subfloor and notched the joists to run ¾" supply pipes from the sink to a whirlpool bathtub, then to the shower. At the bathtub, we used reducing T-fittings and elbows to create ½" risers for the tub faucet. Solder caps onto the risers; after the subfloor is replaced, the caps will be removed and replaced with shutoff valves.

At the shower location, use elbows to create vertical risers where the shower wet wall will be constructed. The risers should extend at least 6" above the floor level. Support the risers with a ¾" backer board attached between joists. Solder caps onto the risers; after the shower stall is constructed, the caps will be removed and replaced with shutoff valves.

Plumbing a Basement Bath

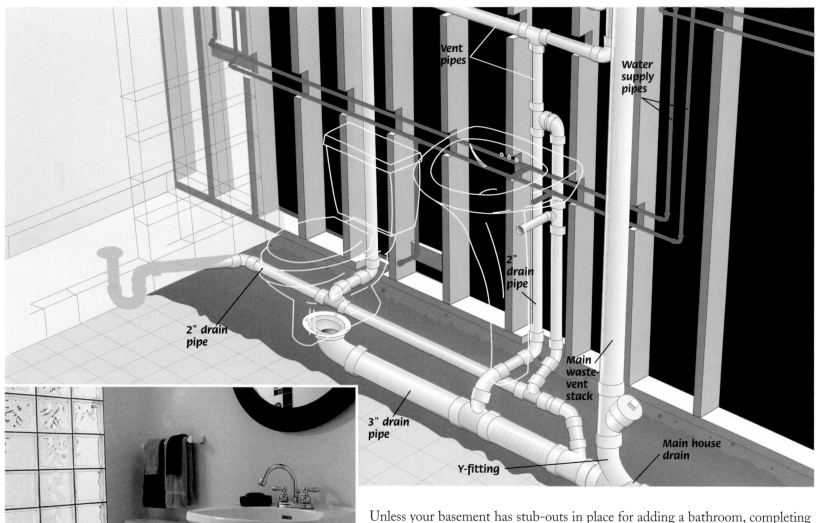

Labels on the illustration: Vent pipes · Water supply pipes · 2" drain pipe · 2" drain pipe · 3" drain pipe · Main waste-vent stack · Main house drain · Y-fitting

Plumbing rough-ins *for our demonstration bathroom include a 2" drain pipe for the shower and sink, and a 3" drain for the toilet. The drain pipes converge at a Y-fitting joined to the existing main drain. The shower, toilet, and sink have individual vent pipes that meet inside the wet wall. From there, a single vent extends up to the attic, where it joins the main waste-vent stack.*

Unless your basement has stub-outs in place for adding a bathroom, completing the rough-ins usually requires breaking up a portion of the concrete floor and digging a trench for the toilet and shower or bath drains: To simplify this laborious process, it's best to arrange the bathroom fixtures in a line along one wall. Another consideration is the location of the bathroom. The fixtures must be close enough to the main drain tie-in that the fixture drain lines maintain a downward slope of ¼" per ft.

In some basements, the main house drain does not extend through the basement floor but instead makes a turn above the floor and begins its run out to the city sewer. In this situation, a basement bathroom requires a sewage ejector to collect the waste from each fixture and pump it up to the main drain.

In this project overview, the in-floor drains feed into a main drain nearby and are vented by a pipe that ties into the main waste-vent stack in the attic. To accept the new drain tie-ins, the main drain and main waste-vent stack are cut into, and new fittings are added. The project also includes the construction of a 2 × 6 "wet wall" for housing the pipes.

Plumbing a Basement Bath

Outline a 24"-wide trench on the concrete where the new branch drains will run to the main drain. (In our project, we ran the trench parallel to an outside wall, leaving a 6" ledge for framing a wet wall.) Use a masonry chisel and hand maul to break up the concrete near the stack.

Use a circular saw and masonry blade to cut along the outline, then break the rest of the trench into small chunks with a jackhammer. Remove any remaining concrete with a chisel. Excavate the trench to a depth about 2" deeper than the main drain. At vent locations for the shower and toilet, cut 3" notches into the concrete ledge, all the way to the wall.

Cut the 2 × 6 framing for the wet wall that will hold the pipes. Use pressure-treated lumber for the bottom plate. Cut 3" notches in the bottom plate for the pipes, then secure the plate to the floor with construction adhesive and masonry fasteners (see pages 323 to 324). Install the top plate, then attach the studs.

Assemble a 2" horizontal drain pipe for the sink and shower, and a 3" drain pipe for the toilet. The 2" drain pipe includes a solvent-glued trap for the shower, a vent T, and a waste T for the sink drain. The toilet drain includes a toilet bend and a vent T. Use elbows and straight lengths of pipe to extend the vent and drain pipes to the wet wall. Make sure the vent fittings angle upward from the drain pipe at least 45°.

Continued on next page

Plumbing a Basement Bath (cont.)

Use pairs of stakes with vinyl support straps slung between them to cradle drain pipes in the proper position (inset). The drain pipes should be positioned so they slope ¼" per ft. down toward the main drain.

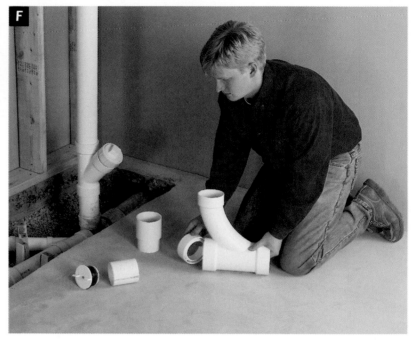

Assemble the fittings required to tie the new branch drains into the main drain. In our project, we will be cutting out the cleanout and sweep on the main waste-vent stack in order to install a new assembly that includes a Y-fitting to accept the two new drain pipes.

Support the main waste-vent stack before cutting into it. Use a 2 × 4 for a plastic stack, or riser clamps (see page 84) for a cast-iron stack. Using a reciprocating saw (or snap cutter, for cast iron), cut into the main drain, as close as possible to the stack.

Cut into the stack above the cleanout and remove the pipe and fittings. Wear rubber gloves, and have a bucket and plastic bags ready, as old pipes and fittings may be coated with messy sludge.

I

3" × 3" × 2" *reducing Y*

Test-fit, then solvent-glue the new cleanout and reducing Y assembly into the main drain. Support the weight of the stack by adding sand underneath the Y, but leave plenty of space around the end for connecting the new branch pipes.

J

Working from the reducing Y, solvent-glue the new drain pipes together. Be careful to maintain proper slope of the drain pipes when gluing. Be sure the toilet and shower drain stub-outs extend at least 2" above the floor level.

K

Check for leaks by pouring fresh water into each new drain pipe. If no leaks appear, cap or plug the drains with rags to prevent sewer gas from leaking into the work area as you complete the installation.

Continued on next page

Plumbing a Basement Bath (cont.)

Run 2" vent pipes from the drains up the inside of the wet wall. Notch the studs and insert a horizontal vent pipe, then attach the vertical vent pipes with an elbow and vent T-fitting. Test-fit all pipes, then solvent-glue them in place.

Route the vent pipe from the wet wall to a point below a wall cavity running from the basement to the attic. NOTE: If there is an existing vent pipe in the basement, you can tie into this pipe rather than run the vent to the attic.

If you are running vent pipes in a two-story home, remove sections of wall surface as needed to bore holes for running the vent pipe through the wall plates. Feed the vent pipe up into the wall cavity from the basement.

Wedge the vent pipe in place while you solvent-glue the fittings. Support the vent pipe at each floor with vinyl pipe straps. Do not patch the walls until your work has been inspected by a building inspector.

Cut into the main stack in the attic and install a vent T-fitting, using banded couplings. (If the stack is cast iron, make sure to support it adequately above and below the cuts, as demonstrated on page 84.) Attach a test T-fitting to the vent T, then join the new vent pipe to the stack, using elbows and lengths of straight pipe as needed.

Shut off the main water supply, cut into the water supply pipes as near as possible to the new bathroom, and install T-fittings. Install full-bore control valves on each line, then run ¾" branch supply pipes down into the wet wall by notching the top wall plate. Extend the pipes across the wall by notching the studs.

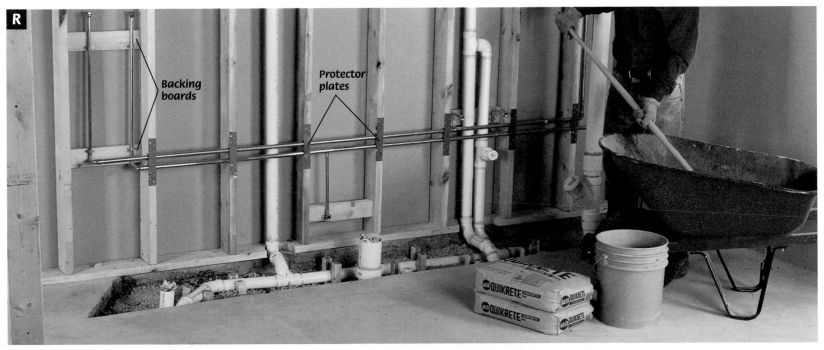

Use reducing T-fittings to run ½" supply pipes to each fixture, ending with female threaded adapters. Install backing boards, and strap the pipes in place. Attach metal protector plates over notched studs to protect the pipes. After having your work approved by a building inspector, fill in around the pipes with dirt or sand, then mix and pour new concrete to cover the trench. Trowel the surface smooth, and let the concrete cure for 3 days before installing the fixtures.

Building a Shower

Showers can be built in different sizes and configurations, but the basic elements remain the same; most have a supply system, a drain system, and a framed alcove.

The supply system: The shower arm extends from the wall, where an elbow fitting connects it to the shower pipe. The pipe runs up from the faucet, which is fed by the hot and cold water supplies. Most building codes require shower faucets to be equipped with anti-scald devices (see page 483).

The drain system: The drain cover attaches to the drain tailpiece. A rubber gasket on the tailpiece slips over the drain pipe, leading to the P-trap and the branch drain.

The alcove: The alcove is the frame for the stall, with 2 × 4 walls built to fit around a shower base and blocking to secure the plumbing. The base sets into a mortar bed for support, and water-resistant wallboard or cementboard covers the alcove walls.

The easiest way to finish a shower stall is with prefabricated panels. For a custom finish, ceramic wall tile is the most popular choice. Though water-resistant wallboard is the standard backer for prefab panels, always check the manufacturer's recommendations. Ceramic tile should be backed by cementboard (see pages 204 to 205). Some building codes require a waterproof membrane between the studs and the wallboard or cementboard in shower stalls.

The type of shower base and wall finish you use will affect the installation sequence. Some bases are made to be installed after the wallboard or cementboard; other bases should be installed first. If your base is going in after the wall surface, be sure to account for the thickness of the surface material when framing the alcove.

Tools: Circular saw, drill, plumbing tools, hacksaw, channel-type pliers, trowel, level.

Materials: 2 × 4 and 1 × 4 lumber, 16d and 8d nails, plumbing supplies, shower base, rag, dry-set mortar, soap.

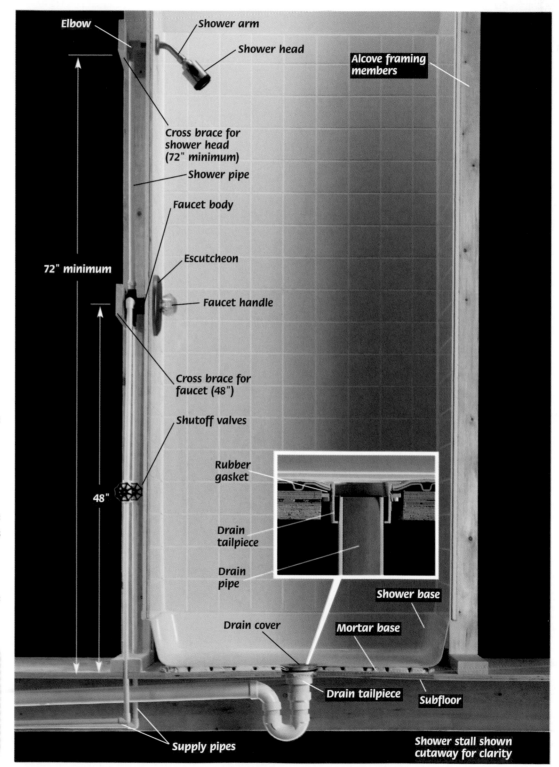

Elbow

Shower arm

Shower head

Alcove framing members

Cross brace for shower head (72" minimum)

Shower pipe

Faucet body

Escutcheon

72" minimum

Faucet handle

Cross brace for faucet (48")

Shutoff valves

Rubber gasket

48"

Drain tailpiece

Drain pipe

Shower base

Drain cover

Mortar base

Drain tailpiece

Subfloor

Supply pipes

Shower stall shown cutaway for clarity

Framing a Shower Alcove

A

Measure the shower base, and mark its dimensions on the floor. Measure from the center of the drain pipe to ensure that the drain will be centered in the shower alcove. Install blocking between the studs in the existing walls to provide a surface for anchoring the alcove walls.

B

Build 2 × 4 alcove walls just outside the marked lines on the floor. Anchor the alcove walls to the existing wall and the subfloor. If necessary, drill holes or cut notches in the bottom plate for plumbing pipes.

C

In the stud cavity that will hold the shower faucet and shower head, mark reference points 48" and 72" above the floor to indicate the locations of the faucet and shower head. For taller users, you may want to install the shower head higher than 72".

D

Attach 1 × 4 cross braces between studs to provide surfaces for attaching the shower head and faucet. Center the cross braces on the marked reference points, and position them flush with the back edges of the studs to provide adequate space for the faucet body (inset) and shower head fittings.

E

Following the manufacturer's directions, assemble the plumbing pipes and attach the faucet body and shower-head fitting to the cross braces. (See pages 78 to 81 for information on working with plastic plumbing pipes.)

Installing a Shower Base

A

Trim the drain pipe in the floor to the height recommended by the manufacturer (usually near or slightly above floor level). Stuff a rag into the drain pipe, and leave it in place until you are ready to make the drain connections.

B Locknut Sealing gasket Drain tailpiece

Prepare the shower drain tailpiece as directed by the manufacturer, and attach it to the drain opening in the shower base (see inset photo, page 468). Tighten the locknut securely onto the drain tailpiece to ensure a waterproof fit.

C

Mix a batch of dry-set mortar, then apply a 1" layer to the subfloor, covering the shower base area. Mortar stabilizes and levels the shower base.

D

Apply soap to the outside of the drain pipe in the floor and to the inside of the rubber gasket in the drain tailpiece. Set the shower base onto the drain pipe, and press down slowly until the rubber gasket in the drain tailpiece fits snugly over the drain pipe.

E

Press the shower base down into the dry-set mortar, carefully adjusting it so it is level. If directed by the manufacturer, anchor the shower base with screws driven through the edge flanges and into the wall studs. Let the mortar dry for 6 to 8 hours. Attach the faucet handle and shower head after the shower walls have been finished.

Installing Bathtubs

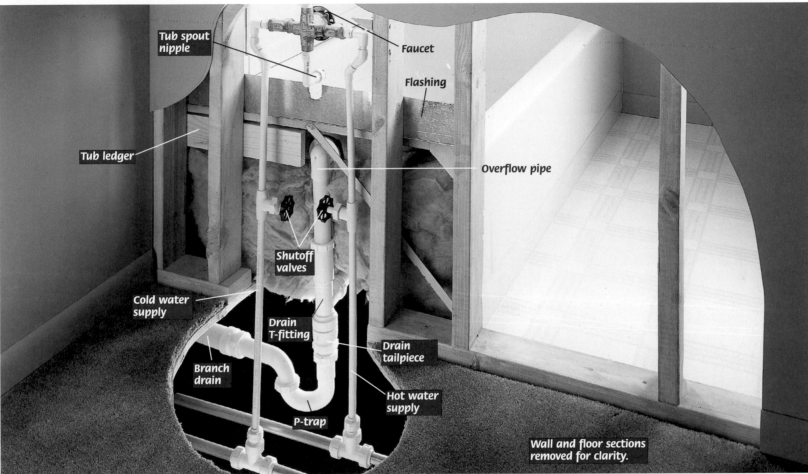

Tub spout nipple

Faucet

Flashing

Tub ledger

Overflow pipe

Shutoff valves

Cold water supply

Drain T-fitting

Drain tailpiece

Branch drain

Hot water supply

P-trap

Wall and floor sections removed for clarity.

The supply system for a bathtub includes hot and cold supply pipes, shutoff valves, a faucet and handles, and a spout. Supply connections can be made before or after the tub is installed. The drain-waste-overflow system for a bathtub includes the overflow pipe, drain T, P-trap, and branch drain. The overflow pipe assembly is attached to the tub before installation.

The development of modern plastics has created a new generation of tubs that are strong, light, and easy to clean. Even if your old fiberglass or cast-iron tub is in good condition, you might consider replacing it with a newer model that's made to resist stains and rust.

Take care when handling a new bathtub, since the greatest risk of damaging it occurs during the installation. If the inside of your tub has a protective layer of removable plastic, leave it on until you've completed the installation. Also set a layer of cardboard into the bottom of the tub for added protection while you work.

This project shows you how to install a standard bathtub into a framed alcove. If you're building a new alcove, follow the tub manufacturer's specifications regarding its size. As with a shower alcove, you can finish your tub alcove with ceramic tile or prefabricated panels (see page 468).

Create an access panel behind the bathtub's water supply valves and

drain connections to provide access for future alterations or repairs.

If you are installing a new bathtub that will also be used as a shower, purchase a combination tub-shower faucet that has a port on top for connecting the shower pipe. Most codes require that these faucets be equipped with anti-scald valves (see page 483), so check with the local building department before buying a faucet.

Tools: *Plumbing tools, channel-type pliers, hacksaw, level, circular saw, drill, screwdriver, adjustable wrench.*

Materials: *Plumbing supplies; tub protector; drain-waste-overflow kit; shims; 1 × 3, 1 × 4, and 2 × 4 lumber; galvanized deck screws; plumber's putty; dry-set mortar; trowel; soap; 1" galvanized roofing nails; 4"-wide galvanized roof flashing; silicone caulk.*

Tips for Installing Bathtubs

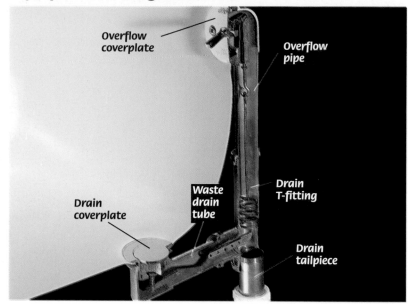

A **drain-waste-overflow kit** with a stopper mechanism must be purchased separately and attached to the tub before it is installed (see pages 473 to 474). Available in both brass and plastic types, most kits include an overflow coverplate, an overflow pipe that can be adjusted to different heights, a drain T-fitting and tailpiece, a waste drain tube, and a drain coverplate that screws into the drain tube.

Build a deck for a drop-in style tub or whirlpool (see pages 478 to 481). Used frequently with whirlpools, most decks are finished with cementboard and ceramic tile after the tub or whirlpool is installed.

Installing a Bathtub in an Alcove

A

Attach the faucet body and shower head to the water supply pipes, and secure the assemblies to 1 × 4 cross braces before installing the tub. Trim the drain pipe to the height specified by the drain-waste-overflow kit manufacturer.

B

Place a tub-bottom protector, which can be cut from the shipping carton, into the tub. Test-fit the tub by sliding it into the alcove so it rests on the subfloor, flush against the wall studs.

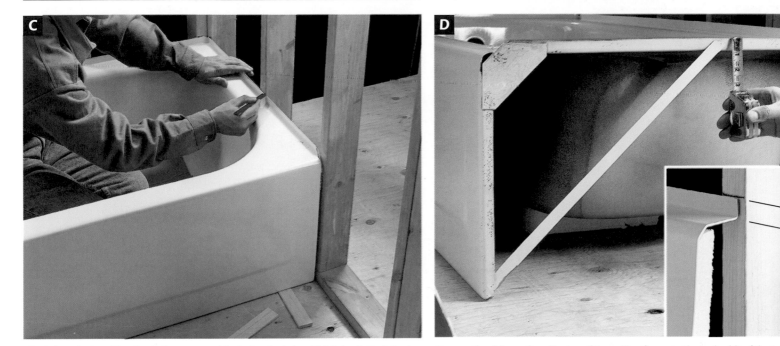

Check the tub rim with a level. If necessary, shim below the tub until it is level. Mark the top of the nailing flange at each stud. Remove the bathtub from the alcove.

Measure the distance from the top of the nailing flange to the underside of the tub rim (inset), and subtract that amount from the marks on the wall studs. Draw a line at that point on each wall stud.

Cut ledger board strips from 1 × 4s, and attach them to the wall studs just below the marks for the underside of the tub rim (step D), using galvanized deck screws. You may have to install the boards in sections to make room for any structural braces at the ends of the tub.

Adjust the drain-waste-overflow assembly (usually sold as a separate kit) to fit the drain and overflow openings. Attach the gaskets and washers as directed by the manufacturer, then position the assembly against the tub drain and overflow openings. Prop up the tub on 2 × 4s, if necessary.

Continued on next page

Installing a Bathtub in an Alcove (cont.)

Apply a ring of plumber's putty to the bottom of the drain coverplate flange, then insert the drain piece through the drain hole in the bathtub. Screw the drain piece into the waste drain tube, and tighten until it is snug. Insert the pop-up drain plug.

Insert the drain plug linkage into the overflow opening, and attach the overflow coverplate with long screws driven into the mounting flange on the overflow pipe. Adjust the drain plug linkage as directed by the manufacturer.

Use a trowel to apply a ½"-thick layer of dry-set mortar to the subfloor, covering the entire area where the tub will rest.

Lay soaped 1 × 4 runners across the alcove so they rest on the back wall's bottom plate. The runners will allow you to slide the tub into the alcove without disturbing the mortar base.

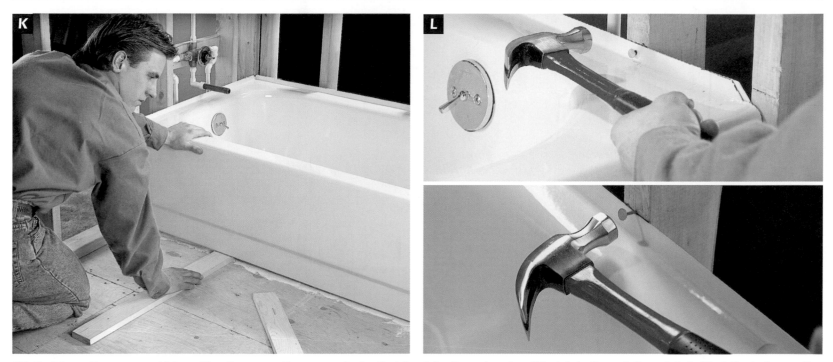

Slide the tub over the runners and into position, then remove the runners, allowing the tub to settle into the mortar. Press down evenly on the tub rims until they touch the ledger boards.

Before the mortar sets, nail the tub rim flanges to the wall studs. Attach the rim flanges either by drilling pilot holes into the flanges and nailing with galvanized roofing nails (top), or by driving roofing nails into the studs so the head of the nail covers the rim flange (bottom). After the rim flanges are secured, allow the mortar to dry for 6 to 8 hours.

Attach 4"-wide strips of galvanized metal roof flashing over the tub flange to help keep water out of the wall. Leave a ¼" expansion gap between the flashing and the tub rim. Nail the flashing to each wall stud, using 1" galvanized roofing nails.

Adjust the drain tailpiece so the overflow assembly will fit into the P-trap (you may have to trim it with a hacksaw), then connect it, using a slip nut. Install the wall surfaces, then install the faucet handle and tub spout (see pages 482 to 483). Finally, caulk all around the bathtub.

Installing a Whirlpool

Installing a whirlpool is very similar to installing a bathtub, once the rough-in is completed. Completing a rough-in for a whirlpool requires that you install a separate GFCI-protected electrical circuit for the pump motor. Some building codes specify that a licensed electrician be hired to wire whirlpools; check with your local building inspector.

Select your whirlpool before you do the rough-in work, because exact requirements differ from one model to another. For installations in existing bathrooms, where space can be tight, many whirlpool manufacturers now offer tapered designs and tubs in various heights.

One of the best ways to choose a whirlpool is to visit a showroom and sit in several models. The tub should be comfortable to enter and exit; it should also fit your body comfortably when you are seated. Check whether the whirlpool offers grab bars to assist your entry and exit.

Select your faucet to match the trim kit that comes with your whirlpool. When selecting a faucet, make sure the spout is large enough to reach over the tub rim. Most whirlpools use "widespread" faucets because the handles and spout are separate and can be positioned however you like, even on opposite sides of the tub. Most building centers carry flex tube in a variety of lengths for connecting faucet handles and spouts.

Tools: Framing square, circular saw, drill & spade bits, jig saw, hacksaw, trowel, screwdriver, staple gun, straightedge, utility knife, tiling tools, caulk gun.

Materials: 2 × 4 lumber, 10d nails, ¾" exterior-grade plywood, galvanized deck screws, dry-set mortar, 12" wood spacer blocks, 8-gauge insulated wire, grounding clamp, paper-faced fiberglass insulation, cementboard, ceramic tile materials, silicone caulk.

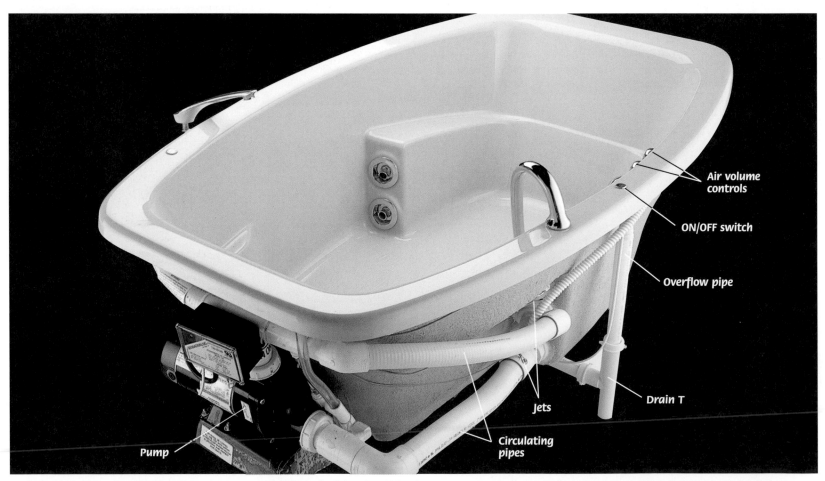

A whirlpool circulates aerated water through jets mounted in the body of the tub. Whirlpool pumps move as much as 50 gallons of water per minute to create a relaxing hydromassage effect. The pump, pipes, jets, and most of the controls are installed at the factory, making the actual hookup in your home quite simple.

Optional Whirlpool Accessories

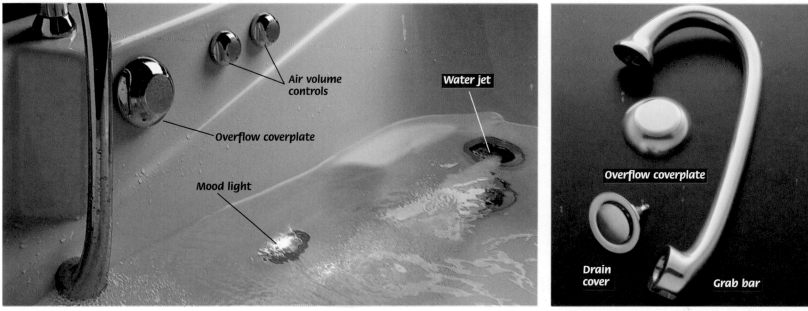

Mood lights are sold as factory-installed accessories by many manufacturers. Most are available with several filters to let you adjust the color to suit your mood. Mood lights are low-voltage fixtures wired through 12-volt transformers. Do not wire mood lights or other accessories into the electrical circuit that supplies the pump motor.

Trim kits for whirlpools are ordered at the time of purchase. Available in a variety of finishes, all of the trim pieces except the grab bar and overflow coverplate typically are installed at the factory.

Making Electrical Hook-ups

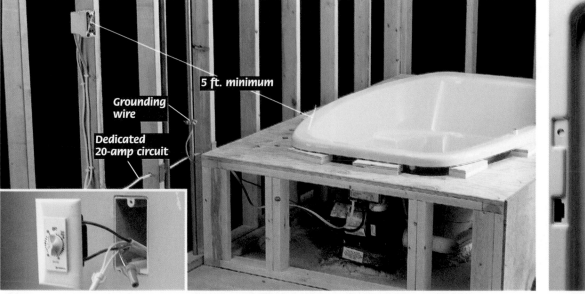

The electrical service for a whirlpool should be a dedicated 115- to 120-volt, 20-amp circuit. The pump motor should be grounded separately, typically to a metal cold-water supply pipe. Most whirlpool motors are wired with 12/2 NM cable, but some local codes require the use of conduit. A remote timer switch (inset), located at least 5 ft. from the tub, is required by some codes, even for a tub with a built-in timer.

A GFCI circuit breaker at the main service panel is required with a whirlpool installation. Always hire an electrician to connect new circuits at your service panel, even if you install the circuit cable yourself.

Installing a Whirlpool

A

Outline the planned location of the deck frame on the subfloor. Use the plumbing stub-outs as starting points for measuring. Before you begin to build the deck, check the actual dimensions of your whirlpool tub to make sure they correspond to the dimensions listed in the manufacturer's directions. NOTE: Plan your deck so it will be at least 4" wide at all points around the whirlpool.

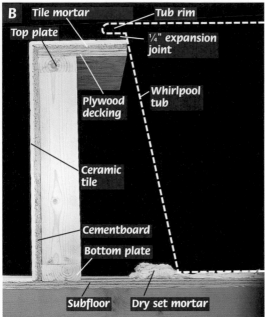

B

Tile mortar — Tub rim
Top plate
¼" expansion joint
Plywood decking
Whirlpool tub
Ceramic tile
Cementboard
Bottom plate
Subfloor — Dry set mortar

Cut top plates, bottom plates, and studs for the deck frame. The height of the frame should allow ¾" for the plywood decking, ¼" for an expansion gap between the deck and the tub rim, and 1" for the cementboard, tile, and mortar.

C

Access panel for pump motor

Assemble the deck frame. Make sure to leave a framed opening for access panels at the pump location and the drain location. Nail the frame to the floor joists and wall studs or blocking, using 10d nails.

D

Cover the deck frame with ¾" exterior-grade plywood, and attach it with galvanized deck screws spaced every 12". Using a template of the whirlpool cutout (usually included with the tub), mark the deck for cutting. If no template is included, make one from the shipping carton. (The cutout will be slightly smaller than the outside dimensions of the whirlpool rim.)

Drill a starter hole inside the cutout line, then make the cutout hole in the deck, using a jig saw.

Measure and mark holes for the faucet tailpieces and spout tailpiece according to the faucet manufacturer's directions. Drill the holes with a spade bit or hole saw.

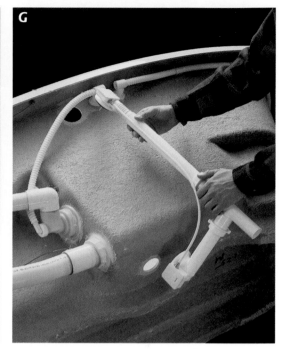

Attach the drain-waste-overflow assembly (included with most whirlpools) at the drain and overflow outlets in the tub (see pages 473 to 474). Trim the drain pipe in the floor to the proper height, using a hacksaw.

Apply a layer of dry-set mortar to the subfloor where the tub will rest. Make 12" spacer blocks, 1¼" thick (equal to the expansion gap, tile, mortar, and cementboard; see step B). Arrange the blocks along the edges of the cutout.

With a helper, lift the tub by the rim and set it into the cutout. Press the tub into the mortar base until the rim rests on the spacers at the edges of the cutout area. Align the tailpiece of the drain-waste-overflow assembly with the P-trap as you set the tub in place. Avoid moving or shifting the tub once it is in place, and allow the mortar to set for 6 to 8 hours before proceeding with the installation.

Continued on next page

Installing a Whirlpool (cont.)

Adjust the length of the tailpiece for the drain-waste-overflow assembly, if necessary, then attach the assembly to the P-trap in the drain opening, using a slip nut.

Inspect the seals on the built-in piping and hoses for loose connections. If you find a problem, contact your dealer for advice. Attempting to fix the problem yourself could void the whirlpool warranty.

With the power off, remove the wiring cover from the pump motor. Feed the circuit wires from the power source or wall timer into the motor. Connect the wires according to the directions printed on the motor.

Attach an insulated 8-gauge wire to the ground lug on the pump motor.

Attach the other end of the wire to a metal cold water supply pipe in the wall, using a grounding clamp. Test the GFCI circuit breaker.

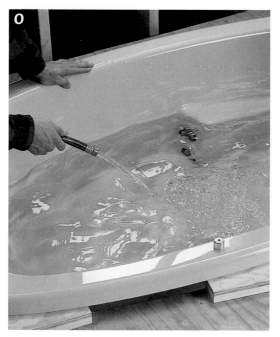

Clean the tub, then fill it so the water level is at least 3" above the highest water jet.

Turn on the pump and allow it to operate for at least 20 minutes while you check for leaks. Contact your whirlpool dealer if you find any leaks.

Staple paper-faced fiberglass insulation to the vertical frame supports. The facing should point inward, to keep fibers out of the motor. Do not insulate within 6" of pumps, heaters, or lights.

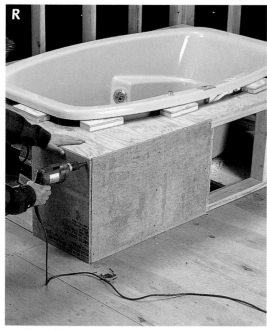

Attach cementboard to the sides and top of the deck frame if you plan to install ceramic tile on the deck. (See pages 428 to 429 for information on cementboard installation.) Use ¾" exterior-grade plywood for the access panel coverings.

Attach the finish surfaces to the deck and deck frame, then install the grab bar and the faucet and spout. For instructions on installing ceramic tile, see pages 426 to 431. Fill the joints between the floor and the deck, and between the tub rim and the deck surface, with silicone caulk.

Installing Faucets & Spouts

Bathroom sink faucets come in a variety of designs, materials, and prices. Better faucets are made of solid brass, while less-expensive models may be made of other metals surface-coated with chrome.

The handle is one of the most distinguishing features of the faucet. Variations include single handles, double handles, or electronic sensors in place of handles. Most types are available in a range of designs, from modern to antique.

Whenever possible, install a faucet before installing the sink. This will allow you the greatest freedom of movement for making connections.

Tools: Basin wrench, screwdriver.

Materials: Plumber's putty, Teflon® tape, supply tube couplings, pipe joint compound.

Bathroom sink faucets *come in many styles, allowing you to match the decorating theme of your bathroom. A basin wrench (inset) enables you to reach faucet locknuts from inside cabinets.*

Installing a One-piece Faucet

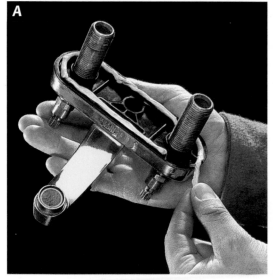

A

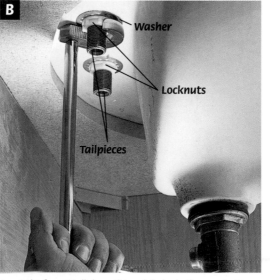

B Washer

Locknuts

Tailpieces

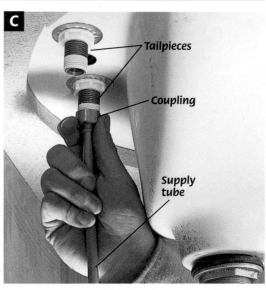

C Tailpieces

Coupling

Supply tube

Apply a ring of plumber's putty around the base of the faucet body. (Some faucets use a gasket that does not require plumber's putty—read the manufacturer's directions carefully.)

Insert the faucet tailpieces through holes in the countertop or sink. From below, thread washers and locknuts over the tailpieces, then tighten the locknuts with channel-type pliers or a basin wrench until snug.

Wrap Teflon tape around the tailpiece threads, then cut supply tubes to fit (see page 77). Attach the supply tube couplings and tighten them with a basin wrench until snug. Connect the drain linkage (see page 485), then attach the faucet handles and trim caps.

Installing Tub & Shower Faucets

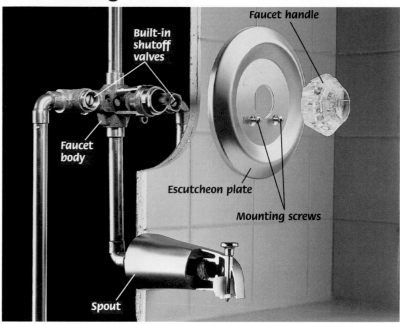

Single-handled faucet: Open the built-in shutoff valves, using a screwdriver, then attach the escutcheon plate to the faucet body with mounting screws. Attach the faucet handle, then attach the spout (see below) and trim cap. NOTE: Attach the faucet body before installing the wall surface (see page 469).

Anti-scald valves are safety devices that protect against sudden changes in water temperature. They are required by most codes for faucets in showers and combination tub-showers. Once installed, faucets with anti-scald valves look like standard faucets (inset).

Installing a Tub Spout

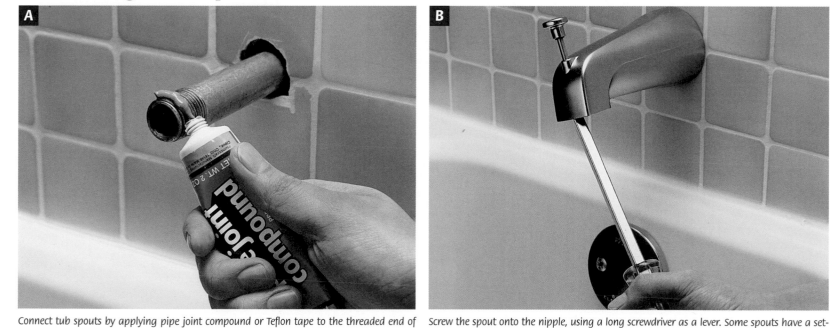

Connect tub spouts by applying pipe joint compound or Teflon tape to the threaded end of the spout nipple that extends from the wall.

Screw the spout onto the nipple, using a long screwdriver as a lever. Some spouts have a set-screw on the underside that must be tightened.

Installing Vanities & Sinks

Many vanity tops installed today are one-piece, or *integral* sink-countertop units made from cultured marble or solid-surface material. These are easy to install and convenient to use, as the sink edge is flush with the counter-top. However, you may want to install a laminate or tile countertop with a separate self-rimming or under-mount sink.

Pedestal sinks are freestanding units that do not have vanities.

Prebuilt cabinets *are inexpensive and simple to install. Most manufacturers sell several cabinet types in the same style and finish. When pricing prebuilt cabinets, remember that faucets and vanity tops are sold separately.*

Tools: Level, drill, sawhorses, basin wrench or channel-type pliers, caulk gun, circular saw, ratchet wrench, jig saw with down-cutting blade.

Materials: Wood shims, 2½" wallboard screws, trim, finish nails, Teflon tape, plumber's putty, faucet, tub & tile caulk, sink-drain assembly, cardboard, 2 × 4 lumber, framing nails, water-resistant wallboard, lag screws and washers.

Installing a Vanity

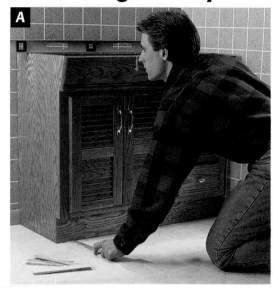

A

Shim below the vanity until it is level. The back of the cabinet should be flush against the wall. If the wall surface is uneven, position the vanity so it contacts the wall in at least one spot and the back cabinet rail is parallel with the wall.

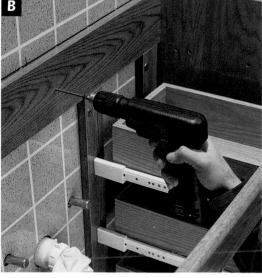

B

Locate the wall studs, then drive 2½" wallboard screws through the rail on the cabinet back and into the wall studs. Drive screws at both corners and in the center of the back rail.

C

Attach any trim and molding required to cover the gaps between the vanity and the wall and between the vanity and the floor. (Small gaps may be filled with caulk instead.) To install two or more cabinets, see pages 402 to 409.

Installing an Integral Sink-Countertop

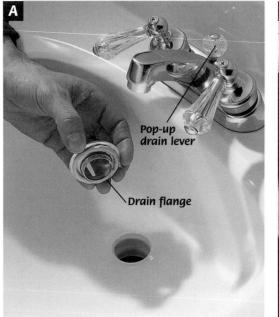

A

Set the sink-countertop onto sawhorses. Attach the faucet (see page 482), and slip the drain lever through the faucet body. Place a ring of plumber's putty around the drain flange, then insert the flange in the drain opening.

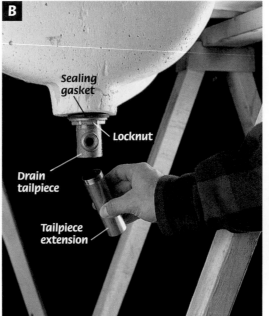

B

Thread the locknut and sealing gasket onto the drain tailpiece, then insert the tailpiece into the drain opening and screw it onto the drain flange. Tighten the locknut using channel-type pliers. Attach the tailpiece extension.

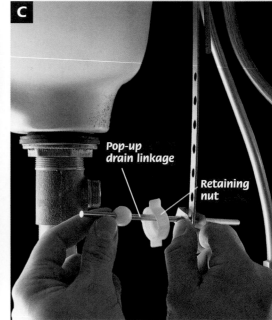

C

Attach the pop-up drain linkage to the tailpiece of the sink. Tighten the retaining nut to secure the linkage.

D

Apply a layer of tub & tile caulk (or adhesive, if specified by the countertop manufacturer) to the top edges of the vanity and to any corner braces.

E

Center the sink-countertop unit over the vanity, so the overhang is equal on both sides and the backsplash of the countertop is flush against the wall. Press the countertop evenly into the caulk.

F

If the cabinet has corner braces, drive a mounting screw through each corner brace and up into the countertop. Cultured marble and other hard countertops require predrilling and plastic screw sleeves.

Continued on next page

Installing an Integral Sink-Countertop (cont.)

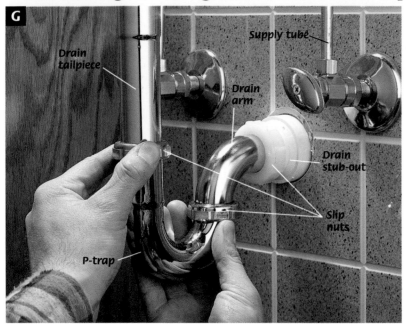

Drain tailpiece
Supply tube
Drain arm
Drain stub-out
Slip nuts
P-trap

Attach the drain arm to the drain stub-out in the wall, using a slip nut. Attach one end of the P-trap to the drain arm, and the other to the tailpiece of the sink drain, using slip nuts. Connect supply tubes to the faucet tailpieces (see page 482).

Seal the gap between the backsplash and the wall with tub & tile caulk.

Installing a Drop-in Sink

Use a template that is ½" narrower than the sink rim to mark the countertop cutout. Drill a ⅜" starter hole, then use a jig saw to make the cutout (see page 348). For countertop-mounted faucets, drill holes for the tailpieces, according to the faucet manufacturer's directions.

Apply a ring of plumber's putty around the sink cutout. Before setting the sink in place, attach the faucet body to the sink or countertop (see page 482), then attach the drain flange and the pop-up drain assembly (see page 485).

Set the sink into the cutout area, and gently press the rim of the sink into the plumber's putty. Hook up the drain and supply fittings (step G, above), then caulk around the sink rim.

Installing a Pedestal Sink

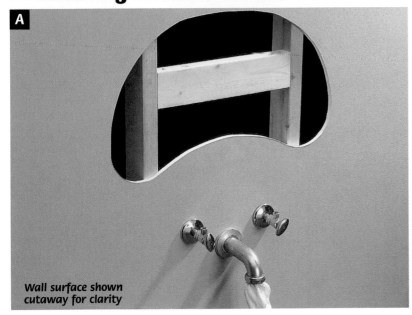

A

Wall surface shown cutaway for clarity

Install 2 × 4 blocking between wall studs, behind the planned sink location. Cover the wall with water-resistant wallboard (see page 205).

B

Set the basin and pedestal in position, bracing the basin with 2 × 4s. Outline the top of the basin on the wall, and mark the base of the pedestal on the floor. Mark reference points on the wall and floor through the mounting holes found on the back of the sink and the bottom of the pedestal.

C

Set aside the basin and pedestal. Drill pilot holes in the wall and floor at the reference points, then reposition the pedestal. Anchor the pedestal to the floor with lag screws.

D

Attach the faucet (see page 482), then set the sink on the pedestal. Align the holes in the back of the sink with the pilot holes drilled in the wall, then drive lag screws and washers into the wall brace, using a ratchet wrench. Do not over-tighten the screws.

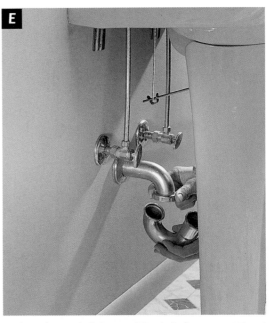

E

Hook up the supply fittings and the drain (see pages 482 and 486). Caulk between the back of the sink and the wall.

Installing Toilets

Building codes now require the installation of water-conserving, low-flow toilets in all new construction and bathroom remodeling projects. Low-flow toilets, which use only 1.6 gallons of water per flush, are available in gravity-flush and pressure-assisted models.

Gravity-flush toilets work much like old models, but with a more efficient water flow. Pressure-assisted toilets use pressurized air and water to flush wastes. There is great variety in price, style, and function, so inspect several models for efficiency before choosing a toilet. Also measure from your bathroom wall to the floor bolts on the toilet flange to determine whether you will need a 12-inch or 14-inch offset model.

Like standard toilets, low-flow models are available in both one- and two-piece units. Two-piece, vitreous china toilets are the least expensive, and gravity-flush models cost less than pressure-assisted varieties.

> **Tools:** Adjustable wrench, ratchet wrench or basin wrench, tubing cutter, screwdriver.
>
> **Materials:** Wax ring & sleeve, plumber's putty, tank bolts with rubber washers, supply tube, coupling nuts, seat bolts and mounting nuts.

Install a toilet by anchoring the bowl to the floor first, then mounting the tank onto the bowl. China fixtures crack easily, so use care when handling them.

Installing a Toilet

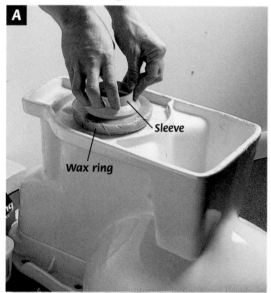

A

Turn the bowl upside down, and place a new wax ring and sleeve onto the toilet horn. Apply a ring of plumber's putty around the bottom edge of the toilet base.

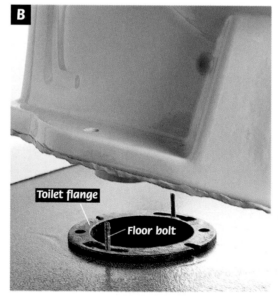

B

Position the toilet over the toilet flange so the floor bolts fit through the holes in the base of the toilet. The flange should be clean, and the floor bolts should point straight up.

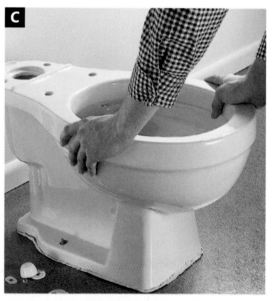

C

Press down on the toilet bowl to compress the wax ring and plumber's putty. Attach washers and nuts to the floor bolts and tighten them with an adjustable wrench until they are snug—do not overtighten. Attach the trim caps.

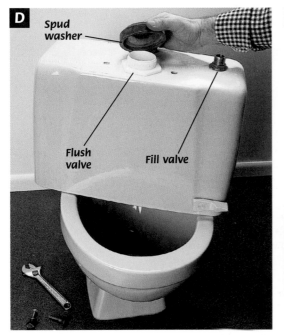

D **Spud washer** **Flush valve** **Fill valve**

Turn the tank upside down, and set the spud washer over the tailpiece of the flush valve. Turn the tank right-side up. NOTE: With some toilets, you will have to purchase a flush handle, fill valve, and flush valve separately.

E

Set the tank onto the bowl, centering the spud washer over the water inlet opening near the back edge of the bowl.

F **Rubber washer** **Tank bolt**

Shift the tank gently until the bolt holes in the tank are aligned over the bolt holes in the bowl flange. Place rubber washers onto the tank bolts, then insert the bolts down through the holes in the tank.

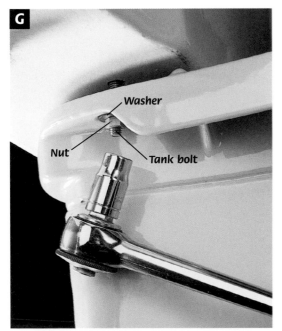

G **Washer** **Nut** **Tank bolt**

From beneath the bowl flange, attach washers and nuts to the tank bolts, and tighten them with a ratchet wrench or basin wrench until they are snug—do not overtighten.

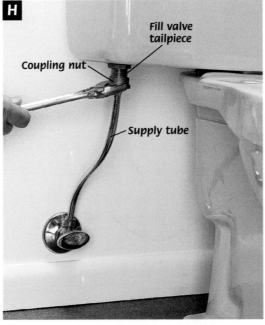

H **Fill valve tailpiece** **Coupling nut** **Supply tube**

Cut a piece of supply tube to fit between the shutoff valve and the toilet tank. Attach the tube to the shutoff valve, then to the fill valve tailpiece. Use an adjustable wrench to tighten coupling nuts until they are snug.

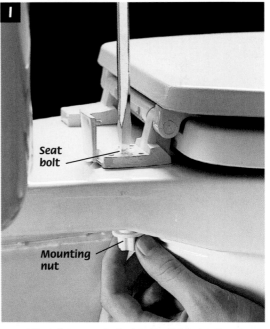

I **Seat bolt** **Mounting nut**

Mount the toilet seat onto the bowl by tightening the mounting nuts onto the seat bolts from below the seat flange.

Installing a Bathroom Vent Fan

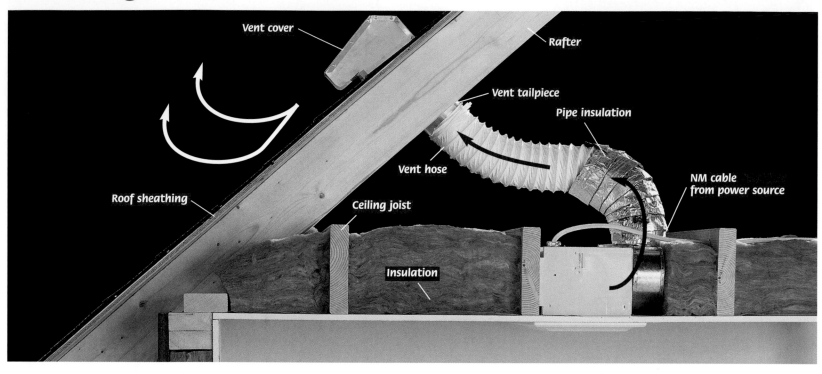

Vent cover

Rafter

Vent tailpiece

Pipe insulation

Roof sheathing

Vent hose

NM cable
from power source

Ceiling joist

Insulation

A bathroom remodeling project is a good opportunity to add a new vent fan or replace an existing fan with a quieter, more efficient model. Most building codes require a vent fan in any bathroom without natural ventilation. Fans with only a light fixture usually can be wired into a main bathroom electrical circuit, but units with built-in heat lamps or blowers require separate circuits.

Most vent fans are installed in the center of the bathroom ceiling or over the toilet area. Do not install a fan over the tub or shower area unless the unit is GFCI-protected and rated for use in wet areas.

If the fan you choose doesn't come with a mounting kit, purchase one separately. A mounting kit should include a vent hose (duct), a vent tailpiece, and an exterior vent cover.

Venting instructions vary among manufacturers, but the most common options are attic venting and soffit venting. Attic venting (shown in this project) routes fan ductwork into the the attic and out through the roof.

Always insulate ducting in this application to keep condensate from forming and running down into the motor. And carefully install flashing around the outside vent cover to prevent roof leaks.

Soffit venting involves routing the duct to a soffit (roof overhang) instead of through the roof. Check with the vent manufacturer for instructions for soffit venting.

To prevent moisture damage, always terminate the vent outside your home—never into your attic or basement.

You can install a vent fan while the framing is exposed or as a retrofit, as shown in this project. Refer to the Wiring section of this book for help with running circuit cable, installing an electrical box, and making basic electrical connections.

Check the information label attached to each vent fan unit. Choose a unit with a fan rating at least 5 CFM higher than the square footage of your bathroom. The sone rating refers to the relative quietness of the unit, rated on a scale of 1 to 7. (Quieter vent fans have lower sone ratings.)

Tools: Drill, jig saw, combination tool, screwdrivers, caulk gun, reciprocating saw, pry bar.

Materials: Wallboard screws, double-gang retrofit electrical box, NM cable (14/2, 14/3), cable clamp, hose clamps, pipe insulation, roofing cement, self-sealing roofing nails, shingles, wire connectors, switches.

Fan rating
(cubic feet
per minute)

70
C.F.M.
AT .10 WG
4.0
Sone
rating

C-K3285 SONES

Installing a Bathroom Vent Fan

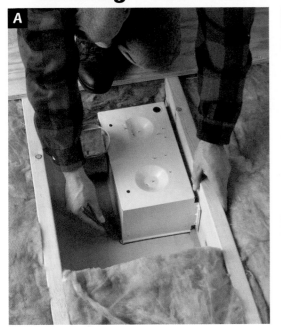

Position the vent fan unit against a ceiling joist. Outline the vent fan onto the ceiling surface. Remove the unit, then drill pilot holes at the corners of the outline and cut out the area with a jig saw or wallboard saw.

Remove the grille from the fan unit, then position the unit against the joist, with the edge recessed ¼" from the finished surface of the ceiling (so the grille can be flush-mounted). Attach the box to the joist, using wallboard screws.

VARIATION: For vent fans with heaters or light fixtures, some manufacturers recommend using 2 × lumber to build dams between the ceiling joists to keep the insulation at least 6" away from the fan unit.

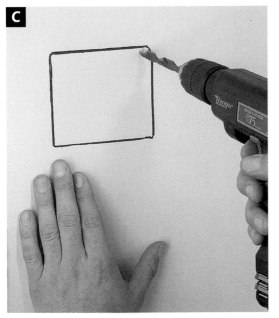

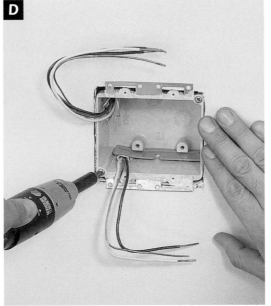

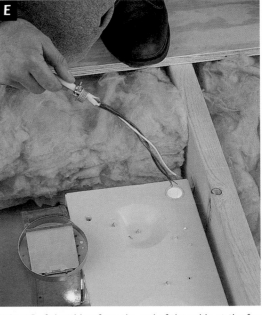

Mark and cut an opening for the switch box on the wall next to the latch side of the bathroom door, then run a 14/3 NM cable from the switch cutout to the fan unit. Run a 14/2 NM cable from the power source to the cutout.

Strip 10" of sheathing from the ends of the cables, then feed the cables into a double-gang retrofit switch box so at least ½" of sheathing extends into the box. Clamp the cables in place. Tighten the mounting screws until the box is secure.

Strip 10" of sheathing from the end of the cable at the fan unit, then attach a cable clamp to the cable. Insert the cable into the unit. From the inside of the unit, screw a locknut onto the threaded end of the clamp.

Continued on next page

Installing Bathroom Vent Fan (cont.)

Mark the exit location in the roof for the vent hose, next to a rafter. Drill a pilot hole, then saw through the sheathing and roofing material with a reciprocating saw to make the cutout for the vent tailpiece.

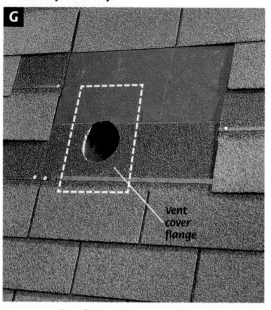

Remove a section of shingles from around the cutout, leaving the roofing paper intact. Remove enough shingles to create an exposed area that is at least the size of the vent cover flange.

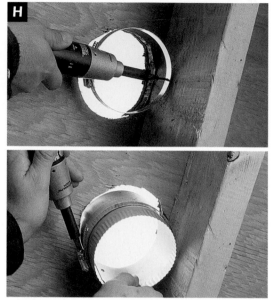

Attach a hose clamp to the rafter next to the roof cutout, about 1" below the roof sheathing (top). Insert the vent tailpiece into the cutout and through the hose clamp, then tighten the clamp screw (bottom).

Slide one end of the vent hose over the tailpiece, and slide the other end over the outlet on the fan unit. Slip hose clamps or straps around each end of the vent hose, and tighten the clamps.

Wrap the vent hose with pipe insulation. Insulation prevents moist air inside the hose from condensing and dripping down into the fan motor.

Apply roofing cement to the bottom of the vent cover flange, then slide the vent cover over the tailpiece. Nail the vent cover flange in place with self-sealing roofing nails, then patch in shingles around the cover.

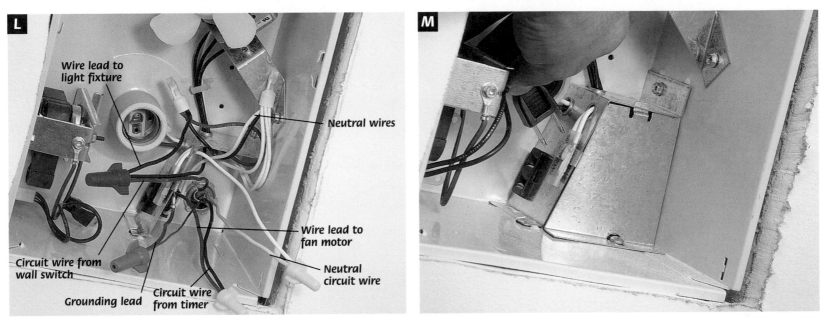

L — Wire lead to light fixture; Neutral wires; Circuit wire from wall switch; Grounding lead; Circuit wire from timer; Wire lead to fan motor; Neutral circuit wire

M

Make the following wire connections at the fan unit: the black circuit wire from the timer to the wire lead for the fan motor; the red circuit wire from the single-pole switch (see step N) to the wire lead for the light fixture in the unit; the white neutral circuit wire to the neutral wire lead; the circuit grounding wire to the grounding lead in the fan box. Make all connections with wire connectors. Attach the coverplate over the box when the wiring is completed.

Connect the fan motor plug to the built-in receptacle on the wire connection box, and attach the fan grille to the frame, using the mounting clips included with the fan kit. NOTE: If you removed the wall and ceiling surfaces for the installation, install new surfaces before completing this step.

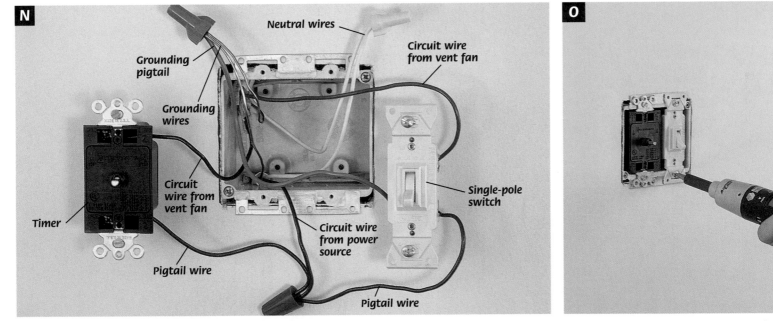

N — Grounding pigtail; Neutral wires; Circuit wire from vent fan; Grounding wires; Circuit wire from vent fan; Single-pole switch; Timer; Circuit wire from power source; Pigtail wire; Pigtail wire

O

At the switch box, add black pigtail wires to one screw terminal on the timer and to one screw terminal on the single-pole switch; add a green grounding pigtail to the grounding screw on the single-pole switch. Make the following wire connections: the black circuit wire from the power source to the black pigtail wires; the black circuit wire from the vent fan to the remaining screw on the timer; the red circuit wire from the vent fan to the remaining screw on the single-pole switch. Join the white wires with a wire connector. Join the grounding wires with a green wire connector.

Tuck the wires into the switch box, then attach the switches to the box and attach the coverplate and timer dial. Turn on the power.

Installing Grab Bars

Installing grab bars in the bathroom is one of the most effective ways to improve safety in your home. In addition to preventing slips and falls, grab bars help people steady themselves in showers and lower themselves into tubs, and they promote independence in the bathroom, where privacy is especially important.

Now standard features in many homes, grab bars are available in a variety of colors, shapes, and styles; some are textured for better gripping. Grab bars should be 1¼" to 1½" in diameter and extend no more than 1½" from the wall. They must be able to support 250 pounds, so it's important to anchor them properly.

The easiest way to install grab bars is to screw them into wall studs or into blocking or backing attached to the studs. Most grab bars require three screws at each end. When anchoring a bar to studs, use #12 stainless steel screws; drive screws into the center of the stud using two of the three screw holes at each end. Secure the third screw with a standard hollow-wall anchor. For other situations or where no framing or backing exists, there are specialty anchors available for securing bars (see page 495). In tubs and showers, always seal bar flanges with caulk to prevent water from entering the wall. Test all installations by pulling on the bars.

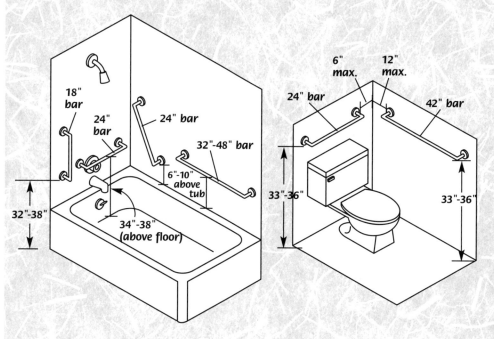

◄ Where to Install Grab Bars

The following suggestions for grab bar placement include some ADA guidelines and recommendations from universal design specialists. You may want additional grab bars in other locations.

Tub/Shower
- Vertical bar (18" long) at entrance to tub; bottom of bar 32" to 38" above the floor.
- Horizontal bar on control wall: 24" long; 34" to 38" above the floor.
- Horizontal bar on back wall (32" to 48" long): 34" to 38" above floor for shower only; 6" to 10" above top of tub for bath only.
- Angled bar: 24" long; bottom end 6" to 10" above top of tub (not necessary in stand-alone showers).

Toilet
- Horizontal bar at side: 42" long (min.); 12" (max.) from the back wall; 33" to 36" above the floor.
- Horizontal bar behind: 24" long (min.); 6" (max.) from the side wall; 33" to 36" above the floor.

Installing Blocking or Backing ➤

If you are remodeling your bathroom and will have the wall framing exposed or are building new walls, add blocking or backing for securing grab bars. Blocking is a good option if you know where the bars are going. Use 2 × 6 or 2 × 8 lumber to provide room for adjustments, and fasten the blocks to the framing with 16d nails. Note the locations of your blocking for future reference.

An alternative to blocking is to cover the entire wall with ¾" plywood backing, which allows you to install grab bars virtually anywhere on the wall. Secure plywood backing to the wall framing with screws.

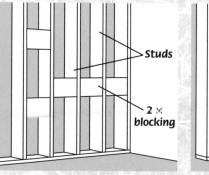

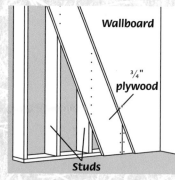

Grab Bar Anchors

Wall anchors are available for a variety of grab bar applications. Make sure the anchors you use can support 250 pounds (contact the grab bar manufacturer for the recommended anchor for your project). Always follow the manufacturer's instructions when installing anchors.

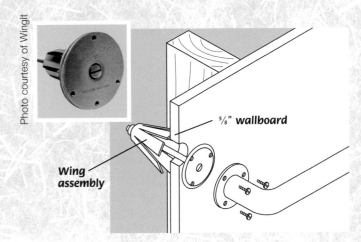

Photo courtesy of WingIt

Wing assembly

⅝" **wallboard**

◄ *WingIt™* anchors are heavy-duty hollow-wall anchors designed to support grab bars that can't be secured to framing or backing. When installed in walls of ½" wallboard with ceramic tile or in a ¼"-thick fiberglass tub surround, WingIts hold up to 1000 pounds; in ⅝" wallboard alone, 450 pounds; and in ½" wallboard alone, up to 250 pounds. Once installed, the anchor's wing assembly is 3" in diameter, so the bar must be located where no stud interferes.

For installation, WingIt anchors are prepared for insertion and temporarily mounted to the grab bar, then are inserted into 1¼" holes. Waterproof adhesive rings hold the anchors in place, and the bar is removed. A tap on the center bolt springs the wing assembly, and the bolt is tightened to draw the wing to the back of the wall. The grab bar is fastened to the anchor mounting plates with stainless steel screws.

➤ *Toggler®* brand SnapToggle™ anchors help secure grab bars to steel studs. This additional reinforcement is important because bare screws can strip or pull out of light-gauge steel. At each end of the bar, one SnapToggle is used to secure the top of the mounting flange to the stud. For the remaining two screws at each end, one is driven into the stud, if possible, and the other is secured to the wall with a SnapToggle or other anchor.

The steel end of the anchor is inserted through a ½" hole drilled through the center of the stud. A collar is slid along the straps of the anchor to snug the steel end against the backside of the stud. The straps are then broken off, and a ¼"-20 stainless steel bolt is inserted through the grab bar flange and screwed into the anchor.

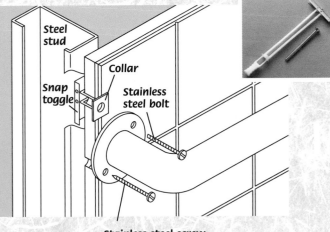

Steel stud

Snap toggle

Collar

Stainless steel bolt

Stainless steel screw

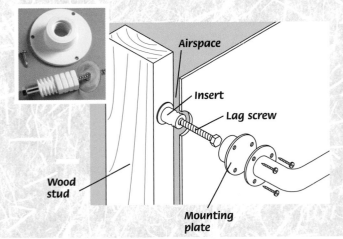

Airspace

Insert

Lag screw

Wood stud

Mounting plate

◄ *Solid Mount™* anchors are designed to secure grab bars in fiberglass tub-surrounds, which present a challenge to grab bar installations because of the airspace between the surround and the wall framing. The Solid Mount system uses a plastic, threaded insert to span the airspace and is secured with a lag screw driven in the wall framing. Once the stud's exact center is located, a 2" dia. hole—centered over the stud—is drilled through the fiberglass. The insert of the Solid Mount is cut to the correct length (based on the airspace), then secured to the stud with a ⁵⁄₁₆" lag screw. Finally, the anchor's mounting plate is threaded onto the insert and the grab bar is secured to the plate with stainless steel screws.

INDEX

ℱHOTO CREDITS & CONTRIBUTORS

Photo Credits

Christian Korab
Minneapolis, MN
© Christian Korab: p. 445T

David Livingston
www.davidduncanlivingston.com
© David Livingston: pp. 363L, 363TR

Karen Melvin
Architectural Stock Images, Inc.
Minneapolis, MN
© Karen Melvin: p. 216 for Tim Hartigan,
p. 362B for Knapp Cabinetry & Woodworking,
p. 444 for William Beson, p. 445B

Melabee M. Miller
Hillside, NJ
© Melabee M. Miller
p. 360 both for Geraldine Kaupp Interiors

Robert Perron
Branford, CT
© Robert Perron: p. 332 both

Roger Turk
Northlight Photography, Inc.
Southworth, WA
© Roger Turk: p. 362T

Contributors

Access One, Inc.
800-561-2223
www.beyondbarriers.com

Andersen Windows, Inc.
800-426-4261, ext. 1232
www.andersenwindows.com

**Architectural Products by Outwater
/ ORAC DÉCOR**
800-835-4400
www.outwater.com

Bruno Independent Living Aids, Inc.
800-882-8183
www.bruno.com

Dura Supreme, Inc.
320-543-3872
www.durasupreme.com

Frigidaire
800-FRIGIDAIRE
www.frigidaire.com

General Electric Appliance
800-626-2000
www. geappliances.com

**Heatilator
a division of Hearth Technologies, Inc.**
800-259-1549
www.heatilator.com

Kohler Co.
800-4-KOHLER
www.kohlerco.com

Kolbe & Kolbe Millwork Co., Inc.
800-955-8177
www.kolbe-kolbe.com

KraftMaid Cabinetry, Inc.
800-571-1990
www.kraftmaid.com

Kwikset Corporation
714-535-8111
www.kwikset.com

Marvin Windows and Doors
888-537-8268
www.marvin.com

Pass & Seymour/legrand
800-223-4185
www.passandseymour.com

**SunTouch Floor Warming
a division of Watts Heatway**
417-522-6128
www.suntouch.net

The Bilco Company
203-934-6363
www.bilco.com

The Stanley Works
800-STANLEY
www.stanleyworks.com

The Swan Corporation
800-325-7008
www.theswancorp.com

U-Line Corporation
414-354-0300
www.u-line.com

Velux-America, Inc.
800-688-3589
www.VELUX-AMERICA.com

WingIt Innovations, LLC.
877-8WINGIT
www.wingits.com

ADDITIONAL RESOURCES

General

American Institute of Architects
800-364-9364
www.aiaonline.com

American Lighting Association
800-724-4484
www.americanlightingassoc.com

American Society of Interior Designers
202-546-3480
www.asid.org

Association of Home Appliance Manufacturers
202-872-5955
www.aham.org

Certified Forest Products Council
503-590-6600
www.certifiedwood.org

Construction Materials Recycling Association
630-548-4510
www.cdrecycling.org

Energy & Environmental Building Association
952-881-1098
www.eeba.org

International Residential Code (book)
International Conference of Building Officials
800-284-4406
www.icbo.com

Light Gauge Steel Engineers Association
615-279-9251
www.lgsea.com

National Association of the Remodeling Industry (NARI)
847-298-9200
www.nari.org

National Fire Protection Agency
617-770-3000
www.nfpa.org

National Kitchen & Bath Association (NKBA)
800-843-6522
www.nkba.org

National Wood Flooring Association
800-422-4556
www.woodfloors.org

North American Insulation Manufacturers Association
703-684-0084
www.naima.org

Tile Council of America
864-646-8453
www.tileusa.com

U.S. Environmental Protection Agency— Indoor Air Quality
www.epa.gov/iedweb00/pubs/insidest.html

Universal Design

ABLEDATA
800-227-0216 (phone)
301-608-8958 (fax)
www.abledata.com

Access One, Inc.
800-561-2223
www.beyondbarriers.com

Adaptive Environments Center, Inc.
617-695-1225 (phone)
617-482-8099 (fax)
www.adaptenv.org

American Association of Retired Persons (AARP)
800-424-3410
www.aarp.org

Center for Inclusive Design & Environmental Access
School of Architecture and Planning— University of Buffalo
716-829-3485 ext. 329 (phone)
716-829-3861 (fax)
www.ap.buffalo.edu/~idea

The Center for Universal Design
NC State University
919-515-3082 (phone)
919-515-3023 (fax)
www.design.ncsu.edu/cud

NAHB Research Center
800-638-8556 (phone)
301-430-6180 (fax)
www.nahbrc.org

National Resource Center on Supportive Housing and Home Modification
University of Southern California
213-740-1364 (phone)
213-740-7069 (fax)
www.homemods.org

Trace Research & Development Center
University of Wisconsin—Madison
608-262-6966 (phone)
608-262-8848 (fax)
http://trace.wisc.edu/

U.S. Department of Housing and Urban Development
Office of Policy Development and Research
HUD User
800-245-2691 (phone)
301-519-5767
www.huduser.org

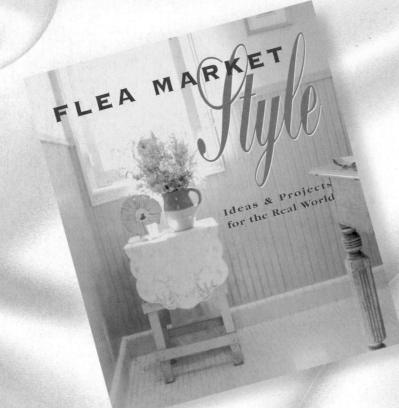

Also available

- Basic Wiring & Electrical Repairs
- Advanced Home Wiring
- Home Plumbing Projects & Repairs
- Advanced Home Plumbing
- Complete Photo Guide to Home Repair
- Carpentry: Remodeling
- Remodeling Kitchens
- Bathroom Remodeling
- Flooring Projects & Techniques
- Easy Wood Furniture Projects
- Built-In Projects for the Home
- Refinishing & Finishing Wood
- Designing Your Outdoor Home
- Building Your Outdoor Home
- Landscape Design & Construction
- Complete Guide to Building Decks
- Building Porches & Patios
- Exterior Home Repairs & Improvements
- Home Masonry Repairs & Projects
- Stonework & Masonry Projects
- Complete Guide to Home Masonry
- Complete Guide to Creative Landscapes
- Complete Guide to Painting & Decorating
- Building Garden Ornaments
- Fences, Walls & Gates
- Finishing Basements & Attics

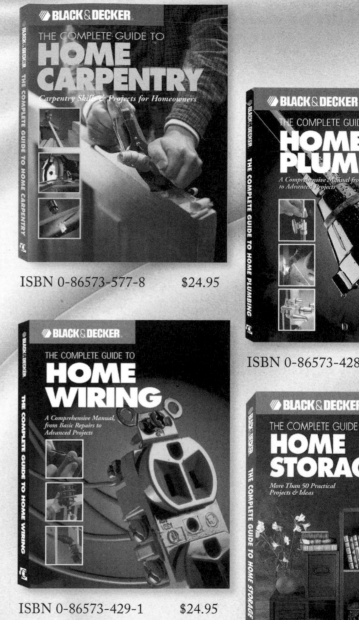

ISBN 0-86573-577-8 $24.95

ISBN 0-86573-428-3 $24.95

ISBN 0-86573-429-1 $24.95

ISBN 0-86573-581-6 $24.95

CREATIVE PUBLISHING INTERNATIONAL

5900 GREEN OAK DRIVE
MINNETONKA, MN 55343

WWW.HOWTOBOOKSTORE.COM

Drill Bit Guide

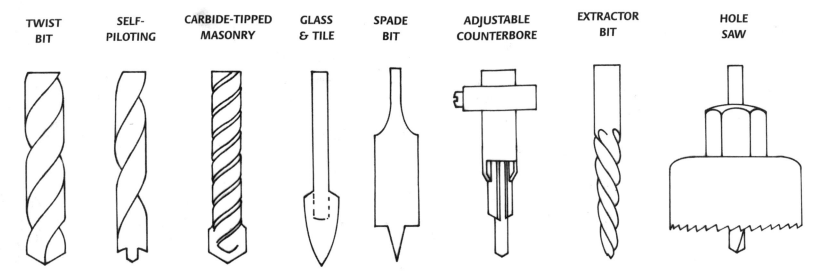

TWIST BIT	SELF-PILOTING	CARBIDE-TIPPED MASONRY	GLASS & TILE	SPADE BIT	ADJUSTABLE COUNTERBORE	EXTRACTOR BIT	HOLE SAW

Counterbore, Shank & Pilot Hole Diameters

SCREW SIZE	COUNTERBORE DIAMETER FOR SCREW HEAD	CLEARANCE HOLE FOR SCREW SHANK	PILOT HOLE DIAMETER	
			HARD WOOD	SOFT WOOD
#1	.146 (9/64)	5/64	3/64	1/32
#2	1/4	3/32	3/64	1/32
#3	1/4	7/64	1/16	3/64
#4	1/4	1/8	1/16	3/64
#5	1/4	1/8	5/64	1/16
#6	5/16	9/64	3/32	5/64
#7	5/16	5/32	3/32	5/64
#8	3/8	11/64	1/8	3/32
#9	3/8	11/64	1/8	3/32
#10	3/8	3/16	1/8	7/64
#11	1/2	3/16	5/32	9/64
#12	1/2	7/32	9/64	1/8